Along with Jacqueline Bouvier Kennedy, John F. Kennedy, and Lyndon B. Johnson, these eleven individuals who gathered at the dedication of the Ronald Reagan Library in November 1991 occupied the White House from 1961 through 1993. These leaders from the World War II generation were raised in a country with a powerful consensus about marriage and morality but presided over the nation as the consensus shattered. *(Bush Presidential Library)*

AFFAIRS *of* STATE

THE RISE AND *REJECTION* OF THE
PRESIDENTIAL COUPLE
SINCE WORLD WAR II

by

GIL TROY

THE FREE PRESS

New York   London   Toronto   Sydney   Singapore

THE FREE PRESS
A Division of Simon & Schuster Inc.
1230 Avenue of the Americas
New York, NY 10020

Manufactured in the United States of America

10   9   8   7   6   5   4   3   2   1

Library of Congress Cataloging–in–Publication Data
Troy, Gil.
    Affairs of state : the rise and rejection of the presidential couple
since World War II / Gil Troy.
        p.   cm.
    Includes bibliographical references and index.
    ISBN 0–684–82820–0
    1. Presidents—United States—History—20th century.
    2. Presidents—United States—Family—History—20th century.
    3. Presidents' spouses—United States—History—20th century.
    4. United States—Politics and government—1945–1989.
    5. United States—Politics and government—1989.   I. Title.
E176.1.T78   1997
973'.099—dc20   96–32795
                                                          CIP

To LINDA

for teaching me how to build a modern partnership
rooted in biblical standards:
"My beloved and I are for each other. . . ."
Together, we'll "flourish among the lilies."

—Song of Songs 6:3

We had been married for thirty-one years and were full partners in every sense of the word. Together we had planned and consummated a successful campaign for the highest office in our land.

—Jimmy Carter describing his wife Rosalynn on Inauguration Day, 1977

CONTENTS

SEARCHING FOR PERFECT COUPLES
IN THE SHADOW OF FDR AND ER

Something new is unfolding in American politics. There is an increasing tension between private life and political life, especially for those couples who call the White House home. It is not simply a women's issue, though it addresses the changing role of American women. It is not just a First Lady issue, though it remains unclear just how to define that extra-constitutional position. Nor is it just a presidential issue, though the president is the one who must face the voters. And it is not just a Hillary Clinton issue, though it is no accident that the first First Lady of the baby-boom generation has been so controversial.

I

In the half-century since Franklin and Eleanor Roosevelt occupied the White House, the concept of the First Couple has emerged. Until this extraordinary duo transformed American politics, while some First Ladies received more attention than others, no one really thought about the presidential couple. The President was the president, and his wife was an accessory, one of the many flourishes that helped paint a presidential portrait. The title "First Lady," like the position, is an extra-constitutional improvisation. It seems to

1

have been used as early as 1863 and became popular after Charles Nirdlinger's 1911 play about Dolley Madison, *The First Lady in the Land.*

Traditionally, First Ladies could be popular or unpopular, influential or irrelevant, more helpful or less helpful, but they did not define their husbands. Edith Galt Wilson's emergence as "Mrs. President" after Woodrow Wilson's strokes in 1919 was considered aberrant. After Theodore Roosevelt and his brood overran the White House in the early 1900s, Americans began to pay more attention to the First Family. They did not, however, talk about the "First Couple," or the president and his wife as a unit.

In 1948 and 1952, respectively, Harry Truman and Dwight Eisenhower each discovered how important a high-profile wife could be on whistle-stop campaign trips. *Newsweek* deemed Mrs. Truman part of the "Presidential trademark," suggesting the importance of consumerism and the growth of media in this appeal. By the 1970s and 1980s, it seemed that both the Carters and the Reagans had established a co-presidency, with the president's wife as the second most powerful person in the White House. And so today Americans scrutinize presidents and their wives in unprecedented ways, speculating about the marriage, the working relationship it creates—or hides—and the joint image the couple projects. This scrutiny involves more than idle gossip about two of America's leading celebrities; it has become a critical part of American politics.

It is tempting to define the First Lady as a Rorschach test for American attitudes toward women, to link the rise of the presidential couple with the rise of feminism, and leave it at that. It appears that the feminist battle cry of the 1960s has come true: the personal has become political. As women entered the public sphere, the search for female role models and women in power often led to the First Lady's headquarters in the East Wing of the White House. More and more political couples, including conservative Republicans like the Doles, the Quayles, and the Gramms, are in two-career peer marriages. Fewer and fewer American families approximate the 1950s cliché of working dad, stay-at-home mom, and 2.2 kids that politicians have long tried to invoke. Even more significant, many in the "chattering classes" have repudiated the ideal itself.

Nevertheless, the First Couple did not rise—and fall—in tandem with the women's movement. On some level, the personal has always been political for American presidents, who serve as both head of government and head of state. Since George Washington, Americans have preferred that their president be an ideal man with an equally ideal family. The White House itself, situating the chief executive and living national icon "above the store," has muddied the boundaries between public and private for nearly two centuries. In a 1993 case seeking to clarify whether Hillary Rodham Clinton was a government "officer or employee," the majority of the United States Court of Appeals for the District of Columbia declared, "We do not think the presidency can be so easily divided between its substantive political and ceremonial functions."

Furthermore, the emphasis on the political couple predates the resurgence of modern feminism. The staid Trumans and Eisenhowers faced unprecedented demands to promenade as a couple amid the great burst of postwar domesticity. In the 1950s many corporations began interviewing wives before hiring executives. "A good wife can't help a husband as much as a bad wife can hurt one," the sociologist William H. Whyte, Jr., warned. By 1960 the *Ladies' Home Journal* proclaimed, "Politics today is a husband-wife partnership." Such cooperation was seen not as a mark of liberation but as an appropriate extension of wifely duties.

Other changes have also focused unprecedented attention on the First Couple. The rise of the trillion-dollar "nanny" state and the corresponding expansion of the executive branch made the federal government the focal point of public life and plunged politicians into Americans' private lives. A voracious and intrusive media needed simple characters to report the complex stories emanating from Washington that interested more people than ever before. And a new kind of political culture confused fame with leadership, exposure with a democratic dialogue.

In fact, the rise of the presidential couple is most closely linked with the rise of the mass media and the new political culture it spawned. The Kennedys were particularly successful at a game that all presidential couples since the Roosevelts have had to play. In many ways the First Couple is a media construct, a colorful vehicle that serves reporters' needs in a world where the media dominates the public square.

Both partners now build one political image. Yet Americans' ambivalence about marriage, family, and power makes for an unstable game. Presidential couples who appear too perfect, like the Nixons, are rejected as unreal, victimized by what the historian John Demos calls the "anti-image" of the modern American family. Presidential couples who promise "two for the price of one," as the Clintons did, run into atavistic fears of unelected women seizing power. The sexual revolution helped rouse American conservativism; today, millions champion the old-fashioned ways even as they live modern lives. Modern Americans yearn for the traditional ideal but assume the worst; they suspect seemingly happy families and condemn unconventional ones; they want equality but find the traditional sex roles soothing.

Important questions lurk beneath all the ambivalence and posturing. What standard should the new presidential couple embrace? Can we properly speak about a "co-presidency"? If so, what does it mean?

After researching in ten presidential libraries in nine states, I have concluded that it means trouble. First Ladies have become prime political targets, attacked, ridiculed, and grilled about their childhoods, their child rearing, their marriages, their fashions, and their philosophies. It is a thankless task. Often it seems that a First Lady cannot do anything right: Nancy Reagan was too trendy, Barbara Bush, too frumpy; Rosalynn Carter was too powerful, Pat Nixon, too passive; Betty Ford was too outspoken, Bess Truman, too discreet. Their spouses have rarely fared better: as husbands, Ronald Reagan was too dependent, Richard Nixon, too independent; Lyndon Johnson was too demonstrative, George Bush, too reserved; Jimmy Carter was too solicitous, John Kennedy, too selfish.

America's dissatisfaction with its First Couples has a simple cause. Just because Americans demanded that a First Lady share the spotlight with her husband did not mean that Americans expected the First Couple to share power. Article II, Section 1, of the United States Constitution states it clearly: "The executive Power shall be vested in *a* President of the United States of America" (emphasis added). The intensity of the attack on ambitious First Ladies reflects the tenor of the contemporary debate about sex roles, but the fundamental problem has remained the same for over two centuries. Co-presidencies should be about joint image-building, not power-sharing.

Modern First Ladies—and especially the powerful ones—have been electorally problematic. They often do more harm than good. Hillary Rodham Clinton has taken solace in the fact that her predecessors were pilloried for all kinds of sins, especially when they refused to remain behind the scenes. Betty Ford hurt her husband's Presidency, even as she charmed the media. Reporters deemed Rosalynn Carter "fuzzy" at first, because her versatile and controversial role as an "extension" of her husband was not easily stereotyped. And Nancy Reagan was attacked so fiercely during the first year of the Reagan administration that many aides suggested she hide from the public. A modern First Lady cannot hibernate, but when outside she needs to watch her step.

This book is about both image and substance. It is about image insofar as the First Couples have sought to fulfill Americans' unrealistic standards for the presidency, and for all married couples, in a turbulent era. Today spouses often do what political parties once did, helping to define the country's leader in an accessible and standard shorthand. As partisan identity declined, presidents instinctively offered up their wives to help forge ties with millions of voters in this mass democracy. As a result, the modern presidential couples have been pressured more intensively than ever to embody an ideal at a time when this same ideal has been both repudiated and revered.

On the substantive side, this book is a story of increasing First Lady involvement in politics, and voters' rejection of that involvement. The continuing traditionalist strain in American politics burlesques powerful First Ladies as "Lady Macbeths" and their compliant husbands as "Casper Milquetoasts." Eventually, each couple has learned this lesson. Thus the amusing, inside-the-Beltway guessing game about how much "pillow talk" is swaying the president on any given day or any given issue needs to give way to a broader historical understanding of how couples as different as the Reagans, the Bushes, and the Clintons ended up following strikingly similar marital protocols in the modern White House.

II

The rise and rejection of the First Couple is rooted in the extraordinary White House tenure of Franklin Roosevelt and his wife, Eleanor. From 1933 to 1945, separately and together, they challenged Americans' assumptions about government, marriage, and society. By inserting the federal government into the American home, Roosevelt revolutionized both. The state became "domesticated" as it usurped parental functions relating to economic welfare and education. This expansion of the state weakened the family's institutional functions, making family ties more based on emotion—and thus more unstable—than ever.

Roosevelt also domesticated the presidency. Building on the tradition of charismatic and heroic predecessors such as Abraham Lincoln and Theodore Roosevelt, playing to the newsreel cameras, the radio microphones, and a cadre of loyal reporters, imprinting his personal stamp on federal largesse from Social Security to rural electrification, Franklin Roosevelt forged personal links between the White House and every American home. With the president more central in Americans' lives, his private life became more relevant. He personified the nation.

In turn, even one of the Roosevelts' sharpest critics, Westbrook Pegler, acknowledged in 1942 that Mrs. Roosevelt "personifies the presidency as an office." Eleanor Roosevelt tried to argue that "you don't elect the woman nor the family when you elect a man President." Still, more than any of her predecessors, she helped bring the presidency to the people.

While their political fates were linked, and they had been married since 1905, the Roosevelts were mismatched. He was ebullient, flirtatious, charming, wily, dilettantish, and pragmatic; she was insecure, starchy, awkward, direct, conscientious, and idealistic. He was a playboy; she confessed to having "an almost exaggerated idea of the necessity of keeping all of one's desires under complete subjugation." Franklin's affair in 1918 with Lucy Mercer, then Eleanor's secretary, ruined the marriage. Franklin and Eleanor only stayed together to raise the children, preserve his career, and keep his allowance, which his mother threatened to cut if they divorced. Mr. and Mrs. Roosevelt became "business partners," their son James said, occasionally warm but always guarded. The sham marriage scarred the children, who would embarrass their parents with divorces, minor scandals, and a flamboyant incompetence. When polio crippled Franklin in 1921, Eleanor nursed him, but she continued building her own life as an activist, journalist, and educator.

In the White House, both Roosevelts became very popular but also made bitter enemies. The President used his wife as a "trial balloon" for radical ideas and as an emissary to the disadvantaged, and she capitalized on her proximity to power. A full-time "do-gooder," Eleanor could not enjoy a "glorious" winter day without wondering "what this weather means to those who are poorly fed, poorly housed, and poorly clothed." She barraged Franklin with memos, lectures, and dinner guests to advance her agenda. She was his "spur," not his partner; she often felt like "a hair shirt"—an abrasive garment worn as penance.

The First Lady's liberalism threatened to alienate large segments of the Democratic party, but the President calculated that party loyalty would limit defections from conservatives and Southerners. Opponents saw through the strategy, even if they remained in the party. One 1944 handbill mocked the strategy by depicting Franklin saying to Eleanor, "You kiss the Negroes and I'll kiss the Jews and we'll stay in the White House as long as we choose."

Reporters knew about the Roosevelts' strained alliance. Many heard rumors about the Mercer affair—or the tale that Franklin once rang in the White House for Eleanor, only to learn she had been out of town for three days. But the Roosevelts benefited from the genteel journalistic ethos that upheld the culture of appearances.

Both Roosevelts reinforced this journalistic reticence by seducing the press. Eleanor mimicked her husband. She held regular press conferences, although she limited hers to the "news hens" who covered the East Wing, where the First Lady's social secretary and two aides worked. The women covering the First Lady considered themselves a "breed" apart from the men covering the West Wing, where the Oval Office was located. These tough professionals endured the disdain of their male colleagues and proudly bore their nickname.

Together, Eleanor Roosevelt and some of the news hens tried to make women "newsworthy"—although society reporters resented the First Lady for not generating social news. A collaborator rather than a combatant, Eleanor told the thirty-five newswomen at her first press conference, "You are the interpreters to the women of the country as to what goes on politically in the legislative national life and also what the social and personal life is at the White House." In the ensuing decades, this journalistic power to create political personalities would mushroom.

As they dished out the society pablum their editors demanded, grateful newswomen protected their shot at an occasional front-page story. Partially as a result, Elliott Roosevelt noted that his mother "managed to conceal her personality completely. She pictured herself as a calm, contented woman deeply concerned with the world and her family. We read her articles and marveled how she created the image of a total stranger, not the detached, harried, fault-finding wife and parent we knew."

The debate about civilian defense mobilization highlighted the complications surrounding the Roosevelts' public and private roles. While Franklin was a capitalist and an individualist trying to fix the system, Eleanor was a radical collectivist. By 1940 the President and his aides were inching away from the First Lady's ambitious statism. The President established the Office of Civilian Defense in May 1941 to lay the groundwork for American intervention in the European war. Mrs. Roosevelt believed that civilian defense should include "progressive social legislation"; the OCD, she felt, should spearhead a "people's movement" to bring "better nutrition, better housing, better day-by-day medical care, better education, better recreation for every age."

In appointing New York's pragmatic Mayor Fiorello La Guardia as director, the President silently repudiated his wife's expansive vision. Eleanor criticized La Guardia for inspecting "fire-fighting equipment" rather than "building morale" through ambitious social programs. La Guardia invited her to become assistant director. Franklin remained "completely neutral" on the subject, though he said "it would help Mayor La Guardia." The wily President was encouraging his wife while avoiding responsibility for it. Eleanor's friends believed that the President "was glad to channel her energies into one area so that she would leave him alone in other areas." The First Lady could be a terrible nag.

Eleanor Roosevelt had expanded her mandate cautiously. Despite her doddering facade, she understood that First Ladies were to be seen at social galas and by their husbands' sides, not heard in policy debates. First, "plain, ordinary Mrs. Roosevelt" acted as her handicapped husband's "eyes and ears" by traveling on his behalf. With the government tackling "humanitarian issues" such as housing, nutrition, and health, Eleanor became the nation's caseworker. This was not a modern, feminist impulse. Since the turn of the century American women had the special honor of projecting what the sociologist Theda Skocpol calls "maternal values" onto the political "agenda." Crusading for social justice was women's work. By the end of 1933, Eleanor was receiving five hundred letters a day. Her progressive zeal for reform, combined with her aristocratic commitment to feminine "uplift," pushed her from advice to advocacy.

The symbolic power of her office, her daily newspaper column, and reporters' interest in White House life gave Mrs. Roosevelt a "white glove pulpit," as one of her successors would term it. In 1939, when the Daughters of the American Revolution banned the black singer Marian Anderson from Constitution Hall, Mrs. Roosevelt resigned from the organization. She then lobbied Secretary of Interior Harold Ickes to permit a Marian Anderson concert at the Lincoln Memorial, which drew seventy-five thousand fans.

Loyal newswomen applauded Eleanor's transformation from caseworker to crusader. By 1939, 67 percent of Americans polled approved of her, while 58 percent approved of her husband. She convinced herself "that people no longer considered me a mouthpiece for my husband but realized that I had a point of view of my own." A formal job with the OCD threatened her independence. "I don't want to do it but . . . I'll have to try," Eleanor told friends. "Just at the moment I feel very low."

On September 29, 1941, the First Lady of the United States walked briskly from the White House to the OCD offices in Dupont Circle. She promised to be "on the job" every morning, and soon she was supervising "every activity which Mayor La Guardia did not want in his part of the program." Nevertheless, she was not just another volunteer "dollar-a-year man." The *New York Times* announced her appointment on the society page.

The President's plan failed. Roosevelt found himself caught between his self-righteous First Lady and the self-promoting mayor. "I can't take Eleanor and La Guardia," he complained, as he sent a mutual friend to "keep them away from me and reconcile their differences." La Guardia's inability to hold two full-time jobs exacerbated the tensions. After Pearl Harbor, Franklin eased La Guardia aside and hired James M. Landis as the director of OCD.

La Guardia's eclipse made Eleanor more influential in the agency and a more prominent target. The job suited her; she was everyone's maiden aunt. Her frumpy cotton stockings advertised wartime limits on nylons. Daily calisthenics and dance sessions demonstrated her faith in "improving" both body and mind. She staffed the OCD with "Eleanor's people": the activists, Hollywood actors, unionists, and artists who formed a competing liberal court to Franklin's bureaucratic toadies. Her division produced a thirty-two-page booklet detailing an "uplift program" of book drives, swimming lessons, pro-democracy courses, and group-relations seminars.

Eleanor's fame led both critics and supporters to exaggerate her power. Columnist Raymond Clapper would call her a "Cabinet minister without portfolio—the most influential woman of our times." The previous Democratic administration had ended with charges that Edith Wilson had usurped power and lied about Woodrow Wilson's illness. Attacks on Mrs. Roosevelt as "Madam President" stirred memories of that "petticoat presidency," especially considering President Roosevelt's infirmities.

Mrs. Roosevelt, like Mrs. Wilson, outraged Americans by violating the genteel boundaries of the First Ladyship. Critics suggested that the First Lady stay home "and tend to her knitting as an example for other women to follow." Women, especially upper-class matrons, were particularly vehement on the subject. Barbara Pierce Bush "grew up in a household that really detested" Eleanor. When girls like Barbara were warned not to be outspoken or they would wind up like Eleanor Roosevelt—"too tall, too unattractive, too strident for any man"—the society's fear of powerful women was clear.

This misogynist fear reinforced the long-standing fear of overweening executive power. Even though Americans accepted surprisingly monarchical touches in their chief executive, they worried about a dictator subverting their fragile republic. With each new presidential initiative, with each unprecedented term, opponents feared that Roosevelt would become another Adolf Hitler. "He is the one whom the founders feared," the *Saturday Evening Post* thundered in 1940, "I, Roosevelt." In this scenario, Franklin's queen engineered his power grab.

In fact, Eleanor was less influential than most believed. She was more Lady Godiva than Lady Macbeth, more crusader than power broker. Franklin disliked her nagging. "First things come first," he would sigh. Rather than admit her impotence, Eleanor played the supportive wife, claiming, "Although I might present the situation to him, I never urged on him a specific course of action, no matter how strongly I felt."

Still, New Deal opponents accused both Roosevelts of exploiting the emergency to "further socialize America." The Southern Democrats and Republicans attacking the OCD revealed deep anxieties about the cost of the war, the New Deal's social agenda, the imposition of wartime rationing, and the centralized and federalized culture of celebrity created by Hollywood and the New Deal. Senator Hugh A. Butler, a Nebraska Republican, said that "if the communities wish to organize dancing and calisthenics, I am sure they can do it themselves without direction from the throne."

The attacks also expressed frustration with the sagging war effort. On February 6, 1942, the House of Representatives banned using defense funds for "instructions in physical fitness by dancers, fan dancing, street shows, theatrical performances or other public entertainment." The verdict was clear: Congress considered the First Lady and her friends frivolous.

The First Lady had overstepped. Eleanor later said she had never endured such "unfavorable press." Congresswoman Mary T. Norton defended her as "a woman who has done more for the womanhood of this country than any other woman of my time." Norton agreed that "we cannot turn all our efforts toward making armaments and building ships if the morale of our country is not taken care of." Still, the assault destroyed Eleanor's delusion that she could act independently of her husband. The director of the OCD, James Landis, admitted that having the First Lady "as an assistant director" was "a perfectly impossible situation." Every time she took "a position," it "involve[d] the president." On February 12, therefore, she resigned. Eleanor learned that "as long as I held a government position, even as a volunteer, I offered a way to get at the president."

Of course, Eleanor vowed "to go on fighting for the things in which I believe." She assailed the "small and very vocal group of unenlightened men" who are now "able to renew, under the guise of patriotism and economy, the age-old fight of the privileged few against the good of man." But Eleanor had been cowed. She made sure to embrace some traditionalist positions in the next few weeks, condemning women who wore slacks and advocating joint filing by married couples—which, because it bumped them into higher tax brackets, discouraged some women from working at all. In a March press conference she would say, "I guess I'd list myself as a housewife—with some experience in writing a column and in speaking—and that's all."

Eleanor had learned her lesson. In an interview with the *New York Times* in 1924, she said she had noticed that men tell their wives: "Lead your own life, attend to your charities, cultivate yourself, arrange your teas and dinners, bring up the children, run the house and be happy. One thing only I ask of you, and that is that you keep out of my business and keep out of politics." The experience at OCD, she wrote, "convinced me that being in the White House would prevent me from doing any real job in World War II." Nevertheless, she spurned the advice of the American Legion commander who suggested she help the war effort by "keeping quiet for the duration." She would continue championing radical policies but would try to avoid making her role the issue.

Within weeks, Eleanor was representing the President in Great Britain, trying to integrate housing projects in Detroit, and advocating a full draft of all civilians to deploy home-front workers effectively. As a result, her hate mail peaked between 1942 and 1943. The FBI reported that many Southerners considered Mrs. Roosevelt "the most dangerous individual in the United States today."

Eleanor's standing with the President suffered as criticism mounted. Franklin Roosevelt preferred to surround himself with flirtatious women and fawning men. Eventually he would deputize his daughter, Anna, to serve as his political wife. "She exercised far greater influence than Mother ever had, and she became what Mother never truly was—a conduit to the President," Elliott noted. In November 1943, Franklin rejected Eleanor's plea to attend the Teheran summit, insisting on "absolutely no women." She was crushed. More and more, Franklin instinctively opposed whatever Eleanor advocated.

Both Roosevelts had boxed themselves into an empty marriage. Eleanor sensed the desolation beneath Franklin's gaiety and flirtatiousness. "He was a very lonesome man," she said shortly after he died. "I wish I had been able to be closer to him, to comfort him sometimes, but I suppose that could not be." Many of her own writings describe herself as a tired, dispirited, abandoned, pinched Puritan. Contemporary admirers often have to do analytical somersaults to get beyond her direct and self-damning descriptions. She would confess to having "lived those years very impersonally. It was almost as though I had erected someone a little outside of myself who was the president's wife. I was lost somewhere deep down inside myself."

Franklin Roosevelt helped forge a "personal" and "public" presidency at the center of American political life. The Roosevelt Presidency suited an emerging mass-media, popular-culture-drenched polity where image was a critical source of political capital. Although Thomas Jefferson, Andrew Jackson, and Theodore Roosevelt, for example, each defined particular moments in American history, John Quincy Adams, Millard Fillmore, and Rutherford B. Hayes had not. After the New Deal, it seemed, every president came to Washington with a cultural agenda and a renewed mandate to serve as the national icon. The need to define the times while leading the nation gave presidential spouses unprecedented prominence in helping their husbands establish a political identity and thrust the presidential couple into the increasingly bitter culture wars that engulfed postwar America.

Eleanor Roosevelt demonstrated the potential of the First Lady as activist, as inspiration, and as celebrity. In the new mass political culture blooming in the 1930s and 1940s, an outspoken First Lady charmed millions. There was no way to be sure, but Democrats assumed this popularity translated into votes. Eleanor also represented the feminist impulse toward individual liberation and self-fulfillment that would become so essential in the future.

Eleanor's frustrations with Franklin and the vicious assaults she endured offered a warning against flirting with power that would often be overlooked. Most Americans remained uncomfortable with real power devolving toward the presidential spouse. And the coming era of mass politics, mass media, and weakened party loyalty would require more of a joint effort from a couple as they played on a more unified national scene. The run-down White House and the awful food served at the presidential table symbolized Eleanor's dereliction of wifely duty. Even an eleven-year-old visitor like Jacqueline Bouvier found the Roosevelts' White House "rather bleak." Years after her 1940 visit she still remembered the broken furniture, the mismatched decor, the lack of an effective guide.

Eleanor herself remained steeped in Victorian values. She preached about the importance of serving one's husband as she asserted her independence. In 1932 she wrote that "even if a woman has the most definite ideas, she must never try to persuade her husband to do anything he does not consider right. . . . She should never nag her husband . . . ; nor need she make [their differences] public." Though she violated these rules repeatedly, she genuinely believed in them.

Mrs. Roosevelt remained tethered to her husband. Her fame derived from his; her influence depended on his whims. She believed that "like many other women, very little that I have done in life seems to have been done as a matter of choice." After he died, she conceded, "It is wonderful to feel free."

Eleanor's Victorian rhetoric underscored the novelty of the Roosevelts' marriage, as well as their mixed legacy. While many reporters and liberals celebrated this bold, outspoken activist, millions of Americans yearned for a traditional, reassuring couple at 1600 Pennsylvania Avenue. Eleanor Roosevelt's immediate successors, Bess Truman and Mamie Eisenhower, tried to model themselves on Mrs. Roosevelt's demure predecessors—and they were duly applauded for their discretion. Nevertheless, the demands of reporters, citizens, and their husbands, all dazzled by Eleanor's legacy, thrust these First Ladies into policy issues and political controversy far more frequently than either would have liked. Even in the "retro" Truman and Eisenhower White House, then, the presidential couple began its inexorable march forward, though the story picks up steam in 1961.

The two tortured Roosevelts set high standards for all of their successors. Rosalynn Smith Carter learned from Mrs. Roosevelt "that there was more to being the wife of the President than sitting back in the White House and enjoying the nice life." Betty Bloomer Ford was impressed "that a woman was finally speaking out and expressing herself rather than just expressing the views of her husband." Similarly, Ronald Reagan "idolized" FDR. "During his Fireside Chats, his strong, gentle, confident voice resonated across the nation with an eloquence that brought comfort and resilience to a nation caught up in a storm and reassured us that we could lick any problem." Both Roosevelts were master illusionists and taught their successors the importance of maintaining an effective public image—whatever sordid realities lurked in the background.

III

The Roosevelts' joint leadership project inspired a generation of presidential couples raised on common ideals, united by dramatic experiences, and uniquely faithful to a vision of their country as a place of middle-class prosperity, genteel sensibilities, bourgeois morality, and democratic principles. After the Trumans and Eisenhowers, the seven presidential couples from 1961 through 1993 courted, married, and began families during the dramatic days of the Depression, World War II, and the cold war. In fact, the first of these couples, the Kennedys, was the last to be married, in 1953. All the men except Ronald Reagan served in the Navy. (Reagan, who never saw combat, was an Army man). All the women except Betty Bloomer Ford attended college, and all established their first homes far away from their families. These fourteen Americans—along with millions more—embarked on their lifetime marital adventures with detailed road maps that emphasized devotion to family, church, community, nation, and God, along with precepts such as fidelity, honor, grace, patriotism, self-control, and faith. Even if these individuals did not always do the right thing, they entertained few doubts about what the right thing to do was.

In their youths, a black-and-white world gave contrasting directions to "all-American" white boys and girls. Boys were raised to succeed. The entire country seemed hooked on the notion that hard work and high ideals would yield male greatness. "In this as in all the many letters I have written you there is the same theme: I love you; I believe in you, I expect great things of you," Rebekah Baines Johnson wrote her son Lyndon. For Dick Nixon's thirteenth birthday his grandmother gave him a portrait of Abraham Lincoln, upon which she inscribed Henry Wadsworth Longfellow's "Psalm of Life": "Lives of great men oft remind us/We can make our lives sublime. And, departing, leave behind us/Footprints on the sands of time."

For these future leaders of America, childhood dreams of greatness matured into a will for power. There was no room for self-doubt in this "American Century." In early 1960, John F. Kennedy would explain his presidential run by saying, "I look around me at the others in the race, and I say to myself, well, if they think they can do it, why not me?"

Americans believed that, as one women's club preened, "men are God's trees; women are his flowers." Men sought achievements, while young ladies cultivated "improvement." Women were raised to be self-sacrificing. Looking back on their childhoods from a computer age, many would recognize they were "programmed for marriage." "Now, Nancy," Edith Luckett Davis would tell her daughter, "when you get married, be sure to get up and have breakfast with your husband in the morning. Because if you don't, you can be sure that some other woman who lives around the corner will be perfectly happy to do so." Husbands were treasures to be pampered and guarded, especially if they were good providers like Nancy Davis's stepfather.

The mid-twentieth century was the age of the "companionate marriage," a voluntary partnership rooted in mutual love but not equality. The institution of marriage anchored individuals' lives and the society at large. When conflicts arose or deviations occurred, indirection was preferred to confrontation. "'Let well enough alone' is a fine matrimonial slogan," preached Dorothy Dix, the advice columnist of the 1920s.

All these mutually reinforcing institutions and ideals rested on a bargain. Those who invested their lives with industry, love, and faith could expect returns in the form of a happy life, a prosperous career, and a harmonious family. There was no need to dwell on feelings and motives; by maintaining appearances, Americans would be able to attain the good life.

The seven girls who grew up to live in the White House from 1961 to 1993 learned their lessons particularly well. Remarkably for the time, only Barbara Pierce grew up with what a later generation called an "intact" family—and when Barbara was twenty-five, her mother died in a car accident. In an era when the annual divorce rate hovered between one and two per thousand persons, both Nancy Davis and Jackie Bouvier were children of divorce. In an era when the average life span jumped from fifty-four years in 1920 to nearly sixty-three in 1940, Lady Bird's mother died of a fall down some steps, Rosalynn Smith's father died of cancer when she was thirteen, and when Betty Bloomer was sixteen her father died of carbon monoxide poisoning in a suspicious accident. By the time she was seventeen, Pat Ryan was an orphan: When she was thirteen her mother died of liver cancer, and four years later her father died of the same tubercular encephalitis that killed one of Dick Nixon's brothers.

Such family tragedies forced these women to assume heavy burdens in their youth and inured them to the draining demands of political wifehood as adults. Pop psychologists would call most of these women "enablers"— people whose need to be needed perpetuated behaviors on the part of their loved ones that were exploitative or self-destructive. When her mother died, Pat Ryan became the "woman of the house," responsible for "washing, ironing, everything." She learned to be systematic, persistent, and upbeat. "Life was sort of sad, so I tried to cheer everybody up," she recalled. "I learned to be that kind of person."

Nonetheless, these women were swept by the winds of change that were blowing through American culture in the 1920s and 1930s. Most of them ended up being bolder, less conventional, better educated, and more mobile than their mothers. Pat Ryan, Betty Bloomer, and Nancy Davis sought adventure in New York City before they married—Pat as an X-ray technician, Betty as a Martha Graham dancer, and Nancy as a Broadway actress. Eventually both Pat Ryan and Nancy Davis would appear in the movies—Pat as an extra, Nancy as a star—and both Pat and Lady Bird Taylor would train to become teachers.

For the men and the women of this generation, the outbreak of war in 1941 derailed their career plans and accelerated their emergence into adulthood. The bombing of Pearl Harbor united Americans as never before. On top of a common culture of appearances and unifying technologies like radio and the movies, Americans now shared a goal.

The nation became as important as the family, the church, and the school. More than a "war to end all wars" or a fight for democracy, this was a war for the American home, a war for Americans' consensus culture. Fittingly, the artist Norman Rockwell would reduce President Roosevelt's Four Freedoms to domestic tableaus. The American family had become the front line in the fight for freedom. Women were told that their contributions were as important as those of the men. Throughout the war, magazines would run features on "How America Lives" and address articles to "you" about "your" feelings, as if everyone from coast to coast shared the same experience.

The search for consensus blinded Americans to the contrasting lessons the war taught men and women. As replacement workers, women learned to apply their domestic skills beyond the home—while still making sure that they remained attractive and their homes functioned. Fashion editors offered "do's" and "don'ts" about the wearing of hair, makeup, jewelry, and clothing on the job. At home, women could not change their "defense haircut," but the *Ladies' Home Journal* urged them to slip out of their coveralls and into "pretty prints" that are "nonmussable, and feminine as a flower garden." As soldiers fighting a brutal war, men discovered that they often had to shed the genteel restraints of the home to succeed in the "real world." Thus women learned to do double duty while men learned to lead double lives. The ideology of the companionate marriage could not contain the conflicting marching orders or the resulting power imbalance. This generation began the greatest marrying spree in history intoxicated by a potent brew of romance, idealism, egalitarianism, patriotism, and sexism.

After the war, all Americans craved a normalcy that had been out of reach for decades. Women left the work force, although an unprecedented number continued to work. Marriage rates and birth rates soared. The postwar euphoria climaxed with the Kennedy administration, as middle managers mimicked John Kennedy's James Bond urbanity and their wives replicated Jackie Kennedy's glamour with bouffant hairdos and $39.99 mass-produced knockoffs of her $7000 Somali leopard coat.

John Kennedy recognized that the joint image of the First Couple helped shape the president's image and could attract some votes. The revolutions in feminism, media technology, and journalism that would build the American obsession with its First Couple had begun. Nearly one-third of America's married women were in the work force. Television was in 87 percent of all homes. Print reporters were trying to justify their jobs by jazzing up stories and bringing their readers behind the scenes. Democrats marketed "Jack and Jackie" aggressively to these anxious journalists and a willing public. As America moved toward a public-relations presidency, the First Lady became the president's most important PR flack.

IV

"History! . . . It's what those bitter old men write," Jackie Kennedy mourned days after Jack's assassination. "No one'll ever know . . . about Jack." Mrs. Kennedy had summoned the author and Kennedy acolyte Theodore H. White to Hyannis Port late on November 29, 1963, explaining, "I kept saying to Bobby, I've got to talk to somebody, I've got to see somebody, I want to say this one thing." Mrs. Kennedy wanted to make sure that "other little boys" would learn to "see the heroes" in history, just as the young Jack had. With White's editors at *Life* holding the presses at a cost of $30,000 an hour, with a thunderstorm battering the house, Jackie rambled. She remembered hearing the sound of a car backfiring, trying to stuff her husband's brains back into his skull, kissing his foot as it dangled out of the white sheet before they placed his "little . . . naked" body into the coffin, having a policeman pull off her gloves, which had "stiffened with blood."

Amid these chilling details, she offered her message, a "line from a musical comedy" that was "all I keep thinking of." She recalled the drafty nights at the White House when she would get out of bed and play some songs "for him" on "an old Victrola." He loved the musical *Camelot* "and the song he loved most came at the very end of this record, the last side of *Camelot*, sad *Camelot:* . . . 'Don't let it be forgot, that once there was a spot, for one brief shining moment that was known as Camelot.'"

This most enduring of legends, wrapped in the glamour of a 1961 Broadway hit starring Julie Andrews and Richard Burton, suited the image Mrs. Kennedy created that week. In its democratized, Americanized version, Camelot was a never-never land of high ideals and virtuous pursuits, a civilized bastion uphold-ing the best Christian ideals against pagan enemies, a perfect parallel for an America that considered World War II and the ensuing cold war proof of its pu-rity. Like all great myths, this one was elastic enough to accommodate a seamier underside of illicit passions and tragic mistakes. Even in her tearful Hyannis Port interview with one of her husband's knights, the widowed queen noted that the wedding ring that was now the "closest thing I have to a memory" of him her in-sensitive beau had bought "in a hurry in Newport" just before they married. "It wasn't even engraved to me" when he gave it, she added, saying, "I had to put the date in" later. White's article omitted this vignette.

Jackie Kennedy's interview may have been the most notable action taken by a First Lady in modern American history. It defined her husband's admin-istration, her husband's life, and their decade of marriage. The interview was excruciatingly intimate—so much so that White kept the transcript private until 1995, after he had died and Mrs. Kennedy had been dead for a year. At the same time, it was exceedingly influential. Even after revelations of CIA assassination plots, Mafia ties, Bay of Pigs incompetence, girlfriends galore, pill-popping, presidential temper tantrums, and un-First-Lady-like petu-lance, the Kennedy myth endures. It is precisely this endurance that under-lines what First Couples best produce: *image,* not political substance.

Today, even as Camelot continues to bewitch millions, it symbolizes America's moral bankruptcy to many others. The rejection of the presidential couple is rooted in the unelected nature of the First Lady's position and in-tensified by the fact that in the three decades following Kennedy's murder, the storybook values went awry. Ultimately, *Camelot* recreated the story of the Garden of Eden, offering a morality tale wherein a bad marriage de-stroyed utopia, as Queen Guinevere's illicit love for Sir Lancelot ruined the kingdom. Not only did millions in the World War II generation fail to fulfill the conventional ideals, their deviations invalidated the standards. The "we" generation spawned the "me" generation.

World War II forged an unprecedented sense of national unity, but it also unleashed powerful forces that would buffet the White House—the new keystone of American political culture. Good old-fashioned American values clashed with the egalitarian march of progress. As Americans' cultural consensus shattered, the White House—the people's home—became the focus of much anxiety. Modern American politics featured many King Arthurs sidetracked by their love for a woman or too many women, from Jack Kennedy to Gary Hart to Bill Clinton. There were also many Guineveres caught in the crossfire between personal desires and political demands, between their own needs and their husbands'.

Looking back, "the Sixties" would become a convenient marker for the many changes women experienced that actually began during World War II. As men and women renegotiated the fundamental principles of their lives, they looked to their leading national icons, the First Couple. In this revolutionary era, the always potent mix of sex and power proved particularly volatile. The elegant parsing each American couple did in private did not translate easily onto the national stage. Betty Ford, Nancy Reagan, and Hillary Rodham Clinton, among others, were polarizing figures far more controversial than their husbands—lavishly praised or pilloried for what they revealed about modern American womanhood.

More often than not, Presidents and First Ladies tried to reflect back what they perceived to be the present consensus when they would have been more successful conjuring up the past. Gradually, many liberals recognized what many conservatives had long argued, that "values matter most" and that a preoccupation with individual rights and liberation undermines community. These realizations, along with the conservative revolution of the 1980s and the long-standing republican fear of untrammeled power, doomed the vision of the egalitarian presidential couple. Even as individual political couples felt compelled to organize their lives in modern ways, most of their constituents demanded politicians who represented the old-fashioned American home.

To the extent that Camelot retold the story of Adam and Eve, it should have warned the First Couples—and especially the First Lady—to avoid overreaching. Despite all the changes that transformed modern America, presidential couples remained imprisoned by tradition. Historically, the ladies of America had great power to raise their children, run their homes, and even reform American politics as what Progressive women called "housekeepers for the nation." Nevertheless, American women, particularly upper-class ladies, had rigidly circumscribed roles. First Ladies similarly had vast power and clear limits. Their very proximity to power and unelected status compelled them to tread softly. The couples who violated acceptable bound-aries triggered great controversy, culminating in the rejection of the Carter, Reagan, and Clinton co-presidencies.

The Kennedys' Camelot showed what the American First Couple could be: a moral unifying force, celebrating America's elected king and his consort queen, exemplifying America the beautiful. The Roosevelts' tenure antici-pated what the American presidency would be: an effective focal point for a powerful nation-state and an institution barraged by competing interest groups, contradictory expectations, and cynical reporters wherein America the beautiful warred with America the dysfunctional—and the second most powerful person was unhired and unfireable. It is easy to understand why the First Couple could go astray in the confusion; why presidents would assign political tasks to their spouses, why the spouses would misinterpret the media demands and the feminist desires, and why both members of the couple would be swept up by change and blind to the continuities. Perhaps, after the Carters, Reagans, and Clintons learned their lessons the hard way, future couples will prove better students of history. But history's lessons are com-plex. Even as they pioneer the new millennium, Americans remain culturally conservative; even as the temptations to forge an equal White House part-nership continue to grow, the institutional limitations will not die.

1

"JUST THE WIFE OF THE PRESIDENT"

On the Trumans, Privacy, and Gentility

On October 1, 1945, Congressman Adam Clayton Powell fired off a telegram to President Harry S. Truman: "REQUEST IMMEDIATE ACTION ON YOUR PART IN THE SITUATION OF MY [wife] HAZEL SCOTT PIANIST BEING BARRED FROM CONSTITUTIONAL HALL BECAUSE SHE IS A NEGRO." A Harlem Democrat, Powell was challenging segregation in the nation's capital. He had encouraged his wife to book her Washington, D.C., debut at Constitution Hall, run by the Daughters of the American Revolution. Six years earlier, the DAR had barred Marian Anderson from singing there, prompting Eleanor Roosevelt's resignation from the organization. Now, Congressman Powell decided, the time had come to test the Roosevelts' successors.

Ten days later, Powell raised the stakes. He had heard that Truman's wife, Bess Wallace Truman, would be attending a DAR tea. Powell begged Mrs. Truman to follow Mrs. Roosevelt's example by boycotting the tea. He wired to her, saying, "If you believe in 100 percent Americanism you will publicly denounce the DAR's action." Powell sent a similar message to the President.

Powell had only been in Washington since January. He had never met the President or the First Lady. Those who knew the Trumans could not have been surprised by the couple's reactions to Powell's attempt to impose modern political obligations on the First Lady. Bess Truman was no Eleanor Roosevelt.

I

The Powell controversy unfolded against a backdrop of Bess Truman's distaste for politics, Harry Truman's guilty devotion to Bess, and Americans' changing attitudes about race, women, and presidential leadership. As their daughter, Margaret, explained, Bess "decided she was not going to let a congressman tell her where she could have a cup of tea." Bess was a genteel woman anxious for privacy. Harry knew she would not be rude to score political points.

The President's aides were worried. The controversy upset the Democrats' uneasy alliance linking blacks, liberals, and Southern whites. It also pitted the Trumans against the Roosevelts. Eben Ayers, a press aide, remembered a "lengthy discussion" the morning of October 12 that continued until "the President made it clear" that Bess "was irked at the request and the controversy and was going anyway and that he could do nothing about it."

That day, both the President and the First Lady responded to Powell. Truman championed civil rights—within limits. He affirmed that "racial discrimination" should not be a "state policy." But the President could not interfere "in the management or policy of a private enterprise such as the one in question" (he was too cautious to name the DAR directly). State-sponsored racism was unacceptable; private discrimination was out of reach.

Bess sidestepped civil rights questions to defend her privacy and gentility. Her response demonstrated the graceful style she learned from her mother. Bess pointed out to Powell "that the invitation to which you refer was extended and accepted prior to the unfortunate controversy which has arisen." A lady never addressed the details of any unpleasantness; using circumspection and the passive voice avoided confrontation. She added, "Personally I regret that a conflict has arisen for which I am in nowise responsible." Still, she deplored "any action which denies artistic talent an opportunity to express itself because of prejudice against race or origin."

Mrs. Truman attended the tea. To arrive on time, she abandoned her husband during a matinee. Newspapers the next day pictured Mrs. Truman entering the Sulgrave Club like a small-town aristocrat with an elaborate corsage, a big necklace, and a fancy hat. When a reporter asked whether she would accept future invitations from the DAR, she huffed, "Why not?"

Reporters enjoyed seeing, "MRS. TRUMAN IN SPOTLIGHT MUCH AGAINST INCLINATION," as a *Denver Post* headline said. Congressman Powell and Miss Scott were less amused. They had no patience for genteel distinctions between public and private. Scott claimed that Mrs. Truman "gives sanction" to "reactionary and vicious" actions. Powell responded to President Truman graciously but argued that Constitution Hall's tax exemption made it "a public institution." Turning to the First Lady, Powell concluded that her "excuse

. . . doesn't bear up when compared with Mrs. Eleanor Roosevelt's" actions in 1939. He jabbed: "From now on, Mrs. Truman is the last lady."

Harry Truman exploded. The Missouri farmer who would integrate the military with one presidential order blasted Powell in a staff meeting as "that damn nigger preacher." Truman barred Powell from the White House, including the annual reception for members of Congress. The President also channeled Harlem's patronage through Powell's rival, Congressman William L. Dawson of Chicago.

Unwittingly, the Trumans had played into Powell's hand. They ignited a nationwide debate about segregation. Newspapers in the 1940s were still provincial, more likely to cover the Junior Jaycees' backing of a bond election than a feud over the First Lady's tea partners. The *New Orleans Times-Picayune*, for instance, ignored the incident. Other papers, including the *Washington Post*, treated it as a women's issue suited to the society page. Yet most American newspapers covered the story on October 12, and most treated the Trumans as heroes caught between Powell's rabble-rousing and the DAR's racism. The *Washington Evening Star*'s front page declared: "TRUMAN ASSAILS CONSTITUTION HALL RACIAL POLICY." The *Kansas City Star* defended the DAR's "American" right "to be foolish or narrow," while attacking Powell's boorish behavior as "the type of thing that retards progress toward improving race relations."

Passions seethed beyond the polite headlines and balanced editorials. Blacks and liberals denounced the DAR. Adam Clayton Powell exulted that the three leading candidates for mayor of New York agreed to address a protest meeting. Many liberals attacked the DAR's private status. As Powell noted, Constitution Hall enjoyed tax breaks. Congressman Emanuel Celler proposed revoking the DAR's congressional charter, mischievously suggesting that the bane of most liberals—the Committee on Un-American Activities—investigate the DAR for illustrating "the Hitler philosophy of *Herrenvolk* [a nation of masters] and *Sklavenvolk* [a nation of slaves]."

Celler's maneuvers outraged Southern congressmen, who were already fuming about Powell's insult to the First Lady. Congressman John Rankin of Mississippi had condemned the "communistic attacks" on the DAR and had defended Mrs. Truman as "one of the finest women who ever graced the White House." The assault on the DAR's tax exemption sent Rankin back into the well of the House, defending Washington's broadly accepted, hundred-year-old "policy of segregation." In the Senate, Theodore Bilbo of Mississippi defended "the patriotic and American stand of the DAR in refusing to let their hall be used as a boogie-woogie reception room for this jazz queen from the island of Jamaica."

Most liberals tried to avoid attacking Mrs. Truman as they attacked the DAR. One of the most prominent, Eleanor Roosevelt, was particularly uncomfortable. She could not ignore the crisis, but how could she condemn her successor? In her column "My Day," Mrs. Roosevelt, herself a lady, simply referred to "this recent controversy" and condemned the "agreement among all Theatre owners of the District of Columbia." She called on the DAR to "lead" the "glorious crusade" for desegregation.

Despite such graceful dodges, the controversy centered on the First Lady. The Committee of Catholics for Human Rights urged Mrs. Truman to resign from the DAR "because of its undemocratic, ungodly policy of race discrimination." Powell too kept up the pressure, suggesting that "the war hasn't helped a bit" in the fight against intolerance. "Even the President can't do anything about it. He hasn't even the power to control his wife."

In hundreds of letters swamping the White House, both supporters and critics placed Bess Truman at the heart of the fight. Most correspondents also agreed that Mrs. Truman's action "condone[d]" the DAR policy and revealed her "stand on the Negro situation." Female fans and critics treated the First Lady as their special representative. "The American public has come to regard the wife of the President of the U.S. as an example of the highest type of American womanhood," said one woman from Queens. "By accepting the DAR's invitation," Mrs. Truman "failed to uphold the[se] ideals." Other women believed that the First Lady fulfilled feminine ideals by minding her own business. "Thank God for your independent mind, it does us women proud, and your womanly attitude in being JUST THE WIFE of the President, and mother to a wonderful daughter, and not trying to enter politics," a Brooklynite wrote.

Blacks, wives of World War II veterans, and northeastern ethnics, especially Jewish women, led the attack against the First Lady. Mrs. Charlotte Rosenthal of New Jersey, the wife of a veteran, said: "All this horror was brought about because when Hitler came into power, the *safe* people like you—Middle West non-Catholics who never have to fear persecution . . .—gave the same kind of smug lip service that you give." Others suggested that Mrs. Truman take tea with Mrs. Roosevelt instead of the DAR ladies. Eleanor Roosevelt's ministry to previously disenfranchised groups, along with their own experiences during the war, emboldened these citizens to make demands both on the new First Lady and on American society. The First Lady, it appeared, was no longer a free agent; she belonged to the American people.

Most of these obligations were cast in terms of Bess Truman as First Lady alone. Only rarely did someone refer to "the Trumans" or the "administration," as if the latter belonged to both of them. Bess Truman was seen as someone who contributed to the presidency and the nation, but operated independently.

While Bess Truman's critics were predominantly northerners, most of her defenders came from the South and the West. They labeled Mrs. Truman a private citizen who was free to associate with whomever she pleased. Other defenders, especially women, praised the First Lady's gentility. "At last we have a lady in the White House," one cheered. "One has to live up to an approved standard in ideals," another wrote.

Many women rejoiced that Bess Truman was *not* Eleanor Roosevelt. Mrs. Truman's passivity was dignified, while Mrs. Roosevelt's many activities were "cheap" and "ridiculous," either too political or too commercial. A neighbor from Kansas City saw the difference between the two First Ladies reflected in their families. Writing to Bess, she hoped "that you stay out of strikes and picket lines and continue to make a home for your family. I'm sure if you continue as you have begun the country will take a new pride in the first family, and we will not hear of divorces and scandals etc. about them."

Many of the "pro" letters degenerated into ugly attacks on Powell or his race. Nevertheless, they received the same ladylike acknowledgment from Mrs. Truman's secretary. Often lacking the subtlety of political speeches or newspaper reports, these letters showed how the idea of gentility and the lines between public and private in the United States were linked to the problem of race. Racial discrimination was not a wart on the body politic that could be detached easily, as so many liberals believed. Rather it was a cancer that could only be removed painfully, with some powerful toxins that would generate their own dangerous side effects. Bess Truman's world of grace was also a world of intolerance; one had developed with the other.

This incident demonstrated the extent to which the First Lady's job description had changed. With the president beginning to tackle complex personal issues such as racial discrimination, his personal life would come under greater scrutiny—his personal example would become more relevant. Presidents and their wives would not be able to crusade for freedom in public while perpetuating the problem in private. Nor could First Ladies hide as easily behind a frilly veil of feminine prerogative to avoid the challenges of modern politics.

The criticisms did not sway Bess Truman. When her friend Mary Paxton Keeley urged her to leave the DAR, Bess would have none of it. "I agree with you that the DAR is dynamite at present but I'm not 'having any' just now," she wrote. "But I was plenty burned up with the wire I had from that——in NY."

Bess was too ladylike to fill in the blank, but her friends and family noticed her fury. Her daughter, Margaret, later wrote: "Much damage was done, not to race relations but to the Truman partnership. There could not have been a worse beginning to her first ladyship, as far as Bess was concerned." The controversy intensified her desire to avoid reporters and escape the White House as often as she could.

The skirmish over the DAR escalated into what one reporter called "the battle of the women." Frustrated women reporters began sniping at Mrs. Truman, pronouncing themselves "profoundly disappointed" with the uncommunicative First Lady. Readers and some columnists rallied to Mrs. Truman's defense. "For Heaven's sake, is it not a relief to NOT hear the First Lady talk—especially about herself?" one reader wrote. Unwittingly, Bess Truman had tapped into a broad public frustration with Eleanor Roosevelt and with an expanding definition of news that celebrated personality and trivia over politics and substance.

The Trumans would not and could not imitate the Roosevelts. The Roosevelts dwarfed them. The Roosevelts were richer, more imperious, more energetic, more famous, and more controversial. Franklin Roosevelt was a barrel-chested playboy with an infectious smile; Harry Truman was a pint-sized, bespectacled, nondescript midwestern burgher partial to blue-serge suits. Eleanor Roosevelt would need twenty Army trucks to move out of the White House; Bess Truman barely filled one truck.

Rather than competing with his predecessor, Truman played the farm boy. Truman replaced the politician's characteristic litany of success with his own distinctive litany of failure. His resumé became his mantra, an easy way of marveling that he, Harry Truman, occupied the Oval Office. His bankrupt haberdashery became the most famous men's clothing store in history. "Well, what is wrong with being the average man?" he asked. "I say it's good." "After a diet of caviar, you like to get back to ham and eggs," Truman's aide Harry Vaughan remarked.

As the Powell affair demonstrated, the expectations of elite Washington—including the press corps—diverged from the bulk of the population. President Roosevelt had played well to both worlds, though Eleanor had not. Measures of popularity in those days were crude, but it was clear that she was most popular among liberals and intellectuals. Truman, by contrast, saw himself as the "people's President" in the populist traditions of Andrew Jackson and Theodore Roosevelt. He would estimate that "the lobbyists" infesting wartime Washington represented "fifteen million," leaving the remaining "150 million" with "only one man, the President." More quietly, Bess would take a traditional, contrasting position to Eleanor's activism—and emerge more popular and less troublesome.

Despite her wealthy background, Bess Wallace Truman helped prove that Harry Truman was a man of the people. The simple, gray-haired matron with a pronounced chin and soft eyes had remained so obscure as the vice president's wife that reporters were caught with "their pencils down" when Roosevelt died. A Democratic party press release offered a folksy biography of Mrs. Truman that mistakenly identified her as a former teacher. Reporters played the Cinderella angle, sending Bess from "her preferred cloak of obscure housewife" in a "maidless" five-room, $120-a-month apartment on Connecticut Avenue to her "new and glamorous role . . . as First Lady" in the White House. Most profiles portrayed Bess as a "model wife" devoted to her husband and daughter. Some described her as "trim" while others found her "plump," but all found her perfectly average. This happy homemaker knew her place. "A career for myself? Never! I have the only one I want," she said. Still, Bess was a political wife; she "helped her husband in his work . . . in addition to keeping house." Bess demurely minimized her role, but Harry insisted, "She is invaluable to me."

Such profiles reinforced the impression of both Trumans as "100 percent Americans." Harry was a real man, direct, hardworking, and disciplined; Bess was a real lady. Headlines proclaiming "NEW FIRST LADY: NO SEEKER OF SPOTLIGHT" set Bess up as the welcome antidote to Eleanor Roosevelt, whose outspokenness and unconventional family had annoyed millions.

Reporters delighted in the romantic story of the Trumans' lifelong love affair. The Trumans were "childhood sweethearts" who met in Sunday school. "I cannot remember when my husband was not part of my life. . . . He was my only beau," Bess had said.

The story the Trumans fed and the reporters spread was compelling, but inaccurate. Born in Lamar, Missouri, in 1884, Harry was the scion of one of Jackson County's wealthiest farming families. His family moved north to Independence when he was six. Harry grew up in houses large enough to accommodate his family of five and a family of servants. Old "Four Eyes" Truman was bookish, a "mama's boy," and not very popular with most lads. His knowledge and amiability earned him some status on the schoolyard (and probably saved him from many beatings), but it was lonely being a self-confessed "sissy."

As part of their effort to give Harry some "town schooling," his Baptist parents sent him to a Presbyterian Sunday school, where "a little blue-eyed, golden-haired girl" mesmerized him. He sat behind Bess Wallace from the sixth grade until high school graduation. "She never noticed me," he claimed, although "on occasion" she let him carry her books home.

Bess Wallace was from a prominent family that disdained the Trumans. According to Bess Wallace's childhood friend, Mary Paxton Keeley, the Presbyterian Wallaces were more "top-drawer" than the Baptist Trumans because of religion, not class. So Harry's pursuit of Bess is not a tale of love across the railroad tracks. Rather, it is a reminder of the prejudices that divided many small towns in the supposedly monolithic world of white-bread America. Bess's mother, Margaret Elizabeth Gates Wallace, was known as "the queenliest woman Independence ever produced." Bess's father, David Wallace, was the grandson of the town's first mayor, but he had to rely on his wealthy father-in-law to foot the bills.

Bess grew up as a charming mix of tomboy and town belle. As she mastered tennis, baseball, and mumbletypeg (a game of flipping a pocketknife into wood), she learned how to act like a proper young lady. In all the retrospective glances at this woman who became so famous, no hints emerged of impropriety. But trouble lurked beneath the sculpted veneer. David Wallace was bankrupt; as he took refuge in alcohol, his wife retreated into her own shell of propriety. Dinner was always served on time, with proper etiquette and beautiful linens to smooth over family fissures.

Early one Wednesday morning in June 1903, when Bess was eighteen, David Wallace woke up, dressed, took a revolver, walked into the bathroom, and shot himself. Mary Paxton found Bess wandering outside, silently clenching her fists. Mrs. Wallace hustled her family off to Colorado Springs for a year. On their return the Wallaces moved into the fourteen-room mansion of Bess's maternal grandfather.

Bess's refusal to talk about the suicide—and her fear of such a discussion—was so great that it would repeatedly threaten Harry Truman's political career. Truman almost refused the vice-presidential nomination in 1944 to protect his wife. After the convention, an aunt told the Trumans' daughter that Bess feared reporters would disclose how "your grandfather died." The twenty-year-old Margaret thought he had died of a heart attack. When she asked her mild-mannered father about it, Harry grabbed her and barked, "Don't you *ever* mention that to your mother."

As the Wallaces struggled to rebuild their lives, the Trumans were suffering as well. John Truman speculated his fortune away on grain futures in 1901, losing almost forty thousand dollars. In 1902 the family moved to Kansas City, and Harry went to work rather than college. By 1906 John Truman and his flock had retreated to his in-laws' farm, a reversal that led to a perpetual feeling of financial inadequacy. Truman's quest would prove that there are none so poor as those who once were rich.

Their respective traumas derailed Bess Wallace and Harry Truman just as they were entering the adult world. It would take almost two decades for either to get back on track. Now, when Harry visited his hometown, he must have felt doubly excluded—he was a farm boy stuck in Grandview. His cousins, the Nolands, lived across from the Gates mansion on North Delaware Street. One summer evening in 1910, Harry jumped at a chance to return a cake plate to the Wallaces. This visit lasted two hours, well beyond the obligatory politeness. Harry asked Bess if he could call again, and she agreed. When Harry returned to his cousins, he confessed his ulterior motives. "Well, I saw her," he exulted, warning his cousins that he would be making the four-hour trip to Independence more often.

Bess kept Harry on the defensive at first. Harry filled his letters to her with self-deprecating comments, calling himself a "clodhopper," "empty head[ed]," and unworthy of both her letters and her friendship. Decades before Woody Allen was born, Harry Truman played the schlemiel. He tried to laugh away his insecurity. In so doing, he sustained the long-standing frontier tradition whose great practitioner, Abraham Lincoln, was one of Harry's heroes.

To woo his love to the farm, Harry built a tennis court, then suffered as it became overgrown from underuse. When Bess promised to visit Grandview, then canceled, Harry could barely contain his disappointment. "I really worked all day Sunday getting that court ready for you," he wrote after one such blow. "We also had a supply of watermelons on hand."

The serious farmer and the athletic town belle made a curious duo. He slaved all week, struggling with mounting debts, uncooperative workmen, and the weather. In the meantime, Bess played tennis, socialized with her friends, and tended to her family. Harry's life seemed the more onerous, but he was reasonably satisfied. Bess led a life that seemed superficially fun but emotionally was more trying. She would rarely talk about their long courtship after they married.

In 1914, as Bess began to look kindly on Harry's repeated offers of marriage, calamity struck. John Truman died. Harry feared that he would never leave the farm. He felt guilty that he had encouraged his girl to "become engaged" and then did not "follow up such things with the proper sort of jewelry," but he was "$12,500 worse off than nothing." On the farm Harry was not as "rugged" as his brother or father; in town, he was neither athletic nor wealthy. Harry saw himself as "a guy with spectacles and a girl mouth." With his head full of adventure stories, he dreamed of "doing the Sir Lancelot" to justify Bess's love. This combination of masculine insecurity, financial pressure, and hungering for glory could have been a recipe for lifelong frustration. World War I, however, gave Harry a chance to break free of the farm, prove himself, and justify his best girl's love.

When Harry Truman enlisted, he felt "that I was a Galahad after the Grail and I'll never forget how my love cried on my shoulder when I told her I was going. That was worth a lifetime on this earth." Harry thrived in the Army, while Bess pined for him. For the first time in their seven-year courtship, Harry was the reassuring one, and Bess was on the defensive. Since her father's death, Bess had tried to avoid being dependent on a man. The discovery that she was indeed so reliant, and that he could end up in a grave in France, must have been devastating.

In September 1918, seventeen years after enrolling in the National Guard, a year after joining the Army, and weeks before the war ended, Captain Truman finally got his first taste of battle. "It really doesn't seem possible that a common old farmer boy could take a battery in and shoot it on such a drive," he exulted. Truman's encounter with death emboldened him. After hundreds of letters he finally wrote: "I'll never cease loving you."

Harry Truman came home on May 3, 1919. On June 28, Bess Wallace married him in Trinity Episcopal Church on North Liberty Street. The sissy bookworm was now a farmer and a fighter; the tomboy was a lady. Still, within their marriage Harry would continue to be the bookish one, the sentimental one, the talkative one, while Bess continued to be the athletic one, the tough one, the silent one.

The newlyweds happily joined in America's march toward postwar normalcy. For all its uniqueness, their relationship conformed to the modern ideal of the "companionate marriage" rather than a patriarchal arrangement of separate spheres, with the wife serving the husband. Harry never understood why they had waited so long to get married—and Bess never explained it. They ignored the past and made theirs a typical, democratic love story between a rough-hewn country boy and a refined city girl.

II

The Trumans lived the life of the town grandees. The local paper covered Bess Wallace Truman's social activities; Harry Truman joined various civic, fraternal, and veterans' organizations. After the tumult of the war, Bess was happy to return to the calm rhythms of life along North Delaware Street, with the family dinners, the club meetings, and quiet evenings on the porch with Harry. Harry and Bess kidded each other a lot. Typically, Harry needled "Bessie" until she stopped him with a sardonic remark or a piercing glare.

Truman's failure in his quest for a fortune is familiar, but his success is often overlooked. Even after his haberdashery failed, Truman remained confident that he could settle his debts. Harry would not sacrifice his reputation in the cloistered world of the Missouri elite for temporary financial relief. Truman's sense of his own standing as well as his ability to think long term would guide him throughout his political career.

In 1922, Truman ran for Western Judge of the Jackson County Court as an ally of Tom Pendergast, the boss of the Kansas City machine. Harry had always dabbled in politics. His emergence as a professional politician at the age of thirty-eight seemed a natural step to the Nolands and other friends. The Pendergasts were not in the business of propping up failures. They turned to Truman because of his pioneer roots, his war record, and his profile as a young leader. After becoming presiding judge in 1926, Harry brought to Jackson County streamlined budgets, refurbished courthouses, and modern roads. Although he did secure government jobs for his brother and brother-in-law, he refused to allow anyone to steal from the taxpayers—including his patrons.

Politics fulfilled Truman's sense of *noblesse oblige* while allowing him to fraternize with buddies. In his dozens of fraternal organizations, Harry Truman found the camaraderie he missed as a boy. He attended countless meetings, dinners, and yearly military encampments. There he mastered a plain-speaking style, cussing and acting gruff—if no ladies were present.

Bess called many of Harry's fraternal activities "silly." However, she appreciated the need for separate activities and separate vacations; she too had an active social life and club life. While the fraternal organizations sought to escape the civilizing influence of women through ritualistic parties lubricated with booze, the women's clubs celebrated domesticity.

As Harry built up his political career, Bess worked on establishing a home. Bess suffered two miscarriages, one in the spring of 1920 and another during Harry's 1922 campaign for county judge. Margaret was born in 1924, just months before Harry lost an election and spent two years pursuing various financial schemes. She grew up in a house full of doting adults. Harry played the pushover. He always had an extra quarter for "my girl" and was satisfied as long as she was "as good as she's nice looking." Bess, prodded by her mother, was the disciplinarian. "Don't spank the baby too much!" Harry, the "sentimental" one, would tease.

Just as Harry oscillated between a tough masculine exterior and a softer feminine interior, Bess alternated between appearing approachable and being formidable. She enjoyed old friends and a good joke, but she could be as haughty as her mother. Many of Harry's closest friends "never" considered calling her anything but "Mrs. Truman." Bess often rebuked Harry, who would backpedal, apologize, and only on occasion mischievously ignore "the Boss." Harry was a powerful politician dispensing millions of dollars at work, but a henpecked husband and son-in-law at home. Harry lacked the money that might have freed him from his mother-in-law, who never approved of her daughter's "downward" marriage.

Bess grudgingly accepted Harry's career choice. She guarded her privacy and her prerogatives as a lady, but she also advised her husband and proved adept in sniffing out men who could injure him. In 1934, when Pendergast designated Truman to run for the Senate, Harry readily agreed. Bess feared for her privacy.

In Washington, Bess entered an exclusive world filled with teas, receptions, clubs, and formal calls. Despite the "warmth and hospitality" she found in this city of nomads, she missed home. Harry was busier than ever, balancing statewide responsibilities with the full legislative burdens of supporting Franklin Roosevelt's New Deal. Together with their young daughter, the Trumans were "cooped up" on the upper floor of a small apartment at 3106 Tilden Street. Bess decided to go home to Independence as often as she could; she took Margaret for the first of their lengthy stays in June 1935.

Harry hated the arrangement. He felt "like a lost soul." Bess missed Harry too. Juggling two homes was exhausting. In anticipation of one trip to Independence, Bess explained to Harry's cousin Ethel Noland, "I am so anxious to see all of you—have been for ages—but how I dread it. It was terribly hard not to go back with Harry in May." Bess occasionally adjusted her schedule when his pleas became frantic, but she usually tried to stay as long as possible at her home in Independence.

On the job, Harry relied on Bess. He trusted her savvy with job holders, and he praised her as a "genius" at handling reporters. Bess became Harry's favorite ghostwriter and the disciplinarian in his Senate office. When she was away, he kept her informed of events in the Senate. He often used his letters to her as an opportunity to clarify his thoughts—although he rarely asked for advice. She acted as his eyes and ears at home.

The periodic family exodus to Independence heightened the separation between Harry's male-centered political world and his female-centered domestic life. When Bess and Margaret left Harry on his own, he joined other Washington widowers in parties, card games, and political events. Harry was so wary of getting into trouble, or incurring Bess's wrath, that he avoided women as much as possible. Reathel Odum, who worked for Truman in the Senate, recalled that the senator was uncomfortable around his female aides. "He never did swear in front of us girls," she insisted. When she brought him a message at his desk, "He'd twist his ring and look up at you and kind of hurry you out. . . . There were only four women in his life, Mrs. Truman, Margaret, his mother, and his sister, and the rest of us were just office workers."

During Harry's brutal primary reelection battle against Governor Lloyd Stark in 1940, Bess and Margaret performed "untold and yeoman service." Bess urged Harry to keep the fight clean, fed him one-liners, and tried to tone down his language, but publicly she remained silent. Good political wife that she was, Bess said she wanted more women in politics. She, however, was content with "seeing the senator is provided with good meals and comfortable surroundings when he's at home, as well as looking after the needs and desires of Margaret."

During Truman's second term, both became more enmeshed in Washington. Harry rose to prominence as a "senator's senator." Bess became so helpful—and money became so tight—that he would put her on the payroll. Harry chaired the Special Committee to Investigate the National Defense Program, popularly known as the Truman Committee; now his purview was national. With her husband traveling so much, Bess became more involved in the running of the office. Harry Truman considered his prominence a joint achievement. "But Mommy, I've wanted so badly to make good in the Senate so you and my sweet baby wouldn't be ashamed of me," he told Bess in May 1942. Two months later he swooned, "When a man gets the right kind of wife, his career is made—and I got just that."

By the time the 1944 Democratic convention began in Chicago, Harry Truman offered a plausible alternative as vice president to the controversial incumbent Henry Wallace: Southern but progressive, pro–New Deal but thrifty. Harry's name had been bandied about for weeks. Truman understood that with an ailing sixty-three-year-old polio victim heading the ticket, the nomination could send him into the White House.

As early as 1943 Harry had dismissed a vice-presidential draft, telling one colleague "that I had only recently become a Senator and that I wanted to work at it for about ten years." In early 1944 he explained to others, "I've talked it over with Bess, and we've decided against it. I've got a daughter and the limelight is no place for children." He told yet another friend that he could not afford to run. Finally, he told the party chairman Robert E. Hannegan that the post was too minor.

Tom Evans, a drugstore magnate from Kansas City, recalled Harry explaining that "I've had the boss on the payroll in my Senate office and I'm not going to have her name drug over the front pages of the paper and over the radio." Herein, Harry was telling his friend half the truth: he did not want publicity for his wife, but more because of her father's suicide than the Senate salary. Evans estimated "a dozen senators and fifty congressmen" had their wives on the payroll.

Harry probably would have sacrificed his ambitions for Bess, but he preferred not to. Despite Harry's "every effort," President Roosevelt ordered him to run for vice president. After Harry was nominated, the Trumans needed ten policemen to wade through the crowd. Bess snapped: "Are we going to have to go through this all the rest of our lives?" Harry was silent.

The 1944 campaign justified some of Bess's worries. Although the press ignored the suicide, Margaret, unbeknownst to Bess, discovered the truth about her grandfather's death. In another indignity, *Life* magazine photographers invaded the Gates mansion. The resulting article embarrassed Bess by declaring the house "gloomy Victorian" and portraying the rugs as "well-worn." Reporters also inquired about the $4,500 Bess earned each year from the Senate. Rumors had it that Harry hired Bess so they could meet their 1942 tax bill. Henry Luce of *Time* began to call her "Payroll Bess," prompting Truman to start spelling the venerable editor's last name "L-o-o-s-e." "Certainly my wife works for me. And she earns every cent I pay her," Harry said. "She is my chief advisor. I never write a speech without going over it with her. I have to do that because I have so much to do and I never make any decisions unless she is in on them. She takes care of my personal mail."

After the election, the Trumans ended up in the eye of the Washington social storm. Yet they lived simply, and their telephone number remained listed. Margaret remembered the vice presidency as a happy time, but Bess resented the impositions on her time, and Harry felt he had too much time on his hands. He had minimal contact with President Roosevelt. Writing one evening at the end of March 1945 to Ethel Noland, Bess sketched out a typical domestic scene, with each member of the Truman clan off in a different direction: "Marg has gone to a picture show and Harry to a poker party. Mother is practically asleep in her chair—so it's very peaceful." That peace would not last.

III

When they entered the White House, the Trumans became American icons. Millions questioned Harry's qualifications. Still, millions more welcomed an "old-fashioned" President and First Lady. World War II had threatened the simple, turn-of-the-century way of life Harry and Bess exemplified. The GI Joes wanted to ape the doughboys. From coast to coast, from newlyweds like the George Bushes to longtime partners like the Lyndon Johnsons, couples looked to the Trumans as models, and built lives around the example Harry and Bess set.

The Trumans missed their privacy. "It is a peculiar American complex to want to know what their President eats, how he sleeps, when he gets up, what meat he prefers etc.," Truman complained. Only from the perspective of the intrusive 1990s would the Trumans appear to have it easy. Harry could not walk to the bank without creating a traffic jam on Pennsylvania Avenue; when his motorcade made a necessary pit stop, the proprietor would put up a sign saying "President Truman Stopped Here." Bess could not prepare a menu without worrying about the example it set amid wartime shortages, while Margaret could not go on a date without prompting talk of a White House wedding. When his mother visited and saw the hoopla she yelled: "Harry, if you are President, why can't you shoo all these people away?"

Outsiders were not the only ones disrupting the Trumans' lives. On becoming President and First Lady, both Harry and Bess became subject to pressures that changed their partnership. Bess could no longer serve as Harry's primary adviser or supervise his small staff. Each was sucked into a different vortex of institutional responsibilities and personal aides.

As President, Harry was commander in chief of more than twelve million soldiers and guardian of a $200 billion economy. His days were filled with policy briefings, formal meetings, official ceremonies. He signed his name an average of six hundred times a day. To get the job done, Harry Truman had "a valet, four ushers, five butlers, seven or eight secretaries, a dozen or so executive assistants, an assistant president—three of 'em in fact," as well as ten cabinet members and 3.8 million employees in the expanded executive branch he inherited from Roosevelt.

This presidential domain was almost exclusively male, just as Harry Truman liked. The ribaldry, the card playing, the stiff drinks at any hour "because it is after 12 o'clock somewhere in the world" were part of the job. Truman used these activities to make friends and appease enemies, just as he used his colorful tongue to assert power. Such uncouth behavior was not appropriate in front of ladies, Truman believed; women therefore could not be around him while he worked.

As a reformed "sissy" always catering to strong women, Truman needed the respite from the "weaker" sex. Women seemed to bring out his vulnerability. Harry indulged his "sobsister" side in private, especially when writing letters. Otherwise, such emotions were too threatening to a macho politician trying to prove he was one of the boys.

Harry found it easy to divorce the two spheres. He would embrace his old Army buddies in public, or slap a crony on the back, but he would not touch women. He even kept his distance from his wife in public. When they went to the movies, Harry would reach for Bess's hand only after the lights were dimmed.

Two Harry Trumans emerged as President. The public Truman was temperamental and decisive, if anything overly rigid and verbally violent. He bombed Nagasaki after bombing Hiroshima, faced down Joseph Stalin, Douglas MacArthur, and Joe McCarthy, cussed a lot, and "gave 'em hell." The private Harry was sweet and loving, if anything too prone to self-doubt. This Truman called his wife "The Boss" or "Sweetie," delighted in his nonagenarian mother and his twenty-one-year-old daughter, never shouted at home, and was henpecked by his mother-in-law. Bess had learned to put up with the political Harry, partially by monitoring him. But she undoubtedly preferred the private version.

Bess was also swept up by institutional forces. Her staff included the chief usher, the social secretary, the housekeeper, and a bevy of clerks, typists, maids, and butlers. While running the White House, Bess also tended to a host of First Lady functions and tried to keep in touch with the folks back home.

Despite these demands, Bess's agenda was clear. She wanted to avoid the public and devote herself to her family and her Red Cross volunteering with the Senate Ladies Luncheon Club. Mrs. Truman would not emulate Mrs. Roosevelt. The White House news hens tried hardest to hold Bess Truman to Eleanor Roosevelt's standards. Many of these career women had languished in the pink ghetto of the society pages, reporting the static world of parasols, evening gowns, and teas. Knowing that a passive First Lady could deprive them of their ticket to the front page, the newswomen begged Mrs. Truman to keep the weekly press conferences and make some news.

On the train back from the Roosevelt burial, Bess cried: "I don't know what I'm going to do. . . . I'm not used to this awful public life." She asked Secretary of Labor Frances Perkins, "Do you think I ought to see the press?" Perkins said no, explaining that Mrs. Roosevelt had a "special talent for publicity." Relieved that she was not "going to be forced into this," Bess had Miss Perkins repeat her advice to the President. Harry agreed: "There's no reason why you should do it, Bess."

On becoming First Lady, Bess inherited some of Mrs. Roosevelt's aides, notably Edith Helm, who headed a nine-person White House social office. Most of these holdovers assumed that the First Lady would follow in Eleanor

Roosevelt's footsteps. They feared that an uncooperative First Lady might generate bad publicity. After three weeks in the White House, Bess allowed her aides to answer a few of the questions cascading into the White House. The answers confirmed Bess's plans to avoid press conferences and to maintain a normal life for herself and her daughter. A week and a half later, Bess "began her social life as First Lady," according to the *New York Times,* by appearing at a luncheon at the American Newspaper Women's Club.

These genuflections toward this most important constituency did not satisfy the newswomen. One reporter asked: "Mrs. Truman, how are we ever going to get to know you?" She replied, "You don't need to know me. I'm only the President's wife and the mother of his daughter!"

Eventually Mrs. Helm; Bess's secretary, Reathel Odum; the new press secretary, Charles Ross; and Ross's aide, Eben Ayers, arranged a tea for the newspaper women at the end of May. Mrs. Truman would answer questions for half an hour. "All questions relating to public affairs would be barred," Ayers noted in a memorandum, "and inquiries would be limited to personal and social matters."

Bess learned from Harry to be hostile to the profession but polite to the professionals. Truman understood that "in the long run," a president's "powers depend a good deal on his success in public relations." Bess claimed not to have "any use for" most of "the news gals," but she became friendly with Bess Furman of the *New York Times,* among others. Once Mrs. Truman sent a quartet of dismissive, one-sentence answers to questions Furman had submitted. With these curt replies from the First Lady came a more graceful postscript from the private lady: "Am hoping for the greatest success for your new book! Sorry to have kept you waiting for these few answers. Bess T."

Bess was more enthusiastic about her duties as the nation's "leading hostess." The First Lady attended hundreds of dinners, teas, and receptions, and she hosted dozens more. Washington society was Victorian. "Woman's real power in the political scene—with a handful of exceptions—is still where it always has been: behind the man," Doris Fleeson wrote in *McCall's* in 1951. Male politicians only tolerated "women who are feminine and well-bred in the best sense of those difficult words."

A permanent government of wealthy matrons wielded power through their parties. They monitored Truman Administration activities—just as they had those of previous administrations—to find desirable guests. In a city where money was less important than access to power, social cachet was a crucial currency. Invitations to the right parties could accelerate an official's ascent; prominence in the society page often paid dividends on the front page. Washington was no longer the small village it had been before the New Deal. Politicians needed opportunities to meet each other and form alliances.

The White House revolved in its own social orbit, occasionally intersecting Washington society. President Truman did not attend parties elsewhere, because he believed "nobody" could host a function with the president "except the president himself." The First Lady was queen of this social universe. The Trumans understood that "a White House dinner is rarely purely social." As diplomats, congressional leaders, bureaucrats, and other powers mingled, "quite a lot got said and done."

As chief clubwoman of the United States, the First Lady hosted receptions for hundreds of associations, and she spurned thousands of other offers. The centralization of power in the federal government prompted local clubs to confederate and establish national headquarters in Washington. Bess Truman sponsored dozens of such organizations, from the American Academy of Poets to the World Peace Garden Association.

Hosting was exhausting work. Bess came to dread attending "one of these dismal teas." "My arm is a wreck this A.M.," she moaned after a "horrible" reception where she shook 1,341 hands. The President estimated that he shook ten thousand hands in 1947, and "Bess was about five thousand ahead of me." He sighed: "I used to like to meet people. Now I almost hate the sight of 'em."

During each social function, the dowagers watched for any *faux pas* they could smooth over and gossip about later, while newspaper women looked for stories. The reporters pounced on any lapses that pegged Mrs. Truman as a hick. After Bess hosted a dinner party for the press at seven o'clock in November 1945, one newswoman sniffed that this "dinner hour [was] more favored in Independence, Mo. than in larger cities."

Newswomen now monitored the First Family around the clock, not only when the First Lady entertained. The Roosevelt family's antics, and the politicization of private life during the war, had expanded the definition of news. The White House became "America's most ornate, complex and inescapable gold fish bowl." Bess happily yielded the spotlight to her daughter and her mother-in-law. Indeed, many Americans vicariously adopted the President's daughter. They bombarded the Trumans with names of potential suitors and requests for a White House wedding. "We have watched with keen interest your lovely family circle, and admire the fatherly relationship existing between you and your charming daughter, Margaret," said a typical letter to Truman. "We . . . feel that it is about time our 'first daughter of the land' should treat us to a romance that would be of 'particular' interest to the citizens of the United States." Such requests prompted the *Saturday Evening Post* to describe Miss Truman as "an item of public property looking for a little privacy."

Harry Truman appreciated his family's help with the image-making burden. The war was not yet over, but the demobilization had begun. Germany surrendered, the Potsdam conference with Winston Churchill and Joseph Stalin was convened, Hiroshima and Nagasaki were bombed, Japan surrendered, and the United Nations was established at San Francisco—all in Truman's first six months.

For her part, Bess was fed up—and homesick. She disliked the pomp and pace of White House life. She worried about Margaret being dazzled by the dowagers who entertained the President's daughter in the style to which they wanted her to become accustomed. And she resented her exclusion from Harry's work.

Bess decided to spend the summer of 1946 in Independence with Margaret. Harry did not want to be abandoned, and so they resumed their argument from the Senate days. Their letters were unusually testy, but still affectionate and solicitous. Both felt guilty. Apologizing to his daughter that he would not be home for Christmas Eve of 1946, Truman admitted, "I have a job to do and it comes first. . . . Your pop, for some unknown reason, can't be a skirt even at the risk of making you and your mother unhappy." Both Harry and Bess understood that their choices hurt the other.

From the time Bess left Washington on June 1, Harry whined about his loneliness. Sometimes she consoled him but she often rebuked him, fearing that he was drunk one night when he called or worrying that he was spending too much money. Whenever his wife and daughter were away, Harry repeated the ritual he indulged in during his army service, his summer encampments, and his Senate days: He pestered his staff for the mail. When no letter arrived from his sweetheart, he would be cranky. If a letter arrived, he would smile, and his subordinates would breathe easily. Everyone who worked with Harry Truman knew that for all his macho pretenses, he was a sensitive man.

As President, Harry finally felt comfortable enough to reveal this softer side in public. He would often rush home to greet his wife when she returned from Missouri, and he would even peck her on the cheek. After a two-month separation, the President told reporters "that he had no other plans for the day than to sit at home 'and look at' Mrs. Truman." Coming from a man of his generation with an admittedly small "demonstrative bump," such exhibitions were all the more endearing.

In mid-July, Truman traveled for three weeks to the Potsdam conference held just outside Berlin. Harry noted in his diary that Bess "wasn't happy about my going to see Mr. Russia and Mr. Great Britain—neither am I." Rather than worrying about Stalin or Churchill or the postwar world, the President worried about his wife. "I'm sorry if I've done something to make you unhappy," Harry wrote Bess. "All I've ever tried to do is make you pleased with me and the world. I'm very much afraid I've failed miserably." Whenever Harry feared he was "in trouble" with Bess, he searched for gestures to prove he was worthy of her. After one transatlantic phone call from

Berlin to Independence, he confessed, "I spent the day . . . trying to think up reasons why I should bust up the conference and go home."

The same impulses that made Harry an honorable husband shaped many of his moves that first year in office. He resisted seduction, be it in the form of political cravings, subordinates' flattery, or wanton women. "It isn't polls or public opinion of the moment that counts," he would say. "It's right and wrong leadership—men with fortitude, honesty and a belief in the right that makes epochs in the history of the world." Watching Truman face down Roosevelt's disciples, congressional critics, and Japan's leaders, Americans learned not to underestimate their new President.

As Truman governed in Washington, Bess and Margaret tried to relax in Independence. Upon returning home, Margaret "relapsed into a seersucker dress and didn't do anything for a solid week." Things had changed, even at home. The house was "bedlam," Bess complained, and she was on a "merry-go-round" for most of the summer. Reporters marveled at how unassuming the Truman ladies were as they shopped, attended church, and visited friends. At the shops in the square, clerks bowed and scraped before the new First Lady. "None of this nonsense," she said. "I haven't changed. I'm still Bess Truman of Independence, Missouri." Longtime neighbors, of course, were on the lookout for any sign that the Trumans were "highhatting" them. While walking into the Kansas City Women's City Club that summer, Bess overheard a lady scoff: "Imagine a President's wife looking like that—wearing a seersucker of all things." Mrs. Truman, in a rare breach of decorum, snapped back, "And why shouldn't a President's wife wear seersucker if she wants to? Why should she look different from anyone else?"

Pressed by events, Bess hastened her return to Washington. She was with her husband the night before the United States dropped the second atomic bomb on Japan. Five days later, they celebrated V-J day, the official end of World War II. Harry and Bess waved and flashed V-for-victory signs at a crowd outside the White House. The celebrants shouted "President Truman forever!" Bess whispered, "Perish the thought."

For all her public domesticity, Bess was a formidable behind-the-scenes force when she chose to be. Early in the administration, Harry's Army buddy Eddie McKim suggested some changes in the First Lady's offices. According to Reathel Odum, Mrs. Truman asked her husband, "What was Eddie McKim doing over here? We run this ourselves." Roberta Barrows, the secretary to the appointments secretary, "was scared to death of Mrs. Truman." Barrows "got plenty of calls from Mrs. Truman, and they were sharp. . . . 'Don't tie the President up on a certain hour'—that kind of thing," especially in the afternoon, when Bess hoped to grab some hours with Harry.

Throughout 1945 Bess continued to scowl around the White House,

often exasperated with her husband about his many absences and her mani-
fold duties. Bess insisted on spending Christmas in Independence, and Harry
kept postponing his plans to join her and Margaret. Finally he flew through
a sleet storm so intense that all commercial aircraft had been grounded. The
New York Times labeled the flight "one of the most hazardous 'sentimental
journeys' ever undertaken by an American Chief of State." Harry arrived in
time for Christmas, feeling heroic. Bess, who hated airplanes and must have
been terrified, lambasted him, telling him he could have stayed in Washington for all she cared.

Two days later Harry had to jet back to Washington to face down his secretary of state. On the plane, the President wrote a blistering letter to his wife
and sent it. The next day, he called Margaret in Independence and told her to
intercept the letter at the post office. "It's a very angry letter and I've decided
I don't want her to see it. Burn it," he commanded. This family rift traumatized Margaret. "I had never before in my life concealed anything important
from my mother," she recalled. "I could not imagine why Dad had sent her
an angry letter."

That same day, December 28, a despondent President wrote Bess:

> You can never appreciate what it means to come home as I did the other
> evening after doing at least one hundred things I didn't want to do and have
> the only person in the world whose approval and good opinion I value look at
> me like I'm something the cat dragged in and tell me I've come in at last be-
> cause I couldn't find any reason to stay away. I wonder why we are made so
> that what we really think and feel we cover up?

Harry was doubting his abilities and could not cope with Bess's disapproval at
this critical time. "You, Margie and everyone else who may have any influence
on my actions must give me help and assistance; because no one ever needed
help and assistance as I do now. If I can get the use of the best brains in the
country and a little bit of help from those I have on a pedestal at home, the job
will be done." If not, Truman whined, all his critics would be proved right.

This letter was in Harry's desk when he died twenty-seven years later. It
was probably not sent, although Margaret called this "one of the most important letters of both their lives." Nevertheless, the impasse between the
Trumans ended. Margaret recalled that the First Lady returned to Washington "in a much improved mood. . . . The air had been cleared of her smol-
dering resentment."

The President had to subdue Secretary of State James Byrnes while still
reeling from his argument with Bess. Just after his return from the Moscow
Council of Foreign Ministers meeting, Byrnes had sent a vague report that
Harry felt treated the President like a disinterested business partner. Truman
also felt that Byrnes was "babying the Soviets." On December 29, Truman

ordered his secretary of state to report to the presidential yacht *U.S.S. Williamsburg*. Accounts vary about what transpired. Truman claimed he read Byrnes "the real riot act"; Byrnes described a "cordial meeting." Six years later, Truman produced a blistering letter he said he had read to Byrnes a week later. Byrnes said "such a letter was never sent to me, nor read to me." Truman's innate courtesy often prevented him from lacing into subordinates while his macho self-image led him to "vastly exaggerate" his "report of his bark," as Dean Acheson, then undersecretary of state, put it. Truman was having a turbulent Christmas week. It seems that being in the doghouse with his wife clouded the overwrought President's judgment—and his memory.

As the Trumans approached their first anniversary in the White House, the tension of the first nine months had eased. Harry was still overwhelmed with crises, and Bess was still protecting herself and Margaret from the press, the public, and the matrons, but they had settled into a routine.

Typically Bess awoke at seven o'clock, two hours after Harry. They had breakfast together at eight; by then, Harry had taken his morning stroll and spent an hour at the Oval Office. At nine o'clock, when he met with his staff, she worked on her correspondence and her official duties, supervising the housekeeping, planning social affairs, and conferring with the chief usher, the social secretary, the housekeeper, and her personal secretary.

One o'clock was lunchtime. If Bess did not have a women's luncheon, they ate together. Harry then napped briefly, and returned to the office until five or six. Bess reserved afternoons for personal matters. Between four and six Mrs. Truman often had a reception, up to three a day during the social season. If both Trumans were free, they sipped "dry Old Fashioneds" (bourbon garnished with orange slices) and chatted. At seven in the evening they ate dinner. If they had no engagements, and no concerts were available, the Trumans would read and gab all evening—he with a stack of papers, she with the sports pages or a mystery. Once or twice a week, Harry slipped out for a late-night stag poker game with old cronies and pet advisers.

White House staffers were struck by how much the "Three Musketeers" enjoyed being together as a family, listening to music, bantering, and occasionally indulging in a watermelon-seed fight. The domestics joked about the time Bess came back from Independence, and the next day one of the Trumans' bed slats was broken. The President strutted around all morning; Bess blushed.

The Trumans did not gossip much about politicians or talk politics. Bess demanded discretion. "If I expressed an unkind opinion of someone . . . I was summarily silenced," Margaret said. When he sat with his family, Harry wanted a break. "Besides," Margaret added, "a President's family is not his Cabinet."

By now, Bess had convinced her staff that she would not mimic Eleanor Roosevelt. Her aides devised protocols to insulate the First Lady. Form letters declined interviews because "Mrs. T does not make known her views on pending public questions." Another letter forwarded to the executive office the hundreds of requests from citizens, especially women, for help in navigating the bureaucracy. This "relieve[s] Mrs. Truman of appearing to intervene in any way in official matters," a memo explained. Such brush-offs were "the rule in the old days," the memo contended, adding, "it was only during Mrs. Roosevelt's time that the wife of the President dealt directly with the Departments."

By April 1946 Bess felt free to take one of her first White House initiatives—she hosted her Tuesday Bridge Club from Independence. The gesture was benign, midwestern, simple, gracious, and popular. Such peacetime indulgences were replacing wartime sacrifices. The four-day trip to Washington included a formal dinner, a sail on the presidential yacht, and a concert at Constitution Hall. Both the ladies from Independence and the ladies of the press delighted in this colorful exercise of what the *Pittsburgh Post-Gazette* called "small-townish behavior." Harry was cast as the long-suffering husband who "got out of the house for as long as he could," according to *Life*. He had gone off to dedicate the Roosevelt library in Hyde Park. "A public which wishes the President wouldn't put so many of his Missouri pals into office will love the way the First Lady invited these Missouri gals into her parlor," the *Post-Gazette* concluded.

That spring, Bess joined 644 other leading Americans in an emergency committee to fight hunger. Bess asked Harry to back the effort; he told her to take the lead. Before going home in June she signed a "Pledge of the American Housewife" to "conserve any and all foodstuffs which the starving millions of the world need." Bess pushed her staff to "set a good example," and as a result, steaks routinely offered to the White House by sycophantic restauranteurs were now returned. Bess preferred parading as "America's Number One Housewife" to messy confrontations about race.

Bess returned to Independence in 1946 reasonably satisfied and also proud of Margaret, who had just graduated from George Washington University. Once again Harry stayed in Washington, and once again he sent forlorn letters and counted the days until her return. As always, Bess lectured Harry from afar, and he alternated between pining for her and appeasing her. "It was nice to talk with you even if you did give me hell for making mistakes," he wrote after one tiff. "Looks like I'm a natural for making them." Still, as he would admit during yet another absence in November, "even when you give me hell I'd rather have you around than not."

Bess's belligerence betrayed her jumbled emotions. Nothing seemed right. In Washington, she would "get awfully tired . . . of all this hullabaloo," as she told Mary Keeley. At home, she told another friend, she rarely wanted to return to the White House, "but my conscience is beginning to really annoy me. Then, too, I'm getting tired of Harry's asking, *'When are you coming?'*"

Despite pining for his "sweeties," Harry rarely vacationed with them. In 1946 he took a two-week cruise. Thereafter he frequented Key West, Florida. He would spend 175 days of his Presidency at Key West. Whenever Bess saw him sagging she sent Harry south "alone," accompanied by his aides and dozens of "press boys." Bess explained to one reporter that husbands had "more fun" when they vacationed without their wives. The news hen concluded: "Bess Truman is a very wise little woman."

At his winter White House, Harry found the "absolute privacy" he craved and the camaraderie he relished. A thousand miles from his women, Truman could curse and hold marathon poker games, as he had in his encampments. Harry loved playing the bad boy, letting his beard grow out or lazing about in his bathing trunks.

Harry Truman's commitment to what a later generation would call "male bonding" was extreme. At one annual party, White House correspondents sang to the tune of "I'm Just Wild About Harry": "I go swimmin' with Harry/That's one thing Harry enjoys/'Cause there's no wimmin'/To spoil his swimmin'/He just invites the boys." Yet his letters suggest he missed Bess's support. Five days before her return in 1946, Harry told Bess some of his summertime troubles, including carping from liberal "crackpots," Secretary of Commerce Henry Wallace's insubordination, the prospect of losing Congress, tensions with Russia and China, "another round of strikes," and intra-Cabinet squabbling. "But you'll say, well you brought it on yourself and so I have no consolation whatever," he sighed.

By the summer of 1946, Truman was worrying about the 1948 election. Truman began juggling the conflicting roles of statesman and politician. He promulgated the Truman Doctrine and the Marshall Plan to check communism abroad while monitoring his election prospects at home. Truman was torn. His aide Clark Clifford recognized that Truman's "greatest ambition . . . was to get elected in his own right. . . . especially because he had been so criticized." His sense of duty also compelled him. Harry knew that Bess wanted to go home, and he too occasionally yearned to retire. "I'd be much better off if I were out or licked and I suspect you and Margie would be much more pleased," he told Bess. A January 1948 poll predicting his reelection upset Bess. Truman explained, Eben Ayers recalled, "that he did not think Mrs. Truman would like to see him beaten, but that she would give everything to be out of the White House."

Ultimately Truman decided to run, for "the welfare of the country." Characteristically, he described his political ambitions as contrary to his own desires. The small-town boy played the unwilling leader, as reluctant as George Washington had been.

Many Democrats questioned whether he should run, and they doubted he could win. Truman's popularity was sinking. Challengers ranging from former vice president Henry Wallace to General Dwight Eisenhower loomed. Bess hedged her bets. In 1947 she suggested that the family spend Christmas in the White House. If Truman did lose, Christmas of 1948 would be glum.

The upcoming campaign caused Bess to relax her fight against publicity. In the fall of 1947 she once again canceled formal dinners because of the European food emergency, but she promised to host more receptions. During the 1947–1948 social season, the Trumans entertained 31,336 people in groups ranging from 20 to 1,500. They accommodated 159,456 sightseers in July and August. Stung by widespread claims that she was frumpy, Bess also began losing weight and sprucing up her wardrobe. She was learning to play the celebrity game. In 1946 a reporter wondered why Margaret had not returned to Washington. "Better tell her" that Margaret was finishing voice lessons, Bess told Miss Odum. "God only knows what they may be saying. I'd prefer telling her it's *none of their d——business.*"

In late 1947, Bess finally allowed Mrs. Helm and Miss Odum to read answers to forty questions reporters had submitted. *Time* called the answers "terse, tart and revealing." Bess had twelve "no comments," refusing to discuss Margaret's critics, her pride in her husband, and whether she would make any speeches. She gave six "no" and seven "yes" answers, affirming that she followed the news, that she worried about Harry's safety, and that she was interested in White House history while denying that she would want Margaret to be First Lady, that she would have wanted a son to be president, or that she would want to be president. Other questions elicited one-sentence replies of no more than twenty words—saying, for example, that the most important qualities for a First Lady were "good health and a well-developed sense of humor."

Bess was steeling herself for another campaign. Her mother was ailing, yet for once Harry's needs would take priority. Bess pressured Margaret to suspend her burgeoning singing career in anticipation of an active fall campaign. Bess doubted that Harry would win, but she was determined to stand (and even run) by his side.

In June 1948, Harry Truman took a cross-country "nonpolitical" trip. He began rehearsing the "off the cuff" speeches he would deliver so effectively in the fall. During one day of campaigning in Washington state, Governor Mon Wallgren introduced Bess and Margaret before introducing the President. The cheers the First Lady and First Daughter received inspired the President to work their appearances into his routine.

Throughout the spring and summer Bess urged Harry, one aide recalled, "to run the way he did when he was campaigning for county judge." It was a "people's crusade" to "give 'em hell." Bess and Margaret were essential props in this all-American festival. As he whistlestopped across America, Harry would speak briefly, then end with a smile. "And now, howja like to meet ma family?" he would ask, and bask in the applause as he introduced "the Boss"—Bess—and "the Boss's boss"—Margaret—and each smiled and waved. He could be on his way in ten minutes. "Mrs. Truman and Margaret certainly stole the hearts of the people as we went along," an aide, William Bray, said. The silent, beaming "Truman ladies" became "a Presidential trademark," *Newsweek* would conclude, an essential "part of his appeal."

"It never occurred to us that we provided any political capital," Margaret claimed. "We had just come along to look after Dad." In fact, though, the family scene resurrected Americans' idealized past. "It put the nation's First Family on a comfortable footing with millions of Americans whose own home life they saw reflected there," *Newsweek* said. Americans needed reassurance after a war of fighting fathers and working mothers. Truman's family tableau both offered a vision of normalcy and humanized the President.

Truman's campaign literature was equally reassuring. One biography hailed Bess and Harry as "children of the sturdy stock that had its roots in the Missouri frontier country. . . . Harry Truman is cast in the American mold," it exclaimed. "His was the accepted American success story. . . . the result of honesty, integrity, and hard work." Mrs. Truman emerged as the model wife, "her husband's complement in every way," a sounding board, and a good homemaker. "Mrs. Average American likes the way Mrs. Truman conducts herself, Miss Teen-Ager admires daughter Margaret as a wholesome ideal, and as for Pop, when he sees the presidential grin on Mr. Truman's face, he doesn't stand in awe of the Chief Executive," the *Smithfield Herald* in North Carolina exulted. "His first reaction is, 'That fellow Harry Truman looks like a regular guy—I think I like him.'"

Over 31,700 miles, in thirty-five days of campaigning, the Trumans brought their whistlestop campaign to millions. Two Bess Trumans were on view. At times she was the small-town matron, hushing her husband when he called her "the Boss." She played den mother to the President and his entourage. She tended to her husband and the aides, reporters, dignitaries, and technicians who crowded the train. "Our job was to render the situation normal," Margaret wrote. Anybody "who needed an aspirin or a button sewed on" turned to the First Lady of the United States of America.

At other times, Bess was the savvy behind-the-scenes pol who projected a homey image. As usual, she was Harry's toughest critic; she edited his speeches, shaped his appeals, and disciplined him when he told a mother-in-law joke or acted undignified. Bess also politicked more than she ever had, meeting with reporters and politicians' wives. Visiting former vice president John Nance Garner in Texas, Bess even gave a brief speech. "Good morning, and thank you for this wonderful greeting," she said, then sat down.

The campaign exhausted Bess. "I don't seem to stay in one spot long enough to get my mail straightened out," she grumbled. She also worried.

During the summer, she and Margaret painted the kitchen in the Gates mansion, anticipating a return home.

But for Harry—with Marg and Bess at his side, the doubters back in Washington or retired, only true-blue advisers abroad, and crowds hailing him—the campaign was a lark. He deployed a lifetime's worth of conversational and political weapons: his ability to bond with men, his down-home way with crowds, the false modesty that built him up as he celebrated those around him—especially his wife and his daughter. Significantly, one of the most celebrated campaigns in American history produced no stirring oratory. But people remembered Harry's tone. Bess occasionally put her foot down, and by the time they reached Lima, Ohio, she forbade him from calling her "the Boss," but that too was fitting. Harry Truman finally was the Boss.

IV

The election victory gave a new legitimacy to Truman's Presidency. Both he and Bess would come into their own in 1949. At Missouri's inaugural gala Harry reprised his now-famous family act, introducing "the Boss" and "the Boss's boss" to wild applause. The Trumans hosted the first integrated inauguration, as they bullied local restaurants to accept black guests. With this action, which was not well publicized, Bess Truman silently refuted Adam Clayton Powell's charges that she was a racist.

During their first three years in the White House the Trumans had suffered through leaks, holes in the floors, and "more noises than a subway." In his second term, Harry moved his family across the street to Blair House to allow for a White House renovation that appealed to Harry's sense of history. He loved tooling around the hollowed-out shell, consulting with architects and bantering with the workmen. Bess enjoyed living in Blair House, which was a more intimate space than the decrepit executive mansion.

The inauguration also marked a new stage in Bess Truman's relations with the press. Reporters complained less about her reticence; they celebrated her influence in private and her grace in public. In early 1949 the major glossy magazines profiled "The President's Boss," as *Look* put it, or what *Collier's* called "Harry's Boss Bess." The articles cannibalized Mrs. Truman's 1947 responses to the forty questions, as well as other brief statements dating back to 1935. Margaret Truman, who loved interviews, helped. "She's far more than a boss," Margaret told *Look*. "She's everything in this outfit. Dad and I think it is time some of the public understood Mother better."

As always, Bess personified genteel values: "Dignity, reserve, conservatism." The "self-effacing First Lady" was "the same lady" she always had been, devoted to her family. For anxious Americans, *Look* defined her best qualities negatively: "She doesn't try to save the world, nor to look like a Powers model. She's the very opposite of the brittle career woman." And yet, the profiles emphasized, this seemingly "demure housewife . . . takes an active interest in her husband's career." After underestimating Bess, reporters now exaggerated her influence. Bess had become Harry's secret weapon in 1948, instrumental behind the scenes and popular. The 1948 campaign exemplified "simple American ideals," the *McCall's* profile concluded, championed by "a lady who stubbornly believes that the good life of a family need not be lost in the duties of a First Lady."

These "in-depth" portraits kept the First Lady's secret. Her father's death was mentioned, but there was no talk of a suicide. Journalists at the time bleached such unpleasantness out of the news. Similarly, reporters kept the Trumans ordinary by downgrading her family riches to "comparative wealth" and reducing the difficult Senate years to a "happy" time. Characteristically, the profiles focused on Bess as mistress of her separate sphere, rather than on the two Trumans as a couple. Profiles of Bess dealt with Harry in as perfunctory a manner as the profiles of the President dealt with the First Lady.

Republicans and Democrats wanted to repudiate Mrs. Roosevelt's example and restore the First Lady's nonpartisan status. When an investigation discovered that Harry's aide Harry Vaughan gave Mrs. Truman a freezer, the most partisan Republican in the Senate defended her: Joe McCarthy called Bess one of the "finest things about the White House" and "the type of lady who is incapable of doing anything improper."

Margaret, in the meantime, was building a singing career. She had coped nicely with her difficult position, enduring many articles complaining that she dressed too simply, that her nose was too big, and that, as the *Saturday Evening Post* said, she "does not, as a rule, photograph well." But these catty comments usually accompanied praise for sticking to her small-town ways against the lures of high society. Before Margaret's radio debut, the Trumans tried to preserve the dignity of the presidency and Margaret's unspoiled image. Reathel Odum read a statement that Miss Truman "wishes to be accepted as a singer on her own merit." The President greeted his daughter at the Silver Spring depot "so they couldn't take pictures of her coming home— maybe that is going a little too far but we don't want The White House used as a promotion by anybody," Harry explained.

As a singer, Margaret demonstrated more poise than talent. "Would she be making successful public appearances at her present stage of development if she were not the daughter of the President of the United States?" a critic asked in *Life*. "The answer is simply no." Bess Furman defended Margaret in the *New York Times Magazine*. The loyal newswoman praised Margaret's discipline and insisted that she had chosen "a career in which her position is about as much of a liability as an asset."

With the start of the new term, Margaret moved to New York City, with

Reathel Odum as her chaperone. Living in Manhattan, sampling its nightlife, and shuttling back to Washington to meet Winston Churchill or the President of Brazil took the Independence out of Margaret's image. People began to see a spoiled celebrity who was famous for being famous or, in this case, for being the daughter of someone famous.

The Trumans were also worried. Bess had overcome her doubts and was encouraging the career. She was grateful, she told a friend, that Margaret "is really *interested* in *something* & is not content to sit around in Wash[ington] . . . it becomes very deadly in a hurry." Harry feared Margaret was becoming spoiled. As he always did when he wanted to discipline his "baby," Harry sent her a letter preaching the values of hard work and modesty and reaffirming "the womanly ideal which her mother and I sought to hold up to her from the days of her childhood onward."

Despite the sniping, in retrospect 1949 would appear to be the high point of Truman's tenure. Problems seemed soluble, the President seemed capable, and his family was happy. Harry's thirtieth-anniversary greeting to Bess, on June 29, lacked the usual apologies. Once again Bess was home, but Harry seemed less forlorn. As always, the shadow of "business failure . . . political defeat . . . almost starvation in Washington those first ten years and then hell and repeat from 1944 to date" haunted Harry. But, he rejoiced, "those dear to me" had not been "made to suffer for my shortcomings. . . . There is no one in the world . . . who can look down on you or your daughter." Harry hoped for "thirty more [years] equally as happy without so much responsibility."

Even Bess complained less. Harry's sly reference to their honeymoon trip in his anniversary wish particularly pleased her. Often, in bleaker times, Harry had urged Bess to "Remember . . . The Blackstone, Port Huron and home." This time he added, "Maybe in 1953 we will be able to take that trip over again." Harry knew that Bess longed for him to retire.

By April 1950, Harry had decided. He rehearsed the reasons in a memorandum, for he had to convince himself that "eight years as President is enough." The Twenty-second Amendment (limiting a president's tenure in office, which would be ratified in February 1951) would not apply to him. By resisting the "lure in power" that was as compelling as "gambling and lust for money," he evinced self-control and made his retirement seem honorable. Margaret was "sure Dad showed this magnificent statement to Mother and I am equally sure that she glowed as she read it."

As a mark of the calm in both the Truman Presidency and the Truman household, Harry flew down to Independence on June 24, 1950, for an early celebration of his thirty-first anniversary with Bess. Since moving to Washington, their regular summertime separations had forced them to celebrate most anniversaries by mail. Unfortunately, North Korea invaded South

Korea that week, sending Harry back to Washington and the Truman Presidency into a tailspin.

The Korean War, which eventually involved 5.7 million American troops and cost 54,426 American lives, traumatized the nation. Truman's administration seemed out of control. The fall of China, Senator McCarthy's anticommunist crusade, inflation, a wave of labor strikes, and the continuing struggles with the Soviet Union all took on a more ominous edge. Once again, Harry Truman grappled with multiple crises that thrust Bess to the sidelines. With generals, admirals, diplomats, and aides bustling about, shuttling from Blair House to the Oval Office, Harry had less time for his wife.

The Trumans also suffered a bout of illnesses. As Harry reported to his cousin Ethel in mid-September, another cousin, Ralph Truman, "had something resembling a stroke last week," Harry's brother Vivian "passed out a few days ago," and "Bess told me last night the Mrs. Wallace is in a bad way. No one seems to be able to take all the blows but your cousin HST," Harry complained.

In November, with the Korean War blazing, two Puerto Rican nationalists stormed Blair House. They killed a policeman and wounded two others before one of them was killed and another was wounded. Harry and Bess were upstairs; Harry scoffed that his "name" was not on any "bullet." But the death of the guard, Leslie Coffelt, devastated the President. "I want no more guards killed," he said as he agreed to be driven across the street in an armored car. "I'm really a prisoner now," he sighed.

Bess had always been the "worrier" in the family, forcing Harry to call whenever he arrived at his various destinations. This trauma intensified her feelings. She just wanted to go home.

Following the assassination attempt, the midterm elections strengthened the alliance of conservative Democrats and Republicans blocking Truman's "Fair Deal" legislation. That same November, three hundred thousand Chinese troops tore into the United Nations army in Korea, destroying General Douglas MacArthur's dream of sending American troops home for Christmas. Two days later, Truman mishandled a question about nuclear weapons. Critics concluded that he intended to unleash atomic warfare in Korea; Prime Minister Clement Attlee rushed over from England to confer. "I've worked for peace for five years and six months," the President moped, "and it looks like World War III is here." Amid these crises, a heart attack killed Charlie Ross, the trusted press secretary who graduated with Harry and Bess from Independence High School in 1901. The Truman Presidency hit rock bottom.

At first, Harry's posture as a regular guy in over his head helped him connect with the American people, even as some sneered that "To err is Truman" and sang "I'm just mild about Harry." Korea silenced the laughter and the cheers. In a world on the brink of nuclear disaster, "averageness" lost its luster.

The night Ross died, the Trumans escorted Prime Minister Attlee to hear Margaret sing at Constitution Hall. The *Washington Post*'s review the next morning concluded that Miss Truman "cannot sing very well." The music critic Paul Hume said she is "flat a good deal of the time" and "communicates almost nothing of the music she presents." General George C. Marshall said the only thing Hume did not criticize "was the varnish on the piano."

This was the last straw. Harry had long harbored guilt that, as he told his cousins, "I've made all my family . . . as much trouble as if I'd robbed the biggest bank in town, pulled a Ponzi, or taken the savings of all the widows and orphans in Missouri." He considered reporters like Hume "paid mental whores." Harry had to defend his women against these sinners.

Truman dashed off a letter to Hume and had a White House servant mail it; he did not want his wife or his aides restraining him, as they normally did. The President of the United States called Hume worse than a "guttersnipe" and threatened that, if they ever met, the critic would "need a new nose, a lot of beef steak for black eyes, and perhaps a supporter below!" Hume released the letter to the press.

Truman's advisers—and his wife—were horrified as the resulting brouhaha touched on some of the key tensions in his Presidency. "It was Harry Truman, the human being who wrote that letter," he said, by way of defense. But the lapse was particularly problematic in the nuclear age. The violent language suggested instability, not a natural release of tension. Harry Truman, who had spent years studying the biographies of great men, knew that private reactions were seen as indicators of public action. Increasingly, Americans were linking intemperate behavior in personal affairs with such behavior in public service. People asked if a man who could not hold his tongue with a critic could manage difficult subordinates like Douglas MacArthur, let alone wily adversaries like Mao Tse-Tung? If Truman overreacted to this minor incident, would he overreact in Korea too? In this, one of the first presidential character crises of the atomic era, Harry Truman was found wanting.

Yet Harry knew what he was doing, and he refused to apologize. "Well I've had a grand time this day," he smirked as he watched the "stuffed shirt critics" condemn the Hume letter. He enjoyed turning away from Korea and playing to the men at home as the protector of the womenfolk. The language of the letter, calling Hume "an eight ulcer man on four ulcer pay," was a display of masculine dominance, a flashing of presidential teeth.

Truman calmed his aides by predicting that 80 percent of his mail would approve. He was dead right. Fathers in particular appreciated the President's dilemma. "The President's action exemplifies the American way of life and his reaction to a harmful attack is exactly what any two-fisted red blooded, American father['s] would be under the circumstances," the *New York En-*

quirer cheered. "The trouble with you guys," Harry chided his staff, "is you just don't understand human nature."

Such displays failed to reverse Truman's slide in popularity. As the war dragged in Korea, as he engaged in a crippling struggle with General MacArthur, and as McCarthy hunted for more communists, Truman's reputation sagged. His approval ratings plunged from a high of 87 percent in July 1945, as World War II moved to a victorious close, to 26 percent in February 1951. Truman had gone from exceeding low expectations to disappointing many high expectations.

With her husband preoccupied and her daughter gallivanting in New York, Bess yearned for Independence. She had to bring her ailing mother to Washington. Since David Wallace's suicide, Bess had dutifully protected her crotchety mother. The move would add to the Trumans' turmoil.

Even when she had been healthy, Madge Wallace had little patience for her son-in-law. "Mrs. Wallace always thought Harry Truman wouldn't amount to anything," the President's valet explained. "It galls her to see him in the White House, ruining that prediction." At best Mrs. Wallace ignored Harry, as when she wrote Mary Paxton Keeley from the White House in 1946: "It is lovely to be here with Bess and Margaret, but I get very homesick sometimes." More often, she patronized the President. As she became more senile and less inhibited, she became more hostile.

Still, Truman "treated her with royal respect at all times," according to the Trumans' physician, Dr. Wallace H. Graham. Truman distanced himself from the irascible Mrs. Wallace, referring to her as "the mother," or "the grandmother" in his letters and diaries. When he spoke of his house on North Delaware Street, he still referred to it as "the Gates house."

All these tensions overwhelmed Bess. Her desk was "piled high," and her plans "seem to be constantly knocked in the head. Don't get the idea that I'm feeling sorry for myself," Bess insisted in the summer of 1951. "I'm just mad about it."

V

The Truman marriage was under great strain. Bess believed that the only solution was to retire, but she feared Harry might reconsider. Both Trumans knew that a premature announcement would make Harry a lame duck. They kept their plans to themselves.

By 1952 Truman was searching for a replacement. He met with Illinois Governor Adlai E. Stevenson in early March. At that meeting, according to Truman, Stevenson urged the President to run again, arguing that only he could win. "My wife and daughter had said the same thing to me an hour before," Truman noted in his diary. "What am I to do?" It is hard to believe that

Bess encouraged him to remain. Either her protective instincts had been mobilized by the attacks on Harry, or Harry heard what he wanted to hear—and wanted to run again.

In March, even Bess was pulled into the public game of speculation. While showing news hens the refurbished White House, Bess was asked if she "would like to spend four more years here." She answered: "Not yes or no—you won't catch me on that one." "You could stand it, though, if you had to," another asked. "Well, I've stood it for seven years," Bess snapped. Americans loved hearing such expressions of loyalty. "Nothing could have been more human and wifely, and for it we like Bess Truman more than we always have," the *Detroit Free Press* gushed.

Truman's retirement announcement at the Jefferson-Jackson Day Dinner on March 29, 1952, thrilled Bess. Now Harry could not reconsider. "Suddenly her step grew lighter," a family friend John Synder observed. Shrewd observers recognized that Bess Truman had "made one of the historic decisions of 1952." "No one, but no one, ever makes up Harry Truman's mind—except Bess," one friend had said after the dinner. Others noted that Harry's stated desire not to "be carried out feet first" sounded like Bess. Harry contemplated running for the Senate, but Bess insisted they return to Independence.

With his term in office ending, Harry relished the refurbished White House, his gift to posterity. Truman exhibited the mansion in a television special. The Harry Truman who invited Americans into his temporary living quarters for a look-see, though, was not the Harry Truman who bullied critics and played poker. This was the soft-spoken Harry, the mild-mannered Harry, the private Harry, the piano player who lacked the macho edge of the Hume episode or the 1948 campaign. This was the Harry with whom Bess had fallen in love, the bookish farmer, the mama's boy.

For all of Harry's successful image-making, for all his perseverance through the end of World War II and the start of the cold war, for all his skill in facing down critics (including Douglas MacArthur), the Presidency ended on a triumphal note for Bess, not for him. Many of the Truman-era retrospectives praised Bess. The news hens might not have liked her, as a more traditional contrast to Eleanor, but they had to acknowledge her popularity. Dorothy McCardle of the *Washington Post* yearned for a First Lady who would "take those invisible 'no comment' signs down from the distaff side of the White House and put out the latchstrings for Mrs. and Miss America." Yet even McCardle acknowledged that Mrs. Truman had "won thousands of admirers for the dignity she has brought to the role of First Lady."

It was a phenomenon that would resurface with the Johnsons, Nixons, Carters, and Bushes. The President had many critics, yet in 1952 his wife attracted kudos as "one of the finest women of our time." The adjectives piled high: genuine, gracious, loyal, poised, sweet, calm, kindly, thoughtful, Christian, decent, dignified, and dutiful. These were the attributes of the "Republican Mother" of the Revolutionary War, commissioned by the nation to "form its manners and character," in the words of one signer of the Declaration of Independence, Dr. Benjamin Rush. Bess was cheered for all that she had not done—she had given no speeches, started no crusades. First Ladies, it seemed, should be seen and not heard. "The nicest thing about her is that . . . you would scarcely have known that Mrs. T. was on board," one columnist in the *Louisville Courier-Journal* said. "She has not preyed upon the presidency." In short, Bess Truman had not been Eleanor Roosevelt. "The contrast between Bess and Eleanor," the *St. Louis Post Dispatch* proclaimed, "is easy on the eyes, easy on the ears, and easy on the nerve centers."

During Harry's final speech one lady cried, "I don't care what they say about Mr. Truman, but everyone loves Mrs. Truman and Margaret." The family's nonpartisan popularity allowed citizens to find common ground during tumultuous times. Bess and Margaret gave disaffected Americans a benign address in the White House. Patriots could disagree with Truman, but like his family.

Some of this popularity did reflect, and reflect on, important personal characteristics of the President. If Bess and Margaret were distinguished by their "humanness," as B. C. Forbes wrote in *Forbes,* that was also one of Harry's most appealing traits. Even his loudest critics conceded that he was a nice guy. A White House stenographer said, "He's the only man I've ever known or ever met that didn't have a mean bone in his body."

Bess and Margaret, like all wives and children, provided glimpses into the husband's character. If that was not enough to keep his party in power, it did help detoxify the atmosphere. Conservative publications like the *Los Angeles Times,* which hated Truman, eulogized Bess as a way of thanking them both. Unlike her predecessor, Bess had remained on a high enough plane to insulate her from her husband's troubles. Both Dwight Eisenhower and John F. Kennedy would make full use of this nonpartisan podium. Ultimately, in fact, this nonpartisan slant would become the means for Harry Truman's historiographical rehabilitation. As Truman's stock rose, he would be remembered less for particular policies and more for his character and style.

When the Trumans arrived in Independence, ten thousand people greeted them at the railroad depot, and another five thousand massed at their front gate. "That home town reception was worth all the effort," Truman said, "all the trials. Never has there been anything like it in Independence or any other ex-president's home town." Bess told her husband: "If this is what you get for all those years of hard work I guess it was worth it." Harry Truman had made history, Bess Wallace Truman was home, and their hometown embraced them both.

In May 1955, a little more than two years after the Trumans left the White House, a television crew invaded the house on North Delaware Street. Harry and Bess Truman had agreed to appear on the popular CBS show, "Person to Person." Instead of the regular host, Edward R. Murrow, their daughter, Margaret, interviewed them via a remote hookup in New York. It was a typical family scene. Harry was amiable; Bess, more clipped and sardonic but still gracious; and Margaret played to the cameras. Despite Margaret's warning, "No kibitzing, mother," the three bantered for much of the half hour. When Harry claimed to have "mowed the lawn once," Bess deadpanned, "I don't remember the 'once.'" When Margaret asked her mother a political question, Harry interjected, "You know your mother never talked politics."

The interview played out a central tension in Truman's Presidency, as modern technology transmitted an old-fashioned scene to millions of homes. Similarly, Harry and Bess represented the sensibilities of the past; Margaret Truman symbolized the technologically sophisticated, celebrity-soaked culture of the future. Harry and Bess Truman were comfortable with nineteenth-century gentility, with ideals of duty, integrity, and silence. Those values faded in a world where publicity was king, where openness was more important than discretion, fame more cherished than honor. The Trumans had preserved their privacy to an extent, but it was a holding action their successors would find harder to duplicate. The Trumans could still count on a cultural consensus that upheld their values, but the seams were beginning to show. Questions about how a culture of grace could survive amid a politics of publicity were shoved under the rug.

On television Harry praised his First Lady in clichéd terms: "She was a wonderful influence and a wonderful help. A President is in a bad way if he doesn't have a First Lady that knows her job and is a full support to him. She's the greatest help a President can have—mine was." Truman told Americans what they wanted to hear. This message would become more popular over the decades. As Americans of later generations searched for influential First Ladies, some would see Bess Truman as a power behind the throne, a little lady with lots of pull limited by sexism.

In fact, until near the end, and excluding the 1948 campaign, Bess Truman privately hurt Harry Truman's Presidency as often as she helped. If her primary functions were to support her husband and maintain his home, she failed frequently. "He can't be happy without her," Margaret Truman said of her parents in 1952, yet Bess often deprived Harry of her presence and her approval. She was a recurring source of guilt and tension. Rather than working together as a couple, the Trumans often functioned as two solitudes; each had a competing agenda. Rather than being a "helpmeet," Bess Truman was a pain in the presidential neck. All too often, when the President of the

United States and the leader of the free world should have been puzzling out affairs of state, he worried about being in the marital doghouse.

Bess and Harry were sufficiently trained in the small-town codes of silence to hide their marital discord from the press. With minimal maneuvering, her trips home became examples of devotion to her mother, not instances of jumping ship. For all their complaints about public intrusions, the Trumans maintained their privacy, and the family thereby remained popular.

The subterfuge succeeded for the same reasons that the culture of gentility operated so effectively—the rules were clear, and the demands obvious. Steeped in the values of home, church, and school, the Trumans knew how to tailor reality to fit the desired appearances. Their partnership was forged in the mores of small-town America, a place where regardless of the emotional realities of the partnership, the desired appearances remained clear. Unlike the unconventional Roosevelts, the Trumans sustained contemporary social expectations.

The subterfuge also succeeded because underneath the tension that could have made headlines and set tongues wagging, the Trumans really did have a strong marriage; they really did try to live by those eternal values a later generation would mock. In hiding signs of temporary tensions, the Trumans were keeping their short-term image more in line with the longer-term truth. Even in the 1940s and early 1950s, the presidential couple found themselves entering an Orwellian world of press scrutiny where only by lying could they convey the truth—or at least contain the great but transient stresses of their presidential years.

Later generations would dismiss this as image-making, as hypocrisy. In fact, the Trumans were maintaining boundaries and living out their own ideal of themselves. To the extent that all interactions are performances, Harry Truman earned applause for being a man's man who knew how to treat a lady. His refusal to cuss in front of women was a mark of civility, not dishonesty. For the Trumans' successors, the script would become murkier, and the performances correspondingly more baroque.

2

"IKE IS MY CAREER"

The Eisenhowers at Home in the Fifties

When Dwight Eisenhower swept the Democrats out of office in 1952, guardians of gentility celebrated the end of Democratic dowdiness. After the election, Emily Post called the reporter Nanette Kutner. "Please, if you get the chance, tell Mrs. Eisenhower what a perfect hostess I think she'll make," said America's courtesy queen. "The White House has been dead for a long, long while." A week later Mamie Eisenhower told Kutner, "I got a real lift from your account of the conversation with Emily Post. Of course, being mistress of the White House is a terrific responsibility, and I am truly grateful for my Army wife training."

Dwight and Mamie Eisenhower considered themselves well-trained for the White House. For more than ten years they had been one of the most famous couples in America, and for more than thirty years they had been serving their country in the Army. Mamie and Dwight were used to promenading as a couple; Mamie was resigned to sharing her man with the public. But neither realized how much they now had to sacrifice. Government had grown tremendously during the past two decades, as had the public demands on the presidential couple. Bess Truman had learned that a First Lady could not just be "mistress of the White House"; her elegance had to be mass-marketed. The celebration of 1950s domesticity would further burden the First Couple. Even the best "Army wife training" could not help Mamie prepare for the daily demands for interviews, endorsements, political stands, and help with the welfare state. Dwight Eisenhower would find his most intimate body functions publicized and his conservative values challenged.

The Eisenhowers were not the placid all-American couple reigning during the placid 1950s, as myth would have it. They did remain popular amid political strife, and they often conveyed the impression that their marriage was blissful. Many of the skills each developed to sustain the marriage proved useful in politics. But Ike and Mamie sold their marital fantasy to a nation that still believed the presidential couple could live up to its billing. The Eisenhowers were the most successful presidential couple in the postwar era—even surpassing the Kennedys—because the Eisenhower marriage thrived in public and in private. Life in the White House improved their marriage, and the Eisenhowers sincerely believed the ideals they upheld. The Eisenhowers tried to be a younger, more heroic version of the Trumans. They too wanted to repudiate the Roosevelts' legacy, but they could not escape the increased expectations. Still, his marriage, and his wife's success as First Lady, helped President Eisenhower keep his popularity ratings averaging 64 percent.

I

The Eisenhowers' "training" for the White House began in childhood. Along with the Trumans and others of their generation, the Eisenhowers were raised to act proper in public. Both Dwight Eisenhower of Abilene, Kansas, and Mamie Doud, of Denver, Colorado, came from homes easily characterized as all-American. The Eisenhowers may have been poorer than most Americans, and the Douds were wealthier, but both families steeped their children in the social consensus that diluted class and most other differences, but not race.

Born in 1890, Dwight was the third of David and Ida Stover Eisenhower's six surviving children. Arthur, Edgar, Dwight, Roy, Earl, Milton, and their parents shared a two-story white frame house of 818 square feet—an area smaller than the office Dwight later occupied in the Pentagon as chief of staff. Eisenhower remembered his parents as "ideal" partners who filled their traditional roles: "Father was the breadwinner, Supreme Court, and Lord High Executioner. Mother was tutor and manager of our household." Most of the Eisenhower boys preferred their mother to their father. David Eisenhower was a cold, methodical, and beaten man who had gone bankrupt before Dwight was born. He worked six days a week in the Belle Springs Creamery and withdrew into his books when he came home. Ida Stover Eisenhower kept her six boys out of trouble with a stream of aphorisms and biblical citations accompanying the farm chores she assigned on their three-acre homestead. "We were needed," Dwight later recalled, arguing that too much leisure bred juvenile delinquents in the 1950s.

Together, the authoritarian father and the preachy mother rooted their children in bedrock values of sobriety, industry, honesty, and discipline. Dwight's upbringing was filled with Wild West playacting, sandlot baseball, schoolboy crushes, the occasional brawl, and the "three R's" drilled in at the local schools. "Our family life was free from parental quarrelling and filled with genuine, if not demonstrated love," Dwight recalled. "I never knew anyone from a divorced family until I went to West Point. Responsibility was a part of maturing. Concern for others was natural in our small community. And ambition without arrogance was quietly instilled in us by both parents."

Dwight inherited his parents' universalist approach to religion while dispensing with the pacifism and puritanism of their Mennonite sect, the River Brethren. As his other brothers did, he began smoking, drinking, and gambling as an adolescent. He did not join a church until he was elected President. But he remained pious on a national secular level, praying and functioning as the nation's chief minister on the eve of the D-Day invasion and at his inauguration.

Dwight's severe upbringing taught him self-control. He often wrote down the names of people he hated and placed them in his desk drawer. This admittedly artificial practice helped him manage his temper; Eisenhower needed a will of steel to hide his volcanic emotions with a smile. His ailments as President—heart trouble, stomach trouble, and a stroke—were the maladies of the overworked and repressed executive. His smile wooed millions as his occasional tantrums cowed subordinates.

At Abilene High School, Dwight was a competent student and a great athlete. This son of poor fundamentalists was particularly shy with girls. He compensated by playing the "tough cooky," as one schoolmate recalled. Edgar and Dwight—known as "Big Ike" and "Little Ike"—never ran from a fight. Their hostility to erudition eased the pain of social exile. One boyhood friend did not remember "the grin that has become world famous," but instead recalled "a grimace of intense determination."

After graduating in 1909, Dwight worked for a year to send Edgar to college. He applied to the service academies for a free education. When Dwight left for West Point, his pacifist mother said goodbye, watched until he was out of sight, then, Milton recalled, she ran into the house and "bawled like a baby."

Cadets at "Hell on the Hudson" endured a harsh diet of tradition, patriotism, and secular piety. The young roughneck did not appreciate West Point's discipline. Graduating sixty-first in a class of 164, Ike would rank ninety-fifth in conduct. He was most interested in playing football. "Daredevil Dwight, the Dauntless Don" was mischievous and relaxed with his buddies, disdainful of eager beavers, and awkward around girls. He preferred poker to socials. At one dance, the chaperons reprimanded him for whirling a professor's daughter around too vigorously. A few months later, he met the same young lady and could not resist the impulse to swing her around again. Sergeant Eisenhower was demoted to private, confined to the barracks area for a month, and forced to walk punishment tours.

After graduating, Dwight joined the 19th Infantry at Fort Sam Houston, near San Antonio, Texas. He kept his reputation as a popular guy disdainful of girls. One Sunday afternoon in October 1915, some buddies tried to break his resolve. They introduced Second Lieutenant Eisenhower to Mamie Doud, whose wealthy family summered in Denver and wintered in San Antonio. Nine months later they were married.

Mamie Geneva Doud was born in Boone, Iowa, in 1896, the daughter of Elivera Mathilde Carlson and John Sheldon Doud. Mr. Doud owned a successful meat-packing firm and retired at the age of thirty-six. He moved his family west and eventually settled in a large house at 750 Lafayette Street in Denver. Mrs. Doud raised her daughters to be genteel; the second daughter, Mamie, was particularly dainty. Before moving to Denver, Mamie and her older sister had raced up the 365 steps of the Cheyenne Monument at an altitude of seven thousand feet. Eleanor collapsed with a heart attack. The family began going south during the winter because of Eleanor, who would die at age seventeen. Mamie's fear and guilt led to a lifetime of rest and hypochondria.

The Douds were aristocratic, churchgoing, and fun-loving. Their proper, urbane midwestern Presbyterianism lacked the intensity and sobriety of the Eisenhowers' frontier evangelism. Mamie spent a year at the Wolcott finishing school, whose motto was "Noblesse Oblige." She took dancing lessons from a lady who always wore long gloves and ball gowns. At the same time, the Douds reveled in America's burgeoning popular culture. They enjoyed vaudeville, local plays, Broadway touring companies, and the fabulous Elitch's Gardens amusement park. Mamie's father called her "Puddin'" after Mark Twain's foolish character Pudd'nhead Wilson; she nicknamed him "Pooh Bah," from the bossy character in *The Mikado*. Once, in the middle of a particularly vigorous turkey trot with her uncle Joel Carson, the uniformed attendant foreshadowed Dwight's problems at West Point when he interrupted the couple. "The management requests that you dance a little less spectacularly," the chaperon said.

Mamie's reputation as the "belle of the block" followed her to San Antonio. At the age of nineteen she had a sultry yet innocent look that reminded many of the movie star Lillian Gish. A coquette well aware of her charms, Mamie knew how to keep the young men at bay. Her family's front porch filled with gentlemen callers; she was encouraging enough to keep them coming while sufficiently demure to maintain her honor.

The pampered maiden and the rough-hewn soldier were an unlikely pair only by today's standards of peer marriage. Ike's reputation as "the woman-hater of the post" intrigued Mamie. He enjoyed meeting this "vivacious and attractive girl, smaller than average, saucy in the look about her face and in her whole attitude." Mamie considered this tall, blond, smiling soldier "just about the handsomest male I had ever seen."

Eisenhower uncharacteristically invited the young lady to accompany him on his inspection rounds. Mamie was wearing low French heels, hated walking, and had a date. Yet she agreed. In the fort, the young lieutenant insisted that she look straight ahead, as "the boys are not too careful about pulling down the shades." Mamie scanned a row of open windows, grinning while Ike squirmed. "If that isn't just like a woman," Ike laughed.

Ike asked Mamie for a date. She was booked for the next month but invited him to drop by unannounced in the afternoons. "You know Ike is as persistent as the dickens, once he makes up his mind," Mamie would beam. "He simply outpersisted the competition," she said.

This handsome couple enjoyed a mutual attraction. Ike considered the gay young girl raised on vaudeville a welcome antidote to his dour relatives. Mamie found Ike self-confident, determined, and fun, unlike "all those lounge lizards with patent leather hair" courting her. The no-nonsense second lieutenant budgeted carefully for their dates around San Antonio.

Eisenhower enjoyed being surrounded by an energetic and loyal brood once again. The Douds lived in a grand house not far from Fort Sam Houston, with servants and fine china. John Doud warned that he would not subsidize the couple; Ike would have it no other way. Mamie "did not have the vaguest idea of the value of a dollar," or how difficult it would be to live on Ike's Army salary.

Ike and Mamie were engaged on Valentine's Day and married on July 1, 1916, in Denver. Mamie's marriage to "a nobody from Kansas" shocked her hometown crowd. The nervous bridegroom arrived at the bride's home two hours early. He refused to sit down for fear of creasing his formal dress pants.

After two days at Eldorado Springs, the honeymooners went to Abilene to meet the Eisenhowers. Mamie charmed the younger ones by rejoicing that she finally had brothers. She proved less effective with her husband, who went off to play poker. Mamie sulked all afternoon until she called Ike to demand his return, but Ike never quit when he was down. "Come now or don't bother to come at all," Mamie yelled and hung up. Ike returned with his winnings after two o'clock in the morning. Mamie considered the ensuing shouting match the worst fight of their marriage. Every word reverberated through the cramped Eisenhower house.

Forty years later, Earl teased that "Dwight has reformed: he has changed from all night poker to 12 o'clock bridge." David and Ida Eisenhower must have been humiliated. Their sons had "never heard a cross word pass between them," and they abhorred gambling. They had extended themselves to host their genteel daughter-in-law, only to see their son act loutish. Committed to appearances, Eisenhower never mentioned the tiff. In his memoir, he described a stopover in Abilene only lasting eight hours.

For Mamie, the row was an eye-opener. "Your husband is the boss—and don't forget it," she would counsel future brides. There were other painful discoveries. Ike's two-room bachelor quarters in Fort Sam Houston did not even have a kitchen. Having grown up shuttling between two elegant houses, Mamie would endure thirty-seven different government homes ranging from a shack to a palace.

The first time Ike packed his bags to go on maneuvers, Mamie asked, "You're not going to leave me this soon after our wedding day, are you?" In words she would often quote, he said, "Mamie, there's one thing you must understand. My country comes first and always will. You come second." "It was quite a shocker for a nineteen-year-old bride," she confessed. She would always resent those who assumed that as an Army wife, "you must be used to Ike being away." She said, "I never got used to him being gone. He was my husband. He was my whole life."

Both struggled with their frustrations and their tempers. Once, while arguing, Mamie slammed Ike's hand as it rested on a table. Their rings collided, and the amethyst in her replica of his West Point graduation ring shattered. "Just for that, young lady," the husband scolded his wife, "you can pay for it yourself." Mamie repaired the ring with money she had been hoarding from a wedding gift, "although parting with those dollars almost killed me," she later said.

A monthly salary of $167.67 did not go far. Mamie, by her own admission, was a "spoiled brat." Ike taught her how to cook basic dishes—he had learned when his mother was quarantined to treat his brother Milton's scarlet fever—but he did not teach her how to manage the household. "Half the trouble in most marriages comes from the way money is handled," her father had warned. "Your job is to make whatever he provides be enough." Mamie learned how to manage the finances, later boasting that she and Ike were never in debt.

Ike and Mamie also had fun. The Eisenhowers were an attractive, extroverted couple. They were often the toasts of his military post, playing cards, leading sing-alongs, or entertaining in their various dwellings. During a stint in Paris their apartment would be dubbed "Club Eisenhower." Their happy public moments balanced the occasional storms at home.

During World War I, Ike was stuck training troops in the United States while many of his comrades fought in Europe. On September 23, 1917, while Ike was on a training exercise, Mamie gave birth to a son, Doud Dwight. John Doud granted Mamie an allowance of $100 a month for the new expenses. At the tank corps training center in Camp Colt, Gettysburg,

Pennsylvania, Ike was promoted to lieutenant colonel. The Eisenhowers lived in a grand white house that Mamie considered their "first real home."

At their next posting, in Camp Meade, Maryland, the Eisenhowers suffered what Ike would call "the greatest disappointment and disaster in my life." Three-year-old "Icky" died of scarlet fever in Ike's arms. Neither Ike nor Mamie ever "recovered," Eisenhower admitted; he simply "had to learn to accept [it] or to go crazy." Mamie took to her bed while her son lay dying. "It was ironic, I have thought many times, how I faced it alone at his birth, and again, at his death," she sighed.

A year later, in January 1922, Eisenhower was posted to Panama—one of the Army's ways of helping a couple recover. Ike enjoyed his work with General Fox Conner, but the bat-infested shanty disgusted Mamie. Both were still mourning. Ike suffered silently, working harder and harder, and Mamie grieved openly, becoming more and more morose. Senior Army wives looked after junior wives; Virginia Conner saw the Eisenhowers drifting apart and counseled Mamie to woo her husband back. "You mean," Mamie asked, "that I should *vamp* him?" Mrs. Conner replied: "That's *just* what I mean. Vamp him!" For this, Mamie was well-trained. A new hairstyle gave her short hair with bangs, which became her trademark. "Mamie did win back her husband and probably saved her marriage," Mrs. Conner said. "Had she not acted at that crucial time, the separation might well have reached the point of no return." Divorce was not an option, "but a cold, lifeless marriage could have resulted."

By the summer, Mamie was on her way back to Denver to give birth. Ike arranged a leave and was present for the birth of John Sheldon Doud Eisenhower, their only surviving child. Still traumatized by Icky's death, Mamie would be a terribly anxious mother; Ike would be a reserved and forbidding father.

The Eisenhowers continued to move around. Mamie had adjusted to Army life, but Ike feared that his career was stalling. He had never seen combat, and his country was isolationist. Mamie rarely meddled in Ike's career. Her husband told her, "The office is mine, the house yours," and she often uttered the Army wife's mantra, "I'll go wherever is best for you." Mamie often heard about her husband's activities by gossiping with other wives. On rare occasions she offered advice, sometimes selfishly—as when she blocked his transfer to the Air Corps or lobbied for a posting in Paris. More often, she sacrificed her feelings for his career.

Ike felt guilty about Mamie's sacrifices. He indulged her even as she exasperated him with her frequent trips to Denver, her refusal to have more children, and her chronic ailments. He bought "minimum accommodations for myself, no matter what I bought for her" when they traveled. Ike shielded Mamie. When he had his appendix out, he did not tell her until after the operation.

Ike buried his frustrations in work. "Only a man that is happy in his work can be happy in his home," he said. Like his parents, he presented a public model of marital harmony. Their son John said, "They never quarreled in front of me."

Mamie's painful initiation into marriage shaped her view of the institution. Her "first and most important rule" for a "happy marriage" was recognizing the husband as "the head of the house." She believed that "being a wife is the best career that life has to offer a woman," and that success came from "wit and straight thinking and a good deal of adapting on both sides." Mamie viewed her "job" as a "joy." Her tasks included stretching the dollars, "keep[ing] the house orderly," remaining presentable around the house, serving a hot breakfast every morning, and "do[ing] my best to help him achieve whatever his ambition might be." The lines of authority were clear in this officer's household. "I never told him anything," she claimed. "He told me."

Such grace, such deference, testified to Mamie's breeding. Many observers paid Mamie the highest possible compliment to an Army wife, or any wife in the first half of the twentieth century—as one aide, Kevin McCann, said, "It would have been Colonel Dwight David Eisenhower if it weren't for Mamie." This anticipated the compliments many would offer when Ike entered politics. John Eisenhower said his mother took "full credit for smoothing the edges off the rough-and-ready Kansan and for teaching him some of the polish that later stood [him] in good stead."

Unfortunately, this philosophy came at great psychic cost. Even John Eisenhower said, "The loving relationship between Ike and Mamie . . . was, however, rarely smooth." Publicly, Mamie remained the gay, lithe belle of Denver. Yet her stormy marriage triggered frequent retreats to *her* "command post"—her bed—and caused a deep sorrow beneath the bubbly veneer. "There were a lot of times when Ike broke my heart," Mamie later confessed. "I wouldn't have stood it for a minute if I didn't respect him. . . . I didn't want to do anything to disappoint him."

This "ideal" Army couple, who were also a characteristic couple from their times, illustrated the powerful cultural code that remained operative through the 1960s. Dating and marriage were as confusing as ever, but common rituals and expectations helped men and women cope. Within marriage, the commitment to appearances—as intense on an Army post as in any small town—helped, as did the virtual ban on divorce. Whereas today's peer couples are often harmonious at home yet lead what Lewis Mumford called an "encapsulated life . . . within the cabin of darkness before a television set," the Eisenhowers functioned better in public. And traditional marriages, even when strained, were neither as brittle nor as empty as many later decided. The traditional marriage could contain conflict. It offered couples an incentive to cooperate through the fear of shame, as well as a vehicle for resolution via the ideology of feminine compliance. The result, in the Eisenhowers' case, was a robust relationship. Not all marriages are placid; the same two-some that established Club Eisenhowers from post to post could break a ring in a fit of temper and mourn their son separately. Their love was strong enough to contain tension, loss, anger, along with affection, warmth, devotion. No one could claim that Mamie and Ike were perfectly happy, but no one should underestimate their love for each other and their devotion to the institution throughout their married life.

"Ike was my career," Mamie would preen, knowing that Ike was un-demonstrative but not uncaring. Columbia University granted him an honorary degree in 1947. Mamie, along with 650 others, rose when he marched down the aisle. As he passed his wife, the general broke formation, took her hand, and said, "Don't you ever stand up for me, Mamie."

II

World War II catapulted Dwight Eisenhower from his rut as a paper soldier to commander of the world's most powerful military force. As an impoverished son of the heartland, he symbolized the American dream soldiers were defending. Still impish enough in middle age to be described as "Gen. Ike's Pin-Up Girl," Mamie became the queen of America's war widows. She was well cast as the selfless coquette, teaching women to remain feminine as they filled in for the menfolk.

Eisenhower was operating in a theater. He understood that without good press, "American soldiers would not know they had an American commander interested in their welfare." Whereas 100 American journalists had covered the first world war, 500 to 700 American reporters covered this conflagration. Daily circulation of newspapers rose from 42 million in 1941 to 46 million in 1944. Americans were addicted to extras and radio bulletins. In modern America, heroes became celebrities; by 1945 at least three Eisenhower biographies and a movie would be in the works. "Soooooo—you see: song, poetry, news-shows, conversations, papers—everywhere—your name is on everyone's lips," an old flame reported in 1943.

Never before had a commander at war faced such an onslaught of publicity. Ike feared that any perceived "attempt at self-glorification" would doom multinational cooperation. Stymied by censorship and Eisenhower's reticence, reporters covered the supporting players in Eisenhower's personal and professional dramas. Ike lived in Telegraph Cottage, a villa south of London, with a colorful cast straight from a war movie. The multiethnic crew included Mickey McKeogh, an Irishman from the streets of New York; John Moaney, a black who would remain Ike's valet for decades; Kay Summersby, a wispy chauffeur and secretary; and Telek, a feisty puppy. Picturing the

Supreme Commander of the Allied Expeditionary Force in Western Europe in his wartime household enhanced his role as a father figure protecting millions of GIs. Eisenhower's "family" also served as a role model to the soldiers, who were trained to consider each other as kin—at West Point, cadets' roommates were known as "wives."

If her husband was Everyman made good, Mamie was Everywoman coping. Together, Mamie and Ike offered a dramatic contrast to the most famous couple in the land, the Roosevelts. Both the President and the general were famous for their grins, yet the polio-crippled Roosevelt had grown grayer over the years while Ike appeared robust. The dour First Lady had only recently stopped wearing an ugly black hairnet around town; Mamie was pretty and perky, always gaily dressed. The Roosevelts personified a decaying northeastern patrician class; the Eisenhowers, the boundless opportunities of the frontier. The Roosevelts were bold and unconventional; the Eisenhowers eschewed controversy and embraced the traditional sex roles.

The public demands to be the ideal wife only intensified Mamie's pain. Mamie had to assume a brave front when her fears about losing Ike made her "a nervous wreck." Whenever she left her apartment she was on display. It was one thing to pose for photographers as she volunteered at service canteens and for the Red Cross, but most coverage was "entirely too personal." She feared embarrassing Ike and undermining the war effort.

Mamie holed up in Washington's Wardman Park Hotel. Her days were filled with card games, cocktails, volunteer work, Spanish classes, lunches, and "hen parties" with her "gang" of Army wives. It was, as *Life* would say, "one of the longest bouts of mah-jongg in history."

Even before Ike left in 1942, Mamie took refuge for two months with her sister "Mike" Moore in San Antonio. At the end of the visit, "Mike" told Ike that Mamie was feeling better, "her nerves were fairly good, . . . she'd gained weight and had done *little* tipping of the elbow which helped a lot." Over the next three years Mamie proved less abstemious, beginning on most days at lunch with two or three shots. She endured chronic headaches, could not sleep, and rarely kept her food down. She lost thirty pounds the first year Ike was away, and she did not regain them until after the war. Rumors circulated that she had been treated for alcoholism. But in the 1940s appearances had to be maintained; reports of the Supreme Commander's wife drinking would have made too many GIs worry about their own sweethearts' excesses.

Ike felt guilty about the "calamitous" impact his success had on Mamie. With the husband overworked and guilt-ridden, the wife lonely and depressed, relations between the Eisenhowers deteriorated. Their letters became skirmishes in their decades-long war. They missed each other and accused each other of neglect. In December 1943, General Eisenhower teletyped his wife that after no letters for "over three weeks . . . I had come to believe that you had retired into a convent." Mamie insisted she was averaging three letters per week.

For three long years Mamie wallowed in loneliness, self-pity, and jealousy. She feared that Ike had not only abandoned her but replaced her. The more reporters played up the familial angle in covering Ike's entourage, the more Mamie stewed. Ike had clearly taken a shine to his attractive aide, Kay Summersby. Frustrated by his "rather lonely life" abroad, he yearned for "feminine companionship." The witty, gay, aristocratic Irishwoman may have reminded Ike of the Mamie he met in 1916. But now, almost three decades later, Mamie was frail, while Kay was vigorous; Mamie was nervous and provincial, while Kay was brash and sophisticated; Mamie was demanding, while Kay was fun; and Mamie was three thousand miles away, while Kay was next door. Kay would recall Ike saying to her: "Kay, there's nobody . . . I can talk to freely. They all ask to be promoted, or if I talk to the wrong person, what I say is reported all over the world. I know that I can let my thoughts flow with you." In Africa, Italy, France, Germany, and back home in London, Kay accompanied the general. Gossips on both sides of the Atlantic speculated about a sexual relationship. "Leave Kay and Ike alone," one general said. "She's helping him win the war."

Many wives worried that their soldier boys would stray, just as many soldiers worried about their wives' fidelity. The macho posturing of the barracks, the rejection of civilian constraints, the loneliness and the fear, all undermined traditional morality. Until the end of her life, Mamie would insist that nothing untoward happened between her husband and his chauffeur. "Of course, I don't believe it," she told an old friend. "I know Ike." But during the war, Ike had to reassure her repeatedly. "I love you all the time," he wrote in February 1943, "don't go bothering your pretty head about WAACs—etc. etc." Two years later he wrote: "Stop worrying about me. The few women I've met are nothing—absolutely nothing compared to you, and besides I've neither the time nor the youth to worry about them. I love you— always." Another time he moped in the age-old lament of husbands, be they innocent or guilty: "Apparently you don't choose to believe anything I say."

When the war ended, Ike retreated from Kay. Kay, who fell for her boss after her American fiancé died, was shattered. In 1948 she published *Ike Was My Boss,* a chaste rendition of their intense relationship. Ike feared that the publicity would refuel the rumors, but Summersby's wholesome account fit with the ethos of the time. Throughout the war, the rumors were relegated to hints in gossip columns and insinuations in mainstream articles that placed Kay prominently at Ike's side. Reporters had no interest, though, in knocking down the all-American hero they created. Besides, talk of sexual peccadilloes was not suitable for family magazines and newspapers. America's fragile wartime morale could not sustain an honest conversation about the illicit liaisons on the battlefront and on the home front.

That Ike had a wartime affair became widely believed only after the sexual revolution spread cynicism throughout the land. In Merle Miller's 1973 bestseller, *Plain Speaking*, Harry Truman claimed that Ike planned to divorce Mamie to marry Kay. Three years later, desperate for cash as she lay dying, Kay wrote *Past Forgetting: My Love Affair with Dwight Eisenhower*. This steamier book came out posthumously under her married name, Kay Summersby Morgan. Kay did not mention a plan for Ike to divorce. Still, in 1979 an ABC television miniseries treated Kay as the general's mistress.

To counter these claims, John Eisenhower published his father's wartime letters to his mother. Ike's son was forced to admit that "no one alive can say that isolated incidents as described by Mrs. Morgan positively did *not* happen." Still, he found Kay's stories exaggerated. John portrayed his father as a devoted husband and an honorable man.

While popular opinion was deciding that Eisenhower had betrayed Mamie, most historians agreed with John Eisenhower. It is hard to believe that a man with Ike's sense of honor and concern about public appearances would court disaster with a wartime romance. It is even harder to believe that he would be so cruel as to send his son John with his wife and mistress to the Broadway show *Oklahoma!* when Kay visited the United States. It is more plausible that Ike was trying to quash Mamie's jealousy and get two women who were close to him acquainted with each other.

Men like Eisenhower often had surrogate wives like Kay at work. One can fault Eisenhower for being insensitive to appearances and for committing a kind of psychological adultery with Kay, but he was in a difficult situation. Exiled from home, overworked, in need of support and the kind of grounding that men of his generation could only receive from women, Ike turned to Kay—but kept his honor. "Some men are so built that they like to have a different drag for every hop," Ike wrote John in 1943. "I think the whole family from which you spring is a bit on the intense side and centers on one thing at a time, be it a girl, a horse, a game or just loafing." This stick-to-it-iveness may have explained Ike's concentration on Kay as well as his fidelity to Mamie. To the extent that Ike resisted temptation he illustrated his love for Mamie and respect for marriage. He also showed that Ida Eisenhower's maternal lectures about self-restraint worked.

The Eisenhowers' wartime experience illustrated the complicated calculus of sacrifice. General Eisenhower faced death but enjoyed a sense of control; his wife enjoyed physical safety but endured a psychological purgatory. This sense that women had to be worthy of the "real sacrifices" men were making made many "widows" feel guilty about their despair. In keeping with the ethos of their generation, many repressed these feelings or expressed them indirectly, as Mamie did.

When the war finally ended, Ike praised Mamie for "having done a tip-top job in her position at home." The Eisenhowers were thrilled to be reunited, but each recognized that the other had "changed terrifically." "Neither of us really knew what the other went through," Mamie confided to her neighbor Perle Mesta. Surrounded by an entourage, an aura, and ever-escalating demands, Ike "belonged to the world and not to me any more," Mamie sighed. It would take time to heal their marriage, as it would many other veterans' relationships. In a conscious counterpoint to his official family's adoring memoirs, Mamie referred to that time as "my three years without Eisenhower."

The Eisenhowers had to readjust to each other and adjust to their celebrity. Mamie was bred to be on display, but the public scrutiny was relentless and vulgar. She did not want to share Ike any more. Ike enjoyed some of the adulation and the money—finally he could shower Mamie with gifts, including her first fur coat. Yet he had lost his autonomy. "It seems that everybody can enjoy 'freedom of speech' except me," he moped. Ike's fame seemed to have a life of its own, taking the Kansas farm boy to the top job in the U.S. Army in 1945, the presidency of Columbia University in 1948, the leadership of NATO in 1951, and—barely eight years after the war ended—the White House.

Ike worried about Mamie's veto at every step along the way. Notwithstanding her rhetoric about always following Ike, Mamie was whiny, strong-willed, needy, and frail. At first she refused to leave her wartime bastion in the Wardman Park Hotel. "We had almost to take her physically and transport her" to the chief of staff's luxurious quarters at Fort Myer, the Eisenhowers' doctor recalled. The general was flabbergasted. He could not recognize that Mamie was having trouble leaving her cocoon. Ike's biggest "doubts" about becoming president of Columbia University concerned "the possible volume of social duties devolving on Mrs. Eisenhower." He told Tom Watson, the IBM president and Columbia trustee, that "although extremely capable she is not too strong; consequently she has to pace herself and watch her health."

The daily requests for appearances, interviews, and charity sponsorships overwhelmed Mamie. "Ho Hum, I'm a rotten liar," she chirped as she instructed her secretary to deflect yet another demand. Mamie wanted to "stay out of the public eye." She socialized with friends and spurned big parties. When Ike headed NATO in Paris, wags joked that "there is about as much chance of getting the General and Mamie to a cocktail party as of getting Stalin or the Pope to a fancy-dress ball at the Ritz."

Reporters pestered her, eager to profile the "woman behind the happy grin that Dwight D. Eisenhower wears." Mamie aggressively embraced the wife's passive role. "I am perfectly satisfied to be known as a housewife," she said. Mamie rooted "a whole philosophy of life" in the traditional division of labor: "A woman's primary job is to remember the little things which can contribute so much to the happiness of others." She loved to tell about the time Queen Elizabeth greeted her at Balmoral in Scotland. "The first thing the Queen asked me was had I brought along a hot-water bottle." Such attention to detail was the key to gracious living.

Mamie Eisenhower became a champion of American domesticity. She taught housewives how to make their men happy. Her husband had led the men to war; Mamie would ensure their warm welcome home. Magazines filled with examples of patriotic housewives praised Mamie as "a good wife, a good mother, and a good American." In making the traditional sex roles patriotic, Mamie and her countrymen exorcised the spirits of the war. Ike was back home, and everything in America should return to normal.

Mamie loved America's new consumerism. Between 1946 and 1950, as Americans bought more than 20 million refrigerators, 5.5 million electric stoves, and 11.6 million television sets, the Eisenhowers went on their own shopping spree. Mamie had deferred her dreams longer and had a husband who was now richer than most Americans. She became famous for her silk bed jackets, for her Mary Chess Yram scent, and for painting her bedroom—wherever she lived—in "her pet interior-decorating scheme" of Williamsburg green and rose. When the Eisenhowers went to Europe in 1951, Mamie took thirteen trunks and twenty-five other pieces of luggage containing, among other items, twenty-one pocketbooks and ten evening bags. "As an American woman I have always valued my right to pretty clothes," she declared in a message supporting National Fashion Press Week. Mamie's changing publicity shots contrasted the austerity of wartime with the profligacy of the peace. When she posed for the November 1950 issue of *McCall's*, she was no longer wearing the simple gay frocks or sensible suits of the 1940s. Dressed in a low-cut elegant gown, her neck, ears, and wrist glittered with large and expensive jewelry.

The Eisenhower marriage recovered slowly, and the campaign to draft Ike for president threatened their fragile peace. Supporters appealed to Ike's Achilles' heel, "the all-important item of duty." "These days we never seem to be free of someone nagging and yelping at us that we have a duty to do this, a greater one to do that," Ike moaned. Surprisingly, though, the pressures of deciding to run, campaigning, and then moving into the White House would come to unite Mamie and Ike. Their marriage, like those of the Johnsons, Bushes, and Clintons, would blossom in the presidency. The White House would finally heal the wounds of war.

This marital healing, in part, reflected the cold war's politicization of domestic life. Americans believed that domestic weakness, be it corruption in Washington or marital discord at home, threatened their country's standing in its life-and-death struggle with communism. Many, like the Eisenhowers, responded to the challenge; by tailoring a life to an ideal standard, they ended up approximating it.

For ten years, Dwight Eisenhower had been built up as a hero. He was comfortable with kings and the scourge of dictators. Now he was no longer Every-man, but a great man. Though magnified, he had been humanized as well. In this emerging celebrity era, articles, newsreels, and radio shows celebrated him while exposing the virtuous man "behind" the smile. Americans felt they knew Ike—they were on a first-name basis—and they could trust him. The pro-found bonds between a leader and his followers had intensified. Americans knew his wife, his brothers, his late mother, and his son. "Thru the articles written about you I feel as though I know you," a Minnesotan wrote to Mamie.

Like Harry Truman, Ike worried that "this whole business is so tough on my family." He resented the focus on "personalities rather than principles." Even once he decided to run, he found himself "really dread[ing]—for the first time in my life—the prospect of coming back to my country." And he is-sued strict orders to keep the family out of politics.

Mamie claimed she "would never presume to advise" Ike about running. She steeled herself against the inevitable. Their friends Bill Robinson and Cliff Roberts visited Paris to push Ike. Mamie cried, "Bill, what have you done to us?" Imitating his wife's tendency to succumb to stress, Ike developed a bad cold and conjunctivitis. By June 1952, however, he was ready.

As Ike planned the campaign and worried about what to say, Mamie planned the move and worried about what to wear. "My mind is in a tizzy thinking about all the packing," she told a friend. "You know how much a gal can accumulate."

Ike would crusade for Abilene's traditional values. "If each of us in his own mind would dwell more upon those simple virtues—integrity, courage, self-confidence, an unshakable belief in his bible—would not some of these problems tend to simplify themselves?" he asked at his hometown campaign kickoff. This appeal became more compelling after Ike captured the Repub-lican nomination and learned he would be facing Governor Adlai E. Steven-son of Illinois. Stevenson was divorced; according to *Time*, only 31 percent of voters surveyed would definitely vote for the most qualified candidate if he were a divorcé. Having a loyal wife at his side boosted Ike's standing.

Of course, an ex-wife was better than a drunken wife or a betrayed woman. The Eisenhowers' united front negated the Kay Summersby rumors and demonstrated Mamie's sobriety. During the campaign for the nomina-tion, some delegates inquired about Mamie's drinking. Ike nonchalantly said, "Well, I know, that story has gone around, but the truth of the matter is that I don't think Mamie's had a drink for something like 18 months." Mamie never posed for a photograph with a glass in her hand, even if she was sipping Coca-Cola. Too many people would misinterpret the contents of the glass.

Ike worked Mamie into his act. Together, they made the campaign train a rolling Club Eisenhower. Like Truman and his "boss," Ike ended each whistlestop by saying, "And now meet my Mamie." Mamie said she always knew where she stood with Ike: "If he's a little bit miffed he'll say, 'And now here is Mrs. Eisenhower.'" When Ike flew to New York for the Alfred E. Smith memorial dinner, Mamie stayed aboard. Aides praised Mamie as the first candidate's wife to campaign "on a train all alone." The ovations surprised Mamie—and Ike's handlers. They were discovering that the ubiquitous "I Like Ike" buttons told only half the story. As *Life* proclaimed, "THEY LIKE MAMIE, TOO."

Mamie refused to deliver speeches. "I leave all the talking to Ike," she would say. The one time she addressed an issue she babbled: "Of course the Korean war must be settled soon, but of course we don't want peace at any price." One reporter who feared yet another silent First Lady quipped: "Mamie is now working a full 16-hour day not making speeches and not taking stands."

On the campaign train, Mamie was as nurturing as Bess Truman had been. Women appreciated how well this town belle turned Army wife "talked lady-talk." Mamie occasionally criticized a speech if she felt Ike was not being himself. Her mother, Mrs. Doud, who was known affectionately as "Min," was the more frequent and tougher critic. Mamie most preferred to play "the sweetheart." Campaign rallies featured two songs, "The Sunshine of Your Smile" and "Mamie, What a Wonderful Word is Mamie."

Citizens who failed to see Mamie and Ike in person still could see them together. Some of Ike's pioneering TV commercials featured his wife talking about the high cost of shopping. Political wives were prized commodities in the brave new world of television cameras and consumption values. Radio ads and press releases about "Mamie Eisenhower . . . Bride" were campaign commercials masquerading as household tips.

Even Democrats acknowledged Ike's greatness and celebrated Mamie. Some observers called Mamie's radiant ability to "win the crowd" a "sort of unspoken communication that only women seem to master." Such attitudes, typified by Ike's discomfort with focusing on personalities, viewed the spread of personality and emotional appeals as part of a weakening, a feminization, of American politics. Others acknowledged that voters of both sexes responded to charismatic appeals. "This feeling" both Eisenhowers evoked, "however illogical, is an extremely important political fact," a reporter in *Life* insisted.

As with the Trumans, most profiles focused on either one member of the couple or the other. Ike appeared to be the typical husband, happy to delegate household matters to his "helpmate." Mamie emerged as the ideal wife with great range, a "homebody" both glamorous enough to greet Queen Elizabeth and practical enough to be a good mom. This woman knew her place. One friend assured *Time* readers that "Mamie won't be an Eleanor. She isn't a girl who wants publicity." *Life* predicted she would have "all the highly commendable dignity of Bess Truman enlivened with a touch of Ethel Merman on the side."

The campaign drained the Eisenhowers. By mid-October Mamie had swollen ankles, unaccustomed as she was to walking so much. The campaign had two plans every day—one if she felt well enough to appear, one if she did not. She said: "I do all I can but I can't do any more than I can do, because if I do I'll be sick, and if I get sick I'll be a burden to Ike, and I can't be a burden to Ike." Mamie was less successful in pacing her husband. By the end, Ike was the sick one.

While Mamie fought to preserve her strength, Ike fought for his soul. After meeting with Republican pols, Ike grumbled: "All they talked about was how they would win on my popularity. Nobody said I had a brain in my head." Periodically, he defied his advisers and ghostwriters to appear independent. Reading one itinerary, he chuckled: "Politics is a funny thing. Thirty five pages to get me into Philadelphia—the invasion of Normandy was on five pages." As President, Ike would often shelter his popularity by distancing himself from politics and politicians.

Mamie's politicking "astonished" Ike. Mamie herself admitted she was acting "out of character." She took credit for helping to win that "all-important . . . family vote." It was hard to believe that the frail "Mrs. Ike" generated so much excitement among Republican matrons at a rally in Boston that the *Boston Herald* compared it to "a bunch of bobby soxers greeting a matinee idol." The analogy was telling. Americans had learned from Hollywood how to worship fame.

After the dowdy Eleanor Roosevelt and the frumpy Bess Truman, many women looked forward to having a chic First Lady again. Some begged Mamie to change her childish bangs, but most applauded her taste. "Fashion needs 'living dolls' to animate it," one reporter said, rejoicing that both the fifty-eight-year-old Mamie and the twenty-six-year-old Elizabeth—who was set to become queen in June 1953—would be trendsetters.

The accolades Mamie attracted made Ike proud, if a bit unsettled. James Reston of the *New York Times* estimated that "Mamie must be worth at least 50 electoral votes." In a conversational ritual of the times, friends praised the wife for outdoing the husband. "I think she is mainly responsible for the victory," Ike's close friend, General Alfred M. Gruenther, Jr., declared. Such praise could make insecure husbands jealous. In October one friend told Ike, "You're doing a splendid job. There's only one person who's doing a better one." The general frowned. When the friend said: "Mamie," Ike replied: "You're damned right. I go off and make a speech, Mamie just goes out and says, 'Hi, folks,' and she gets better applause than I do."

Protocol compelled women to deflect these compliments. "You are a dear," Mamie told Gruenther, "but we both know that the real reason . . . was that the American people responded so enthusiastically to Ike's sincerity." Throughout their tenure, the Eisenhowers would be told, as one fan would telegram: "HISTORY KNOWS THAT NO MAN EVER BECAME GREAT WITH-OUT THE HELP OF A WOMAN." The companionate marriage emphasized in-terdependence; the Eisenhowers together were greater than Ike himself.

For all their teamwork, the Eisenhowers kept to their separate spheres. Politicos now encircled Ike. On election night, Ike and his aides sat in one room in the Commodore Hotel. Mamie was upstairs in another suite with a dozen ladies. Sitting on the floor, watching the television announcers pro-claim her husband President of the United States, Mamie felt lonely and cried.

Mamie Eisenhower had become too shrewd a politician to reveal such an-guish in public. Her ebullience was central to her appeal, just as Ike's smile was to his. The Eisenhowers proved to be as heroic in peacetime as they had been during the war. Mamie's mass-marketed femininity helped women dis-tance themselves from the war's spartan demands to ration and to work; Ike's masculinity helped protect veterans from going soft.

Only a war hero could have gotten away with the widely reprinted photo-graph of Ike and Mamie in their jammies, which first appeared in October. The two seemed elegant yet accessible. Ike appeared confident, robust, and still somehow dignified. Mamie's warm smile, polished nails, satin night-gown, and bracelet with a big "IKE" charm qualified her as the perfect wife. *Life* ran the photograph side by side with an advertisement of a housewife sit-ting at her Mary Proctor Hi-Lo Ironing Table. "NOW . . . END IRONING DRUDGERY FOREVER!" the ad proclaimed. The three beaming smiles, the three waving hands, epitomized the Eisenhowers' promise of postwar pros-perity and domestic bliss.

Both Eisenhowers understood that this popularity would only last if they did not seek it. Most reporters "will eventually turn upon a man who shows any indication of courting them in his own self-interest, no matter how 'col-orful' they may deem him at first," Dwight had noted during the war. Mamie kept a dignified reserve from reporters and speechmaking, while Ike dutifully grumbled about the hoopla. Somewhat defensively, he insisted that he cam-paigned not on personalities but on "convictions." Yet even Mamie would admit that Ike's "sincerity" carried the day. It would be his most powerful tool as President.

III

Ike and Mamie were now America's leading and representative couple. Ike joined his wife's Presbyterian church to set a proper example. After church on the morning of the inauguration, Ike said to Mamie, "You always have a kind of special sense of propriety in such matters. Do you think it would be ap-propriate for me to include a prayer in my Inauguration Address?" With Mamie's encouragement, Ike composed a prayer in ten minutes.

After taking the oath of office and before offering his prayer, Ike broke another precedent. He kissed his wife on the cheek. Such touches helped make the day "a real homey homecoming," the *Washington Post* rejoiced, continuing three months of gushing tributes.

Most new residents enter the White House with enthusiastic reviews; the Eisenhowers elicited particularly rhapsodic coverage. "This is a different kind of story," Jay Franklin, a former New Dealer turned Eisenhower devotee, would write in 1953.

> It is the tale of old stock, solid Americans in every part of a large country, working and living and trying to do their duty to their nation and their family and their God. It is the America of Currier & Ives . . . the small towns where girls in pigtails play hopscotch and learn to cook and go to Sunday schools, where small boys whoop and scuffle in the piles of autumn leaves around the Soldiers monument, and neighbors need not lock their doors at night. . . . It is the salt of the American earth, the essence of our society, the hope of our future, the very best we have.

The sexual division of labor was a key part of this appeal. An AP dispatch defined Mamie as "a remarkable woman in an unremarkable way," the "guardian of Ike's health, social assistant and home maker." The couple's traditional "teamwork" reaffirmed for the *Wichita Eagle* "that the home is the center of our civilization" and suited an administration "with its accent on the unity of the people as the only basis for solving America's problems." Mamie updated the line she had used since World War II, saying, "Ike runs the country and I turn the lamb chops." The President usually withdrew into a vague but enthusiastic endorsement of his wife as his "invaluable . . . indispensable partner." In later years Ike explained that "Mamie's biggest contribution was to make the White House livable, comfortable, and meaningful for the people who came in. . . . She exuded hospitality."

In fact, being First Lady entailed more than "turning lamb chops," which never had been Mamie's forte. "Ike and I have been quite busy," she told a friend after the first month, "he with conferences and meetings and planning—I with luncheons, benefits, receptions, picture-taking and such." "A smile," she sighed, "is very necessary in this job."

The "White House takes quite a bit of housekeeping," Mamie learned, but she claimed "that is what I enjoy." The 107-room, 16-bath executive mansion had 18,694 pieces of china, glass, and silver, received a thousand letters in an average week, and hosted six hundred thousand visitors a year. Seventy-two servants staffed the mansion. "I am never happy until I know exactly how and why things are done in any home of mine, but I am little by little taking hold of the reins," Mamie reported after a few weeks.

Mamie had feared she was too much the "little violet" to be a great hostess, but she came to enjoy "meet[ing] people from all over the country." She sponsored dozens of organizations and greeted thousands of visitors from the Maryland Women's Council, the National Institute for Dry Cleaners, and the International Chamber of Commerce. Short breaks helped Mamie cope with receiving lines of up to six hundred people. "I feel that I have shaken millions of hands!" she exulted, proud of her stamina.

Mamie's enthusiasm was infectious and endearing. During the Truman administration gossips had told how one guest overheard Mrs. Truman asking after a reception, "Who was that dowdy bunch of women?" Now, when reporters asked about her mother's claim that she had never said, "Well, I'm glad that's over!" after a big party, Mamie exclaimed, "How could I? I love people too much."

The President's men worried about Mamie's relations with the press. She disliked reporters and politicians, and barred them from the Eisenhowers' Gettysburg, Pennsylvania, home. Eisenhower's aides also wanted to protect Mamie. They announced that the First Lady avoided "personal involvement in matters of public policy," would "not take part in any TV or radio program," would not make speeches, and would not "make out of town appointments." The administration even prohibited reporters from quoting Mamie directly. Staffers advised "Mrs. Ike" and her social secretary, Mary Jane McCaffree, that any deviations from these "ironclad" rules would establish a "precedent" Mamie did not want and cause requests to "come flooding in."

By keeping Mamie more like Grace Coolidge than Eleanor Roosevelt, the administration solidified its identity as the conservative rejoinder to the New Deal. The President's unwillingness to dismantle the welfare state made symbols all the more important. Besides, Mrs. Coolidge's reticence suited the protocols of the Eisenhowers' relationship. Neither Ike nor Mamie wanted her doing his work for him. She just wanted to "look after Ike." She banned shop talk at home; he kept home life away from the office.

Still, no one wanted to fight with reporters. Mamie distinguished herself from Bess Truman and Eleanor Roosevelt by holding a press conference for men and women. It only tantalized reporters because she never held another one. For the next eight years they pressed the First Lady for material. "Every woman will be fascinated with the details of the service" at a state dinner, editors from *Time-Life* claimed. "Do let every day people know more about you!" Helen Reid of the *New York Herald Tribune* begged her friend. Mamie tolerated coverage of her public activities; however, as the assistant press secretary Murray Snyder reminded Mrs. McCaffree in 1955, reporters were "denied access" to Mamie's "reactions as First Lady, her philosophy as a mother, housewife, soldier's wife." As a result, Fleur Cowles of *Look* sighed, reporters relied "on stale and by now overworked features." A portrait of Mrs. Eisenhower could "only" be a "rewrite job."

In the 1950s, politicians still had more power than those who covered them. Mamie and Ike could keep reporters at bay, choosing which scraps to throw at them. Reporters were more likely to collaborate with politicians than expose them, to defer to politicians rather than confront them. The leading journalists of the day, Walter Lippmann, Arthur Krock, and James Reston, were courtiers, not scolds.

Mrs. Eisenhower did make the occasional public service announcement, just as Mrs. Truman had done. These nonpartisan, patriotic appeals usually were addressed to women. The First Lady began a $93 million American Red Cross drive by appealing to American mothers' readiness to "respond to any call which promises greater protection and happiness for their families."

The "constant merry-go-round" was "tiring," but Mamie paced herself. She tried to spend every morning in bed, and every now and then did not get up all day, especially during the summer. She told her staff "that every woman over fifty should stay in bed until noon." After the President asked her to host one dinner too many, she erupted: "Now look here, Ike, I'm doing everything I can to make this thing go. Don't push me any harder because I just won't be able to take it."

The White House hired a half-dozen stenographers to help with Mamie's growing correspondence. Officially, however, she had just one aide, Mary Jane McCaffree. The *Congressional Directory* of 1953 set a precedent by listing McCaffree as "Acting Secretary to the President's Wife." This listing presaged the expanded staffs of the future. For now, when citizens called a staff for the First Lady monarchical and expensive, White House aides were happy to say that "Mrs. Eisenhower has only one secretary."

Despite their lack of access, reporters conceded that Mamie's popularity and her charm made for good stories. "IKE'S MAMIE ENDEARS HERSELF TO AMERICANS," headlines proclaimed. Dowagers grumbled that Mamie entertained infrequently and lacked sophistication. Nevertheless, they acknowledged her grace and her command of the social scene. General Henry Aurand would deem her "as gracious a First Lady as had been in the White House in a long time. If we define it by what we call 'gracious' in my younger days." Mamie had discovered a key to First Lady success: Go retro. Americans always praise a First Lady who exudes older values and virtues.

Still, a First Lady of the 1950s faced certain modern demands. Every week, hundreds of letters arrived addressed to Mrs. Eisenhower. Only since Mrs. Roosevelt had First Ladies received so much mail. Many were requests for autographs and photographs, a mark of the First Lady's growing celebrity. Others were heartbreaking personal appeals, a mark of her increasing politicization as well as of the traditional assumption that good works were a lady's domain. Widows, mothers, daughters, and grandmothers asked the First Lady to help search for a son who was missing in action, to increase an elderly mother's public assistance, to determine why a husband at Goodfellow Air Force Base in Texas had not been paid, to secure special permission for a sergeant on duty to get married, to arrange housing in a government project, to expedite a GI loan to purchase a home, or to explain why the Bureau of Internal Revenue disallowed a deduction of $536 for a husband's part-time work. Other letters were more policy oriented, demanding equal treatment for all disabled veterans, urging the continuation of rent control, or asking that college boys be drafted into the Korean War before fathers. Each request was duly forwarded to a government agency, many of which had not existed the last time Republicans ruled: the Economic Stabilization Agency, the Selective Service System, and the Federal Security Agency, for example. After two decades of Democratic rule and a world war, Americans relied on the federal government in unprecedented ways. They turned to the First Lady as first mother, a crucial ally in promoting the nurturing qualities of the federal government.

This combination of femininity's traditional allure and modern government's activist "nanny state" was powerful. At times, Mamie's retreat from these substantive issues made her appear frivolous. Her public role as the merry hostess could reinforce this impression. Her bangs, her charm bracelet commemorating key moments in Ike's career, and her expensive dresses became regular conversation topics. She frequented lists of the "ten best-dressed women" in America. A *Better Homes and Gardens* profile concluded: "Propped up on the rose-colored satin bed, with a matching pink ribbon in her hair, Mamie resembles nothing so much as the last bonbon in the box."

The First Lady reveled in triviality. Each week Mamie wrote to dozens of friends. The notes blathered about her health, Ike's health, her mother's health, the grandchildren's antics, her exhaustion, his exhaustion, her card games, his card games. Mamie detailed her quests for the perfect dress, for the ideal flourish at Gettysburg. Royalty came and went, wars were declared and averted, but Mamie ignored them, busy forming Scrabble "words in my sleep all night instead of canastas and bolivias" or "mulling over my wardrobe—and Christmas shopping" in August. The visit of the chancellor of Germany merited a mention because Frau Adenauer "brought me the loveliest Frankenthal figurines"; after the Republican convention renominated her husband in 1956, Mamie delighted in "the purple satin dress I wore . . . it is always a gamble to know what to take on such a trip." "The latest news is that [her grandson] David has lost his first tooth," she reported on March 31, 1954, as her husband faced an outcry over American hydrogen bomb tests and the Russians stirred trouble in East Berlin. When world events intruded, Mamie bristled. "Because of the Israeli condition we cut our vacation short," she complained to her friend Mabel in February 1957, as the Suez crisis flared again.

In the end, Mamie's obsession with minutiae triumphed over its critics and grounded the Eisenhowers. Her chitchat kept her on par with her friends, charmed millions, and distracted her husband. In a world of nuclear wars and round-the-clock servants, Ike appreciated Mamie's light touch. Ike was used to the male insularity of the Army and did not solicit Mamie's advice; instead he craved her humanity, the reality check she offered the President. Mamie could no longer make her husband do the dishes weekly, as she had at Columbia University and in Paris, but she kept him aware of daily life. No matter how high they soared, both Eisenhowers remained down-to-earth. As contemporaries said, they "walked with kings and talked with queens but still retained the common touch."

Ike needed Mamie in the White House. "This is a slave's life," he complained. A president could not even escape the workload by walking alone on the streets. Rather than viewing the White House as a jail, though, the Eisenhowers made it their refuge. They enjoyed the protection after ten years of prying eyes and pawing hands. They hosted old friends, watched television, and screened movies. "At last I've got a job where I can stay home nights and, by golly, I'm going to stay home," Ike said. Mamie was thrilled. Many prudes were shocked to discover that the First Lady and the President slept in the same bed—although they often formally had separate bedrooms. Mamie explained that she liked to reach over in the middle of the night "and pat Ike on his old bald head anytime I want to."

Mamie would not waste their precious evenings together lobbying. The President occasionally said he would ask Mamie about a controversial decision, but that may have been a way of buying time. Like his wife, Ike was a master of indirection. Mamie only entered the Oval Office four times in eight years—"and each time I was invited," she insisted. In 1,400 pages of White House memoirs, Ike would mention Mamie only 51 times.

Instead of Mamie, Ike's brother Milton was the President's confidant. "To me, he wasn't the President of the United States, he was a brother whom I respected and loved very deeply," Milton would recall. "Therefore, he could think out loud with me." Given Milton's experience in government, Ike's discomfort with women, and the protocols of the Eisenhowers' marriage, the younger brother was a better policy "spouse" than the wife.

The Gettysburg farm symbolized the Eisenhowers' newfound harmony. Ike would "rebuild that house completely as the one thing I can do really to satisfy her." He also wanted "to give her an outside interest that will pull her away from Washington occasionally." This thank-you to his wife proved expensive, as Mamie scoured the world for fine fabrics and beautiful furniture. Costs soared, an exasperated Ike would recall, when "Mamie occasionally forgot a detail or two" in her planning, including central air conditioning and properly placed electric switches. Still, they both loved their "dream house." Mamie was delirious. By 1957 she could say that she was "loath to leave Gettysburg. The peace and quiet of our farm is ideal and the fact that it is our first real home means much."

Here, too, the Eisenhowers paralleled one of the great trends of their times. The 1950s were the heyday of the single-family tract house. "No man who owns his own house and lot can be a Communist," said the master builder William J. Levitt. "He has too much to do." Mamie epitomized the suburban housewife who made decorating and shopping full-time occupations, just as Ike played the role of the overworked husband trying to earn enough to finance all the chintz and satin.

Like so many of their peers, the Eisenhowers played marital hot potato. Each claimed the other was "the boss." The Eisenhowers' struggle paralleled that of another popular couple, television's Lucy and Ricky Ricardo. In both the Ricardo home and the White House, the wife subverted the husband's apparent authority: Lucy through buffoonery, Mamie through coquetry. When Lucy feared she was losing Ricky, she concocted harebrained schemes to make him jealous; when Mamie had feared she was losing Ike, she "vamped" him. Mamie even hosted the cast of "I Love Lucy" at the White House and was mentioned in an episode about golf widowhood. Yet the real-life Ricardos subverted traditional sex roles, just as the Eisenhowers reinforced them. Desilu Productions was a joint venture, and after their divorce in 1960, Lucille Ball eclipsed Desi Arnaz. The Eisenhowers, on the other hand, were the real thing. "I never pretended to be anything but Ike's wife," Mamie said.

IV

Both Mamie and Ike felt swept up by forces they could not control, schedules and responsibilities they could not avoid. Even brief escapes became vital. One afternoon, when rain canceled his golf match, Ike looked out the Oval Office window and moaned, "Sometimes I feel so sorry for myself I could cry."

Whereas the Trumans had shuttled between Independence and the White House, the Eisenhowers roamed around America, fleeing to Maryland, Pennsylvania, Colorado, and Georgia. Camp David, just ninety miles from Washington, was convenient but too imperial. Gettysburg was the most sentimental option, but it often entailed too many chores. Denver was the regular venue for the Eisenhowers' summer vacation. Mamie felt free to collapse in her girlhood home and "ward off public invasions of our privacy there." Only after three weeks of "complete rest" in 1953 could Mamie report, "Today is the first day that I have felt like a human being and am anxious to get my hair done and go for a drive some place." Unfortunately, Denver's high altitude strained Mamie's heart.

The Eisenhowers found the most excitement at the Augusta National Golf Center in Georgia. This playground for two hundred wealthy couples symbolized the Eisenhowers' ascent to the top of American society. Members of the club contributed $200,000 to stock "Ike's Pond" with fish and build the six-room, two-story "Mamie's Cabin." Here is where fellow sufferers helped Mamie cope with the burdens of golf widowhood. She enjoyed the opportunity to "be alone when you want to [b]e—and yet there are always friends available if you are inclined to be sociable." In anticipating a "dash" to Augusta for a golfing weekend, Ike confessed, "I am almost like a little boy in my anxiety to get started."

Such enthusiasm was uncharacteristic. Despite his famous smile, Ike inherited his dad's remoteness. A lifelong struggle with his temper, thirty-six years in the Army, and a decade on the world stage made Ike more aloof. "Anglo-Saxon men usually find it difficult to exchange direct expressions of sentiment and affection. I am as subject to this inhibition as is any other person," he stiltedly confessed to his friend Bill Robinson, publisher of the *New York Herald Tribune*. With Mamie, Ike was not demonstrative and did not chitchat. Mamie's weakness and Icky's death made Ike more reserved. At one point after the war, as Kay Summersby carried on about her dead fiancé, Ike mused: "Makes one wonder whether any human ever dares become so wrapped up in another that all happiness and desire to live is determined by the actions, desires—or life—of the second."

This reserve, combined with many moves over the years, sent Ike into the White House with few lifelong friends nearby. His disdain for politicians kept him from socializing with them. Yet he and Mamie were sociable people. Increasingly, the Eisenhowers turned to "the Washington gang" of magnates and power brokers they befriended in the late 1940s, most of whom belonged to Augusta. These people were more glamorous, more wealthy, and more available than the old Army buddies. These "congenial friends" flattered and financed the Eisenhowers. All were on call, ready to mobilize one of their private jets whenever the President wanted a foursome of golf or a rubber of bridge.

Dwight Eisenhower had a poor boy's fascination with rich people. Great wealth was one thing that still impressed him—and that he had not attained. With the farmhouse renovations costing nearly $215,000, Mamie and her husband envied their friends' bankbooks. Cash flow became so tight in the White House that Ike made a payment on the farm for Mamie's birthday; it usually came out of her account as "boss of the money." The Eisenhowers' friends racked their brains for ways to please the President and his lady. Mamie's offices in the East Wing became a clearinghouse for tens of thousands of dollars' worth of gifts. Cases of scotch, sides of beef, crates of fruit, and the finest leather, silver, and gold goods flowed into the White House.

Ike and Mamie usually reciprocated on a smaller scale or with one of Mamie's charming thank-you notes.

Furnishing the Gettysburg farm became a nationwide project. Corporate America sent a 1,300-pound Black Angus cow and 150-pound calf from the Brandywine Angus Breeders Association, two thousand flower bulbs from some Washington florists, a $3,000 putting green from the Professional Golf Association, a $25,000 power-tool shop. Leading fund-raisers sent antiques and a Black Arabian filly. Most Americans considered this largesse a hero's due. The *Minneapolis Tribune* reported: "Each mention of the Black Angus gift herd at Gettysburg appears to provoke more offers."

"The gang" opened the Eisenhowers to a world of private planes and country estates. Members boasted that they never asked the President for a favor; none ever initiated a discussion about politics or policy. The members of the gang wanted only one thing from the Eisenhowers: friendship with "the outstanding American at the time" and his wife. Reminiscing about one visit, Ike praised "the informality of the occasion, the free exchange of views among good fellows, with no pressures or exhortations marring the quality of a pleasant conversation."

The friends heaped compliments on the Eisenhowers as enthusiastically as they heaped gifts. When "the boss" made a good shot, they blew their cart horns. Every toast—and there were many—praised Ike and Mamie for their patriotism and their love. Everything the Eisenhowers did or touched was the nicest, the finest, the best.

Even though no one from the gang lobbied Ike, they shaped his Presidency. In choosing this group of friends, Ike embraced the mores of America's smug WASP elite. Their rigid world had many rules and no room for self-doubt. They luxuriated in their preeminence. People were expected to know the right thing to do, and to socialize with the right people. Regarding one weekend, Priscilla Slater doubted that anyone was invited to be with the Eisenhowers "but the only members who turned up were those who knew in their hearts they would be welcome."

The President hosted many members of the gang at his periodic "stag dinners." Ike would invite up to sixteen leading Americans for a "personal" discussion. Mamie went to bed early or screened a movie. As Ike's chief of staff Sherman Adams recalled, "These evenings were never devoted to abstract discussions nor was the conversation ever highly intellectual." Ike enjoyed demonstrating his manhood through the kinds of ritualized activities Ernest Hemingway celebrated. Ike liked "stag" vacations but usually settled for segregated activities. "The men" played golf or bridge, while "the girls" played Scrabble, bolivia, or canasta. The men talked about tax breaks and horse breeding; the girls traded fashion tips and pictures of grandchildren. The men and women only joined together for meals. One of the wives, Nettie

Jones, resented the constant sexual stratification, saying that she had "never been made to feel like such a wallflower."

Ike had become particularly cautious around women since the Summersby episode. With women present he was courtly, polite, and unwilling to curse; like Truman, he preferred to keep them away when he was working or playing. Ike idealized women and dismissed them. He considered them "beautiful, intelligent, charming, attractive, and altogether super-human," bringing a "far more idealistic attitude toward political activity than do men." But he also wanted no part of their "gabfests" filled with "gossiping and giggling." Feeling himself and other men obligated to indulge feminine frivolities, Eisenhower did not consider women oppressed. In 1954, an adviser suggested the President support an equal rights amendment to the Constitution. Ike revealed his own sense of the balance of power within his marriage and within his social circle when he asked, "Where are they unequal?"

The few women who did work for Ike certainly were unequal. He never called any of them by name, except for his secretary, Ann Whitman. To Ike and his friends, secretaries were simply tools; a great one such as Ann was a "most devoted friend and slave," as the president of the Frankfort Distillery, Ellis Slater, put it. These attractive "career gals" threatened Mamie and her friends. Mamie treated the servants in the mansion warmly, and the secretaries in the West Wing coolly. When Ann Whitman first began working for Ike during the 1952 campaign, Mamie tried to get her fired. Ann remained until after Ike retired to Gettysburg, when the pressures of working so close to Mamie became unbearable. Ann had grown to love Ike and had seen her own marriage founder as she worked around the clock. She left bitter and feeling used. "One of the most decisive purposes that has ruled my life is a determination never to give any real friend the right to believe that 'I have let him down,'" Ike said in 1955. His buddies rarely felt let down by him, unlike the three most significant women in his adult life—Mamie, Kay Summersby, and Ann Whitman.

Mamie and "the girls" enjoyed their perches on the pedestal. After years of living in her husband's military world, Mamie must have relished watching Ike enter her family's aristocratic world. She also enjoyed the adulation. Priscilla Slater praised the First Lady as "feminine, really luscious looking, dainty and loveable, appealing in an almost childlike way. . . . She has a forceful personality, but her warmth and affectionate regard for her friends more than makes up for her decisiveness." Mamie appreciated the companionship, the breaks from routine, and the way the men kept Ike close to home. "Mamie wants her soldier boy around, and Ike likes to be around her," one of the gang told a reporter. "So when you play bridge, you play at Ike's place."

Mamie and "the girls" also served as willing audiences to their men's hijinks, the practical jokes, the surprise parties, the little ditties set to old standbys. The whole world was their yacht club. Mockery camouflaged their sentimentality. Ike, for example, might praise Mamie's "years of endurance of a husband of doubtful disposition and uncertain temper." "It's the levity, the crabbing at each other, the apparent disgust at a partner's poor play or shot that brings the laugh that makes for the fun," Ellis Slater rejoiced. When Ike exploded after a bonehead bridge play, Mamie sulked; his buddies laughed off the tantrum, but they also tried harder.

Alcohol fostered the hilarity. Sly jokes about the "Cheer Water" and "my favorite 'essence'" added to the fun and made these pillars of the community feel naughty. In June 1956 Mamie thanked Alfred M. Gruenther, a peripheral member of the gang, for "bring[ing] me the wonderful usual welcome gift"—some Barclay's bourbon. "I know it will brighten my spirits immensely!" Such partying demanded discretion, since millions of Americans were still dry. When five hundred cases of California champagne were donated for Eisenhower's second inauguration, hundreds of letters protested the invasion of demon rum into the White House. Also, Mamie was still dogged by rumors of alcohol abuse. In 1953 word spread through Washington's black community "that colored servants smell liquor on her breath." In 1959 the *National Enquirer* claimed that, at a party, the First Lady "boozed it up so much that the hostess tried to cut her off" and that the President "was obviously embarrassed by his soused spouse."

The White House never addressed these rumors publicly, although the press secretary, Jim Hagerty, assured inquiring citizens that the claim was "a downright lie." The Eisenhowers' friends said a heart murmur and Meniere's disease—an inner-ear imbalance—made Mamie wobble when she walked. Merriman Smith, the hard-edged senior White House correspondent, dismissed the rumors after watching Mamie "nurse an old-fashioned all night long." "An alcoholic can't do that," he concluded.

The gang usually played to Ike's nonpolitical and imperious side; they too disdained politicians, reporters, and public opinion. They cheered him when he said, Slater recalled, that "the things he would stand for and do would be for the good of the whole country—if that meant losing votes it would be just too bad." In 1954 the oil baron Pete Jones noted that the President had not yet called anyone an SOB. "How different," they all murmured, remembering Roosevelt's partisanship and Truman's vulgarity. "Here in the White House," they rejoiced, "are intelligent people, kind and gentle."

His new friends' aristocratic distance confirmed Ike's instincts to avoid challenging Senator Joseph McCarthy. Ike said he would not use "the office of the Presidency to give an opponent the publicity he so avidly desires." In the end, Joseph Welch, an attorney with similar sensibilities but more courage, helped bring McCarthy down. Welch posed a question Ike could have posed to his fellow Republican years earlier: "Have you no sense of decency, sir, at long last?"

By 1956 Eisenhower had changed his rationale for entering politics from a sense of duty and a concern for world peace. As he told his brother Edgar, "The only reason I got into politics in the first place was to attempt to bring the United States around to understand the virtues of progress along a straight, clearly-defined road, rather than one that veered constantly and always to the left." Ike blasted "centralization of power in Washington, inflation with rising living costs, and federal ownership of an increasing number of types of utilities."

Regarding civil rights, members of the disproportionately Southern gang of Ike's friends viewed blacks as a breed apart. After a vacation at Treasury Secretary George M. Humphrey's thirteen-thousand-acre plantation, the guests and "the help" gathered to send off the President. Mamie shocked Ellis Slater by shaking the hands of the "colored" servants. "It was wonderful to see their broad smiles and white teeth," he added. Such people would encourage the President to stand fast against "the militant advocates of racial equality." This sort of private handshaking was the closest Mamie would come to taking a stand on civil rights.

Amid plush surroundings, the gang's cultural conservatives often decried the decline of civilization. One July weekend at Camp David, the Eisenhowers, Humphreys, Joneses, and Gruenthers bemoaned the divorce epidemic that had hit at least a million ex-GIs. They congratulated themselves that none of them had been divorced. Enamored of sweet ballads such as "Jeannie with the Light Brown Hair" and "My Old Kentucky Home," they tended to ignore Frank Sinatra and Benny Goodman, let alone Elvis Presley and Little Richard. To young people, therein were laid the seeds for revolt—and reason to view Eisenhower as sclerotic.

The Eisenhowers and their friends spent a great deal of time bashing the press. Ike disliked reporters. He considered their concern with "so-called human interest" vulgar, and he often complained that "things of importance to the Administration and the country are not being properly placed before the public." The *Washington Post*'s insinuations about Mamie's drinking and her inactivity so enraged him that he forbade Mamie from reading the paper—although she arranged to read it on her own.

Still, Eisenhower worked hard to maintain his popularity. He wooed the press, in his way. His two campaigns pioneered in the use of television and utilized the latest advertising techniques. His administration began broadcasting press conferences, prompting howls from reporters that this "important and established publicity medium" would become a "show" and lose its "spontaneity." His party chairman, Leonard Wood Hall, understood that each presidential broadcast had to be "a production." To illustrate his point, Hall mounted an elaborate "Salute to Eisenhower" in January 1956. The closed-circuit TV special, complete with "pretty lady singers" and a short but moving speech by the President, raised over five million dollars. "They got all the impact as though the President were there in person," Hall said of the sixty-three thousand people who watched at fifty-three different dinners. The President privately embraced Hall's "politics is show business" philosophy while publicly disdaining it.

A broader, more popular, more frivolous culture was overwhelming the WASP gentility that had dominated America for over a century. Americans still appreciated leaders more than celebrities, ideas more than images, but their priorities were changing. In 1958, pollsters asked which famous people Americans would most like to have to dinner. Only one celebrity, Will Rogers, made the top twenty, and he was seventeenth on the list, behind Winston Churchill, Jesus, eight Presidents, and two First Ladies—Eleanor Roosevelt and Mamie Eisenhower. That same poll foreshadowed the coming celebrity-oriented culture when it asked respondents to name the authors of thirteen statements. Nearly three-quarters of those surveyed knew that the Lone Ranger said, "Hi, Ho Silver," and nearly two-thirds knew that Mae West said, "Come up and see me sometime." Barely one-third could identify Franklin Roosevelt as the man who said, "The only thing we have to fear is fear itself," and only 14 percent remembered that Woodrow Wilson wanted to make the world "safe for democracy."

The Eisenhowers helped reconcile the conflicting cultures, albeit temporarily. The widespread use of "Mamie" and "Ike" heralded the new, mass politics suited to this emerging leisure culture, while the Eisenhowers' conservative principles and proper behavior reassured traditionalists. A poll taken at the beginning of the administration found that a plurality approved of calling the President "Ike," by 47 percent to 38 percent; yet a plurality disapproved of calling the First Lady "Mamie," by 44 percent to 40 percent. The older the respondents, the more likely they were to object to this undignified intimacy. Fifty percent of the respondents between the ages of twenty-one and twenty-nine preferred the use of "Mamie," while half of the respondents older than fifty objected.

The longer Ike stayed in office, the harder it was for him to balance the old ways and the new. Mamie helped, balancing consumerism with elegance, mass appeal with gracious living, and populism with elitism. By the end of the administration the Eisenhowers would remain popular, but they would be identified with the politics and culture of yesteryear—where they and their friends belonged.

V

On September 23, 1955, Ike suffered a heart attack in Denver. The President's press secretary, Jim Hagerty, explained that the President was in Mrs. Doud's home. As the *Washington Post* reported, Hagerty "said he assumed that the President had called to her room from his bedroom near hers." Either Mrs. Doud insisted that her daughter and son-in-law use separate bedrooms or Mamie knew Ike was sick because they were in the same bed—but at a time of presidential illness, his aides did not want to upset the nation's moralists.

Once the President stabilized, his physician, Howard Snyder, had to calm a jittery First Lady and an equally nervous public. Snyder waited a day before telling Mamie that it was a heart attack rather than indigestion; he then announced the news to the nation. Years before, Ike had told Hagerty that in the event of illness, "Don't you put me in the spot that Mrs. Wilson put President Wilson." In the three decades since her husband's strokes, Edith Wilson's "regency" had been blamed for many disasters, including the collapse of the League of Nations. Now Ike commanded, "Tell the truth." Daily medical bulletins included exact dosages of medication. The zealous aides even announced Ike's first bowel movement, an important sign of health to cardiologists. The President later complained that this detail carried " 'realism' a bit too far."

Mamie had to prove that she was not another Mrs. Wilson. Instead, she played Florence Nightingale with a touch of Lucy Ricardo. Mamie was so devoted that she did not leave Ike's side for nineteen days, but loopy enough that she had a pink toilet seat installed in her hospital suite. Mamie earned praise as "the ideal wife," steadfast, comforting, inspiring, and humble. "I am sure the doctors all agree that you were the best medicine in the world for the President," gushed Harry Bullis, the chairman of the board of General Mills.

Traditionally, women were supposed to replace their husbands in the event of illness or death. Becoming a "deputy husband" was one of the few paths women could take across the rigid sexual boundaries. The backlash against wartime working women, however, had swept aside this venerable notion. Mamie knew that a woman's place was by her sick husband's side. "You are a gallant soul and I am sure your wisdom does more than anything else in bringing back health to your great man whenever it slips," Helen Reid would write Mamie after Ike's stroke in 1957. This attitude placed great faith on a woman's ability to heal her husband—and great pressure on her when he flagged.

Ike played his role well, too. He was supposed to be the "model patient," stoic and anxious to return to work. He told his chief of staff, Sherman Adams, "Funny thing, if the doctors here didn't tell me differently, I would think this heart attack belonged to some other guy."

The public responsibility and acclaim helped Mamie through a difficult time. She lost ten pounds during the first two weeks. To one of Ike's Army buddies she uttered what could be the caregiver's credo, evidence of the roller coaster such diseases triggered: "When he feels good, we all do. When unhappy, so are we all." As a tonic, Mamie signed replies to every one of the eleven thousand letters she and Ike received. A haze of pleasantries hid her pain. "We conversed daily on a wide range of subjects," Ike recalled, "but on none that might encourage emotional outbursts." Here Mamie demonstrated the power of banality. Her inanity soothed Ike, herself, their friends, and the nation.

Mamie was also fortified by Americans' mystical faith in the presidency. Less than a week after the heart attack, when Dr. Snyder could still only speak about "if and when he returns to his desk as President of the United States," Mamie did not doubt her husband's recovery. She wrote a friend: "I have tried to keep in mind that the President is the image of God and therefore perfect, and this is most comforting to me."

Mamie conveyed this belief to her husband as well. "Mamie, above all others, never accepted the assumption that I had incurred a disabling illness," he recalled. "While solicitous above all for my health and welfare, she . . . retained the conviction that my job as President was not yet finished." An odd role reversal occurred: with Ike frail, Mamie became solicitous. Now she was the one to mask emotions, hiding from her fears of losing Ike by talking about finishing his mission.

In the ensuing five years, Ike would undergo abdominal surgery due to ileitis and suffer a stroke. Mamie would smother her husband, worrying when he ate too much, slept too little, or worked too hard. She would outlive Ike by a decade. During each presidential health crisis, Ike's aides would follow the pattern set in Denver, with full briefings and clear lines of authority; in contrast, Mamie enjoyed a woman's prerogative to silence. In August 1957, Hagerty released a four-sentence statement that Mrs. Eisenhower "underwent an operation for a benign condition." Few newspapers offered any details. The *Des Moines Register* did identify the surgeon as a gynecologist, explaining that "a gynecologist is a specialist in women's ailments."

Initially, the heart attack convinced Mamie that Ike had to retire. Two weeks before it occurred, in fact, Ike had decided not to run again in 1956. As Ike recovered, though, Dr. Snyder told Mamie that idleness might be more damaging than the stress of the presidency. Mamie insisted that Ike make his own decision, and she denied influencing him in any way. But as Ellis Slater predicted shortly after the heart attack, "Mamie's judgment will prevail, aided of course by his own innermost desire."

By encouraging Ike to run again, Mamie revealed how much the Eisenhower marriage had healed in the White House. She was no longer so fixated on keeping Ike to herself. Now her love for her husband led her to tell him just what he wanted to hear, even as she yearned to retire. This First Lady loved her husband as he was, not as she wanted him to be.

The skirmishing between the Eisenhowers, of course, continued. After his heart attack, the President wanted to go south for Christmas. As he reported to Nettie Jones, though, "Mamie simply will not go." She wanted to celebrate Christmas with their family—and they did.

The 1956 campaign featured a rematch between Ike and Adlai E. Stevenson. Ike insisted that his advisers take advantage of Mamie's popularity. "Mamie is a wonderful campaigner and, I truly believe, the best vote-getter in the family," he boasted. The Women's Division of Citizens for Eisenhower-Nixon used Mamie's popularity to justify a bigger role for women. Republicans recognized "the vital importance to this country of her role, and the heart-warming way in which she has filled it." Deeming Mamie "the ideal with which every woman can identify herself," the campaign praised her "fine" example "as a wife, mother, grandmother, helpmate, patriotic citizen" and her "delightful, modest and gracious . . . personality." Republicans, especially women, were commanded: "BRAG ABOUT OUR MAMIE!"

Again, it worked. Mamie campaigned silently by Ike's side, waving but not speaking. Her popularity enhanced his, and he easily beat Stevenson.

Although after the election Ike and his advisers claimed his victory ratified their policies, the second term would prove them wrong. The Democrats carried both the House and the Senate, making for four years of divided government. Foreign policy crises erupted in Lebanon, Taiwan, Berlin, and Cuba, a fact presaged by the crises in the Suez and Hungary that marred the last month of the reelection campaign. Eisenhower's health sagged. Both he and Mamie were criticized for some of their leisure activities, especially, as the 1957–58 recession sobered Americans during these legendary "Happy Days." By 1960, the 1952 image of the glamorous couple had faded. Ike and Mamie would still be popular, but they would be seen as doddering, gray grandparents, worthy of respect—and retirement.

In September 1957, opposition to the integration of Little Rock's Central High School compelled President Eisenhower to send in the National Guard. Ike's nationalism and his respect for the law overcame his caution. He told the public that the troops were not intended "to enforce integration, but to prevent opposition by violence to orders of a court." He justified his move to his conservative gang, on their terms, as an economically rational decision, rather than an idealistic or a nationalistic one. Ike warned "that all this anti-Negro agitation here" hurt America's ability to market goods in Africa and Asia.

Ike's conservatism, though, was not up to mastering the upcoming challenges. Less than two weeks after the Little Rock clash, the Soviet Union launched the first man-made satellite, *Sputnik I,* into space. This communist coup proved even more unnerving than having the commanding general of World War II deploy troops on American soil. *Sputnik* became a symbol of American decline, as an aging, frail President came to epitomize a country whose greatest triumphs might be in the past. Even his popularity dipped. Ike began 1957 with 79 percent approval, by mid-October it was 57 percent. The public reaction depressed Ike. "Alleged inter-service rivalry, guided missiles, *Sputnik II,* Little Rock, Syria, and a variety of other problems seem to clog my memory these days," Ike wrote an old friend.

These crises made Ike more anxious for diversions—while making his recreation politically dangerous. During the first term, Ike's golfing inspired confidence; only 17 percent of those surveyed in 1953 felt the President devoted "too much time" to his golf game. Many Americans were enjoying extended leisure for the first time in their lives and wanted their President to have some fun, too. In his second term, however, Ike's athletics became politicized. When aides publicized his once-secret golf scores to demonstrate his vigor, supporters worried the President was "overdoing" it, and Democrats scoffed that the doddering Eisenhower golfed while the world burned. Adlai Stevenson's 1956 campaign against Eisenhower used Ike's golfing to define him as a "part-time" president serving the rich. This criticism lingered throughout the second term.

Reporters also looked more closely at the ethics of the Eisenhower administration. In February 1958, Ike took a 2,945-mile detour west to Arizona on his way north from Georgia to Washington so Mamie could go with her sister and Priscilla Slater to Maine Chance, Elizabeth Arden's "luxurious beauty resort." There Mamie occupied a seven-room cottage especially decorated for her, with a bedroom in green and pink and a direct phone link to the White House. Her retinue of fifteen aides occupied another seven-bedroom house. Reporters pounced on this example of the Eisenhowers' extravagance, claiming that the President's plane should not be used for such indulgences. Ike and Mamie no longer appeared to be so ordinary. Jim Hagerty seethed: "I think when the President of the United States wants to go any place with his wife, that is his business and nobody else's." Harry Truman volunteered that critics should not attack a president through his wife and that the First Couple's personal life should remain private.

The Eisenhowers were tiring of life in the "squirrel cage." When Mamie shopped in a chain store, the National Federation of Independent Business protested. Her social secretary claimed that the Eisenhowers "deal almost exclusively with independent stores in and around the Washington region." When Mamie crossed a picket line to shop at Bonwit Teller in New York, union members protested. The assistant special counsel to the President asserted that Mrs. Eisenhower had "entered the store, not to shop, but only to visit a personal friend."

These attacks on the Eisenhowers' activities illustrated journalists' growing boldness. The press used these invasions of privacy to challenge the administration's character and some fundamental tenets of the WASP elite. Eisenhower and his colleagues appeared too refined to meet challengers like Joe McCarthy, too elitist to work in a world of emerging minorities, too old to face the challenges of modern America. One young speechwriter, Stephen Hess, would recall that "the last years of the Eisenhower administration" were spent "mopping up," and that they lacked the tension and "bubbling" of a new administration.

Just as Mamie had fit into the glamorous popular image of the first term, she symbolized the extravagant and sclerotic second term. Fewer articles described her as looking "younger than her calendar years," while more played the angle of "Grandma Lives in the White House." The Eisenhowers were still popular, but the President was losing control. By the end of 1958 his chief of staff, Sherman Adams, would be forced to resign for accepting free hotel rooms and a vicuña coat. Adams's gifts were a fraction of the Eisenhowers' take—but for now the First Couple remained untouchable. In the November congressional elections, the Republicans suffered their worst defeat since the Depression. Ike considered this "the worst year of his life," Ellis Slater reported, "the time when 'All Hell broke loose.'"

Even the impression of the Eisenhowers' marriage changed. The postwar divorce wave made many experts view marriages more clinically as a "contract" between "fallible" human beings. "Living together is synonymous with 'working out problems,'" one therapist, Karl Menninger, wrote in *McCall's* in 1955. A 1960 profile of Mamie in *Better Homes and Gardens* would note: "The Eisenhowers ha[ve] had their difficulties, but nothing worse than could be expected by most couples."

Still the Eisenhowers remained united, publicly and privately. Some First Ladies would become more popular as their husbands' administrations floundered; Mamie's image remained linked to Ike's. They faced her operation, his ailments, and her mother's deteriorating health together. Ike would often grumble about Mamie smothering him, but he appreciated it. Mamie did withdraw from more official tasks. When Ike decided on a series of farewell tours around the globe, Mamie stayed at home, letting her daughter-in-law, Barbara, substitute. "Barbara has been an excellent representative of the 'feminine' side of the family!" Mamie boasted. Barbara's trip, and John's assignment as a staff officer for his father, triggered a spate of profiles about the younger Eisenhowers.

This desire for a leader from the GI Joe generation strengthened Richard Nixon's position as Eisenhower's heir. Publicly the young, earnest Nixons enacted the benign, paternal relationship many postwar veterans and their wives felt they had with the Eisenhowers. Privately the Vice President did not have an easy time working with Ike. A grocer's son from Southern California, he did not socialize easily with the white-haired millionaires the poor boy from Abilene befriended. Nixon was stiff where Ike was smooth; Nixon could not forget his class resentments, whereas Ike refused to remember them.

Nixon had proved himself loyal and statesmanlike during Ike's illnesses.

He had also done Ike's bidding as the GOP hatchet man, campaigning incessantly with his wife, Pat, loyally at his side. Still, Ike treated his partisan subordinate coolly. In 1956 the President tried to drop Nixon from the ticket in exchange for a Cabinet appointment, but Nixon refused to withdraw. Eisenhower did not have the heart to fire him, especially because Mamie and others appreciated Nixon's loyal service. The popular perception that Nixon "does not like and understand people" disturbed the genial President. Ike's disdain in turn strengthened Nixon's resolve to prove himself by reaching the White House as well.

In the 1960 campaign, both Republicans and Democrats agreed that it was time to change. Accepting the Republican nomination, Nixon delicately said that "the next President will have new and challenging problems." Despite his loyalty, Nixon failed to secure a proper blessing from Eisenhower. In a poignant moment where public and private needs clashed, Ike planned a final campaign swing for his vice president. Mamie begged him not to go; a previous trip had boosted his blood pressure. Desperate, Mamie went behind Ike's back, saying to Pat Nixon that Ike "was not up to the strain." Dr. Snyder agreed, telling Nixon "to either talk him out of it or just don't let him do it— for the sake of his health." Nixon asked the President to shelve his plans; the election was close enough that anything, including Ike's passivity, could be blamed for the loss. Nearly a decade later, in 1968, Ike would endorse Richard Nixon before the Republican National Convention, partially as a favor to his grandson David, who was in love with Nixon's daughter Julie. That effort, doctors said, triggered Ike's fifth and ultimately fatal heart attack.

As he aged, Dwight Eisenhower preserved his popularity with Mamie's help. He remained among America's ten most admired men until his death in 1969. A month after his vice president lost the 1960 presidential election, Ike enjoyed an approval rating of 59 percent, though only 20 percent predicted he would be remembered as a "great president." Despite Eisenhower's popularity, Nixon had entered the 1960 campaign with a party crippled by its years in power. From 1953 to 1960 Republican strength in the House had dropped from 199 to 153 members, and in the Senate from 47 to 35. The number of Republican governors plummeted from 25 to 14, and the number of states where Republicans controlled both houses of the legislature fell from 26 to 7. Eisenhower's "hidden hand" strategy to distance himself from partisan politics had worked—and devastated his party.

The Eisenhowers left the White House tired but satisfied. His relief at ridding himself of "my constant problems" tempered his distress at Nixon's election loss. Mamie had begun doubting that Ike would be healthy enough to move to Gettysburg. Finally, though, she and her soldier boy were going home.

The Washington years had allowed the Eisenhowers to rebuild their marriage. Mamie was the President's loyal consort: self-sacrificing, uncomplicated, unthreatening, and noncontroversial. She was not interested in his power, only his welfare. These qualities made her an ideal First Lady, and they solidified her status as one of America's most admired women through the 1970s. In contrast, in the decade after Truman retired, Bess Truman made Gallup's top ten list only once. Mamie Eisenhower's zest as a hostess made Bess Truman seem brusque. To millions of women who valued hospitality, Mamie's contribution was palpable. "It was wonderful to be able to come and see you and to feel the warmth that you have brought with you into the White House," the highborn Betsy Whitney told Mamie.

The demands on the presidential couple were mushrooming. The press had already demonstrated how a couple could be reduced to whatever box was convenient. When reporters needed a perfect couple in the early 1950s, they found the Eisenhowers. A few years later, when reporters needed a couple that weathered storms yet stayed together, they found the Eisenhowers again. In the future, reporters would not have trouble defining both Bess and Mamie as contrasts to Eleanor, making them seem very similar when they—and their marriages—were quite different.

The Eisenhowers and the Trumans were sufficiently steeped in their own values that they could distance themselves from the demands the press placed on the presidential couple. Yet neither Harry Truman nor Dwight Eisenhower could resist posing as a representative American. Both knew how to use their wives—Truman to prove he was ordinary, Eisenhower to transcend partisanship. Both instinctively understood how to bleach out deviations from the norm. Married couples at home in Abilene, Independence, or anywhere were just as adept at maintaining appearances.

Presidents of the next generation would be less successful in protecting their privacy. They would face a more powerful press, and personal popularity would be associated more closely with political success. Also, sex roles would be less clearly defined. Fewer First Ladies would succeed even in establishing the barriers Mamie and Bess had. More and more, presidential couples would feel compelled to woo reporters, not shoo them away. And First Ladies would be steadily pulled into the political fray.

3

THE KENNEDYS

"A Magic Moment in American History"

Barely six months after the Eisenhowers retired to Gettysburg, President and Mrs. John F. Kennedy visited Paris. One million people mobbed the streets, shouting *"Vive Zha-kleen! Vive Kennedy!"* Jacqueline Bouvier Kennedy was enchanting. Reporters catalogued each fetching gesture, every costume change. "De Gaulle and I are hitting it off all right, probably because I have such a charming wife," Kennedy told an aide. The President graciously introduced himself as "the man who accompanied Jacqueline Kennedy to Paris." The First Lady was thirty-one years old.

The outpouring continued at the superpower summit in Vienna. Mrs. Kennedy shared the spotlight with her Russian counterpart, Nina Khruschev. The huzzahs were for them both, the radiant Barbie doll told the dour babushka. The venerable liberal Max Lerner deemed Jackie one of America's "secret weapons," proof "that life can be gracious" only amid freedom. In the 1940s Franklin Roosevelt refuted communist ideology with the Sears catalogue; in the 1950s Richard Nixon used the American kitchen; now, in June 1961, President Kennedy offered his wife.

Along with McCarthyism and air raid drills, the Kennedys' renown was a cold-war phenomenon. The vigorous Kennedys seemed nothing like the elderly Eisenhowers; the Old World put a new light on the former debutante's aristocratic airs and expensive fashions. Conspicuous consumption appeared patriotic, constructive, and—thanks to an extraordinary economic boom—accessible. Newly prosperous Americans loved having a President and First Lady so well suited to be the king and queen of the free world.

Despite the public acclaim, only half of the presidential couple succeeded. Soviet Premier Nikita Khruschev lambasted John Kennedy at the summit. "He savaged me," Kennedy confided to James Reston of the *New York Times*. After hosting the President the next day, Prime Minister Harold Macmillan wrote to Queen Elizabeth: "For the first time in his life Kennedy met a man who was impervious to his charm." For months afterward, Kennedy feared an outbreak of nuclear war.

The Kennedys could not live up to the wholesome front they presented in Europe. The President envied Jackie's popularity, and he criticized her for traveling with thirty-five trunks of clothing. The Kennedy entourage included Dr. Max Jacobson, a doctor who injected Mr. and Mrs. Kennedy with a "pick me up" cocktail of amphetamines and steroids. The President needed "Dr. Feel Good" to cope with back pain. The First Lady further brightened her mood by remaining in Europe, doing the cha-cha in Greek nightclubs as her husband limped around on crutches in Washington. Jack could not lecture his wife about marital propriety though. He later told Macmillan that "if I don't have a woman for three days, I get a terrible headache."

Such revelations would be routine twenty years later, making the Kennedys' apotheosis puzzling. How did a playboy and a dilettante caught in a sham marriage seduce the nation? Apologists could justify the personal sins of a Franklin Roosevelt or a Richard Nixon by pointing to political achievements such as Social Security or détente. But John Kennedy's greatest political achievements were personal; Americans loved the Kennedys for who they were—or at least who they seemed to be. Yet Kennedy and his wife were nothing like their shining images.

I

Even at the time, the Kennedys' popularity was surprising. John Kennedy won the presidency by the slimmest margin in the twentieth century. Many initially doubted the very traits they now praised. Some considered him a rich Catholic upstart with an amoral father. Even his family first thought him too shy and too sickly; he had already received last rites four times. In turn, Jack had feared his own wife was too aristocratic for politics.

The Kennedys' popularity was a fluke, but it was a fluke that had been in the making for years. The Kennedys constructed a fantasy that tapped into deep communal longings. Their story shows how much Americans crave an ideal, even when the contours of the ideal are uncertain. How should the presidential couple behave? No one knew. Still, the Kennedys were neither superheroes nor con artists; they were not the only rich and ambitious family in America. They succeeded as a result of effort, skill, luck, and a chameleon-like ability to master social forms.

John Fitzgerald Kennedy was born in 1917 into a family organized along conventional lines. The home was the woman's power base, the bastion of refinement she created. Rose Kennedy and her husband, Joe, saw themselves as "individuals with highly responsible roles in a partnership that yielded rewards which we shared." Her job was to maintain order, harmony, and grace in the home. Even when a car accident gave her "a good-sized gash in my forehead," she told her high-flying husband "what a fine day it was." In the 1930s Rose would become one of America's most famous household "executives," hailed for raising nine children scientifically.

This conventional family, however, had exceptional aspirations. Rose Kennedy called Joe "the architect of our lives." He designed, she said, "the perfect family—boys brilliant, girls attractive and intelligent, money, prestige, a young father and mother of intelligence, devoted exemplary habits." As an Irish Catholic trying to break into a largely Protestant elite, Joe Kennedy learned the value of appearances. You could betray your wife as long as you remained married; you could smuggle liquor as long as you kept a respectable job as a bank president. Rose Fitzgerald Kennedy's prudishness and piety underlined this emphasis on appearances. She chose to ignore her husband's ugly behavior. Jack felt she spent more time tending her wardrobe and her sacraments than her children.

Jack's years at Choate Preparatory School confirmed the lessons he learned, at home and in church, about the importance of appearing earnest. Jack hid his derelictions with an engaging personality and a winning smile. He maintained his sunny disposition despite being sickly. Home movies of the young Kennedy show a tan, lithe adolescent playing tennis barefoot at the family's Hyannis Port compound. He moves smoothly, easily, without a care. When the camera zooms in on him, he bursts into a smile.

Joe Kennedy's stint as America's ambassador to the Court of St. James from 1938 to 1941 made the Kennedys "America's best known large family," according to the *New York World-Telegram*. Reporters characterized the children as energetic and unspoiled. Rose appeared "equally at home as the suburban matron or as hostess to the King and Queen at a state dinner." The Kennedys' Irish Catholic roots and sheer size helped them exemplify democratic ideals of tolerance and success despite their wealth.

As a member of the Harvard class of 1940, the likeable and easygoing Jack was known as the "Mayor of Mount Auburn Street," the commercial strip near his Winthrop House dormitory. He knew how to use his family name. Jack exploited his father's contacts to prepare and publish his senior thesis, *Why England Slept*, which became a bestseller.

During World War II, the Kennedy connections helped Jack see combat despite his frailty. His friend John Hersey's melodramatic *New Yorker* article redeemed Jack's failure as the skipper aboard PT-109. Jack called the ensuing publicity—which his father stoked—a "lucky" break, although the memory of his two dead comrades "rather spoils the whole thing for me." Typically, the book the Kennedys assembled after Joe, Jr.—Jack's older brother—died in the war was titled *As We Remember Joe*. The Kennedys were always obsessed with perception.

This sickly second son raised in a competitive household, dominated by his father, alienated from his mother, and eclipsed by his older brother tried to prove that he, too, was macho. In dating, he sought conquest rather than intimacy. "Once I get a woman," he said, "I'm not interested in carrying on, for the most part. . . . It's the chase I like—not the kill!" His sister Kathleen once warned a beau: "The thing about me you ought to know is that I'm like Jack, incapable of deep affection." Jack's reputation ruined his relationships with well-bred women. "It's certainly amazing how all these girls are so strong for me—and then marry someone else," Jack moped on hearing of one ex-girlfriend's engagement in 1943. Quick assignations with wanton women were less painful, easier to manage, and more thrilling.

Jacqueline Lee Bouvier was also raised in a world that emphasized appearances over integrity. Born to John Vernou Bouvier III and Janet Norton Lee on Southhampton, Long Island, in 1929, Jackie was the oldest of two sisters. The Bouviers' marriage was a decadent upper-class alliance between his social standing and her newer money. "Black Jack" Bouvier was a womanizing drunkard. Years later, when Jack Bouvier met his prospective son-in-law, the two men would talk about "politics and sports and girls—what all red-blooded men like to talk about," Jackie recalled; she found the two "very much alike." With these degenerates as models, no wonder Jackie doubted that "there are any men who are faithful to their wives." She told friends, "men are such a combination of good and bad."

While Joe Kennedy compensated for his infidelities by educating his children, "Black Jack" abdicated. Jack's antics culminated in posing with his wife and mistress for a newspaper photographer. The headlines in the New York papers about the Bouviers' divorce in 1940 only deepened the humiliation. Long after she married the wealthy Hugh D. Auchincloss, Janet remained embittered.

Jackie and her sister, Lee, grew up in a world of mansions and stables, of calling cards and servants. The headmistress of Miss Chapin's School in Manhattan urged Jackie to master feminine arts such as penmanship and deportment. Comparing her beautiful pupil to a "thoroughbred," Miss Ethel Stringfellow lectured: "You're well built and you have brains. But if you're not properly broken and trained, you'll be good for nothing." To preserve gentility, a young lady had to crusade for taste, actively cultivating beauty. The contrast between the cultivated arts instilled at school and her father's debauchery was striking. Jackie became emotionally remote even as she mastered the social forms.

A fellow high school student at Miss Porter's School in Connecticut found Jackie to be "prissy, bookish and bossy"; her classmates nicknamed her "Jacqueline Borgia." But another side of Jackie emerged as well. Jackie feared becoming like her mother, who replaced her dependence on "Black Jack" with an equally debilitating dependence on the staid Hugh Auchincloss. The social tumult of war emboldened Jackie to reject conventional expectations. She could be saucy, rebellious, and funny. She smoked, wore outrageous hairstyles, and organized pranks. In June 1947, Jacqueline announced in her senior yearbook her ambition in life: "Not to be a housewife." This impressionable eighteen-year-old had absorbed the contemporary conceit that even once the war ended she could be a Wonder Woman, the Amazonian super hero DC Comics developed in the 1940s.

For all her schoolgirl iconoclasm, though, Jackie was thrilled to be named "The Queen Deb of the Year of 1947" by Igor Cassini, the Hearst gossip columnist. Cassini called the Vassar freshman "a regal brunette who has classic features and the daintiness of Dresden porcelain." Such qualities attracted many suitors. Jackie was flirtatious yet prim. A breathy and little-girlish way of talking masked her intelligence. In search of a career and fiscal autonomy, Jackie would also study at the Sorbonne and at George Washington University. She received her B.A. in 1951.

In 1952 Jackie became the *Washington Times-Herald*'s "Inquiring Photographer." Frank Waldrop, the paper's executive editor, asked Jackie when she was hired if she just wanted to "hang around a newspaper until she got married." She insisted she wanted a career, but she was engaged within months. According to the fiancé, John G. W. Husted, Jr., Janet Auchincloss sabotaged the engagement because she feared he would never make enough money for her daughter.

Jackie posed questions to passersby, snapped their pictures, and printed their answers. Among her questions: "Which First Lady would you most like to have been?" "Would you like your son to grow up to be President?" "Should a candidate's wife campaign with her husband?" "If you had a date with Marilyn Monroe, what would you talk about?" "What prominent person's death affected you most?" Once she asked two congressional pages and two politicians what they thought about each other; the two politicians were Richard M. Nixon and John F. Kennedy.

Despite interests in journalism and academics, Jack ended up in politics. His oldest son's death imposed the elder Joe Kennedy's expectations on Jack. "I can feel Pappy's eyes on the back of my neck," Jack told one Navy buddy;

the Kennedys would soon be "trying to parlay a lost PT boat and a bad back into a political advantage." Shocked at her scrawny brother's yellowish skin, Eunice had asked, "Daddy, do you really think Jack can be a congressman?" Joe offered what could have been the Kennedy motto: "You must remember, it's not what you are that counts, but what people *think* you are."

John F. Kennedy built his political career on his war record, his family name, and his sex appeal. "Men who pushed back the Japanese . . . men who stormed into blazing Normandy . . . are now fighting a different kind of campaign—a political battle on behalf of a young man who at one time during the war was reported killed in action," his 1946 congressional campaign proclaimed. In California, Richard Nixon campaigned in his Navy uniform; two years later, in Michigan, Gerald Ford's headquarters would be a reconstructed Quonset hut.

Since women received the vote in 1920, politicians had wondered how to woo "the weaker sex." In a speech to the League of Catholic Women, Jack recognized women's potential as a voting bloc. "Women compose the majority of voters now," he said. "Women control 50 percent of the wealth of this state, they spend about 85 percent of the money spent, and they inherit 75 percent."

Next to Jack's own "matinee idol" appeal, the "comely" Rose Kennedy was his most formidable weapon in his grab for female voters. Living link to the colorful politics of her father the legendary Boston mayor and congressman "Honey Fitz," homemaking whiz, friend to the Queen, papal countess, Gold Star Mother (one who had lost a son in war), and doyenne of Cape Cod and Palm Beach, Rose was a paragon of gentility, piety, patriotism, and success. Rose could talk simply to her Irish cousins or don her pearls to tell society women about meeting the Queen. She and her daughters hosted as many as 1500 ladies at "Kennedy teas."

These teas portrayed Jack as a gay blade, not a rake. "Every woman either wants to mother him or marry him," campaign workers beamed. With his mother and sisters as chaperons, Jack could make his sex appeal wholesome.

Jack proved to be an excellent politician. His charisma could not be manufactured or bought. His diffidence enhanced his appeal and neutralized fears of a Kennedy power grab. It also distinguished the son from his hot-tempered father. Being "cool" was beginning to be a virtue, proof of sophistication and self-control. The poised, Harvard-educated naval war hero represented a new breed of assimilated ethnics emerging from war.

Congressman Kennedy quickly established his reputation on the Hill as a Casanova. For the next decade and a half, Jack would flirt with the possibility of scandal. That he avoided exposure enhanced his sense of invincibility and made him more reckless, but it also said more about the times than about the man. Washington was still a cozy place; relations between politicians and reporters were more fraternal than adversarial. Just as Harry Truman preserved his military machismo in the 1920s by singing bawdy songs at the American Legion, many cold-war pols proved their machismo through promiscuity. Reporters would not expose Kennedy, Nelson Rockefeller, Estes Kefauver, Lyndon Johnson, and other philanderers for fear of weakening national morale.

Congressman Kennedy was a playboy, but he was also hardworking. His spotty attendance record reflected his speechmaking and globetrotting, not laziness. In 1952 the three-time congressman ran for the Senate. His campaign literature ascribed to him the qualities of a Hemingway hero—or of Dwight Eisenhower. Proclaiming "MASSACHUSETTS *NEEDS* A MAN LIKE THIS FOR U.S. SENATOR," pamphlets boasted that "in his every public and private act—he has *PROVED* his ability to *THINK* clearly, *SPEAK* frankly, *ACT* courageously, *SERVE* well but humbly and *LEAD* fearlessly."

After three tryouts in the Eleventh Congressional District, the Kennedy ladies took their act statewide. Seventy thousand women from across the political, social, racial, religious, and ethnic spectrums attended a Kennedy tea. Thousands more had "Coffee with the Kennedys" by watching one of two half-hour television programs broadcast throughout the state. On these programs, Rose and her daughters chatted about the family, displayed the index cards she used to keep track of the Kennedy clan's health and education, and reminisced about the heroic death of Joe, Jr., and Jack's brush with disaster at sea. When the "girl talk" ended, Jack ambled onto the set and answered questions called into the studio. Awed by Kennedy's magic on the air and in person, one Republican wondered, "What is there about Kennedy that makes every Catholic girl in Boston between eighteen and twenty-eight think it's a holy crusade to get him elected?"

The impression that "the family steamroller . . . swept him into the Senate" upstaged Jack's hard work. At the start of the miraculous postwar economic boom the Kennedys proved that domestic virtue spawned worldly success. Wealth was liberating, not corrupting. The Kennedys were "part of a new aristocratic tradition," the *New York Post* claimed, one of public service and private virtue despite being raised in "baronial splendor." "Potentially America's most celebrated and important family," the Kennedys were the darlings of glossy magazines.

While the thirty-five-year-old Jack benefited from his reputation as what the *Saturday Evening Post* called "The Senate's Gay Young Bachelor," it was time to settle down. The new senator feared being dismissed as a lightweight. The 1952 campaign proved that a helpmate like Mamie Eisenhower could lure thousands of votes, while Adlai Stevenson's divorce made him appear unreliable. "A politician has to have a wife," Joe Kennedy said, "and a Catholic politician has to have a Catholic wife." Deferring the announcement until after the *Saturday Evening Post* profile had celebrated his bachelorhood, Jack Kennedy announced his engagement to Jacqueline Bouvier on June 24, 1953.

Jack and Jackie met in 1951 when the reporter Charles Bartlett and his wife hosted both of them for dinner. Jack invited the twenty-year-old brunette for a drink. She demurred; a boyfriend had sneaked into her car and was waiting for her. Over the next two years, they had "a very spasmodic courtship," Jackie would recall. Jack "spent half of each week in Massachusetts" campaigning: "He'd call me from some oyster bar up there, with a great clinking of coins, to ask me out to the movies the following Wednesday in Washington." Jackie teased Jack through her column. She posed questions about the nature of marriage, and whether the "Irish are deficient in the art of love." She translated books from French for the senator, edited position papers, and even worked on a term paper for his brother Teddy.

Jack was not about to woo Jackie or any other woman too ardently. "He's not the candy-and-flowers type," Jackie would tell a reporter. Jack asked so many friends whether he should marry Jackie that one suggested he "put the matter before the Senate for a vote." After they were engaged, Jackie told reporters that "since Jack is such a violently independent person, and I, too, am so independent, this relationship will take a lot of working out." If Jackie was moodier than Jack would have liked, she was at least cultured and intelligent. If Jack was less romantic than Jackie would have liked, he was at least successful and sober. He had money, she had class, and both were Catholic. Jackie worried that she was too scrawny for Jack's taste. That was central to her appeal. Jack wanted to sleep with buxom movie stars; he wanted to marry a thin, elegant equestrian. "I have never met anyone like her," Jack told his aide Dave Powers.

This "most eligible and wealthy" senator's engagement to a "New York debutante" made front pages across the nation. A typical announcement of 161 words mentioned both families' wealth five times. This marriage was made in public. Jackie had to know she was marrying Jack's family and his career; her private life would be public fodder for the rest of her days.

The young lovers posed for the photographers, but neither seemed giddy. Jack had proposed long distance when Jackie was covering the coronation of Queen Elizabeth; after Congress recessed, he went off to Europe without her. "No man in love does something like that," Janet Auchincloss snapped. That summer, Jackie spent a weekend in Hyannis Port with her fiancé. The twosome, however, was a threesome. A *Life* photographer followed them for an exclusive photo spread about their courtship.

Jack and Jackie seemed to be the "perfect couple," Clark Clifford recalled. America's aristocrats applauded Jack's engagement to this "little peach." "She has brains, charm, character: what more can a man hope to find?" one minister asked.

Jack's friends sent condolences as he embarked on this "risky" enterprise. "GREATEST BLOW [TO] FEMALE[S] SINCE VALENTINO PASSING," teased a Navy friend, Red Fay. Jackie and her set were equally cynical about matrimony. Years before, she toasted the marriage of one of her classmates by writing, "But watch yo' step honey on that path of roses/There's more thorns 'neath them thar leaves than you knowses."

Jack responded to these half-hearted wishes in kind, refusing to betray any vulnerability. Jack joked with Red Fay that marrying "means the end of a promising political career as it has been based up to now almost completely on the old sex appeal." Asking for help in managing "the bride's mother," Jack sighed, "As I am both too young and too old for this—will need several long talks on how to conduct yourself during the 1st 6 months."

The public nature of this private wedding complicated the planning. Jack seemed most concerned with dispensing magazine rights. Jackie and her mother wanted a quiet affair without "vulgar" reporters; Jack and his mother expected a "public" event that befit a potential president. Joe Kennedy settled the dispute and produced a spectacle.

The wedding was a milestone in American Catholics' quest for acceptance. Archbishop Richard T. Cushing officiated on September 12, 1953; Pope Pius XIII sent a special blessing. Eight hundred guests filled St. Mary's church, and fourteen hundred guests celebrated on the lawn of Hammersmith Farms, the Auchincloss estate. Three thousand spectators gawked. Jack's secretary, Evelyn Lincoln, noticed that "the Senator was used to crowds, but Jackie backed away." The newlyweds worked the reception line for two hours. Rose Kennedy could not "think of a more appropriate introduction to her new life as the wife of a political figure."

The "storybook wedding" climaxed the efforts by both the Kennedys and Jacqueline Bouvier to reinvent themselves. The Kennedys were no longer strivers; they now set the standards. Jackie was no longer a poor little rich girl humiliated by scandal and short on cash.

II

On that September day, Jack and Jackie helped expand the American dream. The facade they constructed cloaked philandering, alcoholism, and family strife. Jackie said they were two icebergs, "the public life above the water— the private life is submerged." The Kennedys fulfilled a social fantasy of money, power, fame, and sex on such an overblown scale that when their cover was blown, faith in the politics of appearances would shatter.

Many guests knew they were minor actors in a public charade. The first years of marriage were sobering. Jack's sisters mocked "the Deb"; in return, Jackie called Eunice, Jean, and Pat "the rah-rah girls." And Jackie could not tame her thirty-six-year-old playboy. Most humiliating of all, one of Jack's friends noted, were those moments "when she found herself stranded at parties while Jack would suddenly disappear with some pretty young girl." Jackie would pretend not to notice. She retaliated by pouting about imagined slights.

Jackie did try to confront Jack's other mistress—politics. A month after the wedding, Jackie wrote a poem about Jack saying, "He would find love/He would never find peace/For he must go seeking/The Golden Fleece." Jack worked ten- to twelve-hour days, gave up to seven out-of-town speeches a week, and studied speed-reading in Baltimore one night a week. The former career girl now dreamed of "a normal life with my husband coming home from work every day at five." Squelching her contrarian instincts and intellectual pretensions, Jackie tried to be the perfect 1950s spouse. She ran Jack's errands, cooked his meals, and begged his secretary to "send" him home earlier.

Jackie not only had to fill this unfamiliar role at home, she had to flaunt it. Six weeks after the wedding, the newlyweds appeared live on the CBS television show "Person to Person with Edward R. Murrow." Sitting on a couch in their Boston apartment, the senator looked vigorous and ready to pounce; his bride looked fragile and in need of protection. When the ex-war correspondent asked, "Which requires the most diplomacy, to interview senators or to be married to one?" Jackie faltered. Jack jumped right in, "being married to one," he chuckled.

Jackie often felt hounded. She sought release in shopping sprees, outraging her husband with extravagant purchases. She also teased her husband through reporters. Many stories about the handsome senator and his beautiful wife contained a zinger from Jackie that the reporters neutralized. In 1957 she would tell *Time* magazine, "If I were drawing him, I'd draw a tiny body and an enormous head." The reporter used this cruel jibe against an infirm husband to hail Jack's "intellectual qualifications."

Jack assumed Jackie's remarks were unintentional and demonstrated her political tin ear. The quips fed the debate about whether Jackie was a political asset. A four-page memorandum detailing Kennedy's "unusual qualifications" as a vice-presidential candidate in 1956 briefly mentioned the senator's "beautiful wife" as an "added attraction." Planning his 1958 reelection campaign, though, Kennedy turned on his wife in a roomful of people. "The American people just aren't ready for someone like you," he snapped. "I guess we'll just have to run you through subliminally in one of those quick flash TV spots so no one will notice." Jackie burst into tears and left the room.

In their first two years together, Jackie miscarried, and Jack struggled with Addison's disease and two spinal operations. He missed the entire 1955 Senate session. As "the Deb" tended to Jack's oozing wound and buoyed his spirits, the Kennedy women saw a resilience underneath the porcelain. Jack, too, reevaluated Jackie. "My wife is a shy, quiet girl, but when things get rough, she can handle herself pretty well," he said.

Jackie encouraged Jack to begin writing *Profiles in Courage*. Although his ghostwriter Ted Sorensen did much of the heavy lifting, Jackie fetched books from the library, edited Jack's prose, and shaped the ideas. The Pulitzer Prize–winning portraits of eight statesmen championed a bureaucratic masculinity that suited the bedridden veteran and his domesticated peers.

When Jack recovered, he reverted to his earlier behavior. Jackie missed his companionship and his dependence. "In some ways it was better when Jack was ill," Jackie told reporters a year later. "I'd see more of him. Now he is either out working or, when he is home, sitting in a chair and reading like mad." The crisis was over. Jack did not need her—for now.

As he sought the 1956 vice-presidential nomination, Jack bought Hickory Hill, a $125,000 estate in Virginia. Jackie was pregnant again; if she could not have her man at home, she could at least have a grand house. Kennedy's men tried to convince the presumptive Democratic nominee, Adlai Stevenson, that he needed a "videogenic," charming, young, moderate, northeastern Catholic running mate. Stevenson recognized Jack as " 'the All American Boy' type candidate." The columnist Doris Fleeson noted: "Kennedy is young and personable and has a beautiful wife."

Jackie, who feared miscarrying again, did not want to fly to Chicago for the convention, but Jack insisted. Sorensen quoted polls estimating that "from 1/6 to 1/4 of all voters . . . would be more favorably inclined toward a candidate who had a family." In 1952, more than twice as many women as men had switched from the Democratic party to Eisenhower. With Jackie at his side, Jack would work his magic with women voters while standing for hearth and home.

Jackie did her duty. She and Jack endured a convention-eve interview on NBC. Asked about her ambitions for Jack, she said, "Just whatever he has for himself, I have for him." When asked if she advised him, she said; "No, I wouldn't dare." Jackie later told reporters that "during the whole five days of the convention I never saw him except when he wandered by our box." Once again, Jackie disciplined her husband publicly yet subtly.

Kennedy lost the nomination but solidified his standing as a "national celebrity." "His was the one new face that actually shone," the *Boston Herald* reported. Americans witnessed "his charm, his dignity, his intellectuality, and, in the end, his gracious sportsmanship." Still, Jack had never lost before. He sulked on a Mediterranean cruise with his brother Teddy and some beauties. While Jack was at sea, Jackie suffered a second miscarriage; she woke in the hospital to find Bobby, not Jack, at her side. Embarrassing headlines proclaimed "SENATOR KENNEDY AT SEA, LACKS NEWS OF WIFE." Jack resented the interruption, and his conversation with Jackie by ship-to-shore radio was curt. Senator George Smathers warned Jack that voters might punish a man who "seemed" to desert his wife when she "needed him," so Jack returned home. He bristled when the hospital spokesman blamed the stillbirth on "nervous tension and exhaustion following the Democratic Convention." "What else do you expect?" Jackie barked.

Jack and Jackie withdrew into separate shells of self-pity. With each of their dreams destroyed, they sold Hickory Hill to Bobby. Jack spent the next two months campaigning and learning how to exploit his star power. When Democrats at a "Ladies Day" rally in Queens Village gave him a frenzied welcome, Jack underlined the comparisons his fans drew between "'Elvis' Kennedy" and America's rock-and-roll king. He said the way Republicans treated Americans reminded him of the Elvis Presley song "You're Just an Ole Hound Dog." Most of the shrieking women were too old to know that their idol had mangled the song's title.

Such efforts strengthened Jack's standing across the nation and weakened him at home; gossips claimed Joe Kennedy paid Jackie to stay married. Jack had little time to indulge his feelings, though, since his 1958 reelection campaign loomed. The Kennedys reconsidered their strategy. With the senator married, was it still appropriate for his family to campaign so much? How could they utilize a wife who, as Jack said, had too much status and not enough quo? On July 21, 1957, a North American Newspaper Alliance dispatch proclaimed: "A vital element has been added to the well-planned and generously financed campaign to make Senator Jack Kennedy President of the United States. The Kennedys . . . are 'expecting.'" Caroline's birth in November helped quash what the report called "some of the recurring rumors that the youthful Mr. Kennedy and his beautiful wife are not getting along so well."

The "team of Jack and Jackie" appeared in almost two hundred cities, up to fifteen times a day. They celebrated their fifth anniversary on the stump in Omaha, Nebraska. Simply but elegantly dressed, with her trademark three strands of pearls, Jackie was pawed and interviewed. She refused to give speeches in English but greeted ethnic communities in Spanish, Italian, and French. "When Jackie was traveling with us, the size of the crowd at every stop was twice as big as it would have been if Jack was alone," Jack's aides claimed, arguing that voters appreciated Jackie's refusal "to put on a phony show of enthusiasm."

Reporters loved Jackie. Most profiles treated this "lithe brunette with elfin charm" as an aristocratic flower blooming in the democratic garden. The Kennedys were praised for living in "a small Boston apartment and an unpretentious Georgetown house," with the missus "doing most of the housework." Such down-to-earth millionaires seemed peculiarly American and most appealing.

Reporters failed to mention that "the petite and lovely senator's lady" was testy. She moped in the limousine waiting for Jack to finish speaking, or read Proust in French as Jack waved madly to the crowd from his motorcade. Aides held Mrs. Kennedy's cigarette as she took furtive drags on it.

The Kennedy publicity machine covered up these lapses. "HIS GREATNESS IS A PRODUCT OF STRONG FAMILY TIES AND TRADITIONS," one reelection pamphlet proclaimed. "The John F. Kennedy Story" printed nine family photos on its eight pages. Film crews followed the Kennedys with orders to film "whenever the Senator appears with Jackie or with an attractive group of women." TV stations loved such footage. In April 1957, Jackie let an NBC crew film her as she walked the dog, dropped Jack's shoes off to be shined, and brought in his dry cleaning. Kennedy's campaign film ended with the senator telling viewers that "I'll take you to my home" to introduce his family. And there was Mrs. Kennedy, in pearls, holding Caroline and offering a breathy and high-pitched "How do you do?" to the people of Massachusetts.

"At Home with the Kennedys," a ten o'clock morning coffee break for the "ladies," replaced "Coffee with the Kennedys." Jackie and Rose exchanged banalities stiffly. With upbeat 1950s family music in the background, the ladies of Massachusetts saw ten minutes' worth of photos and film clips of Kennedys at play. The visit felt as intimate and as benign as the neighborhood coffee klatsch; eventually, the senator arrived to answer questions.

Once again the Kennedys had invited Americans in to chart the family's progress, as the kids started their own baby boom. The bouncy music linked the show with "Ozzie and Harriet" or "Father Knows Best." As in those shows, the women dealt with each other and the children, the men handled the real world, offstage.

Jackie accepted her fate as a political prop, but she wanted to shield her daughter. *Life* infuriated Jackie by photographing Caroline's nursery when she was three months old. Jack mollified Jackie with a trip to Paris and a promise to limit future exposure.

Jack's 1958 Senate landslide ratified his tactics and positioned him as a leading presidential contender. It also proved his aristocratic wife could lure votes. "She is simply invaluable," Jack beamed. Over the next two years John Kennedy benefited from a boom built largely on his own popularity. Jack was the Democratic Eisenhower, beloved for who he was instead of what he believed. Republican polls showed that "Kennedy's strength lies in his personal appeal, the glamour of the publicity he has received, the beauty of his wife, and the zealousness of the efforts by him and his brother to meet the threat of labor rackets."

The shy, awkward, gangly young congressman had become a master campaigner. Jack was never comfortable backslapping and waving, but he was outgoing, charming, and wry. Leslie Carpenter, a reporter who knew "the early Jack Kennedy," would say, "I never saw anyone change so drastically in my life."

Like good makeup, Jackie Kennedy highlighted Jack's most appealing features. Her society background brought class to his wealth, her glamour made him look cool but not cold, and her Continental ways added a touch of savoir faire. Jackie's presence was particularly important to Catholics. Jack wanted to capture the Catholic vote; Louis Harris noted that Catholics praised Kennedy as "a good family man," assuming that reflected a pious life.

Jackie's prominence also inoculated Jack against the inevitable whispers. One Catholic couple living in Georgetown discovered just how impervious the senator was to scandal. Leonard and Florence Kater photographed Kennedy leaving the apartment they rented to his twenty-one-year-old secretary Pamela Turnure at 1:00 A.M. on July 11, 1958. They also recorded the sounds of lovemaking and intimate conversation. Despite taking this evidence to newspapers, television stations, Joseph P. Kennedy, and Richard Cardinal Cushing, the Katers were ignored.

Jack Kennedy knew he could trust the gentlemen of the press to protect his secrets. By the late 1950s he had assembled a formidable staff that planted stories and vetted articles. Reporters socialized with Kennedy and helped him; some, like *Newsweek*'s Ben Bradlee, sent him lengthy memoranda offering political insights.

The senator's prop-stop crusade across America for the 1960 Democratic presidential nomination solidified the ties. The pranks, the rushed dinners, and the late nights energized the reporters. By the end, Theodore White wrote, the middle-aged men covering Kennedy "felt that they, too, were marching like soldiers of the Lord to the New Frontier."

Throughout the 1960 campaign, Jack's image distorted reality. His rival in the primaries, Senator Hubert H. Humphrey, led an exemplary private life, but ran on the issues. One Harris poll found that voters almost "always" called Kennedy a "good family man" but rarely said that about Humphrey.

Nevertheless, this preoccupation with popularity unsettled Jack. His own polls warned that his "personality element" attracted attention, "but it does not do the convincing as such." Many doubted Kennedy. His senatorial colleagues saw a mediocre legislator, a young man on the make. Louis Harris tried to link Kennedy's "youth and liberalism," arguing that this perception of him as "modern" was "the most common really positive side of the Kennedy image." But the candidate had to fill in the blanks, substituting accomplishments for his family's achievements, principles for an appealing personality.

In both the primary campaign and the general campaign against Richard Nixon, Kennedy tried to stir the masses while earning respect. From the time he announced his candidacy in January 1960 through election day, Jack was constantly running toward the presidency and away from the truth. Every day he had to make sure that the public Jack eclipsed the private Jack, that the illusory Jackie compensated for the real Jackie. That year, their marriage often seemed anything but convenient.

Many Democrats wondered "how to generate an excitement" for their cool, technocratic candidate. Eric Sevareid of CBS called Nixon and Kennedy "junior executives . . . clothed in no myth or mystique." Kennedy, with his upper-class ease, could more easily play a role without appearing to play it. He quoted Goethe, Pentagon statistics, and policy analyses. He let those around him pander and treated such appeals as illegitimate. "When you run for the Presidency your wife's hair or your hair or something else always becomes of major significance," Kennedy sighed. "I don't think it's a great issue, though, in 1960."

Kennedy's pose as the cool intellectual helped him maneuver around his Catholicism. He could not declare his religion irrelevant to his public life if he politicized his personal life too much. Also, a philandering politician parading as a family man needed to bar touchy personal issues from the public realm.

Just as both Kennedy and Nixon symbolized the rise of a new generation of cool GI Joes, both "lovely aspirants for the role of First Lady" epitomized the best of American womanhood. A congressman called Mrs. Kennedy "the ultimate political weapon," while President Eisenhower deemed Mrs. Nixon the "most important" of her husband's many virtues. Jackie Kennedy and Pat Nixon reflected contrasting sides of the feminine ideal; if one was the id, the other was the superego of the American home. *Newsweek* called Jackie Kennedy a "stunning egghead." Her life appeared to be every woman's fantasy. Beautiful, well-bred, and rich, she could indulge in eighteenth-century French furniture for her townhouse, an elegant hairdo, a little painting here, a little fox hunting there. Somehow Jackie's lavish lifestyle, combined with the populist nature of her husband's career, made such luxuries seem accessible to ordinary people. The fact that Jackie was "by no stretch of the imagination the conventional political wife" thrilled voters. By the summer Jackie would be a "pace setter" in fashion, her bouffant all the rage. She was pregnant and limited her travels. Her rare appearances triggered rousing welcomes.

Pat Nixon was slim and pretty, but she was "self-discipline[d]" rather than self-indulgent. Everything she and her husband owned testified to their grit, as well as their good fortune to be living in postwar America. Pat enjoyed being "a suburban housewife" running a "large and lively household" with two daughters, three cats, six kittens, a parakeet, and a dog, Checkers. Pat was, *Newsweek* wrote, "the super-duper . . . cool and poised," preaching a gospel of "self control" and self-reliance. She never bought a dress just because she liked it: "I think: Will it pack? . . . Can I wear it a long time?" Pat was as self-promoting as her husband. "We both work hard, we're both self-sufficient, we don't show temper or irritation. We are friendly and try to give off warmth," she reported mechanically. "Pat's only flaw," *Life* said, describing the classic 1950s mom, "is flawlessness."

Pat's use of the plural pronoun distinguished the Nixons from the Kennedys. Pat and Dick cooperated at home and on the stump. *Time* called them "the best-known team in contemporary politics." "I've always been a part of what's done, but a silent partner," Pat insisted. Reporters constantly spied the two exchanging "affectionate glances" and compliments. In his ham-handed way, Dick tried to exploit Pat's popularity. "Whatever you think of me," he often said, "I'm sure you'll agree that Pat would make an excellent First Lady."

In contrast, Jackie was unconventional. While Pat never cracked, Jackie was known to pop off at reporters, aides, and even her husband. At rallies, Jackie would "pull some invisible shade down across her face, and cut out spiritually," Ben Bradlee wrote. The Kennedys did not generate a sense of warmth or togetherness. Before one of their rare joint appearances, one aide reminded the senator to "turn to her with a gesture or a smile." Reporters' stupid questions made Jackie wince. "It's the most important time of Jack's whole life, and I should be with him," she said, trying to be the dutiful wife, but her disdain showed. Pictures of the wispy socialite in a trim black dress posing with a rotund Democratic Committee woman with heavy cat's-eyes glasses and a bulky fur-lined hat spoke volumes. "She breathes all the political gases that flow around us, but she never seems to inhale them," Jack marveled.

Jackie's comments continued to upset Jack. When some pols asked where to hold the 1960 Democratic National Convention, she suggested "Acapulco." Even in her column for the Democratic National Committee, "The Campaign Wife," she jabbed her husband. Caroline, she reported, "keeps seeing her father's picture on lapel pins and bumpers and wondering why so many people are talking about him and why he isn't home more often."

Jackie's wardrobe became the talk of the nation. Matrons fretted about the "shocking pink" slacks she wore while strolling in Georgetown. When asked if she and Rose spent $30,000 a year shopping in Paris, her defense underscored her extravagance. "I couldn't spend that much unless I wore sable underwear," she said. Pat's simplicity threatened Jackie. "I'm sure I spend less than Mrs. Nixon on clothes," she purred. Remembering where Pat Nixon had purchased her 1956 inaugural gown, Jackie added, "She gets hers at Elizabeth Arden." Pat responded that she bought most of her clothes "off the racks." The candidates' wives caused "as much talk on the subject of cash and couture as their husbands provoked on soberer issues," *Life* complained.

It is hard to believe today that, as Louis Harris reported, women voters "in general" preferred Nixon to Kennedy. Harris's poll found that women who were "political romantics" disliked "the image of the Kennedy machine." They preferred Nixon's "image of the clean-cut, quiet, conscientious family-centered public servant." The "conservative anti-Catholic" women of the South also favored Nixon. Jack's attempt to build his credibility and soft-pedal his celebrity appealed more to men. Harris said Kennedy had to equal "Nixon as the self-confident warrior" and surpass "him as the more warm and human warrior." Perhaps women in 1960 could sense a playboy, even if the press kept silent.

Kennedy pandered to women by promising "to appoint a consumer counsel in the office of the President." The counsel would help "housewives" by trying to check the high cost of living. More broadly, Margaret Price, the Democratic vice chairman and director of women's activities, said that "with one-third of this country's work force women, he [Kennedy] would hardly think it appropriate to relegate them to attending teas and fashion shows." Supporters insisted that John Kennedy's "New Frontier is co-ed." As proof, Price noted that "The Kennedy Ladies" attended 112 receptions in fourteen states during the final two months. Price did not realize just how well a bunch of elegantly dressed matrons singing "High Hopes" anticipated the Kennedy administration's approach to women.

Ironically, Jackie's absence from the campaign trail ended up offering reporters and politicians unprecedented exposure to a candidate's wife. When the aspiring First Lady said she felt "so totally inadequate" in her husband's campaign, Lady Bird Johnson proposed that Jackie host political events at home. And so Jackie allowed reporters to watch her in Hyannis Port as she watched the first debate. She also hosted a meeting of the "Women's Committee for the New Frontier" at 3307 N Street in northwest Washington, D.C., where the group identified "four major issues" of special concern to women: "peace, education, medical care for senior citizens and the cost of living." In her living room, Jackie filmed campaign commercials, in English and Spanish, alone and with celebrities like Dr. Benjamin Spock. She also granted interviews to Walter Cronkite, Charles Collingwood, and other reporters. While she grimaced at the reporters' questions and resented their lights and wires, at least she was at home and away from mobs.

Surprisingly, Jackie's standoffishness enhanced her appeal. Her popularity reflected a key lesson that jazz musicians had mastered in the 1940s, "beat" hipsters had learned in the 1950s, and Marshall McLuhan would popularize in 1964: Jackie, like her husband, was cool. "To express a desire or a need for anything is not cool," Americans were learning. In politics, Professor McLuhan would explain, the public filled in the blanks of detached and enigmatic performers like the Kennedys. Jack hid his hunger for the presidency, while Jackie truly dreaded it. Their restraint suited a "cool" medium like television. The passion of the "sharp," well-defined Nixons proved self-defeating. Good-looking couples like the Kennedys, who emphasized vague appearances rather than specific accomplishments or passionate commitments, prospered in America's cool, TV-oriented culture.

In mid-September, the Kennedy courtier John Kenneth Galbraith praised Jackie for demonstrating such qualities on the "Today" show. The professor, however, used traditional terms, characterizing her appearance as "an occasion of rare dignity and good taste." Traditional gentility was more enduring in modern American politics than traditional oratory. "I took your letter with me to Washington and showed it to Jack," Jackie wrote Galbraith from Hyannis Port. "Coming from you it means more than you can imagine."

For all the hoopla surrounding the clash of the wives, women remained secondary characters. At best, the First Ladies-to-be had gone from being stationary props to marionettes, with repetitive motions and easy lines. Even the "ideal wife" of the time, Pat Nixon, avoided speechmaking. Still, a significant change occurred. Reporters demanded separate plot lines for candidates' wives; aspiring First Ladies had to prove the vitality of their partnership by striking out on their own. They needed independent activities that implied deference while allowing their husbands to bask in their fame.

In the end, the impact of the wives remained unclear. It is tempting to pick out the evidence from 1960 that Jackie would be popular, but some still feared that she would be a liability. Her youth, her breeding, and her extravagance were all potential trouble spots. What popularity she had was shallow and volatile.

At one point during the long wait for results on election night, it seemed that Kennedy might even have a landslide. Jackie whispered to him, "Oh, Bunny, you're President now!" But even that moment would be ruined. "No . . . no . . . it's too early yet," Jack hissed. Once the results were in, Jack teased his wife and Ben Bradlee's wife, Toni, who was also pregnant: "Okay, girls, you can take out the pillows now. We won!"

III

John Kennedy entered the White House determined to prove he was smart enough and serious enough for the presidency. He dressed formally for his inauguration to look more mature. He called for a "struggle against the common enemies of man: tyranny, poverty, disease and war itself." Yet signs of Jack's frivolity flourished alongside the solemnity. Just as he had the good taste to invite the eighty-six-year-old Robert Frost to read a poem at the inauguration, he had the bad taste to slip away from his wife at a ball for a quick assignation with the twenty-eight-year-old starlet Angie Dickinson. "This Administration is going to do for sex what the last one did for golf," Ted Sorensen crowed.

John Kennedy's many secrets—about his health, his promiscuity, his father's influence—made him a master performer. What a genteel mother considered "poise," detractors would call "deception" and supporters would call "great P.R." He loved his new administration's style. "Have you ever seen so many attractive people in one room?" he exclaimed at one party.

The new First Lady at once boosted and undermined the President's quest for respectability. Her poise and her interest in the arts would give the administration a sophisticated sheen, but her youth and her celebrity would emphasize his callowness. She refused to remain in the genteel straitjacket imposed on her predecessors, and she clashed with reporters.

Initially, few problems with their glamour were apparent. Anxieties about relying on an untested leader in a treacherous age drowned in a sea of celebrations welcoming the new generation to power. "Jacqueline Bouvier Kennedy will bring youth, beauty and babies to the White House," the conservative *U.S. News and World Report* had gushed during the transition. Barely three weeks after her husband's victory, Jackie gave birth to John F. Kennedy, Jr. As usual, the public celebrations hid private tensions. When Jackie rushed to the hospital three weeks early, her husband was in Palm Beach; Jackie had begged him not to abandon her. "I'm never there when she needs me," the wayward husband confessed.

The birth of "John-John" gave Jackie more cover as she entered the White House. She wanted to be First Wife and First Mother, not First Lady. "Running our home has always been a joy to me," she told reporters. "I feel this is what I was made for." In "our White House home," Jackie would help her husband "refuel away from the tensions of his work." Yet Jackie seemed more like a movie star than "an old fashioned wife." As she nursed her new baby in seclusion, her legend was born. In the three months between the election and the inauguration, she became as celebrated as Elizabeth Taylor and Marilyn Monroe. *Photoplay,* the "daddy" of the fan magazines, would feature side-by-side photographs of Jacqueline Kennedy and Elizabeth Taylor on its June 1962 cover. In boldface type, the headline screamed "AMERICA'S 2 QUEENS," promising: "A comparison of their days and nights! How they raise their children! How they treat their men!"

The preinaugural gala Frank Sinatra hosted celebrated the new links between Hollywood and Washington. The movie colony reflected Jack's values just as the Augusta crowd had reflected Ike's sensibilities. Kennedy gossiped about the stars, read *Variety,* and often frolicked with Sinatra, Sammy Davis, Jr., Dean Martin, and others in the "Rat Pack." Not only did Jack look like Hollywood's idea of a president, he fused two central streams in American culture: He made power glamorous.

America commodified the President and First Lady. Proof of the Kennedys' popularity abounded: in advertisements with Jackie look-alikes, the bestselling "First Family" record albums, Mort Sahl's comical Kennedy routines, the Kennedy board game, the Kennedy paper dolls, the Kennedy coloring book, the President Kennedy salt shaker, and the Kennedy playing cards with family members as jacks, queens, and kings. Jackie's face on magazine covers boosted sales. Many Americans felt closer than ever to the First Family. "Inaugural day, I along with thousands more mothers, were worried about you," one woman wrote Jackie from Detroit. "Were you warm enough? Were you tired?"

The "Jackie Kennedy look" swept America's multibillion-dollar fashion industry. Of twenty-three fashion shows mounted during New York City's Fashion Week in January 1961, all but five mentioned the First Lady-to-be. One New York hairdresser only did "Jacqueline" hairdos all day long. "Women everywhere are rushing to copy your dress, your hair-do, even your very ideas and opinions," businessmen wrote the First Lady, begging her to save their corner of the industry by parading a mink coat, a lace-trimmed dress, or a new hat. Chicago beauticians would crown Jackie one of "the best coiffured women of 1961," along with Princess Margaret, Sophia Loren, and Eva Gabor. The New York Couture Group would label her the world's best-dressed woman.

"There are other things which I think are more important now . . . than my views on fashion," Jackie had said during the campaign. But Jackie was as obsessed with her looks as Jack was with his. She "discreetly" ordered clothing from France and tried to conceal designs of the clothing she wore. Oleg Cassini became her exclusive designer. "Just make sure no one has exactly the same dress I do," she commanded. "I want to be original & no fat little women hopping around in the same dress."

Comparison with Jackie diminished her predecessors. Mamie Eisenhower was caricatured as a frumpy grandmother. Bess Truman became "American Gothic to the core, stubbornly wearing her orchids upside down, curling her gray hair tight the way she'd always done it in Missouri," columnist Dorothy Kilgallen said.

The First Lady's protests that "my motivating force . . . is to be a good wife" only enhanced her appeal. Jackie Kennedy was a woman who had everything—money, brains, sex appeal, power—yet she wanted to be a mom. "If you bungle raising your children I don't think whatever else you do well matters very much," she preached. This career girl turned housewife validated the choice millions of women had made. She was what Betty Friedan would call "the Happy Housewife Heroine." In *McCall's, Good Housekeeping,* and the other mainstream women's magazines, Friedan discovered a prototypical woman who is "young and frivolous, almost childlike; fluffy and feminine; passive, gaily content in a world of bedroom and kitchen, sex, babies and home." "It is now quite all right for a woman to be a bit brainy or cultured as long as she tempers her intelligence with a 't'rific' girlish rhetoric," the *New York Times* reported in January 1962.

During the cold-war clash over ideal lifestyles, both Kennedys became powerful advertisements for American capitalism. If, as one British writer admitted, in the atomic age, "The President of the United States is the President of Britain," his wife was First Lady of the World. Mrs. Kennedy "is a real public relations asset to the nation at a time when we are not doing too well in holding up a favorable image to the rest of the world," the *Minneapolis Star* insisted. The First Lady was a novel weapon in a peculiar war, making inroads against communism by wearing a pillbox hat and redecorating her home.

Traditionally, new administrations enjoyed an extended honeymoon during their first few months. The American people's romance with the Kennedys was exceptional. Reporters repeatedly marveled at the Kennedys' popularity, thereby feeding it. The Kennedys granted unprecedented access to reporters—and TV cameras—to chart their lives. In mid-February CBS News featured "A Day in the Life of President Kennedy," offering "a candid glimpse" of the President's daily routine. Two months later, NBC featured a prime-time interview with the President and Mrs. Kennedy. Kennedy's popularity soared from 69 percent approval in January to 83 percent in May.

Jack confessed, "We couldn't survive without TV." The First Family's "most extraordinary pipeline from their house to your house" showed Americans "how the President runs his administration, [and] how Mrs. Kennedy takes care of the 'living,'" one critic noted. Such exposure gave "everybody" a "piece of the White House," as the President had promised. On Monday, September 2, 1963, "CBS Evening News" marked its expansion from fifteen minutes to half an hour each night by interviewing the President.

Reporters tried to compete with this new penetrating visual medium by bringing their readers to places cameras could not reach. "We interviewed Jackie's hairdresser, her pianist, her caterer . . . [and] even . . . the owner of the local diaper service," Helen Thomas of UPI admitted. Once Thomas called the press secretary Pierre Salinger at three o'clock in the morning to inquire whether one of Caroline's hamsters had died. Jack's weekend activities, Jackie's purchases, Caroline's jokes, John-John's first steps—all were covered meticulously.

Television magnified the impact of the most trivial acts. From Charleston, Arkansas, a mother complained about the President's accent: "My two teenagers thought that Americer, Cuber and Africer must be correct and acceptable if a well educated man like Mr. Kennedy pronounced them this way." In gauging "the enormous personal appeal of the President," Louis Harris said the widespread perception of Kennedy as a "good family man strikes a deeply responsive chord. With it (in a minor note, however) is the sense that the President really cares about people and their lot."

Such scrutiny overwhelmed the White House press office. Pierre Salinger had expected to handle all news about both President and Mrs. Kennedy, but he "found it impossible to jump from an announcement on nuclear testing to a precise description of Mrs. Kennedy's latest hat." He consigned "all questions involving society, zoology, and millinery" to the East Wing. Forty people now helped the First Lady cope with her public duties, including a growing correspondence unit, and a press secretary, none other than Pamela Turnure. The social secretary, Letitia Baldrige, supervised the staff and reported to the First Lady.

Kennedy tried to put his popularity to good use. Although he kept the ideas fuzzy, he revitalized liberalism. Millions believed with him "that things can be improved." The morning after the inauguration, James Meredith applied to become the first black to attend the University of Mississippi. "Negroes are getting ideas they didn't have before," Kennedy's black adviser, Louis Martin, warned in 1962. "Where are they getting them?" Kennedy wondered. "From you!" Martin replied. "You're lifting the horizons of Negroes."

Jack's permissiveness with the press undermined Jackie's efforts to protect her children. In her first NBC interview she complained, "There is so little privacy, I don't mind for myself, but"—she smiled to soften the blow—"[I] think it is very hard with them." Mrs. Kennedy could not even go to the circus without fearing harassment. The interviewer, Sander Vanocur, asked if it was "really possible" to maintain privacy. Sounding patrician, Jackie said, "Well I hoped it was. You ra*w*ther discourage me, Mr. Vanocur." She then whined, "but I hope it is . . . because otherwise how can I bring up normal children?"

Jackie established a private school in the White House for Caroline. By 1963, when Caroline entered first grade, it had twenty students in two classes; the other pupils were children of administration officials and family friends. A tribute to Mrs. Kennedy's desires to be a "normal mom," the school suffered from what one unhappy parent called "the 'hothouse flower' aspect." It was hard to consider a school meeting in the solarium on the third floor of the executive mansion "normal."

The new cult of personality had its problems, evoking concerns about presidential dignity and contempt for the vulgar medium of television. After the Kennedys appeared on NBC, Robert Donovan asked in the *Boston Globe:* "Is President Kennedy lowering the dignity of his office by submitting to interviews in the White House on television programs that are commercially sponsored?" The Republican National Chairman, Senator Thurston B. Morton, and others said yes, deeming such appearances "bad taste."

Public scrutiny was relentless. When Jackie missed church, correspondents demanded she attend; when she went to Mass in slacks, they chided her to dress appropriately; when she dressed formally, the clothes had to be American. In *McCall's*, Clare Boothe Luce dressed down the First Lady for patronizing French designers: "Just as the personal activities of the President can never be dissociated from his role as America's First Citizen, so, too, the personal activities of the President's wife cannot be dissociated from her role as First Lady," Luce lectured. Mrs. Kennedy's task as First Lady "is to form and lead American taste." Jackie's press secretary, Pamela Turnure, responded that Mrs. Kennedy's "official" wardrobe was almost exclusively American, while her unofficial wardrobe "is a personal matter."

Jackie Kennedy tried in other ways to separate her official and personal roles. She rejected the title of "First Lady" as suited to "a saddle horse," preferring the more democratic "Mrs. Kennedy." The "President's wife should be just that—his wife," she insisted. "People must be as sick of hearing about us and [Caroline's pony] Macaroni as I am," she believed. She commanded Pam Turnure to follow a press policy of "minimum information given with maximum politeness."

In contrast, Jack Kennedy and his men in the West Wing tried to merge his official and personal roles. They believed that, as Arthur Schlesinger, Jr., would say, "His 'coolness' was itself a new frontier." Jack knew that the wrong image could undercut his Presidency. In February 1962, *Time* magazine falsely alleged that the President had posed for *Gentlemen's Quarterly.* "What do you mean I posed for them!" Kennedy yelled to Hugh Sidey, *Time's* White House correspondent. "People always remember the wrong things, they remember Arthur Godfrey for buzzing a tower and Calvin Coolidge for wearing those hats and they'll remember me for this." Kennedy's fears suited a leader with so much staked on his personal image, and so much to hide.

Jackie also lashed out at reporters. She called Helen Thomas of UPI and Fran Lewine of AP "harpies." Kennedy worried about Jackie's hostility to the press. "Poor Jack," she sneered. "He thinks if I ignore them he'll be impeached." "The boss can't do a thing with her," Dave Powers sighed. At one dinner, the President grabbed the First Lady by the arm, dragged her across the hall, and commanded, "Say hello to the girls darling."

Many of these "girls" had entered newsrooms during World War II, only to be banished when the men returned. After working for a decade and a half, Helen Thomas was "low man on the totem pole with United Press International's White House news team" and therefore "assigned to cover Jackie." Women reporters and First Ladies were marginal in a world where, the *Washington Post's* Ben Bradlee recalled, "women were treated exclusively as shoppers, party-goers, cooks, hostesses, and mothers."

Mrs. Roosevelt had created occasional headlines. In this new media world, Jackie "was news twenty-four hours a day," Thomas exulted. The fascination with Mrs. Kennedy helped free newswomen from their professional ghetto. Thomas soon became a "regular" covering "Presidential news," even as "women's news" became accepted as "real."

Still, Jackie believed that the nosey newswomen with their off-the-rack dresses ruined White House parties. She tried to gag them. In the summer of 1962, Turnure and Baldrige told a dozen women reporters "to avoid personal contact with the President and Mrs. Kennedy" and their guests. Viewing the First Lady's struggle with reporters, Washington socialite Virginia Livingston Hunt called Mrs. Kennedy "the rudest; most self-conscious First Lady since I came here to live. . . . Do not expect any civility from Jackie unless it suits her."

Jack, too, was utilitarian in his dealings with reporters and sensitive to criticism. Yet he emphasized their generational ties and common interests. One guest of every five at White House luncheons or dinners was a reporter. In February 1963, *Good Housekeeping* printed "The Private Letters of John F.

Kennedy." For six months, the editors and Salinger nursed this puff piece: The magazine got an exclusive, and the President was lionized.

This cozy relationship would not last. That same February, the prickly May Craig asked the President at one of his news conferences about "the practice of managed news." "We've had very limited success in managing the news, if that's what we have been trying to do," he chuckled. Reporters were becoming more aggressive. "I don't believe in managed news at all," Craig told the President. "I thought we ought to get everything we want."

The President occasionally bullied the press. He sent Henry Luce a twenty-four-page analysis finding "an air of sarcasm" in *Time*'s treatment of the Kennedys compared to "sympathy" for the Eisenhowers. When reporters violated his ground rules, he often blasted them. "Ted Sorensen told me yesterday how upset you were . . . and that you tried to get hold of me at the time and that I was lucky you didn't," one photographer groveled.

Salinger mediated between the President and the press; the President mediated between the press and his wife. When Mrs. Kennedy visited Greece in 1963, the President allowed *Look* to send a photographer for a feature on "the President and his son." Kennedy told the editor: "We'd better get this over with quick because when Mrs. Kennedy is around things get pretty sticky."

The Kennedys were often one step away from major scandal. In late December of 1961, the Associated Press reported that "Mrs. Jacqueline Kennedy slipped out of Palm Beach last night and for an hour and a half danced the 'Twist' in a Fort Lauderdale night club." The hip-gyrating rock 'n' roll song and dance sensation of 1960 was such a controversial symbol of youthful subversion that the activist Eldridge Cleaver would call it "a guided missile, launched from the ghetto into the very heart of suburbia." Such revelry appeared particularly inappropriate because the Kennedys were visiting the President's father, who had just suffered a stroke. The story made front pages from the *New York Journal American* to the *Los Angeles Herald Examiner*. All day, radio disk jockeys told the story before playing "The Twist." Raymond J. Connor of the Bronx and others telegrammed the President with warnings: "COMMUNISTS CAN EXPLOIT ADVERSE PUBLICITY OF MRS KENNEDY DOING TWIST IN SLACKS IN A NIGHTCLUB. THEREFORE REQUEST THE WIFE OF THE PRESIDENT OF THE UNITED STATES EXERCISE DECORUM AND DIGNITY IN DISPLAYING HERSELF AS FIRST LADY."

The story appears to have been false. Kennedy's people insisted that witnesses had mistaken Senator Jacob Javits's slim, brown-haired daughter Stephanie for Mrs. Kennedy—although Senator Javits did not have a daughter by that name. The President was livid; he demanded a retraction from the AP. Salinger stopped golfing and began browbeating AP officials, who tarried six hours before retracting the story. The *Journal American* carried the apology on page two, for one edition; the *Herald Express* carried the retraction in its first edition only.

Kennedy's popularity gave him a false sense of omnipotence. He ignored warnings that fourteen hundred exiles could not liberate Cuba. Indulging the dyspeptic masculinity of the barracks, Jack mocked critics of the proposed Bay of Pigs invasion for "grabbing their nuts" in fear. Yet, for all his macho posturing, Kennedy wanted to "keep our hand concealed in this affair." By April 1961, Kennedy had an exaggerated faith in his ability to manage appearances as well. He dispatched Adlai Stevenson to the United Nations to deny American involvement in an invasion. Kennedy also tried to squelch news leaks, asking his staffers, "Is there a plan to brief and brainwash key press within 12 hours or so?"

The night after the invasion, April 18, 1961, could have been a delicious moment surpassing even a James Bond movie. At a reception honoring members of Congress, the President and his tuxedo-clad warriors flitted from tête-à-têtes with the 450 guests to hurried conversations in the corners. By midnight the President was in the Cabinet Room, looking "resplendent," Arthur Schlesinger, Jr., recalled. Unfortunately, Washington was not Hollywood; the invasion was failing. The military men begged the Commander-in-Chief to call in Navy jets and destroyers. "No," Kennedy insisted, "I don't want the U.S. to get involved in this." "Hell, Mr. President," Admiral Arleigh Burke, the Navy chief of staff responded, "we are involved." The Cubans killed 114 exiles and captured 1,189 others. Kennedy's concern with image would lead critics to blame his "political decision" rather than any "military" mistakes.

The Bay of Pigs confirmed critics' fears that Kennedy was too immature, too arrogant, and too self-involved to succeed. All the hoopla about style distracted him. The resulting feelings of invincibility were dangerous in a nuclear age. "Despite himself, even this dispassionate and skeptical man may have been affected by the soaring euphoria of the new day," Schlesinger admitted. Two months later, former Secretary of State Dean Acheson told Harry Truman that Kennedy's preoccupation with "image" was "a terrible weakness. It makes one look at oneself instead of at the problem. How will I look fielding this hot line drive to short stop? This is a good way to miss the ball altogether."

The Bay of Pigs could have ruined the rookie President, but the author of *Profiles in Courage* rallied. Privately, Kennedy blamed others. "My God, the bunch of advisers we inherited," he exclaimed, as he appointed a commission of inquiry to deflect responsibility. Yet the President took the blame in public. At his press conference he barred questions about Cuba. Predictably, a reporter ignored the ban. Jack was ready. "There's an old saying that victory has a hundred fathers and defeat is an orphan," he said, coining the phrase. "I'm the responsible officer of this government." Government by epigram worked. Admirers would label this humiliation "one of his most courageous moments." When polls showed that Americans' approval for their humble commander had skyrocketed to 83 percent, Kennedy learned yet again the power of appearances: "Jesus, it's just like Ike. The worse you do, the better they like you."

On December 29, 1962, Castro finally released the Bay of Pigs prisoners. The President and Mrs. Kennedy welcomed them at Miami's Orange Bowl. Jackie said in Spanish how honored she was to have her young son, John, Jr., along: "It is my wish and my hope that some day he may be a man at least half as brave as the members of Brigade 2506." Even after botching the job, Jack could still score some political points—with Jackie's help.

IV

Despite its relatively happy ending for Kennedy, the Bay of Pigs demonstrated that popularity was ephemeral. Only accomplishments endured. Jackie Kennedy "wants to be as great a First Lady in her own right as Jack is a President," a relative said. Jackie recognized that Americans' fascination with "whatever the First Family likes" gave her great power.

Jackie Kennedy revolutionized the role of First Lady while insisting that she only wanted to be a good wife and mother. Rather than playing to America's matrons, she played to the cameras and the middle-class masses. She combined the well-bred woman's interest in philanthropy, the arts, and entertaining with the suburbanite's zeal for home improvement and PTA meetings. Her four major projects—the White House restoration, a more elegant social season, support for the arts, and Caroline's nursery school—illustrated the mix. Jackie would not humor garden clubs or help the poor. Her efforts revealed a penetrating and effective executive beneath the girlish facade.

Jackie said she wanted "to make the White House the first house in the land" because it "belongs to the people of America." Privately, she refused to live in a house that looked like a "dentist office bomb shelter." When Mamie Eisenhower first showed her the White House, Jackie excused herself and burst into tears. She was determined to make the White House fit for a President—and for a Bouvier Kennedy.

The First Lady began one of the greatest shopping sprees in American history. Exercising "a woman's prerogative," she gave "her new home a new look," the *Boston Globe* noted. Jackie exhausted the annual $50,000 decorating budget within weeks. She set out to organize a fine arts committee, hire a curator, change the laws governing income tax deductions for donations, establish the White House as a museum, supervise production of a guidebook, and raise millions of dollars. She beautified the state rooms and made the executive mansion more like a home, installing a private dining room, a small adjoining kitchen, and a nursery.

Jackie was a hard-driving, bargain-hunting perfectionist. She did what she could to secure this $165,000 portrait of Ben Franklin, that $25,000 red-

and-beige Aubusson carpet. She used all the weapons in a lady's arsenal—flirtatiousness, flattery, secrecy, and the occasional tantrum. J. B. West, the White House usher, learned that her coquettish "Do you think . . ." or "Could you please . . ." was "a command." Before one committee meeting, she praised the chairman Henry Francis du Pont's "brilliant" efforts in acquiring some chandeliers. She then suggested that he circumvent a discussion of "the renovation of China & Gold Rooms . . . as everyone chatters when they leave these meetings."

The restoration was Jacqueline Kennedy's defense against the vulgarity of politics. She waged war against curtains that had "horrible wrinkles" or an "ugly yellow" color. While Jack appeased cigar-chomping bosses, she would hobnob with the gentry. The First Lady protected the White House from crass showmanship. When she saw a congressman posing in the Rose Garden with "an enormous bunch of celery," she stormed into Jack's outer office and dictated a memo saying: "I think it is most undignified for any picture of this nature to be taken on the steps leading to the President's office or on the South grounds. If they want their pictures taken they can pose by the West Lobby."

For all its upper-class pretensions, Jackie's project reflected a middle-class faith in "uplift." Men and women had different tasks in perpetuating society; women cultivated beauty to elevate their husbands and children. "I want every little boy who goes through this White House to get some sense of history, to be shown things and have them explained," Jackie said. "But I also want it aesthetic. Girls must go out and make homes."

Jackie's plans made Jack nervous. He feared that if his aristocratic wife spent millions redecorating both she and he would seem frivolous. The President asked the Washington fixer Clark Clifford to handle the First Lady. Jackie became attuned to appearances. In February 1962, she would ask Clifford how to avoid admitting that they needed to raise two million dollars. "Jack and I agree that figure sounds awful," she wrote. "It could be politically used against us—'palace of the Caesars' etc." Jack became interested once the renovation proved popular; when she found a particularly interesting item, Mrs. Kennedy often rushed to the Oval Office.

Jackie immersed herself in her project. Once, when Dr. Martin Luther King, Jr., came to meet the President in the residence, the elevator he entered went down to the basement first. Jackie climbed aboard, dressed in blue jeans and streaked with soot. "Oh, Dr. King," she gushed, "you would be so thrilled if you could just have been with me in the basement this morning. I found a chair right out of the Andrew Jackson period—a beautiful chair." King sputtered, "Yes—yes—is that so?" Jackie said, "I've just got to tell Jack about that chair." She then caught herself and retreated, saying, "But you have other things to talk to him about, don't you?" As she left, King shook his head: "Well, well—wasn't that something!" King's meeting with Kennedy was more relaxed than their previous interactions had been; such feminine "frivolity" often put men at ease.

East Wing concerns often distracted President Kennedy from West Wing crises. Right after the Bay of Pigs, the President blasted Letitia Baldrige for having too much French on the White House menus. He then abruptly hung up, saying, "Just forget I ever called." "Quarreling over food prices rather than atom bombs" relaxed him, Pierre Salinger noted.

Jacqueline Kennedy's restoration succeeded wildly. The initial printing of 250,000 guidebooks sold out in three months. By 1962 the White House averaged 4,560 daily visitors, up from approximately 3,000 during the Eisenhower era.

On February 14, 1962, Mrs. John F. Kennedy took Americans in 28 million homes on a televised tour of the White House. Four million TV sets more than usual were turned on that night. In her thin, breathy voice and her upper-class accent, Jackie showed the nation the "mahvelous" colors, and the antique "chaiahs" of the redone mansion. Her breeding made her seem qualified to guard the nation's treasures. Most of her performance consisted of beautifully sculpted sentences, compelling facts, heroic stories about rescuing lost pieces of furniture, and charming asides. Occasionally a close-up caught the First Lady loosening her tongue and fighting dry mouth. She worked the names of patrons into her patter—and reshot one take when she overlooked a major donor. When her CBS host, Charles Collingwood, asked about the "relationship between the government and the arts," the knowledgeable, elegant matron turned girlish. "That's so complicated. I don't know," she purred. "I just think that everything in the White House should be the best."

Toward the end of the program, the President appeared. Jack stiffly praised his wife and echoed the middle-class belief that history promoted patriotism. He hoped to "double" the number of visitors to the White House, especially among children. "They'll come home more interested, and they'll become better Americans," he said.

Like Jack's presidential debates, Jackie's tour seemed to justify the television industry. The show won a special Emmy award, and the A.C. Nielsen company boasted that "Jacqueline Kennedy and television br[ought] more people to [the] Presidential Mansion in an hour than visited during its entire 162-year history." Theodore White called it "the most successful nonfiction show" CBS had ever produced. Reporters hailed "a charming woman" who was also "a person in her own right," mixing "fragile loveliness" with "remarkable thoroughness." "I approve of what you are doing to the White House as much as I disapprove of your husband's policies," one Republican wrote.

The White House renovation was Jackie's great gift to Jack—and a source of revenge. She proved she could help his career. While watching the TV special with the Kennedys, the Bradlees sensed that the President envied his wife's performance and disliked his own. As with so many other housewives, the redecorating project gave Jackie a sense of purpose. "I think every woman wants to feel needed," she said.

Jackie's renovation of the White House was popular for many of the same reasons her husband's administration proved popular. The riches they reveled in now seemed accessible. In 1950, 36 percent of the population earned enough income to qualify as middle class or higher; by 1960, the figure was 59 percent. America had become the first overwhelmingly middle-class country in world history. The Kennedys' mass-marketed gentility made many Americans feel prosperous. The *New York Times* claimed that, thanks to the Kennedys, "the average American has a much clearer idea of what it must be like to have everything." From 1950 to 1972, real income after inflation would double. Americans were ready to spend, and the Kennedys showed them the way.

Jackie did not want the White House to be "an empty museum." She wanted to create a democratic Versailles. The Kennedys jazzed up the White House social life. At one event, shocked society columnists counted up to eight shattered precedents as hard liquor flowed, ashtrays appeared, music began before the First Couple arrived, and children attended a reception for new officials—on a Sunday. "Nothing quite so dramatic has happened to the White House since the British came to town and burned it in 1814," conservatives harrumphed. Feeling young, glamorous, and powerful, the Kennedys' guests enhanced the legend of these parties. "It was all so gentle, and reassuring, in that lovely house, so well done and so easy," the novelist Katherine Anne Porter rhapsodized. "What style they had, those young people! And what looks."

Sometimes, though, the parties went too far. Word that the First Lady of the United States and Secretary of Defense Robert McNamara had "twisted" away at a White House party dismayed many older Americans. The timing was particularly bad; as the Kennedys rocked, the Russians released Gary Powers, the American U-2 pilot. Charles Bartlett advised against such behavior: "It's bound to get out and it doesn't seem to me to be worth the price, however small." The President agreed. He was also worried about the wild parties at Bobby Kennedy's Hickory Hill estate. The First Family needed to maintain some sobriety.

The reception honoring Pablo Casals in November 1961 was a quintessential Kennedy event, mixing classical art and movie-star glamour. Jack preferred James Bond novels and Broadway musicals to Shakespeare and symphonies, but he considered the arts "a part of our arsenal in the cold war." Jackie just wanted to civilize her husband and her country. She lobbied for an independent arts agency and a national cultural center in Washington—what eventually became the National Endowment for the Arts and the John F. Kennedy Center for the Performing Arts. Her greatest contribution remained in the realm of public relations. White House aides said the Kennedys triggered a "general ferment of excitement and hope for [a] new era of cultural activity on the part of the general public."

In spreading refinement, however, the Kennedys helped doom it. The new aristocracy of achievement was less authoritative than the older, fixed kind. Wrenched from its moorings, deprived of its most powerful patrons, gentility became more widespread and weaker. Giving gentility to the masses implicitly allowed the masses to reject it. In the ensuing decades, the Kennedy revolution would come to haunt the country.

Jackie assailed gentility by renouncing many of the First Lady's matronly duties. She often begged off from receptions at the last minute; her husband, her mother-in-law, Lady Bird Johnson, or an aide substituted. Mrs. Johnson, the "Second Lady," replaced her more than fifty times. Often Jackie feigned illness, only to appear in the next day's newspapers shopping or waterskiing. In February 1961, Jackie refused to go to a performance the Indian Ambassador hosted. The next day, Tish Baldrige reminded White House aides: "In case any one asks you about Jackie perhaps you better say that she has a cold and the doctor has told her to stay in her room." When she announced her pregnancy in 1963, the President joked, "Now, Jackie will have an excuse to get out of things."

For all her popularity, Jackie Kennedy had little impact on policy. Jack confided not in her but in his brother Bobby and his "Irish Mafia." "My family calls me John's other wife," Dave Powers joked. Echoing Mrs. Eisenhower, Mrs. Kennedy said she talked to the President "about family matters, never about matters of state." Jackie said, "Jack has always told me the one thing a busy man doesn't want to talk about at the end of the day is whether the Geneva Convention will be successful or what settlement could be made in Kashmir or anything like that."

While both Kennedys were ambitious, contemporary attitudes wanted only the man to appear hardworking. Many reporters tailored the Kennedys' image to fit popular beliefs. "She did not court this position as First Lady, and she looked forward to it with anxiety bordering on regret," Jim Bishop wrote. "But once she became immersed in the chores of the White House, she decided to do all, be all, participate in everything, and still save enough of herself to have a family life." In 1000 days, Jackie Kennedy reinvented herself. The petulant snob became a democratic supergirl—thanks to those pesky reporters.

V

Jack's and Jackie's great triumphs during the administration were individual rather than joint achievements. Jackie distanced herself from the struggles over domestic and foreign policy that defined her husband's Presidency; Jack was only a supporting player in the White House renovation and the crusade for the arts. In fact, these model parents, this glamorous couple, often worked at cross purposes. They had been married barely seven years when they moved into the White House, making theirs the youngest marriage in the postwar White House by decades. And despite the unrelenting pressure for them to appear harmonious, deep fissures were often apparent. They led curiously separate lives, more typical of the aristocrats they were than the suburbanites they purported to be.

Observers thought the Kennedys went from triumph to triumph, but Jackie suffered in the White House. In July 1962, Tish Baldrige explained to one of the Bouvier clan that Jackie needed a vacation, having "had one horrible year, as you know, and it has taken its toll on her." Jackie was bred not to demonstrate her despair—except when convenient. Jack once scribbled a wavy line across the page and said that was Jackie. He then drew a straight line through the waves to characterize his own temperament. She was moody; he was even-keeled. It did not make for easy living.

Shrewd observers could find hints of trouble even in the circumspect press of the times. Few pictures showed the two parents and the two children together. Even the Caroline Kennedy comic book illustrated the separate relationships each Kennedy parent had with the youngster. The cover featured a graphic of Jacqueline and Caroline. Inside, a two-page spread focused on "Caroline's Daddy": "President . . . Senator . . . War Hero . . . Conqueror of Pain . . . and *Wonderful Father!*" A separate spread focused on "Caroline's Mommy": "First Lady . . . Model Wife . . . Fashion Leader . . . Equestrienne . . . Socialite . . . and *Wonderful Mother!*" Of nearly sixty images in the comic book, only two pictured the Kennedys as a couple with their daughter. One classic pose of a little girl holding a balloon, escorted on her left by a woman and on her right by a man, showed Caroline leaving ballet class with her nurse and a Secret Service agent.

The Kennedys did not work well together. "You'll find that no *easy* problems ever come to the President of the United States," President Eisenhower had warned. "If they are easy to solve, somebody else has to solve them." Kennedy often made difficult decisions without his wife's encouragement. Jackie, in turn, made decisions about the children and the household without Jack's help. "That's your province," he would snarl when Jackie asked his opinion. She would retort: "Yes, but you're the great decision-maker. Why should everybody but me get the benefit of your decisions?"

The pressure to trumpet their union as a model marriage exacerbated tensions. Jack surrounded himself with sycophants; he prized loyalty. Jackie lashed out at him to prove her independence. Once, when the President dawdled on his way to church, Secret Service agents overheard the First Lady screaming: "Come on now, you son of a bitch. You got yourself into this and you know your public demands it. So get your damned tie and coat on and let's go." At a Lincoln's Birthday celebration in 1963 for eight hundred blacks, Jack asked Jackie to help block photographs of an interracial couple, Sammy Davis, Jr., and Mai Britt. Jackie refused. She threw a tantrum and made only a perfunctory appearance at the gala.

At the start of the administration, Kennedy dispatched his chief of protocol, Angier Biddle Duke, to explain to Jackie "the responsibility of the wife of the President in regards to visitors and things." Jackie claimed she wanted to do "as little as possible. I'm a mother. I'm a wife. I'm not a public official." Jack worried that Jackie would hurt him politically, but Jackie refused to sacrifice her few remaining pleasures. She continued to suit up and go fox hunting, even after hundreds of voters protested against the decadent, bloodthirsty sport. Once, when his wife sported a particularly outlandish hairdo, the President, who feared mockery screamed, "What are you trying to do, ruin my political career?"

Along with so many other young couples, the Kennedys battled about money. The focus on her fashions emboldened Jackie to shop even more extravagantly. She spent over $100,000 in 1961 and 1962 combined. She dismissed Jack's complaints by remarking, "The president seems more concerned these days with my budget than with the budget of the United States."

Jack used intermediaries to avoid confronting his wife. When the king of Saudi Arabia gave Jackie some expensive horses, the President called Ambassador Duke. "Tell her it's hurting me politically," Jack instructed. "The Arabs give her these horses and then Israelis come along with an old Bible worth about $12." Jackie told the ambassador, "I understand what you're saying, Angie, but . . . I want the horses."

The President and First Lady established competing courts. Baldrige said there was a "civil war" between Jack's people in the West Wing and Jackie's people in the East Wing: "The presidential assistants tried to force decisions affecting Mrs. Kennedy on our office without consulting us." Kennedy's macho men had little respect for Jackie's "girls" or their allies. Secretary of State Dean Rusk scorned Arthur Schlesinger by saying the professor was based in the East Wing, "with the women."

Jackie escaped from the tension regularly. She shopped in New York, spent weekends on Cape Cod and in Palm Beach, holidayed on the Riviera, and lobbied for assignments to romantic places. Reporters rephrased Jimmy Durante's Mrs. Calabash television signature to "Good night, Mrs. Kennedy, wherever you are." To justify his wife's gallivanting, the President encouraged her to accept Prime Minister Jawaharlal Nehru's invitation to visit India. The President and the Prime Minister did not get along, but Jackie had charmed the elderly Nehru. Jackie would keep American policy evenhanded by also visiting Pakistan.

The Kennedys labeled the two-and-a-half-week voyage in March 1962 a "semi-official" trip, more than a personal tour but not quite a state visit. Mrs. Kennedy doled out banalities about how "the art of children is the same the world over, as are our feelings for children." The nearly four hundred thousand words of press traffic, and sixty-one broadcasts totaling almost one thousand minutes during her ten-day stay in India were overwhelmingly positive. "You are one half woman, and one half dream," CBS's Walter Cronkite fawned, quoting "India's greatest modern poet," Tagore.

Mrs. Kennedy was demure when she returned home. "It feels unnatural for me to go on such a semi-official trip without my husband," she said. "I have missed my family and I have no desire to be a public personality of my own." She attributed the welcomes she received to the fact that "I was the wife of the President, so the people were showing their affection for him." Perhaps regretting her solo tour, she lamented, "He should have been there to receive it." Her first weekend home, the Kennedys made sure to pose for photographers as they attended church.

Most reporters praised the First Lady for providing such a colorful story; many Americans were less enchanted. White House mail ran two to one against Jackie's pilgrimage. Anticommunists feared that her penchant for luxury and her avoidance of the starving masses made Americans appear decadent. Moralists complained that getting special permission for her party to carry liquor made Americans appear insensitive. But the most common criticism had to do with the estimated cost. The $224,000 covered a three-man camera crew from the United States Information Agency, which produced a sympathetic travelogue eventually broadcast throughout the world. "Has it never occurred to her that she might share her wealth with the unfortunate among our own people, instead of increasing the tax burdens of Mr. and Mrs. Ordinary American Citizen?" a California couple asked.

Furthermore, in Pakistan Jackie insulted the DAR. A reporter asked her about the DAR's claim that buying UNICEF greeting cards supported communism. According to the *Pakistan Times,* the First Lady said the criticism "is mostly confined to old and lonely women and their organizations." When the wire services picked up the report, the White House denied it. The President muttered, "Jesus Christ, I'm going to have to muzzle the First Lady."

Relations with the DAR were already strained because Mrs. Kennedy had spurned the group's 1961 convention, yet hosted a party for newspaper women the same week. The center of gravity had shifted; reporters were more important than matrons. Outraged women tried to teach the First Lady some manners. "The closer to the truth you might have felt your words to be, the less gracious it was of you to utter them," one lady lectured. "I was personally 'hurt' that my idol of women could think of me 'old and lonely,'" a woman from Indiana wrote. All the anxieties about Jackie Kennedy being too hedonistic came pouring out. "Of course, those of us who do service work in these groups do not ride to the hounds in Virginia. If we have pink coats they are products of the home sewing machine and not of Oleg Cassini," one woman sneered. "Our First Ladys [sic] in the past have been such gracious hostesses to everyone. . . . It's a shame you can't be," mourned a Missourian who lived just north of Bess Truman.

Many older, conservative Americans disapproved of the First Lady's behavior. They wanted a genteel matron who upheld tradition, not a bold celebrity. Eleanor Roosevelt may have neglected the white-gloved brigade; Jackie Kennedy insulted them. "Are you as bad as Liz Taylor?" one New Yorker asked. "You should keep out of newspapers & act as a lady." To many, Jackie's extravagant consumerism threatened America's traditional sobriety. Her excesses undermined the President's calls for sacrifice. The then-conservative *Chicago Tribune* attacked "the peacock opulence of Mrs. Kennedy on her recent progress thru India and Pakistan" and asked: "What is our 'Image' before the world to be—that of a lady with a dozen daily changes of wardrobe, spread in color thru the picture magazines?"

These criticisms intensified in August when the First Lady took Caroline to Italy. Normal American families vacationed together, and foreign travel was unpatriotic in any event. The image of their First Lady, in slacks, doing the cha-cha deep into the night with the exotic Count Silvo Medici del Vascello further offended conservative sensibilities. Married women were only supposed to dance with their husbands, especially in such disreputable venues as nightclubs. "DOES THIS SET A PROPER EXAMPLE FOR THE YOUNG WOMEN OF AMERICA?" the Concerned Citizens of America asked. "Has something gone wrong between you and her?" Americans asked their President. The cold war equated domestic harmony and governmental effectiveness. Many wondered: "You are the head of our state. Aren't you the head of your household?"

Meanwhile, women mobbed the President when he swam near Peter Lawford's Santa Monica beach house. Newspapers published photographs of the bare-chested President in swimming trunks alongside pictures of the First Lady modeling her green one-piece suit on the Italian coast. "It appears that all decorum, dignity and decency has been thrown overboard by our President and the First Lady," the executive secretary of the Colorado Baptist General Convention protested. Jack cringed, but Jackie was enjoying herself for the first time in months. Her initial two-week stay in Italy became a month-long jaunt.

Jackie Kennedy was caught in a culture clash. Leaders, especially First Ladies, were supposed to represent transcendent values. Many renounced a celebrity culture that valued fame for fame's sake. Respectable matrons were appalled; many lower-class women were jealous. "I'm just a poor housewife who pays little income tax every year so you will have plenty to throw away, & it makes me *mad*," a woman from North Texas wrote, complaining about the cost of security on the Italy vacation. "I'll never vote for a Kennedy," she vowed.

To millions, Jackie symbolized all that was wrong with the Kennedys—their arrogance, wealth, and dynastic ambitions. Many conservatives who disagreed with Jack politically hated what he and his family represented. The affluent America that reporters applauded terrified others. The *Richmond News Leader* attacked the feminine, glitzy show the Kennedys put on when contrasted with Nikita Khruschev's style. The *News Leader* believed Khruschev indulged the Kennedys because "A Harvard freshman, dancing with the belle of the Vassar ball, does not invade Cuba (except with an autograph pencil). A king and queen of movieland are ideal enemies, in Khruschev's realistic world of brute strength."

The criticisms worried the President. After seeing pictures of his wife swimming with Gianni Agnelli, the owner of Fiat, Jack telegrammed: "A LITTLE MORE CAROLINE AND LESS AGNELLI."

The President never forgot that he had barely won the 1960 election. Jackie's vacation came just before the 1962 congressional elections. Conservatives like Barry Goldwater were making effective attacks on the "headlong national rush for money," the decline of traditional morality, and the growth of federal power. The Arizona senator was anticipating a 1964 campaign posing his "genuine commitment" to tradition against Kennedy's cynicism. In Massachusetts, Teddy Kennedy's Senate campaign absorbed attacks on the Kennedys' arrogance, wealth, and ambition: "We're having more f—ing trouble with this than we did with the Bay of Pigs," the President had exclaimed to his national security adviser, McGeorge Bundy. The chorus of disapproval from the genteel ladies harmonized with the growing populist conservatism. Jackie remained defiant. "People told me ninety-nine things that I had to do as first lady, and I haven't done one of them," she boasted. A month before the 1962 elections, a Gallup poll showed that Mrs. Kennedy remained popular. Respondents most often mentioned her "good looks," her "good personality," and her intelligence. But her actions attracted criticism. Asked "What are the things you like least about her?" respondents mentioned her travels away from her family, her love of the limelight, her hairdo, her clothes, and her undignified behavior.

Jackie's absences justified Jack's dalliances and made them easier to arrange. He maintained his steady diet of sex with stars, subordinates, socialites, and strangers in the White House, at New York's Carlyle Hotel, and at the Lawfords' Santa Monica home. His behavior was so outrageous it can only be explained by resorting to psychological speculation: a desire to defeat his illness; a need to outdo his father and brother Joe while punishing his mother and his wife; a self-destructive streak; a feeling of invincibility. Jack learned from his father that women were commodities to be accumulated, along with money and power. "He was completely driven to dominate them," a friend recalled.

President John F. Kennedy was a sexual outlaw. During the campaign he had feared that "if I win—my poon days are over." Once in office, he learned how to deploy presidential resources to satisfy his cravings. When Jackie was in Asia in March 1962, the FBI director J. Edgar Hoover confronted Jack about the sordid triangle between the President of the United States, Judith Campbell, and a Chicago mobster, Sam Giancana. That day, John Kennedy made the last of over seventy phone calls through the White House switchboard to this paramour. He soon canceled plans to visit the mob-connected Frank Sinatra as well. As overworked aides pimped for the President, they noticed their anomalous situation. "We're a bunch of virgins, married virgins," the secretary of the Cabinet, Fred Dutton, complained. "And he's like God, f—ing anybody he wants to anytime he feels like it." Amid such debauchery, it is ironic how many Americans attacked Jackie's behavior, but not Jack's.

To Jack, it would have been weak, even girlish, to retreat from his womanizing. He linked sex and power. Jackie's behavior confirmed Jack's impression of women. Girlfriends were playthings; wives were ornaments. Jack equated masculinity with strength. He rarely talked about his illnesses. His college buddy Henry James said "he was heartily *ashamed* of them, they were a mark of effeminacy, of weakness." Such attitudes were utterly conventional. One female student at Yale in 1960 claimed that exposure of Kennedy's philandering "will help him. It will show he knows how to get what he wants." In the spring of 1962, a campus poll would find that American co-eds considered their President blessed with more sex appeal than anyone else, including Rock Hudson—an impression confirmed at Kennedy's Madison Square Garden birthday rally in May when Marilyn Monroe cooed "Happy Birthday, Dear Mr. President."

The President's contempt for his wife and his paramours complicated his attempts to gain women's support. Jack built his career on the women's vote at a time when women were becoming more demanding. While Betty Friedan was still unknown and unhappy, many of the ideas that would be attributed to her were spreading. Nostalgic for their wartime jobs; underutilized in a modern home filled with time-saving gadgets; eager, sometimes desperate, to earn added income in a consumer society increasingly addicted to shopping, middle-class women were fleeing their kitchens. Twenty-three million women were working; one-third of all wives had jobs. A new vocabulary recognized the challenges posed by staying home. Women needed "outside" interests while fulfilling their "traditional" duties—just as Jackie Kennedy combined travel with her restoration and her one-note paeans to homemaking.

To address the problem—and pander to women—in 1961 Kennedy appointed Eleanor Roosevelt to head a Presidential Commission on the Status of Women. Mrs. Roosevelt and other leading Democratic women proved most interested in government jobs. Women had been working their way into government for decades. Woodrow Wilson had appointed a dozen women to key posts. Franklin D. Roosevelt made Frances Perkins the first female Cabinet member and recruited female assistant secretaries and appellate judges. Despite their discomfort with women, Presidents Truman and Eisenhower had also broken new ground. Eisenhower named 175 women to "high level" federal posts, including Oveta Culp Hobby to head the Department of Health, Education and Welfare and Clare Boothe Luce as ambassador to Italy.

As "housekeepers for the nation," women were considered supremely qualified to help manage the welfare state. "Certainly there are some areas—those which call for a high degree of human understanding, of skill in person-to-person relations, of caring, if you will, about the welfare of children or older people—in which women may have special qualifications," wrote Margaret Price, the Democratic activist. To staff such "women's jobs," America's unofficial queen, Mrs. Roosevelt, presented the new President with the names of almost one hundred qualified women.

Nonetheless, Kennedy appointed 240 men and only 9 women to key posts. Aides argued that there was "everything to gain and nothing to lose" by appointing women, but Kennedy feared this minefield; when he acknowledged women's aspirations outside the home, homemakers protested that he did not respect them. Activists accused the President of discrimination. "Kennedy never thought of a woman as anything but a sex object," one of the grand Democratic dames, India Edwards, concluded.

Jackie Kennedy's name rarely came up in these discussions about women and the Kennedy administration. Her disdain for politics, and her reputation as both a mother and a "glamour girl," made her an unlikely ally for the female crusaders. Many women did expect Mrs. Kennedy to fight for peace "as a wife and mother." Thousands of letters begged Jackie to "assume the position of First Lady of Peace by publicly condemning the manufacture and use of nuclear weapons." The protests escalated when the White House announced that the First Lady would help launch a Polaris nuclear submarine. Women asked Jackie "how you, who are truly an epitome of American beauty, graciousness and culture," could "lend yourself to the launching of one of these instruments of horror?"

Mrs. Kennedy refused to intrude in such "policy" matters as the status of women. The President, however, picked up the refrain. During the summer of 1963, he met with representatives of seven women's magazines reaching 33 million readers monthly to talk about women and peace. The editors agreed to publish their stories simultaneously in November. "As the mothers of our children, women are most intimately concerned with the future of the human race," the President believed. In treating peace as a women's issue, the President recognized the emerging female political identity. Being ghettoized empowered women. Middle-class housewives were beginning to break out of their gilded cages, opting for political involvement and eventual liberation.

Kennedy's commitment to women's participation was more rhetorical than real. The same week the President preached egalitarianism, Secretary of State Dean Rusk signed the Limited Test Ban Treaty at the Kremlin. The large, all-male American delegation showed that the cold war remained man's business.

Two days after the signing, Jackie gave birth five weeks prematurely. Jackie was vacationing on Cape Cod, and Jack was working in Washington. Jack was with Patrick Bouvier Kennedy when he died two days later at the Children's Medical Center in Boston; Jackie was recuperating on the Cape.

In mourning their son, the Kennedys' cool facade cracked. After the burial mass, the President wept on the coffin. "My dear Jack, let's go, let's go," Richard Cardinal Cushing said as he pulled the President away from the casket. "Nothing more can be done." Bill Walton spent the weekend with the Kennedys. "She hung onto him and he held her in his arms," Walton remembered, "something nobody ever saw at any other time because they were very private people." Instinctively hoping that some good could come from such anguish, observers sensed a new tenderness in the presidential couple. Jackie told Jack that, great as this loss was, "the one blow I could not bear would be to lose you."

Two months later, Jackie was off cruising the Mediterranean aboard the 303-foot yacht *Christina,* owned by the notorious Greek shipping magnate Aristotle Onassis. In the 1950s, Onassis had paid seven million dollars to avert a federal indictment. "Jackie, do you know what you're doing?" Jack asked. "Are you aware of this fellow's reputation?" One Ohio congressman attacked the "impropriety of our First Lady . . . in accepting the lavish hospitality of this international character." A widely circulated photograph caught the First Lady sunbathing in a bikini. "Does this sort of behavior seem fitting for a woman in mourning?" editorialists asked. Once again, the Kennedys were struggling. Jack pleaded for Jackie's return; Jackie ignored him.

When she did return, Jack exploited "Jackie's guilt feelings" to get her politicking. Since September 1962 his popularity had been declining, and by November 1963 only 43 percent of those polled would approve his performance. He feared a showdown with Barry Goldwater, and he did not want to lose the moral high ground. The backlash against Nelson Rockefeller's divorce and hasty remarriage to a divorcée had boosted Goldwater's standing. Republican National Chairman William Miller wondered what First Family life was coming to "with Sinatra types infesting 1600 Pennsylvania Avenue

. . . twisting in the historic East Ballroom . . . [and] all-night parties in foreign lands." *Newsweek* ominously suggested that "Mrs. Kennedy's immunity" to political attack "suddenly ran out."

"I will do anything to help" in the 1964 reelection campaign, Jackie vowed. "I guess if Pierre ends up putting me and the children on the cover of *Look* in a bubble bath, I'll have to put up with it," she told Pam Turnure. Jackie agreed to accompany her husband on a political trip to Texas to help repair their relationship and her reputation.

On the morning of November 22, 1963, a rain-drenched crowd greeted President Kennedy in Forth Worth. They had been waiting for over an hour "to hear him and see Mrs. Kennedy," as Vice President Lyndon Johnson would say. "Where's Jackie?" someone shouted. "Mrs. Kennedy is organizing herself," Jack quipped. "It takes longer, but of course she looks better than we do when she does it." For one last time, Jack played the harried husband, building his wife up while cutting her down.

Jackie's concession placed her by her husband's side when Oswald's bullet shattered his brain. Her presence in the convertible united the two in death as nothing had done in life. "It's my husband, his blood, his brains, are all over me," she told doctors as she remained with the dying President.

The assassination, and the dramatic public spectacle that followed, retroactively exorcised any public doubts about the Kennedys or their marriage. "The manner of the President and his wife to each other was always simple, courteous and loving, without gestures, without trying," Katherine Anne Porter wrote in the *Ladies' Home Journal,* marveling at how their life was "lived hourly in love with joy, yet every duty done and every demand fulfilled." In this, the greatest performance of her life, Jackie acted instinctively—and appropriately. Silently, she paraded around in her blood-splattered dress to "let them see what they've done." Her breeding and hauteur paid off as she telegraphed her anguish while displaying self-control.

Television intensified Jack Kennedy's ties to the people during his life, and it intensified the trauma associated with his death. Jackie Kennedy starred in this modern mourning spectacle. "Mrs. Kennedy achieved on this desperate day something she had never quite achieved in the years she'd been in the White House—[a] state of love, a state of rapport between herself and the people of this country," Lady Bird Johnson noted. "Maybe it was a combination of great breeding, great discipline, [and] great character." Jackie demonstrated the mores of her genteel, aristocratic upbringing on this most modern and vulgar medium. Her poise was a mark of her gentility. Her silence and grace confirmed the wisdom of a social circle that preferred self-discipline to self-indulgence. The matrons of America reconciled with Jackie that November. Yet even as she advertised its virtues, Jackie helped bury this traditional culture. The assassination would be seen as the end of American innocence, the death knell for gentility, as media-magnified social chaos spread and self-expression became the order of the day.

Widowhood made Jacqueline Kennedy the primary keeper of Jack's flame. No longer a thorn in his side, no longer a potential political liability to be neutralized, she guarded his image. Troubled by the meaninglessness of the death—"if it had at least been for his civil rights stand," she mourned—she helped make his death a monument to American idealism. She was the one who offered the defining metaphor for her husband's tumultuous, spasmodic, and ultimately mediocre Presidency. Amid her grief, she called in a trusted reporter, Theodore H. White, to rescue Jack from "those bitter old men" who write history. "And her message was his message—that one man, by trying, may change it all," White wrote. Showing that she had learned from her husband how to market, she offered "Camelot" as the defining image for the Kennedy era. "So the epitaph on the Kennedy administration became Camelot," said White, "a magic moment in American history, when gallant men danced with beautiful women, when great deeds were done, when artists, writers and poets met at the White House, and the barbarians beyond the walls held back."

On January 14, 1964, Jackie appeared on television to thank Americans for the eight hundred thousand condolence letters she received. She made her own attempt to burnish his image. Dressed in black, with a simple hairdo, flanked by Teddy and Bobby Kennedy, she emphasized her husband's two greatest assets: his popularity and his charisma. "The knowledge of the affection in which my husband was held by all of you has sustained me, and the warmth of these tributes is something which I shall never forget," she said. "All his bright light [is] gone from the world," she sighed.

For over a decade, Jackie succeeded in protecting her husband from the historians. In 1965 Arthur M. Schlesinger finished his ode to the fallen leader, *A Thousand Days.* "Now no one will ever be able to hurt Jack because your book is a testament against them—and for all that he could not finish," Jackie wrote. A year later she stopped cooperating and then spearheaded a nasty campaign against William Manchester's elegy, *The Death of a President,* when she feared it might prove too revealing. In a documentary commemorating the tenth anniversary of Kennedy's death, CBS News praised the Kennedys for adding "a touch of royalty" to America. "Someday somebody may separate John Kennedy's wit from his wisdom, his sense of style from the substance," the narrator intoned, but "what his generation remembers is the mixture." To illustrate the point—and the continuing yearning for "Camelot"—CBS showed shots of the President playing with Caroline, the First Lady horseback riding with Caroline, and the Kennedys aboard a yacht, with Judy Garland singing "Somewhere Over the Rainbow" in the background. The documentary talked about crises, especially in foreign policy, but made no mention of womanizing, illegal wiretapping, or shadowy CIA operations and mob connections.

Jack Kennedy's assassination ended an extraordinary idyll in the history of the American presidency. Both Eisenhower and Kennedy seemed to have been universally popular, especially after the assassination obscured Jack's last few difficult months. The Republican grew up as a poor boy in the West; the Democrat was a rich northeasterner. Both, however, benefited from the crusading climate Mrs. Kennedy captured with the "Camelot" label. At the movies, Americans still watched newsreels. These newscasts, with their heroic soundtracks and wry asides, epitomized the midcentury culture in which patriotism invigorated gentility. Eisenhower and Kennedy were both patriotic heroes who transcended their parties, and eventually undermined them.

A cold war fought more with perceptions than with guns magnified and complicated the president's role as national father. Eisenhower projected an easygoing masculinity until he took ill, whereupon he seemed more grandfather than father. Kennedy's callowness, good looks, coiffed hair, and frivolous wife made him dread becoming a symbol of feminization and ridicule. He compensated with an explosive combination of sex, power, and charisma, with vigorous rhetoric about his "new frontier," and with aggressive bursts of masculinity in Cuba and Vietnam, in his bullying of steel executives in 1962 to rescind their price increases, and in the presidential boudoir.

The cold war's lifestyle battle focused on the First Couple at a time when other presidential weapons, like party loyalty, were being dulled. First Couples came to epitomize the administration and the country. The First Ladies played important supporting roles in this world of nonpartisan, cold-war celebrities. They helped define their husbands—literally, in the case of Jack's death. Jackie's actions as First Lady proved controversial; she shifted the First Lady's focus away from the white-gloved brigade toward the American masses. But Americans were still swept up by the fantasy of who she was. Jackie and her husband were products of a new, proud prosperous America whose citizens believed in their leaders and in themselves.

In death and in life, the magical image the Kennedys created generated such excessive expectations that a fall was unavoidable. Both Jack and Jackie profited in the short run from their magical reputations, but the gap between their images and reality was too great. Even without the many skeletons in the Kennedy closet, no mortal could measure up to Jack's billing. The Kennedys' predicament was the predicament of postwar America: Some of the achievements were so monumental, the images so powerful, the ideals so grand that when reality intruded, the drop was precipitous. For a time, the

Kennedys—like their country—would set a high standard that all would aspire to and none could achieve. Ultimately, however, they and their country would produce such disillusionment that both the earnest efforts and the actual achievements would disappear along with the bright, shining, and unrealistic image. Eventually the Kennedys' failures would make Americans doubt that the perfect couple could exist at all.

Just as late-twentieth-century presidents would strive to do right by Roosevelt in the Oval Office, all subsequent presidential couples would strive to succeed as the Kennedys appeared to have at home. But those who followed would also be cursed by both the unrealistic standards the Kennedys set and the ensuing disappointment. First the Johnsons, then the Nixons, and finally the nation would pay a high price for the lies that Jack and Jackie Kennedy lived.

4

"CRAWLING DOWN PENNSYLVANIA AVENUE ON BROKEN GLASS"

The Johnson Partnership During the Assault on Standards

Lyndon B. Johnson had yearned for the presidency, but he never dreamed it would begin like this. The White House photographer recorded the swearing-in of the thirty-sixth President of the United States aboard a grounded Air Force One. The judge administering the oath, Sarah T. Hughes, was one of John F. Kennedy's few women appointees; her presence foreshadowed the real gains women would soon make. The 6'3" President dominates the photo. He is already aware of the "high, forbidding, historic" wall separating him from the others. He raises his right arm and rests his left hand on a Catholic missal, the only holy book Kennedy aides could find on this chariot of the secular state. The new President's receding hairline and hound-dog features make him less photogenic than his predecessor, a harbinger of coming frustrations in attempting to separate appearance from reality as his predecessor had done. To the right of the President, in her trademark pink ensemble—now blood-splattered—stands the new widow, playing her role superbly. She is legitimizing the transfer of power while reminding everyone of the fallen leader. To the President's left is his wife, Lady Bird, at his elbow as she has been for twenty-nine years.

That day, no one could have predicted that the Johnsons would create a new model of an activist presidential couple. The Johnsons would show just how much a president and First Lady could accomplish. Franklin D. Roosevelt's media-magnified, crisis-driven, power-drenched presidential style would peak in 1965 as the Johnsons set out to overhaul their country and save the world. In overreaching, they discovered the limits of the American presidency and of American power. The Johnsons' experience would also show that no matter how forceful and dynamic a modern First Lady was, she remained an extension of her husband.

I

If Jackie Kennedy at that moment represented the American woman transcendent—glamorous, mysterious, remote—Lady Bird Johnson epitomized the authentic American woman—long-suffering, accommodating, loyal, and ready to enter the realm of men. For three decades the Johnsons had sustained the kind of partnership that the Kennedys approached only once, after Jack's back surgery. Jackie could not fathom Lady Bird's wifely ethic. "Lady Bird would crawl down Pennsylvania Avenue on broken glass for Lyndon," Mrs. Kennedy had sneered. The Johnsons had the potential to model a new kind of egalitarian marriage to Americans. Yet, despite a stronger union, they would never achieve the iconic status of their predecessors.

The millions of words eulogizing John Kennedy confirmed the new recipe for presidential success: a winning smile, a beautiful wife, an attractive family, a sense of humor, flights of oratory, and the occasional well-handled crisis. All this panache seemed suited to the political consumers who had emerged since the end of World War II. The image of the presidential couple became a critical source of political currency—but that currency was unstable. Unlike Kennedy and Eisenhower, Lyndon Johnson was a creature of the system that emphasized party and policy. He built his career on "Concession, Patience, [and] Maneuver." Ultimately, Lyndon and Lady Bird were too political, too western, too authentic to thrive in a political culture centered on charisma, popularity, and mawkishness.

Johnson envied and scorned Kennedy's style. As a senator, he distinguished between "show horses" and "work horses." In the masculine subculture flourishing on both ends of Pennsylvania Avenue, "show horses" who played to the masses were feminine. Senator Hubert Humphrey said that comparing Johnson to Kennedy "was like comparing a heavyweight boxer to a ballet dancer." Humphrey called Johnson "a muscular, glandular, political man. . . . a doer. Kennedy was more a talker."

President Johnson hoped to outdo John Kennedy and Franklin Roosevelt; his First Lady wanted to outdo their wives. Lady Bird was a Southern belle conditioned to conceal her talents. "I am suddenly onstage for a part I never rehearsed," she sighed. Even her official biography conceded she had "been a partner in the political life of her husband longer than any First Lady in history." Bird would serve Lyndon and their daughters, Lynda Bird, aged nineteen, and Lucy Baines, aged sixteen: "I will try to be balm, sustainer, and sometimes critic for my husband. I will try to help my children look at his job with all the reverence it is due . . . and retain the lightheartedness to which every teenager is entitled. For my own self, the role must emerge in deeds, not words."

Lady Bird also wanted to be known for her actions instead of her fashions. Mrs. Kennedy's "dazzling" precedent was particularly daunting for the fifty-one-year-old Texan. "Her nose is a bit too long, her mouth a bit too wide, her ankles a bit less than trim, and she is not outstanding at clotheshorsemanship," *Time* would grumble. Lyndon bullied Bird to dress better, to check her hair in the mirror. "You don't sell for what you're worth," he fumed.

The Johnsons lacked the Kennedys' flair, but Lyndon still boasted: "I've got the best wife and the best two daughters in the world." They "never" disappointed him, despite his neglect. The Johnson daughters hosted receptions and met with reporters. They proved less controversial than Margaret Truman. Lynda Bird was bookish, political, steady, and, according to the *Saturday Evening Post*, "voluptuous." After breaking a three-year engagement, she would enjoy publicized romances with the actor George Hamilton and others. Lucy Baines was "pretty as a picture, sweet, thoughtful—and sometimes—exasperating!" Bird said. She would begin spelling her first name "Luci," and offend some Protestants by becoming a Catholic. Raised in the Washington scene, both girls were used to preening and used to serving their daddy. One photographer said that as soon as he raised his camera, "their mouths flew open. It was automatic. They went into smile."

As always, Bird tried to please everyone. In January 1964, she "sandwiched in" a chat with Luci between hosting a lunch for Queen Frederika of Greece, an interview, hours chained to "that tyrant, my desk," and a nine o'clock evening swim with Lyndon. Bird wanted "to give my husband as comfortable and serene a milieu in which to work" as possible.

Bird often soothed her volcanic husband. Clark Clifford recalled Bird interrupting a long meeting after the assassination "to tell him just because he was President was no reason why he didn't have to have dinner." Lyndon valued these intrusions. He mentioned in his memoirs that during the Six-Day War, "Lady Bird brought breakfast to us" in the Situation Room at dawn.

Johnson's aides grew accustomed to the First Lady's presence. One adviser, Joe Califano, recalled how the President held court in bed, with his wife lying "there next to him, bed jacket on, covers modestly pulled up to her chin." Eventually she would say, "Now you boys look the other way," and slip into her dressing room. When Lady Bird came by the office, "Johnson would stop everything," Harry McPherson recalled. "And he'd pull her down and have her sit on the ottoman, holding her hand, touching her back." Matrons criticized these vulgar displays, but Lady Bird shrugged. "It thrills me to pieces," she said.

The Johnsons took pride in their partnership. A CBS report on "The New President" introduced Bird as "a big political asset to Johnson" and someone who "genuinely likes public life." Lady Bird would tell another CBS reporter: "I think he accords me the very considerable respect of thinking I have good judgment and he likes to hear what I have to say. It's good to have one person with whom you can have total [and] complete freedom in what you talk about." Lady Bird criticized when necessary. "I find that after 35 years of living with me, she can still be objective about me," Lyndon would say just before he retired.

This was something novel—not just a Bess Truman helping out or an Eleanor Roosevelt with her own programs, Lady Bird was the first true adviser First Lady to flaunt her influence. "A sturdy political pro," she demanded policy briefings, slipped Lyndon notes saying "let's save voice" when he rambled, soothed victims of presidential tantrums, and helped make personnel decisions. Bird was always on call. As she told the socialite Brooke Astor, "Unfortunately, plans with me have to be made to fit into my husband's schedule—and that often means that mine are done on short notice."

Through hugs, kisses, gropes, waves, and florid prose, the President demonstrated that he valued her advice—and was crazy about his wife. After the emotionally blocked Kennedys, it worked. Americans were pleasantly surprised by an effusive President who praised Lady Bird as "the most wonderful wife a man can have," "my dearest running-mate," and the possessor of "great political instinct." When Dell published a Lyndon Johnson comic book, fifteen frames pictured the Johnsons together campaigning, dining, dancing, and posing with their kids; only three pictured Lady Bird alone. *Newsweek* would soon characterize Jackie Kennedy as "an elusive private being, mysteriously separate from the President to whom she belonged."

Many magazines labeled the Johnsons' "working partnership" a model marriage. It was vibrant, even if occasionally trying. Realism was replacing romance in the women's magazines. *Newsweek* said Lady Bird was not "a woman who sentimentalized marriage, but one who had made it work." Asked how she coped with her husband's demands, Bird would say "marriage, like life, is never static." Lyndon admitted that "I'm not the easiest man to live with."

It was remarkable that an egomaniac like Johnson was identified so publicly with his wife. He sometimes feared that his reliance on his wife was emasculating. To compensate, he would needle her in public or in private.

The judicious, farsighted, disciplined, and demure Lady Bird appreciated her impulsive, shortsighted, wild, and dynamic mate. The manic Lyndon offered fervid praise and bitter rebukes; his effusions helped him assert control. Bird admired "he-men" like her father, a tall, tyrannical merchant. "Oh, he makes me so mad," Bird exclaimed when she needed dental care in Washington and Lyndon insisted they go to Texas. "What are you going to do?" the friend asked. "Well, I have to do what he wants," Bird replied. "Mrs. Johnson has said over and over 'Lyndon stretches you,'" Liz Carpenter recalled. "He stretches you beyond your capacity and somehow in the stretching, you grow."

But a modern First Lady could not just cater to her husband. Lady Bird began trying on different aspects of her new position. She hired a reporter as press secretary and staff director; Liz Carpenter became the first newswoman to run the East Wing. This appointment confirmed that the press now was the First Lady's primary constituency. "I don't have to worry about Viet Nam or de Gaulle," Carpenter would say, "I'm in charge of women, dogs and old brocades"—well aware that such seemingly trivial matters helped determine presidential success. Yet, recalling Mrs. Roosevelt, she understood that "newspaperwomen want an activist first lady." Liz would help make Lady Bird Johnson "the greatest invention for newspaperwomen since the typewriter." This approach repudiated the cold wars of Bess Truman, Mamie Eisenhower, and Jackie Kennedy.

Bird set an extraordinary pace. During one two-week stretch she hosted six receptions, spoke five times during a nine-hour trip to Pennsylvania, granted one television interview, and appeared around town at dinners, luncheons, and dedications. Headlines declared: "SCHEDULE STIRS MEMORIES OF ELEANOR ROOSEVELT."

Lyndon was even more frantic than his wife. "I wanted power to use it," he said. His call for "the Great Society" broadened his "War on Poverty" into an assault on injustice throughout America. Unlike Eleanor, Bird took his program as hers, too. "The bet we are making—the government, I mean . . . is that you can do [all] this without destroying the character and self-reliance of American citizens," Bird wrote.

While the President planned to save America, his wife worked to secure the women's vote. Lady Bird refused to limit herself to desultory receptions with genteel ladies. Jackie Kennedy warned that one could easily get "tea poisoning" at the White House. But "Mrs. Johnson didn't want to have luncheons of people to sit around and talk about their ailments and their bridge games," Carpenter recalled. To attract a "more vital type of woman," Bird invited "can-do" women to monthly "Women Doers" luncheons.

The Ike-and-Mamie monolithic image of the cold-war world was crumbling. More middle-class women wanted to solve Betty Friedan's "problem that has no name." Many were trying to build a home and forge a career. The idea of an "egalitarian marriage" where both partners flourished at home and at work spread. By 1962 Lucille Ball had dumped Desi Arnaz and now appeared as Lucy Carmichael, a widowed working woman irritating her boss instead of her husband. Yet the *Saturday Evening Post* publicized a 1962 Gallup poll that found most married women satisfied and convinced that their "chief purpose" in life was to be good wives and mothers. "The American woman reflects what she helps to create—a God-fearing stable society," Gallup wrote. "And she likes not only the society she is molding but her role in it."

The reigning model for women was becoming schizophrenic. Lady Bird defined the "natural woman, the complete woman" when she delivered the baccalaureate address to Radcliffe College's class of 1964. Growing up in the South, Lady Bird had seen many interdependent partnerships between husband and wife. Even though they appeared frilly, Southern belles were more likely than their northern sisters to be "women doers." Lady Bird called for balance. A woman could be "a wife, a mother, a thinking citizen" without being an overworked "superwoman" or a "long-striding feminist in low heels, engaged in a conscious war with men." Women pioneers, she said, mastered "the dual role"—Lady Bird had learned from Lyndon to dress Southern lessons in western clothing. Bird did not consider intelligence "a threat to your femininity," but she urged her audience to retain "those qualities of warmth and tact and sensibility which a real woman possesses." Lady Bird believed the Great Society could free women too.

John F. Kennedy had paid lip service to women's dilemmas to woo their votes; his wife had mouthed the conventional paeans to domesticity while doing whatever she pleased. The new, earnest First Lady was confronting the questions squarely and offering her life as an answer. "If given a choice between lying in a hammock under an apple tree with a book of poetry and watching the blossoms float down or standing on a platform before thousands of people, I don't have to tell you what I would have chosen 25 years ago," she confessed two weeks after the Radcliffe speech. "But 25 years and the invention of the nuclear bomb have left us no choice." Lady Bird Johnson would spend five years crusading as an independent "total woman" only to discover that when her husband faltered, she did too.

Proving yet again that he was "JFK, with a difference," President Johnson declared himself "unabashedly in favor of women." He saw women as his natural allies in securing the traditionally feminine social welfare agenda of the Great Society. He promised to appoint more women to the government. In a quip that two decades later would be cliché, the President said "A woman's place is not only in the home, but in the House, the Senate and throughout government service."

The search was not always easy. Many women turned down jobs for the sake of their families, and many more had forsaken their professions years before. One local columnist warned women walking through Washington to be "extra careful . . . if they don't get mugged, they may get drafted for a job in government." During that first year, Johnson appointed 69 women to high positions, including the economist Alice Rivlin; he appointed 32 to advisory boards. There were also 418 new appointments to mid-level government jobs and 1,553 promotions. By the end of his administration, Johnson could also point to the 1964 Civil Rights Act, his 1967 executive order against sex discrimination, and four hundred improvements in state laws pertaining to women.

On one level, Johnson's "prowomen feeling" was in character. He idolized his wife and his mother and often told his two daughters that "the great untapped natural resource in the United States today is woman power." At the same time, Lyndon was a "good old boy" who praised old-fashioned housewives while pawing their daughters. "In a day and age when most families feed on television dinners and fruits packaged in cellophanes, it warms the heart of a man when he comes across a woman—like you—who is still capable of putting up a good pickle mustard," he told one of his backers' wives. Lyndon Johnson was a flirt and a philanderer. His male aides called his bevy of beautiful female secretaries "the harem." He boasted of having "more women by accident than Kennedy had on purpose." He inspired his own corpus of stories about presidential lechery, the most famous of which had him jumping into a secretary's bed during a visit to the ranch, commanding, "Move over—this is *your* President."

Lyndon tried to appease Lady Bird by drenching her in macho praise. When showing visitors the ranch, he would come to the master bedroom and proclaim, "Ah've had hundreds of women in my life, but let me tell you, nobody is better in that bed than Lady Bird." After his death, in an age of full disclosure, Lady Bird would obliquely acknowledge her husband's infidelities. "You have to understand, my husband loved people. All people. And half the people in the world were women. You don't think I could have kept my husband away from half the people?" she said in 1987. By then, such confessions were far more accepted than the blanket denials of a Mamie Eisenhower, who disavowed her wartime suspicions and went to her grave insisting that Kay Summersby was simply Ike's driver.

Johnson used his sexuality as a governing tool. "In the Lyndon Johnson era, macho was the order of the day," his press secretary, George Reedy, would write. By holding court in his bedroom, the President linked sex and power. He wanted to prove his potency to subordinates and secretaries. Johnson was equally capable of uttering high-minded odes to the Great Society and grabbing himself to trumpet his considerable endowments.

Johnson wooed voters with the same demonic energy he applied to less savory pursuits. When asked in 1964 why he was working so hard despite a commanding lead, he said that he did not just want the American people to elect him; he wanted them to love him.

In the elaborate dance of deciding to run that year, Mrs. Johnson clearly wanted to return to the White House. Disliking histrionics—"I infiltrate," she purred—she subjected Lyndon to her own version of his persuasive methods. After one exchange, Lyndon acknowledged that "in a few words she hit me on two most sensitive and compelling points," his patriotism and his virility. She also appealed to his grandiosity, his altruism, his sense of history, and his need for control. At the same time, Lyndon shrewdly solicited his wife's adulation and her approval. They both wanted to stay in office; the Johnsons knew how to handle each other.

Ugly personal attacks did make Johnson waver. "I was not thinking just of the derisive articles about my style, my clothes, my manner, my accent, and my family," he wrote. He told his aide Walter Jenkins, "I just don't think a white Southerner is a man to unite this nation in this hour."

Attacks on "the Johnson fortune" enraged him. Muckrakers asked how a lifelong public servant ended up as the second-wealthiest president. Johnson usually claimed that Lady Bird, not he, owned KTBC, the source of the family fortune. But both Johnsons were embarrassed in May 1964 by reports that Mrs. Johnson had black tenant farmers in Alabama living in shanties. Voters told the President, "Your 'war against poverty' should begin in your own family." There were drawbacks to marrying an heiress with too much property in a backwater.

Lady Bird emerged as a formidable politician in 1964. Before the convention, she traveled 35,405 miles by herself and 9,433 miles with the President; after it, she would travel 21,576 miles with the President and 9,943 miles alone. In mid-August she took a three-day tour of Utah, Wyoming, and Montana. Bird celebrated conservation, tourism, and the President's largesse at the Flaming Gorge Dam, a billion-dollar reclamation project. Never before had a woman dedicated a project that big. Lady Bird also boosted two Democratic senators in tight races. "The hustings have never seen the likes of this First Lady—at least not since Eleanor Roosevelt," one reporter cheered.

Television helped Mrs. Johnson reach far more voters than Mrs. Roosevelt ever had. In mid-August Bird showed Walter Cronkite and CBS viewers around the Johnson ranch. She loved this source of "serenity" and "continuity"—a word she repeated three times in one answer, each time deliciously drawing out all five syllables. Ten days later, ABC broadcast Howard K. Smith's hour-long interview with the First Lady, in which Bird called herself "a sounding board" for the President. Any difficult questions elicited a warm smile and a drawn out "Mis-tah Smith," buying the practiced politician time to formulate her answers. She knew her place. "I've spent 30 years learning the particular role of helper; I do not see myself as the one in the front, although I do not pass lightly over my contributions," she said.

Despite her loving references to "Lyndon," the First Lady eclipsed the President in both programs. Similarly, Lyndon's half-hour campaign special ignored Lady Bird. Mrs. Johnson's programs were suitably feminine, focusing on homey touches and seemingly revealing tidbits. The President's film was hard-hitting, issue-oriented, and majestic. Each Johnson stayed on the appropriate side of the sexual divide; Lady Bird's softness, though, humanized the President. "When I . . . heard the First Lady mention that she hates waste and likes to serve corn and tomatoes grown in your own garden, like an ordinary, thrifty housewife, it made me feel very close to her," one viewer wrote.

The First Lady's trips were equally successful. "Mrs. Johnson represents a political asset for the campaign which is unique in Presidential history," Douglass Cater memoed after her western swing. "She comes across as intelligent and knowledgeable and *unlike* Eleanor Roosevelt thoroughly feminine." Cater urged the First Lady to strike out on her own during the campaign.

When the Johnson team was together, Lady Bird was the silent, deferential wife, happy to wave at the crowd and gaze at her husband. But Lady Bird also saw herself as "a link between the President and the people." To fulfill that task, she stepped off the First Lady's nonpolitical perch and traveled on her own, putting up with the "early sun-ups, cold pancakes, and total confusion" endemic to every campaign.

The First Lady's most dramatic effort was her four-day, eight-state, 47-stop, 1,682-mile whistle-stop trip through the South. The fight over civil rights had turned ugly; there were murders in the South and riots in the North. Encouraged by Liz Carpenter and Lyndon, Lady Bird decided to tour the South.

Johnson's aides feared headlines describing a "subdued" or hostile reaction in the President's backyard. Others wondered whether it was unmanly to hide behind the First Lady's skirts. The holdovers from Kennedy's Irish mafia scorned the initiative. "They didn't want Mrs. Johnson to do anything," Bess Abell recalled. "They didn't know any women like her."

With 55 advancemen, 225 reporters, a dozen "Johnson girls," a tape of Carol Channing singing "Hello Lyndon" to the tune of "Hello Dolly," eighty thousand balloons, one hundred thousand whistles, and lots of saltwater taffy labeled "CHOOSE LYNDON," the trip was a splashy, old-fashioned frolic. Lady Bird stacked the train with Southerners. "I am fond of the old ways of keeping up with your kinfolks," she would purr, "of long Sunday dinners after Church—of a special brand of gentility and courtesy—of summertime filled with watermelon cuttings and swimming in the creek."

The President helped launch his wife's journey. He beamed as she confronted the key issue: support for the Civil Rights Act. "We are a nation of laws, not men, and our greatness is our ability to adjust to the national consensus," she said. "The law to assure equal rights passed Congress last July with three-fourths of the Republicans joining two-thirds of the Democrats." Lady Bird thus tackled the most explosive issue of the century directly. Such behavior was rare for any politician.

The whistle-stop tour snared big crowds, front-page coverage in newspapers, and coveted five-minute segments on the network news shows four nights in a row "It's a new 'secret weapon,' as Mrs. Johnson called it—the wife of a candidate and a whole brood of other charming women from all over exuding that special Southern femininity," a New Orleans paper declared. As the President had hoped, Lady Bird's tour galvanized the moribund Democratic effort in the South. "You've put us to work," grateful party leaders said. "We've needed something like this."

Still, the enthusiasm did not mask the tension. A false locomotive preceded the train in case the tracks were sabotaged. In Columbia, South Carolina, hecklers pounded a drum and shouted "Lady Bird, Lady Bird fly away." One man yelled, "What's the matter, can't daddy make his own speeches?" The snubs triggered the backlash the Johnsons expected. This was not the way to treat a lady; men insisted that "chivalry is not dead in the South." Lady Bird would look back on those tumultuous four days as "one of the greatest adventures of my life." Reunited with his wife in New Orleans, watching his wife work the crowd, the President must have been amazed. This Lady Bird was a far cry from the shy consort he knew during his first campaign, terrified of speaking, who simply "packed the bag and washed the socks and reminded him to eat." Lyndon may have seen glimpses of this character in the woman he first met in 1934, but there had been decades when this verve was nowhere to be found.

II

Both Lady Bird and Lyndon grew up in a world where women's power was masked. Southwestern women of the early twentieth century imbibed a powerful blend of rugged pioneering and gentility. The Johnsons had a typical frontier marriage: he was the "warrior," and she was the "worker."

Born on August 27, 1908, Lyndon Baines Johnson was the first of five children of a reserved schoolmarm and an extroverted politician. Rebekah Baines Johnson escaped frustrations with frontier life and her tempestuous marriage by taming and driving her firstborn son. When the eight-year-old quit violin and dancing lessons, his mother pretended he was dead; when he succeeded, Rebekah was Lyndon's greatest fan. Lyndon inherited a love of politics from his father, Sam Ealy Johnson, a popular five-term state legislator. But by the time Lyndon was thirteen, "Mister Sam's" drinking had bankrupted the family. "There was nothing Mother hated more than seeing my daddy drink," Lyndon would later say. At Southwest Texas State Teacher's

College at San Marcos, where he enrolled in March 1927, Lyndon aped his father rather than his mother. He courted people more intensely than he studied. Lyndon also developed discipline, however, the trait his father lacked. As president of the student government, "Bull" Johnson was notorious for his energy, affability, ambition, and dishonesty. He acted like a ladies' man, vainly hoping that the perception would create the desired reality. Lyndon would barrel successfully through life by force of personality, reinventing reality as necessary. By succeeding in "Mister Sam's" chosen field, Lyndon fulfilled his mother's dreams and bested his father.

In November 1931, Johnson moved to Washington, D.C., as a congressional secretary. He lived in the Grace Dodge, home to seventy-five other aides. The first night, Lyndon showered in the common bathroom four times to meet his neighbors. The next morning he brushed his teeth five times at ten-minute intervals. By the time he was twenty-five Johnson had proven himself on Capitol Hill. Back home, meanwhile, his buddies decided "it was high time" he got married.

Lyndon proposed to Claudia Alta Taylor on their second date. A mutual friend had introduced them when both were visiting Austin in the late summer of 1934. Lyndon soon sent her a photograph inscribed: "For Bird, a lovely girl with ideals, principles, intelligence and refinement, from her sincere admirer, Lyndon Johnson." Like his daddy, Lyndon was looking for a mismatch, and like Sam, he would be surprised by what he found.

"I see something I *know I want—I immediately exert efforts* to get it," Lyndon wrote Bird during their whirlwind courtship. For two months Lyndon violated his morning routine and wrote a love letter. "This morning I'm ambitious, proud, energetic and very madly in love," he wrote. "If I had a box I would almost make a speech this minute—plans, ideas, hopes—I'm bubbling over with them." Two months after meeting her, Lyndon married the shy, elegant, ladylike, and usually judicious twenty-one-year old. Cynics would say it was because Lady Bird was the daughter of the "richest man in town." But there was a lot more to Lady Bird than her rich daddy.

The exhibitionist and self-promoting Johnson always stressed how far he had risen from his rocky rural roots. Lady Bird Johnson's psychological journey was more impressive. Pegged in high school as most likely to be an old maid, she never dreamed she would be married to the President of the United States.

Claudia Taylor, born in Karnack, Texas, in 1912, was also the product of a mismatch. Her father, Thomas Jefferson Taylor II, was a forbidding merchant, landowner, and cotton farmer known as "Mister Boss." He parlayed 116 acres of land he bought for $500 in 1899 into a 65,000-acre patrimony. Minnie Lee Patillo, his wife, was a tall, refined Alabama belle who listened to opera records in their horrid Texas hamlet. Emotionally fragile, she wandered around Karnack wearing a turban and long white veils.

It was not surprising that ambitious ruffians such as Tom Taylor and Sam Johnson plucked dainty flowers as brides. Women pioneers had an even greater responsibility than their eastern sisters to civilize their homes. While their husbands tried to create thriving homesteads on barren land, the women of the West recreated what one pioneer called their "holier, more refin'd" empire of piety in a cultural desert.

Minnie fell down the circular staircase in the Taylors' residence, "The Brick House," and died in September 1918. One old friend claimed that Minnie's six-year-old daughter "looked like a little pitiful bird left in the nest" and was nicknamed Lady Bird. The more popular version traced it to a nursemaid when the girl was two or three who exclaimed, "She's as purty as a ladybird." Mrs. Johnson blamed it on "the family nurse . . . when I was a baby, in no position to protest."

Close friends like Virginia Durr attributed Lady Bird's refusal to "give way to emotion" to the early loss of her mother. Eventually, Minnie's "spinster sister," Aunt Effie, moved to Karnack to help raise the child. Aunt Effie was an ethereal, gentle lady in delicate health, "undoubtedly the most unworldly human in the world," Lady Bird recalled. Effie exposed her niece to "books, pianos, sunrises, walking in the woods," and one's duty to help "needy members of the family or the community." Effie's fragility, though, propelled Lady Bird toward "Cap" Taylor. "My father was a very strong character, to put it mildly," Bird said. "And he sort of lived by his own rules."

Shy, insecure, lonely, and peculiar, the princess of Cap Taylor's "feudal" domain found solace in nature. Before high school graduation, she feared that she might be valedictorian; she would rather have "small pox" than make a speech. Decades later, Lady Bird still remembered the exact averages of the two girls who nosed her out by half a point, thus sparing her.

In 1929 Lady Bird arrived at the University of Texas in Austin. There she found something "for every hunger of the mind or for every love of gaytimes." She blossomed, emerging as self-confident, funny, rebellious, and attractive. Bird told some friends "she wanted a nice man and a big white house with a fence around it and a big collie dog." But she also wanted to roam. She took typing and shorthand, secured a teacher's certification, and took a second degree in journalism because "people in the press went more places and met more interesting people."

Bird found Lyndon loud, brash, and "repulsive." Yet there was something compelling about this "excessively thin . . . but very, very goodlooking" twenty-six-year-old. "I just knew that he was different from anybody I'd ever met before—more intense and driving and, somehow or other, more alive." After they met, Lyndon invited Bird to breakfast the next morning at the Driskill Hotel. She was noncommittal. Lyndon sat by the window and waited; when she passed by, he waved her over. He later confessed that without his ambush, "I've always doubted whether she would have really walked in that dining room."

The breakfast "date" lasted for the better part of a week. Lyndon invited Bird for a drive out to the country, and "he told me all sorts of things that I thought were extraordinarily direct for a first conversation." By that evening, Lyndon had proposed. "I just thought it was sheer lunacy," she said. Over the next few days, the two visited his mother, his boss, and her father. At the Brick House, "Mr. Boss" muttered: "Hmmm. You've been bringing home a lot of boys. This one looks like a man."

Lyndon returned to Washington and began a long-distance campaign to woo Lady Bird. Bird read the Episcopal marriage service, contemplating the meaning of the lifelong contract. Studying Lyndon's photograph with her friends, she admitted, "his ears are a little too long," but "he's the only man I've ever met who is taller than my daddy." Thomas Jefferson Taylor was his daughter's yardstick—and Lyndon measured up.

In November, Lyndon returned to Karnack. He said, "We either do it now or we never will. And if you say goodbye to me, it just proves to me that you just don't love me enough to dare to." Bird consented "because I didn't want to let him go either, although I think I realized the hazards of the future more than he did."

On Saturday morning, November 17, 1934, Lyndon called his friend, Dan Quill, to arrange a wedding in San Antonio that night. Lyndon and Lady Bird were four hundred miles away; when they arrived, they had not even bothered to stop in a jewelry store. Quill ran across the street and brought a dozen rings from Sears and Roebuck. Lady Bird settled on a $2.50 special. After the standard Episcopal ceremony, the good reverend mumbled, "I hope this marriage lasts." Johnson never reimbursed Quill.

His new bride thrilled Lyndon. She was dependable, fun, deferential, and "the prettiest girl I ever saw." But once they were settled in a one-bedroom apartment in Washington, Prince Charming became a demanding boor. Lyndon would bombard her with a dizzying array of commands, criticisms, and bear hugs for the rest of his life. He appreciated his wife's refinements, but he did not adopt them. A reverse Cinderella like Mamie Eisenhower, Bird learned to cook, to clean, to budget, and to host last-minute guests. Lyndon molded Bird into the perfect political wife, efficient, flexible, hospitable, well-informed, and obedient. She later reported that Lyndon's thoughts became more important "than my own feelings."

In public, Lyndon humiliated his wife if he disliked her dress, or if she did not fetch him that second piece of pie fast enough. Bird withdrew, as she had in Karnack, hanging on the edges of parties. "Bird," Johnson would call out, "are you with me?" She amused herself, nicknaming her husband "Mein Herr." Decades later, when Lyndon asked why it took two years to replace the Sears ring, she cooed, "Why, darlin', I wanted to be sure the marriage was going to last."

Lyndon was domineering but "emotional and affectionate," more open than his self-controlled wife. "She's the greatest," he would say, "the best wife a man can have." The demanding husband came to depend on the compliant wife. "Never shall I expect so much of any other individual," Lyndon wrote his wife after ten months of marriage, "and Dear, it is most comforting and reassuring to know that you do such a swell job."

The Johnsons had just arrived in Austin, where Lyndon served as the National Youth Administration's Texas administrator. The job placed him at the intersection of state and federal government when the New Deal was nationalizing politics. Lyndon put thousands to work. Bird enjoyed life in Austin; their house was a "beehive." When the local congressman died in 1937, Lyndon was well-placed to enter the ten-man field as a Texas New Dealer. But he needed money. Lady Bird "called my Daddy," who advanced $10,000 against Bird's inheritance. "I kept that deposit slip in my purse until it wore out," she beamed.

Lyndon Johnson spent the next two decades offering first-class constituent services and redirecting federal dollars to his district. Lyndon thrived on Capitol Hill, but Bird's return to Washington was "a nightmare." Lyndon expected her to serve his aides and his constituents; a stenographer's notebook, filled with his commands, became her trademark. Johnson's staff functioned like a small overworked family, with a domineering father and a gracious mother. Lyndon made everyone around him—especially Bird—work for him and confirm his self-perception. He reduced them all to what a later generation would call "enablers." Even friends viewed Lyndon as "larger than life." He entertained, he cajoled, he flattered, he fawned, he whined, he groaned, but he rarely shared. After a lifetime of such relationships, he confessed, "I was always very lonely."

Searching for companionship and settling for conquest, Lyndon often violated his marriage vows. He had an extended affair with Alice Glass, the mistress of the editor of the *Austin-American Statesman,* Charles E. Marsh. Marsh had a thousand-acre estate in Virginia, "Longlea." From 1938 through 1940, the Johnsons visited frequently. Marsh hosted a "salon" of writers, politicians, and tycoons. "I remember Alice in a series of long and elegant dresses," Bird would recall, "and me in—well, much less elegant." Lyndon reveled in the exchanges. Lady Bird languished, saying "Yes, Lyndon," when he bossed her around. Although Lyndon and Alice were discreet, regulars knew about the romance and were "sure" that Lady Bird did too. "I could never understand how she stood it," Alice's sister, Mary Louise, said of Bird. Clad in her drab dresses, clutching *War and Peace* or some other tome, Lady Bird appeared bookish, impractical, and ethereal. She had become Aunt Effie.

When Lyndon made his next bold move, running for the Senate in 1941, Lady Bird remained in the background. Lyndon lost the election by a thin—

and fraudulent—margin of 1,311 votes. "I felt terribly rejected," he said. Lady Bird would "fondly" recall watching "Lyndon in a ruffled, seersucker suit with a very jaunty smile and a jaunty walk—going out to catch a plane to return to Washington." After years of masquerading, she knew "just how much nerve and effort it took to keep up that appearance." Besides, "I can't say that a solid diet of success is good for anybody." After feeling so eclipsed, Bird enjoyed having her husband cry on her shoulder.

The Johnsons' seventh anniversary in November 1941 was sober. The European war worried everyone, and Lyndon doubted his political future. Lady Bird was broken, a shadow of the confident co-ed Lyndon married. She was still recovering from a September operation for a gynecological problem, having suffered three miscarriages already. "This was a sadness," she would say later, drifting into silence. She enrolled in "business school, brushing up on my old college short-hand and typewriting, so I can really be of some use." Unable to be a mother, she figured she might as well be as good a wife as possible.

After Pearl Harbor, Johnson enlisted in the Navy. Preparing for a Pacific inspection tour, the thirty-five-year-old drafted a will in which he left everything to his wife. He also left behind a sealed manila envelope marked "LBJ. To be Opened only by JBC [his aide, John Connally] or LBJ." Inside were four pictures of Alice Glass, whom Lyndon saw in San Francisco before shipping out.

When he went west in early 1942, Lyndon directed that all of his mail go out over Bird's signature. He appears not to have informed his staffers, however, that Bird's role would be anything but symbolic. Lady Bird Johnson was "scared"; her marriage had sapped her confidence. It was hard to go from being the pitiful, compliant wife to a hard-driving, efficient substitute.

Lyndon soon realized that his grant of authority was too vague. In March he urged his wife to be assertive and independent, the qualities he had been squelching: "First you *use* your own judgment and talk to anyone—anytime on anything," he said. "I've come around to thinking your head is better than mine in most things even including so many political matters."

Bird plunged into her "strange new career." In an act of patriotic grandstanding, Lyndon had renounced his congressional salary for the Navy's lower pay. Bird moved in with Nellie Connally, John Connally's wife; Bird and Nellie would boast about being "two of the busiest war widows in Washington." Such gallows humor helped women on the home front cope with their fears. Bird worked from 8:30 A.M. until "Lyndon-Johnson quitting time—which is when everything is done."

It was easy for a bookish Southern belle to distribute pleasantries in her husband's name across the Tenth Congressional District. Bird also had to deliver results. With each new Roosevelt attempt to manage the home front—the War Production Board, the Office of Economic Stabilization—government became more intrusive. Each initiative created new spheres of influence, new headaches, new demands for favors. "More and more I am getting lonesome for Lyndon—or rather it is hardly a personal thing at all but a desire that he be back here in this maelstrom making something really move," she told Lyndon's mentor, Alvin Wirtz. Lady Bird's success created a stir. Jane Ickes, who was often eclipsed by her husband, the Secretary of the Interior, wrote, "You certainly do have what it takes!" Johnson's aide Jim Blundell called Bird "the best damn 'she' congressman in these United States." Friends teased Lyndon about Bird's masquerade. "If Bird keeps up the pace she'll make it hard for you when you get back," Blundell wrote about the 1942 election. By July 1942, President Roosevelt ordered mobilized congressmen to return home, thanks to Lady Bird's lobbying via Sam Rayburn. "What changes hath this one year wrought!" Lady Bird had exclaimed in the spring. She celebrated Lyndon's return as "the grandest day of my life: he looks wonderful and is the same dynamic driving Lyndon as before he went to the wars."

Lyndon quickly reasserted control. When, out of habit, his wife stayed on in a meeting, he said, "We'll see you later Bird." She retreated. Shortly thereafter, when asked if his wife advised him, he answered, "Of course." Then he snarled. "I have a nigger maid, and I talk my problems over with her, too."

World War II did not have the immediate transforming impact on women many expected. After the crisis, most wanted to return to "normal." For Bird and her peers the changes were more subtle, the transformation more gradual. Twenty years later Lady Bird called it "one of the very best things that ever happened to me, because after about three or four months I really felt that if it was necessary I could make my own living." She now had a better "understanding of Lyndon" and "what sometimes seems to me Lyndon's unnecessary irritations."

Their marriage would never revert to prewar conditions. Lyndon remained a bully, but Bird stopped acting like a battered woman. Her cousin said, "He told her how to dress, but she told him when to stop talking."

Bird insisted they settle down. She found a house at 4921 30th Place in northwest Washington, D.C. When she told him about it, Lyndon pooh-poohed her and continued working with Connally. Bird exploded: "Every woman wants a home of her own. I've lived out of a suitcase ever since we've been married. I have no home to look forward to. I have no children to look forward to, and I have nothing to look forward to but another election." Lyndon asked, "What shall I do?" Connally drawled, "I'd buy the house." Eventually Bird gave birth to two baby-boom children, Lynda Bird in 1944 and Lucy Baines in 1947.

Bird, the happy homemaker, had also become a canny executive. In early 1943 the Johnsons purchased KTBC, a radio station in Austin. Political proprieties demanded that Bird apply for the license. She cited her experience running the office and vowed to devote "full time" to the station, even if Lyndon still considered Bird's job to be "running the household and me." In August the station posted an $18 profit; by 1951, it would be worth $439,000. Ten years later, after the Johnsons expanded into TV, their broadcasting empire would be worth millions.

The image of Lady Bird as a businesswoman scouring reports at her dining room table covered up Lyndon's involvement in "our" radio station. "She's any man's equal," one associate would say in 1964, "she reads a balance sheet like most women examine a piece of cloth." Lyndon knew that it was better to hide behind the silk dress of a businesswoman than to abuse the public trust.

In 1948 Lyndon tried again for the Senate. He distributed pictures of his family throughout Texas, pleased that his unmarried opponent "can't do that." Lady Bird's deference made Lyndon look macho, giving him an edge over Governor Coke Stevenson in wooing the "women's vote."

In the Democratic primary on July 24, Stevenson won 40 percent of the vote to Lyndon's 34 percent, forcing a runoff. With only five weeks to undo the governor's lead, Bird organized women supporters and traveled around the state. Lyndon demanded that she speak at the final rally in San Antonio. En route her car overturned, but Bird soldiered on, badly bruised. She only told Lyndon about the accident after the rally. He labeled her performance "the most wonderful, courageous, exciting thing" he had ever encountered. She joked, "All I could think of as we were turning over was I sure wished I'd voted absentee." Lyndon's eighty-seven-vote victory earned him the nickname "Landslide Lyndon."

Both Johnsons enjoyed Lyndon's two terms in the Senate. This period may have been the high point of their marriage. Lyndon dominated the Senate by giving his colleagues "the treatment"—a deft mix of flattery, bribery, and bullying. He became majority whip in 1951, Senate minority leader in 1953, and the majority leader two years later, after a landslide reelection. He was forty-six years old.

Lady Bird became well known around the capital as a "supermom" before the phrase gained popularity. In 1956 *Life* profiled Senator Johnson and praised Bird as "an efficient woman who handles her own widespread business interests (TV-radio stations and ranchlands) as well as the heavy demands of hospitality imposed by her husband's position." Bess Abell, who served as Mrs. Johnson's social secretary, praised Bird's great ability "to compartmentalize her life. We'd be working on something . . . and one of the girls would come in from school, and . . . suddenly all of her attention was devoted to that child." Just as the women's movement would identify this skill as one of the most characteristic and demoralizing aspects of 1950s motherhood, Lady Bird, too, recognized its challenges. "With all the demands on you, you undergo what Anne Lindbergh called 'fragmentation of self,'" she said in 1963. "You just hope that all your efforts add up to something worthwhile."

Lady Bird was often caught between her husband and her children. Lucy and Lynda called themselves "de-privileged" kids, deprived of "a normal home life" by their parents' success. Bird also occasionally protested via the press, as Jackie Kennedy did. When a CBS reporter asked what Lyndon's "worst feature" was, she sent her husband a message. The girls would like to see him show up to some school functions, Bird said, "and I would like it if I knew what time he was coming home for dinner."

Lyndon would not stop. By 1955 he was smoking three packs a day, sleeping erratically, and eating poorly. He insisted on spending the Fourth of July weekend at a patron's Virginia estate, even though it was Lucy's eighth birthday and she was sick at home; Lady Bird remained with her daughter but promised to join him later. On Friday evening, July 1, Lyndon suffered a heart attack.

For the next five weeks Lyndon was bedridden. Lady Bird moved into the room next door to serve her husband. She inserted herself into his affairs as fully as she had in 1942, although she could not appear independent. She began most sentences with "Lyndon said" or "He asked me to tell you." At the end of August the couple flew to Texas for a four-month stay on the Johnson ranch; they had purchased the decrepit homestead in 1951 despite Bird's protests. Lyndon made it into his trademark and the family's "home base." Soon Lyndon's mentor Sam Rayburn would say, "Thank God Lyndon has that ranch. Now he has something else to talk about beside politics." When Lyndon finally returned to the Senate in January 1956, he limited himself to 14-hour days, ate better, stopped smoking, and started napping.

As the leading Democrat in Eisenhower's Washington, Johnson considered himself the obvious party nominee in 1960. He dismissed John Kennedy as a "little scrawny fellow with rickets" and assumed that legislative achievements and party connections would prove more potent than popularity.

While the majority leader rested on his laurels, however, he did refurbish his wife's image for the campaign. Lady Bird now was the dutiful wife who, a Citizens for Johnson press release boasted, had "traded a career for homemaking" and considered "her biggest task" to be "rearing her two daughters." "I'm not deeply informed on political issues," she claimed. Yet Lady Bird was a new kind of political spouse, a "charming and business-wise" woman whose husband "regards her as a reliable 'weathervane' on possible public reaction to his ideas," the press release said. Bird would campaign with her husband because "people feel they can get the measure of a man by taking a look at him and his family." Besides, she lied, "I love it."

In July 1960, when John Kennedy offered Lyndon the vice presidency, both Johnsons were torn. In his self-centered way, Lyndon would characterize this as the third "major crisis" in Lady Bird's life, the other two being "the day I went to war" and "the campaign of 1948." Bird hesitated because "the Hill was Lyndon's life." Ultimately, she would claim, loyalty to the Democratic party compelled "them" to accept the nomination.

When the Johnsons visited Hyannis Port, Bird went off with the women and Lyndon stayed with the men. Still, Lyndon kept asking Bird for information, and she jotted every name mentioned in her notebook. Through it all, Bird "would sit talking with us, looking so calm. I was very impressed by that," Jackie Kennedy recalled, jealous of the Johnsons' partnership and appalled by Bird's rudeness.

The Johnsons fought to keep the South Democratic—which was why Kennedy chose Lyndon. When Texas and six other Southern states stayed with the Democrats, Lyndon took credit. But Bobby Kennedy would only say, "Lady Bird carried Texas for us."

When her husband became vice president, Lady Bird vowed "to help Lyndon all I can; to lend a hand to Mrs. Kennedy when she needs me; and to be a more alive me." Bird loved being at the pinnacle of Washington society. She was used to playing second fiddle, but Lyndon was not; her enjoyment increased his misery. He was no longer the king of the Hill. Kennedy was kind to Johnson, but Kennedy aides—and Mrs. Kennedy—ridiculed "Uncle Cornpone" with his "little porkchop," Lady Bird.

Bird knew that when she married Lyndon she married his political career. She had become so devoted to his career, and so essential to his success, that some scoffed that she cared "more about her husband's career than her husband." In 1963 she would describe her husband as "a wonderful man to live with; an exhausting man to keep up with; a man who has worn well in the 29 years we've been together, and a man from whom I've learned that to put all the brains and heart and skill you have into the job of trying to make your government work a little bit better can be a wonderful life for a man, and his wife." At the end of Lyndon's Presidency, when asked how she became interested in his Great Society programs, she would say, "I married into them."

Although friends marveled at her fortitude, she adored Lyndon and recognized that she, too, profited from the marriage. "Lyndon saw more in me than I saw in myself, and he expected more than I realized I could do." It was, she believed, a fair exchange. Lyndon "bullied, shoved, pushed and loved me into being more outgoing, more of an achiever," while "I gave him comfort, tenderness and some judgment—at least I think I did." Bird was more realist than romantic. "Marriage grows with the years," she said. "We survived so much together—so much good and so much bad. We were better together than apart."

III

Lyndon Johnson's forty-four-state, 486-electoral vote sweep in 1964 legitimized his Presidency and swelled his ego. He pictured "millions upon millions of people, each one marking my name on their ballot, each one wanting me as their President." Yet both Johnsons brooded after the election, especially when their confidant Walter Jenkins left town. Jenkins had been arrested for "disorderly conduct" in the men's room of the YMCA. His behavior was attributed to nervous exhaustion and became an ominous symbol of the high personal cost of serving in the White House.

Christmas, followed by the inauguration, buoyed the Johnsons. Lyndon wanted to implement his Great Society "before the aura and the halo that surround me disappear." His "new agenda" could revolutionize the nation. Bird was ready to help her husband achieve his grand goals. Her political activism was an inevitable spillover of his new government activism; there was too much to do for the First Lady to be passive. She also kept him in line.

Despite their busy schedules, in the White House the Johnsons saw "more of each other than ever before in our married life," Bird noted. They often had breakfast in bed, met for lunch, and ended each day reading in bed together. "Sometimes he passes one or another piece to me or reads something to me and asks: what is your opinion on this?" she told reporters.

Aides attributed many moves in the Johnson administration to Bird's "pillow talk," including the appointment of the first black mayor of Washington, D.C., Walter Washington. During the day, Bird's influence was equally obvious as she passed on appointments, edited speeches, revised legislation, and urged Lyndon to slow down. "I came very late and timorously to the uses of power," Bird postured. In fact, one associate called her "the most consummate politician" he had ever known. "In her quiet way, she made him come to heel," Vice President Hubert Humphrey noted.

Had Lady Bird merely served as Lyndon's shadow president, she still would have been one of the most influential of all First Ladies. But since the war, Bird had been trying to be more independent. "Sometimes I'd like to write—to have a little achievement of my own," she would sigh. Besides, as Liz Carpenter said, being a behind-the-scenes player and a "shake hands with the DAR" kind of First Lady was "not virile enough. . . . Times have gone past tea parties and petit-fours." "She wanted to have a project," Bess Abell recalled, "something that she could identify with . . . something that would be involved in some way in the President's program."

Lyndon agreed. He wanted Lady Bird to use her "power" as First Lady and "not fritter it away." Bird was inspired by Eleanor Roosevelt's example, but wanted to work with her husband. Thus Sargent Shriver, head of the War on Poverty, was able to enlist the First Lady to help the Head Start Program, which funded local programs for underprivileged preschoolers. It exposed needy children to the middle-class values deemed so necessary in the fight against poverty. Lady Bird became Honorary Chairman of Head Start, a title she disliked because "if I take it on, I want to work at it." She appeared on posters, starred in public service announcements, made spot visits.

Bird was happy to serve as Lyndon's bleeding heart. By May 18, President

Johnson could hold a Rose Garden ceremony to announce 1,600 summer grants to help 9,500 preschool centers serve 375,000 children. Bird came to the ceremony five minutes late. Lyndon growled, "Next time be on time when we are holding a meeting which you are going to be in on." While the rest of the country hailed her, Lyndon still manhandled his wife.

Head Start, however, was not Lady Bird's "own" project. Increasingly Bird became identified with "beautification," the attempt to better what a later generation called the environment. A typical Great Society program, "beautification" fostered consensus with a benign, progressive-sounding label that obscured its radical intentions. Beautification, along with so many other programs, brought government more dramatically into American life. Sweetly, subtly, Bird was helping Lyndon advance the presidency as the address for every problem in America, as the all-purpose source of solutions.

Lady Bird's summons to fight urban despair with geraniums made daunting problems appear manageable. She called for community action as an antidote to modern alienation. This call appealed to her particular constituency, women, at a time when many housewives were looking for projects in the community. Her solution combined biblical ideas of concern for others, American beliefs in self-improvement, and radical approaches calling for change through community activism.

A long tradition of women conservationists had preached that "bad physical environment means bad moral environment." But Bird and her allies insisted that their cause was not some feminine indulgence. She winced as critics mocked her work. "Beauty is a fragile word. . . . an almost embarrassing word," she admitted in 1965. She toyed with "environmental quality," and Lyndon called for a "New Conservation," but "beautification" worked. It was punchier, yet more feminine than its clinical-sounding rivals. The term was less simplistic than "conservation," which emphasized preserving land, and less pessimistic than the "environmentalism" of the future, which would try to limit growth. The Johnsons were sophisticated enough to see that progress spawned pollution, but optimistic enough to rely on more flowers and fewer billboards to help. Bird hoped that "a combination of our affluence, our technology and leisure time has given us the courage to use the word right out in public."

Some critics were merciless, but their ridicule provided a convenient cover. Just as a Southern woman often hid behind her frills, Bird advanced a far-reaching program behind all her talk of wisteria and wildflowers. "Getting on the subject of beautification is like picking up a tangled skein of wool—all the threads are interwoven—recreation and pollution and mental health and the crime rate, and rapid transit, and highway beautification and the war on poverty, and parks," she noted in her diary in January 1965. When she published the diary in 1970, Lady Bird excised this passage.

Part of the project involved chairing the Committee for a More Beautiful Capital. The city of Washington, D.C., posed a formidable challenge for beautification. The city was home to 800,000 people, with another 1.5 million living in its suburbs. The Washington of monuments and bureaucrats was the gleaming capital of a superpower; the Washington of slums and poor people was the shame of a nation. The committee established the Society for a More Beautiful National Capital, Inc., modeled after Jackie Kennedy's committee for the White House. More than $2 million in private funds would help "revitalize parks, equip playgrounds, construct fountains, launch plans, support youth employment, and stimulate significant public and business investments as well."

Two factions divided the committee. Mary Lasker and other philanthropists focused on the tourist areas; to them, beautifying national monuments was a way of purifying the nation's soul. Others, such as Walter Washington, then head of public housing for Washington, D.C., wanted to reclaim the inner city. Bird pushed for consensus, making comments that were often so lyrical few could disagree with her. Her light "womanly" touch helped people transcend the tensions—a tactic that would have served her husband well. "A conversation between two people is very simple," Emily Post taught. "You find a topic on which you agree."

The President often distanced himself from what he called "Lady Bird's business." He joked that his naps were interrupted by his wife, "Laurance Rockefeller, and 80 ladies talking about the daffodils on Pennsylvania Avenue" in the room next door. At other times, Johnson called it a joint crusade "to produce the great men and women which are the measure of a great society." When Lyndon was most enamored with beautification—and the program was popular—he took full credit. At a 1967 conference of women fighting the War on Poverty, he claimed that when he ran the Texas National Youth Administration, "the beautification expert in the Johnson family was me—not Lady Bird."

The President's ambivalence about his wife's project complicated the battle to ban billboards from the vast federal highway system. In a testament to the government's extended tentacles, Johnson commanded Secretary of Commerce Luther Hodges to require landscaping on and around all highway projects. The President also proposed legislation to block and move junkyards visible from the highways and limit billboards.

Beautification was no longer benign. The major oil companies, the Outdoor Advertising Association of America, the Roadside Business Association, the National Auto and Truck Wreckers Association, the Institute of Scrap Iron and Steel, and the American Motor Hotel Association all objected as the President and his aides tried to bulldoze the bill through Congress. Lyndon exclaimed: "Why that's Lady Bird's bill!" Pitching it as his wife's bill gave the President a unique prod for reluctant congressmen; he used the First Lady's interest to twist arms while washing his hands of the most controversial elements. "If we don't do this, all the women in the country will be on our backs, with Lady Bird first," he warned.

The East Wing followed up on the West Wing's efforts, contacting garden clubs, conservationists, and editors. As the President bullied, Lady Bird "continued on her own sweet way" charming congressmen, Drew Pearson reported. One congressman sighed, "No one in the Texas delegation likes the bill, but no one wants to vote against Lady Bird."

West Wing aides felt caught between "this remarkably tenacious distaff side of the White House and an absolutely adamant Congress." Small businessmen deluged the Congress with claims that the bill would destroy their livelihoods. Compromise was impossible, however, because it had become "a matter of personal honor to the president," one aide, John Sweeney, recalled. Even when Lady Bird was willing to compromise, Lyndon refused, thundering, "Ain't nobody going to be able to write a headline saying that Congress administers defeat to Lady Bird!"

Placing the First Lady in the center of such a battle was risky. For the first time since Eleanor Roosevelt, both members of the presidential couple endured partisan attack. Many congressmen resented what they called "one of the biggest White House persuasion campaigns of this session." The House of Representatives held a bitter fourteen-hour debate. At one point, Congressman Robert Dole of Kansas offered an amendment to insert the words "Lady Bird" wherever the term "Secretary of Commerce" appeared in the bill, because she was behind the effort. Dole lost. He justified his attack by saying that "when one chooses to step down from the pedestal of the dutiful preoccupied wife of the President . . . and to wade into the turbulent stream of public controversy, one must expect to, at least, get her feet wet."

Although the Johnson administration would count the final bill as one of its fifty greatest accomplishments, the legislation had been gutted. "It is a first step, and there will be other steps," the President said as he signed the bill on October 22, 1965. Ultimately, though, television advertising would discourage more billboards than any federal laws did.

The beautification fight sobered the Johnsons. A billboard appeared in Montana—and was popularized in a Bill Mauldin cartoon—saying "Impeach Lady Bird." "Imagine me keeping company with Chief Justice Warren!" the First Lady laughed. Nevertheless, she became defensive. Chastened by the attacks on his wife, and still embarrassed that the term was too womanly, Johnson would not even mention the highway-beautification bill in the three pages he devoted to "conservation" in his six-hundred-page memoirs. Thereafter, the President was more protective of Lady Bird, Califano recalled, "and he never put her as far out front again." This lesson would be ignored by future activist First Ladies.

A month after Lyndon signed the Highway Beautification Act, ABC broadcast "A Visit to Washington with Mrs. Lyndon B. Johnson" on Thanksgiving Day, 1965. Inspired by Mrs. Kennedy's earlier special, the hour-long program highlighted the contrast between the two women. Jackie had focused on architecture, history, and art, all suitably genteel concerns. Lady Bird offered a touch of history, but much of the special was a brief for beautification.

Bird gave a tour of Washington from sunrise to sunset. Viewers saw the standard shots of monumental Washington: the White House, the Capitol, the Lincoln Memorial. But they also saw jarring shots of traffic jams, junkyards, honky-tonk billboards, litter, pollution, and slums. This travelogue had an edge. Lady Bird was offering a devastating social criticism wrapped in monuments and magnolias and narrated in a silky Southern voice.

As the narrative unfolded, Bird became more passionate and more eloquent. Sweetly, softly, with just a touch of regret, she chided Americans for being wasteful, uncaring, greedy, and sloppy. Lyndon never appeared in the documentary, but she did quote him at the end. "The President has said we must leave future generations a glimpse of the world as God really made it, not just as it looked when we got through with it," she said.

The show garnered high ratings, a special Peabody award, and warm compliments for its "most appealing" host. But most viewers missed the point. They were so taken by Lady Bird's "beauty and poise," they so enjoyed the "excellent view of Washington," that they ignored the social criticism. Ironically, after the legislative fight, Lady Bird's beautification campaign would be dogged by this inability to transcend its feminine, charming, trivial side, making it more popular and less significant.

Still, the special—with the other efforts—helped "sow some seeds of interest in nationwide beautification," as Bird hoped. In retrospect, 1965 would emerge as a turning point. That year, 28 percent of those surveyed deemed air pollution a "somewhat" or "very serious" problem in their area; a year later, the number jumped to 48 percent. The first Earth Day and the environmental movement would soon follow.

Here was a modern First Lady, substantive, ambitious, political, and loyal. Bess spent much of her time away from Harry; Lady Bird only left Lyndon when she peddled his program. Mamie was kept in hams and scotch; Lady Bird received "exquisite edition[s]" of serious tomes. Bird mourned that "this job allows little time for . . . self-indulgence," but she relished the challenge.

All this activity raised the profile of the East Wing. West Wing staffers viewed their neighbors warily; they feared crossing the influential First Lady or tangling with the peppery Liz Carpenter. The President occasionally tried to circumvent his wife by having his aides thwart East Wing staffers. "We didn't like to do it," declared George Christian, the press secretary after 1967. "I tried to stay out of Liz's way."

Lady Bird's aides had the authority to draft speeches without West Wing approval, but they needed help in other areas. They needed to coordinate joint appearances. They needed more storage space for files, more office space for staff, more money for travel expenses, and support for the First Lady's trips. Bird's assistants learned that "In an economy move, it is the East Wing that suffers first." They returned from Texas in July 1965, for instance, to discover their newspaper subscriptions cancelled. Carpenter protested that "First Ladies get very little consideration. They have no salary. They have no military transportation. They still must fulfill commitments in a demanding way to help the President." With "some 50 hungry, eager reporters who cover this side of the house on a daily basis," the East Wing needed respect—and its daily newspapers. "Do you put this press office back on the list—or do I take up whoring to pay for it?" The next day, the crude press secretary could thank the President's aide Marvin Watson "for saving a middle-aged woman from a life of sin."

The First Lady's ambiguous status as an unpaid government official complicated matters. Carpenter found the Secret Service agents insensitive to the itinerary; Secret Service agents found Liz expecting presidential treatment for the First Lady. The tensions over security and logistics prompted President Johnson to suggest that future First Ladies stop flying by commercial aircraft. This shift, partly motivated by security concerns, acknowledged the First Lady as an independent agent and gave her some of the president's imperial prerogatives.

More and more, the First Lady seemed to be working in a political "job" rather than fulfilling a gracious role. "With Mrs. Kennedy and Mrs. Johnson the role of the First Lady has become almost as meaningful to voters as that of the President," a columnist claimed during the 1964 campaign. Most of the First Lady's mail continued to concern anniversaries, birthdays, and desired photographs, but thousands of correspondents detailed local attempts to implement Bird's "green thumb" approach. Two aides worked solely on beautification mail. By 1967 Lady Bird would receive fifteen thousand letters a year about beautification, one-third of her correspondence. Also, more letters than ever directed the First Lady to advise the President about specific legislative stands. Two-thirds of such "eyes-and-ears" mail or "tell-it-to-the-President" letters came from women. For the first time, a weekly report would summarize the First Lady's mail as well as the President's to reflect public concerns.

Like Eleanor Roosevelt, Bird co-opted reporters. She honored them at Women Doers' luncheons, hosted them at cocktails, invited them to White House parties, thanked them for sympathetic stories, and, most important, gave them news. The newswomen helped Bird improve her image. As Betty Beale admitted, "I don't believe in accepting someone's hospitality and then spitting in their eye." They proposed speech topics, tactics, and itineraries. Before a speech, Bird usually discussed the topic with a reporter who specialized in that particular area.

The First Lady's trips emerged as among the most effective weapons in her arsenal. Initially, she justified them with the Roosevelt-era rationale of serving as "eyes and ears for the President." As she grew more confident, she spoke of being the President's "interpreter" or his "extension," representing him to the people. But Bird was more than a conduit or a surrogate. In forty road trips traversing two hundred thousand miles, her trips "focus[ed] the interest of people on . . . what my husband is trying to achieve in his administration." She believed that her 1964 Appalachian trip led to "18 bills" on education. Acknowledging her own power in setting the national agenda, she admitted that her trips had "political tones."

The trips addressed significant yet relatively uncontroversial issues. Bird's love of nature, combined with Liz Carpenter's political theatrics, yielded stunning images of the First Lady navigating rapids, crossing deserts, and hugging children. It was ideal fare for newspapers that were beefing up their women's sections and for newly expanded network news shows. Bird was superb on the stump, warm, gracious, and unruffled. She oohed and ahhed on cue. "I can report from a day with her that her trip deeply moved the Vermonters—whose feelings are not easily set in motion," Walt Rostow told the President.

Out on the hustings, Bird received the kinds of raves Lyndon craved. Her successes, especially as her husband failed, upset the balance of power in their marriage. Lyndon teased Bird about "how many miles I travel," and how when "he wants me to do something for him . . . I am off planting a tree." Bird recognized that "many a true word is spoken in jest. . . . I think he really would like to have me there to talk to a little more." For the first time in his marriage, Lyndon felt upstaged.

These trips created a new forum for First Ladies. For all of Bird's successors, no matter how shy they were, goodwill trips would become a fact of life. The First Lady could no longer remain in the White House greeting guests; she had to seek out supporters across America. The arts of gentility were now secondary—coverage, exposure, and action counted.

Of course, old-fashioned ways would not vanish overnight. Lady Bird was able to complete her image as the "total woman" by presiding over daughter Luci's August 1966 wedding to airman Patrick Nugent, the first White House wedding in fifty-two years. The Johnsons announced that they "do not consider Luci's wedding an affair of state, but rather a family and personal occasion." Reporters, though, demanded full access. "The marriage of a daughter of the President of the United States is a major and significant social news event of interest to a majority of the American people," an NBC producer informed the White House. "Please! Each home will have the TV on when the Princess of our United States is going to be married," an enthusiastic Chicagoan wrote, begging for full coverage. In the end, the ceremony was not televised, partially because the Protestant Johnsons did not want the rococo ninety-minute Catholic nuptial Mass broadcast.

The Johnsons wanted to score points with a humble posture and a glamorous event. The wedding struck the right balance, with seven hundred guests in the church followed by a reception at the White House. A pool of newswomen relayed information to five hundred reporters gathered from around the world. Most reports emphasized the glamour and romance, leavened by a guest list filled with what the *Washington Post* called "uncelebrated middle-class friends and relatives."

Johnson was thrilled. With a wife who functioned more as a political partner than a popular adornment, he needed his children, along with his dogs and his ranch, to humanize his image. The wedding, according to Liz, was "the No. 1 story of the summer." "We have gotten page 1 stories on the wedding for the past three weeks in the *Chicago Tribune*," Liz told the President. "The only way for Democrats to succeed in that newspaper is to either come out for dogs or daughters."

The wedding also put the Johnsons squarely on the side of tradition. The conventional ceremony proved that not all young people were draft-evading hippies. Clark Clifford said that in 1966, "the American people were starved for [such] an occasion."

As the First Lady looked back on the wedding, she had many reasons to feel proud. "She has come of age," said a relative. "Now she is well-dressed, traveled, well-read, and has a large and colorful vocabulary." Bird had emerged as a powerful, effective First Lady, one who would serve as a role model for women and for her successors—even at the cost of some political damage. The anthropologist Margaret Mead deemed Bird the ideal "total woman," weaving together "the several strands of a complicated life," taking "responsibility at home for a husband and children, in the community and in the world at large."

And yet, despite performing superbly, Lady Bird failed to win the hearts of the American people. Many women could not accept her as First Lady. Even when the Johnsons' popularity was at its peak, neither the matrons nor the masses were crazy about her—although few criticized her. Year after year, the East Wing staff cringed as Mrs. Kennedy outpolled Mrs. Johnson in Gallup's survey of "Most Admired Women." Only when Jackie married Aristotle Onassis in 1968 did she lose her status in that survey. Robert Kennedy's widow, Ethel, now topped the list, with Lady Bird fourth behind Rose Kennedy and Mamie Eisenhower. "Something is lacking in Mrs. Johnson," a clubwoman in South Carolina said. "Maybe it's finesse." More sympathetically, a high school history teacher in Maine explained, "What she suffers from is having had to follow a goddess."

Part of the problem was political backlash. First Ladies are not elected, and they make waves when they step into legislative arenas. But another part was personal; Bird was too ordinary to become a star. Her ethic of wifely devotion paled before Jackie's excesses or Mamie Eisenhower's indulgences. "Lady Bird was beige, and beige ladies did not command the cocktail parties of the 1960's," said Johnson's house intellectual, Eric Goldman.

Bird felt uneasy, not just on her own behalf but also on Lyndon's. Stumping through New England with Lyndon in August 1966, she described the "current of feeling that you can almost touch between the President and the crowd. . . . But knowing its power, I can understand something of the danger if that feeling changed to hostility." The danger of such a switch was growing, fueled by dissatisfaction over Vietnam, the cities, and the economy. Even Luci's wedding had been marred by protestors taunting, "Hey, hey, LBJ, how many kids did you kill today?" "I myself did not see the pickets," Bird said. "I understand they were there somewhere." Over the next two and a half years, such protests would become impossible to ignore.

IV

As President Johnson's problems multiplied, the First Lady discovered the limits of her power. The harm a First Lady could do to a President was considerable, while the aid she could give—in public—was limited. Bird did not have enough standing to bolster her husband. In fact, as Lyndon's popularity dropped, hers did, too. Even with a positive press, constructive projects, and a record of devoted service to her husband, the First Lady lacked an independent political identity. Both felt isolated during their final two years in the White House, defeated by a war and a youth rebellion they never understood.

Bird learned how to handle the press from watching Senator Johnson. Unfortunately, these techniques were less effective for a president in the 1960s than for a First Lady or a Senate majority leader. Johnson's familiarity with reporters, his informality, his vulgarity, and his excesses bred contempt, as did her more careful informality. Reporters mocked the President for "swat[ting] Lady Bird so hard on the behind that her feet nearly leave the floor." By 1965 they called the chasm between his tall tales and the truth "Lyndon Johnson's 'credibility gap.'" Both Johnsons suffered from the backlash against Kennedy's "news management." Younger journalists who did not experience the male camaraderie of World War II, and the small but growing number of women journalists, were particularly disparaging. The more he gave them "the treatment," the more they gave him the business.

The rise of television complicated the situation. Print reporters anxious to justify their existence became more probing. The cameras were unkind to the angular Lady Bird, and they were positively cruel to her wrinkled husband. Aides urged Johnson to mimic Kennedy's style, and to recognize that his own "astonishing" accomplishments were less relevant than appearing "relaxed, confident and human," as Jack Valenti advised.

Television's obvious power, and Kennedy's incomprehensible success, misled Johnson. Finding what Liz Carpenter called "a good picture possibility" would not save his administration. His unpopularity stemmed from "ugly problem[s]" that included the escalating war in Vietnam, the mushrooming urban crisis, rising inflation, and the spreading student revolt. The Johnsons' attempt to focus on "quality of life" had failed; Americans needed a safe and peaceful country before they could build a Great Society. A poll in September 1967 showed that 54 percent of those surveyed viewed Johnson less favorably than they had in 1964; his job approval rating had dropped 31 points.

By 1967 the President's political problems had poisoned attitudes toward the First Lady as well. In October Bird undertook a disastrous visit to some college campuses. At Williams College, seventy-five students walked out when she began to speak; at Yale, eight hundred students protested her appearance. The image of protesters shouting "Shame, Shame" at an idealistic crusader calling for America "to grow—with beauty and compassion for every life and its fulfillment" epitomized the tragedy of the Johnson years. No matter what Bird said, no matter what she did, she was considered the enemy because her husband was Lyndon Johnson.

It only made matters worse that Lady Bird was too much her husband's partner to avoid the Vietnam debate. She gamely tried to echo his position. In such an atmosphere, the campus visits were "probably a mistake," she admitted, because she gave the few "dissenters" a large public "platform." The Johnsons were discovering the modern media equivalent of Gresham's law: "the louder voices of hate and anger" shouted down calls for harmony. A "distressed" President told his depressed wife, "I just hate for you to have to take that sort of thing." Bird, who earned high marks for her "poise," remembered struggling to maintain her "dignity. But through every pore, you sense a sort of an animal passion right below the surface."

A week and a half later Bird was on her knees, helping to plant eight hundred thousand daffodil bulbs Mary Lasker donated for Columbia Island, just below Washington's Memorial Bridge. Bird did much better on the "garden club" stage of beautification. Lobbyist, cheerleader, business executive, celebrity, and scold, she helped preserve such national treasures as the Redwood National Forest and the Grand Canyon. She posed with television's favorite dog, Lassie, to fight littering. Suggesting a visit to a nature center in Arizona, Interior Secretary Stewart Udall wrote, "Education-children-nature—an unbeatable combination!"

Yet Lady Bird's prominence inflated expectations. Citizens expected her to control the federal bureaucracy, especially on conservation issues. Crusaders against pornography chided the First Lady for avoiding their beautification campaign concerning "the minds of our youth today." And pushing Lyndon to impose beautification on all federal agencies backfired. Billboard owners worked against her by offering federal agencies free highway advertising for public service messages.

Then a counterattack on the 1965 Highway Beautification Act began. Lyndon had pushed through an expensive, unrealistic, and unpopular bill; his need to prove himself to his wife had actually weakened her precious legislation. Lobbyists chipped away at it. The cost of compensating billboard owners, screening junkyards, and landscaping was estimated as high as $1.8 billion. By 1967 only 600 of 17,000 junkyards had been relocated or screened, and the 1.2 million ugly billboards remained. Both Johnsons felt cornered. Highway beautification was their "baby," but they did not want more bloodshed. Lady Bird learned that it was easier to celebrate beauty than to enact it.

Throughout 1967 the two sides skirmished. The House minority leader, Gerald Ford of Michigan, vowed to repeal the bill. Conservationists lost faith in it. In the end, the President's $380 million budget request for highway beautification dwindled to $85 million. In June 1967 the *New York Times* deemed the act "the biggest legislative flop in the beautification push."

The Federal Aid Highway Act of 1968 proved to be highway beautification's Dunkirk. The lame-duck President and his wife lobbied Congress half-heartedly. Lyndon was distracted. Lady Bird turned to publicity stunts, taking "a leisurely, civilized trip" up the Hudson and unveiling "a new series of stamps boosting beautification." Meanwhile, the House of Representatives voted in July for a $12 billion highway package with no money for beautification. "Everyone is in favor of America the beautiful until it comes time to do something about it," the *Louisville Courier-Journal* mourned. Eventually, House and Senate conferees would agree on a bill allocating token amounts.

The Johnsons' many critics on the left were outraged, particularly by one provision forcing construction of a controversial highway in Washington, D.C., within thirty days. Radicals had long disliked the Johnsons' "garden club" manners, "piddling programs," and "paltry funds" for the environment. These bolder ecologists, who would soon be called environmentalists, demanded a transformation of capitalist society.

Radical environmentalists joined with the major conservation organizations and Secretary Udall to demand a presidential veto. Caught between her embattled husband and her beloved cause, Bird wavered. She funneled briefs from Udall and other opponents to the President, but deferred to her husband when it was time to decide. Eventually the First Lady and the President sidestepped their dilemma; Johnson could sign the bill and prevent the D.C. highway by relying on other regulations. On August 23, President Johnson signed the Federal Aid Highway Act of 1968. He attacked some of the sections as "unfortunate, ill-considered and a set-back to the cause of conservation." Still, he sighed, "I believe the good in this bill outweighs the bad."

The President attended the final meeting of Bird's Committee for a More Beautiful Capital in December 1968. "Thank you for returning my wife to me!" he joked. The Johnsons had considered issuing an executive order continuing the committee. Joe Califano discovered that "the First Lady has never been given official duties by law or executive order, and this would be a break with tradition." Yet the Johnsons had broken many other precedents. Indeed, never before had a presidential couple cooperated so publicly on such a critical issue of governance. The Johnsons were important transitional figures in the environmental movement. In all, Lyndon signed 278 "significant" conservation and beautification measures. Locally, thirty-five states regulated junkyards, and twenty-eight regulated billboards. Hawaii and Vermont banned billboards entirely.

Toward the end of the administration, Lady Bird heard that some Republicans were looking for a similar "gimmick" for Pat Nixon as First Lady. "My face fell," Bird recalled. "Four years of enthusiastic hard work and the lady calls it a 'gimmick!'" Those deeming the beautification effort a gimmick missed its sweep, its ambition, and its centrality to the Great Society. Lady Bird demonstrated a First Lady's great potential for public leadership. She also discovered that there were lines she could not cross; Americans had elected her husband, not her, to pass legislation. The beautification crusade illustrated the dangers in a presidential couple's overstepping—in a wife's becoming too identified with legislation or a husband sentimentally rushing through inadequate bills. But the Johnsons also demonstrated the great potential of a presidential couple to set a tone, to establish an agenda, to lead Americans as a couple.

While the Johnsons failed to achieve their Great Society, they accomplished a great deal. When Lyndon Johnson asked Americans to help the poor, and when Lady Bird asked Americans to beautify their surroundings, the Johnsons were appealing to the public-spiritedness of the majority and solidifying the identity of the newly prosperous millions. Jack and Jackie had shown the middle-class masses what they could buy and what they might achieve; Lyndon and Lady Bird showed how they could participate in civic life and help the few they had left behind.

Yet the searing debate about the Vietnam war upstaged these feats. The Johnsons kept trying to return to domestic questions, to resurrect their Great Society crusade. But they could not shake the Vietnam bugaboo. It hit Bird as hard as Lyndon.

On Thursday, January 18, 1968, fifty Women Doers met at the White House to discuss "What Citizens Can Do to Help Insure Safe Streets." The

President dropped by to encourage "mothers and women" to fight crime. As the President started to leave, Eartha Kitt, a black singer who also played Catwoman on the television hit series "Batman," jumped up and asked, "What do we do about delinquent parents?" Johnson dismissively suggested that "you women" discuss it "and you all tell me what you think."

When the question period began, Kitt exploded, blaming the Vietnam war for juvenile delinquency, drug use, and hopelessness. She gesticulated wildly and approached the First Lady menacingly. Kitt concluded: "They rebel in the streets; they will take pot. If you don't know the expression, it is marijuana. They will smoke a joint and get themselves high as they possibly can in order to avoid whatever it is to get shot at."

As Kitt ranted, the other ladies, dressed in their Sunday best, sat in silence. Lady Bird blushed and trembled. Some claimed that her eyes filled with tears. One East Wing aide sat on the edge of her chair, "ready to beat off Eartha Kitt . . . if she lunged at Mrs. Johnson."

After about five minutes, Betty Hughes, the First Lady of New Jersey, interrupted Kitt. "Anybody who's taking pot just because there is a war in Vietnam is some kind of a kook," she said. Hughes's response, and Kitt's exchange with another guest, gave Lady Bird time to compose her thoughts. Still shaken, she said, "Because there is a war on, and I pray that there will come a just and honest peace, that still does not give us a free ticket not to try to work on bettering the things in this country that we can better."

Kitt's "violent" attack on the First Lady "in her own home" touched a nerve. The White House received thirty-five thousand letters, the overwhelming majority sympathetic to Lady Bird. When Kitt appeared on WTOP radio after the show, 80 percent of the four hundred calls attacked the singer. Some callers were so menacing that two policemen escorted Kitt out of the station building. Hundreds of women called the White House, sobbing, "outraged" by the First Lady's "ordeal," saying, "Mrs. Johnson's humiliation is all our humiliation." The President was furious, and the First Lady was shaken by what she called "a stormy Thursday, a black Friday and a surprising Saturday—when the letters began piling up in the White House." Just like Adam Clayton Powell's attack on Bess Truman, Kitt's attack raised questions about the virtues of politeness versus principle. Politeness still seemed to reign.

Kitt underlined the First Lady's unhappy role as a lightning rod for criticisms against her husband. Martin Luther King, Jr., justified the outburst because the "ears" of President and Mrs. Johnson "are somewhat isolated from expressions of what the people really feel." Less subtly, a "voter" wrote: "Hooray for Eartha Kitt. God bless her. So Lady Bird cried—well doesn't she know that the mothers of 15,000 boys MURDERED in Vietnam by her husband's foreign policy cry every night?"

A vocal minority now espoused new fundamental values. The Harris poll found that these liberal voices came from among "the most affluent, most educated members of the electorate—the 22 percent who earn more than $10,000 a year." Traditionally, "the richer part of society [had] been thought of as being the most conservative and the least likely to push new ideas." This astonishing reversal of class politics would have profound implications for future First Couples; rather than safely playing to the sensibilities of the former conservative elite, presidents and their wives would need to appear both hip enough to mollify the most articulate Americans and traditional enough to remain popular with the rest of the electorate.

To these new activists, niceties seemed irrelevant in the face of "genocide." By 1968, Bird's social criticism seemed tepid and cosmetic. One Californian demanded, "Stop cultivating flowers and cultivate young minds starving for justice." Many young rebels believed that "uplift" perpetuated the dreaded "status quo" by focusing on nonessentials. "THE FIRST LADY OF THE UNITED STATES SHOULD BE BETTER ABLE TO COPE WITH A RUDE EMOTIONAL PRESENTATION OF A VALID IDEA THAN TO REACT AS THOUGH HER MAID HAD SPILLED SOUP ON SOMEONE," one woman telegrammed the President.

For the majority, this was the last straw. Thousands of Republicans told Mrs. Johnson they disagreed with her husband, but they respected the presidency. Republican Congressman George Bush of Houston attacked the "disgraceful" new morality: "There seems to be a tendency these days toward excusing bad manners in the name of protest, and worse, there seems to be a tendency on the part of the protesters to feel that personal attacks on the President and his family are very much in order." Agnes Meyer of the *Washington Post* said "the quality of being a lady is not the meaningless outmoded ideal it is often considered to be in our morally impoverished era. . . . It infers a high standard of behavior, complete self-control and genuine seriousness tempered by understanding and compassion."

Many Americans resented Kitt's rudeness without realizing how much the Johnsons had politicized the First Lady's position. Nancy Dickerson noted on NBC that the luncheon came the day after Lyndon attacked crime in his State of the Union address, and "was typical of the way the Johnsons work together. He states the issue. . . . And she does what she can to follow through," making particular efforts to mobilize "a good deal of woman power." Even the reaction to Kitt's outburst was skillfully managed. Carpenter invited reporters to monitor phone calls—once she saw that most callers supported Lady Bird.

Ironically, attacking Lady Bird showed respect for the new kind of First Lady role she was pioneering. "If Mrs. Johnson was embarrassed, that's her problem," Kitt said, surprised by the political warhorse's fragility. "After all, the Johnsons are our family and as the head of the nation, who better to discuss the subject with?" Under other circumstances, Lady Bird and Lyndon would have been flattered. First Ladies no longer were as disengaged as even Bess Truman had been.

There was another lesson latent in the incident. Activist First Ladies offered a new line of attack on presidents. The intense emotions between husband and wife make presidents vulnerable; Kitt and other critics stalked Lady Bird to hurt Lyndon.

By 1968 the Johnson White House was a besieged fortress. Even innocuous luncheons exploded into controversy ignited by Vietnam. Bird found herself constantly "pushing against the wall of gloom," worried about her husband and her country. Lyndon worked harder than ever, trying to solve all the problems and restore his popularity.

As Lyndon Johnson faced his greatest crisis, his top deputy failed him. Lyndon's demand for total devotion over the years made Lady Bird his cheerleader. Sharing his vision of the Great Society, Bird fed Johnson's idealistic self-image, the part of his identity that allowed him to bully and lie and bomb, convinced that he was working for the greater good. She accepted his rationalization that the problem was perception, not policy. "Surely the war took more lines in the paper and minutes on the TV. But this other great tide surged forward too," she would say. Surrounded by "yes men," Lyndon needed Bird to jolt him from his self-defeating patterns, but she could not see the problem clearly either. When Lyndon asked "Why don't people, especially young people, really jump into the poverty program, roll up their sleeves and get it roaring like we did back in the New Deal?" she shrugged her shoulders, equally mystified.

Lady Bird's steadfast efforts spun the web of self-delusion around the Johnsons even tighter. She helped garner compliments from Walt Rostow and other devotees that "there had never been a President and First Family that better stood for the very best that is in us." Such compliments kept the President on his path, no matter how disastrous.

Bird definitely wanted Lyndon to retire in 1969, but he vacillated. She doubted they could "endure" four more years in the White House. But Bird knew better than to nag her husband. Arguments that he was not up to the challenge physically or politically might push him to run, as they had in 1964. Lyndon later said he appreciated that "in all our conversations about declining to run in 1968, Lady Bird had always been most deferential. She never took the lead in these discussions or forced an opinion or a point of view on me." Deftly, cautiously, Bird handled Lyndon.

Lyndon finally announced his retirement on March 31, 1968, after ordering a bombing halt "to deescalate the conflict" in Vietnam. The master politician hoped that such a linkage would make him appear statesmanlike. Even that night, Lady Bird "wasn't really 100 percent sure" he would go through with it "until the words came out." When reporters asked him, "What role did Mrs. Johnson play in your decision?" Johnson replied, "The same role she plays in every decision I make—a very important one."

Few realized how much Bird helped shape the speech itself. Her revisions typified her contributions to Lyndon's career; she avoided the policy details and focused on politics and the big picture. She pushed the President to invoke themes of self-sacrifice and patriotism, to work in references to World War II. When the text complained that a bold fiscal "action" to fund the war "has not been taken," Bird insisted that the culprit be identified. The final draft complained that "Congress has not acted." Bird always wanted to make Lyndon Johnson look as good as possible.

By the spring of 1968, most of Bird's efforts were as futile as her husband's. The Johnsons had lost their mandate to remake America from the top, gradually, benignly. Ironically, the President and First Lady of their generation most sympathetic to the rights revolution—to the expansion of opportunities for women, the poor, and minorities—were ruined by the passions they helped unleash. This ending was fitting. Ultimately, the concatenation of social movements known as "the Sixties" produced tremendous social change, great cultural chaos, and a resurgent conservatism that would threaten many liberal achievements, including the welfare state and civil rights. In the coming decades, these dueling legacies would bewilder the Johnsons' successors.

Watching Lyndon's retirement speech, the fifty-five-year-old First Lady felt the same commanding, dynamic force that initially drew her to him. "The speech was magnificently delivered," she applauded. "Those who love him must have loved him more. And those who hate him must at least have thought: 'Here is a man.'" After thirty-four years, Cap Taylor's assessment of Lady Bird's beau still resonated more loudly than both the vocal antiwar protesters and the large, more muted, backlash against Lyndon's grandiose Great Society.

5

"STAND BY YOUR MAN"

From the "Pat and Dick" Show to The Final Days

On election night of 1968, Richard Milhous Nixon and his family holed up on the thirty-fifth floor of the Waldorf Astoria. "Pat and the girls"—Tricia and Julie—were in one room; Dick and his advisers were down the hall. Through the long night, neither he nor his staff contacted the family. Nixon said he "knew how worried they would be" and "did not want to make them feel that they had to keep up a cheerful front for my sake." At three in the morning, Nixon "allowed myself the luxury of self-assurance. I had won the Presidency." As Dick called leading Republicans, his family languished. At six o'clock, television anchors announced that Mayor Richard Daley of Chicago was still holding back precinct votes. Pat Nixon feared a repeat of 1960, when similar shenanigans threw the election to Kennedy. According to Julie, Mrs. Nixon rose "and went into the bathroom. We could hear that she was sick to her stomach." Only two and a half hours later did the President-elect come down the hall to his family. The reunion was sober. "But Dick, are we sure of Illinois?" Pat demanded. Once assured, the next First Lady of the United States burst into tears.

The coming six years would be filled with such moments. Lyndon Johnson had demanded his family's complete participation; Jackie Kennedy had fought for privacy. Richard Nixon would want his wife and daughters close by while keeping his distance from them. His treatment of his family convinced his critics he was a heartless Machiavellian, eager to exploit his family but unaware of their needs. To others, such moments revealed a vulnerable, insecure, and awkward yet loving family man, trying to shield his family and himself from his brutal profession.

While headlines emphasized what was new and outlandish in American life, shrewd politicians emphasized that which was enduring and reassuring. The year of the great rebellion, 1968, produced a most conservative chief executive. Richard Nixon heralded "the Sixties"' conservative revival. He and his loyal wife Pat represented many of the constants in America during this time of great change. Ultimately, however, Nixon proved to be a typical conservative of the cold-war era, helping to subvert the accepted social order despite remaining unyieldingly traditional in his rhetoric.

Just as the Nixons felt caught between the reserve of the past and the exhibitionism of the present, they were unsure whether to model themselves on their mentors, the Eisenhowers, or their rivals, the Kennedys. By 1969 Pat had withdrawn too far from Dick's political career for a Johnson-style partnership. But Dick recognized the changing standards for couples, and he tried to exploit them politically. Pat was the last First Lady able to stay far in the shadows—like Mamie Eisenhower—yet she was as political as anyone among the new presidential couples. Despite Richard Nixon's tragic flaws, she showed one successful solution to the problem of new couples—appear nonpolitical for political purposes, like the Kennedys.

I

Richard Nixon was too emotionally clumsy and too hidebound to pioneer a new era in gender relations. He was born in Yorba Linda, California, in January 1913 to a pugnacious father and a serene Quaker mother. He was the second of five boys. Dick reduced his childhood to "three words . . . family, church and school," all preaching the ethic of "honesty, hard work, do your best at all times." Frank Nixon's grocery would succeed modestly, but it entailed long hours. Dick rarely waited on customers and would not wear a grocer's apron. Even when he washed the dishes at home, Hannah noticed, "Richard always pulled the blinds down tight so that people wouldn't see him."

Dick distinguished himself from his volatile father. Frank was handy, Dick was all thumbs; Frank would squeeze his nieces, Dick avoided touching women in public, including his wife. Richard Nixon respected his mother's self-control. He would recall that "in her whole life, I never heard her say to me or to anyone else, 'I love you.' She did not need to. Her eyes expressed the love and warmth no words could possibly convey."

Hannah raised her son to be sober. "He wasn't a little boy that you wanted to pick up and hug," one cousin recalled. The deaths of two brothers—seven-year-old Arthur in 1925 and twenty-four-year-old Harold eight years later—reinforced Dick's determination to succeed. He tried, Hannah recalled, "to be *three* sons in one," striving to compensate his parents "for our loss."

At Whittier College, Nixon was disciplined, intelligent, and ambitious. His football coach, Wallace "Chief" Newman, encouraged him to be relentless, thundering, "Show me a good loser, and I'll show you a loser." Dick "never could get up the nerve" to ask girls for dates; he stepped on their feet when he danced. He took refuge in the life of the mind. His intellectual exploits, along with his term as student body president, won him admission to Duke University Law School.

After graduating with honors in 1937, Dick returned to Whittier, where he joined the city's oldest law firm. The young Quaker squirmed when he sifted through the sordid details of divorce cases. Early in 1938 Dick tried out for a play, hoping to bump into a new teacher in town. The handsome bachelor whose broad smile filled out the puffiness of his cheeks was charmed by the "beautiful and vivacious young woman with titian hair." He offered her a ride home, which she accepted, and a date, which she rejected. "I'm very busy," she said. Dick exclaimed: "You shouldn't say that because someday I am going to marry you!"

The stranger to whom Nixon proposed was Thelma Catherine "Pat" Ryan. Beyond the movie-star looks, trim figure, and reddish-blond hair, Nixon sensed a grace that he lacked and a tenacity he could match. Born in a miner's shack in 1912, Pat grew up on a farm in Artesia, California, with three brothers, an older sister, a genteel German immigrant mother, and a volatile Irish-American father. Pat's life had also been burdened with responsibility and punctuated by tragedy. When Pat was thirteen her mother died, and she began to run the house. Four years later her father died. Pat learned to smile through her heartbreak.

Both Pat and Dick were restrained. "Her life is a classic example of triumph over adversity," Dick would say. After half a century of marriage, he would praise his wife by comparing her to "an athlete [who] comes back to win after suffering a defeat." Pat was equally sober in her assessment; in 1952 she described her husband of a dozen years as "a quietly determined fellow."

In the early 1930s Pat worked for two years as an X-ray technician in New York, where she learned to smoke, drink, and flirt. By 1934 Pat had returned home to finish her education at the University of Southern California, thinking that she "didn't want to marry early." Living with her two brothers, Pat again ran the house. One professor recalled that Pat "stood out from the empty-headed, overdressed little sorority girls of that era like a good piece of literature on a shelf of cheap paperbacks."

Teaching offered a respectable career for an ambitious young woman who felt she "had not lived yet." Unfortunately, Whittier proved stultifying, and so every weekend Pat returned to Los Angeles. Dick Nixon, an earnest, driven, insecure provincial, could not compete with Pat's sophisticated city beaux. Yet the quiet, even grim, determination each had drew them together. While others may have scoffed at Dick's willingness to chauffeur "Miss Vagabond" to Los Angeles to date other men, she respected his persistence. Often, walking in the mountains or reading in the sunshine, Pat and Dick simply shared the silence. Gradually, their friendship blossomed.

Pat and Dick married in a Quaker ceremony on June 21, 1940. Dick vowed to prove himself worthy. "You are a great inspiration to me, and though you don't believe it yet, I someday shall return some of the benefit you have conferred upon me," he said after their engagement. Pat began to remember the courtship as mutual and prolonged only by their poverty. Still, Pat's first birthday present to her husband was a foot-high ceramic knight. "It reminds me of him," she would say, conscious of how quixotic his quest to woo her had first been.

In the Quaker way, the Nixons' partnership was more equal than others. Both dreamed of escape; Pat called herself "just a gypsy at heart." By the fall of 1941 Dick had secured a government job at the Office of Price Administration. After Pearl Harbor, Dick's mother wanted him to keep "our Quaker principles" and become a conscientious objector. Pat, though, encouraged him to enlist and to break free of Hannah Nixon. As an aspiring politician, "a student of history," and a patriot, Dick decided to fight. Dick's identity as a cosmopolitan American eclipsed his identities as a son and a Quaker.

The war was "the break point" with the past for Nixon and millions of his peers. Three of four Quakers would not seek an exemption from the draft. The military wanted to "break down the wall of timidity which has encircled many of our present day youth" and produce, as one Navy guide put it, "a fearless, courageous combatant." Dick's first week in basic training was "the longest I've ever known." He told Pat, "those navy chiefs—they put you in your place and that is good for anybody."

The war made many men gruff yet sentimental, and many women self-reliant yet dependent. After one brief reunion, Dick wrote Pat: "Coming back I looked at myself in the window and thought how very lucky I was to have you. I certainly am not the Romeo type and you are so beautiful." Once overseas, "Nick" Nixon further distanced himself from his roots by cursing, parading around bare-chested, and gambling. While relishing his freedom, Lieutenant Commander Nixon wrote his wife every day for fourteen months. "Please say it always," he admonished Pat about saying "I love you," for "you are the only one for me, it's been that way from the first." She began her lipstick-dabbed letters "Dear Plum."

After a series of white-collar jobs, Pat ended up as a price economist with the Office of Price Administration in San Francisco. Despite the hoopla, not all

"Rosies" actually riveted; almost a million women had civil service jobs. Pat enjoyed contributing "to the winning of the war." "Your job is far more important than mine was at OPA," Dick wrote, slightly jealous. "I like to tell the gang how smart you are as well as being the most attractive person they'll ever see."

During the war women achieved "liberation" and "self-fulfillment" without equality. No matter what they did, men did more. Most Americans viewed women's entry into the work force as temporary. "A woman is a substitute, like plastic instead of metal," a War Department brochure proclaimed. When Dick was ordered home in the summer of 1944, Pat's response captured the ambivalence many wives felt as their tenures on factory floors and at typewriters ended. She wrote: "These many months you have been away have been full of interest, and had I not missed you so much and had I been foot loose, could have been extremely happy. So, sweet, you'll always have to love me lots and never let me change my feelings for you which has [sic] been so beautiful all these years." Pat and millions of other women would spend decades trying to feel as liberated when their husbands were home as they had when their husbands were overseas.

Dick Nixon came home on July 17, 1944, with lieutenant's bars, two battle stars, and a commendation. He cleaned up his vocabulary and reverted to his civilized, closed Quaker self. Still, he was more worldly. One of his relatives noted that Dick had "learned how to get along with people. . . . He was really much more humble; I mean he saw how the other half lived." The Nixons settled in Maryland for the duration of the war.

The wartime drama, for all its pain, liberated the Nixons and solidified their partnership. Their affirmations of love and dependence were now mutual. Dick had pulled himself from his mother's orbit; in Whittier, Pat would have always remained a junior partner and an outsider. As they contemplated their future, the chances of a mutual partnership seemed strong.

In the fall of 1945 some Whittier businessmen recruited Dick to run for Congress. "I could see that it was the life he wanted," Pat recalled, "so I told him that it was his decision, and I would do what he liked." The Nixons flew to Whittier. When one executive asked Dick to become "our candidate," Dick excused himself to find Pat, then returned saying "they" would run. By ostentatiously seeking out his wife and speaking in the plural, Dick reassured Pat that "they" were a "team."

Nixon's literature compared this "working wife and sailor husband" to "other young 'war couples.'" To complete the picture, Tricia Nixon was born in February 1946; three weeks after giving birth, Pat was back campaigning. The Nixons blurred patriotism, partisanship, and sentimentality. Dick proclaimed that Tricia "will grow up in the finest state of the union, in the greatest country on earth, and when the time comes she will register and vote Republican." The Nixons showed that women could participate in the postwar world and know their place. Pat attended women's coffees, coordinated the volunteers, and did secretarial work; she refused, however, to give speeches.

"Pat and Dick" would become one of the most famous "teams" in American politics. Pat felt needed and Dick appreciated her efforts. He would boast "that Pat not only goes along for the scenic effect but that she also goes as my secretary." Yet while publicly parading their partnership, the Nixons privately were learning some new rules of disengagement. There were new men in Dick's life, and he had to make harsh decisions that he would not discuss with his bride. A streetwise pol, Murray Chotiner, became a key Nixon adviser and Pat's rival.

This separation worsened in Washington. Pat plunged into motherhood while Dick had little time for fatherhood. Pat was neither as independent as she had been during the war, nor as central as she had been during the campaign. In the middle of Dick's 1948 reelection, a second daughter, Julie, was born at Washington's Columbia Hospital. When pregnant, Pat had finally crashed and complained about the loneliness. Dick promised to be more solicitous, but he would break this promise throughout fourteen years of continuous campaigning.

Usually Pat refused to complain; she simply took on more responsibility. This world of infinite demands terrorized a perfectionist like Pat. Even in 1946, matrons had sniffed that she did not "know what color finger-nail polish to wear." Pat wanted to draw down the blinds and hide. Instead, she walled off a part of herself, as she had done in childhood.

Meanwhile, Dick became a leading anticommunist. He ran for the Senate in 1950 against Congresswoman Helen Gahagan Douglas, a Hollywood leftist married to Melvyn Douglas, a Jewish actor. Pat's presence tempered the ferocity of Dick's attacks and underlined his wholesomeness. The Nixon campaign sent out a postcard picturing Dick at home, hugging his wife and two daughters; an inflatable cowboy "Bop Bag" was at their feet. The postcard warned, "The vote you cast, or do not cast, may determine the fate of our American way of life." And so Dick Nixon fought communism with an arsenal of postwar domestic artifacts: blond children, a slim wife, toy cowboys, and lawn furniture. The approach was cloying, irrelevant, and effective, as Dick won by 680,947 votes. During one TV appearance, cameras caught two-year-old Julie picking her nose. The tomfoolery about the wife and the kids was serious business. Nixon joked, "Julie honey, you have either just won or lost me the election."

By 1952, when Dwight Eisenhower designated Nixon as his running mate to mollify right-wing Republicans, the Nixons had their act down pat. "My husband and I always campaign together as a team. I go around with him and talk to the women," Pat said. A *Time* cover story called the thirty-nine-year-old senator the candidate who "seemed to have everything—a fine TV manner, an attractive family, a good war record, deep sincerity and religious faith, a Horatio Alger-like career." *Time,* the *American Weekly,* and the *Saturday Evening Post* told how Dick hosted a picnic in his office one Sunday; Pat and the girls sat on a blanket on the floor while Dick worked at his desk. Pat said this "special treat" revealed Dick's success in integrating child rearing into a busy life. In fact, it revealed Pat's frustrations with her workaholic husband.

These frustrations, swept away by the post-nomination euphoria, burst through when Dick was accused of having a secret $18,000 fund his business backers donated to cover extra office and travel expenses. Other politicians had similar funds. Still, protesters pelted the Nixons with pennies. Pat developed a stiff neck, and Dick considered resigning. Pat warned: "If you . . . crawl away. . . . Your life will be marred forever and the same will be true of your family, and particularly, your daughters."

Nixon secured half an hour of television time to justify the fund and describe the Nixons' modest finances. Such candor was unheard of in the 1950s. "Why do you have to tell people how little we have and how much we owe?" Pat asked. "People in political life have to live in a fish bowl," Dick lectured. The personal attack demanded a personal response. Having marketed their private life so successfully, Nixon had to use similar techniques to salvage his political career.

Thirty minutes before airtime, Eisenhower sent word demanding that Nixon resign at the end of the broadcast. Dick wailed, "I just don't think I can go through with this one." Pat steadied him. Before 58 million Americans, Dick detailed their assets, their debts, Pat's "respectable Republican cloth coat," the legitimate expenses the money covered, and a lovable "black and white spotted" dog named Checkers he received as a gift. Stiffly he introduced Pat, her face frozen in a half-smile: "She's a wonderful stenographer," he said, but with "so many deserving stenographers" around he never put her on the payroll. In this classic of cold-war politics, after he listed his possessions Nixon shifted back into campaign mode and blasted "the crooks and the Communists" for ruining America.

Pat sat onstage "like a wax figure," afraid of showing "too much emotion." She later regretted not doing more, but the editor of the *Long Beach Independent Telegram* said that "the character in her face, the picture of a loyal wife backing up her husband," was enough. Americans were learning that a good wife "is a vital factor in the attainment of [a man's] objectives." Eventually Pat would realize that "the wife of a candidate will always be beset by these if's, these backward looks."

Almost two million telegrams demanded that Nixon stay on the ticket. The speech climaxed the Nixons' six-year campaign to represent their generation as many veterans identified with Nixon's financial plight. "Dick and Pat are just a couple of all-American kids who didn't know what they were letting themselves in for when they got into politics," one supporter said. Offers to raise "A Dollar for Pat" to pay off the Nixons' debts poured in. Dick's crowds—and his press entourage—swelled.

The speech helped give birth to a new ethos; personality and personal disclosure would become increasingly important in politics. Yet just as the Nixons' image as a political team jelled, their partnership ruptured. The "Fund Crisis" intensified the power struggle that began when the Nixons moved to Washington. Dick's success cost Pat her freedom. Dick responded to the public embrace; Pat would never forget the humiliation. She would retreat into her shell, doing her duty joylessly. The crisis only lasted a week, but Dick recognized that "Pat and I were to live with its consequences for the rest of our lives."

After the Eisenhower landslide, the "Pat and Dick" show was staged at home instead of the stump. The Nixons' seven-room brick house at 4801 Tilden Street NW, became one of the most famous homes in America. "You do not live in a mansion and you make your own coffee," one visitor exclaimed. The Nixons were America's suburbanites-in-chief; they helped indoctrinate thrifty, sober Americans into the culture of consumption. Never before had a vice-presidential couple played such a role as cultural leaders.

Each domestic task Pat undertook was seen as a mark of her virtue; every item she consumed was a mark of their prosperity. Profiles detailed the chores this "homebody in the public eye" completed. Pat maintained her image by forbidding photographs of her maid. As Mamie Eisenhower grew into her role of the nation's grandmother, Pat was named Outstanding Homemaker of the Year in 1953, Mother of the Year in 1955, and the "nation's ideal wife" by the Homemakers' Forum in 1957. "I love my home," she beamed. "It is important to us to have happy homes throughout the nation."

In fact, though, this homemaker was unhappy. Dick was "sometimes moody," rarely around, and usually remote. Pat was overworked, isolated, and bored. "All the useless gadding I am expected to do" was tiresome. At one party, Pat cut Dick off by passing out Chiclets and chirping, "Here, take one of these, it's better than the baloney he puts out." When Dick missed a Brownie meeting at his home, nine-year-old Julie asked, "Why can't he work like the man in the grocery store and come home every night at six?"

Dick used his domestic image to rehabilitate himself. Reporters met the first of many "New Nixons" as the street fighter became a statesman. "I've got a temper—I expect I got it from my father," he confessed, but "I've found that a restrained, tolerant, courteous approach is the best." Nixon was trying to imitate the two most important women in his life, Hannah and Pat. "Some people are not as friendly and sweet as others," Pat would advise one daughter attending sleep-away camp. "The main thing is to treat them in a friendly fashion and stay your own sweet self rather than becoming like them."

The Nixons' relationship with the Eisenhowers remained proper, not warm. Dick served as Eisenhower's jack-of-all trades, ready to mediate with Congress in the morning, host a diplomat in the afternoon, then represent the President at a reception at night. Within a year Nixon was labeled the "assistant President," the most effective vice president ever. Still, many Republicans wanted to dump him from the ticket in 1956. Dick contemplated withdrawing. Despite her desire to return home, Pat urged him to fight. The Nixons' friend Jack Drown noted, "Any time you pressured Pat, her Irish came out . . . thank God."

As usual, Pat did her duty on the campaign trail. She consented to hold a news conference, but she would not "discuss politics." It was hard to claim that the endearing details she offered about domestic life were not "political." A "teammate" who campaigned across the country, granted interviews, and sought to gain votes by personalizing her husband was certainly political; she just was not issue-oriented. For the next four decades, politically active spouses like Pat would become more familiar, but they would still be tiptoeing around the confusing terminology and ambivalent attitudes about spouses in politics.

Pat's life had become an elaborate masquerade. In the spring of 1958 she sprained her back and was immobilized for days. Americans were beginning to attribute such maladies to emotional strain. That August a doctor in *McCall's* warned that "anxiety, suppressed rage, fear, and stress over domestic or marital difficulties" caused "severe back pain."

All the talk about being Dick's partner boxed Pat into a demanding role. As the Eisenhowers slowed down, the Nixons had more dinners to host and more overseas trips to make. Just as Dick had to pose in his backyard playing with the girls to bolster his claim to be the full 1950s man, Pat had to prove she was the total woman. One *Life* photo spread showed her shopping in a supermarket, making a hat, and tickling Julie, followed by photographs of her hosting a diplomat, working in Dick's office, giving interviews, and visiting India, Japan, and Vietnam.

Still suffering from the back strain, in May 1958 Pat joined Dick on an arduous eighteen-day trip to South America. In Caracas, Venezuela, protesters mobbed the Nixon motorcade. Years of training paid off that day, as both put on poker faces. Nixon recalled thinking, "I must be as cold as the mob was hot." He saw Pat in her limousine "talking to the Foreign Minister's wife as calmly as though the trouble was no worse than an afternoon traffic jam." Only when newsmen cheered her later did Pat's eyes fill with tears. Dick's Air Force aide would pay Pat his highest compliment, saying, "She was as brave as any man I ever saw."

Nixon's effectiveness abroad all but guaranteed his nomination as the Republican standard-bearer in 1960. Much as Pat wanted to retire from politics, she wanted her husband to be happy. She began emphasizing their teamwork on the campaign trail rather than her exploits at home. "I think we've had enough of this kitchen thing, don't you?" she told photographers who wanted her posing in an apron yet again. Well aware of her rival Jackie Kennedy's disdain for the vulgar hordes, Pat claimed, "The trips are not hard on me because I enjoy people."

Despite her fine political ear, Pat would have difficulty striking the right note in 1960. She still refused to give "political" speeches, saying, "My husband attends to the political end." But she freely chatted about politics with reporters. Similarly, she claimed that "I never exactly advise Dick, because he doesn't need advice." But she insisted that she was "in on" the strategy, "and it's more than just listening in."

Beneath the smiles, Pat often felt like a pawn rather than a partner. The campaign decided to celebrate "Pat Week." "When you elect a President, you are also electing a First Lady whose job is more than glamour," the campaign press release proclaimed, "she represents America to all the world." Pat was not consulted about her "week," which she feared would upstage the candidate. As usual, however, she did her duty despite her qualms. "The teas and coffees had all been announced," she explained.

Both Nixons kept up a grueling pace. Jack Sherwood, who campaigned with them throughout the decade, said Dick "would snap when the campaign became too much and let off steam," but Pat "did not show tension at all." She refused to dwell on mistakes, or speculate about how she would act as First Lady, declaring, "I always live for the present."

Nixon's loss shattered his family. During the concession speech the cameras zoomed in on Pat's anguished attempt to fight back tears; Pat felt violated. Her display of emotions, though, helped Dick maintain his composure. Dick decided that women "find it much harder to lose than do men." They get "involved more deeply and emotionally because women basically are more idealistic than men are." Julie said that 1960 "disillusioned" Pat "beyond redemption. She saw a stolen election and could not understand why so many were indifferent." Julie and Tricia sent their Christmas gift money to the Chicago Recount Committee.

Nixon cashed in, joining a law firm and becoming an author. He earned more his first year as a private citizen than he had earned in fourteen years as a public servant. Still, it all "seemed unexciting and unimportant" to him. Pat, in contrast, enjoyed "the first private life we had ever known as a family."

The respite was brief. Dick happily succumbed to pressure from California Republicans to run for governor in 1962. Even though his advisers believed he had "already" decided to run, Dick made a great show of calling a "family council." Pat pleaded with her husband, "Let's be a private family." She also warned that the move was politically unwise. Dick ignored Pat's advice. He doubted her conclusions because he knew she wanted to avoid another race. The result was a humiliating defeat and Nixon's "last press conference." After

Dick vowed that reporters would not have him "to kick around any more," Pat shouted "Bravo" at the television set at home. After the election, however, Tricia noted, "There was a sadness and the sadness went on for years."

Richard Nixon was no longer the young crusader. He was now a man of crises, of pain. Pat was now the long-suffering wife of an also ran, the victim of Richard Nixon's ambition. Rumors spread that Pat contemplated divorce. Marital strife had destroyed the presidential hopes of Dick's rival Nelson Rockefeller; instead, Dick would live on Pat's terms during what she called their "six-year vacation" in New York. They moved into a $425,000 ten-room apartment off Fifth Avenue. Stripped of his staff, his power, his future, Dick was thrown back onto his wife. Pat helped out at the office, fielding phone calls as "Miss Ryan" and assuring callers that she would see that the message reached somebody "close to Mr. Nixon." Dick was miserable, but Pat loved shopping at Bloomingdale's without being recognized.

Gradually Nixon rebuilt his public career, this time without his wife. During the 1966 congressional elections, Nixon stumped for candidates. Pat felt guilty that she rarely accompanied Dick. During one vacation at Key Biscayne, Pat asked Julie and Tricia whether she was "a failure to Daddy."

Buoyed by the Republican success in the 1966 elections, Nixon considered himself the candidate of destiny in 1968. Who better than Eisenhower's heir to solve the problems of the Vietnam War? Who better than a symbol of 1950s fatherhood to discipline the rebellious baby boomers?

Nixon surrounded himself with an energetic corps of former allies and advertising executives. These professionals had no patience for wifely meddling. Once again, months after he told his "oldest friends and closest advisers" to "proceed," Dick convened a family council to decide his future. This time, Pat refused to partake in the charade. "Whatever you do, we'll be proud of you. You know we love you," she said.

Dick needed his family's help to present a "New Nixon." His daughters would humanize him. Julie said, "The public image of Daddy is that he is not sensitive. Actually he is very sensitive. He knows how mother feels without her telling him." Tricia, Julie, and Julie's fiancé—Ike's grandson David Eisenhower—would help Dick connect with the baby boomers. The three youngsters would also offer a wholesome contrast to the hippies.

Pat was no longer Dick's partner or the prototypical housewife. She was "a volunteer for Nixon—his eyes and ears with the women voters." She pasted on her smile, packed her sensible suits, and armed herself with platitudes. She would campaign forty thousand miles, mimicking Lady Bird by celebrating "women achievers" along the way. Pat recognized that a revolution was brewing. In 1960 she talked about cooperation between men and women; now she appealed to women like her, who derided "women's liberation" but wanted more respect.

Political spouses could no longer be benign. Most reporters covering Pat were more radical than their readers. Her stamina, her self-sacrifice, her poise, now seemed to stem from "low self-esteem." Her claim in 1960 that "I may be dying, but I certainly would never say anything about it" was reprinted often. *Newsweek* described her as "the public man's dream—a seemingly selfless, super-efficient helpmeet with just enough grace and style to impress the provinces without inspiring jealousy." A decade earlier, the same descriptions had been laudatory.

Pat resented the condescension. During an interview with Gloria Steinem, she exploded: "I never had time to think about . . . who I admired, or to have ideas. I never had time to dream about being anyone else. I had to work. My parents died when I was a teen-ager. . . . I've never had it easy."

Pat's tirade reinforced Dick's attempt to divide the spoiled baby boomers and their parents. Rather than snarling, "the New Nixon" used his stiffness as a weapon in the cultural war against the hippies. Dick defined his family as "happy" because both his parents "were deeply devoted to the children," who responded to "this sense of self-sacrifice." The appeal worked, barely: Dick won by a slim margin of a half-million votes out of 73 million cast. Julie recalled that when the Nixons boarded an Air Force jet Lyndon Johnson sent to take them on vacation, the Nixons embraced, and "my father swung Mother around in a Pirouette."

II

Richard Nixon carried the scars of his long quest for power into the White House. He wanted to be more stylish than Kennedy, more revolutionary than Johnson, more popular than Eisenhower. He would fail at all three. Nonetheless, his ambitions would transform the White House, including the East Wing, into an elaborate public relations operation—and the First Couple into a deliberately political faux image of conventionality.

Nixon entered office after a year of war, riots, and assassinations. The new President promised to heal the nation, but he remained a pit bull. "A President must come through as very strong, bold and even ruthless," Nixon told his chief aide, H. R. Haldeman. Nixon meant to achieve harmony by crushing the Viet Cong, the students, and the "liberal media."

Nixon wondered how "to really convey the true image of a President to the nation"—his Quaker subconscious stressing honesty twice as he schemed. Television cameras, he realized, could circumvent biased reporters. Dick deluged his aides with tidbits about the "little acts of kindness" he might do in a day, including calling people who are "down." Yet after two years, he would whine that "we come across as a cold, businesslike, no-nonsense Administration, which from the standpoint of those qualities that appeal to most Americans means nothing less than zilch." Just as with his family Dick could not balance intimacy and self-control, as President he could not convey sufficient "warmth" and "strength."

Nixon suffered from the continuing backlash against Kennedy's news management and his own well-deserved reputation for posturing. While celebrating his sincerity, the President told Haldeman, "We should only do things that help on the PR impact." Echoing Dean Acheson's analysis of Kennedy, Nixon uttered what could have been his own epitaph. On the "Today" show he preached: "When Presidents begin to worry about their images" they become like bad athletes, "so concerned about what is said about them . . . that they don't play the game well."

Nixon's relations with the media had an "Alice Through the Looking Glass" quality; reporters tried to elicit evasions they could discredit while the President tried to appear authentic. When Helen Thomas asked about his favorite songs, Dick vetoed the East Wing staffers' answers, "God Bless America" and "America the Beautiful." He chose "Thank Heaven for Little Girls" instead. His aides noted that, with their replies, "it is a bit as though we are trying to make him look like a super-patriot and nothing else."

Nixon needed his family to illustrate his warmth. He also expected Pat and the girls to outdo the Kennedys, gaining popularity painlessly. The President directed his staff to "hypo coverage" of the First Family—using slang for the jolt drug abusers received when they used hypodermic needles, which later would be known as "hype." What the Kennedys did instinctively—and, in Jackie's case, ambivalently—the Nixons would do deliberately and thus less effectively. Nixon peddled the "First Family" to take pressure off the First Lady and appeal to youth.

Nixon demanded that the East Wing ignore Washington matrons and entertain the masses. He wanted experts handling his family's "TV just like mine," believing that "nothing [was] worth a damn unless nat[iona]l coverage" was achieved. Thus, "teas, etc." were "not worthwhile." The First Lady's mandate was to help make her husband more popular, not to be genteel. When Barbara Walters wanted to interview the First Lady, the President insisted that the questions have "*no* substance." Nixon expected the East Wing to pitch ideas to reporters and set their agendas. We "need to do [a] better job of forcing *our* pic[ture] opp[ortunities]," he told Bob Haldeman. "Only give them the one pic[ture] we want."

The First Family's appearances required careful planning. By the end of the first term, Pat would travel to 23 foreign countries and 107 American cities, Tricia to 3 foreign countries and 65 U.S. cities, and Julie to 4 foreign countries and 84 U.S. cities. The Nixons appreciated Lyndon Johnson's "gift" authorizing the use of military jets for the First Family. Security concerns, scheduling demands, and the desire for privacy kept the First Family away from commercial flights. This shift made the First Lady's operation more formal, more systematic, and more imperial.

Dick was obsessed with the way he appeared to "history." His exaggerated sense of decorum intensified his long-standing aversion to public displays of affection. Stilted interactions with his wife fed the popular perception of the two Nixons as "automatons." Now, at a time when even the perfect television couple, Mike and Carol Brady, shared a bed, separate bedrooms in the White House, at Key Biscayne, and in San Clemente set tongues wagging. Dick's fear of acting undignified would encourage speculation that his marriage with Pat was loveless, drained by the years of loss.

These perceptions would vex Nixon. He often was told that Pat was a "great asset," and her solo trips would reflect well on him. Yet while his wife often made him look good, their marriage often made him look bad.

Their many responsibilities spun Pat and Dick off into different orbits. They logged very little time together during their White House years. The few times the Eisenhowers communicated via memo, their tone was ironic, but the Nixons often communicated that way. After moving into the White House, for instance, "The President" sent a memo to "Mrs. Nixon" regarding "RN's room." Dick informed his wife of twenty-eight years that the President "needs a bigger table on which he can work at night. The table which is presently in the room does not allow enough room for him to get his knees under it."

In addition, the President and the First Lady often communicated through their staffs. During a morning briefing, Dick might tell Haldeman to have his secretary Rose Mary Woods "call PN" to inform her that the President was planning to go to Camp David. Pat had a testy relationship with Haldeman, the President's official "wife." In a White House obsessed with public relations, Haldeman and his men encroached on the First Lady's traditional domain. The President made his chief of staff, for example, worry about the distribution of Christmas cards and gifts to Nixon's relatives. The personal notes that Mamie Eisenhower distributed haphazardly, Nixon's men organized dispassionately.

Dick always withdrew from Pat when he was overworked or anxious; in the White House, he was perpetually overwrought. When he relaxed, Dick preferred to bask in his millionaire friend Bebe Rebozo's adulation instead of navigating the more nuanced relationship with Pat. The Nixons left most White House dinners by eleven o'clock at night, ostensibly to accommodate guests who would not leave until the President did. Dick usually then returned to work. Hours after the Nixons left one state dinner, Julie saw her mother standing at the top of the Grand Staircase, still dressed. "She was swaying to the faint sound of music coming from the Grand Foyer where some of the guests were still enjoying the dancing."

Usually, though, Pat was too busy to be lonely. "I looked at each day in the

White House as a new day," she said. "I didn't think about the day before. I just accomplished what needed to be done." This philosophy of denial buried the pain of the past and neutralized the pain of the present.

Lady Bird Johnson had tried to free her successor from any expectations. Nevertheless, the new consensus demanded that a First Lady find a "project." A week after his inauguration, Nixon told Haldeman to have the chief domestic policy adviser, John Ehrlichman, "get PN going on *her* program." Such reductionism insulted Bird; she had tried to launch a crusade, not a sideshow. Pat, meanwhile, was not a crusader by nature. "I just want to go down in history as the wife of the President," she insisted during the campaign. She did not want to undertake one "Project A."

Mrs. Nixon spent hours each day answering her mail. An average week brought in 2,200 letters; other weeks could bring in as many as 3,500. Aides had to be familiar with the federal bureaucracy, the President's programs, and the First Lady's "policies and principles," the First Family staff manual directed. Many citizens credited the First Lady with solving their problems. This care with correspondence reflected Pat's Capitol Hill roots, where such constituent services were essential. For decades, Americans had been turning to the First Lady's office for help. Finally, a First Lady responded.

Pat's old-fashioned ways upset reporters. Mrs. Nixon "is very busy, but all she's doing is running a parade of groups through to serve them tea and cookies," Liz Carpenter complained. "Eighty-five newswomen" needed "real" news to get published or get aired.

The First Lady's benign pursuits solidified her image as "Plastic Pat," the "tragic epitome of the captive political wife." The term described a woman who bent to her husband's whims, yet appeared inflexible and lifeless. The nickname echoed students' rejection of mass-produced artifice, as well as feminists' repudiation of housewives. In criticizing the First Lady, reporters also demonstrated their hatred for the President. They wondered whether Pat's "feminine spirit [had] been burned out by that long climb beside Dick Nixon to 1600 Pennsylvania Avenue."

Pat had been performing the same script for decades. For some members of the media, it was now obsolete. In 1970, in the *New York Times Magazine,* Judith Viorst claimed to speak for the "many people" who recoiled from "the public Pat," asking, "Who is this woman who has yet to be caught with a smudge or a spot or a wrinkle, whose hair never blows in the breeze?" It was too threatening for Viorst and many other radicals to believe that Pat Nixon might be happy. Viorst jeered, "How many women—in Middle or any America—would want her life?" Viorst and her "sisters" would have been appalled by the real answer.

"Plastic Pat" had trouble "humanizing" her husband, who was also skewered for being unreal. "If the President does have an unseen human side . . .

it is a desperately held secret," John S. Carroll wrote in the *Baltimore Sun* three months after Viorst's outburst. Such writers concluded that because Pat and Dick did not reveal their love in public, they did not love each other at all. No matter how many close friends characterized the Nixons' relationship as "warm and loving," most reporters described them as "people who have lost whatever they once had between them." The Nixons were chided for being undemonstrative—and, even worse, boring.

Increasingly, reporters focused on their subjects' inner lives. The growing appetite for "all news, all the time" demanded more filler while the "adversary culture"'s assault on objectivity and "the establishment" created a more penetrating journalism. In 1968, the *Washington Post* changed its "for and about women" section into a "Style" section. Ben Bradlee did not want to chronicle matrons' activities; he wanted to explore "how men and women lived" during a time of cultural ferment. The new liberal elite was now more newsworthy than the older, conservative generation. Reading the New Journalism of Tom Wolfe, Jimmy Breslin, and Norman Mailer, watching the innovative underground press, reporters "jazzed up" their own writing. Many celebrities obliged by revealing themselves, but traditionalists and politicians resented these invasive lines of inquiry.

With no Kennedyesque sexual escapades to reveal, journalists blasted the Nixons' reserve. Dick said, "Pat is really a very shy person. She steels herself for the public bit and, like other people when they're doing what doesn't come naturally, perhaps she puts up an extra-bold front. She may seem more composed, even cool, than someone careless and easy about meeting the public." Pat dismissed the "new journalism" and the new belief in "letting it all hang out." She clung to her traditional faith in appearances and actions. "I think people are able to judge others by what they do," she said. "That's what's important, not character analysis and personality assessment."

Reporters searching for a colorful political spouse built up Martha Mitchell, the wife of Attorney General John Mitchell. Martha Mitchell was outspoken, ebullient, honest, and photogenic, as well as unstable, manic, and alcoholic. These traits made her a superstar in the new Washington. Journalists starved for a colorful personality encouraged her. Her attacks on student protesters, Vietnam war critics, and Washington hypocrisy made headlines. By the end of 1970 she enjoyed name recognition among 76 percent of Americans, a level 58 points higher than the secretary of state. By the end of 1971, she would rank eighth on Gallup's list of most admired American women. Reporters saw a "delightful" "live-wire celebrity" with "star quality" who shared their commitment to "unfettered expression." Pat saw an erratic woman who did not realize when the media mocked her and whose mental deterioration was furthered by all the attention. Pat snubbed Martha Mitchell, even as Dick applauded her pluck.

Attacks on Pat infuriated the President. Calling his wife "too good to be true" acknowledged that "she happens to have the virtues" her critics lack, he fumed. She had "guts, character, determination"—the traditionally masculine qualities Dick most desired in himself. Nixon claimed that his wife and daughters took the criticism "much harder" than he did. Reporters "don't bother me," he insisted, despite having "the most unfriendly press in hist[ory.]" As usual, Dick expressed his deepest emotions through his wife and daughters.

Eventually, Pat embraced "volunteerism" as her project to still her critics and appease her husband. Dick's inaugural address had asked Americans to enlist "in those small, splendid efforts that make headlines in the neighborhood newspaper." Dick selected the popular former football coach Bud Wilkinson to quarterback the volunteer drive. The Nixons trusted individuals to solve problems; they would showcase "small projects" rather than the "large Federal projects" the Johnsons loved. Their commitment to fostering individual volunteers was as central to their critique of the Great Society as the notion of beautification was to the Johnsons' vision.

Championing volunteerism allowed Pat to repudiate feminism in a genteel way. Echoing her husband, she begged "every woman in the United States" to engage in "those small, splendid efforts that can turn the power of woman into positive human values." Saying that "there is in a woman's mind and heart the power to change the world" implied that women did not have to burn their bras to improve society. Pat appealed to the "silent majority" of white-gloved ladies in the heartland. They welcomed Pat's message that they could lead meaningful lives without becoming liberated. "Few pursuits are more feminine or more fitting for a First Lady," the president of a hospital auxiliary in Middletown, New York, cheered.

The First Lady's call for volunteerism suffered most from a lack of focus. Pat and her aides scurried about, helping poor kids here, elderly widows there, dabbling in literacy crusades, urban planning, postal academies for inner city education, and environmentalism. But after a year in office, Pat's staff director, Connie Stuart, had to turn down a $100,000 donation from Dick's patron William Marriott for Mrs. Nixon's projects, "since most of them haven't even gotten off the ground."

The push for volunteerism did, however, silence some of the First Lady's critics by getting her on the road. In mid-June of 1969, Pat and Julie visited ten "vest pockets of volunteerism" in the far West. Anticipating the President's call for a "New Federalism" that summer, Pat called these local programs "the answer to our problems here in America." Elated reporters tried to encourage more trips; all of a sudden, "plastic Pat" became a "model of warmth and graciousness." Meanwhile, Pat continued doing what she had always done. "If she keeps up the pace . . . she could possibly provide Richard Nixon with another, Republican version of F.D.R.'s Eleanor," Lenore Hershey wrote in *Ladies' Home Journal.* This fantasy was the news hens', not the Nixons'.

For all the talk about Pat being a "traditional" First Lady, this trip *was* modern. As her husband did with the Great Society, Pat conserved Lady Bird Johnson's innovations by imitating her predecessor. Road trips became a part of the First Lady's routine, and Pat participated in "pseudo events"—stunts staged for media coverage—to advance the President's policies and score political points. Each "working trip" had an "overall objective." Pat had to "be photographed in situations that would identify her" with various issues, one aide noted. If she visited a strip mine, she cared about the environment; if she visited an art museum, she cared about culture. Gone were the days of Eleanor Roosevelt freelancing against her husband's wishes or Bess Truman's and Mamie Eisenhower's splendid isolation in the White House or elsewhere.

At the White House, as the President explained on "60 Minutes," Pat brought to entertaining "a touch that only a woman can give." For the public, he sighed the world-weary sigh of the American husband and said, "My advice is often asked, but not very often is it taken." In fact, Dick monitored social affairs obsessively. "In the White House we, of course, must exercise *absolute* control," Haldeman thundered. The President dictated the pace of the service, the flow of the people, the shape of the tables, the duration of the program, the choice of china, and the type of wine. Pat and her aides usually deferred to the President. Pat knew that once Dick identified a problem, her advice would be neither "asked" nor "taken."

White House social life unnerved Dick Nixon, the outsider. He remembered how dowagers in the 1950s sniffed that he was too stiff, and Pat was too "middle class." State dinners were theatrical pieces to showcase the First Family and reaffirm patriotism, faith, and sobriety. He instituted regular Sunday worship services in the White House to appear pious without having to mingle in public. He also concealed the fact that hard liquor was served at social affairs. "For whatever it may be worth, I want you to know that the good people of Kansas are most impressed with the Sunday morning worship services and with the practice thus far of serving no 'hard liquor' at White House functions," Senator Bob Dole wrote the President. The Kennedys might know how to dazzle the intelligentsia; the Nixons knew how to play to Topeka.

The Nixons staged some glittering events, including tributes to the jazz musician Duke Ellington and the artist Andrew Wyeth. Still, the *New York Times Magazine* mocked the Nixons' dinners as awkward. "Pat Nixon is as well organized as an IBM 301 computer," a Washington matron said. "She is also as bland as they come." Haldeman brooded that "the Kennedys got all kinds of credit" for what "they did—we get very little for what we've done." The President designated aides to serve as "anecdotalists," recording Nixon at his most human and most commanding. These tidbits would create an alternate record to counter reporters' tendency to focus on controversies and gaffes. Pat Nixon rarely appeared in these reports, except as a wallflower accompanying her husband.

All these activities placed unprecedented demands on the East Wing. The First Lady's operations had always been informal. In the Johnson White House, Lady Bird, Liz Carpenter, and the social secretary, Bess Abell, were old friends who worked well together. They kept their operation well-focused. The Nixon East Wing was chaotic. The press secretary, Gerry Van der Heuvel, the social secretary, Lucy Winchester, and Pat's personal secretary, Bessie Newton, bickered. No one knew, for example, whether a DAR tea was to be handled by the press office or the social office.

Mixed signals from the West Wing further complicated matters. The East Wing and the West Wing interacted as poorly as the First Lady and the President did. Dick vacillated between boosting his wife as an independent executive and undermining her. He told Haldeman that he wanted to "build her staff *very* big." Yet Dick often schemed with Haldeman about ways to "slip" allies and ideas "into [the] PN operation" without confronting her.

The staff chaos outraged women reporters. Their status in the White House depended on an effective East Wing. In June 1969 *Newsweek* skewered the "badly organized" and "closed" operation, quoting unnamed "news hens" who said that the Nixons need "humanizing" and "here we are panting on their doorstep and they are shutting the door in our faces." The newswomen resented "West Wing males" dominating "East Wing operations," White House aides noted. "More than that, they resent incompetent female staff who, by their failures . . . force the men to be involved."

By August of that year the President realized the "PN thing is a real problem." John Ehrlichman analyzed the East Wing. He advised hiring a "chief of staff" with "clear-cut authority." The public-relations prescription was trickier. Ehrlichman and his men acknowledged that "Mrs. Nixon has the most dramatically exciting job of any woman in the country. It may also be among the most difficult." Since the New Deal, "the Nation has grown to expect their First Lady to be an active public personality and busy with newsworthy affairs." In fact, "If the President is the number one news subject in the country, the First Lady can be number two." First Ladies had to use the press as a "public relations arm." The public wants the First Lady "to be an active leader, but only in those areas deemed appropriate for women." She should not "become an assistant President," Nixon's men warned. They were right.

Nixon's men concluded that Mrs. Nixon possessed "all of the positive qualities which the public applauds." She was ladylike, poised, attractive, and dignified; she was not power-hungry. Her biggest public liability was her obscurity—40 percent of the people surveyed in July 1969 had no opinion about her. The solution was "increased, imaginative exposure" through "a sustained news development program for Mrs. Nixon." The First Lady had to start making news while publicly shunning power. In the age of mass media, it was indeed a winning formula.

Ehrlichman's assistant Charles Stuart noted that "Mrs. Nixon's role as the President's wife" was "most valuable" but "also the one most neglected." Because Dick often traveled alone, the First Lady did not have many opportunities to humanize her husband before the American people. "They campaigned together for more than 20 years as 'Pat and Dick,'" Stuart noted. "Don't let Mrs. Nixon disappear now that he has won."

Thus the Office of the First Lady became an integral part of the White House operation. The East Wing was no longer a rogue operation improvised by a determined First Lady and a few aides. In line with Nixon's overall expansion of the executive branch, the East Wing was now given thirty employees, a budget, a staff handbook, and a flow chart—with Haldeman and Ehrlichman just below Mrs. Nixon. One person with two titles, both staff director and press secretary, would be in charge. Combining the tasks suited the administration's priority: "favorable publicity" for Mrs. Nixon. As press secretary, this person would be "the official spokesman for the First Family." As staff director, he or she would set policy for the East Wing, work with the West Wing, and supervise the appointments secretary and coordinator of special projects, a director of press relations, the social secretary, the director of social correspondence, the director of social entertainment, and two dozen assistants. The Office of the First Lady became a key vehicle for improving the President's image.

In an administration filled with advertising men, the woman designated to revitalize the East Wing was Constance Stuart, a thirty-one-year-old public-relations executive and the wife of the architect of the renovation, Charles Stuart. The voracious media had to be handled by a professional—not by a matron, not by a news hen. Stuart instituted press briefings twice a week—the first regular briefings since Eleanor Roosevelt's Monday morning sessions. A fourth person would now be injected into the Nixons' "triangle" with Haldeman. Connie Stuart expected that Mrs. Nixon might approach her about a problem "and I could get to Bob, and maybe we could work out whatever the difficulty was before it got to the husband and wife level."

The President summoned Connie Stuart to the Oval Office during lunchtime her second or third day on the job. For half an hour, as the President of the United States ate his cottage cheese and pineapple, he talked about his wife: "She matters to me. She matters professionally, and you work hard, young lady. Make sure you do the right job."

Richard Nixon's vast presidential PR project had engulfed the East Wing. Pat still refused to "have just one project" and sometimes spoke about tackling the environment—a reminder of the continuing criticism that she was too diffuse. Still, things were improving. Pat was third on Gallup's list of most admired women in 1969, behind Mamie Eisenhower and India's Prime Minister Indira Gandhi but ahead of Jackie Onassis, Rose Kennedy, Ethel Kennedy, and Lady Bird.

III

After one year in the White House, both Nixons still felt misunderstood. The press continued to depict him as a stiff loner and often ignored her. Noting that 54 percent of the people approved of Mrs. Nixon and only 6 percent disapproved, Dick called his wife "an asset we should use more."

Critics attacked "the largest, most expensive press or public relations staff ever assembled to promote the public image of a President's wife"—but it seemed to work. Stuart forced the *New York Times* to follow up its claim that Pat bought $19,000 worth of clothing with an article called "Mrs. Nixon's Wardrobe: Effortless Bargains." Mrs. Nixon, with her image-makers' help, began to engender the kind of love her husband never could.

That spring, Stuart's operation paraded Pat on a four-day swing to colleges in March and a two-day trip to Peru in June. Nina Totenberg in the *National Observer* dismissed the student trip as "The Selling of the First Lady 1970," prompting Nixon to order Connie Stuart to "pull the Jewish dame" out of Pat's press pool. Yet both expeditions attracted great coverage and triggered more welcomes for a "new" Pat Nixon who was "warm," activist, and "unwound." Most of the First Lady's "college tour" avoided campuses; rather, she visited with students working on volunteer projects in communities. The trip was part of the President's effort to bypass the protesting minority and reach the "silent majority."

Three months later, Pat's trip to Peru earned even more accolades. During the 1950s Dick and Pat had perfected their globe-trotting routine: He met the leaders, she visited hospitals. During the Nixon administration, though, Pat often traveled alone. An earthquake on May 31 had killed fifty thousand people in Peru. Since a military coup there in October 1968, relations had soured. Instead of sending his controversial vice president, Spiro Agnew, Dick decided that Pat was "ready for another country swing." He wanted to "make a real show of it—supplies, etc.," noting that the trip "must only have one star," his wife. Nixon told Haldeman to "orient" the trip "to TV—not writing press." Pat brought nine tons of supplies and $30,000 in donations, including a "little check from Dick." The trip moved Peruvians, scared the Russians, and impressed Americans. President Juan Velasco Alvarado said, "To have President Nixon send his wife here means more to me than if he had sent the whole American Air Force." *Time* praised "the first such foreign mission ever undertaken by a First Lady."

Pat did not, however, let Dick make all her decisions. She often vetoed proposals, especially for TV specials. She also rebuffed Dick's repeated attempts to commission a biography of her. The press yearned for such integrity in the President—and disdained it in the First Lady.

Tension flowed between the two wings of the White House. Haldeman and Ehrlichman had filled the First Lady's offices with intelligent, assertive women. Stuart tried to make the East Wing more independent; she demanded mess privileges and other perks for more staffers. As the 1972 campaign loomed, the President considered the First Family too important to be left to the East Wing, but few wanted to tangle with the women who worked there.

Both factions were hostile. "The attached schedule proposal went through several hands on the West Side before it arrived on my desk today, but it still is a good idea," Connie would sneer to Mrs. Nixon. When Haldeman wanted professionals to produce the entertainment at receptions, Stuart objected. Haldeman told his aide Alexander Butterfield: "Suggest a meeting with Lucy, Connie, Carruthers, Goode, you & me"—typically, the "girls" were called by their first names, the men by their last names.

Throughout 1971 Haldeman and the President talked about firing Stuart, yet she lasted to the beginning of the second term because Mrs. Nixon wanted her. Gwen King, the director of correspondence, said that Stuart was "persistent and probably bugging people" in the West Wing. "Her job was to do a good job for the First Lady, and she knew what the First Lady wanted."

The lacunae in the Nixons' relationship exacerbated the tension. Dick avoided confrontations with Pat. When Ehrlichman came up with an interesting plan for the Washington mall, Nixon said that he *"must sell PN on it."* "You see the president did not speak to her much," observed Alexander Butterfield. "They would never speak in the helicopter [to Camp David], ever. . . . They lived in separate houses down in Florida." They relied on their staff to resolve problems.

A "passive-aggressive" personality, Pat used her silence effectively. Aides never knew whether her silence reflected oblivion, agreement, or anger. She exploited her husband's fear of conflict and guilt about her predicament to get what she wanted without overstepping her bounds. Pat preferred to deploy Connie Stuart rather than combat the President or his aides directly. As a result, while some considered Pat a cipher, others recognized her genius.

Pat's silence confounded observers speculating about the First Lady's influence on the President. She avoided "questions of big policy, like the war," Stuart noted. While reporters chided Mrs. Nixon for being passive, most Americans still wanted a traditional First Lady. Citizens asked Pat "about Tricia, David and Julie more than anything else." During Stuart's four years in the First Lady's office, "the most requested picture" would be one of the Nixons' three dogs.

Mrs. Nixon was neither as central as Mrs. Johnson and Mrs. Truman nor as peripheral as Mrs. Kennedy and Mrs. Eisenhower. In the White House, she was cut off from her husband more than she ever had been, yet the new logic of the First Couple propelled her into public affairs and public relations. Her many years as his partner gave her standing. Pat offered advice about all kinds of image-making details; Nixon often began his morning meetings with Haldeman incorporating some advice from his wife or responding to a complaint she had. She was just as concerned with politics and appearances as he was. During their rare moments together, though, Dick did not want to talk politics with Pat.

Pat was too loyal to confront her husband in public; she was more effective by affecting disinterest. "I do not think you can have two voices in an official family," Dick said. Pat did privately—and unsuccessfully—push Dick to appoint a woman to the Supreme Court and to help pass the Equal Rights Amendment. In public, however, Pat did the President's bidding.

Nixon venerated women but did not fully respect them. He often praised his saintly mother, his self-sacrificing wife, and his two lovely daughters, but in a way that strengthened his fragile masculine identity. If Hannah Nixon was a saint, her son was a real man in the real world. If Pat and her daughters suffered when he lost, Dick proved his grit.

Nixon appreciated women's political power. As a congressman he appealed to women by praising Pat, and as a senator he backed the Equal Rights Amendment. In 1968 Nixon promised that his administration would not be "blind . . . to the great contributions that women can make." As President, he appointed women to score political points, but he kept them out of his inner sanctum. He mastered the cant of egalitarianism, listing his token appointments while insisting he only hired on merit.

Behind the scenes, Nixon and his men refused to take women seriously. In 1969 Nixon reported to his all-male Cabinet about "a group of women" who protested "our failure to hire enough women." Nixon then asked the Republican National Chairman Rogers Morton, "You want to say something to that, Rog? I told them you were responsible." According to the Cabinet secretary, "Amid the laughter, Morton grimaced and said he thought that was a dangerous responsibility. But the President gave him no relief. 'You, Rog,' he said, 'are in charge of women.'" The changing sexual landscape unnerved Nixon and his "boys club."

As with his campaign to appear warm, Nixon went through the motions but remained unconvincing. Cracks that "I want a woman to be a woman," and rumors that the President joked about how Gloria Steinem looked at a conference, seemed to reveal the "real" Nixon behind the posturing. With women holding only 1.5 percent of the top jobs in the federal government and few key positions in the White House, the President of the National Organization of Women Wilma Scott Heide labeled the Nixon administration "an affluent white male club"—a new kind of political epithet.

Nixon did not recognize sexism as a systemic problem; he dismissed "women's libbers" because women "do all right in this country." Political confusion compounded his ambivalence. He wanted to "make political hay" on the issue and directed Haldeman to "grab [the] ball on the whole women's business. See that women are properly recognized." But he did not know how to keep Republicans' "white-gloved" constituency while wooing the "women's libbers."

Characteristically, Nixon tried to mollify both factions. He employed more women than his Democratic predecessors had, but he celebrated the housewife more enthusiastically than he hired women. At a time when Pat was most estranged from his work, Dick resurrected her image as an equal partner. He defined "being a political leader's wife" as "a profession" and called Pat "a high-ranking executive in the Nixon organization." He was "proud of the women in our Administration who don't hold office but hold the hands of the men who do." He publicized occasional working sessions he held with the Cabinet husbands and wives.

Just as women were rejecting the subordinate status as the "wife of," Nixon and other men tried to bolster it. While most feminists complained that wives remained subordinate, others applauded female influence, however acquired. Barbara Bush would remember one Cabinet spouse meeting when her husband was Nixon's United Nations ambassador as "the silliest thing in the world. . . . we felt like dolts—sitting in the back row."

Publicly, Pat agreed with Dick that the women's issue was overblown. "Women have equal rights if they want to exercise them," she proclaimed in 1969. "I just don't feel there's any discrimination." Pat's benign pro-womanism led Nixon and his men to cast her as the "First Woman," the spokesman for feminine self-respect. The First Lady could help divide the women's movement at a time when moderate women complained that feminists refused "to separate specific women's rights issues, which a majority of females can support, from broad ultraliberal social philosophy."

Nixon preserved Pat's credibility as the First Woman by encouraging her disagreement on some issues. She visited day care centers—a bold move when many still viewed day care as a license for maternal neglect. He also had Haldeman "get a story out" that Pat and the girls were the "strongest advocates" for a woman on the Supreme Court. Even if he did not appoint a female justice, women would know they had friends in the White House.

Nixon's Supreme Court maneuvers were better received in the press than at home. When the President nominated two male justices on October 21, 1971, Pat confronted him. Finally, Dick waved her off, saying, "We tried to do the best we could, Pat." That evening, Haldeman told his boss that the announcement "scored another ten strike." The President replied, "Well, probably so, except for my wife, but boy is she mad."

The President was equally crafty on the delicate question of the Equal

Rights Amendment. In 1951, when the ERA was an antidiscrimination statute, Nixon found it easy to co-sponsor it. But the rise of feminism generated a backlash. Nixon—and millions of others—feared that the amendment would be a Trojan horse, imposing unwanted social changes behind benign language. Now he wondered how vigorously to embrace it.

On February 1, 1972, after the House passed the amendment and the Senate Judiciary Committee began hearings, Julie and Pat spoke with Dick about the ERA. Following the Nixon family protocol for addressing important issues, Julie wrote her father a note demanding vigorous support for the amendment. The next morning, Nixon's secretary Rose Mary Woods wrote to John Ehrlichman: "Last night the President asked that I again send you a note saying 'we absolutely must push this Women's Rights Amendment.' This was after a discussion with Mrs. Nixon and Julie."

But the President stalled. Eventually he sent a letter supporting the ERA to the Republican leader Hugh Scott four days before the Senate approved the amendment. Once it passed Congress, however, Nixon refused to pressure individual states.

Julie's appeal to her father on the ERA reflected the Nixon daughters' intense involvement in their father's administration. Many supporters in 1968 told Nixon they approved "your adherence to your sacred marriage vows" and the way "your wife and daughters were examples of admirable womanhood, suitable for residence in the White House." Americans "want to think that" the President is "a human guy who likes his wife and kids and a good time," Nixon acknowledged. The Nixon girls were proud to be "square." Both Tricia and Julie knew how to parade around as what *Newsweek* called "the embodiment of most of the ideals embraced by Mr. Nixon—wholesomeness, loyalty to family and country, piety and old-fashioned all-American *goodness*."

The Nixon girls could not go overboard in embracing traditional values. "They should not be portrayed as paragons of virtue, because in this day and age paragons are not popular," Stuart warned Haldeman. In the 1960s, what historian John Demos calls "an 'anti-image' of the family" had emerged: "Domestic relationships look dangerously like an encumbrance, if not a form of bondage inhibiting the quest for a full experience of self." Nixon therefore tolerated some dissent from his daughters to enhance their credibility. Tricia admitted that women endured discrimination. Asked if she thought her father was appointing enough women, Julie said "No, I don't. And neither does my mother." To soften the blow, Julie called feminists too "strident" and accused them of "alienating a lot of women and most of the men."

The Nixon children were particularly important in an administration with a shy President and a reserved First Lady. By proving that they had not been reduced to "appendages to his career," they rehabilitated the President.

As a result, their outings received a "full effort" from the East Wing, including briefings beforehand and a "press bus, wire care and press advance woman" on site, Connie Stuart assured Haldeman. While they often sounded alike, Tricia and Julie were different. Tricia, according to the President, was more of an "introvert," while Julie was "an extrovert." Despite her limited public schedule until she graduated from college in the spring of 1970, Julie gradually upstaged her older sister.

In addition to mobilizing White House resources to advance the daughters when they traveled, Nixon had his best men trying to figure out what kinds of jobs his daughters should take. Such official concern illustrated a new level of politicization of the presidential family. In the White House and in the press, the daughters were treated as extensions of the President himself.

The desire to exploit Nixon's daughters, and the considerable East Wing resources their activities required, became clear when the President announced Tricia's engagement in March 1971. Tricia's fiancé was Edward Ridley Finch Cox, a Harvard Law student and a descendant of signers of the Declaration of Independence. Initially Tricia wanted a small wedding, but she soon changed her mind, saying, "We both thought it fitting and appropriate to share it with so many of the American people." The wedding would help reveal Nixon's "human side." Haldeman said the President considered the June 1971 event "the biggest news story going today." Since Nixon and his men had already lost confidence in Connie Stuart—she was "too emotional," the President said—Haldeman designated Alexander Butterfield to "keep a hard look on all the handling of events and publicity."

Connie Stuart half-jokingly encouraged the happy couple "to elope." More than a hundred chefs, florists, seamstresses, painters, calligraphers, and press aides tried to mount a tasteful spectacle with four hundred guests, sixteen hundred reporters, and 60 million TV viewers. The wedding on June 12, 1971 was well-staged and well-received. "It may be the closest thing Americans have, or want, to a royal occasion," Dan Rather declared on CBS. The day went smoothly. The President actually danced with his wife in public.

The wedding solidified the Nixons' image as what Dick would call "America's First Family you can be proud of." The wedding also gave them a chance to reassert old-fashioned traditions focused on love, romance, and place-settings. The Nixon administration scored one of its greatest PR successes.

As they waltzed across the White House floor, Pat and Dick "were beautifully, and simply, happy," the President would recall. Yet just before the wedding, Nixon directed Haldeman "to begin a totally oriented commitment of relating everything we do to the political side, without appearing to do so." The wedding spectacle might charm millions, but it would not appease critics. News of the nuptials would compete on the front page of the *New York Times* with news about a leaked "Vietnam Archive" that would become known as the Pentagon Papers. After two and a half years, Nixon was still haunted by the Vietnam War and the student rebellion.

Pat Nixon built on her achievements with a well-publicized solo tour in August 1971, her first in over a year. Mrs. Nixon visited new park sites created when federal park officials returned 4,249 acres of land to the states. The trip advertised Dick's desire to shrink the federal government, as well as Pat's interest in "improving the quality of life for the American people."

The trip provided footage and an excuse for an hourlong ABC television special, "A Visit with the First Lady." Broadcast in September, the program portrayed Pat as a gracious and assertive First Lady traversing America, running the White House, and relaxing in San Clemente. Virginia Sherwood treated Pat as Dick's emissary and portrayed the Nixon marriage as a warm partnership. Always more functional than sentimental, Dick said he often told candidates, "first pick the right wife, because the wife as a partner in a campaign is an enormous asset. [She] doesn't make as much news . . . but the wife has an enormous impact in bringing the man, the candidacy, to people that the candidate is unable to reach." The First Lady appeared down-to-earth as she hugged children and mugged for the cameras. "I don't have a personal maid who travels with me, because I'm a do-it-yourself person," she said, echoing her theme from the 1950s. Julie praised her mother "for not trying to be made into a certain image, or trying to become an Eleanor Roosevelt." Nixon and his men were so pleased that they pressured ABC to rebroadcast the program.

A month and a half later, after he announced his diplomatic breakthrough with China and his wage and price freeze began to take effect, the President's job approval rating in the polls rose to 54 percent, the highest in a year. Contrasting the "mannequin"-like Pat of the 1968 campaign with the gracious and energetic First Lady of 1971, *Time* proclaimed, "Pat Nixon has changed again." Dick felt that his family PR campaign, his bold moves, and even his occasional abuses of power were bearing fruit.

In December the Nixons tried again to appear warm. "Christmas at the White House with Julie Nixon Eisenhower" marked the third year in a row that the White House became a seasonal broadcast studio. In 1971 Julie took CBS viewers "upstairs" to show that her house is "like any home in the United States with mothers and sons and daughters doing most of the labor and the father coming in at the end for a few final finishing touches." Sporting a colorful smoking jacket he only wore "at Christmas," the President was jocular, just a bit stiff and a touch sweaty on his nose. Here was Nixon as the head of a cozy, devoted family, calculating that his family's love made him lovable.

Looking over the Nixon family's string of successes in the latter half of 1971, Special Counsel to the President Charles Colson told the President that "the image of the First Family as it has recently emerged—warm and appealing—may well be one of the most important political developments of your Presidency." Colson praised the family, and Mrs. Nixon particularly, for finally conveying "the human side of the President" after three frustrating years stymied by the "hostility of the media." Mrs. Nixon "has come across as a warm, charming, graceful, concerned, articulate and most importantly, a very human person. . . . Men often judge other men by the character of their wives." All in all, Colson concluded, "Mrs. Nixon has had a very significant and very positive impact on the country."

IV

Pat was now crucial to the reelection campaign, beginning with a trip to Liberia, Ghana, and the Ivory Coast in January 1972. Pictures of a glowing First Lady wrapped in a bright-blue lappa cloth during a tribal ritual were transmitted throughout the world. Walter Cronkite of CBS stressed the substantive nature of the trip. Pat showed "she was not just the wife of the President of the United States—but her country's official representative," briefed by Henry Kissinger and "carrying a message" from her husband to Liberia's president.

For her efforts, Pat received a love note from Dick, in his fashion. "The TV coverage, particularly by CBS, was outstanding," he cabled. "Everybody here believes sending you on the trip was a ten strike. Tricia, Julie and I are saving all of the good clips for you. Love, Dick."

The trip solidified Pat's image as what the *Philadelphia Inquirer* called "the first lady of diplomacy." "If we can't improve the President's public image in the next 120 days, what do you say we drop him and run Mrs. Nixon instead???" one aide teased. Colson begged the President to use Pat more: "She is an enormous asset. She can do things you can't do; her moves will not be instantly labelled political, as yours would; she has the ability to project warmth and to create empathy." Colson said Pat's trip "has had a far reaching impact in changing the public impression of you and the Administration. The warmth of the First Family and the public affection for Mrs. Nixon, Julie and Tricia can be, if properly developed through the rest of the year, that 'something extra' that makes the critical difference." Pat sent a copy of Colson's memo announcing his "discovery" of the First Lady's potential to her best friend, Helene Drown. Pat scribbled: "Thought you'd be amused at late recognition!"

The First Lady's African journey in January fed the excitement about the Nixons' trips to China in February and the Soviet Union in May. Initially, the President had expected to leave Pat behind. This kind of "big league" diplomacy was for men, especially when the slim, blond, well-coiffed First Lady might appear too "bourgeois" for Chinese tastes.

But Pat lobbied to go to China. Dick realized "the picture of the American President being received by a million Chinese is worth 100 times the effect of the communique." The President told Haldeman and Kissinger that "Mrs. Nixon would provide one opportunity for getting 'people pictures' that would be very difficult to get otherwise." Haldeman noted that "if she is not along, he will have to go out and make more of an effort for contact with the people for picture purposes." In an age of media diplomacy, the First Lady was "good for TV etc."

Pat knew her place. If Pat "goes, she goes solely as a prop," Dick said. In planning her itinerary, Pat sought out "events interesting for TV coverage." "Of course, I wouldn't say anything to spoil the good work Dick has done," she told reporters. "My role is a supporting one."

Richard Nixon called his Peking visit "the week that changed the world." He had demonstrated his "unusual world statesman capability" and what he called "the personal qualities of the man," meaning himself. Pat sparkled in China; her hosts were restrained but gracious. She loved "every minute of it," as she visited a glass factory, a people's commune, and a children's hospital. Publicly, the defining moment of the summit came when the Nixons visited the Great Wall of China. The photograph of the beaming presidential couple in fur-lined coats, towering over their Chinese hosts while standing on the enduring symbol of Chinese xenophobia, illustrated the great breakthrough. Pat's presence helped Dick get the picture he needed.

By the end of June, the East Wing had collected dozens of tributes to the First Lady who "pictorially . . . stole the show" from her husband "in China and Russia." Nixon's long-term strategy was succeeding; Pat's TV exposure made her the object of fascination. Dozens of smaller, more conservative newspapers profiled her. These articles found the First Lady warm, friendly, and "average . . . a typical example of our femininity at its best. She isn't too sleek and too chic," the *Sioux Falls Argus-Leader* said. Pat was "ideal," neither "a bit much for many tastes" as Mrs. Kennedy was or "ineffective" as Mrs. Johnson was. As always, it was easier to define what Americans did not want in a woman or a First Lady than to identify what they did want. In 1972 a Republican politician, Margaret Heckler, would call Pat "the No. 1 liberated woman." These missives from the heartland illustrated the gap between the "Washington gals'" liberal assumptions and the "silent majority."

In publicizing his wife and children, Nixon deliberately politicized them. By July the First Family was at the center of the President's reelection efforts; Julie and Tricia had appeared on TV shows covering an estimated "75% of the nation's major media markets." After Labor Day one pretense was dropped: the Nixon family travels were billed to the campaign. Between the convention and the end of October, Julie would travel 38,234 miles; Tricia, 33,445 miles; and Pat, 22,375 miles.

In a mark of journalism's new cynicism, reporters often debunked the First Family efforts while reporting them. "President Nixon continues to stay away from any active campaigning, but today Mrs. Nixon went on a six-day tour," NBC reported in September. "She said she wants to bring the White House to the people, [but] another way to say it is she's campaigning for the reelection of her husband."

Still, the surrogate strategy worked. Often the networks and newspapers reported the President's nonpartisan activities, then "twinned" stories about Mrs. Nixon with the Democratic nominee, George McGovern. Thus the President appeared presidential and the First Lady took on the challenger.

The Republican National Convention in August sometimes felt like a "Sadie Hawkins" rally, devoted to the First Lady instead of the President. A Republican National Committee Women's Division brunch at the Fontainebleau Hotel in Miami Beach honored the First Lady. The theme was "Women of Achievement." Nixon's top women appointees modeled "replicas of inaugural gowns" and were "escorted by high administration officials," meaning men. The Nixon camp still did not know how to reach out to feminists.

The convention's ten-minute video "Tribute to the First Lady" praised Pat Nixon as the ideal woman: "Out of her desire to serve . . . she emerged as a force in her own right." Actor Jimmy Stewart's twangy narration celebrated the Nixon "partnership. . . . She believes in him, she's always there. Companion, helpmate, campaigner." The closing shot offered a rare shot of the Nixons on the beach, with Pat's head cradled on Dick's shoulder.

Fittingly, Mrs. Nixon received her most enthusiastic ovation alone, her face beaming, her arms outstretched, her hair perfectly in place. As Republicans cheered the transformation of "Plastic Pat" into superwoman, her husband watched alone from Camp David. The President recorded in his diary his proud but hardheaded assessment as the cameras panned from his "graceful and gracious" wife to their smiling daughters and sons-in-law: "No First Family ever looked better than they did. No family looked more the all-American type than they did."

Yet the Nixon efforts were undermining the traditional deference given to First Families. During Pat's first extended solo campaign trip in twenty-six years, a seven-state, 5,500-mile tour to take "the White House to the people," frustrated reporters bushwhacked the First Lady. A "press coffee" in Chicago became a press conference: Reporters grilled her about Vietnam, abortion, amnesty, the Watergate scandal, and equal rights for women. Pat was both too discreet and too disengaged to answer most of the questions. "All I know is what I read in the paper," she claimed, although she conceded she "would be willing to die to save freedom for [the] 17 million people of South Vietnam."

The incident disrupted the lovefest between Pat and the press. The President banned future press conferences, seeing that "it doesn't develop the story that we want." At one of Mrs. Nixon's events shortly thereafter, the host would say, "The only question we will entertain is 'Can we take another picture please?'" Fortunately, by the end of the tour, after Pat endured gale-force winds in Montana, snow in Wyoming, and 102-degree temperatures in California, most reporters again praised her as a "trouper." "I do or die. I never cancel out," the First Lady said.

The Democratic nominee's wife crossed over the line into unabashed political advocacy; Eleanor McGovern's willingness to confront the issues prompted comparisons with an earlier Eleanor. Pat's silence contrasted with her rival's eloquence. "Never before in the history of U.S. politics have the wives of two presidential candidates squared off so directly," a *Time* cover story on the battling ladies proclaimed. "While Eleanor was playing the themes, Pat was off playing the heartstrings in her self-appointed role as Dignified First Lady."

The 1972 campaign vindicated both the President and his First Lady. Together they had captured the great American middle. Eschewing the Johnson example of a joint crusade for justice, they peddled the Eisenhower message of old-fashioned values with Kennedyesque public relations techniques. Millions of Americans in the early 1970s thirsted for the kind of reassurance Dick, Pat, and the rest of the Nixon clan offered. Characteristically, the President also threw in his own Nixonian twist, an ugly undercurrent pitting the Nixons' silent majority against the dreaded McGovernites. This "us versus them" backlash would help destroy his Presidency but shape the contours of American political debate for decades. It would serve as a model for the Reagans' upbeat conservatism and fuel dozens of crusades in local, state, and national politics. In 1972, meanwhile, Dick won the most popular votes ever cast for a candidate, and the second largest number of electoral votes. At the end of the year, Pat headed Gallup's most-admired-woman list for the first time.

The Nixons welcomed 1973. A peace agreement was in sight; Pat could relax a bit while looking forward to retirement. As Dick had noted on election day, "The only sour note of the whole thing, of course is Watergate. . . . This was really stupidity on the part of a number of people."

V

"We shall answer to God, to history, and to our conscience for the way in which we use these years," the President intoned in his second inaugural address. That night, in his diary, Dick expressed his relief that "Pat did not kiss me" after the swearing-in. Sometimes "these displays of affection are very much in place, as was the case election night," but "on this occasion I didn't really think it quite fit." Yet he also complained that Americans still did not perceive him to be warm. "The staff just hasn't been able to get it across and so I am going to have to do all of these things publicly which demonstrates that."

Pat was ready to relax. "I've been campaigning all my life for Dick or somebody else, and I'm not going to do that anymore," she had told Connie Stuart during the campaign. "I want to enjoy my family; . . . I'm going to go out for lunch; I'm going to shop." When Stuart resigned, Pat did not replace her. Pat wanted the East Wing to be an intimate enterprise. She had accepted Ehrlichman's expansion only as long as it was necessary.

Gradually, the staff dwindled. Coral Schmid's position had evolved with the office. As special projects director, she helped Pat shop for a focus; as appointments secretary, she helped the First Family campaign. Now, after she resigned, her positions disappeared. Mrs. Nixon asked Schmid one last time whether there was a good "slogan or phrase for a special project" that would focus the East Wing. "Mrs. Nixon, you care about people. You do not need a special project or a catchy slogan," Schmid insisted.

Pat became her own chief of staff. She supervised a press secretary, Helen McCain Smith, and the social secretary, Lucy Winchester. Gwen King remained in the correspondence office and took over some of Stuart's administrative duties. Where Stuart had a staff of nine, Smith had a staff of three. "It's so quiet in the East Wing you can hear the hiss of a hairspray can," one reporter would write in May.

In paring down her staff, Pat was sending her husband a message; she disliked Dick's dependence on Haldeman. As Julie recalled, Pat and her daughters feared that by the time decisions trickled through the "overworked" chief of staff to "his young aides. . . . Much of the sensitivity and thoughtfulness we saw in my father was squeezed out." Pat realized that Dick would not brook any criticism of his system, but she continued to squabble with Haldeman. Since 1969 she had stopped Haldeman from redesigning Air Force One without adequate space for her and from imposing elaborate uniforms on White House guards. Now Pat scotched Haldeman's plan to consign junior staff members to a small dining room in Camp David. Knowing that it was futile to talk to her husband, Pat and Bebe Rebozo arranged for the President to see the awkward arrangement himself, then order the changes.

The Watergate scandal confirmed Mrs. Nixon's fears about Haldeman. Pat and Dick considered the June 1972 break-in to the Democratic headquarters at the Watergate office complex politics as usual; Dick resented the "double standard" that countenanced Kennedy's wiretaps, Johnson's abuse of the FBI, Roosevelt's and Eisenhower's taping systems. Pat defended Dick as a good man and a great statesman victimized by overzealous aides, hypocritical Democrats, and partisan reporters.

By the spring of 1973 a Senate subcommittee had begun preparing for summer hearings, and presidential counselor John Dean had warned of a "cancer within, close to the Presidency." During Easter vacation in Key Biscayne, Dick contemplated firing Haldeman and Ehrlichman for engineering the coverup. He brooded for hours. Pat tried to comfort him, but he spurned her. While watching a movie one night, Julie blurted out, "Mother's trying so hard to make things right, and you don't realize it. It's hard for her too." Only after the movie ended—and his daughter feared that she had overstepped— did the President admit, "You're right; it's hard for her too. I'll try." Julie thought "because both my parents were very private people, their relation-ship was a delicate, polite one that did not allow for much second-guessing."

On April 30, 1973, the President announced the resignation of Haldeman and Ehrlichman. The "cancer" was malignant; Dick "felt as if I had cut off one arm and then the other." After the speech, the President of the United States shuffled off to bed and muttered, "I hope I don't wake up in the morning."

Usually the President enjoyed fielding phone calls after a speech, but after the April 30 speech, Pat took the phone calls. "She was marvelous; *she* was re-assuring *them!*" exclaimed Paul Keyes, a television producer. "If I had a prob-lem, I'd like my wife to be like Mrs. Nixon." The next day Pat ate lunch at the White House mess for the first time. "She was full of cheer," an aide told a reporter, "and it was a great morale booster."

Her husband's great failure brought Pat back into the center of things. Nixon's presidency would soon hinge on Americans' faith in his integrity. Having constructed them as "props" illustrating his personal side, President Nixon would need Pat and the girls now more than ever.

While maintaining a facade of unity, however, the Nixon family fractured. Tricia and Ed were living in New York, hoping for some privacy. Dick with-drew. He doubted "the girls'" ability to help him in this rough fight, and he was embarrassed.

Three weeks later, the Nixons hosted the largest sit-down dinner ever held at the White House, for returning prisoners of war and their spouses. Nixon, Kissinger, John Wayne, and Bob Hope fêted America's newest war heroes. Irving Berlin led the crowd singing his patriotic ode, "God Bless America." Later, at one o'clock in the morning, Dick summoned Tricia, Julie, and David to the Lincoln sitting room. He asked if he should resign; he had broached the subject three weeks before at Camp David. Then, as now, his family said no. They still believed in his innocence and his mission. He would not mention the subject to them again for over a year.

By the summer, the pattern for the next twelve months had been set. Each new revelation of wiretapping, payoffs, abuse of power, and lies triggered a round of denunciations, followed by a series of denials, retreats, and justifica-tions. Publicly and privately, Dick became more withdrawn and more tense. Pat maintained her chipper facade. Julie emerged as what *Newsweek* called "her father's No. 1 defender."

After the "Saturday Night Massacre" of October 20, 1973, Julie defended her father's "balance." "I really admire him for not taking things in a personal way," she said. "It's a really silly situation, he's feeling sorry for us and we're feeling for him." "Richard Nixon could not be as bad a man as they say if he inspires so much love from his daughter," one Democrat said.

David Eisenhower also assured reporters that his father-in-law was calm and steady. In early 1974, David faced reporters in a press conference. As one of them recalled, they fired a barrage of questions: "Is the President drinking too much, sleeping too little, going to resign, guilty of tax evasion and obstructing justice, in a manic depression, about to suffer the breakup of Patricia's marriage, a friendless loner and tone deaf to advice?" Such questions would have been off-limits only a few years earlier—especially for the President's son-in-law.

As the Watergate story metastasized, Pat became isolated and miserable. The prolonged exposure in this case dwarfed the week-long Checkers crisis, which had soured her on politics for life. By the end, the probe would smear everything the Nixons had built. Jewels from the Saudi Arabian king that an aide neglected to log correctly, tax deductions for Dick's pre-presidential papers, gifts Bebe Rebozo gave to Pat, and the $17 million the government spent running the "Western White House" at San Clemente and the compound in Key Biscayne would all become grist for the reporters' and prosecutors' mills. Tricia's marriage, which was toasted throughout the world in 1971, would set tongues rattling two years later. By April 1974, the more retiring of the Nixon daughters would feel compelled to write in the *Ladies' Home Journal:* "Ed and I *did* pay our proper taxes. We *do* love each other. We are *not* divorcing. We *do* believe in Daddy as ever."

Pat could not even suffer in silence; she was on display whenever she left her private quarters. "Everything's going to be all right," became her mantra. "My mother is at peace with herself," Julie explained. In fact, though, the composure was stoic rather than serene. Over the years she had admitted, "I keep everything in." Pat was not going to start sharing feelings now.

"No matter what I do I can't win," Pat sighed. "If I give the press all the tidbits about people and issues, they would say I was talking too much. And if I give them nothing, they accuse me of . . . being capable only of small talk." Pat was enough of a professional to recognize that this dilemma had nothing to do with Watergate. It was the lot of the political wife.

As one Nixon man after another was disgraced, one perky, loyal, all-American wife after another suffered as well. Only Martha Mitchell publicly expressed the wives' feelings, ranting that the President "knew all about" Watergate. Reporters rallied around their creation, especially as they decided that the revelations vindicated her. UPI's Helen Thomas called her a "heroine." A writer in *McCall's* praised her as a "unique phenomenon: a political wife who has an identity of her own." The reporter wondered why a woman like Martha Mitchell, "who *does* have some needs," was considered crazy while Pat, "having no visible, separate needs . . . qualifies as healthy, normal and mentally sound." Millions of other Americans, including the First Lady, pitied Martha Mitchell. "Moutha" Mitchell divorced, was diagnosed as an alcoholic, and suffered a nervous breakdown.

In January 1974 the President proclaimed that "one year of Watergate is enough." The administration decided Watergate was just another public relations problem. Mrs. Nixon consented to an interview with Walter Cronkite to assure Americans that the President "sleeps well." As every good wife should, Pat Nixon would stand by her man, as Tammy Wynette's now-famous 1968 hit said. A few days later, Tricia and Ed worked the crowds at Lafayette Park across the street from the White House, Julie visited the Environmental Protection Agency—which her father had created—and Pat posed with poster children. Everything appeared normal.

Pat also played up her role as First Housewife. The Arab oil boycott in fall 1973 introduced Americans to fuel shortages and energy conservation. Pat helped advertise the idea "that the conservation of energy begins in the home" and taught housewives how to shop sensibly.

In March 1974 Pat reprised her role as "Madame Ambassador" with a six-day trip to Venezuela and Brazil. NBC's Tom Brokaw said "all of this is part of the White House plan to demonstrate that the President is concerned with other matters than the impeachment investigation." In 1974, all journalistic roads led to Watergate. Reporters covered "the mood of the family" wherever the Nixons went. Pat complained, "It doesn't matter what we're doing—the press is just looking for cracks."

Pat flew from South America to Nashville to meet Dick at the dedication of the Grand Ole Opry. Even this televised event, in the heart of Nixon country, went wrong. Nixon was unusually effusive. He tried out a yo-yo and played "God Bless America" on the piano, followed by "Happy Birthday to You" in honor of Pat's sixty-first birthday. When Dick finished playing, Pat extended her arms to embrace him. Dick rose from the piano, turned away, and walked toward center stage, leaving his wife alone and grimacing.

Nixon's aides had long worried about his tendency to neglect Pat in public. His media expert Roger Ailes advised Haldeman in 1970 that the President "should talk to her and smile at her" more, adding that "women voters are particularly sensitive to how a man treats his wife in public." Still, when the Nixons were more popular, reporters overlooked the mishaps. Now such moments convinced critics that the Nixons' marriage was empty. Despite his family's devotion, Richard Nixon became the embodiment of the neurotic, repressed, loveless American who needed "liberation." Pat told her assistant Gwen King that "the public statement that the President was ignoring her was much more hurtful than the oversights themselves."

Six weeks after Pat returned from South America, President Nixon released transcripts of Watergate-related conversations he had secretly taped.

The tapes "should have been destroyed like love letters," Pat would say. "My mother's greatest regret in the aftermath of Watergate was that my father did not consult her about the tapes before their existence became common knowledge," Julie wrote. "How could any individual survive a public reading of private conversations?" Even though Dick shunted her aside, Pat blamed herself for not saving her husband from himself.

Nixon's exaggerated sense of propriety, combined with his need to swagger behind closed doors, made it essential to hide this public man's private self. Many New Journalists felt vindicated. The tapes justified their focus on the man, not the issues, and their obsession with uncovering the truths behind social appearances. After years of crusading against the student rebels' "adversary culture," Nixon handed them a great victory. The transcripts made the Nixons' "'cloth coat' morality" seem shabby. Even Nixon's friend the Reverend Billy Graham mourned, saying that he found the transcripts "profoundly disturbing. . . . We have lost our moral compass."

Millions abandoned the President. Pat was "puzzled" why Republican leaders did not rally to Dick's side. "No," she said when asked if Dick would resign. "Why should he? There's no reason to." When Helen Thomas pestered her once too often, Pat clenched her fist and snarled: "You know I have great faith in my husband. I happen to love him."

In defeat, Pat continued to reflect well on Dick. While reporters scorned this "lifelong bride of crisis" seeking refuge in "small talk," millions of Americans applauded her. Pat received five hundred letters of support a week, with few condemnations. Four months after her husband resigned, Pat would be the most admired woman in *Good Housekeeping*'s poll of its readers and come in third in the annual Gallup poll, behind Israeli Prime Minister Golda Meir and Betty Ford. Pat Nixon would remain on the *Good Housekeeping* list for the next decade and a half. When she suffered a stroke in 1976, more than a quarter of a million Americans would send her get well cards.

"How can they admire me and say the things they do about Dick?" Pat wondered. In fact, both Nixon-lovers and Nixon-haters sympathized with the First Lady. "Most people . . . do not have an easy life. . . . Pat relates to these people and they to her," Dick would say. Being a political spouse, like being a housewife, no longer seemed glamorous. It was now an "ordeal."

In May 1974 Dick's loyal secretary, Rose Mary Woods, sighed, "If there is a hell on earth, we are living through it now." Sometimes the President insisted on proving his enemies wrong; he negotiated with the Soviets and brokered a Mideast settlement. At other moments he indulged the emotions that had always raged within him, becoming weepy, self-pitying, and sloppy. Even Julie would admit that her father "*was* drinking a little more than he ever had before, but at dinnertime, when he was trying to unwind."

The capital filled with rumors about a drunken President who might start a war to save his mandate. After Vietnam, the student revolt, the rise of investigative journalism, and the revelations of the tapes, anything seemed plausible. As impeachment proceedings in the House of Representatives accelerated, Nixon's chief of staff, Alexander Haig, asked the President's physician to withhold all tranquilizers. Secretary of Defense James Schlesinger remained in Washington; he instructed all military commanders to disregard White House orders lacking his countersignature. Schlesinger "had seen enough so that I was not going to run risks with the future of the United States."

Pat was philosophical. "Politics is a funny business," she had said in 1972, explaining that "you're up one day, down the next." "Dick has done so much for the country," she told Helene Drown. "Why is this happening?" Drown would tell Julie: "Your father never had a better admirer. At times she would tell me she was 'angry' or 'furious' about a decision, but always, overriding it all, was a tremendous respect for him." "In the pre-Watergate years she had seemed fragile," Julie said of Pat. "We had worried about her and wanted to protect her. Now she was the strongest of all."

Nevertheless, Pat could not fulfill her main task. During this final crisis Pat and Dick could not face each other. She opposed resignation, but she began packing their belongings. Dick would say: "With us sometimes, as it is between people who are very close, the unspoken things go deeper than the spoken. She knew what I was going to do." She was too hardened to comfort him; he was too embarrassed to turn to her. In his guilt at disappointing her, then withdrawing from her, Dick would always say that Pat suffered the most.

On August 2, 1974, the President decided to resign. He told Julie, who told Pat. Showing that her faith in Dick was more than an act, Pat asked, "But why?" Julie explained that Dick was about to be impeached. Julie would remember her undemonstrative mother's tearful hug as "perhaps the saddest moment" of the final days. Nixon had spent a lifetime posing as a fighter; now he had to convince himself that resigning was not gutless. Dick showed his family transcripts of the "smoking gun tape" of June 23, 1972, wherein he connived with Haldeman to use the CIA to block the Watergate investigation. On July 24 the Supreme Court had decreed that this tape and others had to be released. Turning to his wife, filled with self-pity, Dick mumbled, "I don't know what I'm going to do, but I know you will all stand behind me."

Despite the evidence, the family convinced Dick to release the tape "and see the reaction to it." Clearly, the isolation had distorted the Nixons' judgment. The June 23 tape destroyed the President's remaining support in Congress; only seven senators would promise to vote against an impeachment conviction.

This time there was no family debate. Dick took charge. He called Rose Mary Woods into his office and asked her to tell the family that he would be resigning. When Dick walked into the solarium on August 7, he noticed his wife's telltale sign of tension—the way she held "her head at the slightly higher angle." She embraced Dick and said, "We're all very proud of you, Daddy." Dick responded stiffly, and a bit abstractly, "No man who ever lived had a more wonderful family than I have."

Against this backdrop of silent suffering punctuated by some bursts of warmth, Pat may have snapped. Rumors claimed that a White House maid heard Pat tell Dick, "You ruined my life." If true, this was a momentary outburst by a woman in pain, not her epitaph for their marriage. Either way, Nixon knew that he had. "Well, I screwed it up good, real good, didn't I?" he told his family.

Richard Nixon's elaborate finale mixed his public and private worlds, building on his experience as the great sentimentalist of modern American politics. That night, when he sat with his family before the speech, he brought in his favorite photographer, Ollie Atkins. "Ollie, we're always glad to see you, but I don't think we need pictures now," Pat said. The President overruled his wife. The resulting picture captured the Nixon clan at the point of crucifixion, all smiling for the camera—except Pat, who is staring lovingly at her husband as if they were still celebrating their 1946 victory. Pat would detest this picture, saying, "Our hearts were breaking and there we are smiling." The old trouper had run out of patience.

The next day, Nixon planned an intimate farewell to the White House staff. The First Lady begged, "Oh, Dick, you can't have it televised." Julie sighed, "She was to the end a private person." Her husband was a public man, suffering with his loved ones through this "public death."

Nixon's farewell displayed the kind of generosity he usually lacked during his political career. With his wife and daughters breathing heavily to suppress their tears, the President urged, "Always remember, others may hate you, but those that hate you don't win unless you hate them, and then you destroy yourself." The President blessed his parents, especially his mother. Yet even now, when it would have been in the spirit of his maudlin meanderings, Richard Nixon could not praise his wife. Helen McCain Smith suspected that "he knew that there is a limit to what Pat can endure—and still keep her head high." Remembering election night in 1960, neither Pat nor Dick could bear another photograph of Pat in tears. Julie thought it had more to do with her father's composure than her mother's; mentioning Pat "would have been asking too much of any man." Judging by his track record, it is perhaps most likely that Richard Nixon forgot. As she returned to California, the overlooked Pat had the unenviable task of consoling him.

Dick would apologize in his memoirs. He claimed that mentioning the family "would be too painful for them and for me." This decision proved yet again that this most private of men was poorly positioned to preside over the nation's transition from a culture of appearances to one of exhibitionism.

Pat's composure during the resignation solidified the impression she had spent five years trying to change. "The image of the plastic Pat may be frozen into the public mind for all time now," *Time* magazine speculated a few months later. Both she and Lady Bird Johnson would be remembered as "brides of crisis." The Johnsons and the Nixons, having tried so hard to represent their nation, would come to epitomize the ugliness, the burdens, and the failure of traditional values.

Pat and Dick, the poor kids from the gritty underbelly of Southern California, mastered the archetypal behaviors of the great American middle only to fail in their attempt to defend them. Feminists considered the old paradigm oppressive; reporters deemed it stale. As a result, Dick's attempt to be a tough guy appeared ruthless, and Pat's attempt to be a benevolent lady appeared masochistic.

This would be Richard Nixon's greatest punishment, for which he could receive no pardon. His disgrace boosted his domestic foes—the loud minority of hippies, reporters, feminists, and New Leftists. The legacy of the self-styled law-and-order President would be one of disrespect for the law and rampant disorder. For many, "Watergate" would offer an easy answer to the perplexing social and cultural dilemmas "the Sixties" generated. It would illustrate why the personal should be political, the press should be intrusive, authority should be questioned, and morality should be recalibrated, as Nixon's conservative revival went into a dramatic, albeit fleeting, eclipse.

The wounds Pat and Dick inflicted on each other healed during their years of exile. Dick said "those first four years in San Clemente were profoundly difficult." The Nixons suffered legal troubles, illness, and depression. At one point, Pat would plead with Julie to leave David alone in Washington to study for his law school exams. She whimpered, "You have only one person to take care of there but two broken people here."

Pat's only solace was her freedom from public life. Never again would she submit to a reporter's scrutiny or be forced to deliver a speech. Dick claimed his only solace came from the opportunity he and Pat finally had "to spend a lot of time together. . . . We've discovered, in this time of crisis, that we need each other. . . . I don't know what history will say about me, but I know it will say that Pat Nixon was truly a wonderful woman." Dick would spend the rest of his life trying to rehabilitate his image; Pat would remain universally popular until her death.

6

THE FORD INTERREGNUM AND THE
PRIMAL SCENE OF PRESIDENTIAL
POLITICS

The nation never elected Gerald R. Ford to the Presidency or even the vice presidency—Richard Nixon appointed him under the terms of the 25th Amendment after Vice President Spiro Agnew resigned in October 1973. Many Americans never forgave Ford for pardoning his predecessor within weeks of becoming President. Today his brief interregnum is often overlooked—Stephen Skowronek's recent analysis of presidential politics mentions the thirty-eighth President of the United States by name only once in 446 pages. Yet President Ford was so successful in helping the nation heal after Watergate that he came within one percentage point of beating Jimmy Carter in 1976. And during Ford's two-and-a-half-year stint, his wife, Betty, became the most controversial First Lady since Eleanor Roosevelt. Peddling their marriage as a "normal" partnership struggling with the challenges of raising a modern family, Betty Ford inserted herself at the flash point of the country's social upheavals. Rather than repudiating the new values sweeping the nation, she embraced them. In so doing, she may have cost her husband the White House in 1976 and the historical respect his administration is now often denied.

The Fords were mismatched. He was "square," whereas she was hip. He loved peppy classics from *Oklahoma!;* she liked melancholy pop songs, including "Bridge Over Troubled Water." Still, the marriage worked. As Jerry would explain, "A successful marriage cannot thrive on simply a mutuality of interests. . . . There must be understanding, compassion and emotion which fit under the umbrella of love." Through his workaholism, her breakdowns, his condescension, and her anger, Betty and Jerry remained in love.

By 1975 Betty Ford had emerged as an outspoken feminist activist. Her candor unsettled the President and his advisers. They feared alienating conservatives who were already disenchanted by the fall of Vietnam, the liberal beliefs of Vice President Nelson Rockefeller, and Ford's commitment to the Nixon-Kissinger policy of détente with the communists. The First Lady's adoring press coverage only complicated matters. East Wing aides felt emboldened. West Wing aides smoldered.

The two factions clashed at Camp David in June 1975. Eric Rosenberger, the director of the press advance staff, told Sheila Weidenfeld, the First Lady's brash press secretary, "We run the show." The White House needed "a unified effort, not 2 operations going in different directions." The President and First Lady had competing needs. As Rosenberger would remind his staff, "Our job is to cover the President, not Mrs. Ford."

Betty moved into the White House in August 1974 with a vague feeling of solidarity for her "sisters" and a growing awareness of women's special burdens. When pressed about the push for equality, she acknowledged that "some women are a lot smarter than men" and should enjoy equal opportunities at work. But she always added, "If a woman wants to be a homemaker and wife and mother, that's fine too." Along with her husband, Betty Ford supported the Equal Rights Amendment but would not crusade for its passage. At first, she believed lobbying was beyond her jurisdiction.

Women's issues were tricky. In his first speech to Congress, Ford vowed to be "the President of black, brown, red and white America, of old and young, of women's liberationists and male chauvinists and all the rest of us in between"—a mark of how quickly feminism had inserted itself into the debate, and how polarized both extremes appeared to most Americans. It often seemed that the more influential feminist ideas became, the less popular feminists became.

Millions of women like Betty were becoming independent without calling themselves feminists. *Time* would conclude that in 1975 feminism "transcended the feminist movement" and achieved "general—and sometimes unconscious—acceptance." A Harris poll found that 63 percent of Americans surveyed favored "most of the efforts" to "change women's status in society," with only 25 percent opposed. In 1970 a similar poll found Americans divided, with 42 percent in favor and 41 percent against.

With Betty "drilling in" to Jerry that "53 percent" of the registered voters were women, he recognized them as a formidable force. He endorsed the ERA and International Women's Year. He strengthened the "Office of Women's Programs" that Richard Nixon established in 1973 as a beachhead for women in the West Wing.

Betty's interest in women's issues had intensified. As with millions of others, her "consciousness raising" resulted from her entry into the work force, as it were. Her role as First Lady drew her into the fight for the ERA, especially after her bout with cancer in 1974 taught her the power of her new position.

Betty checked into the hospital on Friday night, September 27. The next morning, as the President was working in the Oval Office with his aide Bob Hartmann, the phone rang with news that the surgeons had removed Betty's right breast and lymph nodes. The President excused himself briefly, then returned to his desk, his face contorted and his eyes red. Echoing the burgeoning movement toward male sensitivity, Hartmann said, "Go ahead and cry. Only strong men aren't ashamed to cry. You're among friends." "Bob, I don't know what I'd do without her," the President of the United States sobbed. Hartmann reassured his boss, "Just thank God they found it so soon." Then the men returned to themselves. "It was over," Hartmann recalled. "We went back to work."

Jerry's reaction proved his devotion. "I had never seen my husband so upset," Betty would say. At the hospital, the Fords did not discuss the breast removal: "Because we couldn't undo what had to be done, there really wasn't much sense in discussing it." Jerry embraced Betty and reassured her; now, she would characterize their troubled union as "an ideal marriage."

The Fords publicized intimate moments to illustrate Betty's recovery. After one visit, Jerry marked Betty's progress by playing the harried husband, saying she "reminded me of things I have neglected around the house." Such glimpses of the playful First Couple eased the nation's anxiety.

While presidential illnesses had attracted in-depth coverage since Eisenhower, First Ladies' ailments had been covered discreetly until now. In the age of full disclosure, the White House was candid, the press insatiable. The Fords' personal trauma became a national event; Betty would receive more than fifty thousand cards. The Fords were both humanized and glorified, struck by common tragedy yet made to appear larger than life.

Betty's illness marked a growing sophistication about public health. A disease so scary that many whispered its name was partly destigmatized. Rather than focusing on the fear of illness, on the embarrassment of losing a breast, Americans talked about prevention. Checkups increased by 300 to 400 percent. A spokesman for the American Cancer Crusade reflected the optimistic American approach to disaster, saying, "It's a tragedy for Mrs. Ford, but she may have saved an awful lot of women's lives." Among the women getting mammograms was Mrs. Nelson Rockefeller, the wife of Ford's new vice president. Within a month, Happy Rockefeller had also undergone a mastectomy,

Overnight, Betty Ford became a national hero for having "saved many lives," for her "remarkable . . . spirit," for teaching about faith in God, love of family, and the need for personal vigilance about one's health. Betty was justifiably proud of her gift to millions of women. The experience would define her tenure as First Lady. "Lying in the hospital, thinking of all those women going for cancer checkups because of me, I'd come to recognize more clearly the power of the woman in the White House." The power was educational, not political; it stemmed from her fame rather than her influence. "I felt I hadn't even begun to work effectively for the causes—the Equal Rights Amendment, mental health, the fight against child abuse, the fight against the abuse of old people and retarded people—that I cared about." As a cancer "survivor," Betty Ford felt "reborn." She left the hospital determined to use this extraordinary platform.

Betty agreed to chronicle her experience for the 6.8 million readers of *McCall's* in its February 1975 issue. But aides said that she tired of entering a room and having everyone glance at her chest, searching for signs of the missing breast. She ended her article by declaring, "This is the last time I will discuss the mastectomy. I want to get back to the support for fields I have previously committed myself to. I can't afford to let this episode become the focal point of my life. I had no choice; it was something I *had to do.* It is over now." It was time to shape her role as First Lady.

It was also time for this unelected wife of an unelected president to insert herself in national debates over personal and political events in unprecedented ways. When Betty returned to work, she reevaluated what one aide called the "policy and practice" that kept First Ladies from becoming "involved in pending legislation." Betty's rhetoric shifted as well. She still preferred to speak about "a liberated woman" rather than a "feminist," but she was bolder: "A liberated woman is one who feels confident in herself, and is happy in what she is doing. She is a person who has a sense of self. I think it all comes down to freedom of choice."

Only five more states had to ratify the Equal Rights Amendment by 1979 for it to become part of the Constitution. In 1975 two consultants, Doug Bailey and John Deardourff, asked Mrs. Ford to help refute the charge that Republicans opposed the amendment. Sheila Weidenfeld, the First Lady's press secretary, saw that the ERA campaign could "defin[e] Mrs. Ford's areas of interests." She told Betty, "Your stressing how much you enjoy being a feminine wife and mother—and still believe in the ERA—would greatly help." And so the First Lady went to work.

Betty's efforts received maximum attention with minimal energy. She sent a few letters and called a handful of wavering legislators—one in Illinois, two in Missouri, and so on. In her low-key, midwestern way, she never told them how to vote. She assured one Missouri legislator: "Oh, I'm not a wild-eyed liberal on this. I enjoy being a wife and a mother and all those things." "I must admit I was complimented," said the Illinois state senator. "I have never been called by a First Lady before."

Many of Betty's targets resented her effrontery. Three of the four senators she approached in Florida would not even return her call. White House mail ran three to one against Betty's lobbying. Her critics condemned her for fostering a "dangerous, anti-family proposal" that would put American girls in unisex toilets, communal showers, and mortal combat. They attacked her for abusing her position, sacrificing her dignity, intruding on states' prerogatives to ratify amendments, and "using taxpayers' dollars to lobby" because she phoned from the White House. For the first time since Eleanor Roosevelt's day, pickets gathered on Pennsylvania Avenue to protest against the First Lady. The signs demanded: "BETTY FORD GET OFF THE PHONE!"

Betty's ERA escapades proved to many White House aides that First Ladies should be seen and not heard. When a state did not ratify the amendment, she and her husband looked weak. "BETTY FORD FAILS TO SWAY ARIZ. ON ERA," one headline read. Even worse, Betty's activities were costing the President votes. One Republican woman warned, "Betty is becoming very unpopular with many women because of her constant promotion of the ERA."

The attacks solidified Betty's identification with feminism. She defended her "right" as a citizen and a woman "to express" an opinion. Echoing Sojourner Truth, the slave who demanded equal rights, Betty Ford justified her feminism by saying, "Why not? I'm a woman, aren't I?" Besides, the phone calls were covered by a flat rate. Forgetting her initial, First Lady–like reticence, she vowed "to stick to my guns."

Many editorialists demanded "Speech Freedom for Mrs. Ford." Betty's defenders tailored the role of the First Lady to feminist sensibilities and media needs. Utilizing the language of the women's movement and of the therapeutic culture, the *Providence Bulletin* said that Mrs. Ford's "self-expression gives added dimension to the function she serves. The individual emerges from the shadows of the President's alter ego." "To deny her the right to address an issue of national concern would be to relegate her, at least symbolically, to the second-class status that the ERA will end," the conservative *Los Angeles Times* argued. An Ann Arbor newspaper rejoiced that Betty refused to "play 'wife of the president' and let hubby take the stands on important issues." Modern First Ladies, it seemed, were supposed to be fighting for "human dignity and freedom" rather than simply "setting fashion trends and . . . decorating the White House."

At Sheila Weidenfeld's urging, Mrs. Ford confronted the critics by admitting that the White House mail was mostly negative. "Those who are for

[ERA] sit back and say 'good for her—push on,' " Betty scolded. Soon, hundreds thanked her for inspiring them "to stop sitting back." Many women felt close to the candid First Lady. "Consider yourself hugged," one woman wrote. Within three weeks, "support mail" outnumbered "anti-ERA" mail by three to one.

The chairwoman of the National Organization for Women, Karen De-Crow, claimed she was "absolutely delighted" with Mrs. Ford's leadership but still felt ambivalent. "As a feminist," she said, "I would be happiest if there was a woman as President speaking from the White House." As more First Ladies would take on this role as "first woman," feminists would continue to squirm. Depending on "the wife of" someone rather than a woman who achieved on her own was embarrassing but useful.

It was hard to balance the needs of the married couple and the political team. The President needed support on a touchy issue like abortion; his wife needed to express herself. The role confusion was ceremonial as well. At the signing of the executive order proclaiming International Women's Year, protocol had the President of the United States seated as Mrs. Ford approached—even though polite husbands usually stood for their wives. Betty bent down to kiss Jerry; remembering where they were, however, she stopped and extended her arm for a handshake. Still seated, he clasped her right hand with his left hand, making for a more intimate touch than a formal handshake without violating propriety.

After the ERA push in early 1975, Weidenfeld began arranging more interviews for Mrs. Ford. The First Lady now had something to say, but deciding where to say it was not easy. Barbara Walters wanted Mrs. Ford to lead a tour of the private quarters for "Today," but the First Lady was "a disaster before 10:00 A.M." CBS wanted her to appear on "Face the Nation," but the format was "too formal." Weidenfeld preferred "60 Minutes." This CBS "magazine" heralded the revolution in television news toward longer, more "investigative" pieces. Its producer Don Hewitt wanted to "take informational programming out of the ratings cellar" by focusing on "current manners, morals and mores." Networks would learn that news did not have to be a money-losing public service. First broadcast periodically, "60 Minutes" would secure a regular weekly spot in the fall of 1975. By 1979 it would be television's top-rated show, reaching 76 million households.

Reporters flush with power after Watergate wanted a First Lady who validated their lifestyles and made "good copy." The "60 Minutes" emphasis on "personal journalism" would portray Mrs. Ford as she "really" is, Weidenfeld said, but "nobody at the White House"—including Betty—agreed. "60 Minutes" was the flagship television show of the adversarial culture, hostile to authority. The media had a particular agenda, an approach to news. Reporters were disproportionately liberal and "modern" in their lifestyles—one 1972 study found that more than three-fourths of television correspondents no longer lived with their first wives. Still, the bias was more structural than political. Reporters were primed for stories, for action, for controversies, and for criticism. "Every news story should, without any sacrifice of probity or responsibility, display the attributes of fiction, of drama," instructed NBC's Reuven Frank, a pioneer of the half-hour evening news show.

Weidenfeld quelled White House anxieties by granting the interview to the urbane Morley Safer instead of the pugnacious Mike Wallace. The interview was postponed repeatedly in the spring of 1975. The CBS crew attributed the wait to Betty's rumored "drinking problem."

Betty disarmed her critics with intermittent candor. She admitted that she drank "occasionally, with my husband." She told reporters about the tranquilizers she took; for the rest, she trusted the reporters' sloppiness and discretion. Hints crept into dispatches about "halting speech," a distracted stare, "a strained smile," a mispronounced word, or a canceled event. But most journalists preferred to tell the story of the open and feminist First Lady in bloom rather than that of the erratic and sedated political wife.

The Fords did admit that Betty's health was frail. Michael Ford would describe a typical evening in the White House study: "My dad will work in his chair," and "my mother will sit in her chair and she'll read or maybe she'll watch TV or she'll just kind of reflect on things." Barbara Walters recognized that "reflection" as the "zombie"-like state of a substance abuser exhausted by her efforts to keep up appearances during the day. Walters would ask the First Lady about rumors that she spent hours staring out the window. Betty deflected the inquiry, saying, "Well, I like to look out and have the view of Pennsylvania Avenue so that I can see the world is going on."

The day of the interview in July 1975, Betty told Safer, "Look, you can ask me anything you want and I'll tell you the truth." On camera, she began by saying, "I told my husband if we have to go to the White House, okay, I will go. But I'm going as myself. . . . And if they don't like it, then they'll just have to throw me out." Such defiance betrayed the alcoholic's fear of an unnamed "they" who might expose her.

In fact, both Jerry and Betty Ford spent much of their lives fearing that various secrets behind their normal veneers would be exposed. Betty Bloomer, born in the Midwest in 1918, studied dance in the late 1930s with Martha Graham in New York. When Graham did not choose her as a main dancer, Betty acceded to her mother's wishes and returned home to Grand Rapids. Betty blamed the end of her career and her subsequent bondage as a housewife on her mother's nagging rather than her mentor's rejection.

At home, Betty was known as a "swinging gal." "Briefly, I was the Martha Graham of Grand Rapids," she recalled with a mix of pride and resignation. In 1942 Betty married William Warren. Warren was dashing, alcoholic, and unreliable like her father had been. After the war, Betty was "ready for a house and children," but Bill did not want to settle down. By 1947 the Warrens had separated.

"It taught me," she sighed, "that there are some people you just can't change." Betty returned home, a twenty-nine-year-old divorcée. She planned never to marry again—or to discuss the divorce, which became a major topic of conversation in 1974.

Meanwhile, across town, Gerald Ford, Jr., was struggling with his own baggage. Thirty-five years old in 1948, the tall, blond lawyer was the toast of the town. An Eagle Scout, a University of Michigan football star, a Navy officer, he had worked his way through Yale Law School. But Jerry's life had a complexity that belied his all-American image. He still carried a flame for his ex-girlfriend Phyllis Brown, a New York model. And he was burdened with the knowledge that his father was not his real father and his real name was not Jerry Ford but Leslie King, Jr.

Jerry claimed that he did not discover his true origins until one day, while working at the local dairy shop, a tall blond man walked in and said, "I'm Leslie King, your father." "It was a hell of a shock for a 16-year-old kid," Ford recalled, although when he was thirteen his mother had mentioned an earlier marriage. Sparing her child the sordid tales of abuse that led her to leave her first husband after sixteen months, Dorothy said that "things just didn't work out." Dorothy Gardner King's attempt to start a new life in Grand Rapids had succeeded, as Gerald Ford, Sr., married her and raised her young boy as his own. After King's visit, Dorothy spent the next nine years trying to collect child support from her ex-husband.

For an ambitious young man in a small town, this imbroglio must have been excruciating. If his origins were not "all American," the rest of his life would be. His college football coach would say that Jerry "comes as close" to being the "all-American boy" as "anybody I ever coached."

Industrious and justifiably wary of romance, Ford dated casually through college. While at Yale Law School in the late 1930s—having turned down offers to play professional football—Jerry fell "deeply in love for the first time in my life." The relationship foundered when Jerry graduated and decided to practice law in Grand Rapids. The free-spirited Phyllis Brown knew she "would never be happy as a Congressman's little wife." Jerry mourned her for years. While he served in the Navy during World War II, Lieutenant Ford's main love was for his ship, the U.S.S. *Monterey*, and his hatred was for the enemy. Subsequently Jerry peppered his speech with nautical metaphors, resurrecting the heroic times that earned him ten battle stars.

After the war, Jerry returned to his law practice and his moping. "When are you going to start dating again?" Mrs. Ford asked her thirty-four-year-old son. "When are you going to settle down?" During the summer of 1947 he met Betty Bloomer Warren at a party. Her broad smile and apple cheeks reminded Jerry of Phyllis. Betty always liked "handsome blond men," but she was not yet divorced and feared a scandal. Jerry convinced her to meet for "twenty minutes," which became an hour. They began seeing each other. "He wanted a companion, and I filled the bill," Betty would say coldly. "As for me, . . . I enjoyed his company and his friends."

By February 1948 Jerry proposed. His proposal was typical: shy, remote, "low-key," practical, one-sided, calculating, and reflecting his commitment to his true love, politics. "I'd like to marry you, but we can't get married until next fall and I can't tell you why," he declared. Betty would have to wait five months before Jerry "admitted that he loved me." Politics would dictate the timing of their marriage, as it would so much else in their future. Jerry Ford was going to run for Congress as a Republican against a five-term Republican incumbent. He ran his insurgent campaign from a rebuilt Quonset hut repainted red, white, and blue.

Politics shaped the Ford marriage. Jerry dashed out of the wedding rehearsal dinner to make a speech, and he rushed in late to the ceremony itself—from the stump—wearing muddy shoes. Dorothy Ford was furious; Betty pretended not to notice. What Betty called their "complete farce of a honeymoon" was punctuated by campaign appearances. As the newlyweds returned to Grand Rapids, the groom rushed off to a rally. Years later, Betty remembered how "a fantasy of me in a hostess gown, soft music on the radio, icy martinis, the smell of a delicious roast filling the apartment . . . died a-borning." Jerry's "first dinner at home" consisted of a can of tomato soup and a toasted cheese sandwich.

For the next three decades, Betty and Jerry would march to different beats while keeping their marriage intact. Betty gave birth to three boys and a girl, while Jerry became a leading House Republican. Press profiles throughout the years celebrated the Fords' traditional marriage. Jerry was "a combination of Mr. Clean and John Glenn," while Betty was the "thinking man's version of Rita Hayworth." He was "a man's man"; she was "the prettiest congressional wife." They headed "as good-looking a family as anyone would want to see." She would be pictured making pancakes, lounging at the beach club with her husband, skiing with the family, and modeling gowns. One newswoman found "the secret of Ford's ability to get things done . . . in the way his wife runs the home, a happy, well organized beehive."

Yet there were cracks in the Fords' facade. Each triumph for him was a setback for her. "The Congress got a new Minority Leader," Betty would say of 1965, "and I lost a husband." Jerry traveled as many as 258 days a year. Betty "felt as though I were doing everything for everyone else, and I was not getting any attention at all." One night, Betty rolled over in bed, saw Jerry, and asked "What are *you* doing here?" Sometimes, Betty sneered about "the ego massage" politics gave him. Sometimes Jerry snapped when Betty ran late, "but mostly I bottled up my misery," she recalled.

In 1964 Betty pinched a nerve in her back. The child of an alcoholic, she hid her pain with a smile and took refuge in the bottle—a drink at five o'clock to lighten the mood, a nightcap to relax, a spoonful of vodka in her morning tea to give "a warm, mellow feeling." "The loneliness, the being left to yourself at night, is what makes marriages crack, makes liquor more attractive," she would later say. She swelled from a size 6 to size 10. A photo at the 1965 inaugural showed that the lithe model was now a jowly matron.

After Jerry became House minority leader, Betty woke up one morning and began crying uncontrollably. Her husband, who was conferring with President Johnson aboard the presidential yacht, rushed home. Betty began seeing a psychiatrist twice a week and taking medication. Her psychiatrist was "a sounding board," she would explain. "It siphoned off the pressures." Despite the political risk, Jerry also visited the psychiatrist. The doctor wanted to see the two together, but Betty refused, without explaining. She may have feared a situation where her feelings of anger could surface and not be controlled. To "weather the storm clouds that are inevitable in an intimate relationship," Jerry would write, "there must be a belief on the part of both that there is nothing of a higher priority than the sanctity & continuation of the relationship." At this flash point, both implicitly agreed that sustaining the marriage was more important than "letting it all hang out." Later Betty said that she and Jerry never contemplated divorce: "We would get mad at each other. But we were in love and we were committed."

Betty had to overcome her generation's prejudice against psychiatry. Americans were ashamed of mental illness, even though the percentage of individuals seeking professional help at some time in their lives was doubling from 14 percent in 1957 to 26 percent in 1976. Betty would conclude that "there was nothing terribly wrong with me. I just wasn't the Bionic Woman, and the minute I stopped thinking I had to be, a weight fell from my shoulders."

Betty absorbed the modern psychiatric and feminist tenets that women who only served others shortchanged themselves. The women's movement taught her that "a lot of women go through this. Their husbands have fascinating jobs, their children start to turn into independent people, and the women begin to feel useless. . . . Sometimes the body makes you pay for what the head is struggling with." Studies were confirming Betty Friedan's claims, finding that housewives were disproportionately "psychologically distressed." Almost 5 million abused alcohol, and 31 million—42 percent of the population—had used tranquilizers. Radical feminists denounced housework as "shit work," while most women acknowledged "mixed feelings."

Jerry felt guilty; he had reduced a bold and beautiful dancer into a drunken suburban housewife. His explanation was circular: "My hands were full," he claimed in his memoirs. "As Minority Leader, I was making about two hundred speeches a year, most of them out of town." Gerald Ford could not begin to explore the demons that compelled him to take on so much.

The great disappointment of Jerry's career heralded Betty's salvation. When the Nixon landslide in 1972 failed to produce a Republican Congress, Jerry realized he would never become Speaker of the House. He promised Betty he would retire in January 1977.

Richard Nixon's designation of Jerry to replace Spiro Agnew as vice president in October 1973, however, threatened the Fords' agreement. Michael asked his father, "Are you sure you want to put her through this?" When Jerry asked, "Is it okay?" Betty sighed "It's always okay." She figured, "If I could take 25 years, I could stand three more." After the announcement Nixon said to Betty, "It's all yours." She replied, "Mr. President, I don't know whether you're offering congratulations or condolences."

Under the Twenty-fifth Amendment, the Senate rather than the people would ratify this vice president; Jerry endured an investigation instead of a campaign. During the background check conducted by 359 FBI agents, the Fords disclosed Betty's psychiatric treatment. "It had nothing to do with Jerry. It was just his dumb wife," Betty said. This sassy style betrayed her anger but would make her famous. Betty admitted she took tranquilizers: "Otherwise, I find that I become tense when I realize how much there is to do in one day." Reporters occasionally saw her sipping a vodka and tonic. She uttered the mantra of the recovering substance abuser, "I live from day to day." Still, she insisted that she spoke haltingly only because she chose her words carefully.

Betty's candor, combined with changing attitudes toward drugs, housewives, and mental illness, shaped her image. A year and a half before, the discovery of Democratic vice-presidential nominee Thomas Eagleton's electroshock treatments provoked outrage. Now, Betty Ford was welcomed as a symbol of the sacrifices political wives—and many other housewives—made.

The Fords' marriage was judged on new terms as well. "As I look around and see" other marriages, Jerry said, "I just thank God Betty and I were so lucky to get together." Marital success now required endurance, not perfection; it was work, not play. Betty preached that "a successful marriage is never really the 50-50 proposition it's chalked up to be. We settled for a 75-25 deal. Sometimes the 75 would emanate from my side. Sometimes it would have to be Jerry's gesture."

Where reporters once saw self-confidence in Betty, they now sensed "loneliness and vulnerability." Reporters were admitting that political wives hated politics. Frustrated with Pat Nixon's stoicism, the newswomen embraced the "Second Lady." A bit defensively, Betty responded, "You can't say I don't like politics. . . . I would have moved out by now if I didn't like it." She still believed that "husbands come first."

For all her apparent comfort with her psychological struggles, Betty Ford remained ashamed. Rather than admitting that since the mid-1960s she had been visiting psychiatrists on and off, she minimized her experiences and exaggerated the cure. In different interviews she said she began seeing a psychiatrist "when my husband became minority leader" in 1965; "five years" after her pinched nerve, which would be 1969; and "about a year ago," which would have been 1972—even as she led another reporter to believe "she hasn't been going for almost a year now." She also claimed that her visits lasted for "two years," for "three years," and "for a couple of years, off and on." When, as First Lady, she would rejoice before the National Association of Mental Health Centers that visits to psychiatrists were no longer a "hush, hush" thing, Betty still claimed that "my problems were physical," although, she said, the sessions "were beneficial."

Reporters did not notice the discrepancies, and most remained unaware of her divorce. Betty and Jerry Ford, still harboring secrets, were cast as honest contrasts to the devious, repressed Nixons. Jerry played the white knight—albeit clad in plaid golf wear—to Richard Nixon's dark knight; Betty played Mary Richards to Pat Nixon's "Stepford Wife." Even the Ford kids were easier to take than the Nixon girls. The Fords were all-American if rambunctious "B" students, not straight-A "goody-goodies."

When Nixon's chief of staff, Alexander Haig, tried to negotiate with Jerry about the resignation, Ford's chief aide, Robert Hartmann, warned his boss to stay away. Any kind of discussion would be improper and threaten Ford's reputation. Hartmann often clashed with Mrs. Ford, but for once he was glad that Jerry relied on his wife. Jerry freely acknowledged Betty's influence, knowing that great duties "would fall on my shoulders and to some degree on hers." He told Haig, "I've talked with Betty and we're prepared, but we can't get involved in the White House decision-making process."

When Richard Nixon resigned on August 9, Betty Ford considered it "the saddest day of my life." Gerald Ford feared he might "break down" during his "inaugural speech." Instead, the ten-minute "straight talk among friends" was a masterstroke. "In other times, Gerald Ford's expressions of old-fashioned virtue, honesty and the Golden Rule, and a human prayer for help might be brushed aside as political boilerplate," William Greider wrote in the *Washington Post*. "Friday, people savored his words and thirsted to believe them."

Ford promised an "openness and candor . . . in all my public and private acts as your President." The Ford family underlined Jerry's "Mr. Nice Guy" image. Jerry's private virtue became a harbinger of his public success. Trivia illustrating the Fords' "close-knit and informal" family clogged the airwaves. Americans heard about the annual ski trips to Vail, the kids' blue jeans, Jerry's habit of making himself breakfast every morning. Twenty-four-year-old Mike, a married divinity student; twenty-two-year-old Jack, a park ranger;

eighteen-year-old Steve, a ranch hand; and seventeen-year-old Susan, a blond high school senior, became famous overnight. "The nation's new First Family is a bunch of squares," the *Washington Star* exulted.

Betty Ford was hailed for raising a fine family while her husband worked the rubber-chicken circuit. She presented herself as "a plain, country girl" living a "typical suburban life." She deferred to Jerry, saying, "I do give him my ideas, not as an adviser, but as a typical housewife would." Betty would be "more folksy" than "Plastic Pat," making the White House "instead of an iceberg, a more cozy, typical American home."

The Fords' public displays of affection delighted reporters. Neither as vulgar as Lyndon Johnson nor as cold as Richard Nixon, Jerry Ford loved his wife. He gently guided her through the reception after the swearing-in, and patted her backside at home with the TV cameras rolling. The Fords moved their king-size bed into Pat Nixon's bedroom; they would be the first presidential couple to bunk together since the Eisenhowers. Headlines leered: "FORDS MOVE—LOCK, STOCK AND BEDS." "We've been doing it for 25 years and we're not going to stop now," Betty said. "I think it's silly not to; besides, it's such a long walk."

Jerry and Betty Ford offered a joint platform to an anxious nation. They hoped to give the country "the same feeling that we have had as a family, a feeling of unity and harmony and warmth." The Fords were not the perfect couple the Nixons tried to be. The divorce, the pills, and the psychiatry made the Fords seem "normal." A Washington psychiatrist speculated that "Middle America is giving up its romantic love affair with the 'ideal family' in the White House," especially after Nixon's "uptight" family "has given us the biggest scandal." "Life is made up of problems," Betty said.

Many people, especially intellectuals, bought the feminist and countercultural argument that "the traditional family structure is not good for human beings." Once "building blocks" of the nation, American families were now perceived as "encounter groups" that unleashed primal emotions. At the same time, the epidemics of divorce, drug abuse, alcoholism, led Americans to recalibrate morality. "Divorce has become socially acceptable," *Parade* magazine would conclude in 1975, pointing to Betty Ford's experience, among others; "it no longer connotes scandal." By 1993 Senator Daniel Patrick Moynihan would label this acceptance of "much conduct previously stigmatized" as "defining deviancy down." "Skeletons" once hidden "in closets"—a nineteenth-century phrase—became "problems" to be "worked through," a late-twentieth-century social worker's jargon.

This "anti-image" of the family changed attitudes toward political wives. In 1972, under Gerald Ford's supervision, the National Republican Congressional Committee had produced a ten-page "Wives' Manual" detailing how to be "a credit to your husband and the party." "NEVER DETRACT FROM HIM," the manual demanded. "Steer clear of controversial statements." In the age of Martha Mitchell, such instruction was necessary. The Ford White House endorsed the guidelines: "This behavior may not be liberated, but . . . it works." In October 1974, *Time*'s cover story on "The Relentless Ordeal of Political Wives" stereotyped the genteel all-around helper as the walking wounded. Political wives, it seemed, became withdrawn like Pat Nixon; alcoholic like Senator Ted Kennedy's wife, Joan; or troubled like Betty Ford.

Women reporters searching for role models loved the Fords. Jerry's habit of making his own breakfast was seen as a triumph for women's liberation. Barbara Walters told Mrs. Ford that her honesty "meant a great deal to other women who also have day to day problems." At the end of September, Betty appeared before Republican women in Chicago; the banner behind her said, "YOU'VE COME A LONG WAY BABY." She beamed: "This does a lot for the ego. It gives me an independence after years of just coping."

Encouraged by the First Lady and the sexual revolution, reporters posed questions they would not have dared to ask ten years before. A proposed interview with the President about "women" for *McCall's* illustrated just how "political" and how "personal" the questioning had become. Winnie McLendon wanted to ask about hiring women in government, whether Mrs. Ford's feelings of worthlessness were "the very root of the women's movement," and end with questions about abortion, "your hopes for Susan," the "ingredients in a good marriage," and whether he had ever been approached by "women attracted to men of power."

The President wisely avoided such inquiries, but his wife was less discreet. A *Newsweek* cover story about the Fords quoted Betty telling a friend, "I've been asked everything except how often I go to bed with my husband." Asking for trouble, she added, "If they had asked me, I would have told them." A week and a half later, when she used the same line on Myra MacPherson of the *Washington Post*, MacPherson asked, "What would you have said?" The sassy First Lady replied, "As often as possible!"

Such talk disgusted millions of Americans. The chorus of approval Betty heard from the networks and the big city newspapers did not resound in America's heartland. The Fords fielded complaints about their children's "'hippie' or 'barnyard' clothes," the number of women wearing "pants suits in the White House," a "highly undignified" photograph of "President Ford's feet on the desk in the Oval Office," and the President's use of the word "helluva" on TV. "Please realize we want to have some feeling of high regard for the office of President," a Floridian wrote. Another man mourned, "It seems as if the good old days when ladies were mothers and wives is gone." Reflecting the elite media's disdain for "mainstream" America, Barbara Walters scoffed, "Many people, it seems, feel that Presidents' wives shouldn't need tranquilizers, and shouldn't have nerves."

Betty did not understand why this "job" was unsalaried. She vowed to "lobby" for a salary after she left office. This call for wages recognized the expansion of the East Wing, and it jibed with feminist calls to compensate housewives. "Now their service is treated like an extension of domestic work instead of the public relations job it usually is," Pat McCormick of the National Organization for Women said, endorsing Betty's proposal. "It's important for all women to have their own identity and to achieve economic independence." Aides dismissed this call for a salary as a "light-hearted response" to a question, but Mrs. Ford was serious. She repeated her call periodically.

If Betty Ford had received a salary, she would have been docked pay for dereliction of duties. Between her osteoarthritis, her chemotherapy regime, her periodic depressions, her daily tranquilizers, and her drinking, her aides never knew if the First Lady would show up to an event—or what her mood would be. Not since Jackie Kennedy had there been such a mercurial First Lady. After the surgery, such "fragility" could be attributed to her chemotherapy, although the East Wing usually emphasized Betty's speedy recovery. Reporters watched the First Lady for signs of illness, fatigue, drunkenness, or drug abuse.

The Ford children also endured intense media scrutiny. Susan Ford modeled a ski outfit for the *Ladies' Home Journal*'s January 1975 cover, but the accompanying article chided her for tolerating her boyfriend's "sexist attitudes." If Susan was too conventional, like her father, Jack Ford was too much the swinger, like his mother. Jack palled around with George Harrison, Bianca Jagger, and Andy Warhol. He endorsed amnesty for draft evaders, sanctioned premarital sex, criticized his father for possibly subjecting Betty to a presidential run, and all but admitted he smoked pot. When asked if he indulged, he grinned, "Uhhh, you know. . . . I would rather not say anything."

This backdrop guaranteed probing queries about the Fords' "manners and morals" when Betty Ford finally met with Morley Safer. The August 10, 1975, edition of "60 Minutes" was fast-paced and filled with the "sex appeal" Don Hewitt demanded. Safer asked Betty about the burdens of being a political wife; if she worried about Jerry succumbing to "some of the attractions in this city"; about the President's habits she "liked least"; and about psychiatry, the ERA, abortion, and her influence on the President. Betty rehashed many of the lines she had been saying for months. Spunky as always, after confessing "perfect faith in my husband" she said she was "glad to see him enjoy a pretty girl," but "he really doesn't have time for outside entertainment. Because I keep him busy."

Two-thirds of the way through, Safer asked, "What if Susan Ford came to you and said, 'Mother, I'm having an affair?'" "Well, I wouldn't be surprised," Betty said. "I think she's a perfectly normal human being like all young girls, [and] if she wanted to continue I would certainly counsel and advise her on the subject, and I'd want to know pretty much about the young man that she was planning to have the affair with; whether it was a worthwhile encounter or whether it was going to be one of those"—Betty wisely did not finish her sentence. She did add, "She's pretty young to start affairs." After Betty conceded that Susan was old enough, Safer sharpened his question. He asked if Betty would be "surprised . . . given the way . . . you brought these kids up." She responded, "No. I think there's a complete freedom among the young people now." Recalling her past she reflected, "Perhaps there would be less divorce." Mrs. Ford went on to speculate yet again that "all" her kids had "tried marijuana," and to admit that Betty Bloomer probably would have tried it.

Mike Wallace introduced the next segment, which focused on the royal family. "It goes without saying that no British reporter could ever have as frank a conversation with Queen Elizabeth of England," he said. "And though there has been criticism the last quarter century of an imperial presidency in the United States, the Ford family seems to be doing its best to turn that notion around." Clearly, in the moral universe of the media, candor was good.

Watching the broadcast with his wife in Vail, the President of the United States disagreed. Like Betty, Jerry expressed his anger through humor. When he heard the answer about Susan, he threw a pillow at his wife, saying, "You just lost me ten million votes." He soon raised it to "twenty million." At the end he stormed out, a detail Betty confessed to her friend Peggy Whyte but, in a rare moment of discretion, hid from reporters.

In fact, the Fords' public peace was as fragile as Betty's mental state. Both Jerry and Betty remained angry. All too often Jerry was exasperated with his wife's antics, and Betty was seething about some real or imagined slight. When a reporter asked Betty where she would like to have a dream vacation alone with the President, she exploded, "I can't ever see the two of us going off alone. We'd probably kill each other." Betty was often jealous of Jerry, who flirted shamelessly with pretty women. A mock briefing paper prepped the President for a meeting with Mrs. Ford "to try to explain" a well-publicized photograph "showing you about to give an enthusiastic kiss to an attractive young lady member of the Longview Rangerettes." The three "talking points" were "Yes dear," "Yes dear," and "Yes dear."

"SUSAN HAVING AN AFFAIR? IT DOESN'T BOTHER BETTY FORD," the *Herald-Journal* of Logan, Utah, declared on its front page. Other papers reported that Mrs. Ford "endorsed premarital sex and use of drugs, as well as abortion." Millions were appalled. A Mormon elder, a Roman Catholic bishop, the Greater Houston Clergy Association, *The Sound of Music*'s Maria Von Trapp, judges, legislators, mayors, and even Dear Abby, blasted the First Lady. Each news cycle spewed new attacks and defenses. CBS ran a sexy picture of Susan Ford while reporting she had "nothing" to tell her mother—"not yet, that is." This image of a kittenish coed seemingly encouraged by her hussy of a mother fed the story.

Betty Ford's "60 Minutes" interview became a cultural Rorschach test, a canvas for expressing attitudes about "the Sixties." On "Today," a psychoanalyst applauded her nonjudgmental parenting. The minister at Washington's National Cathedral said the First Lady helped "us to demythologize our taboos." Grace Slick of the acid rock band Jefferson Starship praised the First Lady, saying, "I thought, wow—she's gonna start steppin' out on the old man. Smoke a little dope. Have some parties." Critics repudiated Mrs. Ford and the sexual revolution she now embodied. William Buckley of the *National Review* blasted rationalists, Freudians, behaviorists, and Mrs. Ford for trying "to rewrite the operative sexual code of Western Civilization." The columnist George Will feared that such disclosures would make reporters "the super-policemen of tomorrow, lording it over a society in which all privacies and intimacies are public."

Nearly two weeks later, Gerald Ford was still trying to clarify the "misunderstanding." A Sindlinger poll taken the day the interview aired and repeated two weeks later showed that his popularity had dropped from 55.3 percent to 38.8 percent. The President said that "Betty meant we're deeply concerned about the moral standards" in the family. Feminists snapped that husbands should not speak for their wives. Besides, Myra MacPherson's profile in *McCall's* made it clear that Betty Ford meant what she said.

"The Blooming of Betty Ford" celebrated America's outspoken First Lady. Instead of a demure midwesterner whose diffidence diluted the impact of her words on TV, the image of a brash power-monger leaped off the glossy pages. Alongside recipes for potato-and-leek soup and cauliflower cheese—marks of the old *McCall's*—MacPherson wrote that "Betty Ford freely admits to smoking, being divorced, seeing a psychiatrist, drinking with her husband and—heaven forfend—sleeping with him." MacPherson repeated Betty's line about wanting to sleep with Jerry "as often as possible." Betty added, "I guess if you're President, that part of your life is—I guess you're supposed to become a eunuch." Regarding her cancer, Mrs. Ford asked, "Which would you rather lose—a right arm or a breast?" The First Lady sounded like the boozy wife who speaks the unspoken at her husband's office party.

In *McCall's*, Betty appeared obsessed with power. She remained deferential on most issues, yet on women's issues she boasted that "if he doesn't get it in the office in the day, he gets it in the ribs at night." She said she "got a woman in the Cabinet" for the first time in twenty years. "Now I'm working on getting a woman on the Supreme Court," she claimed. But if "pillow talk" influenced presidential personnel, Americans had every right to peer into the presidential boudoir. The all-too-graphic phrase made the personal very political.

MacPherson made Betty Ford into a feminist reporter's ideal. Betty's life demonstrated the value of renouncing conventional morals and exposing one's intimate self to the media. "A quiet, unremarkable, slightly overweight housewife who volunteered little [in a 1970 interview] except to say the Fords were conventional" had become a self-assured powerhouse. Betty's openness supposedly made her more popular and more serene. MacPherson even claimed that Mrs. Ford "never once minded the excessive publicity about a very private illness." The media commitment to "letting it all hang out" brooked no ambivalence. *McCall's* hit the newsstands on August 19. "MRS. FORD DOES IT AGAIN—SPEAKS OUT FRANKLY ABOUT SEX," the local newspaper in Vail screamed. Betty disagreed with Jerry that these revelations cost him votes, saying, "Well, he has to rib me a little bit." The networks fed the controversy and encouraged the First Lady. CBS broadcast only one "man on the street" reaction: "I admire her for saying what she thinks." ABC News proclaimed, "the First Lady has been making almost as much news as the President." The natural order was upset. Reporters were thrilled.

That week, Andy Warhol's *Interview* magazine published Jack Ford's complaints that his Secret Service bodyguards intimidated potential dates. He also complained that in the White House, "you never know when you're going to be walking around in your boxer shorts and there's 15 people getting the special upstairs tour." In fact, a year later, Steve Ford would have to smuggle a young lady friend out of the Queen's Bedroom without bumping into Barbara Walters's televised tour.

The Fords were no longer the "Brady Bunch." After Jack said he smoked marijuana, the President of the United States felt compelled to announce that he "never" used the stuff. Ford also conceded that he would not "be very popular at home" if he tried to stifle his family. Betty said that Jack's "announcement"—calling it a confession would be too judgmental—"was a great relief to many parents because they then said, 'our children aren't perfect either, they're normal.'"

By October, the East Wing would count 23,308 "con" and 10,512 "pro" letters. Betty had shoved the White House into the nationwide fracas about morality. The letters revealed a deep chasm in American culture, as well as conflicting definitions of a First Lady's role. Some said Mrs. Ford surrendered her "private identity": "You are, because of the position your husband has assumed, expected and officially required to be PERFECT!!" Others disagreed that a First Lady had to play "Miss America grown up."

The "pro" letters invariably championed Betty Ford as a new kind of First Lady: humane, candid, "real," and "hip." The writers embraced the new ideology of candor emerging out of the 1960s. "Truth is the ultimate standard of morality," one man wrote. To many women, this candor was a central part of Betty's liberation, as well as their own refusal to be "doormat[s]" any longer.

Mothers wrote heartfelt letters detailing their discoveries that "if I didn't get flexible with the ways of today, I could just stay 'fixed' and never understand my children or their world at all." Women needed new compasses for what *Ladies' Home Journal* called this "gray, no-woman's land in-between the morality of their mothers and the very different standards for their daughters." Many appreciated Betty Ford's common sense.

Critics, however, felt betrayed. Most expected the First Couple to defend "morality." Forty-four percent of those surveyed still believed premarital sex was "always" or "almost always wrong." "Any president who has a family with such low morals, is in my mind, not fit to be in the position you and your family are now in," one teenager wrote. This morality was central to America's civic religion. "Permissive sex will eventually destroy good homes, which in turn will destroy the very foundation of good government," some Kansas women mourned. Thousands of letters invoked religion. "God is affronted to have the First Lady of this land say" that an affair could be "a worthwhile encounter," a woman from Las Vegas wrote. "Fornication is fornication."

After stewing for weeks, Betty responded with a 250-word letter that the *New York Times* printed in full. Betty was defensive and empathetic. She called for tolerant attitudes, not promiscuous behavior, noting that she and her husband had "lived twenty-six years of faithfulness in marriage." The disagreements with "many of today's generation," she wrote, "must never cause us to withdraw the love, the counseling and the understanding that they may need now more than ever before."

To moderate her image, Betty accepted an award as "homemaker of the year" at a conference on "Identity in Homemaking" in September. Workshops on homemakers' legal rights and mental health reflected how dramatically women's lives had changed. Betty praised the "profession" of homemaking. Her career and her family had given her "the best of two worlds," she said, adding that a "sense of self" was critical no matter what a woman did.

Mrs. Ford and Sheila Weidenfeld felt vindicated weeks later, on November 10, when a Harris survey confirmed one of the central facts of modern politics: Notoriety feeds popularity. Sixty-four percent of those surveyed now agreed with Mrs. Ford. Louis Harris proclaimed her "one of the most popular" First Ladies ever. This poll spawned the myth that Betty was a political asset and that the "60 Minutes" fiasco ended well. She stopped apologizing, instead developing a new answer to "the question": "I certainly don't expect this to happen in our family, but if it did, I would certainly treat Susan with compassion and do everything I could to help." Outspokenness became Betty Ford's "trademark," her "project." Betty's candor helped caricature her predecessors: in contrast, Pat Nixon was robotic, Lady Bird Johnson's beautification was frivolous, and Jackie Kennedy was dilettantish.

Reporters desiring outspoken First Ladies lionized Betty Ford. *Newsweek* named her "Woman of the Year" in a cover story entitled "Free Spirit in the White House." *People* named Betty—and not Jerry—one of its "25 Most Intriguing People"; she appeared on the cover beside Cher and Woody Allen. The title of the *People* article summarized the new image and ethos: "THE PRESIDENT'S SECRET WEAPON IS A REFRESHING LADY HIGH ON BEING HERSELF."

Betty Ford viewed 1975 as her coming-out party. In fact, Mrs. Ford's candor may have killed her husband's chances of winning in 1976. At best, Betty neutralized some hostility to Jerry, but few liberals would vote for a president they disliked because they liked his wife. "If only you could have been the wife of one of the candidates I avow!" a New Yorker mourned. In the Roosevelts' day, Franklin used Eleanor as an emissary to key constituencies, but in an age of mass politics and weakened parties Betty Ford was not much help. Even the Harris poll noted that segments of the public least likely to back her husband most supported Mrs. Ford. "Gerald Ford is much too square to pull in the liberated vote," the *Dallas Morning News* grumbled.

The critics were more passionate than the fans, and more likely to switch their votes. The First Lady's mail opposed her by two to one; the President's mail was more overwhelmingly critical, by 237 to 20 the first week, 2,119 to 76 the second week, and 628 to 63 the third week. "We think this error is much more serious than anything that President Nixon did," a Southerner threatening to "sever our connections" with the party, wrote Ford's campaign manager. "Your statements on '60 Minutes' cost your husband my vote," one woman wrote. "Until now I thought we had someone in the White House who thought along the same lines that I did."

Betty Ford alienated the President's right flank just when he needed to shore up conservative support. Ronald Reagan, the right-wing populist former governor of California, was tempted to seek the Republican nomination. The "60 Minutes" flap weakened the President with Reagan's core constituency: small-town Republicans in the South and West, rural voters, and the elderly. Many Bible Belt voters were particularly outraged, and they helped make the South the region where Reagan did best in 1976. In late September, Reagan's wife denounced "the new morality" for young people in what she called her first formal speech ever. Nancy Reagan's talk had the desired effect, garnering headlines saying, "MRS. REAGAN, MRS. FORD DISAGREE ON SEX."

That November, Reagan launched his challenge. In his memoirs, Jerry would jump in the same paragraph from discussing Betty's interviews to discussing Reagan's rebellion—although without blaming her explicitly. The Reaganites would distribute leaflets saying, "Betty or Nancy? A Definitely Different Point of View." To the extent that the "60 Minutes" controversy encouraged Reagan's run, it helped cripple Ford going into the general campaign against Jimmy Carter. With his party reeling from the Nixon resignation, the fall of Saigon, the rise of stagflation, and the energy crisis, Jerry Ford had no margin of error. He would lose that contest by less than 2 million votes out of 80 million cast.

The consensus culture of the 1950s had degenerated into a polarized society. Most of the elite, as well as the media, demanded "normal" politicians who confronted the messy cultural realities emanating from the 1960s. These elites became obsessed with their feelings and projected intractable private issues like abortion into the public realm. In contrast, millions of Richard Nixon's "silent majority" demanded "normal" politicians who maintained appearances and upheld tradition. In the ensuing "culture wars," each faction demanded obeisance from politicians, who struggled to fit their life stories into cultural shorthands satisfying to both. The gap was often so dramatic, the cultural confusion so great, that many politicians did not even know if they succeeded. Betty's fans believed she was popular, just as her critics believed she was unpopular. Betty became a heroine to her staff and many feminists—and an entertaining source to reporters—but remained a dangerous, unstable, and shrewish wife in the eyes of the President's men.

Like other First Ladies, Betty came to personify unappealing aspects of her husband's character. Polls showed that the three biggest criticisms of the President were that he "hasn't the ability for the job," was "ineffective," and was "weak." Strong women were presumed to have weak husbands. Indeed, even Betty's friends dismissed the President. "Unlike her husband who has survived in politics via compromise, waffling, and 180-degree turns, Betty Ford is a woman of candor, forthrightness and honesty," Lloyd Shearer wrote in *Parade*.

With Betty mimicking the brazen lead character of "Maude"—the "All in the Family" spinoff that was television's fourth most popular show in 1975—Jerry resembled Maude's hapless and whiny husband, Walter. During the last half of the year, the First Lady repeatedly upstaged the President. In December, footage of Betty hamming it up with dance students "stole the diplomatic show from her husband on his otherwise forgettable Chinese journey," the *Daily News* reported.

More than most Presidents, Jerry Ford's image was linked with his wife and children. *Time* marked Ford's first anniversary in office by running a family photo on the cover. *Time* attributed Ford's popularity to "the change of tone he has brought to the White House," achieved with "the invaluable assistance of his close-knit but independent-minded family." At that time, in late July 1975, *Time* declared that "few people crack jokes any more" about the President's clumsiness. Gerald Ford was "in command."

But Ford's popularity soon went into free fall. By November, when Reagan challenged Ford, *Newsweek* reported that the President "carries about him an aura of vulnerability that runs beyond his daily accident report." In its year-end issue, while hailing Mrs. Ford as one of twelve "women of the year," *Time* chronicled the President's stumbles. President Ford did occasionally trip over his words—and his legs. But once reporters decided he was clumsy, they seized on examples. In October 1975, "NBC's Saturday Night

Live" debuted, with the comedian Chevy Chase caricaturing "President Klutz." "Saturday Night Live" and Chase became famous at the cost of Gerald Ford's dignity.

Betty Ford did not make her husband "the country's leading target of jokes," but she did not help. With his wife shooting her mouth off and his son jet-setting, the President no longer seemed commanding. "Since you can't control your wife, how do you expect to control the country?" one Republican asked. Betty fed Jerry's "stumblebum" image by calling him "accident-prone" in *People* and saying that he knocked over a "bouquet of flowers" on their first date—a story she had not told before.

By Christmas 1975, Ford's crusade to restore the presidency was stalled. He had brought openness and credibility to the office without respect and dignity; the nefarious Nixon and the megalomaniacal Johnson had been replaced by a clown. At the same time, the "Imperial Presidency" suffered an additional blow: John Kennedy's escapades were exposed, and Americans got another disconcerting look behind the scenes at 1600 Pennsylvania Avenue.

As part of the Watergate backlash, a Senate Select Committee on Intelligence Operations investigating the CIA discovered President Kennedy's affair with a Mafia moll. Chaired by Senator Frank Church, a Kennedy acolyte, the committee sanitized the report by referring to a "close friend of President Kennedy." On December 15, 1975, William Safire announced in the *New York Times* that the "close friend" was "a beautiful girl who divided her time between the Chicago underworld leadership and the President of the United States." "The private life of any public figure is nobody's business but his own," Safire conceded. "But when the Nation's Chief Executive receives even a few calls from the *home telephone* of the leader of the Mafia in Chicago, that crosses the line into the public's business."

By 1975 the Johnson and Nixon failures had magnified the legend of Camelot. Some authors described Jack's philandering, Jackie's petulance, and the family's arrogance, but the accounts were drowned in a sea of tributes to those now-magical "Thousand Days." Even after Watergate and Vietnam, reporters respected this legend. According to the *New York Times,* most journalists agreed that "private behavior should remain private when it does not affect the conduct of public business."

That December, the story of the mistress, the Mafia hoods, and the President dominated the media. *Time* printed a side story about "Jack Kennedy's Other Women." The article mentioned the two secretaries, "Fiddle" and "Faddle," who did not type much; Jackie's discovery of a pair of panties that were "not my size"; and Jack's liaisons with beauty queens, including Marilyn Monroe, who supposedly whispered, "I think I made his back feel better." The article was salacious, many complained, and was not related to "presidential performance."

What *Newsweek* called "a kind of gentlemen's code of silence" was broken. Having been caught covering up for a politician, reporters would no longer be so discreet. Over the next few months, articles describing marijuana parties and orgies painted what the *National Enquirer* called "a shocking picture of life behind the scenes at Camelot." Just as the Kennedys had symbolized America's hopes and dreams in the 1960s, they came to epitomize America's fears and sins in the 1970s. By 1980, the best a Kennedy sycophant could offer would be Harris Wofford's half-hearted defense that "I never personally saw any evidence of John Kennedy's extramarital relationships." Wofford advocated "a reasonably skeptical" approach: "Discount 90 percent but rule nothing out. Applying that formula to John Kennedy leaves a remarkable residue of fire under all the smoke."

The 1975 disclosures triggered a revolution in journalism. Coming after Senator Edward Kennedy's cowardice at Chappaquidick—which in 1969 was viewed as an abuse of power, not a case of debauchery—Watergate, Congressman Wilbur Mills's dalliance with a stripper, and the Betty Ford interview, reporters became more inquisitive. Editors became more willing to publish intimate details of a politician's life. As the Kennedy revelations emerged, correspondents debated how to report President Ford's drinking habits. In November 1975, *Newsweek* speculated about the link between Ford's "painful" speeches and his social habits: "He enjoys a pre-prandial drink with the boys, like any politician on the road, and occasionally shows it in his post-prandial speeches." "We didn't say the President was a drunk," Washington bureau chief Mel Elfin insisted. "It was a question of whether the President has a drink or two."

Three weeks later, ABC's "Good Morning America" reported that the *National Enquirer* was exploring whether the President had a drinking problem. "Respectable" journalists often reported the coverage of a rumor, thus spreading it without assessing it. Other journalists refused to speculate "publicly." Aides called the ABC report to the President's attention, trusting him to get the message and hide his tracks better.

The reports, however subdued, warned that character was a two-way street. The press would not just accept the President's word that he was decent. The boozy intimacy between politicians and reporters was ending. Mel Elfin articulated the new ethos: "Character will become central. We have overlooked those things in the past, and it is not good enough anymore."

"What used to be called gossip is now called information," Richard Cohen of the *Washington Post* noted. "Tidbits" now offered "insight into character." At a time of growing moral relativism, a new Victorianism emerged in public life. Reporters decided that "a man who cheats on his wife (and vice versa) is more likely to cheat on his constituents than is a man who respects his given word." The feminist notion that the personal is political, the Freudian idea that sex motivated human behavior, the fear of unstable leaders triggering nuclear holocaust, and the countercultural belief that leaders were fallible and American society dishonest gave the search for dirt intellectual respectability. The anguished response to *Time's* gossipy article in 1975 soon seemed quaint. Dozens of newspapers imitated the *Washington Post* and created a "Style" section. Profiles of politicians in newspapers and on television proliferated.

This obsession with personality was not just another aberration of "the Sixties." In an increasingly anonymous and urbanized secular society, Americans forged an artificial sense of community by focusing on politicians and celebrities. The more Americans withdrew into their own worlds, the more they indulged their own emotions, the more they would focus on their leaders' private lives. With vital connections between individuals attenuated, these ersatz bonds grew in importance. The retreat from a politics of issues to a politics of personality reflected the shift from the traditional culture of sacrifice to the modern culture of indulgence.

As the United States prepared to celebrate its bicentennial, its citizens witnessed the primal scene of presidential politics. Americans peeked into the presidential bedroom, invited by Betty Ford and justified by what they could learn about Kennedy's trysts, Nixon's demons, and other indiscretions. For the next twenty years, they would continue scrutinizing the most private reaches of every public figure's life.

While Betty Ford showed how First Ladies could be popular, she undermined Jerry's attempt to be the nation's "moral leader." In September 1975, Ford's aides proposed mobilizing the "silent majority," who resented big government's undermining of "neighborhood, community and family." Ford could attack busing, the "strange or offensive textbooks" polluting American schools, "sex education," and the "liberal chic, women's lib content" imposed on "traditional educational programs." It could have been a winning program, as Ronald Reagan would demonstrate in 1980. But Jerry could not tackle these social issues without appearing to declare war on his wife.

At the start of 1976, Jerry's approval ratings dipped below 40 percent; Betty's ratings continued to rise. Looking back, 1975 emerged as "the first year Mrs. Ford was freed from being a political wife," Weidenfeld rejoiced. Yet Betty's evolution from suburban housewife into Woman of the Year hurt her husband. Betty now had to campaign for him, not for her own "self-worth."

During the 1976 campaign Betty danced, mugged, hugged, hobnobbed, and mouthed niceties. In Texas she took the moniker comedian Flip Wilson gave her, "First Mama," and stumped over "CB" radio. The division of labor in the Ford family became clear: Jerry governed, and Betty campaigned.

People greeted Betty with an enthusiasm her husband did not generate— but his opponent, Ronald Reagan, did. Women, in particular, were thrilled to see her. One Republican woman in Concord said, "It's physical. When she walks into a room every woman there clutches her bosom." Others simply reveled in the reflected glow of an entertaining celebrity. People were celebrating her aura, not her accomplishments.

In a personality-oriented political culture shaped by personality-obsessed journalists, Betty Ford had become "the President's biggest asset." She was tailor-made for *People,* a weekly founded in 1974 to focus on "individuals rather than issues," which was already selling more than a million copies an issue. Campaign buttons subordinated the President, roaring, "ELECT BETTY'S HUSBAND" AND "KEEP BETTY IN THE WHITE HOUSE."

Reporters made much of the fact that Betty's poll ratings were higher than her husband's, yet such comparisons were specious. Mrs. Ford received a 58 percent approval rating, whereas Mr. Ford received only 46 percent, but they were judged on different scales. Even with her success, the President Ford Committee banned Betty and her son Jack from Bible Belt states like North Carolina.

On most days during the primary fight, Betty Ford loved campaigning. Solo campaigning allowed her to help her husband without deferring to him, and the adoring crowds roused her. After initially feeling "sick" to her stomach when she had to speak, she "became so involved I stopped thinking about my stomach and carried on like the rest of the troops."

As her poll ratings soared, and as the President beat Reagan in New Hampshire, Florida, and Illinois, Betty's standing improved in the White House. For once, her success coincided with Jerry's; he was proud of her, and grateful. "He used to take her for granted," one friend noted. "Now he stands back and looks at her in awe." Jerry was a better congressional candidate than a presidential campaigner, and he often stiffened up in big crowds. Betty spent more time on the road than he did. Her activism underscored his pledge "never to neglect my first duty as President."

Betty's popularity stemmed from her persona, not her politesse. She demonstrated her poise in June 1976 at a Jewish National Fund gala in New York. The JNF's president, Dr. Maurice Sage, suffered a fatal heart attack while introducing the First Lady. As Secret Service agents and the various doctors in the house ministered to the fifty-eight-year-old rabbi, Betty Ford led the three thousand diners in prayer. This riveting demonstration of Betty's faith and power was broadcast throughout the nation.

By the time the Republican convention met in mid-August, the President had 1,102 delegates to Reagan's 1,063. Ford needed twenty-eight of the ninety-four remaining uncommitted to clinch the nomination. Betty was proud of her contribution and thrilled by the latest polls: she enjoyed 71 percent approval, up from 50 percent in September 1975. Two-thirds of those surveyed did not believe that Mrs. Ford was too active and should stay behind the scenes; 48 percent even said they approved of her answer to the "Susan question." Her popularity stemmed from her support for the ERA, of which 73 percent approved, and her courage, particularly in facing breast cancer and responding to the JNF emergency, which 86 percent praised. A year's worth of media adulation and crowd-pleasing bore fruit. Yet, again, hers was not the electable popularity of a leader—and Jerry failed to generate that on his own.

With the President in Washington, Betty worked the convention. She surrounded herself with celebrities, including the singer Sonny Bono. The first night, a resounding ovation for Mrs. Reagan eclipsed Mrs. Ford's entrance into the arena. The next night, when Mrs. Reagan entered, Betty began dancing with the singer Tony Orlando. This display triggered a huge and much-needed Ford rally; it also made for great television. Later, the First Lady and the singer did "the bump" on stage. A widely distributed photograph showed Orlando, with his long hair, thick mustache, mod vest, loud bell bottoms, and platform shoes, extending his buttocks at a pronounced angle toward the First Lady of the United States. Betty Ford, looking like a chic matron with her bouffant hairdo, accepted the bump without protruding as much as her partner. Still, it was too much.

Reporters loved the spectacle, but voters were ambivalent. Conservatives upset by the First Lady's "sleazy little exhibition with that gigolo" became angrier when they read about the "Battle of the Wives." Betty told *Time* something about the Reagans that some friends said about her: "I just think when Nancy met Ronnie, that was it as far as her own life was concerned. She just fell apart at the seams." Soon the White House released its latest apology, saying that "Mrs. Ford, too, was disturbed by media accounts of events at the Republican National Convention which implied a lack of graciousness on her part regarding Mrs. Reagan." The letter claimed that Mrs. Ford could not see across the arena and had no idea when Mrs. Reagan entered.

At the convention, Betty shared the stage with her family, who appealed to "ticket splitters." Noting that the Reagans were also busy, ABC News announced that the "family campaign no longer appears to be optional. People expect it. It gives them a chance to see whether a particular family will provide a good First Lady, interesting children, and even a lovable first dog."

The convention climaxed with a tribute to Gerald Ford, the family man. Cary Grant praised the Fords as a warm family who would unite "not only your party but the entire country." He then praised Betty Ford for using "pillow talk" to "advance women's progress." Grant's crack about how "women have always been one of my favorite causes too" underlined how inappropriate it was to ask an aging celluloid Casanova to introduce the feminist First Lady. Republicans again seemed torn between wooing "women's libbers" and pleasing the "little ladies at home."

After the First Lady spoke briefly—and haltingly—a short film offered "the television viewer" an "emotional, accurate and revealing . . . vision of

Gerald Ford, the man." One scene, filmed amid great tension, showed the wholesome First Family at Camp David: Susan, Jack, Betty, and Jerry sat at the kitchen table and talked stiffly about how natural they were. The Fords insisted that a man who was "open" and caring with his family would be open and caring as a president. Shots in the Oval Office also tried to show a determined leader, who was "with it" enough to hug his vice president, but "tough" enough to send in the Marines when local Cambodian forces seized the *Mayaguez,* an American merchant ship.

Humanizing the President trivialized him; showcasing his family and emphasizing his warmth made it harder for him to appear tough. He came across as a modern "touchy-feely" dad rather than an inspiring leader. Jerry Ford appeared good, not great.

The Republican convention set the tone for the national campaign. Ford's election effort alternated between selling Jerry as a nice neighbor and as a great president. The First Family's "principal task" would be "to reinforce those personal qualities of the President that we are trying to get across to the electorate." Throughout the fall, the Ford family proved that as a series of five-minute commercials would boast, "sometimes a man's family can say a lot about a man."

"What a *team* effort that was!" Jerry would exult. There were no limits to what the Ford family would do to draw "wide media attention"—and, they hoped, votes. The Fords' celebrity status and their proximity to the President made them doubly valuable. The *New York Times* found "the emphasis on family as a vehicle for portraying character . . . so pronounced that the President almost appears to be riding the coattails of his attractive children and wife."

In this final act of the Ford drama, Betty returned to her role as the dutiful wife. No one from the Ford campaign dared demand that the First Lady be docile, but it was time for Betty to coast on her reputation for outspokenness without upstaging her husband. "There's no reason I have to answer a question just because they push me into it," she said of reporters. She would campaign "as his wife," trying "to communicate him to the people" rather than addressing "the issues."

Still, Betty Ford was far more political than most of her predecessors. "I am not the luncheon and bridge club type," she insisted. "Not that I don't like bridge. But when I do something I want to have a purpose and to get a sense of accomplishment."

The President recognized that if Betty were too subdued, reporters would turn on her—and him as well. Now that she was neutralized, he began to build her up. The President praised his wife for "educating me" about the need for the ERA. Using the kind of sarcasm that listeners perceive but readers do not, he added, "She had to work on me in her loving, persuasive way but I'm glad she did." Jerry told ABC that "Betty has had an impact on some of the decisions I have made in the White House . . . she has [a] good feel for the way people feel throughout this country." The President portrayed his family as a vigorous kitchen cabinet that refused to be a collective "yes man." A new age had arrived; Nixon, Johnson, and Kennedy rarely boasted of sharing power with their kin.

The columnist Ellen Goodman blasted this posture, attacking Ford's novel campaign poster picturing the President and First Lady together. Goodman resented the crass appeal to liberals that said "Jerry couldn't be all that conservative if he is married, and lovingly so, to Betty." Noting Ford's dismal record on women's issues, Goodman said, "Ford and his staff seem to treat her opinions with an 'Isn't she cute when she's mad' attitude." In fact, "as warm and thoroughly alive and likeable as she is, Mrs. Ford has no more political power than did Bess Truman." In an age of feminism and of growing doubts about the welfare state, First Ladies often would seem more liberal than their husbands.

In the *Washington Post,* Jeanne M. Holm, Ford's "special assistant for women," defended the President's record on women's rights and endorsed the notion of a co-presidency. "When I look at that campaign poster with Betty Ford standing at her husband's side I wonder why it hasn't been done before," Holm wrote. The presidency, she said, was a package deal: "We tend to forget that when we elect a President in this country we also catapult an entire family into the White House."

The election was so close that Susan Ford went to sleep with the outcome still in doubt. The next morning she came into the bathroom where her mother was dressing and singing to herself. "Mom, did we win?" Susan asked. Betty responded, "No, you kids got a father back, and I got my husband back." Susan "burst into tears." Once again the Fords were out of sync. Betty was relieved "that our ordeal was over"; Jerry was "crestfallen." Exhausted and hoarse after a two-week final blitz, Jerry could not even read his concession statement. He asked Betty to read it, giving her one last opportunity to upstage him.

The Fords left the White House amid a wave of gratitude from a healing nation. Jerry wanted to be remembered as a "nice person, who worked at the job, and who left the White House in better shape than when I took it over"—and he was. Betty wanted to reject the First Lady's genteel straitjacket. "My advice to anyone as First Lady would be to be herself. . . . No one should have to live up to a standard." The Fords' return to private life was eased by a lucrative "his-and-hers" book contract from Harper & Row and *Reader's Digest.*

Betty Ford's appeal was not universal. Many continued to believe that the roles of "First Mama" and First Lady were incompatible. Even as they relished the gossip, millions of Americans still did not want too close a look into the First Couple's bedroom or psyche. Sheila Weidenfeld smoldered as she realized on the last day of the Ford administration that Ford's aides "*still* did not believe that a strong First Lady could be a Presidential asset—that to him the ideal presidential couple was composed of one leader and one follower." Weidenfeld concluded that the President also did "not understand it. . . . He loves his wife. He was proud of her popularity and found it politically useful," but he "thought of it as 'cute' as opposed to public recognition of her great inner character."

More than "male chauvinism" accounted for this perception. Ford and others in the West Wing better recognized the risks inherent in Betty Ford's prominence. They knew the damage she had caused. They saw the letters of complaint, the desertions from the party, the subtle way Reagan had exploited the situation. Her effusions, coupled with the Kennedy revelations, diminished the presidency and the country.

General popularity did not translate into political strength. Older, less educated, more conservative women—the backbone of the Republican party—disliked the First Lady. The "beltway" being constructed around the capital city would soon offer a useful metaphor to help distinguish between media adulation and actual votes. The polls reflected this split. From a cross-section of the entire population in 1976, the Gallup poll put Betty Ford at the top of the "most admired woman" list and Pat Nixon only twelfth. That same year, *Good Housekeeping's* more genteel readers selected Pat Nixon as their most admired woman, with many mentioning her "ladylike" behavior. Betty was a distant second, except among readers "under 25." In a poll of *National Enquirer* readers, 65 percent surveyed selected Pat Nixon as their favorite among the last seven First Ladies. Eleanor Roosevelt ranked a distant second and Betty Ford ranked fifth, with barely 4 percent.

Betty Ford was the neurotic, wounded political spouse reporters thought they saw in Pat Nixon. Mrs. Nixon and Mrs. Ford offered dramatically different images—of silence versus candor, stoicism versus activism, and 1950s idealism versus 1970s cynicism. In his 1976 acceptance speech, President Ford boasted of ending "the polarization of our political order." The culture, however, remained split. The 1960s had not transformed American political culture so much as divided it. Americans would spend the next three decades trying to reconcile traditional culture with the new sensibility. The growing backlash against feminism and the sexual revolution added a touch of hysteria to the enduring fear of an unelected queen. Time and again, members of the presidential couple would find themselves torn between traditional values and modern media demands, between the kind of couple the Nixons tried to be and the kind of couple the Fords actually were.

7

"WHO ELECTED HER?"

The Carters' Co-presidency

On July 21, 1976, reporter Robert Scheer and *Playboy* editor Barry Golson interviewed Jimmy Carter at his home in Plains, Georgia. As the Democratic nominee escorted the reporters to the door, Golson said, as an afterthought, that most of his friends remained uneasy about Carter's "rigid Baptist faith." Carter said his faith kept him humble; no one could meet the "impossible standards" Jesus set. "I've looked on a lot of women with lust. I've committed adultery in my heart many times," the "born again" candidate confessed. "Christ says, Don't consider yourself better than someone else because one guy screws a whole bunch of women while the other guy is loyal to his wife." After proving that he was not a prig, Carter said that his "religious beliefs" would "prevent" him from taking "on the same frame of mind that Nixon or Johnson did—lying, cheating and distorting the truth."

A "bunny" about to disrobe graced the cover of *Playboy*'s bestselling November issue, along with the words: "NOW, THE *REAL* JIMMY CARTER ON POLITICS, RELIGION, THE PRESS AND SEX. . . ." In a forum offensive to left-wing feminists and right-wing moralists alike, Carter opened a window on his sexuality, talked dirty, and called the most recent Democratic president a liar. *Playboy*'s clever public-relations campaign would attract an estimated 25 million readers, quadrupling its usual circulation. Jimmy Carter had stumbled on a way to outdo Mrs. Ford's "60 Minutes" flap.

The *Playboy* firestorm revealed Hugh Hefner's triumphs in the war on conventional morality he launched in December 1953. *Playboy* embodied the sensuality of the consumer culture and the promiscuous commitment to indulging one's impulses, be it in the department store or the bedroom. Exposure had eclipsed discretion; piety had become synonymous with sanctimony. The personal had not only become political, it threatened to become paramount. During this time, Jimmy Carter, a man of essentially conservative rural values, had become a liberal political husband with an astonishingly political wife.

I

Jimmy was born in 1924, the first of the four children of Earl and Lillian Carter. Earl was a tough, extroverted agricultural entrepreneur who bought up hundreds of acres of rich, red Georgia soil. Still, the Carter homestead had no electricity and an outdoor privy stocked with old Sears catalogs for toilet paper. Jimmy would claim that "the greatest day in my life was not being inaugurated President, it wasn't even marrying Rosalynn, it was when they turned the electricity on our farm." Until then, "my life on the farm . . . more nearly resembled farm life of fully 2,000 years ago than farm life today."

Earl called his eldest son "Hot," for "Hotshot," "because Daddy never assumed I would fail at anything." Jimmy worshiped his forbidding daddy, "hunger[ing] . . . for just a word of praise" from Earl. Still, Jimmy's father was more attentive than his mother. Lillian Carter was an acid-tongued, self-involved nurse, more interested in ministering to the neighbors than in caring for her family. "Miss Lillian" often left a note on a desk reminding the four children to do their chores. Jimmy recalled teasing her "that we thought that desk was our mother for a long time."

Jimmy tried to be the farm boy Earl demanded, as well as the bookworm Miss Lillian expected. He relished the "feeling of exclusive masculinity" when Earl took him hunting. Jimmy knew that "it would have been considered effeminate, or even depraved," to mention his qualms about killing animals, yet Lillian preyed on this weakness. Gleefully, she characterized her son as "terribly sensitive," remembering when "his daddy shot a bird, and he cried." For his part, Earl ate in silence, staring straight ahead as Lillian and the children read during meals.

Jimmy's life "centered almost completely around our . . . own home. . . . We felt close to nature, close to the members of our own family, and close to God." The nearby town of Plains—with a population of six hundred—was a "metropolitan" center; it had six churches, three black and three white. "We were very attentive to the proprieties of Plains," Jimmy would recall. "We never failed to be at Sunday school on time." Jimmy and his wife Rosalynn laughed off reporters' nosiness in the late 1970s, saying, "We grew up in Plains where everybody always knew what you were doing."

The outbreak of World War II when Jimmy was seventeen confirmed his desire to "go to Annapolis." As a child, he secured a copy of the Naval Academy's brochure and "planned my studies . . . accordingly." When he entered Annapolis in 1943, his possessive mother called it "the saddest day we had up until then."

The Navy was the most aristocratic of the services. It attracted patricians like John Kennedy and bounders like Richard Nixon. It was an odd choice for a farm boy from a landlocked town in the South. The training pounded in discipline while beating out differences. Midshipman Carter's refusal to sing General Sherman's battle hymn, "Marching Through Georgia," earned vicious paddlings. He took lessons in ballroom dancing, deportment, mathematics, weaponry, engineering, religion, and character. Navy training had to produce genteel killers, deferential commanders, cooperative risk-takers, competitive team-players, and aristocratic democrats; a generation raised on a culture of appearances could handle these paradoxes. More motivated by ambition than patriotism, Jimmy persevered. Graduating 59th in a class of 820, he served with distinction for eight years.

When Earl succumbed to cancer in July 1953, Jimmy felt guilty that they had drifted apart. Lieutenant Carter abruptly resigned his commission and came home to "assume some of the responsibilities that had made Daddy's life so admirable." In the 1960s the Carter peanut warehouse, which had yielded less than $200 in profit in 1954, boomed. By 1970 it would be worth over half a million dollars.

"There was only one thing his father had done that Jimmy hadn't—become a member of the state legislature," his cousin Hugh Carter said. In 1962, Jimmy saw himself as "a naive" citizen "who wanted to be part of the new openness and reform in the life of my state and nation." Typically, Miss Lillian was more skeptical about her son's decision to run for the state senate. "I think he got bored," she said.

After two terms in the state senate, Carter lost a last-minute gubernatorial bid in 1966. Unaccustomed to failure, exhausted, twenty-two pounds lighter, and $76,000 in debt, Jimmy broke down. His sister Ruth counseled, "You've got to be less self-centered." While walking in the woods, Jimmy reflected on a sermon that asked, "If you were arrested for being a Christian, would there be enough evidence to convict you?" Struck by all the visits he had made "for myself" while campaigning and the few visits he had made "for God," Jimmy renewed his Christian faith.

Jimmy joined the estimated one-third of Americans who were "born again." An evangelical movement emphasizing one identifiable moment of renewed commitment was revitalizing American Christians—often, this commitment accompanied a rejection of hedonism and materialism. The emphasis on a personal relationship with Jesus suited an era of disillusionment with institutions and of fascination with the self.

Jimmy became more spiritual but remained competitive; he would trust in the Lord without relying on Him. Jimmy believed in the same ethos that drove Richard Nixon and millions of others on football fields and in offices, "'You show me a good loser and I will show you a loser.' I did not intend to lose again." In 1966 Jimmy had run the kind of campaign Miss Lillian raised him to run: a principled if bloodless effort promising an engineer's efficiency and an officer's integrity. In 1970 he would try to be the kind of good ole' boy Earl raised. Carter slammed his rival Democrat "Cuff Links" Carl Saunders as too rich and too cozy with blacks. Jimmy campaigned as a good Christian, a peanut farmer, a ninth-generation Georgian; in short, as his brochures pronounced, "our kind of man, our kind of Governor."

In office, the populist became progressive. Jimmy's inaugural speech, which reached out to blacks, landed him on the cover of *Time* as a son of the new South. Governor Carter was more the engineer than the farmer, more the stiff officer than the friendly neighbor. He streamlined state government, but he failed to establish a rapport with his old colleagues in the legislature.

Limited to a single four-year term, Carter spent the last half of his tenure planning a presidential run. When he told Miss Lillian he was running for president, she scoffed, "president of what?" But as his aide Hamilton Jordan learned, "All you ever had to do for Jimmy Carter was to tell him something was impossible and he would usually do it."

Only Rosalynn Smith Carter had more faith in Jimmy than he himself had. Their marriage had matured from a tense alliance between a Navy boy and a schoolgirl to a warm and effective partnership. Jimmy said he could not have run for office without her support at home, at the warehouse, and on the stump.

The ties between the Carters and the Smiths were profound. Rosalynn's mother, Frances Allethea Murray Smith, had named her fourth child Lillian Allethea after the family's benevolent neighbor; Miss Lillian helped nurse Rosalynn's father, Wilburn Edgar Smith, when he was dying of cancer; and Jimmy's younger sister, Ruth, was Rosalynn's best friend. The night in late 1940 that her father died, the thirteen-year-old Rosalynn stayed with the Carters.

Rosalynn, born in 1927, had been raised to suffer silently, work diligently, and believe deeply. Her widowed thirty-four-year-old mother went to work and left her oldest daughter in charge of three other children. "My childhood really ended at that moment," she mused. Rosalynn learned from her mother "that you can do anything you must do." Rosalynn knew she had to "appear to be strong. But I wasn't. Underneath I felt very weak and vulnerable." Despite her sacrifices, Rosalynn "felt very guilty" that she was not helping enough. This exaggerated sense of responsibility dogged her for decades

The timid girl blossomed at school. She "had visions of becoming an architect, a stewardess, an interior decorator, even a famous artist." Rosalynn graduated as valedictorian of Plains High School in 1944, three years after Jimmy was salutatorian. Her speech echoed the contemporary commitment to "building bodies and minds and so forth," she recalled.

The shy Rosalynn felt inadequate around her privileged "best friend," Ruth. "She was beautiful, I was ordinary. She was popular, and though I wasn't a wallflower, my prom card wasn't always full," Rosalynn said. Rosalynn's crush on Ruth's brother complicated matters. Jimmy "never paid much attention to her"; he claimed she had only "been around our home a few times," even though she visited there regularly.

Although Jimmy began dating when he was thirteen, he "never had any real sweetheart." Just before returning to Annapolis for his final year in the fall of 1945, Jimmy claims, he was "cruising around in a rumble-seated Ford with a friend of mine" and they casually asked Ruth and Rosalynn to the movies. Rosalynn insists the "friend" was Ruth's beau and that Jimmy "got out" of the car, "walked across and asked me to go to the movie with him"— making it a "first date." The date came after Ruth, Rosalynn, and Jimmy had spent the day cleaning the Carters' pond house. When faced with his wife's version, Jimmy protested, "Ruth talked me into it. Rosalynn and Ruth had been planning, plotting that for a long time."

Whatever the origins, both agree that at the end of the evening, Jimmy kissed Rosalynn. "I had never let any boy kiss me on the first date," she recalled; her mother "hadn't even held hands with Daddy until they were engaged! But I was completely swept off my feet." Jimmy told his mother, "She's the girl I want to marry." Both Miss Lillian and Mister Earl, though, expected Jimmy to marry someone more suited to their station. A lifelong power struggle began. When Jimmy was commissioned into the Navy, both Rosalynn and Lillian would rise to pin his insignia on him.

Jimmy and Rosalynn had only "seventeen real dates" before they married on July 7, 1946. Once Rosalynn decided to marry, "I never did think about what other kind of vocation I would like to have." "War brides are as much a phenomenon of war as uniforms on the streets," the *Ladies' Home Journal* noted. The Carters married in the Smiths' Methodist church, but Rosalynn became a Baptist to please the Carters. The newlyweds now had to get to know each other. Rosalynn was just "a child," she would later say; Jimmy would admit he was "very domineering and demanding." Jimmy teased her that the "only reason" she married him was to escape Plains. Both, however, were determined to make the marriage work. Back home, the Carters would recall, "Divorce was considered to be a terrible sin that was committed only in faraway places like New York and Hollywood. Marriage vows were assumed to be absolutely binding for life."

Shortly after their engagement, Jimmy had sent Rosalynn *The Navy Wife,* a guidebook that she "studied to the last detail." Rosalynn became the "resourceful, efficient and brilliant general" in the "field of homemaking" the Navy expected. She missed Jimmy when he shipped out and "felt overwhelmed but Jimmy never seemed to worry about me." Jimmy had "no patience with tears, thinking instead that one makes the best of whatever situation—and with a smile," Rosalynn learned. The Navy also expected "a cheerful agreeableness rather than a resigned stoicism," she read in the guidebook. "Somehow, the Navy wife manages."

Things became harder to manage as Rosalynn gave birth to three boys in different ports. Jack was born in Portsmouth, Virginia, on July 3, 1947; Rosalynn marked her and Jimmy's first anniversary in the hospital. Chip was born in Honolulu in 1950, and Jeff in New London, Connecticut, two years later. Through it all, Rosalynn willed herself to become the ideal Navy wife: "She loves to travel, enjoys different people, changes of scene; but most of all, she loves the Service," the manual gushed. When Jimmy decided to move back to Plains in 1953, though, she resisted. The Carters argued "violently." "But Jimmy would have none of it," Rosalynn recalled. "His mind was made up, and he is a very stubborn man."

Both Miss Allie and Miss Lillian sensed Rosalynn's rage. Miss Lillian stopped the couple from moving into her home "because no house is big enough for two women." Apparently, no town was either; Miss Lillian soon took the extraordinary step of leaving Plains to serve as a housemother for a fraternity in Alabama.

As Jimmy built the business, Rosalynn helped. Miss Lillian seethed that Earl had never made her a partner—"I was just his wife"—but Jimmy made his wife "a co-partner." Rosalynn learned accounting and soon had a better grasp of the firm's finances than her husband did. Jimmy was "a hard teacher. He tells you how to do it and then he hasn't time to answer your questions. You have to figure it out from there." Jimmy later tried to endear himself to feminists by saying his partnership with Rosalynn "was a rare thing." Rosalynn considered such participation completely natural. Family life in the South, like the economy there, was closer to pre-industrial times, when women were integrated into the economic structure. Rosalynn had grown up without the "stereotype . . . of Southern belles," and with the reality of the working poor: "Women just worked and helped their husbands."

Rosalynn was proud of her contributions. "I was doing something more important than cooking and washing dirty blue jeans," she said. She "never really thought" she could advise her husband, "but I did, and I think that out of that there came a mutual respect and understanding between Jimmy and me that we might never have had otherwise." The Carters "were not only building a business. We were really building our marriage, too."

Jimmy the Baptist was the visionary, always ready to gamble. Rosalynn the Methodist was the skeptic, constantly asking, "Can't we relax and leave well enough alone for a while?" But Jimmy never stopped expanding the business, and he never stopped partaking in community service, church work, and night school courses. "Everything that could be done, I tried to do it," he said.

Although Rosalynn claimed the Carters "grew together—as full partners," Jimmy remained the boss. He decided to run for the Georgia senate in 1962 without consulting his wife—he simply announced it on his thirty-seventh birthday. Looking back, desiring a more egalitarian image, he would claim that such a unilateral move "would have been inconceivable in later years."

After Jimmy won, Rosalynn managed the business alone for the three months a year that her husband tended to state business. She "felt very, very important, because he couldn't have done it all if I hadn't managed the business." She was "more a political partner than a political wife." The added duties liberated her from "frivolous" tasks she disliked. She now rushed through her Christmas list, because "I wasn't trying to be perfect anymore."

When Jimmy ran for governor in 1966, he drafted his wife and the rest of the family into the campaign. Rosalynn was terrified. Once again she would have to teach herself. Unlike most political couples, the Carters usually traveled separately. With only three months to promote their obscure candidate, she recalled, "we had to go in different directions." In Georgia any kind of family campaigning was novel. "People had never seen the family of a gubernatorial candidate, and we could always get our picture on the front page."

Jimmy used Rosalynn as a surrogate, not a prop, insisting that his wife make speeches. At first she got sick to her stomach before speaking, but eventually she managed. Her brothers and sister could not believe that their reserved sister was speaking in public. Rosalynn repeated Jimmy's mantra: "It's just whatever you put your mind to." Rosalynn's emergence as a speechmaker would symbolize to her and to her family how she grew as Jimmy's wife, and as his running mate.

Jimmy's post-election depression intensified when Rosalynn entered the hospital for gynecological surgery. Recovering from her illness and his defeat, and planning a four-year crusade for the governorship, the Carters went off on a retreat. The two were growing ever more dependent on each other. "If it appears that they are a tight little unit, complete within themselves, with no real friends other than each other, it's because they are," one acquaintance said. Nine months after the retreat, Rosalynn gave birth to the couple's only daughter in October 1967.

Amy Carter was born into a family already embroiled in the 1970 race.

When Rosalynn went into labor, Jimmy was doing some early campaigning eighty miles away. When Amy was two, her mother was campaigning full-time. Rosalynn struggled with the working mother's dilemma: "Every time I came home she [Amy] had changed, and it was always sad to go off again." The anxiety, the guilt, the exhaustion, and the work itself made her consider the campaign "the hardest thing I'd ever had to do in my life." The family effort completed Jimmy's image as what his pollster called a "stylistic populist." The Carters shook hands with more than half the voters in Georgia—over six hundred thousand people.

Rosalynn had to develop her own political identity on the stump. When one mother explained how hard it was to care for a mentally retarded child, Rosalynn found her cause. Later that day, she crossed paths with her campaigning husband and slipped onto the receiving line. Before Jimmy recognized her, she said, "I want to know what you are going to do about mental health." Without missing a beat he replied, "We're going to have the best mental health system in the country, and I'm going to put you in charge of it."

After Jimmy won, Rosalynn "panicked." Jumping "from the simpler life of being a wife and mother in Plains . . . to being the First Lady of Georgia" traumatized her. "The move to the White House later was much easier for me." Before she could figure out how to be a governor's wife, however, Rosalynn had to contend with a more familiar problem. Miss Lillian moved into the governor's mansion, saying Rosalynn was too unsophisticated to be the state's hostess. Jimmy, as usual, was silent. Rosalynn finally confronted her mother-in-law. Miss Lillian could always "come and visit," but the governor's wife would run the mansion.

Rosalynn was equally resolute in defining her mandate. She considered herself a working woman who "hadn't planned to spend all my time pouring tea." She wanted to advise Jimmy, pursue some projects, serve as hostess, and yet somehow "let Amy be a normal child." Rosalynn could only achieve all this by refusing to be a typical First Lady. She established an office in the house and hired a secretary. Her parties would run smoothly but they lacked flair; she tried to accept the fact that "I would never be perfect." Nervous and despondent, Rosalynn renewed her faith, trying to release her problems to Jesus as Jimmy did.

Experience helped, too. The Carters learned that their instincts to wear jeans and entertain informally appeared refreshing. After years of intimidating farmers into dressing like city folk, urban Americans were dressing like farmers.

After four decades of responding to her mother and then her husband, Rosalynn finally had the self-confidence to start projects on her own. Rosalynn realized that "a First Lady can pick and choose her projects and do almost anything she wants because her name is a drawing card." She was particularly proud of her work on her husband's mental health commission, which multiplied the number of community mental health centers, day care centers, and training centers in Georgia from 23 to 134.

Still, Rosalynn's priority remained advising and boosting her husband. In the statehouse, as in the warehouse, Jimmy dreamed and his wife doubted. He also relied on her judgment in assessing personnel—she could sense disloyalty. Rosalynn used her mandate as a devoted wife to help in all facets of Jimmy's career. She was not afraid to disagree with him; she just refused to fight in public.

The Carters' only public spat occurred when the Georgia House of Representatives considered ratifying the Equal Rights Amendment in January 1974. The progressive in Jimmy supported the measure, but his populist political antennae sensed trouble. Trying to finesse the issue, he told a crowd protesting against the ERA, "I am for it—but my wife is against it!" That night, a friend confronted Rosalynn at a concert. Enraged, Rosalynn blurted out to her husband, "How could you?" Jimmy "just grinned." She decided that her husband had heard her criticize Gloria Steinem's pro-ERA march and mistook that for opposition. The next day, Rosalynn wore her "I'M FOR ERA" button. The measure failed, but Jimmy succeeded in muddying his tracks.

This contretemps aside, the Carters left the statehouse and entered the presidential run as "a team." Reporters and feminists treated Rosalynn's story as a tale of one woman's liberation. But the story was more Southern than Northern, more rural than feminist. Neither a traditional political wife nor a modern career woman, Rosalynn was Jimmy Carter's political partner. "The things that he does are important," she said, "but there is also a place for me to do the things that I'm interested in." Rosalynn, like many other Democratic wives, was following in Lady Bird Johnson's footsteps. Republicans tended to resist these kinds of political partnerships.

II

The Carters' presidential campaign applied the techniques of the 1970 Georgia governor's race nationally; Carter and his family would take "my campaign to the people." Jimmy promised to cure America after a decade and a half of corruption and incompetence. Carter ran to be the nation's paragon. "There must be no lowering of these standards, no acceptance of mediocrity in any aspect of our public or private lives," he insisted.

Jimmy tried to reject the excesses of the 1960s—the moral relativism, the family breakdown, the rampaging bureaucracy—while embracing popular products from the era—the emotional exhibitionism, the rhetoric of love, the passion for social justice. As an obscure outsider hyped by an amateur "Peanut Brigade" of friends and relatives, he also repudiated Nixon and his slick pols. Hipsters sneered, "How can you put confidence in a man who's been faithful to the same woman for 30 years?" But this cultural conservatism helped make Jimmy popular.

His was not a reserved conservatism; Jimmy could be as open—and indiscreet—as Mrs. Ford. He affirmed the media's dogma that a democratic leader should expose himself. The guarded, intense Southerner created a false intimacy with his broad smile and his carefully rationed revelations. George Will noted that his "most detailed campaign document *is* his autobiography."

Advertising his traditional marriage and his egalitarian instincts, Jimmy called his wife "a substitute candidate . . . a perfect extension of me." "I'm not doing this only for Jimmy," Rosalynn insisted, "there are lots of things I can do as First Lady." Jimmy sent her and their son Jack's mother-in-law, Edna Langford, to Florida to "make friends." Ros spent seventy-five days in Florida and visited more than one hundred communities in Iowa, the site of an early presidential caucus. In all, she would reach forty-two states.

Rosalynn Carter proved how much political wives could help. She explained, "I can call attention to Jimmy. Then when people hear his name again, they'll listen." Always well-briefed, Rosalynn reached out to Jimmy's core constituencies, especially blacks. She elicited the kind of reaction Betty Ford's aides imagined the incumbent First Lady received. "I'm going to vote for him," one young waiter in Orlando said after meeting Rosalynn. "Any man with a wife like that has got to be all right."

Her tension and her drip-dry dresses often made Rosalynn appear severe. Jack Ford passed her in a television studio and exclaimed, "That's one cold lady." Others found her as "tough-minded," "ambitious," and "humorless" as Jimmy. With a limited stable of Southern stereotypes, reporters began calling her the "Steel Magnolia," a tribute to her soft drawl and intense determination.

Rosalynn did not see herself as a feminist or a steely Southern belle; she was just doing what her mama and her neighbors did. When she hosted Rosalynn on her television show, Dinah Shore noted that working "does nothing to rob you of your femininity." When her fellow Southerner agreed, Shore concluded, "Equal rights and women's liberation appeared in the South without people making a big issue out of it."

Shore and others could not help asking Rosalynn how much "do you have . . . to do with Governor Carter's decisions?" Such questions always made Rosalynn cringe. She disliked being underestimated but did not want to overstep. She sat in "on all the strategy meetings." "Jimmy always listens to me," she said, although "he doesn't always take my advice." The Carters had a candid marriage. "We have always argued and debated about issues," she said. Her refusal to disagree with her husband publicly made it easy to underestimate Rosalynn's influence.

Rosalynn was also upstaged by Jimmy's colorful family. The Carters proved that eccentric extended Southern clans like William Faulkner's

Snopes and television's Beverly Hillbillies were not only found in fiction. Contributing to the Fords' debate about conventional behavior in the 1970s, Jimmy's brother, Billy Carter, exclaimed: "My mother joined the Peace Corps when she was 70, my sister Gloria is a motorcycle racer, my other sister, Ruth, is a Holy Roller preacher, and my brother thinks he is going to be President of the United States! I'm really the only normal one in the family."

Miss Lillian happily presided over the ménage—and diverted attention from Rosalynn. Reporters acknowledged that Jimmy's mother "became the darling of the media—the most candid, refreshing, and unpredictable personality of the year." Asked by a reporter to "define [a] white lie," she purred, "Do you remember when you came in the door a few minutes ago and I told you how good you looked and how glad I was to see you?"

Jimmy understood that his colorful kinfolk helped make him famous and underlined his promise to restore old-fashioned values. Every family tidbit he offered had a moral. He acknowledged his sons' experimentation with marijuana to illustrate their ability to "work with drug addicts with a feeling of understanding." He admitted that he and Rosalynn argued, then claimed that they resolved disputes by praying together at the side of their bed. When asked about this, and not told that Jimmy was the source, Rosalynn scoffed.

As the Carter juggernaut shifted from the primary to the general campaign, reporters began to scrutinize the Carters more carefully. Miss Lillian now came across as haughty, selfish, and mean. Billy came across as alcoholic, racist, and mean. His older brother began to appear self-righteous, shifty, and mean. Those who read the full *Playboy* interview saw a carefully packaged candidate who became prickly when pushed. Still, most reporters would not dismantle the image they helped construct over so many months. James Wooten of the *New York Times* was overheard saying, "I sound like I admire the Carter people; actually I despise them. . . . Southerners know he isn't a good ole boy or poor—he's the patrician of the town. His language is so subtle and smart. He thinks he's 99 percent smarter than anybody who's around him."

Carter revealed his less appealing side when he advocated maintaining the "ethnic purity" of some neighborhoods. The phrase appeared to be shorthand for segregation. Jimmy at first refused to disavow the remarks. Only when Rosalynn explained just how bad he had sounded did he try to remedy the situation. "When Jimmy gets stubborn, there is just one person who can handle him and that is Rosalynn," his cousin Hugh Carter would say.

The *Playboy* interview also caught Carter in the act of being himself. His need for approval and his desire to appear open and plebeian made him talk dirty. In an interview with Norman Mailer, Carter had uttered a four-letter expletive that the *New York Times* rendered as "——." Such slips were unavoidable after a twenty-two-month talkfest in which the candidate had peddled his personal life and beliefs. "Jimmy talks too much, but at least people

Franklin and Eleanor Roosevelt set the standard for modern presidential couples. Both Roosevelts were master illusionists who taught their successors the importance of maintaining a glowing image — whatever sordid realities lurked in the background. *Above*, the two often unhappy, often sparring partners present their public face: aristocratic yet ebullient, warm, and approachable. *(Franklin D. Roosevelt Library)*

World War II was a war for the American home, for Americans' consensus culture. General Dwight Eisenhower and his perky wife Mamie — pictured *above right* with statues of her two soldier boys, "Ike" and their son John — became national icons. They personified the sacrifices made at home and abroad. *(Dwight D. Eisenhower Library)* The war's canonization of domesticity helped trigger the greatest marrying spree in American history: 1.5 million soldiers tied the knot between the attack on Pearl Harbor and VJ Day. Lieutenant George Bush married his sweetheart Barbara on January 6, 1945 *(Bush Presidential Library)*; Ensign Jimmy Carter married Rosalynn Smith on July 7, 1946. *(Jimmy Carter Library)*

The conflicting demands of the Roosevelts' outsized legacy and Americans' desire for an old-fashioned presidential couple dogged Harry and Bess Truman. As the photo *right* from the 1944 Democratic convention in Chicago makes clear, Harry's nomination as Franklin Roosevelt's running mate upset Bess. Her unhappiness would distract Harry throughout his turbulent administration. Still, during the 1948 presidential election, *below*, Bess ("the Boss") and her daughter Margaret ("the Boss's boss") did their duty and became part of the "presidential trademark." *(Harry S. Truman Library)*

Only a war hero could have gotten away with this widely reprinted photograph (*above*) from October 1952 of Ike and Mamie Eisenhower in their jammies. *Life* ran the picture alongside an advertisement showing a housewife sitting at her Mary Proctor Hi-Lo Ironing Table. The two beaming smiles, the two waving hands, epitomized the Eisenhowers' promise of postwar prosperity and domestic bliss. In the White House, the Eisenhowers rebuilt their marriage after years of strain and gently guided the nation. Eventually Ike's illnesses, followed by various domestic and foreign upheavals, made the Eisenhowers seem doddering, though still popular. *Right*, Mamie escorts Ike out of Walter Reed Hospital after his June 1956 ileitis operation. (*Dwight D. Eisenhower Library*)

The seven presidential couples who occupied the White House from 1961 through 1993 courted, married, and began families during the dramatic days of World War II and the cold war. The 1961 inauguration marked the transition from the now stale Eisenhower years to the dazzling thousand days of John and Jackie Kennedy. Viewing the inaugural parade, the President and Mrs. Kennedy, Vice President and Mrs. Lyndon Johnson were flanked by heroes of the older generation, including Joseph P. and Rose Kennedy on the left and the Trumans one row behind on the right. The press hordes below signified the increasingly intrusive media stalking First Couples. *Below*, one photographer captured Jack and Jackie in an intimate pose during a 1962 state dinner, revealing the Kennedys' powerful mix of materialism, glamour, charisma, and sexuality. *(John F. Kennedy Library)*

Jackie Kennedy was a rather controversial First Lady. She hated reporters for publicizing embarrassing moments like the one pictured *above*. Jack was driven to distraction by Jackie's airs, her refusal to play politics, and her insistence on indulging in aristocratic sports like fox hunting. Still, despite the tensions between them and with reporters, the Kennedys transmitted a magical image of a happy family, as evidenced by the photo *left* taken on September 30, 1963. As usual, Jack and Jackie are staring at the cameras, not at each other. *(John F. Kennedy Library)*

In the most influential action taken by a modern First Lady, Jackie Kennedy shepherded the nation through the trauma of Jack's murder, then labeled her husband's administration with the lasting appellation "Camelot." Jack's successor, Lyndon B. Johnson, was sworn in by a woman judge on Air Force One. If Jackie Kennedy at that moment represented the American woman transcendent — glamorous, mysterious, remote — Lady Bird Johnson epitomized the authentic American woman — accommodating, loyal, and ready to enter the realm of men. *(Cecil Stoughton/Lyndon B. Johnson Library)*

The Johnsons appeared to be an ideal First Couple — cooperative, experienced, loving. But his grand dreams of a Great Society, and her influential role as his adviser and the champion of beautification, faded amid the controversy and pain of urban riots, the Vietnam war, and student rebellion. Rather than serving as a model for future co-presidents, the Johnson experience served notice that, even in an age of rising feminism, First Ladies could be only as successful as their husbands. (Yoichi R. Okamoto/Lyndon B. Johnson Library)

From the start of his political career, Richard Nixon shamelessly exploited his family. In this postcard (*right*) from his winning 1950 Senate race, Dick Nixon deployed an arsenal of postwar domestic artifacts: blonde children, a slim wife, and an inflatable cowboy "Bop Bag." *(Richard Nixon Library & Birthplace)* Two decades later, after finally winning the presidency, Nixon was still using his family. During a CBS Christmas special in 1971 (*below*), the President, wearing a colorful smoking jacket he wore only "at Christmas," was jocular, just a bit stiff, and a touch sweaty on the nose. Here was Nixon as the head of a cozy, devoted family, calculating that his family's love made him appear lovable to the public. Ever eager to give her husband the spotlight, Pat the faithful wife sat on the floor, gazing lovingly at her man. *(National Archives)*

THE NIXONS—PAT, JULIE, DICK AND TRICIA

Dear Friend:
Every California family has a real stake in the coming election. The vote you cast, or do not cast, may determine the fate of our American way of life.

National observers are agreed that Richard Nixon has done more constructive work to combat Communism than any other member of Congress.

Protect your future. Vote November 7th for Congressman Richard Nixon for United States Senator.

Sincerely,

Frank J. Slavinski

The success of Nixon's administration, however, depended on substantive actions such as détente with China. Standing on the Great Wall in 1972, at the peak of his political career, Nixon needed his wife Pat as a prop. Posing together conveyed his accomplishment to American voters and symbolized a new era in American foreign relations and presidential power. *(Richard Nixon Library & Birthplace)*

Nixon's long-suffering wife, unfairly caricatured as "Plastic Pat," was in fact a warm, vivacious First Lady who thrived in her role as "Ambassador to the World." In Russia, the contrast between the svelte, blonde First Lady and the dour, matronly *Babushkas* made Americans proud, while illustrating the onerous fashion demands made on American women, especially First Ladies. *(National Archives)*

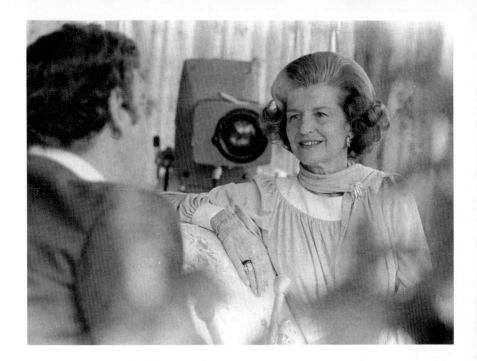

He's making us proud again.

The Fords appeared to be an all-American respite from "Tricky Dick." But by the 1970s, the consensus surrounding the World War II generation was shattering. Many Americans now defined being "normal" as sharing the pain and conflict of modern family life. In her 1975 interview with "60 Minutes" (*above*), Betty Ford spoke openly about sex, drugs, and abortion. The resulting controversy, and her continuing role as "the drunken wife at the company picnic," embarrassed the President. Still, in the new, media-driven culture of exposure, notoriety was often confused with popularity and political power. The unprecedented campaign poster *left* featuring a president and his wife tried to harness Betty's fame. In fact, her actions upstaged, undercut, and distracted her husband and may have cost Jerry Ford the election in 1976. *(Gerald R. Ford Library)*

Jimmy and Rosalynn Carter walked down Pennsylvania Avenue with their daughter Amy during the 1977 inauguration to mark the end of the imperial presidency (*above*). But the Carters' partnership, epitomized by their weekly working lunch, reeked of imperial prerogative (*left*). Many commentators misinterpreted this quintessentially rural and Southern partnership as a feminist statement. (*Jimmy Carter Library*)

As often happened during this age of the co-presidency (*right*), First Ladies thrived at their husbands' expense. By the time of this "60 Minutes" interview with Dan Rather during the 1980 campaign, the cool, open, relaxed candidate Carter of 1976 had become a stiff, gray, closed, and burdened President. Meanwhile, his wife had blossomed. (*Jimmy Carter Library*)

The 1981 inauguration offered Ronald and Nancy Reagan's retort to the iconoclasm of the 1960s as they celebrated enduring American ideals of elegance, conformity, power, success, and money. Parading as the exemplars of traditional values, they posed with their contentious family. The formal portrait *above* hinted at the underlying dynamics by isolating Nancy and Ronnie, whose intense relationship obscured all other ties. While the President's glamour and grandeur enhanced his status, "Queen Nancy" served as a lightning rod for criticism. In March 1982 "Second Hand Rose" wriggled into a frumpy getup at the annual Gridiron press "roast" to change her image (*left*). The resulting turnaround in coverage was a grotesque display of media power. Nancy succeeded because she worshiped the media lords in their own temple and embraced their values, emphasizing entertainment over dignity, cynicism over sincerity. (*Ronald Reagan Library*)

The Reagans celebrated old-fashioned virtues but created a modern peer marriage. Most photographs of this warm, spontaneous couple showed them touching, hugging, glancing at each other. The Reagans' joint radio speech against drugs in 1982 (*above*) highlighted Nancy's unlikely role as a modern mainstream feminist and a pioneering First Lady. Nancy balanced her central role in the war against drugs and in her husband's administration with an intense wifely devotion. *Below*, Nancy gazes at Ronnie as he entrances the country once again with his signature brew of patriotism, melodrama, nostalgia, optimism, and idealism. *(Ronald Reagan Library)*

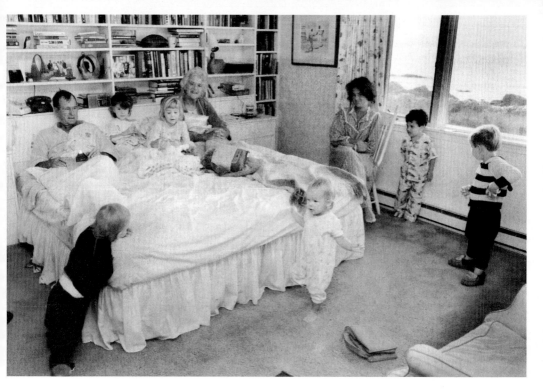

George and Barbara Bush heralded a WASP restoration led by "the real Reagans" — a genuine war hero married to a traditional wife who raised a warm and loving family. This intimate shot from 1987 of Vice President and Mrs. Bush, their daughter Dorothy, and only six of their ten grandchildren at the time in Kennebunkport, Maine, set the tone for his presidency. *(Bush Presidential Library)*

In public, the Bushes endorsed the separate spheres illustrated by this Oval Office scene, where he tended the office, she minded the family, and Millie the dog stood watch. This traditional arrangement contributed to Barbara's great popularity, even though such distinctions were impossible to maintain in the modern White House. Barbara, too, was an active co-president, but her grandmotherly demeanor made her seem benign. *(Bush Presidential Library)*

The Clintons inherited this contradictory legacy. They promised a co-presidency, epitomized by Hillary Clinton's role in their health insurance reform plan. *Above*, the First Lady presents their health bill to Congress, flanked by a bipartisan group of legislators including Bob Dole, Bill Clinton's rival in 1996. Fear of powerful women, combined with an atavistic anxiety about unelected presidential advisers, helped destroy the Clintons' co-presidency and their reform scheme. (© *1993 The Washington Post. Reprinted with permission.*) Yet even as Hillary made herself over into a more traditional First Lady and Bill publicly distanced himself from his wife to revive his presidency (*left*), this savvy, well-educated powerhouse still had her husband's ear.
(© *1994 The Washington Post. Reprinted with permission.*)

know he's honest and doesn't mind answering questions," Rosalynn said, squirming. "I trust him completely and it doesn't bother me at all." She blamed the press for going after every blooper.

Rosalynn feared that the campaign was floundering. For weeks she had been hectoring Jimmy to stop playing the liberal and return to his conservative fiscal message. Unlike Jimmy, she recoiled at Betty Ford's candor. Asked on camera if she had ever committed adultery or had lust in her heart, Rosalynn seethed, "If I had, I wouldn't tell you." To yet another question about "lust" she replied, "I think I'd like to talk about . . . aren't there some other issues?"

Carter learned his lesson from the *Playboy* interview. He became more guarded. But the dilemma persisted. Once elected President, Jimmy had to maintain his reputation for candor while upholding the dignity of the office.

In mid-December, Barbara Walters featured the First Couple-to-be on an ABC special, along with one of the reigning couples in Hollywood at the time, Barbra Streisand and Jon Peters. During the Carters' segment, the two appeared dressed casually, he in a cardigan, she in a green dress. The two lounged on their living room couch in Plains, sitting side by side, with Jimmy's right arm on the headrest behind his wife. They appeared relaxed and open, with Jimmy suitably protective of Rosalynn, both ready to share with the American people in what Walters called "a very personal conversation."

Walters peppered the Carters with invasive questions. She asked: "Does he have any irritating habits? . . . Does Mrs. Carter have any irritating habits? . . . What makes your marriage work? . . . Is he romantic? . . . Does he bring flowers and write love letters? . . . Do you ever argue? . . . [Was it true that Jimmy wanted a baby, Rosalynn did not, and] you did it for your husband? . . . Will you be able to wear jeans and walk around in a bathrobe in the White House? . . . Will you join a church near the White House? . . . Will you be bringing your own bed? . . . Do you sleep in a double bed or twin bed? . . . What women did she want to be? . . . What men did she like?" Walters asked about Rosalynn's guilt about abandoning Amy, her conflict with Miss Lillian, her fears that Jimmy might be assassinated, and whether her husband reminded her of Rhett Butler. Rosalynn deflected some of the most invasive questions with a giggle; Jimmy sidestepped. On the sleeping arrangements, Rosalynn modestly volunteered, "When Jimmy was Governor we had a First Lady's bedroom and a Governor's bedroom, and Amy slept in the First Lady's bedroom." Walters pressed, "So, I assume then, that you'll be sharing a room, and the second bedroom will be a bedroom for Amy or recreation or something else." Jimmy chuckled, "We're not about to change after thirty years."

Behind the smiles and the giggles, both Carters were fuming. Jimmy occasionally betrayed his anger with a pursed mouth. After the interview, he said he would never again agree to meet with Walters unless she promised to avoid such questions. But it was hard to limit Walters and her colleagues after indulging them for so long.

III

Jimmy Carter's slim victory over Gerald Ford was celebrated as a triumph of peanuts, Plains, and the people. Lacking a strong power base, a commitment to issues, deep party support, or a broad mandate, Carter had to continue emphasizing "style." His pollster, Patrick Caddell, preached the new gospel that "governing with public approval requires a continuing political campaign." Jimmy had to build on his apparent "concern" with "the average person." Just as Governors Jerry Brown and Michael Dukakis built support with "life style" gestures, President Carter could govern effectively by "cutting back on 'imperial' frills."

Jimmy's attempt to tone down the presidency jibed with his push to economize. The nation was beginning to pay the bills for the Great Society and the Vietnam War. With the budget deficit growing and the value of the dollar declining, a struggle over the size of the government ensued. Carter, the populist engineer, was confident that he could make the government thrifty and efficient. When he strayed, his conservative wife would remind him that "we won . . . because people saw Jimmy Carter . . . does not believe in massive federal spending programs." Unlike most of her predecessors, Rosalynn wanted to emphasize thrift.

Although Gerald Ford had also tried to dismantle the "Imperial Presidency," Jimmy Carter became obsessed with this task. The first movie his family watched in the White House was *All the President's Men,* celebrating the triumph of media skepticism and exposure over Nixonian patriotism and secrecy. The new chief executive called himself "Jimmy," not "James Earl Jr.," and told his staff to "always say 'Rosalynn' instead of 'Mrs. Carter.'" He walked down Pennsylvania Avenue with Rosalynn and Amy after the inauguration to herald a new era of openness.

The walk also confirmed that the President and his wife were partners. Rosalynn was part of his political identity, and his mandate. Jimmy credited her with choosing the verse from Micah in his inaugural address—about aspiring "to do justly, and to love mercy, and to walk humbly with thy God"—and inserting a vow to strengthen the family, "which is the basis of our society." Jimmy would elevate their strong marriage to an ideal one: "We communicated easily, and often we had the same thoughts without speaking. We had been ridiculed at times for allowing our love to be apparent to others. It was not an affectation, but was as natural as breathing." Individually, Rosalynn and Jimmy could be harsh, but together they were delightful. Despite having spent their first eight years together in a military culture that demanded restraint, the pair often kissed, hugged, or touched in public. "Holding hands is something I never even noticed," Rosalynn later confessed. "It just comes naturally."

With the inauguration, Americans happily transformed the Carters from the Snopes to the Waltons. Johnny Carson, the nation's "emcee," found the caustic Miss Lillian "delightful, like everyone's grandmother." *Time* hired a Southern novelist, Reynolds Price, to praise the Carters as a "national family" that would "feed us" with "the stories of care and honest consolation that we've needed for very much longer than was good." Americans needed Plains to be what the historian Betty Glad would call a "rural Camelot." Making the First Family perfect reassured Americans that their families could be perfect, too. It also advertised the administration's vow to "strengthen" the family, "unlike some prior Administrations whose actions through ignorance or indifference damaged families."

After too many months on the road, Rosalynn happily gathered her family around her. Chip took a part-time political job and moved into the White House with his pregnant wife, Caron, who gave birth to a boy in February. Jeffrey enrolled in George Washington University and moved in, along with his wife, Annette. Meanwhile, Amy settled in as the youngest occupant of the White House since John-John Kennedy. "This is home," Rosalynn exulted. To prove that they were "relentlessly just-plain-folks," she and Jimmy posed for *Time* sitting on the Truman balcony in their rocking chairs, "like generations of Southern couples on countless porches of a summer evening."

Rosalynn expected to be an active First Lady, but the East Wing was chaotic, demoralized, and ineffectual. An average of one hundred invitations and up two thousand letters arrived each week. An entourage of 50 to 115 reporters usually accompanied the First Lady on her travels. Carter's transition team concluded that the Office of the First Lady had to be modernized and adapted to Mrs. Carter's "needs." A decade after Nixon's attempt, the East Wing was not yet integrated into the White House bureaucracy. Merging the East Wing and West Wing correspondence sections would improve coordination. The social entertainment office was reduced to accommodate the Carters' desire for a "working White House." Shifting clerical jobs to the West Wing freed "precious physical space in the East Wing" and provided cover for staff increases in press relations, advancing, and "substantive First Lady projects."

The reorganization distanced the First Lady's office from its roots as an ad hoc center for social affairs and family support. Maintaining the tradition of Liz Carpenter and Sheila Weidenfeld, Mary Hoyt combined the jobs of press secretary to the First Lady and staff coordinator. Hoyt and the Carters had more "substantive" concerns for "an active and popular First Lady."

Funding for the East Wing had evolved haphazardly in small, improvised grants buried in larger congressional allocations for running the White House. It was then continued out of "tradition." Officially, though, lawyers concluded that Rosalynn Carter's seventeen aides and the four staffers for Joan Mondale, the vice president's wife, were "illegal employees" because federal employees were not allowed to "work for private citizens." Only on November 2, 1978, would a short amendment to Public Law 95-570 finally authorize "assistance and services . . . to be provided to the spouse of the President in connection with assistance provided by such spouse to the President in the discharge of the President's duties and responsibilities."

These changes invigorated the East Wing while expanding it. In his zeal to establish his wife's credibility, the man who was "de-pomping" the West Wing would be criticized for making the East Wing more imperial. Headlines pronouncing "Rosalynn Carter Wants Bigger Staff" embarrassed the Carters. A public that had spent two years reading about Betty Ford's many activities did not understand why Mrs. Carter needed more help. East Wingers would also have a hard time explaining that their demand for perks and salaries commensurate with their West Wing peers was a matter of respect, not a grab for power. No longer a bureaucratic outlaw, the Office of the First Lady still lacked legitimacy.

The "First Lady-elect," as her aides called her, refused to establish a "projects office." That was how Lady Bird Johnson's environmental crusade had been trivialized. Instead Rosalynn proposed a "Projects, Issues and Research office" to reflect her breadth; its coordinator quickly became known as the "Director of Projects." In fact, Rosalynn needed a project director to help her fulfill "my one and only campaign promise: to study the mental health needs of our nation." She wanted "to take mental illnesses and emotional disorders out of the closet." Jimmy had promised to establish a Presidential Commission on Mental Health, and she expected to be "the chairperson."

A law passed after Robert Kennedy served as his brother's attorney general, though, barred a "public official" from appointing close relatives, even if they served for free. Mrs. Carter could become honorary chairman "if she remained sufficiently removed from the commission's official function," the Justice Department's Office of Legal Counsel warned. She should "avoid being the moving force" but could attend hearings, submit her ideas, offer her support, and solicit support from others. This dodge highlighted the First Lady's anomalous position, even after the recent transformations. It was difficult to translate the fluid and nebulous position of First Lady into bureaucratic imperatives. Legal fictions became essential.

Rosalynn would repeatedly run into such problems. Conflict-of-interest laws, the push to economize, the de-pomping of the White House, and the ambiguity of the position complicated matters. When Rosalynn traveled on official business, for example, the White House could not pay for a private citizen, the Democratic National Committee did not want to underwrite government business, and it was inappropriate and possibly illegal for the First Lady's hosts to pay.

Rosalynn became honorary chairperson of the mental health commission, which President Carter appointed in February 1977. Faced with her "first opportunity" to be seen "operating in a substantive area," Rosalynn vowed to take the lead. Her good friend Dr. Peter Bourne warned that her "entire image" as First Lady was at stake. The commission held public hearings, issued position papers on twenty-four task panels, and relied on more than two hundred volunteers. Deftly, Rosalynn and her aides shuttled between the White House domestic policy staff, the Department of Health, Education and Welfare, the National Institutes of Health, and the relevant congressional committees. The commission produced a voluminous preliminary report by its September 1977 deadline.

Dr. Bourne and Rosalynn had assumed that all this activity would attract "media attention" and generate "public interest." But reporters did not just want an activist First Lady, they demanded she address "sexy" issues. Rosalynn resented her dependence on the media's whims. Mental health should not be "dismissed as a First Lady's 'pet project.'" She refused to hold a Washington press conference until September, when she presented the commission's preliminary report. Now the press was the "captive audience," and she could "raise some questions that are important to *my* work—instead of the other way around."

The commission's final report made 117 recommendations, including 8 "major" ones. The resulting Mental Health Systems Act of 1980 provided $99.1 million to integrate mental health into the broader health care system. Rosalynn ignored the proprieties as she lobbied, becoming the first First Lady since Mrs. Roosevelt to testify before Congress and earning praise for her aplomb. This ambitious mental health project would be only the beginning of her activism.

Rosalynn's "greatest disappointment" was the failure of the Equal Rights Amendment. In 1978, ERA proponents pushed to extend the ratification deadline—they were three states short of final approval. Rosalynn "did just about anything I could think of for the cause"; conservatives felt she did too much, while feminists fumed that she did not do enough. She wondered whether it was "appropriate" for the First Lady to be auctioned off at a dance for the ERA, until Jimmy said, "Well, it's better than being a wallflower!"

Jimmy dutifully supported the drive. The Democrats were trying to deepen what they would call a "gender gap" with Republicans by including women in the party's array of special-interest groups. Besides, his wife and mother left him little choice.

At the Houston conference celebrating International Women's Year in

1977, Rosalynn proudly linked arms with Betty Ford and Lady Bird Johnson. The First Lady worried that the ERA and feminism had a "serious" image problem. "Attention has often centered on those supporters who have appeared to be demanding and strident man haters," she would explain; she wanted to show that "nice women" wanted the ERA, too. Echoing Betty Ford, Rosalynn said, "I am a relatively traditional person. I enjoy my roles as wife, mother, partner and businesswoman. I care how I look—and what I think. I'm not threatened by ERA. I feel freed by it."

The ERA debate provoked a civil war among American women. Two opposing conceptions of "womanhood" clashed. Mrs. Carter's participation in the IWY conference elicited "the most impassioned [letters] ever received on any previous issue," according to the White House weekly mail report. Opponents linked the ERA with gay rights and abortion. "This confusion makes it even more difficult for them to understand how a self-professed Christian and family advocate can support such legislation." Such reactions reinforced Rosalynn's caution and her sense that feminists had lost the heartland.

Rosalynn's status as the "wife of" a powerful person, rather than someone powerful in her own right, unsettled many feminists. Following Nixon's example, Carter assigned women's issues to the West Wing. In 1978 Sarah Weddington became a Special Assistant to the President "to move women into the mainstream of White House and government activities." But even though Rosalynn helped hire this Texas attorney, who had argued *Roe v. Wade,* Weddington distanced her efforts from the First Lady. The newsletter "White House News on Women," which Weddington sent to fourteen thousand supporters, often ignored Rosalynn's activities.

Weddington's fiefdom reflected the mushrooming federal government, as well as women's growing political importance. The burgeoning welfare state continued to thrust the president into previously inviolate areas. While equality for women could be defined as a civil rights issue, identifying preservation of the family as a major Carter administration goal politicized family life in novel ways. This further blurred the division of labor in the White House. The President took a stand on many issues traditionally relegated to the woman's sphere, including adolescent pregnancy, adoptions, child abuse, "early childhood development," "the quality of family life," and nutrition.

Rosalynn avoided being ghettoized into either a single issue or a set of "women's issues." She functioned as Jimmy's chief partner—over and above his close relationship with Vice President Walter Mondale. Hamilton Jordan and other aides respected the First Lady's "keen political antennae" and her power. "I am a political person," she affirmed. "I have influence and I know it!" The President often marked important papers in the upper right hand corner: "Ros, Comment, J." When staffers could not convince Jimmy to do something, they often asked "Ros" to help.

Rosalynn helped temper Jimmy's zeal, from small things like lobbying him to adjust the temperature in the White House back from energy-crisis levels and arguing for the reinstatement of "Hail to the Chief" to bigger ones like begging him to defer some of his unpopular initiatives to a second term. Jimmy never asked, "What do I do about this?" the First Lady said. "Never in his life has he ever asked me that." But the Carters would sit on the Truman balcony and chat. Rosalynn knew that "He would never do it if I said, 'Do this.'" She was most effective suggesting, "Let's not do it this way," especially on political matters.

Rosalynn did not overstep. "Some things I won't even approach him on," she admitted. "I know his mind's made up." She shied away from personnel matters. "I don't even let Rosalynn criticize my staff," Carter would explain. "That's the quickest way she can aggravate me." She avoided economics and defense, focusing instead on social issues, foreign policy, and politics above all. In December 1978, Barbara Walters asked Rosalynn why she never criticized the President. Acknowledging that her agenda was different than the media's agenda to stoke conflict, Rosalynn said, "I would lose all my effectiveness with him."

While Rosalynn downplayed her influence, Jimmy celebrated it. The President told "Barbara" that "I don't hesitate to discuss with her every major decision that I have to make; unless it involves a vital and top secret security point which I do not share with anyone." When pressed for an instance when his wife changed his mind, the President stammered, "I think a change in emphasis, sometimes in domestic programs involving the elderly or mental health, she is a very effective spokesman." By celebrating his wife's influence in general though incoherent terms, Jimmy scored points with women voters; he knew that specifying contributions would undermine his own decisions and image.

The two biggest symbols of Rosalynn's influence were her weekly "working lunch" with the President and her attendance at Cabinet meetings. The regular meals in the President's study began because, at first, Rosalynn barraged Jimmy every night with questions "about the mansion, correspondence, public events, official and personal visitors, and our family budget." Finally, Jimmy suggested that she "save these routine things" for a weekly lunch "so we can do them all in one day."

Even so, the White House "contact master list" logged dozens of meetings between the President and the First Lady each week for strategy sessions, ceremonies, state dinners, lunches, and movies. Several months into the Presidency, Jimmy began waking up at 5:30 A.M. so he could stay home after dinner. He and Rosalynn tried to keep their schedules free after 4:30 P.M. so they could jog, play tennis, swim, or bowl together. During one of the administration's many reassessments, Hamilton Jordan noted that "Rosalynn spends more time with you than anyone." Jordan made the "suicidal sugges-tion" that they lunch "every other week" instead of weekly. Jordan kept his job, but his recommendation was ignored.

Rosalynn's presence at Cabinet meetings proved her unprecedented status. The First Lady tried to minimize the novelty, explaining that the meetings included "secretaries, people whom Cabinet officers have asked to come in to report on some project . . . and lesser government officials." As with the lunches, the Cabinet invitation stemmed from Rosalynn's tendency to pounce on Jimmy when he "got off the elevator." In February 1978 he in-vited her "to the Cabinet meetings, and then you will know why we make these decisions." Rosalynn sheepishly admitted that the invitation was ut-tered "in exasperation," but "I cannot imagine anybody . . . being asked to sit in on Cabinet meetings and not doing it."

There were, of course, limits to the relationship and to Rosalynn's influ-ence. Jimmy was still the President, and both the weekly lunches and the Cabinet attendance originated because Jimmy needed to subdue Ros. One source told *Time* that if she ever was so "presumptuous" as to give the Presi-dent policy advice, "he would cut her off at the knees"; she was merely a "sounding board." In the black-and-white world of reporters, where Ros-alynn was either Lady Macbeth or a decorative Southern belle, Rosalynn's pushing and Jimmy's limits would prove that "theirs is no different from any other Southern marriage," with Jimmy indulging Rosalynn's desire to appear influential. This particular leak was one of many attempts to downplay Ros-alynn's formidable role.

Neither Jimmy nor Rosalynn had a master plan for their partnership; her stature grew in the White House as naturally as it had grown in the ware-house. As both confidante and emissary, she operated with Jimmy's blessing. In the White House pressure cooker, Jimmy naturally turned to her for more and more tasks.

Four months into his term, the President of the United States sent his wife to Latin America. This was not a Pat Nixon–style goodwill tour but a serious attempt to befriend America's southern neighbors. Administration officials repeatedly called the tour "substantive" to impress the First Lady and her skeptical hosts. Many Latin Americans resented the President for sending his wife. Congressman Dante Fascell stormed into one of her baker's dozen of two-hour briefings and barked: "The Latins are macho and they hate gringos and women. What else do you want to know?"

Rosalynn, though, "was *determined* to be taken seriously." She said, "Every one of the leaders wanted to talk to the President of the United States. And who is closer to the President, who better has his ear, than his wife?" She of-fered the broader explanation that "I've always worked," defining her part-nership with Jimmy as one more job in a lifetime of responsibilities.

The First Lady was visibly nervous when she began the two-week, twelve-thousand-mile tour on May 30, 1977 by landing in Jamaica with nineteen aides, nine Secret Service agents, and twenty-seven reporters. Each visit, her aide Rhonda Bush explained, entailed a "substantive bilateral" meeting with either the head of the state or the head of the government, an official dinner, a meeting with Americans, and a "public event" characteristic of a typical goodwill tour. Always the good student, Rosalynn toted around a book with her notes outlining "Jimmy's policy." The First Lady ostentatiously wrote down messages from the leaders that she would deliver to her husband.

Rosalynn Carter proved to be charming, knowledgeable, and formidable. Reporters now had a new angle to play—that the First Lady was competent. "In Peru it was clear that Rosalynn Carter not only knew where she was, but what she was doing," ABC reported, clearly surprised. She told the head of Peru's military junta that if he held democratic elections, she would attend the inauguration. When she fulfilled her promise in 1979, the incoming president embraced her in the middle of his inaugural speech. In Colombia, a reception for "wives only" was opened to government ministers. This shift, State Department diplomats wired back to Washington, "reflected the growing Colombian realization that Mrs. Carter's tour is substantive and . . . not a flying coffee klatsch."

The President was proud of his wife's success, and relieved as well. Just before the trip, he had backpedaled and started emphasizing its ceremonial aspects. But Jimmy needed Rosalynn as his "eyes and ears" at home and his mouthpiece abroad. His big investment in the trip helped it succeed. He had already sent Miss Lillian and Chip to India. Some argued that traditional societies appreciated these marks of the President's personal interest, but other observers disliked these kingly prerogatives. They wondered, is "an Imperial Family taking over where the Imperial President left off?"

Women reporters seemed particularly hostile. One female journalist asked Rosalynn, "Have you felt entirely comfortable with the knowledge you bring to these meetings, to understand what you're talking about?" After the trip, NBC's Judy Woodruff peppered the First Lady on "Today," asking: "What gives you the right to conduct foreign policy? . . . Would Jimmy Carter want to talk foreign policy with the wife of Soviet chairman Brezhnev?" Woodruff tipped her hand when she said, "You were handed an assignment simply because you were the wife of the President—isn't that kind of a setback for the women's movement?" Bristling, Rosalynn sidestepped the question. She insisted that in "every single country I went to, I had leaders of the country say to me 'Mrs. Carter, you are doing great things for women.'" The hostile response Rosalynn often received from feminists explained why she spoke about "women" rather than the "women's movement."

Americans remained unsure what to do with what *Newsweek's* Meg Greenfield called the "unelected kin of elected officials." More were grumbling,

"Who elected her?" even as others viewed the First Lady as "Mrs. President." In the modern White House, "the wife of a President cannot avoid Government service or play only a private role," the *New York Times* proclaimed. Therefore, its editors reasoned, "visible influence" was better than shadowy "pillow talk." The high tide of feminism had shifted the debate to a plane more respectful of women's competence, but the problem raised a fundamental question about the unelected, unappointed, unimpeachable status of the First Lady.

The Carters evaded this question, defusing the issue by downplaying Rosalynn's power. A few months after the Latin American trip, the administration reevaluated its decision to block Israel's sale of twenty-four Kfir fighter jets to Ecuador. Unnamed "sources" credited Mrs. Carter, but Rosalynn's press secretary sidestepped the question. "She talked regularly with her husband on the trip and she's talked to him at some length since she's been home," Mary Hoyt said. Yet somehow, "she wanted to make it clear" to the press and the public that she did not intercede.

This tendency to discount her influence and to support the President publicly proved that Rosalynn Carter was no Eleanor Roosevelt. Nevertheless, the comparison with Franklin Roosevelt's First Lady was irresistible and facile. Jimmy fed it by calling his wife "my Eleanor," a play on the first name Rosalynn never used. Rosalynn dismissed the analogy; she was more supportive, deferential, and powerful than Eleanor Roosevelt had ever been. If anything, Rosalynn was more like Edith Wilson—Woodrow Wilson's second wife and shadow prime minister—or perhaps a more evolved version of Lady Bird Johnson than Franklin Roosevelt's independent crusader.

Leading feminists were enraged. "More than any other president's wife I have seen there is no independent thought or phrasing separate from him," Gloria Steinem fumed. Even East Wing staffers mocked the First Lady's tendency to preface her remarks by saying, "Jimmeh thinks" and "Jimmeh feels" and "Jimmeh says." A White House television correspondent blamed the President: "He is not a totally liberated person. He wants Rosalynn to be active but he wants her to fill a certain role and no more. He wants to be proud of the little woman."

As the memory of their Latin American jaunt faded, reporters grew restive. More and more, they began to write about the First Lady's "fuzzy" image, saying she was as unfocused and as naive as her husband. Rosalynn's predecessors, they complained, "whether or not they had an impact at least had a clear image." Jackie renovated, Lady Bird beautified, Pat volunteered, and Betty spoke out, "but when one mentions the name of Rosalynn Carter, many people draw a blank," reporters charged, annoyed they could not stereotype Mrs. Carter. The reporters wanted the First Lady to be independent, not loyal.

Rosalynn was not interested in being newsworthy. The quotation under her photograph in her junior-college yearbook had said, "There is great ability in knowing how to conceal one's ability." The First Lady certainly refused to feed reporters' appetite for controversy. "That's their identity crisis, not mine," she said, dismissing her critics. Rosalynn had been extraordinarily productive. That first year she visited 16 countries and 21 cities; gave 12 major speeches, 26 media interviews, 21 photo sessions, and 26 press conferences; received 210 hours of Spanish lessons, 10 violin lessons, 8 speed-reading lessons, and 71 hours of briefings on Latin America and Europe; and hosted 17 arrival ceremonies, 8 state dinners, 8 luncheons, 8 teas, and 52 receptions. Of course, she affected disinterest in her image. In fact, she was frustrated by her inability to command attention, especially regarding mental health. Despite her press releases and public meetings, reporters would "always" say, "why don't you do something . . . sexy?"

Most Washington reporters and their "enlightened" peers now condemned intense devotion to one's spouse. One poll found that from 1962 to 1977, the percentage of women who believed that "most of the important decisions in the life of the family should be made by the man of the house" had halved from two-thirds to one-third. Younger, well-educated, and working women—a category that included most reporters—were more likely to be egalitarian. By 1980, only 40 percent of women surveyed would want a "traditional life." A Roper poll concluded that "older, more traditional women are more liberal today even than young radicals were in 1970." Rosalynn insisted, "I do not think that my respect for him—just because he is my husband—diminishes me as a woman."

Despite reporters' unhappiness, a Pat Caddell poll after the Latin America trip found that "Mrs. Carter's rating has increased greatly," from 56 percent favorable in January to 78 percent in July 1977. Rosalynn was popular across the political spectrum; even 60 percent of ardent Republicans approved. Unlike Betty Ford, Rosalynn did not alienate voters, with 85 percent saying that "there is nothing they dislike about Mrs. Carter." Seventy percent of the respondents rated the Latin America trip "excellent or good," an "extraordinary" rating. Of particular interest to strategists was her popularity among core Democratic supporters, such as Jews and blacks, as well as with undecided voters in the 1980 election race. Caddell concluded, "She clearly helps the President across the board." Passing the poll to his wife, Jimmy advised, "Rosalynn—Don't run against your husband!"

Though such applause for her activism would have been impossible in an earlier era, the poll was not the mandate Caddell's client desired. Rosalynn's popularity stemmed from her position, not from particular achievements. Analysis of her mail made that clear. Christmas cards, birthday wishes, and pleas for photographs and personal blessings came in by the thousands; requests for assistance with various personal and bureaucratic problems came in by the hundreds; and issue-oriented letters came in only by the dozens. Less than one-fifth of the 428,282 letters Rosalynn and the First Family would receive in four years would address issues. Barely 5 percent would concern Mrs. Carter's mental health crusade, and only 3 percent would discuss the elderly.

Undoubtedly, despite the jeering, most Americans approved Rosalynn's devotion to Jimmy. In an age of activism, Rosalynn combined new responsibilities with traditional values. Her compatriots among Gallup's ten most admired women in 1980 would include such pioneers as Governor Ella Grasso, Congresswoman Barbara Jordan, Barbara Walters, Jane Fonda, and two prime ministers, Margaret Thatcher and Indira Gandhi. But it would also include Jackie Onassis, Nancy Reagan, and Mother Teresa. Mrs. Carter was caught between Americans' desire for a traditional First Lady, her and her husband's wish for a working partnership, and reporters' need for an outspoken celebrity. Unfortunately, in the media age, the faction that merited the least say—reporters—had the loudest voice.

IV

Rosalynn Carter was not the only one in the family having trouble with the press. Jimmy's broad appeal in 1976 did not translate into an effective governing strategy. His fiscal conservatism alienated Democrats still committed to the Great Society and did not satisfy Republicans yearning for what Tom Wolfe would call the "Great Relearning." The high moral standards Jimmy set only made it easier for reporters to snipe. As the dreaded Washington establishment devoured the self-righteous outsider, the press turned on its creation. Beginning in February 1977, for 46 months in a row the number of negative news stories would outnumber the positive ones. Even Richard Nixon fared better.

President Carter continued to struggle with the different impulses he inherited from his parents. He was never sure whether to play the populist or be a progressive, to pal around with the boys like Mr. Earl or save the world like Miss Lillian. As a result, Jimmy would seem both too demagogic and too principled, simultaneously too sensitive to polls and too committed to his own agenda. America was not yet ready for a "new man" in the Oval Office. In a nation growing ever more aware of "gender"—the modern term for the cultural dimensions of sexual identity—Carter's attributes were seen in sexual terms and rejected by millions.

A former Ford speechwriter, John Mihalec, later noted, "Jimmy Carter first presented himself to the nation as a masculine personality. Naval Academy. Submariner. Nuclear Engineer. . . . But once in office, he lost no time revealing his true feminine spirit." Jimmy was a conciliator. "He wouldn't twist arms. He didn't like to threaten or rebuke." He embraced peace in the Middle East, human rights, the SALT II arms-limitation agreement, and the return of the Panama Canal. At home, Carter reorganized the government, a form of housecleaning, and inflation sapped strength from the dollar, the seminal symbol of American power. "In a sense, we've already had a 'woman' president: Jimmy Carter," Mihalec claimed. "And his feminine style of leadership nearly drove us crazy."

Making his wife so prominent did little to shore up Jimmy's macho status, nor did all his gestures to "de-pomp" and thus defang the presidency. Ironically, the First Lady emerged as the more hard-headed politician. She kept her eye on the polls while Jimmy babbled about high ideals. In January 1979, Jimmy showed Rosalynn the seventh draft of his upcoming third State of the Union Address. Her criticisms anticipated Ronald Reagan's subsequent campaign against Jimmy's impotent Presidency. "The mood of the country is toward less government, cutting taxes, balancing the budgets," she wrote. She urged her husband to stop thinking "that 'we' & government—or government—have all the answers." Rosalynn suggested that the speech "be more demagogic and a 'call to action' to people in our country to assume responsibilities."

The speech Jimmy delivered reflected the conflict between the two Carters, and among his warring impulses. He defined the "problems we face today" as "more complex" than "those that confronted earlier generations." His conclusion that "few of these problems can be solved by government alone" acknowledged the backlash against liberal statism. Yet he claimed that "in our government it is a myth that we must choose between compassion and competence." The problems of the country had become the problems of the man.

Carter's people preferred blasting the media to addressing their boss's shortcomings and their own ineptitude. By 1979, Jimmy's adviser Hedley Donovan would find the press scapegoated "at least six or eight times" in one Cabinet meeting. Vietnam and Watergate convinced reporters that they "are the good guys and the politicians, particularly the President, are the bad guys," Hamilton Jordan mourned. The resulting fault-finding and "cynicism" undermined "respect for all of our institutions."

Jimmy's repudiation of what he called "permanent Washington" deprived the President of a safety net. Rosalynn Carter later admitted it was a "mistake" that "we didn't get involved in the social life in Washington. He felt he was there to run the government and not go out and party every night." Jimmy admitted that "it never has been my nature to be a hail fellow, well met." His no-nonsense wife, with her polyester dresses and interest in policy matters, did not help. At one soiree, a guest spied a "look in Rosalynn's eyes that you see in foreigners who don't speak English very well." The Carters made things worse by gutting the White House "social entertainment office."

With Rosalynn uninterested in formal entertaining, Jimmy evinced a

Nixonian attention to detail in orchestrating social affairs. He combed through the guest lists, complaining of one proposal, "Too many W[hite] H[ouse], N[ational] S[ecurity] C[ouncil] and State [Department] Guests. None from Business and public." He kept an eye on the budget, fearful of entertaining too lavishly, yet he minimized the use of the most important resource—his presence. He would boast in his diary about curtailing "the ceremonial events that Presidents ordinarily attend" and letting "my sons and their wives and Rosalynn" substitute. "The time pressures are so tremendous that every minute's valuable."

The problem was, as the *Washington Post* put it, Americans wanted a chief executive "to look every inch a President, without looking one centimeter a king—to balance the image of a man of the people with the trappings of the most powerful office in the world." Rosalynn agreed that Jimmy overplayed the humility bit, but she also found the press "very cynical." "Jimmy and I are just amazed when we read about ourselves," she said. "Whole books have been written about the family and what we do and say and think by authors we have never met." Proof of the media's cynicism came when she hosted a conference about childhood immunizations. "We didn't read one word about it," she said.

In some ways, the concern with style focused more attention on Rosalynn's substantive programs. Her activities helped define Jimmy. Just as Lady Bird Johnson shared her husband's faith in government programs, Rosalynn shared her husband's ambivalence. Jimmy built his career on Reinhold Niebuhr's insight that "the sad duty of politics is to establish justice in a sinful world." Jimmy's was a politics of cutbacks and tradeoffs. Nevertheless, Rosalynn accepted the First Lady's traditional role as an advocate for "a more caring society." Like Jimmy's though, her attempts to avoid expressing concern by expanding government often failed.

Rosalynn's efforts to help the elderly inevitably launched her into fights for more programs and more government intrusiveness. She would boast about lobbying "for the Age Discrimination Act, which eliminated mandatory retirement at any age in the federal government and raised the age limit from 65 to 70 in the private sector; the Older Americans Act, which . . . authorized substantial increases in appropriations for the various social services and health and nutrition programs for the elderly; the Rural Clinics Act, which expanded medical services to underserved rural areas; and Social Security Reform." Rosalynn's agenda illustrated why First Ladies were often assumed to be more liberal than their husbands. The nineteenth-century "cult of true womanhood" assigned such "soft" concerns to the woman's sphere. Cast as the "heart" of her husband's administration, the First Lady, like many of her predecessors, ended up championing big government.

When Rosalynn tried to avoid expanding the "nanny state," many perceived her efforts to be half-hearted. In the spring of 1978, Rosalynn prescribed individual and corporate volunteerism as the remedy for America's urban ills. While some noticed that the First Lady was trying to tackle America's biggest domestic problems at once, the "Rosalynn Plan" came across as a weak mishmash of Eleanor Roosevelt's advocacy for the poor, Lady Bird Johnson's beautification, and Pat Nixon's volunteerism. A supportive article in the *Washington Post* conceded that "the caution and modesty with which Mrs. Carter approaches most activities could militate against full success."

That spring, Rosalynn's predecessor entered an alcohol and drug rehabilitation center. The loss of her "moment in the sun," along with Jerry's overbooked retirement schedule, made Betty Ford feel that "nobody needed me any longer." Within a week, she went public, releasing a statement admitting, "I have found that I am not only addicted to the medication I have been taking for my arthritis but also to alcohol." Once again, reporters blessed Betty for her "unaffected directness"—and for giving them a great story. Betty Ford would soon become a mythic figure in America's twelve-step confessional culture. Rosalynn would salute Mrs. Ford for helping "make it possible for other spouses not to have to be quite so perfect," even as "Sister Rosalynn" reveled in her own perfection.

Two months later, in June 1978, Rosalynn described her conception of the First Lady's office at the National Press Club. The exiled Russian novelist Alexander Solzhenitsyn had just attacked the "spiritual exhaustion" of Western democracies at Harvard's commencement—a year before her husband's own infamous "malaise" speech. Rosalynn responded that Americans "are not weak, not cowardly, and not spiritually exhausted." She mourned—with some self-pity—that "good works" are "often perceived as, well, boring. . . . Good news doesn't sell."

The face-off between American optimism and Slavic despair, though, did "sell." The speech epitomized the Carters' frustrations with the media. Rosalynn wanted to defend her mandate as First Lady and define her image. Rather than reporting her manifesto for "sincerity and caring and dedication," however, journalists described a showdown between the housewife and the novelist. Reporters wanted conflict and drama, not good works. Still, White House aides told her, "You should do more things like that."

In the *Washington Post* that week, Sally Quinn blasted Rosalynn Carter for seeing her role "as assisting the president, rather than just assuming the role of first lady." Quinn charged that Jimmy "falsely advertised" Rosalynn's influence in 1976 to woo feminists. "Rosalynn Carter has as much influence on Jimmy Carter as the average married woman has on her husband," Quinn claimed. "Which is not to be sneezed at, but hardly to be feared." Quinn and her colleagues disapproved of Mrs. Carter's loyalty, selflessness, and humility. They missed Betty Ford.

Washington insiders preferred the vice president's wife, Joan Mondale.

"Joan Mondale is more identifiable than Rosalynn Carter," Quinn said, despite the fact that Mrs. Mondale had little name recognition and never even made the top twenty of the "most admired" lists Mrs. Carter headed. The *New York Times* said "Joan of Art" had "eclipsed" Rosalynn by becoming "the Administration's leading spokesman for the arts." "If Rosalynn spent all her time thinking and dealing with one issue like Joan," one West Wing aide told *Newsweek*, "she would have a much clearer image." "She's created her own identity which is totally separate from Fritz," said another aide. "Yet by doing so she has been a true asset to him, rather than just a helpmate."

Rosalynn rightly ignored her critics. "I don't think there's any confusion on the part of people in the country," she said. "There may be some confusion on the part of the people who are trying to write about me." Still, with congressional elections looming and Jimmy's polls sagging, she decided to travel more.

In addition to suffering her usual nervousness, Rosalynn took a while to find her pitch on the campaign trail. Many in the West Wing wanted the First Lady to give "a great deal more substantive, factual material than she usually uses, and that gets the tone off for her," a speechwriter explained. Rosalynn was best speaking extemporaneously or answering questions, tasks where she could demonstrate her political savvy. In her speeches she ticked off her husband's successes, yet offered candidates some distance from the ailing administration by calling each Democrat "his own man" who would stand up to the President if necessary.

Rosalynn's range strained the East Wing. Even though she was the first First Lady to work there rather than in the private quarters, the East Wing was a shambles. Critics charged that her aides could not keep up with their boss, that they were still geared to a "tea party lady" approach. Half of her original eighteen aides would leave by January 1979. Having learned that trips needed professional planning, Rosalynn expanded the scheduling and advance office. Still, press relations remained troublesome. Rosalynn's staffers did not know how to get their boss covered in the news sections of newspapers, and she had lost her "natural" claim on the women's pages, which were themselves changing. Reporters grumbled that their deadlines were ignored and that the First Lady was inaccessible.

The relationship between the East Wing and the West Wing also deteriorated. With Rosalynn free to do "pretty much what she wanted," as her aide Kathryn Cade said, she and her staff stepped on many toes. "The relationship between Rosalynn's staff and Jimmy's staff . . . is hate. Hate. Kill. Kill," one insider said.

Just before September, Rosalynn reshuffled her campaign schedule so she could help Jimmy host Israeli Prime Minister Menachem Begin and Egyptian

President Anwar Sadat at Camp David. In July 1978, during one of their many walks at the rural retreat, Jimmy mused, "I don't believe anybody could stay in this place, close to nature, peaceful and isolated from the world, and still carry a grudge. I believe if I could get Sadat and Begin both here together, we could work out some of the problems between them." The sober Rosalynn asked her visionary husband, "Are you willing to be the scapegoat?" He replied, "What else is new?" Quoting the line Jimmy often used to spur her, Rosalynn said, "You can guarantee that you won't fail if you don't try anything. You can also guarantee that you won't succeed." Most experts advised against the summit, but Jimmy persisted.

Jimmy placed great faith in the atmospherics of the summit. He invited Mrs. Begin and Mrs. Sadat along, "so they could ease some of the tension." He assumed their marriages were as soothing as his own; also, Jimmy's admiration for the Begins' warm relationship tempered his distaste for the prickly, obstinate, pedantic Israeli. Given that the President could see "no compatibility at all between Begin and Sadat on which to base any progress," perhaps the wives could help. Jihan Sadat was tending a sick grandchild and did not come, but Aliza Begin accompanied her husband, to Jimmy's relief.

Jimmy also invited the wives so he could keep Rosalynn at his side. Jimmy would describe the First Lady as "a partner in my thinking throughout the Camp David negotiations." Over two agonizing weeks Rosalynn played the many roles she played throughout the administration, as Jimmy's sounding board, tennis partner, stand-in, adviser, and cheerleader. Being barred from the formal sessions made her edgy, though, since she was used to participating. She also felt torn: as her husband negotiated for peace, her daughter was starting a new school. "It was a relief for me to hear Amy's voice on the telephone," Rosalynn would recall. "Talking with Amy made my life seem normal again for the moment."

The Camp David masterstroke showed Jimmy at his best. The warring elements of his identity were in balance—the masculine with the feminine, the populist with the progressive, the charmer with the idealist, the preacher with the engineer, the zealot with the politician. Typically, Jimmy viewed Camp David as a joint achievement. A day after the signing he addressed a special session of Congress; the President of the United States marched in behind Prime Minister Begin, President Sadat, and Mrs. Carter.

V

Raging inflation and an oil shortage wiped out Jimmy's post–Camp David political bounce. Into the summer of 1979 the gas lines lengthened and Americans' mood soured. Just as some Presidents were unduly lionized for economic booms and military victories, others were vilified for crises beyond their control. Jimmy Carter was starting to resemble that other former engineer, Herbert Hoover, the symbol of modern presidential impotence.

In April 1979, Pat Caddell urged his boss to tell Americans that they could no longer expect untrammeled progress and unending prosperity. Three months later, after visiting Japan, the Carters canceled their vacation and rushed to Camp David. Aides submitted a draft for a speech on July 5th about energy. Early in the morning, suffering from jet lag, Jimmy asked Rosalynn her opinion of the speech. "Nobody wants to hear it," she said. "They've heard about new energy programs ever since you've been in office, and prices are still going up." Once again, the First Lady had sensed Jimmy's mood and told him what he wished to hear. He replied, "I decided last night to cancel it." Years later he would claim, "The decision not to make the original, scheduled energy speech was made by me and Rosalynn."

"Rosalynn and I decided before I called the staff that we would stay at Camp David for a few days, and have some people come in whom we trusted to give me advice on where we should go from here," Carter recalled. For the next ten days, Carter and his staff consulted with 150 people from "every segment of our society," Carter boasted. Jimmy relished this "intense reassessment." He winced when he was criticized, but he continued to probe. Part group therapy, part socio-drama, the meetings allowed Carter to remind himself of his initial goals.

The thirty-two-minute speech on July 15, 1979, illustrated the kind of President Jimmy Carter wanted to be. Rosalynn recognized that the Presidency was at stake; her "heart was in my throat all the way through." The television audience, which had dipped to about 30 million for Carter's previous addresses, doubled to at least 65 million viewers. Before submitting his latest six-point program to solve the energy crisis, Carter called upon Americans to forsake "fragmentation and self interest" for the "path of common purpose and the restoration of American values." He ended by amending his autobiography, saying, "I will do my best, but I will not do it alone."

Although he did not use the word, Carter's exhortation would be known as the "malaise speech"; Jimmy Carter would become America's unwelcome prophet of gloom. The press portrayed an ensuing Cabinet reshuffle as a Nixonesque "Saturday Night massacre." Reporters no longer stereotyped Jimmy Carter as naive and indecisive—now he was mean and indecisive.

The Camp David retreat demonstrated the First Lady's prominence. She sat in on all the meetings, and she was rumored to have excoriated certain staffers. In a memo written after the speech offering his services as a chief of staff to restore discipline, Hamilton Jordan wrote his boss, "If you and the First Lady will trust me . . . we cannot and will not fail."

The label hung on the First Lady had already started to change. In May,

Hugh Sidey of *Time* had called her "the second most powerful person in the United States." Sidey deemed Rosalynn the "first woman in the club" of unelected presidential Rasputins such as Clark Clifford, John Foster Dulles, Robert Kennedy, and Henry Kissinger. All of a sudden reporters could find aides who said, "She has more impact on policy than any other President's wife in this generation." Sidey declared the weekly lunches "a unique institution of the modern presidency."

A long-scheduled trip to nine cities in late July made Rosalynn Carter the first prominent administration representative to venture out after the reorganization. The coincidence solidified her new status among reporters. As always, she spoke in the plural, explaining that "we realized that we had the attention of the country. So, we decided that we could really talk about the problems of the country." Resurrecting the line from 1976, the New York *Daily News* proclaimed, "Clearly, the Carters are a team."

The ground was shifting. The style section of a newspaper still called Rosalynn "the dessert after the $500 a plate dinner" at a fancy estate; on the front pages, however, she was "the administration's 'point man.'" With Jimmy's approval ratings down to an abysmal 21 percent, Rosalynn feared being typed as a Scarlett O'Hara to his Ashley Wilkes. "I just have a good relationship with Jimmy," she said. "It's not the position of an adviser. I am a wife. I like to know what's happening. . . . I have never been interested in details, legislation and policy." Her power had been, "uh, exaggerated," she said. Confusing her pronouns undermined her case. To minimize the Cabinet shuffle, she said that "the people that left knew they were going to leave and so I just . . . uh . . . we . . . I . . . uh . . . Jimmy thought and I agreed with him that it was better to do it fast—two days, three days—and that's it, and then we could go forward."

Reporters pounced. They built up Rosalynn's influence, then attacked her for seizing power. "Goddamn it. I voted for Carter, not his wife!" one businessman seethed. A nurse from Arkansas had "visions of the President saying to her every night, 'Rosalynn, I just don't know whether or not I can do this job,'" and Rosalynn reassuring him. By the fall, Rosalynn's approval rating of 59 percent more than doubled Jimmy's—though it was still lower than Betty Ford's August 1976 rating of 71 percent. Rosalynn earned respect but rarely inspired love.

The Carters' defenders argued that it took a strong man to marry a strong woman. Masculinity had to be redefined to accommodate the rise of feminism and the decline of the John Wayne male. The *Daily News* reported that Jimmy appreciated this "precious relationship," saying, "she doesn't dominate my life, I don't dominate hers." The columnist Carl Rowan said calling Jimmy "henpecked" was the "unfairest and silliest" of charges. Rowan concluded, "I'll be damned if I ever want my country run by a President who is too dumb to consult his wife."

The buildup climaxed in the fall, when Jack Anderson's syndicated column declared, "The First Lady . . . is now co-president, with a tremendous impact on U.S. policy." Two days later, the *Washington Post* quoted a Florida Democrat saying of Rosalynn: "I think that she's a co-president. She stands up and says what she thinks." The *Washington Star* soon reported that "To the many 'co-presidency' questions she answers 'those comments are only made by people who don't understand. I can advise him on mental health and aging but I wouldn't presume to advise him on things I don't understand.'" By November, *Newsweek* ran a cover story on Rosalynn Carter, "The President's Partner." Reporters had their hook; Rosalynn now had an image.

This image was nothing but trouble, as it would be for Hillary Clinton two decades later. It made Jimmy appear too weak, and Rosalynn too aggressive. Americans were becoming used to strong women—as long as they remained unmarried. Four of the top ten television shows from 1979 to 1980 featured sassy, independent, and very single women—"Three's Company," "Alice," "Flo," and "One Day at a Time." *Newsweek* asked whether "Lady Macbeth" lurked "beneath the soft voice." The comparison conjured up a long line of powerful and seductive women back to Jezebel in the Bible. More concretely, news that the First Lady hired a chief of staff—Kit Dobelle, who would earn the $56,000 that senior presidential aides received—ignited a firestorm.

Dobelle came aboard to organize the East Wing and work better with the West Wing. The reorganization that began in 1977 culminated in her hiring. Her high salary was supposed to preempt criticism from feminists and mark the emergence of the East Wing as a legitimate branch. Many reporters took advantage of the appointment to trace how Mrs. Roosevelt's three-woman staff became Mrs. Carter's eighteen-person, $650,000-a-year staff. Articles about "The Imperial First Lady and Her Costly Court" fused anxieties about the imperial presidency, the runaway budget, Jimmy's broken campaign promises, the economic crisis, the women's movement, and Rosalynn. One Florida woman wrote: "I am a taxpayer and object to footing the bill for this exorbitant ripoff of Rosalynn Carter. Let her stay at home and take care of that daughter Amy. We did not (the people) vote her in." "You keep on telling us to cut down, why don't you start in your own place?" an Illinois woman asked the President. "Since when does Mrs. Carter have to have 20 secretar[ie]s. Is she running our country or you?"

Going into the reelection campaign, though, Rosalynn would have been happy to double her staff. By the fall of 1979 it was clear that Senator Edward Kennedy wanted to seize the throne from the Georgian outsiders. Thanks to the women in small towns she had befriended in 1976, Rosalynn had recognized the threat earlier than most. She warned Democratic congressional candidates to spurn Kennedy. "It's going to be unfortunate for them if they don't," she said, flashing a hint of steel.

Both Kennedy's challenge and the Carter Presidency were derailed on November 4, 1979, when Iranian militants overran the U.S. Embassy in Teheran and took sixty hostages. Even as voters rallied around their President temporarily, their remaining faith in Jimmy Carter died. Jimmy later compared the crisis to the constant tension he felt when he first came back to Plains and flirted with bankruptcy. "It was a gnawing away at your guts no matter what good, other things were going on."

In early November, amid the distractions of the Kennedy challenge and the hostage crisis, Rosalynn decided to inspect Cambodian refugee camps in Thailand to "call attention to the need for help." Jimmy objected, saying that it was "too dangerous and too politically complicated." Rosalynn responded that the trip was "another example of how you can use the office," one of her aides recalled. If she went to Thailand, Jimmy insisted that she take "some concrete action." He feared another empty gesture.

The slapdash, improvised, fifty-eight-hour trip was a huge success. Shots of the overcrowded, poorly supplied, unsanitary camps made great television. Rosalynn mixed substance with melodrama. She warned the United Nations High Commissioner for Refugees of a greater influx and conferred with the UN Secretary General. All the relief agencies met with her in the White House to coordinate their responses. She rushed $2 million for the camps through the bureaucracy, and her television appearances and commercials helped raise another $60 million. It was, noted her projects director, Kathy Cade, an "extraordinary example of what, if a First Lady is willing to put herself on the line, she can do." By 1979, with this issue, there was no backlash.

The President of the United States welcomed his wife home at Andrews Air Force Base. Edna Langford noted "the eagerness with which they greeted each other, the absorbed way Jimmy listened, the careful manner in which Rosalynn detailed her trip," and thought, *this is their relationship."* The Carters' love sustained them; "their show of mutual affection and respect" was not merely for the public.

It was also characteristic of the Carters to squeeze maximum political advantage out of this humanitarian gesture. As Richard Moe of the vice president's staff emphasized to Hamilton Jordan, *"we should do everything humanly possible to alleviate the suffering, and to be seen doing it."* Perusing the Presidential Proclamation on Kampuchean Relief, the President ordered: "Get Jody [Powell] to Hype this up Here & at State."

Still, the reelection looked like a long shot. Since 1962, Jimmy had been running as the outsider. Even in his one previous reelection effort, for state senate in 1964, he had set himself up as the outsider trying to keep the senate honest. This time he just could not carry it off. Jimmy's competence and integrity were questioned; even his family's reputation was in tatters.

Jimmy believed that the White House "brought my family closer together than we'd ever been before. . . . It was like a team." But Chip's marriage died, wounded by the many women who gravitated toward the President's son in Georgetown bars. Jeffrey and his wife were rumored to have smoked marijuana while being guarded by Secret Service agents. Amy was mocked by comedians and hounded by reporters. No preteen would want to read in the local paper that "the scrawny strawberry blond kid has grown several inches. There is the beginning of a bosom, a hint of a waist."

The damage was even greater in Plains. The media spotlight exposed fault lines among the Carters, and various relatives stopped talking to one another. The media made Lillian's favorite son, Billy, a celebrity, then destroyed him. In 1977 Billy Carter made an estimated $200,000—what Jimmy earned as President. Billy charged $5,000 for appearances where he allowed Americans to enjoy the democratic anomaly that the President's brother was a beer-guzzling, overall-wearing, redneck lout. But Billy wanted to show that he, too, could be a power player. Lobbyists for the renegade Libyan government hired him. In November 1979, Rosalynn called Billy to see if he knew anyone in Libya who might intercede for the hostages. She mentioned the call to Jimmy, who informed his national security adviser. Nothing happened. An observer later said that "if Lady Bird Johnson had interjected herself into the conduct of foreign policy, her husband would have remanded her to the basement for a week."

Billy's failure to register as a foreign agent almost landed him in jail when "Billygate" broke in July 1980. As a result, Rosalynn reported, when "Jimmy should have been working on his acceptance speech for the approaching Democratic Convention, our lawyers had us both searching our diaries and files for any mention of Billy or Libya." The Billy Carter affair would drag on throughout the campaign, making the Carters look amateurish, naive, and unsuited to the presidency. An October 1980 memorandum would "caution government employees against dealing with members of the President's family in ways that create either the reality or the appearance of impropriety."

In 1980, Rosalynn seemed to be the only Carter having any fun. The Carters followed the Nixons' and Fords' reelection tradition of politicizing the First Lady and insulating the President. While her husband brooded in the White House, she stumped; by October, she had appeared in 166 cities and raised $2.5 million. Reporters called her "a virtuoso," and admiring aides called her "the best politician I've seen." After all the failures, she was back doing something she had already mastered. The crowds exhilarated her. "I had to keep reminding myself that it was the position, not me," she said. "Nevertheless, I enjoyed it and always felt 'cheered on.'" Feeding reporters the morsels they desired, Rosalynn began describing situations in which Jimmy would say, "Don't you want me to do what's best for the people of the country?" and she would say "yes, but can't you wait?" until it was politically more palatable. Her confession of spousal conflict tried to set him up as a strong man and a statesman.

The President, the Vice President, and the First Lady were "the principals" in scheduling trips; everyone else was a "surrogate." The First Lady's participation stopped being a novelty. After all, as one Democrat would say, "It's their Presidency." Rosalynn brought crowds "greetings from Jimmy. He said to tell you all hello and that he loves you and cares for you." Rosalynn preempted criticism that she neglected her family to play co-president by mentioning her least controversial relatives: "Amy sends her greetings too. I left her at home this morning playing her violin and my little granddaughter, who is 10 months old, was on the floor playing with Amy's cat." The First Lady praised Jimmy as steady and persistent, whereas he appeared tense and defensive. She joked with reporters, while he avoided them. A photo from New Hampshire showed Rosalynn in a trench coat, flanked by a Secret Service agent, working a line of people on Newport's Main Street with a two-handed handshake. It was a typical political scene—except that it pictured the spouse, not the candidate.

Much of the fight for delegates took place privately. Here, too, Rosalynn was indispensable. Jetting off to Thailand, she scribbled to Carter's political aide Tim Kraft an eleven-page list of names she tried to contact and where they stood. She promised to "call this week-end from Camp David any that you still want me to touch base with." Volunteering his wife for yet another event, Jimmy told Florida's governor, Bob Graham, "I prefer to keep my participation in private sessions with key potential backers to a minimum." "Don't trade Rosalynn in just yet," the *Atlanta Constitution*'s editor, Hal Gulliver, told Jimmy in June. "Wait at least until she finishes winning enough delegates to assure the nomination."

In the White House, Rosalynn pushed her husband to be bolder, and, as she put it, more "demagogic." She blamed his loss in the New York primary on his stubborn desire to do "the right thing" and make budget cuts she begged him to defer. She urged him to be tough on Iran. She first proposed an oil boycott, then advocated a military response. Both understood that if he bombed Teheran, Jimmy could win the election but lose the hostages.

Despite winning the nomination, Jimmy Carter remained under a cloud. Rosalynn, though, continued to shine. In a "60 Minutes" interview before the convention, the contrast and competition between the Carters was obvious. Jimmy looked older, tighter, and grayer than he had four years before. His body language had changed as well. He was no longer open to questions—often in interviews he assumed a defensive crouch, one leg over another, his hands clasping his knee as reporters grilled him about his failures.

Before Mrs. Carter joined the "60 Minutes" interview, Dan Rather asked the President about her. Jimmy described her in more traditional terms than usual, saying that she helped "with crucial delegates in the last few days. She's a good seamstress, she makes a lot of her own clothes, she also takes care of me and Amy and our needs on the sewing machine, but she's also a close friend and a partner, a confidante, and sweetheart. So we kinda share almost everything. Likes to run, likes to swim, likes to fish, also likes to be involved in a political campaign." Jimmy was describing Rosalynn as a supermom, feebly trying to give their relationship the best of the traditional and modern worlds. But Jimmy was also trying, just as feebly, to put his wife in her place.

Once the President and the reporter joined the First Lady, Jimmy withdrew. Rosalynn was pleased with herself, looking comfortable, stylish, and relaxed while Jimmy sulked. She acknowledged her competition with Jimmy when she said, "I don't like interviews with him where he does all the talking and I sit and look at him . . . but when you ask me questions I enjoy that." Now it seemed that Rosalynn, not Jimmy, was the star.

Jimmy Carter's renomination cost him a great deal. Even many who stuck with the President doubted his credibility, his competence, and his commitment to the Democratic party's liberal tradition. Helping his staff forge a "reconciliation strategy," Jimmy's first piece of advice was as follows: "Use Rosalynn more."

During the general election campaign, Jimmy was still reliant on the First Lady, although he was more active. Rosalynn finally seemed to be making peace with her critics, realizing that "I could stay here and pour tea and entertain the guests all day and I would be criticized." Joan Mondale agreed. The "Second Lady" said that "no matter what she does or doesn't do," a First Lady would be criticized. "Rosalynn has a happy solution. . . . She ignores it, and insists on being herself."

Rosalynn felt liberated. Her sinewy speeches were laced with statistics and policy matters. With Jimmy hitting the major media markets, Rosalynn tried to hit two or three secondary markets a day. "She is just like a candidate," campaign aides said. "She can go just about anywhere we can put the President."

Finally, Rosalynn Carter seemed to be the kind of woman feminists desired. Having Ronnie and Nancy Reagan as opponents further enhanced Rosalynn's status among women activists. Nancy's claim that her life began when she married Ronnie enraged women seeking independence, and Ronald Reagan's old-fashioned demeanor and conservative contempt for the 1960s scared many of them.

The Carters underestimated their opponents. Jimmy was sure he could beat the aging movie star face to face. He agreed to debate Reagan despite Rosalynn's objections. Tight-lipped, flashing smiles at inappropriate moments, and looking like a parson, Carter offered fact-filled sermons emphasizing that there are "no simple answers to complicated questions." When he quoted Amy to the effect that "nuclear weaponry" was "the most important issue," the President of the United States looked ridiculous. At rallies, Reagan asked, "Who's running the country?" and his supporters shouted back: "Amy Carter!"

"Damn, damn Khomeini!" Rosalynn would say. "All the understandable disillusionment of the American public fell on us." The Carters never expected to lose. Jimmy's "somewhat artificial cheerfulness" intensified his wife's despair. Almost a decade later, he confessed that "I never admitted how deeply I was hurt and I still find it hard to do so." The Carters "had a few strained and unpleasant moments between us in those early weeks, and now I realize that with my calm and reassuring attitude it seemed to Rosalynn that I didn't recognize her pain." Their friends Betty and John Pope reminded them of their bedrock rural and Christian values, inviting the Carters to come home "and walk along a bubbling mountain creek and pause here and there to watch the freedom and force of the water as it tumbles down Rosalynn Rapids. Then, later, we would climb the highest mountain to be nearer to God."

During the transition, tributes poured in for the presidential couple. Even reporters turned sentimental. They described a "touching" scene when the President bid farewell to Chancellor Helmut Schmidt of Germany, whereupon Secretary of State Ed Muskie put a consoling arm around Jimmy's shoulders. Rosalynn later reported that Jimmy told Muskie, "Sometimes Helmut can be a pain in the ass." Chuckling, the secretary of state had put his arm around the President and agreed as they returned to the Oval Office.

Back in Plains, as the Carters pondered renovating their house, Rosalynn said, "Isn't this a shame—the most important thing in my life right now is whether a walk should be crooked or straight!" With no more goals left in their driven lives, both drifted for a while and bickered frequently until they became authors and activists—sometimes working together, sometimes working separately.

In retirement, Jimmy became recognized as the man of peace he had tried to be, Rosalynn's image as a powerful woman crystallized, and their reputation as a couple grew. Both the male peacemaker and the female powerhouse proved more palatable out of office. When Rosalynn published her memoirs in 1984, *Vogue* called the Carters "the closest working partnership ever to live in the White House." Another reviewer said, "More than a wife, she has been Carter's best friend and most trusted adviser (a remarkable thing in an era that has seen commitment go out of fashion and only lately shows signs of reviving)." Rosalynn proved steadier than the reporters who covered her.

Once again, a First Lady had blossomed as her husband withered. By all rights, Rosalynn Carter should have been an extraordinarily popular First Lady. She was a gracious, effective, and loving spouse in an age which valued equal partnerships. Her agenda offered White House correspondents a host of compelling topics. As First Lady, she successfully avoided any major gaffes or controversies, and millions respected her. But she did not generate the kind of popular enthusiasm that might have buoyed her husband. The masses did not love her. Part of the problem stemmed from the fact that Rosalynn, like Lady Bird Johnson, was "too beige." She lacked the flair for exhibitionism that her husband showed in 1976 and that one needed to star in the media firmament. Like Lady Bird, Rosalynn was also saddled with an unpopular husband. And like Lady Bird—as well as Eleanor Roosevelt—Rosalynn ran into the enduring discomfort with unelected First Ladies seizing power. Increasingly anxious about the changing definition of sex roles, most Americans turned to the White House for reassurance not creativity. Sharing power might help a First Lady make history, but it did not help her—or the president—make many friends. America was not ready for a co-presidency.

8

"DOING EVERYTHING WE CAN"

The Reagan Liberation

There *they* were again, invading Ronnie's ranch. Nancy bristled. The 688-acre mountaintop homestead was the Reagans' refuge, and yet here were those vulgar reporters ruining a photo opportunity in August 1984. CNN's Charles Bierbauer asked if Ronnie could do something to get the Soviets negotiating. Why did they "always impl[y] that he is sitting there doing nothing?" she fumed. The seventy-three-year-old President paused, then asked, "What?" As Bierbauer repeated the question, the woman Ronnie called "Mommy" whispered, "Doing everything we can." The old actor straightened up and repeated his cue: "We're doing everything we can," he smiled.

Reporters did not hear the exchange, but a CNN microphone did. "I wasn't prompting him," Mrs. Reagan said. "I was talking to myself out of sheer frustration." This presidential couple puzzled reporters. Was Nancy Reagan a superficial society queen or a Lady Macbeth? Was Ronald Reagan a doddering marionette or a political genius? The press never could fathom how the Reagans became one of the most popular First Couples, or how the old-fashioned Reagans championed a Carter-style co-presidency. One of the couple's secret weapons was Nancy's unrecognized feminism.

I

When the 1980 Republican convention nominated Ronald Reagan, his entire family joined him on stage. Years later, he would point to the picture and tell his troubled daughter Patti Davis: "Look. We were a happy family." The Reagans' public devotion to the American home stemmed from their lifelong quest for it. Before and after they married, Ronnie and Nancy were often deprived of a conventional life. Each learned from childhood how to compensate for private deficiencies with public illusions.

Born in Tampico, Illinois, in 1911, Ronald Wilson Reagan spent his childhood hiding from the ugly realities of life with a drunken father. He even adjusted his name to improve his image. "Ronald" was not "rugged enough for a young red-blooded American boy," he said; he preferred "Dutch." Dutch's childhood was "sweet and idyllic . . . as close as I could imagine . . . to the world created by Mark Twain in *The Adventures of Tom Sawyer*."

Talk about "imagining" and "creating" betrayed his hand. Even Dutch admitted that the marriage between his refined mother and his hard-drinking father was an endurance contest. "If my father was Catholic, my mother was Protestant," he said. "If he rebelled against the universe, she was a natural practical do-gooder. . . . Perhaps she never understood the reason for his week-long benders once or twice a year, any more than he understood her cultural activities, but they put up with each other."

Lost in his own world, Dutch "loved three things, drama, politics and sports," arenas where he could play the hero. His entry in the 1928 Dixon High School yearbook illustrated his optimistic veneer. His favorite quotation was, "Life is just one grand sweet song, so start the music." But a poem he wrote at the time revealed a darker side: "We hang onto a jaded life/A life full of sorrow and pain. A life that warps and breaks us./And we try to run through it again."

Dutch followed his high school sweetheart, Margaret Cleaver, to Eureka College. By this time Dutch had grown into what one friend characterized as "the perfect specimen of an athlete, tall, willowy, muscular, brown, good-looking." Eureka was the kind of small community where "you couldn't remain anonymous," he recalled. Everyone had "a chance to shine at something and build their sense of self-confidence." Still, the scrutiny could be smothering. Reagan knew "that in the middle of Illinois in 1932, I couldn't go around saying, 'I want to be an actor.'"

Shortly after graduation, Dutch entered "show business" by becoming a radio sports announcer in Iowa. The one cloud during this sunny period came when Margaret sent him a letter "and my fraternity pin and engagement ring tumbled out." Dutch told one mentor he did not care whether he lived or died.

Nearly everyone who met the affable sportscaster liked him, but few became close to him. In 1937 the twenty-six-year-old took a screen test; his agent sold him as a "likeable, clean-cut American" type. When Warner Brothers offered a seven-year, two-hundred-dollars-a-week contract, "it was a fantasy come true." Hollywood's masters of make-believe changed his hair style, tailored his shirts to make him appear better proportioned, and contemplated renaming him. Ronald Reagan sold his handlers on his real name.

Ronnie felt at home in the land of illusions. He was hardworking and reliable, less ambitious and self-absorbed than his peers. In fifty-three films from 1937 until 1964, he played the "good guy" if not always the hero. He called himself the "poor man's Errol Flynn"—handsome enough to swashbuckle, not charismatic enough to star. In the 1930s, Dale Carnegie preached about fitting in, not standing out; Ronald Reagan defined himself as "Mr. Norm," a "plain guy with a set of homespun features and no frills." Ronnie's marriage to Jane Wyman in 1940 appeared to be an American fairy tale, with the square midwesterner redeeming the saucy divorcée. He warned his volatile bride, "We'll lead an ideal life if you'll just avoid doing one thing: Don't think." The studio publicity machines used their stars' lives to confirm Hollywood's idyllic version of married life. A daughter—Maureen—was born and Warner Brothers deemed the Reagans "one of the most important First Families of the film colony."

Ronnie's performance in 1940 as George Gipp in *Knute Rockne—All American* promised to free him from "B movies," but the war intervened. Military service that was limited to making training films in California undermined Reagan's self-image as a macho warrior. As his career stagnated, his wife's boomed. "Now I'm carrying the ball, financially," Jane boasted, intensifying "Captain Wyman's" feelings of inadequacy. "The monastery of movies" began to bore Ronnie; at the same time, the New Deal's taxation and bureaucracy enraged him. He plunged into the politics of the Screen Actors Guild and began distancing himself from the Democratic party.

Trying to reconcile without impeding Jane's career, the Reagans adopted a boy in 1945. Consigned to a nanny, Michael did not help unite his parents. The Reagans separated in late 1947. Ronnie viewed his marital trouble through the prism of his parents' rocky relationship. "This learning to live a lifetime together isn't easy," he said. He wanted to work it out, but Jane refused. "I *was* divorced in the sense that the decision was made by someone else," Ronnie would say. Still, he was crushed; his quest for "An American Life" had been publicly destroyed.

Ronnie first met Nancy Davis during this black period. Nancy had been mistakenly identified as a "Communist sympathizer." The director Mervyn LeRoy interceded for her with the president of the Screen Actors Guild, prodding Reagan to explain the mix-up over dinner. When Ronnie asked Nancy out, each claimed to have an early casting call, in case the date fizzled. They partied until three in the morning, as Ronnie often did. One friend recalled Ronnie saying that, at the time, he awoke one morning "and I couldn't remember the name of the gal I was in bed with. I said, 'Hey, I gotta get a grip here.'"

At dinner Ronnie suggested Nancy change her name. *"But Nancy Davis is my name,"* she said. Ronald Reagan did not realize how hard the young lady had worked to earn it. She was born Anne Francis Robbins, although her mother had called her Nancy. Just as Ronnie's detachment and fantasy life marked him as a child of an alcoholic, Nancy's behavior marked her as a child of divorce. She, too, learned to respond to adversity with fantasy.

When the itinerant actress Edith Luckett gave birth in 1921, her marriage to Kenneth Robbins had already soured. After two years Edith asked her sister to give her "backstage baby" a "normal" childhood. Growing up as one of the few kids in Bethesda, Maryland, whose parents did not live with her, Nancy's childhood was far from normal. "Nancy Robbins, Nancy Robbins," children yelled when inviting her out to play, mocking her different last name. Nancy would resent "armchair psychologists who claim that I was 'abandoned' by my mother," but she did recall crying out when she had pneumonia in 1926: "If I had a little girl, I'd certainly be there if *she* was ever sick."

After Edith married Dr. Loyal Davis and reclaimed her daughter, Nancy worked hard to be "normal." Rather than admitting how difficult it was for a jealous, chubby, and awkward child to earn her forbidding stepfather's affection, Nancy claimed "my father had to earn my love." After she took her stepfather's name at the age of fourteen, Nancy Davis spent years denying that she was born in 1921, that she had contact with her natural father, or that she was born in Queens, the most pedestrian of New York's boroughs. Nancy Davis erased the stain of her mother's divorce by mastering the social graces. "Nancy's social perfection is a constant source of amazement," the 1939 Girl's Latin yearbook proclaimed. "She is invariably becoming and suitably dressed. She can talk, and even better listen intelligently, to anyone."

At Smith College, Nancy "majored in English and drama—and boys." Nancy played the part of Loyal's daughter to perfection, hobnobbing with Ivy League boys in New York—although she would emphasize that she always stayed at a "girl's-only" floor of the Biltmore Hotel. Still, she felt inadequate. She would remember her debut, a sumptuous tea, as "modest." Nancy always adopted her most extravagant friends' standards, finding her own indulgences either inadequate or just right.

The advent of World War II did little to sober Nancy. She was typecast as "the Glamour Girl" in one college production. She sang: "I miss my Nassau winters and Paris in the spring/My butler's making nuts and bolts/They've rationed everything." After graduating in 1943, Nancy worked in a department store and as a nurse's aide. She was engaged briefly but decided to be an actress in New York rather than "lead the life of a sub-deb." The highlight of her New York career was her fling in 1948 with Clark Gable, "the most glamorous and desirable man in the entire world." A chameleon, she admitted, "I wasn't in love with him, but if we had seen more of each other I might have been."

By spring 1949 Nancy had landed an MGM contract, thanks to her new boyfriend and Edith's old friends. Rumors suggested that the woman who told publicists that her goal was "to have a successful happy marriage" was not as pure as she appeared. "I had always heard stories about the wild side of Hollywood," she would recall, "but I never saw much evidence of it."

That year, she charmed Mervyn LeRoy into introducing her to Ronald Reagan. Unlike Jane, "one of the things" Nancy "liked about Ronnie right away was that he didn't talk only about himself." The twenty-eight-year-old "old maid" and the divorcé also shared a common desire to have an old-fashioned family.

But snaring Ronnie was not easy. He would acknowledge that he did "everything wrong." Nancy befriended his children, donned coveralls to fix up his ranch, and canceled her Christmas visit to Chicago to be with her beau. During that Christmas of 1951, Nancy asked Ronnie, "Do you want me to wait for you?" Ronnie said yes, but still no ring was forthcoming.

A few months later, on March 4, 1952, Ronnie and Nancy married in a small ceremony witnessed only by William and Arden Holden. Ronnie vetoed Nancy's plans for a big wedding—partly because he was humiliated at having to repeat this once-in-a-lifetime event, but also because there was not much time to plan a party. On October 22, 1952, Nancy gave birth to a fully formed, seven-pound daughter, Patti. "Go ahead and count," Nancy declared in 1989, after enduring years of snickering that she had forced Ronnie's hand.

Ronnie claimed he just decided in the middle of a meeting to marry. Nancy claimed they "squeeze[d] in" the wedding between film projects. "By then," she postured, "we felt that we were already married, and it was time to make it official." Ronnie counseled his daughter, "Your mother and I waited, no matter how difficult it was sometimes. . . . But we knew it was important to be married first." Patti eventually confronted her father "about the lies" surrounding her birth. "Well," he said, "if the studio hadn't made us change the wedding date, you wouldn't have been premature." Ronnie always remained wedded to his illusions.

Even Nancy admitted that their first year of marriage was "difficult." The Reagans would will themselves to become the ideal couple. Ronnie insisted, "From the start, our marriage was like an adolescent's dream of what a marriage should be."

Once the marriage was sealed, Nancy stopped wooing Ronnie's kids. Maureen called her father's second wife "the Dragon Lady." A decade and a half before America's divorce revolution, Reagan, Davis, and Wyman created a blended family, with devastating results. Reagan's four children would suffer through a half-dozen divorces, bouts of drug addiction, and years of misery.

Even the family Ronnie and Nancy created—with Patti and then Ronald Prescott Reagan, born in 1958—lacked the stability, warmth, and values the Reagans would defend so intensely. Patti remembered a pill-popping mother who was cold and abusive. Still, Patti "preferred my mother's anger to my father's absence. . . . it left a handprint on my face, but at least I could look in the mirror and say, 'Oh there I am. Someone knows I exist.'"

All four Reagan children suffered as the bond between Ronnie and Nancy became so intense it eclipsed all others. Most photographs of the Kennedys caught them looking away from each other, posing; most photographs of the Reagans caught them mooning over each other. In the 1980s the librarian of Congress, Daniel Boorstin, would praise the Reagans as an exceptional "presidential couple," demonstrating a "love" that "isn't seen much around here these days." Ronnie responded, "If Nancy Davis hadn't come along when she did, I would have lost my soul."

Nancy became Mrs. Ronald Reagan as enthusiastically as she had become Dr. Davis's daughter. Hollywood preached that, as Debbie Reynolds told Frank Sinatra in the 1955 movie, *The Tender Trap,* "A woman isn't a woman until she's been married and had children." Nancy would say, repeatedly, "My life didn't really begin until I met Ronnie." Enraged feminists would interpret this line to mean that Nancy lived through her husband. In fact, Nancy believed that marriage was a project wherein both partners built a joint fantasy.

Nancy's enthusiasm for homemaking suited Ronnie's emergence as General Electric's "Ambassador of the Film World." Ronnie's movie career fizzled during the early 1950s, but prosperity returned in 1954 when he began hosting CBS's weekly "General Electric Theater." Nancy and Ronnie came to personify the American dream. The family starred in a Crest commercial, one of many homages to American conformity broadcast nightly. The Reagans built a model "House of the Future" filled with General Electric gadgets. Once, one of Patti's playmates said: "Wow, everything's so perfect. How do you ever play here?" Patti replied, "We don't."

During the Kennedy administration Nancy modeled herself after the First Lady. Ronnie was less impressed with Jackie's husband. He continued questioning the assumptions of the social welfare state and his Democratic party. His growing partisanship soured some GE executives, who canceled his show in 1962.

"Not a day goes by when someone doesn't come to the house and ask Ronnie to run for senator or governor or even President of the United States," Nancy told a friend in 1962. "It boggles the mind but maybe it'll get me out of the car pool." Critics caricaturing Ronnie as an empty vessel would claim that the ambitious Nancy and her conservative stepfather converted the amiable New Dealer, but Ronnie had been interested in politics long before he met Nancy. Also, a woman who ignored politics until she was forty hardly qualifies as a political mastermind. Nancy just wanted to support her husband. "If Ronnie were selling shoes, I'd be out pushing shoes," she would say.

Ronnie emerged into the political limelight with his famous speech endorsing Barry Goldwater in 1964. The speech recycled lines Ronnie had perfected in visits to GE factories and in harangues to friends. Reagan wanted his nation, like his family, to conform to a traditional vision. He entered the California gubernatorial race in January 1966 with a recognition factor of 97 percent.

Having failed to become royalty in Hollywood, the Reagans now had a shot at it in the real world. Nancy did not want voters noticing that the conservative crusader was divorced. "He has *two* children," she told the men stage-managing the campaign.

Many scoffed at the washed-up B-movie actor running for governor, yet Ronald Reagan unseated Democratic Governor Edmund G. Brown by nearly one million votes in a heavily Democratic state. Nancy later claimed that this was "the most difficult time for our marriage." The "roughness" of politics shocked her; she expected "story approval" when she granted interviews.

Nancy made the biggest impression on voters—and reporters—when she watched Ronnie speak. Each time, her outsized hazel eyes seemed to grow even larger, her face glowed. As criticism of "the Gaze" grew, one friend said, "Nancy, people just don't *believe* it when you look at Ronnie that way—as though you're saying, 'He's my hero.'" Nancy responded, "But he *is* my hero."

Nancy's friends had caught her in the act of remaking herself into the ideal political spouse. Nancy refused to acknowledge any deviation from the 1950s fantasy of the happy homemaker. Her decade as an actress became "a stopgap," something to do "until I found the man I wanted to marry." The Reagans' two-and-a-half-year mating dance became a whirlwind romance, wherein they married "a year" after they met.

Ronald Reagan's hostility to "Sixties liberals" during two terms as California's governor from 1967 to 1975 defined his career. He was the conservative Kennedy—charismatic enough for the masses, ideological enough for the partisans. The Reagans' conservatism anchored Ronnie and insulated him from the charges that he lacked substance. Reagan's detractors alternated between dismissing him as an inexperienced actor and caricaturing him as a right-wing lunatic. The attack on his politics gave him credibility, just as his good looks, sunny approach, and Hollywood background made his ideology appear more palatable. Reagan offered Goldwater's conservatism with a smile.

Nancy and Ronnie wanted to be role models, to repudiate the "Sixties" attitudes personally and politically. The governor praised his wife as ardently as she praised him. Asked to describe her, he became embarrassingly intimate:

"How do you describe coming into a warm room from out of the cold? Never waking up bored?" As Ronnie lauded his wife, Nancy wept. When a young woman attacked him for opposing birth control and abortion, he became one of the first American politicians to address this intimate subject. "Sex is not a purely physical act," he said. "It is indeed at the very foundation of our social fabric based on the family unit." Standards, even if not always followed, were better than the alternative—a headlong rush into "hedonism."

The Reagan children, especially the troubled Patti, were not inspiring role models. Fortunately, reporters at the time rarely exposed much of a politician's family life. Still, Patti's betrayal enraged her mother.

At home and in the office Nancy was Ronnie's enforcer: he smiled, and she glared. His faith in his staff and his passivity in the face of conflict frustrated her. Her passion occasionally intimidated him, but he learned to exploit it. Nancy was always looking out for disloyalty. She was suspicious; he was indulgent. Once, after an aide contradicted the governor, Nancy called her husband in his office. Ronnie was with a reporter who heard him say, "Yes, dear" a few times, followed by, "No, dear, I don't think he was being insubordinate. It's just when I say something in Sacramento, and he says something in Los Angeles, we'll have to get together." The reporter decided that Nancy was the power behind the throne.

When Nancy deemed the governor's mansion unlivable, the Reagans moved. She ordered all female aides to wear dresses, not slacks. She supervised the governor's schedule and often adjusted it as his horoscope dictated. Those who crossed her were often exiled. Some called Nancy what Maureen did, the Dragon Lady. Reporters found it difficult to reconcile "the Gaze" with "the Glare." Some said her backstage maneuverings discredited her public persona. But attacks on Nancy for overreaching contradicted earlier attacks on her for being too reverent as well as her full schedule of traditional wifely duties. These twin images of Nancy the devoted wife and Nancy the devious mastermind would dog her for the next quarter-century.

In 1975, as Gerald Ford stumbled his way toward the political center, conservatives pressured Reagan to run for president. Betty Ford's behavior helped convince the Reagans and their supporters that Ford was not the man to revitalize America. Throughout the primary campaign, Nancy stayed at Ronnie's side to highlight her role as a deferential wife who would not embarrass her husband or the presidency. "I simply don't differ with Ronnie on anything significant," Nancy claimed.

Reporters mocked such statements and caricatured Nancy as a throwback. They also characterized her as "the most powerful influence on Reagan." Nancy was equally confused; she resented being called a "homebody" as much as she resented being called Machiavellian. In the reductionist world of reporters, she had to be either all-powerful or deferential.

Ronald Reagan suffered his first and only political loss in 1976. Still, this divorced denizen of the Hollywood fleshpots had established himself as the country's leading conservative. Just as ironically, while fighting the good fight for traditional marriage and the separate spheres, he and his wife found themselves creating a newfangled "peer marriage."

II

Thirteen months after Ronald Reagan won the 1980 election, the December 20, 1981 edition of "60 Minutes" opened with Mike Wallace saying to Nancy Reagan, "You're really hurt by some of the press you're getting." Biting her lip, Nancy said, "Yes." She repudiated her image as a selfish *nouveau riche.* "It's just not true," Nancy declared. "That whole picture kind of started before I ever got to Washington, before they ever knew me."

In 1980, Ronald Reagan's romance with Nancy emerged as a key chapter in his legend. His campaign chairman, Senator Paul Laxalt, had "never seen a wife be more helpful or more totally supportive." Nancy trimmed Ronnie's schedule, supervised his strategy, and moderated his rhetoric. She spent hours at night calling operatives for updates. Ronnie appreciated "Mommy's" collaboration. "When you need help, the gentlest way is through her saying to him, 'Honey, don't do it that way,'" an aide admitted. When staff tensions erupted, Nancy mediated.

Voters rarely saw this side of Nancy. They saw "The Gaze" and heard the little woman vow that her only job would be "supporting him." "She never seems to get an itch, her lips never stick to her teeth, she hardly blinks," Sally Quinn marveled. "Don't her legs ever go to sleep? Haven't they had a terrible fight just before the speech? Isn't she ever bored hearing the whole thing over and over and over?"

When Nancy did leave Ronnie to campaign, they usually rendezvoused at night. On her own Nancy became more dynamic, although she still avoided policy details. Her question-and-answer sessions, campaign aide Peter Hannaford rejoiced, were "as close to living-room conversation as is possible" in an election race. Only when crowds pressed her did a different Nancy emerge—her eyes narrowed, her lips pursed, disgust and fear crossed her face. "Campaigning and warmth aren't natural to her," an aide admitted. Her fear of exposure, her disdain for the masses, and her discomfort with intimacy became clear.

After a few days, Ronnie would demand, "Give me back my wife." When the Reagans reunited, both glowed; he no longer seemed detached, and she no longer seemed brittle. His performance improved. "They had eyes only for one another," Hannaford said. In an age of cynicism about marriage, Nancy's aide Nancy Clark Reynolds was shocked that "when they hold hands it's for real." William Morrow published Nancy's autobiography. Candidate autobiographies were expected, but a spouse's memoir was exceptional. Fifteen years later, Nancy would still be retelling the anecdotes in her book, following the same structure and using the same phrasing. *Nancy* "was all sweetness and light," one editor commented. "And she had this strange feeling that she did not want to be upstaged by Ronnie."

Nancy's persona as "Ronald Reagan's Total Woman" annoyed reporters, "mostly women reporters," she noted. The *New York Times Magazine* identified Nancy as "part of the Him Generation—a woman who, in the words of the Tammy Wynette song, stands by her man." *New York* savaged Nancy's "shamelessly goody-two-shoes autobiography," her retreats to "the Land of Safe Answers" when she was asked a question, her social climbing, and her pose as "perhaps the last perfect great-man's wife."

The cultural clashes of the 1960s swirled throughout the 1980 campaign, making Nancy as controversial as her husband. Both Reagans denounced abortion, premarital sex, and the Equal Rights Amendment. Both, according to Nancy, supported "equal rights for everyone" and welcomed women's "stronger role in our society," but worried that "things" were "out of balance." Insiders like John Sears said Nancy would "soften" Ronnie's stance on women's issues. Nancy, not Ronnie, would eventually consider backing abortions after rape. Yet most reporters preferred to blame Ronnie's chauvinism on Nancy, the traitor to her gender, rather than acknowledge the popular doubts about feminism the Reagans represented.

Nancy resented how reporters "glare at me and say it's somewhat corny that I say my life began when I married Ronnie. . . . Corny? If it is, great— but let's not keep knocking it, or pretty soon we won't have much left to respect in life." Nancy could not see what she had done wrong. "My biggest fault, it seems, was that I was too polite, too much a lady," she moped.

Nancy was right. The hostility toward her was both visceral and palpable. Young women recoiled from her peppy perfection, her gushing tributes to Ronnie, her professed love of the home. Salaried professionals resented the free-spending ways of this woman freeloading off her wealthy husband. Feminists who expected more from a former "career gal" felt betrayed. "Nancy, you are a Smith person, and how can you not be for equal rights for women?" Betty Friedan asked her fellow alumna.

Yet beneath her anti-feminist veneer, Nancy was as political and as outspoken as Rosalynn Carter. Nancy filmed a commercial condemning Jimmy Carter's "cruel" attacks. "I don't often speak out in campaigns but I think this campaign now has gotten to the point and the level where I have to say something," she began. Her voice quivering, she denied Ronnie was a warmonger, saying, "I deeply, deeply resent it as a wife and a mother and a woman."

Nancy understood the public's limits. Asked whether she would be in-

volved in policy decisions she said, "No, no, no." "Well, I try to be supportive of my husband," she purred. "I just do whatever they tell me to do." "If I
were there I wouldn't be sitting in on Cabinet meetings," she chirped, hiding
her enmity with a smile. She also vowed to keep her staff small, a jab at the
Carters' large East Wing operation.

Nancy knew not to talk about personal problems, and she knew how to
blend modern and traditional. "Obviously we talk politics all the time," she
said. "And you can't be married 28 years without each one influencing the
other. But as far as policy-making decisions go, he makes them." Two years
later, Ronnie echoed her views, saying, "You can't have been together for almost 30 years without being an influence on each other. She does not inject
herself and say, 'You ought to sign this or do this.'" The Reagans' qualified
egalitarianism suited a country where 93 percent wanted "more emphasis on
traditional family ties," yet only 21 percent wanted a return to the days of
"spic and span" housekeeping with "women staying home."

Ronald Reagan swept the electoral college vote 489 to 40, though he
barely won half the popular votes. As per tradition, reporters celebrated the
incoming president during the transition; slashing attacks seemed unsports-
manlike. Nancy Reagan, however, became the first modern First Lady vilified
before taking office. A steady flow of articles in November and December
portrayed her as scheming, overbearing, unyielding, and dishonest. "THE
NEW FIRST LADY IS A FORMER DEBUTANTE, BUT WATCH OUT: 'SHE'S A
FIGHTER,'" *People* proclaimed. The most devastating attack came from the
Reagans' hometown, where the society writer for the *Los Angeles Herald-Ex-
aminer* interviewed dozens of Reagan associates who pilloried Nancy as
"more Rodeo Drive than rodeo." Wanda McDaniel portrayed an imperious,
jealous, insecure, and powerful First Lady-to-be who sniped at her "Second
Lady," Barbara Bush, pushed the talk-show host Johnny Carson to cut out
the "Ronnie dyes his hair monologues," never saw her son perform with the
Joffrey II Ballet, and refused to talk about the time when Patti "lived with a
member of the Eagles rock group."

These attacks devastated Nancy; a decade later, the McDaniel article "still"
made her "cringe." Nancy became even warier with reporters, thus alienating
them further. They pounced on her confession that she kept a "tiny little"
handgun in the house when Ronnie traveled, as well as her appearance at the
White House with her society decorator. When Nancy suggested at a
Georgetown party that the Carters should move out early, annoyed Carter
aides fed the line to reporters. Nancy became the Democrats' quintessential
Reaganaut: gun-toting, materialistic, and selfish.

Some feminists caught themselves sympathizing with their *bête noire*.
"Why can we not simply accept the fact of the matter—that savvy political
wives who have been as close to the career as to the man will naturally have

influence and there is nothing sinister about this at all?" one activist asked. The *Boston Globe* columnist Ellen Goodman wondered what Americans wanted: a "First Companion or Co-President, Independent Woman or White Housekeeper?"

Reagan's transition people regretted their failure to manage Nancy's image. But public-relations staffers could only construct an image once the presidential couple defined the First Lady's goals. The Reagan transition team aptly characterized this as "a policy decision," which was "necessarily a personal one, but with significant official implications." "It's a hard job and they've all done it differently," Nancy said of her predecessors. Therefore, she concluded, "I'll be me." Ronnie sent a mixed message. He said Nancy's first job would be "redecorating the living quarters," but he also said that "Nancy knows that her husband is going to use her as a confidante."

The Carters' vulgar male "Georgia mafia" left town; the plutocratic couples closest to the Reagans, known as "The Group," arrived. Tycoons like Alfred Bloomingdale, Charles Z. Wick, Holmes Tuttle, and William French Smith had bankrolled Ronnie's political rise as their wives shopped with Nancy. The women were extravagant, old-fashioned, flamboyant hostesses, deferential to their wealthy husbands—and seemingly happy. They believed they were fulfilled women, unlike the media caricature of dour feminists who deified equity and renounced femininity. "I don't like the Equal Rights Amendment," Martha Lyles, the wife of a Hollywood producer, proclaimed. "*I'm* a woman and *I've* gotten where I want to."

The inauguration gave the bond between Nancy and Ronnie great political and cultural meaning. This warm, loving, spontaneous duo set themselves up as the exemplars of traditional values and the symbols of happy marriage. As much as critics might scoff at the Reagans' politics or style, it was hard to scorn their love affair. Most agreed with *People* that "perhaps" the Reagans' "greatest gift to the style of official Washington will be their unabashedly public romance." Nancy and Ronnie's "very special love story" would inspire at least two books and hundreds of articles about "The First Couple: Mutual Devotion at the Top." Even the *New York Times* would run a front-page article in 1986 about "A Very Special Relationship."

The Reagans often demonstrated their passion. Sending his wife on her first foreign trip, the President whispered, "I love you, be careful," and kissed her four times. During the campaign, one reporter witnessing their reunion after a day and a half joked that Ronnie "gave old Nancy a bite on the neck." All this public intimacy justified the media's invasion of privacy. The Reagans did not object to exposure per se; they just wanted to hide those truths they worked so hard to ignore.

Ronald Reagan became the national father. *Time's* essayist Roger Rosenblatt believed that despite Reagan's failings as a father, his "main characteristics . . .—good humor, modesty, patience—are the attributes of fatherhood at its best." Budget director David Stockman would note the President's "fatherly" tendency to dismiss disputes by saying, "Okay, you fellas work it out." The result in the White House paralleled the result in the Reagan home: Nancy suffered. Staffers feared her, not him, and blamed her rather than him for the tension. Similarly, reporters found it easier to make the well-dressed, sharp-edged Nancy symbolize hard-hearted policies. Ronnie was too affable. He seemed nothing like the greedy TV oil baron J.R. Ewing in "Dallas," the top show in the early 1980s; she seemed eerily similar to the devious Alexis Colby on "Dynasty," which premiered as the Reagans did in January 1981.

Once again Ronald Reagan exceeded his critics' low expectations. The formidable triumvirate running his White House reflected key ingredients in his success. The patrician James Baker linked the President to the Republican corporate establishment, the ideologue Ed Meese helped circulate Reagan's anti-government ideas, and the adman Michael Deaver packaged Ronnie as a Norman Rockwell for the 1980s. Reagan was the most ideological and the most evanescent politician of the modern era. Without the business and conservative grounding, he would have floated away; without the image making, he would have sunk under the weight of his rhetoric. Although he entered office less popular than any modern president, after the first hundred days his approval ratings matched John Kennedy's.

Ronald Reagan was a hero in an age of anti-heroes, an old-fashioned "real" man in an age of wimps. Jimmy Carter's intellectual and spiritual openness, along with his roots in the one American region with a tragic tradition, made him peculiarly vulnerable to the questioning, defensive spirit of the 1970s; Ronald Reagan's intellectual innocence and his hegira to the great American West made him peculiarly resistant to such defeatism. Seeking to conjure up Franklin D. Roosevelt's ebullience, and consciously mimicking western heroes from John Wayne to Clint Eastwood, Reagan united bookish conservative intellectuals and angry blue-collar males against the traditional Roosevelt coalition of progressive intellectuals and labor unions.

Ronnie's avuncular patriotism helped him become the "Teflon" President; his wife's intense domesticity helped her become the Velcro First Lady. "Critics who are disarmed by the President's friendly grin are somehow annoyed by the First Lady's implacable smile of self-assurance," *Newsweek* confessed. Just as Betty Ford's and Rosalynn Carter's reputations benefited from their respective husbands' weaknesses, Nancy's reputation suffered from her husband's strengths. Nancy's $6,000 Galanos dresses, her dinners at Le Cirque while her husband cut school lunch programs, and her "old fashioned" promises "to be the best wife I can to my husband" enraged critics anxious to repudiate her and her family values. Nancy's $800,000 White House renovation triggered stories about excess at a time of austerity, even though the funds were privately donated. "That the first family will not do as the president is asking others to do makes every extravagant gesture of the first lady worthy of reporting," one man wrote to the *Washington Post.* "If nothing else, such stories shed light on the sincerity—or lack of it—of the president's program."

Nancy's visits to hospitals, her support for the Foster Grandparents' program, her attacks on drugs, were called "more ceremonial than substantive." Reporters now longed for Mrs. Carter, who did not just pose for pictures. "She worked hard, she made speeches, she understood issues and she professionalized her staff by paying it more than any First Lady had," one *Washington Post* pundit proclaimed, reversing past criticisms.

The sniping mortified Nancy. Beneath the pasted-on smile and despite her steel spine, she remained the abandoned girl yearning for affection. Her press secretary admitted she read "everything" and watched "at least two news broadcasts a night." "I wish I knew how to develop a thick skin," Mrs. Reagan sighed. Instead, she took many "a long, hot bath, during which I have a marvelous imaginary conversation" with critics. While her lovable husband easily drifted off to sleep, she worried deep into the night. Often, she ate a banana in bed for comfort; apples were too noisy.

Nancy's fragile state impeded her recovery from the shock of Ronnie's shooting on March 30, 1981. At the hospital, Nancy found her husband coughing up blood from a bullet that had barely missed his heart. "Honey, I forgot to duck," he joked. Five hours later, she entered the recovery room where Ronnie was hooked up to machines, struggling to breathe. Nancy cried, "I love you," then grabbed his hand and held it in silence. That night she wrote in her diary, "Nothing can happen to my Ronnie. My life would be over."

Unlike Edith Wilson after Woodrow's strokes, Nancy Reagan let the advisers run the country. Unlike Mamie Eisenhower, though, she ran the Presidency, managing her husband's physical and political wellbeing. Nancy grilled the doctors and controlled Ronnie's schedule. Before releasing one photograph she had the picture cropped to delete the nurse in charge of the tubes draining the President's chest. Thanks to Mrs. Reagan, it would be months before the nation discovered just how close the President had come to dying.

Long after her husband returned to work, though, Nancy remained traumatized. She felt guilty that she had not been with Ronnie when he was shot. She became more dependent on astrologers for scheduling tips. "I think you hold yourself together for a long time because you have to," she would tell Barbara Walters, ". . . and then tears come easily."

"I have a new impression of her," a former "Kennedy Democrat" told Nancy's social secretary after watching the interview. "No longer shall I think of her as cold, icy, controlled. . . . She displayed touching vulnerability." This reaction emboldened Nancy to appear more frequently on television and convinced Michael Deaver and other allies that the First Lady could be rehabilitated.

Nevertheless, the criticism mounted. The Reagans and their supporters lambasted the "liberal media" for attacking Nancy after praising the Kennedy redecoration. In his affable way, Ronald Reagan was continuing Nixon's war on the media. "You are right, what we're getting from the press is dictated by ideology," Ronnie wrote a friend. One study Republicans trumpeted found that 54 percent of reporters were liberal while only 17 percent were conservative, making "today's media elite" one of "the most liberal, anti-establishment groups in American society."

The Reagans appealed to the silent majority of women who were traditional. "I don't mean that women shouldn't have interests outside the home," Nancy said, "I think it's very important that they do. But now I think that women who choose not to have a career feel self-conscious about it, and I don't think that's right."

The firestorm was most intense within the Beltway and among the nation's elite. Even after a year of heavy attack, and despite headlines exaggerating the criticism, only 23 percent of those surveyed in November 1981 had an unfavorable impression of Nancy Reagan. Millions applauded this "lovely, lovely person" with "exquisite" taste, who "goes about the job of being a President's wife." "She dresses like one," a Washington attorney rejoiced. "She acts like one. . . . She undoubtedly cares for the waifs and strays, but she doesn't wear it on her sleeve." "Good Heavens, She's Normal," the conservative pundit R. Emmett Tyrrell exulted. "She does not flop onto the Freudian couch every time some sophomoric reporter fixes an eye on her and inquires as to the existential suffering that throbs within." "I and many like me are tired of the 'age of the slob' and delight in the elegance and high ideals of our first lady," a Virginian proclaimed. "She stands for all of us who put our families ahead of ourselves."

The Reagans knew not to overestimate Nancy's centrality in people's lives or to underestimate her support in the heartland. Nancy tried laughing off her critics. She said at the Alfred E. Smith Dinner in New York that the "Queen Nancy" postcards of her were "silly. I'd never wear a crown—it messes up your hair." In a reference to her lavish White House tableware, she offered to establish "The Nancy Reagan Home for Wayward China." In December the warm reception such quips received emboldened her to bypass reporters and speak to the sixty million or so Americans who watched "60 Minutes."

Nancy Reagan would not repeat Betty Ford's error; her interviewer, Mike Wallace, was an old family friend. "60 Minutes" revealed a warm, intelligent, and coquettish First Lady wounded by her critics. Nancy's feelings were so raw the segment was difficult to watch. To make peace with reporters, she admitted to being defensive. Wallace treated his subject tenderly. He ended by hoping that Americans give Nancy a "fresh look" as a Christmas gift. "That would be nice," Nancy paused. "Look at what I'm really doing," she begged as her voice trailed off.

III

The Reagans began their second year in the White House more worried about her press notices than his. Even with a recession, the President was buoyed by the passage of his domestic spending cuts, tax cuts, and defense spending increases. The "Reagan Revolution" was on its way, but the "bum rap" against Nancy angered Ronnie. "Last year was a lost year," Nancy sighed in early 1982. This old-fashioned First Lady would have to use the modern techniques she honed as an actress and a governor's wife to restore her reputation.

Nancy's predecessors bequeathed her formidable weapons for a public-relations war. Nancy could appear thrifty by scaling back Rosalynn Carter's operation, yet still enjoy considerable resources. Her aides rationed reporters' access to her and choreographed her appearances. Mrs. Reagan reviewed "all major media interview requests." She did not tape local TV interviews at the White House, saving herself for interviews with "national release." Cameramen received detailed instructions to remain "*no more* than seven feet away from Mrs. Reagan" and to arrange special lighting because of her "deep set eyes and fair skin."

Thanks to her predecessors, Mrs. Reagan did not pussyfoot around politics. She avoided "hard news" and, according to her press secretary, Sheila Tate, considered press conferences "more suitable for policy-making individuals." But Tate briefed "East Wing 'regulars'" daily and issued "127 media advisories with regard to Mrs. Reagan's activities" in 1981 alone. Nancy also lobbied openly for Ronnie's 1981 economic reforms. Senate Finance Committee Chairman Bob Dole asked the First Lady to fête the wives of key senators just before his committee voted on the President's budget bill. At that lunch and elsewhere, Nancy mixed chitchat with a hard sell for the debt ceiling increase.

In mid-January, Nancy's New Year's resolution to get along with the press in 1982 weakened when Lesley Stahl of CBS reported that Nancy did not buy many of her designer dresses. The East Wing said the First Lady was promoting the fashion industry—"She has derived no personal benefit." Nevertheless, the 1978 Ethics in Government Act required public officials and their wives to report gifts worth more than thirty-five dollars. Nancy said she donated her used dresses to museums. East Wing aides soon announced that Mrs. Reagan would "no longer accept designer-loaned clothing."

At a Camp David retreat, East Wing and West Wing aides crafted a strategy to rehabilitate Nancy's image. They presented it to the First Lady in February. Her new chief of staff, James Rosebush, would spur the campaign.

Sheila Tate proposed that her boss appear at the Washington press corps' Gridiron Club dinner on March 27. Every year this elite club of sixty members hosted a dinner and roast for six hundred powerbrokers. Tate predicted that reporters would lampoon the First Lady, but Nancy could disarm her critics by joining them.

Nancy was very nervous the night of the dinner. She walked out of the ballroom when the parody began about her "Second Hand Clothes," sung to the Fanny Brice standard, "Second Hand Rose." As the "Gridiron Chorus" finished, the First Lady climbed out from behind a clothing rack. She had wriggled into overlapping frumpy dresses, yellow rubber boots, a mangy boa, fake pearls, and a floppy red hat overflowing with feathers and flowers. The diners burst into applause. Nancy began to sing, to the same tune, "I'm wearing second-hand clothes, second-hand clothes/They're quite the style in the spring fashion shows/Even my new trench coat with fur col-lar, Ronnie bought for ten cents on the dol-lar." As she finished, she tried to smash a china plate. Although the plate refused to cooperate, Nancy received another standing ovation and calls for an encore. She repeated the routine, and this time the plate broke.

The Gridiron Club evening was off the record, so few citizens heard about Nancy's shenanigans. The resulting turnaround in coverage was a grotesque display of media power. Nancy succeeded that night because she worshiped the media lords in their own temple and embraced their values, emphasizing entertainment over dignity, cynicism over sincerity.

Defusing reporters' hostility, though, was not enough. Nancy had to give them something else to write about. For a year, Nancy's two "special" projects—the war on drugs, and foster grandparents—had endured skepticism. Now they loomed as worthy causes and enabled reporters to profile the activist First Lady. Photographs of a bejeweled "Queen Nancy" resplendent in fur were replaced by photographs of a concerned Nancy exhorting teenagers to avoid drugs, or a beatific Nancy hugging a child.

The Foster Grandparents program offered Nancy great photo opportunities with young and old. The program grew in the 1980s from 16,900 foster grandparents serving 50,700 children to 26,600 volunteers and 66,500 children. When Frank Sinatra recorded a song for Nancy's program, the lyrics captured her sentimental approach to social problems: "To love a child you start with a smile and after a while a hug and a kiss; it takes no more than this to love a child." Nancy made public service announcements, talk-show appearances, and visits. She released an entirely ghostwritten 1982 best-seller, *To Love a Child*—although Mrs. Reagan did acknowledge her "co-author's" help.

While Foster Grandparents was a safe, traditional First Lady program, crusading against drugs was risky. One aide called it "a Betty Ford issue." Deaver and Tate urged Nancy to avoid this "depressing" and "unsolvable" problem. Nancy insisted, saying, "I want to do something I'm interested in for four years."

The Reagans wanted to be moral leaders in the war against permissiveness. He did not want to be remembered as the first divorced president; she was still dodging questions about Patti's quick gestation. The drug war would also prove that government could champion morality without expanding. "Money does not buy parent involvement, parent concern, parent knowledge," Nancy said. Her husband could cut the budget and still fight drugs, because responsibility rested with individuals. "Government didn't give birth to the child, parents gave birth to the child," Nancy told Merv Griffin. Such epigrams honored the "social issues" many conservatives felt Reagan abandoned. The war on drugs appeased lifestyle conservatives without hurting Reagan's economic program or exposing the rift between libertarians and moralists.

Nancy spent most of 1982 traveling to drug rehabilitation centers, meeting "recovering" addicts, and perfecting her pitch. If "peer pressure" lured many youngsters into drugs, she would mobilize alternative pressure to keep kids clean by publicizing the stories of former addicts. On the road, these troubled teens—and reporters—met the smart, empathetic, and sentimental woman Ronald Reagan loved. The kids' stories were moving, and her ability to save their lives was humbling. One youngster wrote the First Lady in 1983: "I became a junkie at age thirteen. . . . Mrs. Reagan, I'm sorry you and your efforts weren't there for me three years ago."

With parents, Nancy was sober, informed, determined, accessible, and statesmanlike. She endorsed parents' groups for "zero tolerance." In 1980 there were one thousand such groups; there were nine thousand by the time the Reagans left the White House.

At one of the 110 anti-drug events Nancy starred in during 1984, one girl at Oakland's Longfellow Elementary School asked, "But Mrs. Reagan, what should I say if someone offers me drugs?" As she had been doing for years, Nancy responded, "Just say no, no, no." A few months later, students reviewed the tape of the First Lady's appearance. One twelve-year-old boy suggested to two friends, "Well why don't *we* start a club against drugs and call it 'Just Say No?'" A letter to "Dear Abby" in September 1985 about the clubs prompted ten thousand inquiries. The phrase "Just Say No" was as simplistic and as profound as the rest of the Reagan program. The phrase would sink into popular consciousness, prompting a nationwide youth movement and appearing on t-shirts, baseball caps, even the plastic base of urinals.

In 1983 Nancy targeted Hollywood. She took to the airwaves and lobbied behind the scenes against the glamorization of drugs. Some chastened admen founded the Entertainment Industries Council; in three years, it would boast that "a marked change has occurred in the way the use of drugs are viewed in film and television." Nancy also co-hosted ABC's "Good Morning America," made a public service announcement with National Football League commissioner Pete Rozelle that was broadcast before a record crowd of 112 million people during Super Bowl XVII, emcced a four-hour PBS show, "The Chemical People," and co-starred in a music video, "Stop the Madness," with Kareem Abdul-Jabbar and Arnold Schwarzenegger.

Nancy's appearance on NBC's "Diff'rent Strokes" on March 19, 1983, typified her use of television. The writers of the popular sitcom asked the First Lady to record a scene in her office; Nancy made her appearance central to the plot. In the episode, Gary Coleman's cherubic character, Arnold, exposed drug use in his elementary school, but his principal did not believe it. Nancy Reagan visited Arnold to encourage him. At Arnold's school she staged a miniature version of her "Just Say No" encounters. Some of the youngsters confessed to experimenting with drugs, and they earned a hug from the First Lady.

Nancy's PR genius astonished her allies. Law enforcement professionals called Nancy's Super Bowl ad "the most significant moment in drug education and prevention to date." Her star turn on "Diff'rent Strokes" drew bags of fan mail. "You radiated warmth, love and *genuine* concern," Burt Reynolds wrote. "And for once, the urgent anti-drug message was agreeable to see, and yet aimed at the people who *needed* to hear it."

The Reagans were reestablishing what Secretary of Education William Bennett would call "constructive hypocrisy." Celebrities learned that despite their predilections—Reynolds would soon be addicted to sleeping pills—they should endorse morality. Nancy could guest star on a glamorous TV show which glorified wiseacre kids and was sponsored by Unisom—the "Number One Sleep Aid in America"—as long as she sounded traditional.

Nancy took her campaign worldwide in 1985 when she convened a "First Ladies Summit" of seventeen wives of heads of state against drugs. Later that year she met with thirty First Ladies during the United Nations' fortieth anniversary and had a special audience with the Pope about drug abuse. Reporters treated the summit as a modern Sadie Hawkins Day. Nancy called the summit "a mother-to-mother conference rather than a government conference"; policy issues were avoided. The seventeen First Ladies comprised Nancy's most elite parent group.

Reporters now looked at Nancy with fresh eyes and discovered a delightful woman. "Because there was so much talk about it and it was kind of ridiculed," the old MGM actress stopped putting on "the Gaze" at rallies. On "The Merv Griffin Show" in 1983, Nancy told about one of her worst White House moments, when her skirt fell as she rose to end a meeting. She recovered by saying to her guest, "Well, I'm sure this is a meeting you'll never forget." All of a sudden, Mrs. Reagan was charming instead of frosty.

Nancy Reagan's drug crusade was the most successful First Lady project in history. By May 1986, when five million people would participate in "Just Say No" marches held in seven hundred cities, Nancy would have traveled one hundred thousand miles, made forty-nine speeches, and given 1,254 media interviews. Leftists angered by budget cuts sneered, "If a wife is going to go around grandstanding, that's kind of cute," but she had chosen an issue where her moral leadership counted. Mrs. Reagan helped trigger a sea change in attitudes toward drugs. "Just Say No" was on everybody's lips. Hollywood heroes stopped getting high. Drug use remained epidemic, but the percentage of students using drugs and alcohol dropped from approximately one-third to one-fourth. By 1985, 70 percent of high school seniors surveyed called marijuana harmful, a striking reversal in less than a decade.

Nancy Reagan had chosen her project wisely. She could not buttonhole rich friends to bankroll restorations or beautification. She had been too controversial to hide behind vague calls for "volunteerism" and would not crusade for women or for candor. Mrs. Reagan acted most like Mrs. Carter. Both adopted an "ugly" issue without a clear payoff, but Nancy's success dwarfed Rosalynn's. Nancy was rehabilitated. Even with Ronnie's soaring post-recession, post-reelection popularity, some 1985 polls found the First Lady to be the most popular Reagan.

The contrast between Mrs. Reagan's anti–drug abuse campaign and Mrs. Johnson's beautification revealed vast changes in twenty years. By the 1980s America's problems seemed intractable: Who cared about cleaning parks and rivers when the nation's youth was being poisoned? A new elite had also emerged, as Nancy's celebrities eclipsed Lady Bird's aristocrats.

Just as beautification was central to Lyndon Johnson's leadership project, the drug crusade was central to Ronald Reagan's. The fight against drugs showed the extent of the Reagans' ambition. They wanted to dismantle the welfare state and undo the Sixties without relinquishing the center. In fact, Ronald Reagan tranquilized American conservatism, making it more moderate and more palatable. With drugs, as with so much else, his greatest accomplishments were rhetorical. Reagan inspired voters with his odes to small government and traditional values, but like Eisenhower, Nixon, and Ford before him, he could not resist distributing government largesse. His staff would boast that "total nominal spending in 1984 on *15 key social programs* is *45% higher*" than it was in 1980. Yearly reports trumpeted all the new government programs, from a National Commission on Excellence in Education to an $8.5 billion Superfund program.

Separately and together, Ronnie and Nancy used their popular pulpits and cultural leadership to insulate the President from nasty policy debates about budget cuts and the military build-up. White House aides preferred feeding reporters personal or patriotic stories rather than political or substantive lines. Nancy helped publicize her husband's personal traits to prove he did not hate the poor. "They portray Ronnie as mean and cruel and a noncompassionate man," Nancy complained of the Democrats in 1984. "He's the softest touch in the world."

In an age of weakened political party affiliation, the Reagans deployed all the popular weapons in the modern presidential arsenal to conquer the public. Both seemed eminently qualified to greet Emperor Hirohito, charm the Queen, or greet the masses. Starring in 1982's "Christmas in Washington," "A warm and glorious" celebration bringing "the country together around their fireplaces and television sets," the Reagans deftly blended celebrity worship, piety, patriotism, and nostalgia. Throughout the administration, the Reagans' staged appearances at solemn ceremonies soothed and united the nation. Their comportment at memorials to the 241 Marines killed in the barracks bombing in Lebanon in 1983, and to the seven astronauts killed in the space shuttle *Challenger* explosion in 1986, was always just right—emotional without being hysterical, personal without being intrusive. The Reagans' ability to express the nation's feelings at such moments bonded the First Couple with the American people.

The Reagans talked about values to promote conservatism without unduly politicizing it. Rather than speaking of "the Reagan Revolution," the President talked about "the Great Rediscovery . . . of our values and our common sense." Reagan was fortunate to endure the recession early enough in his first term so that he could take credit for the ensuing economic boom. The return of prosperity gave providential blessing to Reagan's rhetoric about restoring tradition and reviving America. After three failed presidencies, even Democrats praised him for proving that, as Jimmy Carter's policy adviser Stuart Eizenstat would say, "a mortal can handle the job and be successful."

IV

By 1983 Nancy and Ronnie were the most popular presidential couple since the Kennedys. "The public sees the Reagans as a partnership," Reagan's pollster Richard Wirthlin wrote, explaining why the First Couple's poll ratings were in sync. America's excitement about their love affair helped keep the administration afloat even amid policy disasters and personal embarrassments.

The "Great Rediscovery" was more like a clever synthesis. Ronald Reagan repeatedly stole his critics' thunder. He silenced attacks on his war against the poor by maintaining the social "safety net." He sidestepped the divisive abortion debate by endorsing a pro-life amendment to the Constitution but not pushing it aggressively. He would prove that he was not bellicose by befriending Mikhail Gorbachev. And, quite surprisingly, he—and Nancy—would defuse the feminist critique by commandeering part of it.

Throughout the 1980s, women continued marching out of the home and into the office. By 1984 more than half the women in the United States were in the work force and only a third were homemakers. The divorce rate was approaching four of every ten marriages. Yet while women achieved greater equality, feminism was discredited. In 1981, Betty Friedan's call for a new appreciation of the family in *The Second Stage* acknowledged the movement's excesses. A year later, the death of the ERA symbolized the movement's weakness. Many women began to resent feminism as an elitist movement that, as one disappointed activist would write, failed to "provide an adequate response to the problems and challenges that shape their lives" while purporting to represent them.

In the 1960s one aide had noticed a "hormone" gap, whereby women were more likely than men to support the handsome actor; as President, Reagan worried about a "gender gap," whereby women were less likely to support him. In 1980, 54 percent of male voters chose him, compared with only 46 percent of women, the largest difference in decades. Women were considered to be more liberal and more vulnerable to Reagan's proposed budget cuts. Aides urged Reagan to "recognize and salute the changing role of women as a/the principal family bread winner." Like his predecessors, Ronald Reagan routinely listed all his female appointees, met with them, and boasted about how his administration had been better to women than any others. In a characteristically brilliant mix of conservative and liberal symbols, Ronald Reagan appointed a seemingly pro-life conservative as the first female Supreme Court justice.

Nancy also played to the center. "I'm not for marches or placard waving," she said, bashing the bra-burning feminist of popular myth. "I think if we stopped giving all movements a 'stage' on TV, there would be fewer 'performances.'" Yet she was, in her own way, a feminist. She and Ron agreed that more women should participate as equals in the work world and in politics. Nancy co-opted the feminist argument for equality and turned the movement's push for self-determination against its leaders. She rejoiced that "there are so many more choices available to women today," and she regretted that the movement "created a certain amount of pressure to make the right choices." "Feminism is the ability to *choose* what you want to do," she said. "I'm doing what I want to do."

Marriage became a critical battleground. Radicals called it "the hell of false expectations," but 94 percent of women polled still considered marriage "the most satisfying way of life." It needed adjustment, not destruction. In the *New York Times Magazine,* Anne Taylor Fleming said modern women "seem caught between the parts of themselves they can't reconcile—the part that wants a hero for a husband and the part that wants a partner; the part that wants to be the perfect, ever-present mother and the part that wants to be the perfect career woman."

The Reagans' marriage seemed easy. Nancy said, "I consider Ronnie's welfare in everything I think or do"; Ronnie said, "I can't imagine life without her." Subtly, Nancy had adjusted the conventional 1950s equation that marriage "is in reality about a 75-25 proposition (with the wife supplying the 75)," to a more egalitarian formula that "it can be 90-10 and you have to be willing to give the 90 or he has to be willing to give the 90. But it's something you want to do." "Thinking of Nancy Reagan's face, her adoring eyes," Fleming wondered "whether all wives, on some primal, preliberated level, want to be able to look at their husbands that way and feel that way about them, and feel cheated if they don't."

Just as reporters had embraced Betty Ford's candor as a mark of liberation, reporters now embraced the Reagans' happy marriage as a sign of restoration. "The Revolution Is Over," *Time* declared in April 1984. While Nancy's unliberated marriage enraged some women, it inspired millions of others. *Ladies' Home Journal* celebrated the athlete Mary Lou Retton, who was small but not weak, the astronaut Anna Fisher, who worked but was "still" a "happy wife and mother," and Mrs. Reagan, who "reasserted the role of the traditional wife." By the spring of 1985, nearly three-quarters of the women NBC surveyed said Nancy Reagan set a good example for women. In Dick Wirthlin's polls, Mrs. Reagan's highest favorability ratings came from married women, suggesting her utility as a long-awaited role model for the American wife.

The example of the Reagans' marriage also subverted one of feminism's most compelling arguments: that women could only be strong and satisfied by becoming liberated. Feminists disdained women who achieved power through traditional means, but Nancy Reagan was strong and satisfied—as were other prominent Republican women, such as Jeane Kirkpatrick and Phyllis Schlafly. In the early 1990s Susan Faludi would write about a backlash that blamed "women's equality" as being "responsible for women's unhappiness." The Reagan assault was subtler and more effective. It hijacked the most popular elements of feminism while tapping into blue-collar resentments of the upper-middle-class white women abandoning the home for huge salaries and plush offices. Many radical feminists and radical anti-feminists agreed that for all the talk of "universal sisterhood," the feminist movement served a very limited and already privileged subset of women.

Feminism, Reagan-style, promised equality and respect, along with tradition and happiness. Nancy Reagan and the millions she represented accepted the ambiguities, the tradeoffs, and the half-measures. Activists sought clarity.

The 1984 election demonstrated that the gender gap was not as wide or as damaging as predicted. Reagan captured only 55 percent of women's votes, as opposed to 64 percent of men's votes, but 60 percent of married women surveyed chose the President. Reagan was unpopular with black women, poor women, and liberal women—who were disproportionately single—rather than with women overall. Politics, not gender, was at issue. Millions of women cheered Ronnie's policies, his values, and his marriage.

Always seeking to conform to the conventional standard, Nancy Reagan had filled a void. She offered a model of personal fulfillment and public respect. In the future other women would try to differentiate between what Christina Hoff Sommers would call "equity feminism," or the push for equality, and "gender feminism," the more radical movement agenda. In the 1990s younger "Third Wave" feminists, frustrated that their movement was no longer "seen as guaranteeing every woman's choice," would begin searching for a middle path. Nancy Reagan addressed these tensions before many feminists did. Her example demonstrated that women could get self-fulfillment without having to use what thirty-one-year-old Naomi Wolf in 1993 would call "the F-word." The fact that a conservative woman like Nancy Reagan could harness it proved just how much of feminism had seeped into the mainstream and how distorted its public image had become.

Both Reagans began the second term feeling comfortable. The inauguration in January 1985 celebrated Reagan's role in America's comeback; more and more reporters celebrated Nancy's importance to the President and, by extension, the nation. By March 1985 she enjoyed an approval rating of 82 percent.

An hour-long prime-time NBC special in June cheered the new, bold, fulfilled First Lady and her political partnership. The documentary described "Nancy Reagan at the peak of her power, at the peak of her popularity." Praising his subject for embracing modern media values, Chris Wallace concluded that Nancy Reagan had become "liberated . . . committed to securing not only the President's place in history, but also her own."

The documentary climaxed with a warm joint interview at the Reagan ranch. "Mr. President," Wallace asked, "how good a politician is Mrs. Reagan?" Ronnie took a deep breath. Nancy chuckled, "Absolutely sensational, don't you think so?" Smiling, Ronnie said, "You took the words right out of my mouth." Wallace laughed, saying, "I think she's prompting you again." "As the two of them complete a remarkable career in politics," Wallace concluded, "insiders say Mrs. Reagan was indispensable."

The media now seemed determined to turn Nancy Reagan into the secret of her husband's success. Reporters listed all the people she ran out of town, including Secretary of State Alexander Haig, National Security Adviser Richard Allen, and Interior Secretary William Clark. As they had done with Betty Ford and Rosalynn Carter, reporters built up the First Lady at the President's expense.

At the White House, Nancy continued to serve as Ronnie's enforcer. "I think I'm aware of people who are trying to take advantage of my husband," she would say. "I'm a soft touch," the President chuckled, avoiding responsibility as smoothly as he evaded conflict. Chris Wallace had asked Reagan's adviser Ed Rollins, Jr., if he was scared of the First Lady—on camera. The glib consultant sputtered, "Scared, scared, is a fun, funny term. I think, uh, we certainly respect her, and I think that you know, when she has a concern with something it goes to the top of the priority list rather than the bottom."

The new chief of staff, Don Regan, learned quickly that he had to manage the First Lady. Regan thought that Mrs. Reagan was usurping presidential "prerogatives." Some of her demands, including firing Raymond Donovan and Margaret Heckler from the Cabinet, "seemed so far out of her proper area of competence that I was disposed to ignore them." Regan sought a deputy to handle Mrs. Reagan. "When I need something, I'll call you directly," Regan claimed Nancy said. "I don't see any need for an intermediary."

During the first Reagan term Nancy had focused on helping maintain Ronnie's popularity; now she wanted to help secure his historical reputation as a man of peace. She resented the claims that her husband was a warmonger. "You just don't like that said about somebody you love, knowing that it's not true." Nancy often told how the Russian Foreign Minister Andrei Gromyko had asked her to "whisper peace into his ear every night" and she had replied: "Oh, I will. And I'll also whisper in your ear." In fact, Nancy did urge Ronnie to "tone . . . down" his rhetoric and begin negotiating with the Soviets.

Despite the gossip, Nancy never forgot that the President retained the final word. Reagan's occasional need to assert his independence made him stick to his plans and visit a German military cemetery in the spring of 1985. When word leaked that forty-seven Nazi SS storm troopers were buried in Bitburg, most of the President's advisers, including Nancy, urged him not to go. In his diary, the President would blame the press for "stirring up as much trouble as they can."

Ronnie's bullheadedness caused rare sustained tension between the Reagans. "I'm worried about Nancy," he confided to his diary. "She's uptight about the situation and nothing I can say can wind her down." Be it with the press or his wife, Ronald Reagan often assumed his critics were overreacting. On the eve of the trip, the President approached his First Lady. "Are you going with me?" he asked tentatively. "I've been in this thing for thirty years," she replied, "and I'm not backing out now."

In July 1985 doctors discovered a large cancerous polyp in the President's intestinal tract. The operation thrust Nancy back to the traumatic days after the shooting. She hovered around her husband and tried to bar all visitors, forbidding spokesmen to say "cancer" or "massive." Media warnings that Ronnie might not survive outraged her, as did Regan's plan to fly by helicopter to the hospital with Vice President George Bush. How dare he usurp presidential prerogatives, she glowered. When the only photograph the White House released showed Reagan's profile and Regan in full, relations between the image-conscious First Lady and the power-hungry chief of staff ruptured.

As usual, Ronnie appreciated his wife's mothering. In his weekly radio talk, the President sounded fatherly as he urged Americans "to have a checkup." He then praised his wife. "First Ladies aren't elected and they don't receive a salary," he said. "They've mostly been private persons forced to live public lives. Abigail Adams helped invent America. Dolley Madison helped protect it. Eleanor Roosevelt was FDR's eyes and ears. Nancy Reagan is my everything." Nancy sat by her husband, tears streaming down her cheeks, thankful he was on radio and not television.

Less than a month after the President's surgery, doctors removed a cancerous growth from his nose. Nancy again banned the word "cancer," ordering Reagan's spokesman, Larry Speakes, "to say it was a pimple." This evasion triggered a firestorm. Reporters after Watergate always assumed politicians were lying, and they pounced when proven correct. Nancy Reagan's truce with the press remained uneasy. Reporters were reminded of how "fiercely protective" the First Lady was; Nancy remembered how vicious reporters could be. They demanded not only candor but obeisance. After six correspondents grilled her husband about his "pimple," she exclaimed, "Sometimes you wonder if they *want* you to be sick."

What the NBC special had suggested, the President's recuperation proved: Nancy was in control. *U.S. News and World Report* called her "Mrs. President." Aides grumbled about the President's isolation throughout the summer. Some feared that he would not have enough time to prepare for his summit with Mikhail Gorbachev. The columnist George Will agreed that Nancy was essential to Ronnie's success. Reagan's "reassuring serenity," Will wrote, "has much to do with the first person he sees in the morning and the last person he sees at night." Will wondered why it took his colleagues so long to recognize her importance. Then again, he wrote, reporters "often are the last to notice."

Nancy noted that Bitburg proved Ronnie's independence, but she took credit for encouraging his meeting with Mikhail Gorbachev in late 1985. The Reagans approached this first summit in six years as a team. To build a nice atmosphere, Nancy invited Raisa Gorbachev to have tea in Geneva.

The balance of power between the Reagans had shifted. Reporters now described Nancy "as a proven commodity in her ability to grab favorable headlines when the going gets rough for her husband." Nancy had shed her reputation as a battle-axe. The *Washington Post* reported that the First Lady would be "trying to show the 'warm fuzzy' side of the administration." She would play "the hospitable humanitarian/diplomat to enhance Ronald Reagan's image as [the] tough-minded statesman/negotiator."

Don Regan, though, was fed up with the First Lady. He resented her attempt to share the spotlight with the President, as well as her many ridiculous demands. Nancy called Regan one Sunday night at 11:15 and urged him to change the residence the Reagans would use in Geneva. And, "as usual," she consulted with her astrologer about the proper timing for Ronnie's activities.

Regan betrayed his contempt for Nancy's actions when he predicted that women would read about the First Ladies' tea because "they're not . . . going to understand throw-weights or what is happening in Afghanistan." The reputedly unliberated Nancy Reagan was incensed. Nancy wisely claimed she did not see Regan's statement. But when asked "if women concerned themselves with substantive issues," she snapped, "I'm sure they do."

Never before had the pro-forma meetings between the spouses attracted such attention. Sensing tension between the two First Ladies, journalists wrote about the "style wars" between the glitzy Nancy Reagan and the elegant Raisa Gorbachev. "I really think that's a little silly," Nancy chided reporters. With her husband discussing the fate of the world, Nancy Reagan did not want to talk about clothes. She wanted to be taken seriously.

Ironically, the husbands ended up getting along better than the wives. Nancy found Raisa pedantic. After Mrs. Gorbachev harangued the President about Marxist-Leninist theory, Nancy snapped, "Who does that dame think she is?" Meanwhile, the supposedly incompetent President would recall having "the pleasure of going into the room to my team and telling them that it was all settled, that there would be a meeting in '86 and '87, the first meeting in Washington, the second one in Moscow. They couldn't believe it." The Gipper had scored without his supporting line and despite his wife.

Ronnie's magic worked best with strangers. Periodic eruptions throughout their tenure in the White House undermined the Reagans' masquerade as the all-American family. Nancy feuded with Michael and Maureen. Ron would embarrass his parents by taking unemployment when his ballet company went on hiatus, then taking employment from *Playboy* and "Saturday Night Live." These squabbles, however, paled in comparison to Patti's antics. In 1986 she published a "novel" about the neglected daughter of a distracted governor and his social-climbing wife. The book, *Home Front,* caused such a stir that the Reagans felt compelled to submit to a Barbara Walters special on the eve of the Academy Awards. "You'll meet the Reagans as perhaps you haven't before," the interviewer promised her fans.

Barbara Walters's evolution from news reporter to celebrity interviewer paralleled the transformation in TV news. Networks in the 1980s ordered their news divisions to entertain. News shows had to compete with cable TV and with sensationalist "reality-based shows" like "A Current Affair." Walters treated all her subjects alike, be they movie stars or politicians.

The Reagans thrived in this world of "infotainment," a term that became popular in the early 1980s. They happily blurred the lines between politics and popular culture, turning their celebrity into political capital. Appearing with Barbara Walters just before Hollywood's great annual celebration, talking about their favorite movies and their life in the movies from the White House screening room, underlined the Reagans' mastery of American popular culture. Never had a presidential couple dominated American culture and politics so thoroughly.

Nancy did not handle the inevitable question about Patti well. "I tried to be a good mother," Nancy whined. "I don't think anybody's perfect, but then, there is no perfect parent, there's no perfect child." When Barbara asked how Patti's diatribe made her feel, Nancy pursed her lips, looked coldly, and gestured dramatically for Ronnie to answer, as if to say, "What did you expect?" "It was interesting fiction," Ronnie ambled. The presidential couple perked up when Barbara ended with questions about "how . . . you keep the romance in a marriage." Nancy repeated her old saw about how marriage "isn't always 50-50," while Ronnie quoted Clark Gable about the thrill a man gets having that special "someone on the other side of the door . . . listening for the sound of his footsteps."

The "Ronnie and Nancy" show remained popular, thanks to the President's Truman-like abilities to connect with the millions who read the daily horoscope, watched the nightly news, and still believed in the American dream. Just as modern journalists always tried to fold the day's story into a "master narrative" about American society, the Reagans focused on the larger narrative about their lives and their contribution to the nation. For eight years, Ronald and Nancy Reagan would keep their spot at the apex of American popular culture. They continued to inspire adoring articles about their love story, to grant the occasional joint interview, and to make the strategic TV appearance that kept their faces in play and their images intact. Sixty million Americans watched the Reagans on Barbara Walters, while barely a million people received the *New York Times*. The message about "morning in America" was generated by the Reagans and confirmed in the media, day and night, in the upbeat sets of morning television, in the glamorous afternoon soap operas, and in prime-time shows perpetuating the American dream, such as "The Bill Cosby Show." The Reagans' meta-presidency, celebrating America's return and the Reagans' ascendance, dwarfed minor political dramas.

The First Couple's sideshow helped both Reagans retain their popularity during a difficult stretch. Bitburg had been followed by terrorist attacks against Americans on a TWA flight and the cruise ship *Achille Lauro,* Ronnie's cancer, and the *Challenger* disaster. But the worst was yet to come.

V

Both Reagans counted the 1985 Geneva summit among Ronnie's major achievements. He wanted to devote himself to this search for peace, yet domestic needs often diverted the aspiring statesman. Reagan's second term lacked the focus of the first term. His increasing distraction and memory loss were early indicators of Alzheimer's disease. The President and his advisers tried to rekindle the zeal of 1981 and 1982. Over the summer of 1986 Ronnie would join Nancy's crusade, briefly making drugs the "Number One National Problem." But Reagan never found a new policy crusade; instead, the President hid behind his image to keep his Presidency alive.

During the second half of Ronnie's first term, Nancy Reagan had brilliantly rehabilitated herself by avoiding public policy disputes and pursuing her own projects. During the second term, her adoring press coverage and her husband's growing frailty eased her into more and more prominence, more and more power. Ultimately she overreached; the deep-seated fear of an overbearing First Lady would prove more powerful than her good works or her sugar-coated feminism.

Four days after his operation in July 1985, Ronnie wrote in his diary: "I had my first food by mouth." He added, "Some strange soundings are coming from some Iranians. Bud M. will be here tomorrow to talk about it." Reagan hoped for "a breakthrough" to free seven Americans held hostage in Lebanon. These "soundings" led to a series of harebrained schemes to sell arms to Iranian moderates and channel the profits to fund the Nicaraguan Contras. When this "Iran-Contra affair" came to light in November 1986, it pierced Ronald Reagan's seemingly invincible shell. The scandal would also focus attention on Nancy's power. Out of this crucible of criticism a new conception of the presidential couple would be forged.

Nancy blamed the scandal on the second term's second-rate staff. While Ronnie's popularity dwindled, his wife and chief of staff clashed. "Are you still here, Don?" Mrs. Reagan taunted Regan. The battle polarized the White House. "Usually in a big place there's only one person or group to be afraid of," Peggy Noonan would say, "but in the Reagan White House there were two, the chief of staff and his people and the first lady and hers—a pincer formation that made everyone feel vulnerable."

No one could push Ronnie around when he was determined to appear in control, not even "Mommy." The claims that he was easily swayed by Nancy annoyed him. The inherent competition between husband and wife stopped the President from doing what he needed to do. Rumors spread that the President had told his wife to "get off my goddamn back" about Regan. Even if the Reagans did not speak that way to each other, as they claimed, Ronnie resented Nancy's nagging. He would remain loyal to Regan.

The bloodletting in the press and in the White House immobilized Ronnie. After a lifetime of image-building, he dismissed Iran-Contra as a "journalistic firestorm." His ability to disconnect from reality led him to a defense built on two contradictory points. He still boasted about trying to free the hostages and woo the moderates, but said he never negotiated with terrorists. And he claimed ignorance of the financial diversion to the Contras, while insisting he was in command.

Few Americans bought it. After the President stumbled through a press conference in November, doubts about him proliferated. His job approval rating dropped in one month from 67 percent to 46 percent. By March more than half the people surveyed believed Reagan was lying when he said he did not remember being told about the diversion of profits.

Reagan faced his greatest political crisis with the same passivity with which he faced his greatest personal crisis, his divorce. Now he blamed hysterical reporters and zealous aides, refusing to take any actions until the commission chaired by former Senator John Tower reported. Ronnie was "unhappy" and "frustrated that I couldn't get my message across," but not "depressed." Nancy asked Ronnie if he was as unworried as he seemed. "I don't believe I did anything wrong," he replied. "I realize there will be some unpleasant times coming up, but no, I'm not worried." The President of the United States continued to sleep soundly as his wife chomped on bananas into the night.

The new year began ominously. Ronnie's prostate surgery in mid-January of 1987 renewed doubts about his competence and intensified the war between the First Lady and the chief of staff. Nancy focused on the President; she wanted Ronnie to recover completely before he resumed a full schedule. Regan focused on the presidency, seeking presidential action to deflect attention from the scandal. Aides searched for "possible ways to show Presidential activity within the medical recovery limitations." No matter how limited the activity Regan proposed, Nancy vetoed it. "You are not a doctor," she shrieked.

As the weeks dragged on, Regan was surprised at his boss's listlessness. The President, Regan would recall, "seemed uninterested in the fact that the field had largely been left to his detractors at one of the most critical hours of his career." The health crisis on top of the political crisis may have convinced Reagan that age had finally caught up to him.

The hospitalization made Reagan the man look as weak as his Presidency. Since the cancer surgery, Nancy had appeared ever stronger, and Ronnie ever weaker. Although Nancy still enjoyed 60 percent approval, the role reversal unnerved many. The jokes had been around for years, as comedians would welcome "the leader of the free world"—and "her husband." Much of the talk in 1987 had more of an edge. In the macho atmosphere of the White House, staffers expressed their disdain for powerful women and their supine mates by calling Nancy Evita, the Missus, the Hairdo with Anxiety, and— mocking their boss—Mommy or Mommy Dearest.

Such sneers may have emboldened Regan. On February 8th, he scheduled a press conference for the 26th and told Nancy it was "time" for the President "to get the scandal behind him." As the argument became more heated, the First Lady of the United States shouted, "Okay, Have your damn press conference!" "You bet I will," the chief of staff said as he slammed down the phone.

The even-tempered President was "troubled by this kind of temperamental outburst, especially toward Nancy, who has always had only my best interests at heart." When Nancy leaked the news about the tiff, the President was also embarrassed. Approaching the most critical week of his Presidency, with the Tower commission about to release its report, the President had to endure headlines saying, "Reagan Caught in Feud Between Wife and Aide." "Who is in charge?" Democrat Bill Richardson asked in the House of Representatives. "A constituent of mine asked, 'How can the President deal with the Soviets if he cannot settle a dispute between his wife and the chief of staff?'"

Like all good husbands, presidents were supposed to be resolute. Mike Royko of the *Chicago Tribune* suggested that if Reagan commuted to work, "the world would be spared the embarrassing sight of a president caught in the middle and looking as henpecked as Dagwood Bumstead." Royko asked, "Imagine what the American business community would be like if every chief executive's wife spent the day hanging around outside of his office?" It was time for the little lady to remember her place.

The mounting criticism depressed Nancy. After Regan blamed the East Wing for a hiring mistake, Ronnie decided, *"That does it."* He claimed he fired Regan because of the "morale issue" resulting from the attempt to be "deputy president," rather than as punishment for Iran-Contra.

When the President finally fired his chief of staff on Monday, February 23, 1987, Regan blasted Mrs. Reagan. The President said if Nancy had over-reached, it had only been because of his health. "I thought I was Chief of Staff to the President, not to his wife," Regan bristled. The President, though, would not fight. He flashed the same disengaged yet amiable grin he always gave.

Forced by Reagan's defense to declare the President of the United States incompetent or dishonest, the Tower commission condemned his "management style." The "flustered" President still tried to insist that his policy never offered arms for hostages. "Mr. President," Brent Scrowcroft said, "there were occasions when the aircraft loaded with weapons was sitting on the runway, waiting for word that the hostages had been freed."

By Friday Nancy and other key advisers had settled on former Tennessee Senator Howard Baker, Jr., as Regan's replacement. Nancy deprived Regan of the gracious exit he desired by leaking word of Baker's appointment. While Nancy had her first good night's sleep "in weeks," the President regretted Regan's humiliating departure. In his memoirs, Regan would come close to an apology—while absolving his wife of any responsibility—by claiming that "the leak was not intentional."

That Monday, the day Donald Regan had planned to resign, he received some revenge. William Safire of the *New York Times* condemned the First Lady's "coup." Safire began: "At a time he most needs to appear strong, President Reagan is being weakened and made to appear wimpish and helpless by the political interference of his wife." Safire called Nancy "an incipient Edith Wilson, unelected and unaccountable, presuming to control the actions and appointments of the executive branch." The next day, the *New York Times* underlined Safire's argument that strong First Ladies made their husbands appear impotent. Above a front-page article claiming "Nancy Reagan's Power Is Considered at Peak," an article proclaimed: "Poll Shows Reagan Approval Rating at 4-Year Low."

The Reagans remained surprisingly sensitive to criticism. Nancy called Safire's attack "the most vicious and unbelievable article about me I had ever read—and I had read quite a few." Old-fashioned cowboy that he was, Ronnie ignored his wife's role in earning the criticism. He felt, Nancy recalled, that "it was a terrible thing for a man to do to another man's wife."

Now the controversy over Nancy's behavior threatened to upstage Ronnie's efforts to restore his Presidency. His aides vainly struggled to "convey a positive message over the long haul," depicting "the President actively engaged in the process of the government." Even the new chief of staff, Howard Baker, was drawn in by his remarks that when Nancy "gets her hackles up, she can be a dragon." Asked about the statement, Baker backpedaled, saying, "She is a great lady and she obviously has strong convictions. That's what I meant."

"Dragon Ladies," like iron maidens, were unnatural, aberrant, overly powerful women. "Dragon Lady" was the name of a character from the 1930s comic strip "Terry and the Pirates." The many cartoons picturing the First Lady brandishing a sword to protect her husband while he shuffled off to bed, holding cue cards as he delivered a speech, or wearing her husband's pants suggested how unnatural, how castrating, how limiting it was for a woman to wield the kind of power men were "supposed to" enjoy.

On March 4, the Reagans' thirty-fifth anniversary, President Reagan attacked the "despicable fiction" that his wife was "running the government." Telling a reporter "you've touched a nerve here," he grumbled, "the idea that she's involved in governmental discussions and so forth and all of this, and being a kind of a dragon lady, there is nothing to that. No one who knows her well would ever believe it."

Reagan's popularity would recover, buoyed by the fact that only 24 percent of those surveyed believed he was in charge. Reagan knew that Americans liked him more than they respected him. He hated the idea that "Americans were forgiving me for something I hadn't done." The President's apparent distance from decision-making intensified the controversy about his overbearing wife.

The debate that ensued was peculiar. Anti-Reagan feminists defended Nancy against a pro-Reagan conservative columnist. At a time when feminism was on the defensive, this most unlikely heroine gave some women something to cheer about. "Regan once said women didn't understand 'throw weight.' Now we do," one woman rejoiced. "Hooray for our side!" The novelist Joan Didion, who was "not one of Nancy Reagan's greatest admirers," noted that critics were uncomfortable with a powerful woman in the White House. Ellen Goodman complained that this "self-proclaimed traditional wife" who had been pilloried for ignoring politics was now attacked as power-hungry. The unrealistic expectations imposed on the First Lady reflected the unrealistic expectations imposed on all women. The *New York Times* distanced itself from William Safire, its house conservative, and endorsed the Reagans' modern egalitarian marriage. "Spousal advice is part of any marital relationship," an editorial argued, "and so is the right of the partner to ignore that advice."

Life in the White House had raised Nancy's consciousness, to an extent. Nancy called the attack on her an attack on women. She had chronicled—and leaked—examples of Regan's sexism. Now she saw sexism among her critics as well. When Phil Donahue convened a panel of experts who condemned the First Lady, Nancy Reagan harrumphed that none of the panelists was a woman. Nancy Reagan was sounding more like Betty Ford, if not Betty Friedan.

Six years in the White House had also strengthened Nancy's confidence. This time she refused to apologize or change. She was relieved that 63 percent of the public still liked her, even though 40 percent of those surveyed agreed she was too influential. A Gallup poll in June confirmed that her celebrity status was intact: more men selected her as the woman with whom they would most like to spend an evening. Actresses Heather Locklear, Cybill Shepherd, and Lynda Carter were distant runners-up. Still, the criticism rankled, especially considering how much the press encouraged her to exert influence.

The First Lady spent the rest of her husband's tenure justifying her behavior. In so doing, Nancy Reagan became the great theorist of the co-presidency. She first tried to define her role before the American Newspaper Publishers' Association in May 1987. Peddling old acting stories as shamelessly as Ronnie did, Nancy remembered one walk-on role where she emerged from the attic and quickly returned. "There are those who think first ladies should be kept in attics, only to say our lines, pour our tea, and then be put away again." Nancy Reagan was not that kind of woman. She had discovered the First Lady's "white glove pulpit"—"more refined, more restricted, more ceremonial" than the president's "bully pulpit . . . but it's a pulpit all the same."

Furthermore, Nancy acknowledged that the president has many advisers "but no one among all those experts is there to look after him as an individual with human needs." She said: "I'm a woman who loves her husband, and I make no apologies for looking out for his personal and political welfare. We have a genuine, sharing marriage. I go to his aid. He comes to mine. . . . We don't always agree. But neither marriage nor politics denies a spouse the right to hold an opinion or the right to express it. And if you have anything less, it's not marriage, it's servitude."

Subtly, coyly, using the ladylike indirection that feminists disavowed, Nancy Reagan had accepted her mandate. She had hoped to combine Mrs. Kennedy's flair with Mrs. Eisenhower's domesticity, but she ended up combining Mrs. Johnson's crusading with Mrs. Carter's insider status. Traditional wifely devotion justified presidential power-playing within limits. But this seemed to be what the American people wanted. The First Lady offered America's middle-class women an energetic representative who understood that marital partnership did not mean total equality.

Unlike Lady Bird Johnson, Nancy Reagan did not contemplate the nature of society or her role in it. Like most American women, Nancy was a "cultural materialist," tailoring her ideas to fit her changing social and cultural circumstances. Mrs. Reagan simply ratified her role and that of millions of other women. Conservatives rushed forward to defend the First Lady and prove that housewives could be equal partners. "What could be more ideal than to think out loud or to share ideas with someone whose judgment you trust?" the Reagans' friend Charles Z. Wick asked. Senator Alan Simpson of Wyoming exploded, "Only a damn fool would suggest that the wife of the president of the United States has no role whatever in the governing of our country. It might not read that way in the civics texts or statute books, but that's the way it is in the book of real life."

The country's top conservative, Ronald Reagan, agreed. He still said that Nancy was not his "main adviser." She was "a good and faithful wife, and I share secrets with her and my problems and all of that." In *McCall's,* Ronnie glowed, "She has made it so natural for us to be as one that we never face anything alone." The President put his political problems in personal perspective, and suggested how deep his bond was with his wife, when he said: "Nancy worries when she thinks something might upset me or might go wrong. If she would only realize that nothing important can go wrong as long as I have her."

Without using the term "co-presidency," Americans began to recognize that the First Lady was "part of the deal," as Simpson said. Americans were dispensing with the fiction that a president's spouse was irrelevant to this very personal office. The role of the First Lady had been transformed, along with Americans' assumptions about their president's marriage. "When they go up to their living quarters at night, is she supposed to talk about dresses and hairdressers?" A. M. Rosenthal of the *New York Times* asked about the presidential couple. "Any man who married a woman that vapid shouldn't be president anyway." Abigail McCarthy, whose ex-husband, Eugene, ran for president in 1968, agreed: "In the waning years of the twentieth century the national wife cannot be confined to the private sphere."

The Reagans' co-presidency was contradictory but not unclear. It suited a nation in transition. Americans were still defining how full a partner a modern, intelligent spouse was supposed to be—both in the White House and at home. Feminists like Betty Friedan implicitly recognized the problem and suggested "an official job title," a salary, and perhaps "elect[ing] a president and his wife as a team." A *Ms.* editorial agreed that "if being 'the President's wife' is seen as a full-time occupation, the woman in question has little choice but to become involved in her husband's policies."

But the unelected First Lady had to recognize her limits. Americans did not want a zealot lobbying the president in bed. Nancy Reagan appealed to moderate women who were more traditional than feminists, but more liberated than their mothers. Her advice to her successor and to all women championed wives' liberation, if not women's lib. "Do your own thing," she said, speaking the lingo of the era she detested. "Just because you're married doesn't mean you've given up your right to have an opinion."

A *Ladies' Home Journal* poll confirmed the Reagans' instincts that the co-president should avoid power-sharing or freelancing. The women surveyed split over whether a First Lady should give up her career. Nearly 60 percent wanted the First Lady to devote herself to projects, however, and more than two-thirds did not want her publicly disagreeing with the president. In essence, Americans wanted the president to have a junior partner. When asked "which First Lady do you admire most?" 28 percent chose Eleanor Roosevelt, especially Democrats and women older than forty-five; 26 percent chose Nancy Reagan, especially Republicans and women younger than thirty. Nancy's popularity with young women illustrated the Reagans' effectiveness in setting popular standards during a confusing era.

Polls showing Nancy's popularity did not silence her critics. To prove that they were not sexist, William Safire and others said they only objected to Mrs. Reagan's isolating the President, who held three news conferences in 1987 and four in 1988. Safire also rebutted White House attacks by suggesting that "after playing that rough," Nancy "should not seek refuge in feminism or femininity."

As 1987 dragged on, other traumas upstaged Iran-Contra. The wonder couple of the early 1980s now felt cursed. In October the stock market crashed, the Senate rejected Reagan's Supreme Court nominee Robert Bork, Iran attacked an American ship, and Nancy's mother died ten days after Nancy's left breast was removed. "I confess this was a period of time in which I was more concerned about the possibility of an even greater tragedy in my own life than I was about the stock market," Ronnie later said.

Even Nancy's illness triggered controversy. Reporters criticized her decision to have a modified radical mastectomy, which removed most of her left breast, rather than a more limited lumpectomy. Nancy said, "I couldn't pos-

sibly carry on the schedule that I have with radiation." Such a calculus perpetuated the stereotype of Nancy as power-hungry, willing to disfigure herself—to cut out her femininity—to play on the world stage. One breast
cancer expert said that Mrs. Reagan's decision "set us back 10 years." Yet the
number of women seeking mammograms more than doubled in the two
weeks after Nancy's surgery.

While helping his wife cope with her double tragedies, the President of the
United States was overseeing negotiations with the Soviets. When Mrs. Davis
died, Ronnie flew to Phoenix with Nancy, flew back to Washington the same
day to meet the Soviet foreign minister, and returned to Arizona three days
later for the funeral—after an agreement had been finalized and a date for a
summit in Washington had been set. For all the President's power, "there was
nothing I could do to bring happiness to my wife at a time when she desperately needed it."

Upon her return to Washington, Nancy began preparing for the summit,
which took place in December. Whereas in 1985 Nancy's job had been to
temper her husband's militant image, her presence now complicated relations. Reporters searched for signs of friction between the First Ladies. At the
signing ceremony for the INF treaty eliminating intermediate and shorter
range missiles, Nancy made a point of shaking Raisa Gorbachev's hand. She
later explained, "That was my way of saying we too are part of this history
making." Still recovering from her "terrible, terrible" year, Nancy needed to
assert herself more than ever.

The impression of the President as what *The New Republic* called "henpecked, manipulated and oblivious" deepened in 1988, as a series of books
described a genial and disengaged President and his scheming, if quirky, wife.
The blurring of politics and entertainment now hurt the Reagans. Publishers
offered huge advances to presidential aides and relatives to expose the "real"
White House. When such books succeeded, author interviews on TV, book
excerpts in magazines, and stories in the media generated big sales. In their
last two years, the Reagans had to endure Michael Deaver's portrait of a
shrewd First Lady protecting her weak husband, Michael Reagan's account of
how his many parents neglected him and a youth worker sexually abused
him, and former press secretary Larry Speakes's admission that he manufactured presidential quotations. The most damaging revelations came in May
1988, when Donald Regan revealed that an astrologer fed "Nancy the
Harpy" ideas that she imposed on the hapless President.

Donald Regan's revenge was sweet. His best-selling book was excerpted in
Time and made the Reagans a laughingstock. Liberals gleefully seized on the
proof that the President was doddering and wrongheaded. Aware of how
many people believed in it, and unwilling to tempt fate, the President hedged
when asked if he believed in astrology. He artfully insisted that "no policy or

decision in my mind has ever been influenced by astrology," which did not deny Nancy's reliance on the charts. Nancy let it be known that the counsel of astrologers comforted her after the assassination attempt.

As John F. Kennedy had recognized, ridicule was more memorable than praise. Guffaws about "the dipper" and his meddlesome but superstitious wife undid Nancy's image-making efforts. Regan's attack accelerated the pace of revelations and helped define the Reagans' historical image. Once they retired, their poll ratings would plummet month by month—Nancy's more dramatically than Ronnie's—accelerated by Kitty Kelley's lurid April 1991 "unauthorized biography" of Nancy Reagan, "America's most formidable petticoat President." By June 1991, one pollster would conclude that George Bush "benefited from the contrast with Reagan. . . . He isn't extreme, and everybody loves Barbara Bush as much as they hated Nancy Reagan."

Nancy Reagan's consistently strong poll ratings during the Reagan years were quickly forgotten. No one was left to refute the media caricature of the "diminutive, designer-sheathed" Dragon Lady. Her plunge in popularity suggested how thin her support had been, and how much popular approval a First Lady enjoys simply because of the respect given to her office. As Americans reassessed the Reagan era, Nancy Reagan once again took the fall for Ronnie.

Nancy had, in fact, overstepped. Her role in the White House far exceeded the limits she defined. In an administration obsessed with public relations, the guardian of the President's image could meddle everywhere—and she did. Ronald Reagan's emotional remoteness and political passivity drew her toward unprecedented power. The constant carping of critics would build on the 40 percent who feared she was too powerful, wiping out her six-year rehabilitation effort.

The President told one columnist that Nancy apologized for having "brought all this down on his head." The President said he responded, "No, honey, I brought all this down on you by taking this job." The conservative senator Orrin Hatch objected to "ole boys" like Don Regan attacking "a very faithful wife in a very reprehensible sexist way."

Ronald Reagan left the White House feeling satisfied. No President since Dwight Eisenhower had lasted so long in the White House or left on such good terms. "The warmest memories of our life" were "in that beautiful, historic mansion," Ronnie would write. The last two years, though, had robbed Nancy of any satisfaction. She was relieved to be going home.

In the Presidency as in their private lives, Ronald and Nancy Reagan were mood rings, reflecting what they sensed Americans wanted. The Reagans' individual journeys and their marriage made both of them extraordinarily sensitive receptors of conventional wisdom. Their marriage and their co-presidency projected conventional assumptions, in all their messy contradictions. The Reagans' "adolescent's dream of what a marriage should be" exemplified the best of "peer marriage"—deep friendship, mutual trust, and an electric intimacy—in a traditional package. The Reagan co-presidency was a natural extension of that balancing act. It offered wifely devotion, idealistic crusading, and a good story.

The Reagans' glitzy traditionalism, their anti-feminist feminism, their constructive hypocrisy were thoroughly American. Typically, the Reagans epitomized the best and the worst of these contradictions. Even as their romance renewed faith in marriage, their dysfunctional family illustrated the costs of selfishness, materialism, emotional remoteness, divorce, and the kind of exclusive love affair that bonded the couple.

The Reagans were hated and loved for the same reason: their smug commitment to living a perfect life. Unlike the Fords, the Reagans refused to "validate" the new morality. The Reagans' belief in the culture of appearances frustrated moral relativists like Anna Quindlen of the *New York Times,* who argued that "ordinary people" were "sacrificed" on the Reagans' "altar" of "affected perfection," forced to "wonder what character flaw brought them divorces, estrangements," and the like. But most Americans wanted inspiration, not validation. Americans wanted to indulge the new freedoms while perpetuating old ideals—just as they complained that fewer people were willing to sacrifice for their children, even though they were less willing to do so themselves.

The Reagans reflected that ambivalence because they lived it. By crossing wires as they did, they soothed their constituents. The result was a swollen government committed to downsizing, a huge deficit fueling an economic boom, a white-gloved feminism promising self-fulfillment and equity while perpetuating the status quo, a continuing sexual revolution despite a new politics of family values, a popular First Lady who would be remembered for her controversies, and renewed faith in the American way amid a deepening cynicism about American politics.

9

PERFECT COUPLE,
IMPERFECT PRESIDENT

The Bush Restoration

On a cold, crisp January day in 1945, a twenty-year-old naval aviator married his nineteen-year-old sweetheart in her family church. It was a typical wartime wedding. An average of one thousand servicemen were getting married every day; one and a half million soldiers would tie the knot between Pearl Harbor and the end of the conflict. He was a Navy pilot, she was a college coed who worked one summer as a "gofer" in a nuts-and-bolts factory, "much to my mother's distress." She wore a traditional white gown; he wore his Navy dress blues. Her mother had "begged and borrowed shoe coupons" to complete a trousseau amid wartime rationing; his childhood friend burst into the church just before the ceremony, bounding down the aisle to stand up for his fellow officer.

They had met in what he recalled as a "storybook" setting, amid the sounds of Glenn Miller at a Christmas dance in 1941. He had three brothers and a sister, while she had two brothers and a sister. All had been raised the "old-fashioned way."

Less than a year after they met, he was in flight school in Chapel Hill, North Carolina, and she was chafing under the wartime travel restrictions.

During a seventeen-day summertime visit with his family, they became "secretly engaged." They announced their engagement at Christmas 1943—both so young that they required parental permission to wed.

After his plane was shot down over the Pacific on September 2, 1944, she suffered for three days before hearing about his rescue by submarine. The brush with death eliminated doubts about the marriage. They were ready to start their lives, although their wedding was postponed as his homecoming kept being delayed.

The honeymooners spent their first night together in New York City. At Rockefeller Center's magical Radio City Music Hall, they saw *Meet Me in St. Louis*. This delightful movie musical, starring Judy Garland, celebrated the old-fashioned values he had defended and she would cultivate in their new home. This time Garland's character found "Oz" in turn-of-the-century St. Louis, a world of Victorian sensibilities where girls fell in love with and married "the boy next door." In these simpler times, long before world wars and great depressions, the wise grandfather could tell his granddaughter—who had been stood up for the Christmas dance because her beau's tuxedo was still in the tailor shop—"'Tisn't often a pretty girl has a real legitimate reason to cry."

After V-J Day, he rushed through college on the GI Bill as she puttered around the house they shared with twelve other families, learning how to run a home. Their son—and his namesake—was born on July 6, 1946, at the start of the "baby boom" that would spawn 68 million children from 1946 through 1960. She remembered that "I knew he was the most wonderful-looking man I ever saw, but I don't think I knew what love was until we'd been married for five years." Trying to explain, she would stumble: "I mean I think I really loved him, but I don't think I really liked him . . . did not have the depth of love" that later developed. "You shouldn't have to tell that," he protested when she asked him to affirm his love. "You see it. You know it."

She considered returning to college, knowing her father would happily pay tuition. In the end she cast her lot with many of her peers: "I chose, instead, to have a big family." Between 1949 and 1959 she would give birth to five more children, three boys and two girls.

When George and Barbara Bush moved into the White House in 1989, they were the seventh presidential couple whose identity had been forged amid World War II. While John Kennedy had entered office in 1961 promising to apply the soldier's can-do spirit, the Bushes were fighting a rear-guard action, trying to preserve a world that observers now derided as "conservative kitsch . . . an ideal past that never existed."

The Bushes repudiated the Carters' and Reagans' drift toward a co-presidency. "I do not speak out on issues because I am not the elected official. When I am an elected official," Barbara chuckled, "I will speak out and I hope George Bush will do for me what I have done for him." The Bushes embraced the separate spheres. "Bar" said of her husband, "I don't fool around in his office, and he doesn't fool around in mine." Her concerns were "running the house, listening to my children's problems, passing them on to George if they're important." She would not be "a wavemaker"; she would not "lobby George Bush" or his subordinates.

In fact, though, the Bushes could not resist creating a co-presidency. George Bush needed his wife to help embody his values and provide symbolic cover when his policy, or the nation's pocketbook, would not suffice. The Bushes' reluctance to govern together as a couple, and Barbara's reticence, would enhance the First Lady's popularity and power. While Mrs. Bush did not dictate policy, she helped shape public perceptions of the Bush administration. Barbara's emergence as "co-president" despite herself would reveal the unspoken but compelling forces that mobilized modern First Ladies. In many ways, the Bushes would be the perfect couple, even if he was an imperfect president.

As President, George Bush struggled with the dilemma that immobilized him as vice president: How could he assert himself while continuing to benefit by identifying with Ronald Reagan? For eight years, Bush had deferred to Reagan so completely as to risk being eclipsed. Once he became President, Bush overcompensated. Even as he genuflected toward his predecessor's policies, his wife helped underline the contrasts. Her fake pearls, her white hair, her ample figure, and her disinterest in power—along with his enthusiasm for his job—proved that the Bushes of Houston and Kennebunkport were more trustworthy, more authentic, more engaged, and more democratic than the Reagans of Hollywood.

While it is not surprising that the New England Bushes disdained the *nouveau riche* Reagans, it is surprising that Americans fell for such blue-bloods. The matronly First Lady, robust President, and their handsome Yankee brood made many Americans feel good. The compliments heaped on the Bushes disparaged the Reagans. After Bush won, the same reporters who had come to appreciate Nancy's glamour and power began praising what *Time, Newsweek,* the *New York Times,* the *Washington Post,* and the *Atlanta Constitution,* among others, would call the "down-to-earth" First Lady. Women reporters who saw too much of their mothers in Nancy Reagan embraced the grandmother within Barbara Bush. "GOODBYE FIRST FASHION-PLATE—HELLO FIRST GRANDMOTHER!" the *New York Post* proclaimed. Americans saw Mrs. Bush as "the kind of person who would go to the Safeway herself"—despite her eight years of insulation as the vice president's wife—and "the warmest person I've ever met"—despite her sharp tongue. "Bush was the real Reagan," the Republican speechwriter Christopher Buckley would explain. Bush fought in World War II rather than making movies about it; he attended church rather than talking about it; he spent time with his family rather than theorizing about it.

Having been mocked as a "preppie," George Bush was now fêted as a well-bred WASP, born to lead. The Bushes, it seemed, offered a restoration. *Newsweek* invoked the most potent presidential stereotype by calling the Bushes "a WASPy, Republican version of the Kennedys." "Poppy" Bush and his tennis-playing, Brooks Brothers–clad, country-club family belonged in the White House, unlike Hollywood *arrivistes,* Georgia peanut farmers, ex-football players married to divorced former dancers, grocer's sons, or Texas dirt farmers. George Bush's mandate was to apply "WASP virtues" to America's problems.

I

Half a century after they married, President George Herbert Walker Bush and his First Lady Barbara Pierce Bush would seem a lot less "typical" as a couple than they thought they were. He could trace his blood lines to ten presidents; she could trace a more direct connection to President Franklin Pierce. His father was an investment banker in the blue-blood firm of Brown Brothers, Harriman and Company, and went on to become a U.S. senator. Her father worked for the McCall Corporation and would become its president. Both fathers took the same commuter train into Manhattan daily; on the way home, Marvin Pierce disembarked at Rye, New York, while Prescott Bush stayed on for two more stops until he reached Greenwich, Connecticut. Both Pauline Robinson Pierce and Dorothy Walker Bush were strong-willed aristocrats with midwestern roots.

And yet, in 1988 and more desperately in 1992, George Bush staked his presidential campaigns on a generational appeal. He made his and "Bar's" experiences appear standard, as they followed his World War II adventures and GI Bill–financed education by moving with their baby-boomer children out west. While raising a family, George saw himself as a regular guy, living the American "dream—high school football on Friday nights, Little League, neighborhood barbecue."

Bar claimed that she and George rarely debated decisions. She could not remember when George proposed marriage or suggested running for president; they just went ahead. While the Bushes did have their conflicts, they enjoyed a consonance that began with their births—his in June 1924, hers 361 days later.

Although George feared his tall, imposing father, his mother gave him enough self-confidence to fulfill the high standards Prescott Bush set. At Greenwich Country Day School and then at Phillips Academy in Andover, George Bush was a star, what they called an "all-rounder." He made friends easily, starred in sports, and had an irrepressible spirit.

Barbara lacked George's self-confidence. Displaying the self-deprecating wit she learned from her father as protection against her mercurial mother, Barbara would describe herself as "a very happy, fat child who spent all my life with my mother saying, 'Eat up, Martha' to my older sister, and 'Not you, Barbara.'" Even as Barbara blossomed into a comely brunette, she suffered in comparison to her beautiful mother and sister. One friend would recall the teenage Barbara as "really mean and sarcastic," treating her peers as her mother treated her.

Rather than attending a school like Andover, which groomed young men to lead, Barbara went to Ashley Hall in Charleston, South Carolina. There, as one schoolmate would recall, "being bad meant taking off your hat and gloves when you got out of sight of the school." The genteel Southern manners Barbara learned gave her a sense of grace and a useful cover for her wit.

Every Christmas the junior members of this elite mingled in parties after months spent billeted away in single-sex boarding schools. At one dance in December 1941, George would recall seeing "a green dress with red stripes. Beautiful, beautiful girl, kind of vivacious, fighting for her own turf out there on the dance floor, doing her own thing as she's done for the 42 years we've been married." A friend introduced them. They had to sit out the next number, because he could not waltz. After talking for about fifteen minutes, George asked Barbara what she was doing the next night. His fears that the two would "have nothing to say to each other" never materialized; instead, George would tease that Bar has not "stopped talking since." That spring, he invited her to his senior prom and for what turned out to be her first kiss. Barbara would shield the wonder of that moment by quipping that whenever she said, "I married the first man I ever kissed," her children "just about throw up."

Barbara would always gush about how handsome George was—reflecting her joy that her mother's ugly duckling snared such a good-looking man. Her devotion delighted him. When asked to list Bar's best qualities, George emphasized what she did for him. "It all comes together," he would say, "her laugh, her beauty, her love, her being with me through thick and thin. . . . Everything." Spurning her erratic mother's example, Barbara modeled herself on the stoic and giving Dorothy Bush. George and Barbara agreed not to quarrel and not to whine—it was better "to talk about the wonderful part," Bar recalled. Such a strategy was more suited to George's even temperament than to Bar's volatile nature. Over the next five decades, the Bushes would move thirty times. "Nothing will ever get to look the way I want it," she would sigh, "we will move just before I get it perfect." Still, George noted, she never complained, "never" uttered a "selfish word." She said, "Everyplace I am with George Bush feels like home."

At Yale, George made Phi Beta Kappa, captained the baseball team, and was tapped by the elite "Skull and Bones" society. At home, there was little time for fun. Barbara had to share George with dozens of friends. George revealed more about himself at the "LH" (life history) and "CB" (connubial bliss) bull sessions at the "Skull and Bones" crypt than he did to his wife.

After graduation, George abruptly decided to move to Texas. As George built himself up into an oil tycoon, Barbara gave birth to five more children: Robin in 1949, Jeb in 1953, Neil in 1955, Marvin in 1956, and Dorothy in 1959. George set the standards and Barbara enforced them. In fact, when many critical decisions loomed, Bar recalled, "George was in some far-off place trying to find work for his oil rigs." Once home he played the "softie"—just like Gerald Ford, Ronald Reagan, and other politicians who craved affection from their kids and their constituents.

Barbara ran a tight ship. "She always made me feel like a slob," one neighbor confessed. She claimed that "I really love my life," but her years as a happy homemaker took their toll. She chain-smoked, ground her teeth, and deployed a sharp tongue, suggesting underlying frustrations. "Bar, are you sure they know you're joking?" George often asked. Barbara later said her mind was "dormant. . . . In a marriage, where one is so willing to take on responsibility, and the other so willing to keep the bathroom clean . . . that's the way you get treated."

George Bush was one of the first in Midland, Texas, to be worth a million dollars, but he was not a rapacious oil baron. His promiscuous impulse for friendship made legions of fans. His mix of business risk and social conventionality—his gambling in order to conform—characterized America in the 1950s and would typify Bush's political career.

George's conviviality often excluded Bar. She felt jealous and burdened by the many last-minute guests. When she asked what happened on a given day, he would mumble, "Nothing." She learned "to probe a little and listen to telephone calls a lot."

Still, when they most needed each other, the Bushes harmonized. When their four-year-old daughter, Robin, was diagnosed with leukemia, early in 1953, the doctor told them nothing could be done. "There's nothing you can't do something about!" George said. The Bushes flew to New York's Memorial Sloan-Kettering Institute, which George's uncle headed. Barbara forbade any tears around the girl, but found George and others "so softhearted, I had to order them out of the hospital room most of the time." When Robin died in October 1953, George rallied as Barbara "fell apart." "George held me tight and wouldn't let me go," she recalled. Robin's memory forged a "genuine closeness" between them that George hoped they still would feel "when we are 82 and 83."

Forced to be strong for his wife, his family, and the outside world, George suppressed his feelings. He worked more feverishly than ever. He rarely spoke about Robin in the ensuing decades—until the politics of self-disclosure in 1988 forced him to wrench open these feelings and humanize his image.

George developed a bleeding ulcer a few years later. Ulcers were the frantic, repressed businessman's parallel to housewives' neck tension. "Learn to concentrate your energy on the things you *can* change, and don't worry about the things you *can't*," his doctor counseled. Without confronting the most profound reason for his stress, George tried to temper his activities. "No agonizing" became his motto. He never suffered a relapse.

George's ulcer helped reorient him toward civic affairs. The Bushes had moved to Houston in 1959; it took courage for a Connecticut Yankee to try to build a Republican presence in a Democratic Southern state. George Bush's favorite phrase, "Where would we be without friends?" summed up his strategy and his philosophy. He was interested in allies, not ideas.

From the start of his career, George zigzagged from the Republican party's left wing to its right wing. He deeply believed that the Republican party should "emphasize the positive, eliminate the negative." As a county chairman in Houston he stood up to the archconservative John Birchers, who dismissed him as a Rockefeller lackey. In 1964, in his losing bid for the Senate, he embraced Barry Goldwater and later confessed to his minister, "I took some of the far right positions to get elected. I hope I never do it again." Running for Congress in 1966, Bush was noncommittal. "Labels are for cans," he scoffed. He posed as a fresh face, a vigorous representative of the GI Joe generation, in the political tradition of John F. Kennedy.

While Bush tried to play the politics of personality, his patrician upbringing prevented him from getting too personal. During his hard-fought Senate battle, he heeded his mother's lessons and refused to indulge in "braggodocio." He would not talk about his war record, take acting lessons, or hire a voice coach. When his opponent called him a warmonger insensitive to the effects of atomic warfare, including "cancer, leukemia," his aides said, "You could really hit him in the teeth with that . . . you know, leukemia." "I know," Bush replied with his trademark diction. "I'm not gonna bring family . . . bring it up."

After winning a congressional seat in 1966, George Bush settled down in the center. He sent out hundreds of thank-you notes every week, even thanking constituents for their thank-you notes. He received more mail than anyone else in the Longworth Building. Bush identified four "rules of leadership" in Congress: "Never get personal . . . do your homework . . . the American legislative process is one of give and take . . . be considerate of the needs of your colleagues even if they're at the bottom of the totem pole." George Bush would try to follow this recipe for niceness for much of his career—with notable exceptions when campaigning for president and vice president.

In his 1970 Senate race, Bush was suitably moderate. The *New York Times* called him "one of the Republican party's glamour candidates." "At least you're young and alert and modern," one fan exulted. "Well, thanks," Bush said. "I've tried to demonstrate some sensitivity." Bush took $100,000 in "soft" money from Richard Nixon but spurned Nixon's advice to slur his opponent, Lloyd Bentsen. Prescott and Dorothy's son maintained his honor, even as he lost the long-coveted seat and earned Nixon's contempt.

George's entry into politics had shocked Barbara. She had no interest in public life, but she would face whatever challenge George imposed. When the Bushes first moved to Houston, a woman asked her, "Where do you come from?" Barbara replied, "I live in Houston now." "Oh, yes," the matron repeated, "but where do you come from?" Slowly, Barbara said, "Houston is my home now."

When George ran for Harris County chairman in 1962, Barbara trekked with her husband night after night to each of the 210 precincts. To fight the tedium, Bar took up needlepoint. Sitting there needlepointing as her husband spoke was deliciously passive-aggressive; she ignored him while serving up a politically potent domestic image. Barbara needed a secure identity to survive. One photographer in the 1964 campaign looked at her and said, "Would the lady in the red dress please get out of the photo?" This story elicited so much sympathy with millions of women eclipsed by their own husbands that in 1988 she would claim the incident had occurred recently.

Barbara was feeling inadequate at the side of her successful, heroic, and buoyant husband. In campaign photos, the trim, genial-looking Texas transplant with jet black hair hugged a bug-eyed, gray-haired woman some would mistake for his mother. His smile stopped at the lower lip and suggested an aristocratic restraint; hers showed too many teeth and suggested a need for approval. Exopthalmus caused the bug-eyed look and hinted at the thyroid problem doctors would discover in 1989. When they saw such photographs, her children jibed: "Look at mom. She's plugged in again."

The move to Washington in 1967 ended the Bushes' suburban idyll. After a welcome for congressional wives, Barbara noted, "I now expect to be without a husband most of the time!!!" Barbara raced from cocktails to car pools, from the life of a socialite to the life of a housewife. Noting George's unending appetite for socializing, Barbara called him "Perle Mesta Bush," after the legendary Washington hostess. This gender-bending taunt confirmed her role as "the enforcer" and his as the "softie."

In 1970 President Nixon compensated for George's losing Senate bid by appointing him ambassador to the United Nations. Bush may have lacked the killer instinct, but he had what Nixon wanted: "Not brains, loyalty." The UN mixed Third World and communist anti-Americanism with elaborate manners. George Bush befriended everyone while defending American interests. After hours he enjoyed a reputation as a swinger, and he was occasionally seen dining with attractive young ladies at New York hot spots. His social prominence combined with the lack of accomplishments made him one of *New York* magazine's "ten most overrated men."

Even though George left her behind when he gallivanted, Barbara enjoyed the husband-wife teamwork of diplomatic life. The Bushes lived in a plush five-bedroom apartment in the Waldorf Towers. All the Bush boys were in boarding school, college, or the military; only Dorothy suffered, missing her brothers and her friends in Washington. Insensitive to her daughter in some of the ways her own mother had been to her, Barbara shrugged off the frustrations of her "adorable, chunky 12 year old."

Barbara recognized that without the UN position, her husband's need to prove his loyalty could have gotten him mired in Watergate. She would ask, "Were we not the luckiest people in the world?" In late 1972 Barbara urged her husband to reject the demoralizing job as head of the Republican party. But George came home, saying "Boy, you can't turn a president down."

George Bush's luck had run out—temporarily. As Watergate metastasized, he vainly tried to defend the President. In April 1973, Nixon told Haldeman that the party chairman "wants to be helpful but he's a worrywart." Bush finally called for his President's resignation on August 7, 1974. A year later he said, "I wouldn't care if I never see Richard Nixon again"—the harshest words possible for George Bush.

Bush's prominence in the party and distance from the crimes made him the leading candidate to become Gerald Ford's vice president. Bush came so close to getting the job that Ford called George before announcing Nelson Rockefeller's nomination. This time George took a diplomatic post in China as his booby prize. He wanted to get far away from "the stench" of Watergate, one friend said. When Bar found out about George's latest "journey into the unknown," she was flabbergasted. But China would heal their marriage, which suffered while George played the gadabout in New York, then traveled exhaustively for the party. Barbara "missed being with George . . . and the thought of having him to myself sounded like the answer to my prayers."

A photograph of the two bicycling in Beijing captured the joy of this second honeymoon. He looked like a tall, boyish tousled college professor in tweed, smiling through his clenched teeth. Her clothing was casual, her smile was relaxed, and her hair was gray and wavy, freed from the hair-spray helmets of Washington. A portrait of Chairman Mao loomed behind them, underlining the exotic nature of the endeavor. "I think it's great to have a new life every ten years or so," she would say.

Heaven for Barbara, though, was purgatory for George. Henry Kissinger's dominion over the China policy made the former UN ambassador irrelevant. George told one friend that, while idling, "I'm sitting out here trying to figure out what to do with my life."

In late 1975, President Ford broke Bush's reverie by asking him to become director of the Central Intelligence Agency. The Church Committee revelations had placed the CIA on the defensive. Bush was a party loyalist whose integrity was unassailable and whose Yale credentials and Texas machismo guaranteed a natural fit with Langley's Ivy League warriors. Barbara begged George not to dive into another political mess, but once again George knew "there was only one answer I could give."

As George burnished the CIA's reputation, Barbara returned to her empty nest. She felt excluded from his top-secret work. The burgeoning women's liberation movement made her feel "that I hadn't accomplished enough." Had she consulted a doctor, the fifty-one-year-old would have discovered that hormonal changes worsened her depression. But Walkers, Bushes, Pierces, and Robinsons did not discuss such things. Barbara's "'code' told me that you should not think about self, but others. And yet, there I was, wallowing in self-pity." Bar greeted George with nightly crying jags. She contemplated suicide. Eventually she threw herself into volunteer work, which "taught me that I could be good." She would no longer be saddled with "a C-plus in confidence." Barbara would later say this depression rechanneled her energies. She would deem it "the best thing that ever happened to me."

After Jimmy Carter appointed his own man, Stansfield Turner, to head the CIA, George Bush returned to Houston to prepare a presidential run. He planned a "personal, eye-to-eye," Carter-style marathon aimed at his "constituency"—"a big family and lots of friends." But, as Barbara noted, he disliked "'blowing his own horn,' a thing we were taught as children never to do." Asked what his greatest fault was, George sighed, "Oh, Lord. Stretch out on the old psychiatrist's couch." George refused to discuss his daughter's death. "I will never, ever trade on her memory to gain sympathy or to show that I've suffered," he vowed. "So help me God."

Barbara saw that every First Lady needed a project that "should help the most people possible, but not cost the government more money and not be controversial." She chose to fight illiteracy. Only years later would supporters claim that Barbara adopted this cause because her son Neil was dyslexic.

Some confidants feared Barbara's dowdy appearance would hurt George on television. When Barbara heard that a few of her in-laws had wondered, "What are we going to do about Bar?" she was crushed. George refused to discuss the subject. "He has always made me feel loved and just right for him," she would say.

Even while smirking that "her matronly figure . . . reflects the hazards of campaign eating," reporters praised Barbara's sangfroid. The press preferred her witty soundbites to Nancy Reagan's wrath. After months of campaigning, Barbara noted that "the children treated me like an adult for the first time.

Before that, they asked me all the 'peanut butter and jelly' questions and George all the 'steak and potato' questions."

Ironically, the growing respect for Barbara's strength coincided with gnawing doubts about George. In 1980, no matter how much George Bush emphasized his Texas background, reporters typed him as a "preppie," a derisive term just seeping into popular culture. Some called him by the older term "weenie," others used the newer term "wimp."

These well-publicized slurs on his manhood kept Bush campaigning—until he realized that if he continued to challenge Reagan, he risked losing the vice presidency. George never rejected a consolation prize. He had attacked Reaganism as "voodoo economics." He and Barbara supported the ERA and abortion, but George always emphasized relationships over issues. His quick conversion saddled him with a reputation for expedience.

Ronald Reagan and George Bush made peace at the convention while their wives smoldered. George promised to work his heart out for the Republican ticket; Barbara said, "I'll work. But not my heart out." Barbara would later say her mother would "have loved Nancy Reagan. She loved beauty and Nancy Reagan is beautiful." To those unaware of Barbara's feelings about her mother, it was a lovely tribute. Nancy would keep her distance—the Reagans never hosted the Bushes in the White House family quarters.

Over the next twelve years Bar retreated into silence. She deemed questions about "women's issues" "insulting. . . . Surely, you mean inflation and unemployment and energy," she said to reporters, repudiating the feminist notion that women had a separate agenda. As the vice president's wife, her mission was to maintain a low profile. "I am not running," she reminded reporters. "I don't agree with George Bush on every issue, and I don't expect him to agree with me on every issue, and we don't agree with the Reagans on every issue," she acknowledged, "but we are in agreement on most of the important things."

Like her husband, Barbara Bush knew her place. "I'm not going to overshadow Nancy Reagan," she told her advisers. "I'm the second wife. My time will come."

Geraldine Ferraro's selection as Walter Mondale's running mate in 1984 played into Bush's fear that the vice presidency was a passive and effeminate position. During the campaign, George seemed obsessed with his virility, a striking contrast to Ronald Reagan's casual yet robust masculinity. During the vice-presidential debate, Bush condescendingly called the congresswoman "Mrs. Ferraro." The next day, the vice president of the United States boasted to some longshoremen, "We tried to kick a little ass last night." Bush blustered that it was "an old Texas football expression," implying that his opponent was not "man" enough to understand. The Connecticut Yankee's rudeness seemed incongruous. "Let's stop patronizing candidates because they are women," Sydney Schanberg of the *New York Times* pleaded.

Bush's comments were particularly off-putting coming two weeks after Barbara had insulted Mrs. Ferraro. In a discussion about her family's wealth that she retroactively declared off-the-record, Barbara said the Bushes did not deny that they were financially comfortable, "not like that four-million-dollar—I can't say but it rhymes with rich." The quotation reflected a vanishing sensibility, with the aristocrat disdaining the *nouveau riche,* the well-bred woman holding her tongue but betraying her contempt by telegraphing a curse.

The juxtaposition of the two attacks made George Bush look like an overeager teenager defended by his mother. On NBC, Bush squirmed as he admitted that Barbara would "go to bat for me, sometimes more than I'm inclined to myself." Barbara's sharp tongue had finally betrayed her. Such behavior was unacceptable and unprecedented. She apologized to Ferraro.

By the end of the 1984 campaign, the vice president and the reporters assigned to him were at each other's throats. The *Washington Post* compared him to J. R. Ewing's rival in "Dallas," calling George "the Cliff Barnes of American politics—blustering, opportunistic, craven and hopelessly ineffective all at once." The networks gleefully repeated the attack.

Such hostility was politically dangerous and personally unpalatable. After the election, George hired the legendary Lee Atwater to clean house. To make peace, George gave reporters the kind of confession they craved, one that seemed revealing and acknowledged their power. He had been "testy" and needed to control his emotions; he might still "have a little acid start dripping down into the lower duodenum" when criticized, but he would learn to accept it. George Bush was struggling to master the bizarre demands of this confessional political culture. "In the final analysis I gotta be what I am, but I know who I am," he would tell the sycophantic interviewer, David Frost, "and if I gotta fit some mold for some other person, instead of being sore at that person, I'll do my best to help him." Trying to be stoic, he babbled: "I've taken some shots, a lot of 'em and uh, still standing, still pretty strong, chin up."

"The Iran-Contra scandal tortured George Bush. Claiming he was not "in the loop" on this issue undermined his stance as a "hands-on Vice President." If he admitted to knowing about the arms-for-hostages scheme, though, he would be betraying his President. George Bush's bottom line was clear. When asked about the scandal he said, "There's no pulling away from support for a president who has been so fantastically good to Barbara and me." Loyalty—and his political future—would take precedence over the truth.

This craven performance confirmed the worst prejudices about George Bush and his ilk. Bush's blind loyalty, his overeager geniality, and his flamboyant preppiness earned widespread contempt. Watching the moderate vice president try to seize the President's conservative mantle sickened conservatives and liberals. People believed that the six-foot-two, 195-pound former athlete was shorter than the six-foot-one Ronald Reagan. Many Americans still associated height with stature, a linkage that had helped propel George Washington's career.

These doubts about George's character marred what should have been a high point for the Bushes, the opening of his 1988 presidential bid. The week George announced, in October 1987, *Newsweek*'s cover showed the preppie politician grimacing against the wind in his powerboat, with the caption "GEORGE BUSH: FIGHTING THE WIMP FACTOR."

II

George Bush wanted to be President for "the honor of it all." When pressed for a more compelling rationale, he returned to the values of his youth. "We don't need to remake society," he said at his campaign kickoff in October 1987, "we just need to remember who we are." In preparing his acceptance speech that summer, Bush offered a pointillist self-portrait of WASP ideals. He told his ghostwriter, Peggy Noonan, that these words had special meaning for him: "Family, kids, grandkids, love, decency, honor, pride, tolerance, hope, kindness, loyalty, freedom, caring, heart, faith, service to country, fair (fair play), strength, healing, excellence." Yet in order for him to win and uphold these values, George Bush would have to violate many of them.

Modern American politics had become exceedingly personal. Not only did the Bushes have to fight aggressively, they had to expose their personal lives to the kind of scrutiny they abhorred. One typical interview, in *Time*, asked the vice president, "What is the most important gift parents can impart to their children?"; "Does power excite you, stir you?"; "Do you view yourself as a conceptualizer or as a person who recognizes ideas that matter?" George Bush had a hard time exposing his "innermost self." When asked if he was "more a man of action than reflection," the vice president of the United States chuckled, "that's a bit profound for me . . . I'm a Phi Beta Kappa graduate of a good university, but . . . hey man . . . cuc-koo," he said as he goofily rolled his eyes and twirled his finger by his ear.

In the age of the co-presidency, the candidate's wife—as an equal partner—also had to be put "down on the couch," as George mocked it. "I'll do anything you want," Barbara told Roger Ailes, "but I won't dye my hair, change my wardrobe or lose weight." Thus did these two children of the genteel culture of appearances come to indulge in the aggressive cult of exposure.

The Bushes learned to be aggressive in concentrated bursts. This strategy was an outsider's tactic, more typical of bounders like Roger Ailes and Lee Atwater. George Bush's counterattack against Dan Rather during a live televised interview in January 1988 demonstrated his new approach. During the nine-minute confrontation, as Rather grilled him about Iran-Contra, Bush burned up valuable airtime with digressions. "It is not fair to judge my whole career by a rehash on Iran," he said. Then George counterpunched, asking if Rather wanted to be judged by his biggest indiscretion, "by those seven minutes when you walked off the set in New York?" Afterward, Bush compared the interview to "combat." George's hyperbole, and Barbara's admission that they "didn't sleep that night, we just felt so awful," revealed how unnerving this approach was for them. "I thought George was wonderful, but it's such an unpleasant way to make a living," Mrs. Bush sniffed.

George's pugnacity triggered a role reversal of sorts within the Bush marriage. Barbara had to use her grandmotherly image to emphasize George's softer side. "The poet laureate has retired," she said. Instead, she traveled the country with a slide show, talking values rather than issues as she played to Americans' curiosity about this rich and famous politician. Voters saw the vice president at the Western Wall, the Berlin Wall, the Great Wall, as well as photos of "Gampy" in bed with the grandchildren.

Barbara Bush's traveling slide show protected her from the growing debate about the role of a candidate's wife in this "Year-of-the-Spouse." Ann Grimes, a Chicago writer who tracked the wives in 1988, noted that "despite herself, Nancy Reagan's lasting contribution to the advancement of American women was in blowing the lid off the covert way in which political wives, especially First Ladies, operate. The silent helpmate pose . . . is no longer plausible." Barbara refused to attend a forum for Republican wives, calling it "asinine. . . . You don't run for First Lady," she snapped. Besides, she smiled, "If they had a beauty contest, I would not win. If they had a contest for the wife with the best candidate, I would win."

Barbara in 1988 became the ideal political wife. Less brittle than Nancy Reagan, she embraced her husband and their conventional life. "I'm the luckiest woman in the world," she crowed. "I'm Barbara Bush married to George Bush." When asked "How [do] you train to be first lady?" she frustrated feminists by saying, "You marry well." She eschewed any ambitions. It would be "untoward" for her to sit in on Cabinet meetings. George praised Barbara for being a wife, mother, and grandmother rather than a political activist. "What's wrong with being part of the family?" he asked. "Why should that change all of a sudden?"

Barbara Bush had to repudiate Nancy Reagan's approach without repudiating the First Lady. When a CBS reporter asked if she would be like Mrs. Reagan and tell the President what to do, Barbara answered warily, "Well, I'd like to be like Mrs. Reagan, I'd like to look like her, and I'd like to run the White House as she has done. . . . But I wouldn't be like Mrs. Reagan only because I'm larger, different. I'm Barbara Bush."

In the general election battle against the Democrat Michael Dukakis, Bar's stance as the little Missus was just as calculated as Kitty Dukakis's crusade to be an activist First Lady. In two and a half months, Mrs. Bush would travel fifty thousand miles to 92 cities, grant 184 interviews, appear at 77 campaign events, and endure 13 "press availabilities." She campaigned on her own approximately 40 percent of the time. Her weekly campaign diary in *USA Today* treated the quest for the most powerful job in the world as a cross-country tour. The "inside scoop" readers received included Barbara's "No. 1 trick for keeping my sanity": "reading novels" and doing crossword puzzles. Barbara was working hard and using novel techniques to appear passive, deferential, and traditional.

As Barbara's popularity soared, reporters deemed her George's "secret weapon" or "HIS HIDDEN ASSET." Barbara's popularity was particularly impressive in light of the "high negatives" with which she began due to the lingering fallout from 1984. She kept on saying, "What you see is what you get," but her benign, grandmotherly casing housed a tough pol. Off camera, Barbara's haughty demeanor and sharp tongue made it clear that only friendly reporters would get the access they needed to file their stories. On camera, her sweet insistence that "I'm not going to go into that" steered away from controversy.

Barbara's high profile and benign demeanor helped refute festering rumors that George Bush had been carrying on a sustained affair with one of his aides. The aide, Jennifer Fitzgerald, first began working for Bush in China. Fitzgerald's function in the office was similar to Barbara's function at home; Fitzgerald was the disciplinarian, the organizer, the gatekeeper, the heavy. She had earned many staff members' enmity and George Bush's loyalty. "When you have to say 'no,' particularly to friends, there's bound to be some level of frustration," he admitted in 1982. Rumors about a sexual relationship took root, watered by sexist assumptions about assertive career women whose bosses seemed indebted to them and a belief that the youthful-looking vice president would be justified in cheating on his dumpy wife.

Some critics scoffed that a scandal would jazz up Bush's image and prove he was not, as the *Washington Post* put it, a "Wimp, WASP, weenie. Every woman's first husband." Lee Atwater realized that unless the Bush campaign controlled the story and accused opponents of a dirty trick, the rumors would fester. Atwater had *Newsweek* publish an item in June 1987, quoting the President's son George W. answering the "Big A question" with a definitive "N.O." George and Barbara were furious that such lies were even dignified with an answer, but the denials killed the story.

While candidates vowed that they had not slept with anyone outside their marriage, they wanted people to know that they were sleeping with their wives. Michael Dukakis's fifty-two-year-old manic wife, Kitty, said she found him "very sexually attractive." On one occasion when they reunited on the campaign trail, Dukakis was overheard whispering to his wife, "Tonight if I'm asleep, wake me up, don't let a moment go by." Such intimacies were supposed to illustrate Michael's passion.

The Dukakises were so demonstrative in public that the Bushes found themselves faced with what *People* called "the domestic-affection gap." WASP reticence did not score points with reporters. "I'm a feeler and I think George is a feeler too, but I'm not one who wears—I like to kiss *in private* my husband," Barbara said. "I'm embarrassed by people who put on a whole kind of lovey-dovey." She told the *Washington Post,* "You know, we've been married so long we don't do that. It's fake."

The Bushes' activities at the Republican convention illustrated their confusion about their joint political identity. In what many believed to be the best speech of his life, George Bush defended the culture of appearances. "We weren't saints, but we lived by standards," he said. Speaking in the plural, as he and his wife so often did, implied that these values were well-defined, enduring, broadly accepted. These were the tenets, Bush argued, of the virtuous American culture that "lit the world."

Dozens of Bush's relatives overran New Orleans as living proof of the Republican nominee's commitment to American values. The plan was simple, Bush's youngest son, Marvin, explained: considering themselves "very mainstream" with five intact marriages, the Bushes hoped to "bore people to death." Nobody would "out-family" George Bush.

Yet George's fear of losing compelled him and Barbara to violate the very norms they were celebrating. During a live interview with Dan Rather, as Barbara left to allow the two men to talk more seriously, the vice president of the United States patted his wife on the fanny. Even more distasteful, Barbara Bush felt compelled to speak about her daughter's death on national television. In a dramatic speech to the entire convention, Barbara praised her husband as an "extraordinary special man" who was "always there," especially when Robin died. Bar's public sharing of her pain after burying it for decades illustrated the depth of the Bushes' desperation to humanize George and the irresistible demands for exposure in modern politics.

Progressive newspapers like the *New York Times* said that closing George Bush's "gender gap will require opening up policy, not just privacy." Yet by late October, Dukakis's twenty-four-point advantage among women had vanished. One Republican pollster, Linda DiVall, said women turned to Bush most dramatically after the convention due to the "compassion" he represented and the strong leadership he projected.

Amid George Bush's vicious assault on Michael Dukakis, the emphasis on the Bush family was a rare point of light. Marketing his family allowed Bush to stand *for* something, rather than just blasting Dukakis. Prodded by Lee Atwater, George Bush had come to recognize choosing a president as a matter of values—or, as he put it, voting for president is like deciding who "you'd like to have sitting across from you at the dinner table."

George Bush saw campaigning as a break from reality. Once the ordeal ended, he wanted to become friendly again and focus on governing. Barbara used the campaign as her dress rehearsal. She mastered the tactics she would use as First Lady and fed reporters the "master narrative" they needed, about a grandmother supporting her husband in whatever way was necessary.

III

George Bush won resoundingly. For the first two years, both Bushes remained popular as they countered 1960s permissiveness and 1980s greed. Reporters cooperated in this transformation. Vice President Bush's decision to "place his manhood in a blind trust"—as the "Doonesbury" comic strip had so brutally put it—became "a masterful act of political calculation." *Newsweek* did penance for its controversial "wimp" cover by celebrating "THE 'LIBERATION' OF GEORGE BUSH." The article claimed that "the new George Bush looks rugged, even macho, standing chest-deep in the Florida surf with his fishing rod."

Despite her disclaimers, Barbara echoed Nancy Reagan's rationale for a co-president, reserving the right to step in if George was overscheduled or otherwise endangered. "I have never interfered in George's office," she said. "But I mean, I would be a dummy if I wasn't concerned about his well-being. If I think something is wrong, I tell him privately upstairs, and I am very careful to have facts, though, because he's not one who loves rumors." Characteristically tempering her revelation with a loyalty oath, she insisted that she "rarely" disagreed with her husband. "We've been married so long, and we've really grown up together. . . . He's just better briefed than I am."

While George Bush did occasionally consult his wife, he often dismissed her, especially when she volunteered her thoughts. When she asked about his inauguration speech, he laughed her off, saying, "What speech?" Bar responded, "God, George, you've got a big speech coming." She told the story to illustrate her husband's confidence; it also showed his insensitivity and independence.

George was supposed to appear interested in his wife's advice, just as she was supposed to appear uninterested in offering any. Asked after the election if he had received advice, Bush smiled and pointed mischievously toward his wife. Bar arched her eyebrows and prompted him—"Just kidding," she said, fearing attacks on her as a Nancy Reagan–like power behind the throne. "No, she's not," he rejoined.

Barbara Bush tried to inoculate herself against charges of meddling by girlishly playing the fool. During the campaign she sat in on meetings "and did my needlepoint and I listened . . . so I can learn, not so that I can have influence." She confessed to having failed at this open university: "I tried the economy and yawned my way through." Hard numbers, along with defense and foreign policy, were clearly for the men.

Yet too many people had heard George say, "I'll take that one up with Bar and see what she thinks." Also, her insignia was on at least one Cabinet appointment; the prospective secretary of the Department of Health and Human Services, Louis Sullivan, was an old friend. She admitted she offered advice and was "for" Sullivan, but she knew her place. "Show me a wife who doesn't" offer advice, she said, "and I'll show you one who doesn't care very much." Advisers set her up as the house liberal. They credited Barbara with endorsing Sullivan, who was African-American, and for softening George's positions on such "women's" issues as "AIDS, the homeless, civil rights and education." Sheila Tate, working for the transition, told *Time*, "Every time he says 'Head Start' that's Bar."

As Mrs. Reagan had done, Mrs. Bush was expected to steer a middle path, to help close the President's gender gap without turning feminist. The new First Lady would support women's rights, but generically. She chided reporters when they asked her about the Equal Rights Amendment, which she supported in the 1970s, saying, "There we go, asking that question. . . . I'm not against it or for it. I'm not talking about it." Plunging into the mainstream, she said, "I want equal rights for women, men, everybody, equal rights for every American, equal pay for equal work."

Barbara Bush, the traditional homemaker, thrilled millions of women and even evoked grudging admiration from feminists. Rather than focusing on her retreat into separate spheres, many feminists celebrated her graceful acceptance of the aging process. Barbara Bush's rare status as a public woman who looked liked most women her age highlighted the demoralizing effect of the modern beauty obsession. During the 1980s, Linda Evans, Joan Collins, and Nancy Reagan set unrealistic standards for older women. Even many feminists were seduced by this cult of the body; part of "having it all" seemed to be looking like Jane Fonda. Gloria Steinem's bold birthday pronouncement that turning fifty "feels a lot like what forty used to feel like" mocked millions of her sisters who were not as thin, as leggy, or as unencumbered as this feminist icon.

Women rejoiced in every embarrassing sign that the First Lady-to-be was no "social X-ray," in the phrase Tom Wolfe used in *Bonfire of the Vanities*—a book Mrs. Bush read during the 1988 campaign. They toasted the fleshy underarms that flapped as she waved, the matronly swimsuit she hastily covered with a T-shirt, the frumpy off-the-rack dresses, the $95 strands of fake pearls that obscured her wrinkled neck. She proved, the columnist Ellen Goodman noted, that not every successful older couple looked like "a local TV anchor team: a gray haired man and a blond."

Continuing to love a woman whom some mistook for his mother made George Bush appear warmer, more progressive, more humane. It also made the rumors of George's extramarital affair both more believable and more dangerous. If Bush's behavior proved the sexist canard that a post-menopausal woman cannot satisfy her young-looking husband, he would have betrayed not only his wife but millions of others who yearned for validation from the Bush example.

Desperate for role models, these women assumed that Barbara Bush was "happy" despite the wrinkles, "satisfied" with who she was. In fact, these back-handed compliments were humiliating. Such remarks "absolutely devastate[d]" her in 1980, she would recall. A decade and a half later, she would still brood about the time Jane Pauley of "Today" asked if she minded that "people say your husband is a man of the eighties and you are a woman of the forties." This "ugly" question made Mrs. Bush wonder, "Why didn't she just slap me in the face?" Barbara eventually learned to laugh off such comments. She also discovered that her image as a cozy grandmother would make her popular and obscure the barbs that occasionally revealed a prickly, angry, and frustrated woman.

"I don't threaten anyone. . . . I mean kissing me is like kissing your grand-mother," she said. On some level, Barbara Bush recognized that women who appeared sexy or powerful could not get close to the president without un-nerving Americans. Only asexualized matrons could serve their families and assert control without being threatening. Once defanged in public, Barbara could enter the Oval Office as often as she liked.

The Bushes were the cuddliest couple since the Eisenhowers. The defining image the Bushes offered as a couple was shockingly intimate, yet reassur-ingly traditional. They were "morning people" and woke up by six o'clock, reading five newspapers in bed for about an hour. The picture of George and Bar lounging in bed was as arresting as Jack and Jackie posing at a state din-ner, as Ronnie and Nancy hugging at the ranch. It evoked the bedroom scenes between Lady Bird and Lyndon Johnson. But whereas Lyndon John-son used the uncalled-for intimacy to unsettle visitors and assert his royal prerogatives over subordinates, the Bush scene was limited to their children, their grandchildren, their dog—and the occasional photographer.

After the first hundred days spent celebrating the patrician President and his sensible wife, 56 percent of those surveyed said they would rather have Bush than Reagan as president, and 37 percent gave Mrs. Bush an "A," al-most three times as many people who gave her husband the same grade. But the Bushes could not remain passive. Barbara worked harder and faced more controversies than she had anticipated, while George learned that he needed a program, not just a sensibility.

George Bush enjoyed the honors and perquisites of the White House but failed to lead. Just as Barbara distributed a list of rules for the guests at Kennebunkport asking them to come on time to meals and to reuse their towels, George distributed a list of rules for his subordinates to follow. These "Golden Rules" summed up George's decades-long attempt to perpetuate the values he had acquired in Greenwich. The nine-point credo that popped up in government offices in January 1989 emphasized honesty, openness, teamwork, and dignity. The rules were suited for hacks who, as one Bush transition aide admitted, "don't have agendas. They have mortgages. They want jobs." It was a recipe for torpor.

Bush's drift increased Barbara's standing. Staffers hoped she could sway the President or, more frequently, steady him. They already recognized her ability to keep them in line. Barbara was the White House schoolmarm, chiding staffers for sloppy dress, poor deportment, and disloyalty. Away from the television cameras, she was imperious and cutting. "You've got to do something about that hair," she told one staffer; "you're too fat," she told another. "You can't have thin skin and work for her," her press secretary would say. "I think every one was scared of her," one of the President's aides admitted.

Barbara Bush wanted to be a traditional First Lady. She hoped to adhere to the same standards she had applied as a congressional wife to Lady Bird Johnson: being "generous . . . gracious . . . caring." But the co-presidency demanded more. Barbara had to be political and outspoken as well.

To the extent that Bush tried to mollify the right, he dispatched his wife to appease the media and the left. At first, Barbara's cuddly image took the sting out of some of the liberal attacks on the President. Phyllis Coelho, the wife of the Democratic House majority whip, Tony Coelho, said, "If you close your eyes and listen to her you'd almost think she was a Democrat. You just know she cares about the little people."

Barbara Bush inherited from Nancy Reagan a formidable institutional apparatus geared toward activism. Initially, Barbara doubted she needed so much East Wing support. She had not had a press secretary for the previous eight years, and she did not want one now. "Obviously I had not yet realized how much had changed and that everything I said and even thought would be news," she later said. Eventually she hired Anna Perez, an African-American, as a press secretary. Barbara said that George inspired this move, although it perpetuated her image as the house liberal.

Barbara—and millions of others—had incorrectly blamed Nancy Reagan for some of the grand touches of the co-presidency. Barbara succeeded in getting a smaller car than Nancy's black limousine, but the Secret Service would not permit travel by commercial airlines and trains. Barbara insisted, however, on using a twelve-person military jet rather than Mrs. Reagan's larger airplane. Decades as George Bush's shadow underlined Bar's childhood belief in keeping a low profile. "I hate the appearance of thinking I'm a big deal, having an entourage," she said.

During the campaign, Barbara resented the elaborate scheduling. During her first official trip as First Lady, to the Far East, Barbara tried to recapture the spontaneity of her vice-presidential days. She forbade advance people from arranging the trip, calling them back from Hawaii when she heard they had been dispatched. The result was chaos.

Reporters were especially annoyed by the sloppy arrangements. Barbara was trying to negotiate boundaries with journalists whose demands seemed infinite. "Somehow I thought my health was my own business," she complained. The daily "rumors . . . that I'm dying of one disease or another," offended her. She announced that she had been diagnosed with Graves' disease at a lunchtime session with reporters, a setting where Mrs. Bush felt most in control and her interlocuters were on their best behavior.

After thriving on stories generated by Betty Ford, Rosalynn Carter, and Nancy Reagan, White House reporters would not abide a demure First Lady. Correspondents expected a First Lady to come into her own—and feed them copy. "For 43 years Barbara Bush has followed her husband's ambition wherever it led," *People* proclaimed after the election, but "now America's new First Lady will make her own mark in the White House."

When "the Silver Fox" yielded, she regretted it. Early on, she advocated banning military-style assault weapons after five children were slaughtered in Stockton, California. This position was heresy in a White House indebted to gun-control opponents. Barbara knew she had violated the terms of her marriage, which demanded that "I stay out of his business and he stays in mine, I'm afraid." She explained that "I muzzled myself about 1967, when George went into Congress." Anna Perez reminded reporters that "She's not the President of the United States. . . . She says that her opinion is not the one . . . that people should be focusing on." The dean of White House correspondents, Helen Thomas, asked, "What if we think her opinions are important?" Feeling cornered, Perez burst out, "Shame on you!" Thomas snapped, "Shame on me for saying the First Lady has a right to an opinion?"

Barbara received enormous pressure to disagree with George about abortion. Since *Roe v. Wade* legalized abortion in January 1973, it had become one of the most divisive issues in American politics. Activists insisted there was no middle ground—although most Americans found one, approving of the right to choose while disapproving of abortion itself.

This topic, along with such other personal issues in American politics as AIDS and birth control, made George Bush squirm. Growing up in the Bush and Pierce households, one did not even say that a lady was pregnant. In Texas John Birchers had used George's and Prescott's support for family planning as proof of George's liberalism. By 1980 George Bush opposed abortion except in cases of rape, incest, or danger to the mother, but he did not push for a constitutional ban. Extremists on both sides doubted Bush:

Reaganites questioned his commitment to the cause, and liberals hoped he was posturing.

Many in 1980 had sensed that Barbara's pro-choice position moderated George's stand. After George's nomination as vice president, Barbara had wearily said, "People try to nail me on abortion, but I have never given my views on it because it is my husband who is running." Now many feminists resented Barbara's silence. They argued that feeling moderate was irrelevant when the administration was trying to deny poor women access to basic rights. "Bush and his policies slash and burn across the nation, and she follows behind, applying Band-Aids, just as upper-class women have done for generations," one writer mourned. Barbara's silence on the issue also stemmed from the kind of wifely subservience to husbands feminism rejected. At one pro-choice rally in Washington, women chanted, "Free Barbara Bush." Barbara was unmoved. She did not see "abortion, pro or con" as "a priority for me," happily leaving the headaches with "those courageous enough to run for public office."

After George retired, Bar would finally admit she was pro-choice. Offering a glimpse into the realism necessary to sustain a marriage for fifty years, she said, "Both George and I felt strongly about our positions but respected each other's views; there was no point in discussing it every time it came up."

Barbara tried to deflect attention away from divisive issues toward her pet projects, especially her crusade for literacy. She instructed her staffers "that each day we should do something to help others. I didn't want to waste the great opportunity before us." But she warned staffers—and reporters—that "I don't fool around in the U.S. government." Barbara's crusade had credibility because she had been identified with literacy for so long. Commenting on her 71 percent approval rating as "the Nation's grandmother" in October 1989, the *Chicago Tribune* explained that "the causes she champions . . . were not adopted simply to fit the White House role, as had been the case with many First Ladies. . . . They have been concerns of Mrs. Bush for most of her adult life."

Barbara learned from Mrs. Johnson to keep the project "useful," noticeable, and to make sure that "it reflects well on your husband." She learned from Mrs. Reagan to harness popular culture for the public good, although she refused to make a Nancy-like television appearance on the geriatric comedy "Golden Girls." Barbara was more comfortable filming public service announcements than risking the dignity of her husband's office on a sitcom.

The First Lady's most successful stunt for literacy was the publication of *Millie's Book*, a runaway best-seller in 1990. The book was similar to her earlier book about her previous dog, *C. Fred's Story*, which had sold fifteen thousand copies when George was vice president. For Barbara, ghostwriting for a dog was easier than speaking for herself. With 136 pages of text and dozens of glossy color photographs, the book offered a dog's perspective on White House life—the spirited Bush grandchildren, the visiting dignitaries, the servants, the tourists, the beautiful decor. *Millie's Book* revealed just what Barbara Bush wanted to about the Bushes' life. Filled with charming frills that united Americans, it presented the presidency at its most alluring, its most queenly, its most benign.

Although George was ultimately an unsuccessful, one-term President, he and Barbara were a popular couple. They played their roles very well, appearing to maintain a traditional division of labor even as they found themselves thrust into a popular co-presidency. They spoke on the phone frequently, often popped in on each other when hosting special guests, and gleefully waved at each other from their offices. Both took paperwork to the family quarters at night and to Camp David on weekends, where they worked side by side. The *Chicago Tribune* would call them "executive business partners."

Barbara Bush was "having the time of my life" in the White House, as was George. Their feelings of success during the first few months of the administration buoyed their relationship. "I *love* the fact that I don't think I've ever been closer to George," Barbara said, celebrating his proximity to home as well as his growing dependence. Staffers learned not to underestimate the First Lady or her influence. People she suspected of leaking were first frozen out by her, then often fired. The President tried to define the boundaries between their two worlds by saying, "She has been part of everything I do, but she doesn't try to fine-tune my administration or get into the day-to-day business of the presidency." Barbara knew her place. "I probably lobby him indirectly by telling him stories and things I've seen," she said. "He's very interested and very good about listening."

After years of struggle, Barbara Bush was at peace. Some feminists were oddly entranced by this woman, whom others dismissed as a "dinosaur." Sharon Rodine, the president of the Women's National Political Caucus, welcomed a woman who said, "This is who I am and I like myself." Women were realizing they had to make choices, that "they can't have it all." When Wellesley College failed to convince Alice Walker to speak at its commencement, Barbara Bush, the matronly college dropout from Smith, was invited to address the class of 1990.

For Wellesley feminists, though, the cult of Barbara Bush had gone too far. One hundred and fifty of the six hundred seniors signed a petition objecting to honoring "a woman who has gained recognition through the achievements of her husband, which contravenes what we have been taught over the last four years at Wellesley." One coauthor complained that Mrs. Bush "does not voice her own opinion"; another dismissed "nurturing women, women who care, who do volunteer work and charity and da-da-da."

The Wellesley protest struck a nerve. Many men stereotyped these "whining, unshaved feminists" as humorless, sexless, and loveless. A columnist in the *Atlanta Constitution* wondered how many of "these little snot-nosed snobs" would end up leaving "their top floor office suites and go[ing] home to a cat?" Some "longtime feminist[s]" and many professional women turned full-time mothers denounced "the male-clone careerism of today's 'dress for success' feminists." Barbara Bush was the rare American celebrity who championed the home. More than three-quarters of those surveyed deemed her a good role model for young women.

In his tongue-tied way, George Bush suggested that "these young women have a lot to learn from Barbara Bush . . . and from her unselfishness . . . and being a good mother and a lot of other things." Barbara was calm. She understood the students' dilemma. These privileged, mostly upper-middle-class white women were under as much peer pressure to get their M.D.'s and M.B.A.'s as Barbara had been to get her "Mrs." She simply worried that the notoriety was "putting too much pressure on" her upcoming speech.

Bar rose to the challenge. "You need not, probably cannot, live a 'paint by number' life," she said in her address. She urged the graduates to "believe in something larger than yourself," to live lives filled with "joy," and "to cherish your human connections: your relationships with friends and family."

The Wellesley speech may have been Barbara Bush's finest moment as First Lady. Some protesters thanked her for taking them seriously. *Time* noted that Barbara went beyond her "official cause" of literacy to fulfill her "unofficial mission." She showed "that there is honor and a deep, sustaining pleasure in motherhood, that a life-style is no substitute for a life."

Americans were still struggling to make sense of the 1960s. Polls showed that 66 percent of those surveyed did not want women saddled with traditional roles in society, but 69 percent believed that too many children were raised in day care centers. Liberals could point to the attacks on the "Wellesley 150" as part of the "backlash" against egalitarianism. On the right, Barbara's triumph at Wellesley was seen as part of the Bushes' WASP restoration. "I think there's honestly a yearning for old-fashioned warmth and coziness and family, and people who aren't afraid to say they love each other," Barbara observed. "People come through receiving lines and sort of whisper, 'Can I hug you? Thanks for bringing family back.'"

George Bush was "very, very proud" of his wife—and eager to exploit her popularity in the midterm elections. At a four-state fund-raising trip in June, Bush praised "the hero of Wellesley." Mentioning Barbara's name triggered more applause than talking about his summit with Mikhail Gorbachev. Republican candidates eager to grab Barbara's coattails began invoking her name more often, saluting her "almost as a co-President," the *Los Angeles Times* reported. In the fall, the President often joked about how a state chairman would ask for "our No. 1 asset" to campaign and he would respond,

"Sure, what time do you want Barbara to be there?" Indeed, some congressional candidates distanced themselves from the President while seeking the First Lady's help. Barbara stumped for thirty-three candidates in twenty-nine cities. Her speeches often addressed local issues and listed the President's substantive achievements. This was hardly a traditional First Lady, after all.

Such triumphs, and approval ratings over 80 percent, sharpened the demands that Barbara Bush expand her role in the Bush administration. The Wellesley protesters asked the First Lady to "take a definitive stand" on issues such as affordable day care and the wage gap between men and women. "If she lives up to her top billing and expands her role beyond her safe and traditional advocacy of literacy and compassion for the sick, no one doubts her potential for making a difference on some important national and international issues," the *Boston Globe* predicted.

Barbara, however, recognized her limits. If she overstepped, she would lose her credibility with her husband, the people, and the very reporters now begging her for action. The co-presidency only went so far. She attributed her popularity to the fact that "people don't feel threatened by me. . . . I think people think it's nice to think you really love your husband and your children and your dog." Asked about the legacy she hoped she would leave, she said, "I hope people will say 'She cared; she worked hard for lots of causes.'" Barbara knew to step carefully.

IV

The limits of the co-presidency became clear after Saddam Hussein ruined the Bushes' summer vacation by invading Kuwait in August 1990. To the Bushes, August had always meant "R & R at Kennebunkport." Just as the Reagans renewed themselves at the ranch and the Eisenhowers cherished their moments golfing at Augusta, the Bushes treasured their retreats to Walker's Point. Despite a voting address at a Houston hotel, Kennebunkport was home, a vast playground where Bar could garden and shepherd her flock of "grandkids" and George could play tennis, jog, sail, and barbecue with friends. The Bushes' sprawling six-bedroom, six-bathroom, turn-of-the-century home embodied the values of the WASP restoration: nostalgia, gentility, family, modesty, and practicality. Now the compound was particularly important, an informal and dynamic refuge from the White House. Here, the President and the First Lady could be themselves.

Critics blasted the President as looking "callous and ridiculous chasing golf balls and zipping around in your boat" during the tense weeks after the Iraqi army stormed Kuwait on August 2, 1990. Bush shrugged off the criticism; an elaborate communications apparatus always followed the President of the United States. At one point he fielded a call from Egyptian President

Hosni Mubarak while on his powerboat, *Fidelity.* The homey surroundings in which George greeted kings, presidents, and prime ministers strengthened the personal bonds essential to his international coalition.

In fact, the decisiveness Bush displayed during the crisis was forged during that first month in Maine. The daily sports helped relax the President. Away from the palace intrigues of Washington, George felt freer, more confident. Kennebunkport is where "I am really me," George said in 1988. "This is home. This is where I am not frantic. This is base."

Saddam's invasion gave George Bush the opportunity to exercise the kind of leadership he trained for his entire life. George would help exorcise the demons of the Vietnam War, demonstrating how a war could fulfill its objectives, unite the country, and end quickly. In fashioning a vast international coalition, George demonstrated that congeniality could be a handmaiden to statesmanship.

All of a sudden, the Bushes' genteel coastal hideaway became the command center of the greatest international initiative in decades. Daily, George and Barbara alternated between the gentle rhythms of vacation life and the specter of world war, between the needs of four generations and the demands of the world. On August 16, the President of the United States began his day at 5:45 A.M., rushing to the hospital to visit his ailing uncle, John Walker. George arrived minutes after his uncle died. While the President met with his advisers, the First Lady went over to Dorothy Bush's bungalow to break the news. "Meanwhile we had all the little kids cleaning out their rooms," Barbara recalled before she inspected their rooms and sent them to the beach. During the day, the President greeted King Hussein of Jordan, followed by Prince Saud al-Faisal, Saudi Arabia's foreign minister. The First Lady drilled the children on how to greet the monarchs and noted with pride that "when the big moment came they all behaved." That night the President and the First Lady attended a fund-raiser for Dick Snelling, who was running for governor of Vermont, then greeted their son George W. and his wife, Laura, whose children had arrived days before.

These constant shifts from the personal to the diplomatic energized George. The meetings with potentates amid heavy security, the daily briefings on military strategy, and the athletic contests turned Walker's Point into a macho fantasy land. One White House photograph captured the incongruity of the President's vacation. Six top national security advisers sat around with the President on garden furniture, with waves crashing against the dock. The White House chief of staff, the national security adviser, and the secretary of defense wore ties without jackets; the deputy secretary of state wore a vest and a tie; the deputy national security adviser wore a checkered shirt; the chairman of the Joint Chiefs of Staff was in uniform; and the President of the United States, looking commanding and comfortable, was in his presidential windbreaker and a baseball hat. At the meeting, the President gave final approval to call up fifty thousand reserve soldiers. "Some typical summer," Barbara murmured.

There was no room for Barbara in the strategy sessions or on the tennis courts. This was man's work. "It's very hard with 12 people asking if they can have a Popsicle or something at the darndest moments," she confessed to reporters. Diary excerpts she reproduced in her memoirs captured childlike expressions of emotion throughout the crisis. The woman whom her children called "The Enforcer" sounded more like an adoring teenaged fan. As George politicked, Barbara gushed, "I love to hear George talk to his foreign friends: *'François, mon ami. . . .'"* Noting his calm response to media assaults, she beamed, "It takes guts to be George Bush." On January 16, 1991, as the air war began, she exclaimed, "That darn Hussein, he is putting all those children at risk." It was, she would conclude, "the darndest war."

These adolescent expressions revealed both the worshipful way Barbara had always talked about George and the limited emotional vocabulary of her upper-class world. The expressions also revealed her own feelings of inadequacy. At one point she asked her husband how he could put up with the media's distortions. George "calmly" responded, "I know what I am doing, I know what I have to do and I don't worry about what they say." Barbara envied her husband, recognizing that "he is at peace with himself." Her feelings of helplessness intensified on the eve of the battle when she broke her leg tobogganing. George did not even accompany his clumsy wife to the hospital; he continued sledding.

The Persian Gulf victory vindicated George Bush. Newsmagazines portrayed a resolute commander in chief with determined eyes and a strong jaw. His job approval ratings leaped to 91 percent, exceeding Barbara's for the first time since the inauguration. Yet George's decisiveness and idealism in liberating Kuwait highlighted his indecision and cynicism in governing America. *Time* named George Bush 1990's "man of the year," celebrating the resolute statesman and condemning the temporizing politician. At the same time that Saddam Hussein invaded Kuwait, a long-feared recession began. It seemed that while George Bush was suited for foreign policy leadership, he and his white-bread advisers were not determined enough or compassionate enough to face the nation's economic problems, manage the welfare state, and heal a racially divided America.

As the domestic problems piled up, the Presidency became less fun for the entire Bush clan. Dorothy's marriage had dissolved, partially as a result of the public scrutiny she and her husband, Bill Le Blond, endured. Most disturbing were the press attacks on Neil Bush for his role in the downfall of a savings and loan in Colorado. The Bushes were outraged that their son was scapegoated from among thousands of directors of S & Ls. "To feel as a father that you're letting down your son—and I will always feel that way—I hate it," George said. Eventually Neil would pay a $50,000 fine; as his mother mourned, "he lost all his savings, his business, his house, and most important, for a while, his reputation."

Surprisingly, the President himself was slowing down. In May 1991, a cardiac episode led doctors to discover that George also suffered from Graves' disease. When first stricken at Camp David, George reassured his wife and apologized for neglecting her when she was hurt, jibing, "Remembering how sympathetic I was when you broke your leg, I know you'll be caring."

In fact, Barbara was starting to feel neglected by her husband. To the extent that he had decided to pitch himself as a foreign-policy president, she was rendered unimportant. The President saw many of her public-relations activities and domestic crusades as fluff, necessary when campaigning but irrelevant to governing. Her literacy drive, for example, attracted a great deal of public attention but remained merely her pet project. No serious programs with the Department of Education or the domestic policy team emerged.

Rather than trying to work with George more, Barbara tried to play with him. She took up golf, inspired by his occasional taunt, "If you played golf we could go out and play right now." "I want to be with George," she explained. This initiative would be no more successful than Barbara's previous efforts to join George's sports life. At one point he told reporters that her golf game "stunk." One former aide saw the golf lessons as yet another futile attempt by Barbara to be George's partner. "I think she's constantly trying to make the marriage work that way. Do you think they ever sit alone and have dinner? I think she'd like that, but she knows it's not going to happen."

As his Presidency drifted, Barbara and other members of the family tried to spur George into action. She and George W. soured on John Sununu, Bush's chief of staff, long before the President did. Sununu angered many in the White House and the press corps with his abrasive personality, then embarrassed the Presidency by abusing transportation privileges. Unlike her predecessor, though, Mrs. Bush did not want her fingerprints on any dramatic personnel changes. The result was that when Sununu finally resigned at the beginning of December, the story had dragged on too long. Washington insiders whispered about the President's inability to discipline his staff.

With domestic problems upstaging foreign affairs, many Americans doubted their President. Despite his war record and his love for sports, he often seemed soft, uncertain. More and more American men were questioning whether modern life and the feminist movement had made them too accommodating. "What's the matter? Too much yogurt?" barked Robert Bly, the most prominent leader of the "men's movement."

V

George Bush launched his reelection effort shell-shocked. The recession had eroded his standing and his image as a man of action. By late 1991 his popularity had dropped to 46 percent, and his Presidency was in crisis. The press abandoned him. His preppie mannerisms, his tortured syntax, and his manic schedule now indicated incompetence.

Barbara received her marching orders. In the age of the co-presidency, First Ladies were expected to rescue their men. Barbara Bush was the most popular political figure in the United States. Buttons and bumper stickers saying "Keep Barbara in the White House" and "Re-Elect Barbara's Husband" harked back to the Ford era. In his tongue-tied way, blurting out his shorthand notes, Bush would declare, "Message: I care." As he saw his credibility dwindle, he started saying, "Barbara and I care."

When a New Hampshire voter would ask the self-styled "education President" just what he had done for American schools, George Bush said, "I got my wife to demonstrate her concern by reading to children. . . . Barbara's out there, and I'm trying to help as best I can, saying you've got to hold the family together." This was nearly an admission of a co-presidency—the First Lady was "out there," with the President only "trying to help."

The Bushes were on the defensive. Republican challenger Pat Buchanan attacked Bush for abandoning the Reagan agenda, thereby mobilizing New Hampshire's conservative and recession-weary voters. Signs said, "WE LIKE YOU BARBARA! BUT YOU'RE SLEEPING WITH THE ENEMY."

Barbara had to transfer her popularity to George. She wanted to exploit the fact that, as one Republican put it, "if you didn't know him at all you'd assume he was a decent guy because she is." To appear more intimate with voters, she began calling him "George" rather than "George-Bush." "She reminds people how much they like the Bushes," Sheila Tate said. "And that is an important ingredient in reminding them how to vote."

Barbara worried, however, that talking about issues too much would undermine her vow to leave government "to my husband." She had to be influential enough to be taken seriously as a surrogate, but not so prominent as to become controversial. "When you've been married 47 years, if you don't have any influence, then I really think you're in deep trouble," she said, advertising her marriage rather than her pull. When asked, "Do you have any influence?" she answered, "I don't think so," then added, "If I thought someone was ill-serving the President you may be sure I would tell him." She called herself "half-Eleanor, half-Bess. . . . I do a lot of traveling and a lot of programs. . . . I really stay out of government business if I possibly can."

Yet again, the more formidable the First Lady appeared, the weaker the

President seemed. After Buchanan won 37 percent of the vote in New Hampshire, the Bush forces faced the same dilemma the Carter and Ford people had—they needed to peddle the First Lady without eclipsing her husband. This challenge became even greater after the Los Angeles riots in April 1992, when Bush botched another crisis.

Barbara's high profile pushed the campaign "off message." The Republican consultant Mary Matalin blamed the media for making "family" the "centerpiece of our campaign. It wasn't intended to be." Matalin followed "the standard presidential campaign rule" that "you don't focus on cultural issues unless peace *and* prosperity are assured." The 1991–1992 recession, however brief and shallow, made the economy the driving issue. But with Barbara, and against Bill Clinton, George mounted a family-values crusade.

The Republican convention pushed the cultural agenda further. On the eve of the convention, in back-to-back *Newsweek* interviews that touched on abortion, both Bushes tried to mollify pro-choice people without alienating pro-lifers. Barbara's decision to address the issue before cutting it off with her usual promise to detail her position "when I run for office" reflected the Republican strategy to showcase the First Lady at the convention. While the politically active, feminist wife of the Democratic nominee hibernated, the aristocratic First Lady plunged into controversies, granted interviews, and gave a speech to the convention. When Rich Bond of the Republican National Committee said that a Democratic victory would have Hillary "advising [Bill] Clinton on every move," Barbara Bush reprimanded Bond. "I don't like that kind of campaigning," she said, repeating her claim that "there are two people running this year, period." George Bush tried to steer a middle course, saying, "If it was factual and stuff then that's quite different from just attacks on my wife. I think if you're going to be in the issue business, it's fine to talk about issues. Barbara Bush is not in the issue business. She's in something else."

It was becoming harder and harder to define "that something else." During one combative interview, when Mrs. Bush refused to take specific stands, she reminded Judy Woodruff, "I'm not a co-president." Yet she was George Bush's most prominent cheerleader. Barbara acknowledged the absurdity of her position at the start of her nationally televised "conversation" with the American people. "There is something not quite right here," she said, acknowledging the august company she found herself in: "Speeches by President Ronald Reagan, President Gerald Ford, Secretary Jack Kemp, Senator Phil Gramm—and—Barbara Bush?" This was the kind of modesty so essential to her success. Barbara had seven minutes to demonstrate compassion for "crack babies and babies with AIDS," uphold "family values . . . however you define family," and praise "the strongest, the most decent, the most caring, the wisest—and yes, the healthiest—man I know."

Contrasting her husband with the yuppie careerists blighting America, Barbara Bush said that when asked "what accomplishment he was most proud of," George did not mention his military career, his business successes, or his public service, but the fact "that our children still come home." The speech ended with Barbara in her role as "Grandma America," surrounded by her five children, her twelve grandchildren, various spouses, and, in a "surprise" appearance, the President himself.

Barbara Bush's warm, inclusive ode to God, mother, and country was much better received than the more intense speeches of Marilyn Quayle and Pat Buchanan. Like her husband's predecessor, Barbara Bush offered her conservatism with a smile. She appeared tranquil, lacking Mrs. Quayle's anger and Mrs. Clinton's passion.

The prominence of the First Lady and the Second Lady during the convention reawakened debate about the legitimacy of wives as players in what was supposedly "the Year of the Woman." Anna Quindlen of the *New York Times* asked if the message of the Republican convention is "that the way to the podium is to marry well?" Other Democrats, overlooking the sexism of their remarks, sneered that "in trotting out Barbara Bush, the Republican party was lurking behind a woman's skirt." In response, conservatives championed women's liberation but not feminism. Georgie Anne Geyer in the *Washington Times* praised Mrs. Bush and Mrs. Quayle for restoring the "personal-emotional-loving life of woman" that the more "radical job- and gender-oriented feminists" had "degraded." Rather than being women who lived through their husbands, Mrs. Bush and Mrs. Quayle became women who valued family. In the heat of the battle, few feminists conceded that Hillary Clinton also was hoping to assume power simply for having "married well."

While the President's image as a loyal husband was being attacked, the First Lady's image as America's grandmother was also assailed. Reporters began to write critically about Barbara, emphasizing her "prickly" side. *Vanity Fair* described Barbara Bush as a caustic, judgmental, and calculating politician—as testy as Nancy Reagan, and as ambitious as Rosalynn Carter. "She's a good person, she talks about AIDS and stuff," one friend said. "But she's not this *nice* person." George Bush was the nice one. Reporters now caricatured Barbara as an oppressed housewife and a bad mother. *Vanity Fair* reported that the Bushes' ardor had cooled, that their relationship transcended sex—a claim Barbara would single out as one "that hurt me."

In October, *The New Republic* published an article by the mother of one of Dorothy's schoolmates in 1968. Marjorie Perloff wrote that behind the "hallmark picture" Barbara projected was "the reality of a rich woman" who enjoyed "her dogs more than her children, a woman who rarely smiled." Perloff suggested that "the former Bush maids," rather than the First Lady, should take "their bows as the perpetuators of the Bushes' family values."

An intense political and cultural battle was being fought between the Clintons and the Bushes. As voters worried about the economy, many pundits viewed the election as a referendum on the social changes of the last three decades. On Election Day, polls showed that citizens most concerned with the economy voted for Clinton or Perot; those most concerned with traditional values voted for Bush.

Reporters now attacked Barbara for being political and influential. The political consultant Edward J. Rollins called her "far and away the greatest political spouse I've seen." As the *New York Times* said, "She is not fooling anybody about her political sophistication or her role as the keeper of the family grudge file." In noting that "Mrs. Bush masks her anger with far more grace than her husband does," reporters let readers decide whether she was demonstrating gentility or dishonesty. The *Washington Post* was less subtle, concluding one portrait by saying, "What big teeth you have grandma."

Barbara Bush and Hillary Clinton were more central to the campaign than any pair of dueling First Ladies had ever been. Yet the wives' impact was unclear. A *U.S. News and World Report* poll in July said 79 percent of those surveyed claimed that Barbara Bush helped her husband's campaign, while only 38 percent said Hillary Clinton helped Bill. A more detailed late September poll of California voters showed that the incumbent First Lady was much more popular than her rival. Half of the Republicans surveyed said that Barbara Bush made it more possible for them to vote for George, while only 32 percent of the Democrats said that Hillary Clinton made it easier to vote for Bill. This suggested that the wives affected the emotional bond voters wanted to feel with their candidate rather than the choice itself. A popular spouse like Barbara boosted morale, while a controversial spouse like Hillary was less helpful with Democrats and may have prevented some Republicans—only 13 percent of whom liked her—from crossing over. Of course, in the end, any such difference proved insufficient, as Clinton won the three-way race against Bush and Ross Perot with 43 percent of the popular vote.

The constant travel, the mounting criticism, and the sinking effort depressed the Bushes. This uncharacteristic behavior fueled rumors that the presidency had "worn" George down. Barbara looked dispirited as she fought to "restore the good name of the Bush presidency." Her appeal was blatantly political; a substantive stump speech replaced the treacly slide show. Bar boasted about George's legislative successes, his military triumphs, the lower inflation rate, the declining interest rates, the educational improvements—and Millie's latest antics. "Hers is a defiant speech," one reporter noted, "she clearly thinks her man has gotten a bum rap." Looking back on her 320-city, nine-month marathon, she would sigh, "The last campaign just killed me. It was so painful."

The women's rights revolution helped propel the First Couple into the eye of the American political storm, then left the duo as confused as their constituents. In this, "the Year of the Woman," the passive grandmother campaigned till it hurt, and the activist lawyer hibernated for months. At the same time, both the war hero and the draft dodger felt compelled to demonstrate their macho bona fides. For all its successes, feminism still could not liberate the First Lady from the prison of coquetry or the president from displays of false bravado.

On the eve of the election, George told an aide, "We've done all we can, and if things don't go well tomorrow, well then, the people out there just want a new generation of leaders and they just don't care about those old World War II virtues of trust and faith and patriotism." His loss, and the ensuing burst of enthusiasm for the Clintons, turned Bill Clinton's inauguration into a changing of the guard as the World War II pilot passed the torch to the Vietnam-era draft evader. As he gathered his family for the concession speech, George Bush said, "OK, let's go do this with style and dignity." Flying back to Washington, he ordered, "There will be no bawl babies on this plane." Bush would leave the White House still upholding the eternal ideals, still struggling to contain emotions in a world that celebrated indulgence over self-control, revelation over repression.

"DATES WITH THE AMERICAN PEOPLE"

From the Clintons' Co-presidency to First Consort

Thirty years after George and Barbara Bush married, in October 1975, a twenty-nine-year-old law professor married his twenty-seven-year-old colleague. It was a typical baby-boomer wedding. They had known each other almost five years, had lived together during law school, and had deliberated about marrying for months. The average age of first marriage was climbing, along with the average length of courtships and the number of couples cohabiting. He was an aspiring politician, fresh from a vigorous but losing campaign to unseat a congressman. She, too, was impressive, having worked for the House of Representatives Judiciary Committee impeachment inquiry. "Never have I been prouder to be a lawyer and to be an American," she would say of her role in bringing down Richard Nixon. She wore a gown hurriedly purchased off the rack. The dress was old-fashioned to please him, she said. Nevertheless, her Coke-bottle glasses and frizzy hair, plus his wide tie and bushy hairdo, marked them as children of the Sixties. Before the wedding, he told his mother that his bride would keep "her own name." His mother, who had changed her name for three husbands and would soon do so again, cried.

Theirs had not been a storybook courtship. She approached him first at the Yale law library in 1971, saying, "Look, if you're going to keep staring at me and I'm going to keep staring back, we should at least introduce ourselves." From then on, they were attached but often at odds. He was glandular, she was controlled; he had a roving eye, and she was a moralist. If he could have been a barfly in another life, she could have been a nun. Both were ambitious. "All we ever do is argue," he would confide to an old friend shortly after she joined the University of Arkansas law faculty in Fayetteville.

Still, time and again, observers would underestimate the intensity of their bond. He thought she was the smartest person he had ever met; she loved how "he combined an absolutely extraordinary mind with a huge heart. . . . and we just started talking and never stopped." They teamed up for a mock trial at Yale and in Texas for George McGovern's quixotic 1972 campaign, a defining mission for their social set. When she spurned the high-powered worlds of New York, Washington, and her native Chicago, her mentors said she was ruining her life. Years later, explaining why she pursued her beau in his backwater, this ardent feminist and accomplished lawyer would offer a simple and convincing explanation: "I had no choice but to follow my heart."

Disdaining convention, they did not plan a honeymoon. Her mother found this intolerable; in the end, they honeymooned in Acapulco with her family. He brought along *The Denial of Death* by Ernest Becker, which located man's natural "urge to heroism" in his fear of death. The Pulitzer Prize–winning tome, filled with references to Otto Rank, Soren Kierkegaard, and Sigmund Freud, exemplified many baby boomers' quest for meaning in abstractions and proved particularly compelling to a young intellectual whose father died in a car accident three months before he was born.

They postponed having children to build their careers, again like many others of their generation. The fertility rate had now dipped from almost four children for each woman of childbearing age in 1960 to less than two children. They moved to Little Rock when he became the state's attorney general, and in 1979 he became the nation's youngest governor. He was thirty-two. While becoming the first woman partner in Little Rock's leading law firm, she established a national reputation by working with classic liberal organizations such as the Children's Defense Fund and the Legal Services Corporation. In February 1980, after trying for a few years, she gave birth at the age of thirty-two. His mother had named him after his late father. Her parents gave her an androgynous name so her gender would not limit her; their daughter's name was taken from a folk-rock ballad, "Chelsea Morning."

Bill Clinton and Hillary Rodham Clinton would enter the White House in 1993 presuming to represent "our generation" of baby boomers. They immediately would establish a co-presidency based on their egalitarian partnership and characterized by shared power. Yet less than two years later, their co-presidency would be a dud, their health care scheme a dead letter, and his Presidency in shambles. This failure of their power co-presidency revealed their own faults, the citizenry's rejection of their elite values, and the peculiar but clear demands for a political co-presidency characterized by joint image-making but minimal power-sharing.

I

When Bill Clinton began running for president in October 1991 he promised "a new kind of leadership." He introduced Hillary as "my wife, my friend, and my partner in our efforts to build a better future for the children and families of Arkansas and America." On the stump, he exulted, "Buy one, get one free!" She crowed, "If you vote for him, you get me." Their peer marriage heralded an era of joint leadership and reform.

By March 1992, however, the Clintons' generational crusade was stalled, their marriage mocked and pitied. In surveys, only 28 percent viewed Hillary favorably. Over half thought the Clintons had a "professional arrangement." Most Americans first met the Clintons in a fifteen-minute post–Super Bowl appearance on "60 Minutes." Bill acknowledged causing "pain" in the marriage and Hillary huffed, "I'm not some little woman standing by her man like Tammy Wynette." Since then, revelations of promiscuity, draft-dodging, and marijuana usage had burdened Bill with the major sins of his generation.

Clinton gambled his future on the protocols of the celebrity culture. The daily exposés of "Entertainment Tonight" and the weekly scandals in the *National Enquirer* had inured Americans to the sins of the rich and famous. The assumption that "they're all guilty of something" promised redemption, after a confession. Gary Hart, like baseball's Pete Rose, had suffered as much for not apologizing as for any initial crimes. Those who tried to stonewall reporters learned who was the boss. Besides, sins were quickly forgotten in a polity where—according to the yuppie prince of darkness, "thirtysomething"'s advertising boss Miles Drentell—history was last week's cover of *People*. "They don't have pictures," the shameless Clinton bragged to one paramour, unaware she was taping him. In January 1992, he told *Time*, "I wish I could find a way to get all these stories out early so I don't have to deal with them after I'm nominated, when they can be so distracting." Days later, Gennifer Flowers obliged him by describing their "twelve-year affair."

In March, the *New York Times* uncovered the Clintons' money-losing stake in a land deal connected to a failed bank. Aides feared another scandal would knock out their "Comeback Kid." Hillary and her cronies at the Rose law firm began obscuring the links between the Clintons and James McDougal's Madison Guaranty Savings and Loan. At the next debate, former Governor Jerry Brown attacked Clinton's "electability problem" and his "conflict[s] of interest," including "funneling money to his wife's law firm." "I don't care what you say about me," Bill exploded, his Southern accent thickening, "but you should be ashamed of yourself for jumpin' on ma wife."

The next day Hillary snapped: "I suppose I could have stayed home and baked cookies and had teas. But what I decided to do was pursue my profession, which I entered before my husband was in public life."

Despite his unfortunate phrasing, Bill Clinton's vigorous defense of his wife proved that this "New Age" man and "policy wonk" was not a wimp. Periodically over the next four years, he would burnish his image with similarly overheated defenses of her. "Bill: stop trying to have it both ways," William Safire of the *New York Times* would taunt, "you cannot be gallant about a feminist." Even as men and women searched for new standards of behavior, most Americans still relished such chivalry.

Hillary's self-defense was less successful. Since Jackie Kennedy had warned Lady Bird Johnson about the perils of "tea poisoning" in the White House, each First Lady had vowed not to limit herself to serving tea, a symbol of a lady's gossamer shackles. Coming from Hillary Clinton, the vow was a declaration of war on the American home. This savvy pol, perhaps fearing the exposure of her financial schemes, confirmed the mainstream's worst stereotype of a career woman. She seemed self-righteous and contemptuous, like Glenn Close in the 1987 film *Fatal Attraction*. With Bill already the candidate of sex, drugs, and rock and roll, Hillary became, as the *New York Times* put it, "the overbearing yuppie wife from hell."

Yet the Clintons were not facing generational tensions as much as a class war. Bill and Hillary belonged to an elite subset of their generation that had been universalizing their experiences and presuming to speak for their peers for decades. In the 1970s, neoconservatives attacked this "new class"; twenty years later, the historian Christopher Lasch would deride the "new elites . . . the new aristocracy of brains [whose] livelihoods rest . . . on the manipulation of information [and whose] obsession with health and moral uplift [resulted in a] crusade to sanitize America: to create a 'smoke-free environment,' to censor everything from pornography to 'hate speech,' and at the same time, incongruously, to extend the range of personal choice in matters where most people feel the need of solid moral guidelines." As always, the media shorthand was most telling: The 1960s' hippies shaved, traded their dashikis for designer suits, and became yuppies.

"Yuppie," the derisive term for young urban professionals that spread in 1984, made explicit the class tensions that sparked when college students clashed with Nixon's blue-collar "silent majority." Yuppies were defined by their "lifestyle," the trendy phrase itself encapsulating the disdain many felt for these self-indulgent and often self-loathing brats who pursued moneymaking as zealously as they had advocated revolution. In retrospect, millions of bystanders would say they belonged to "the movement"—even though only a quarter of the white population went to college, and only 28 percent of that elite admitted in 1969 to participating in any kind of demonstration. Yet while millions more indulged in some aspect of the yuppie lifestyle, few admitted it. Offering the kind of pedantic sidestep characteristic of her peers—and of the future Clinton White House—Hillary would say, "I'm too old to be a yuppie."

Hillary Clinton was not too old to be a feminist—or to be burdened with the frustrations millions felt with that movement. Her tea-and-cookies quip bespoke the elitist disdain for homemaking that many sensed from feminists and that the conventional wisdom blamed for destroying the American home. One woman wrote that "the women's movement started off on the wrong foot because it ranked women's paid work over unpaid work." Hillary's phrase also reflected the presumption that paid work was a matter of choice, a step toward self-fulfillment rather than the economic necessity it was for most of America's 56 million working women. Now, Republicans gloated, the real Hillary had emerged.

The demonization of Hillary Rodham Clinton had begun. The Clintons' class baggage fed an anxiety about the duo that they clumsily exacerbated. The Clintons posed as the most open public figures since Jimmy Carter—in addition to acknowledging some marital troubles Bill shared the pain of his showdown as a fourteen-year-old with his violent stepfather to connect with his countrymen. Once in office, he would say he preferred briefs to boxer shorts and the First Lady would often tell a too-vivid story about her baby spitting up breast milk from bad breastfeeding technique. Yet while sacrificing their dignity to create a false intimacy on television, both conveyed a sense that they were holding back, that they were somehow insincere.

Questions proliferated about this McGovern organizer turned New Democrat, this Southern governor who boasted about his generation's idealism yet refused to admit he dodged the draft or smoked pot, this Yale lawyer and Rhodes scholar from one of the two most primitive states in the union. Relieved that at least one state ranked lower on most quality-of-life measures, Arkansans often said, "Thank God for Mississippi." With the spouse considered a window onto the candidate, many of these questions settled on Hillary: How could a feminist relinquish a career in the megalopolis and her last name for her man? How could a 1960s liberal who came to fame when *Life* quoted her commencement speech rejecting the "prevailing, acquisitive and competitive corporate life" go corporate? How could any woman put up with her "Bubba's" tomcatting? It was easier to indulge the traditional fear of powerful women, to deem the marriage a sham, to caricature Hillary as an avenging feminist, than to try to understand the enduring if imperfect bond uniting these two complex people.

Hillary certainly was the leftist ideologue her conservative critics made her out to be. Time and again, she had ingested and contributed to the New Left's cornucopia of statist and anti-establishment reform ideas—at Wellesley, at Yale, as children's rights activist Marian Wright Edelman's protégée, and as the chair of the New World Foundation, which funded civil rights crusaders and other New Left darlings, including the Palestinians.

Nevertheless, she was also a conventional daughter of the Midwest, raised on "family, church on Sunday, respect your elders, do well in school, participate in sports." Rather than buying the "anti-image" denigrating the family, she appreciated growing up in a family she described as being "straight out of . . . 'Father Knows Best.'" Unlike many of her peers, she remained a churchgoer. Her Methodist upbringing opened her to the hip call for "service" while rooting her in traditional values of responsibility and temperance. Hillary tried to be an "authoritative" parent to her daughter with the flower-child's name, rejecting traditional "authoritarianism" as well as modern "permissiveness."

Hillary's conflicting legacy made it easier to compromise as so many of her friends did when they matured. She emerged as an odd amalgam, the family's breadwinner and a political wife. In 1980, Bill and "that feminist in the governor's mansion" lost to Frank White and his wife, who campaigned as "Mrs. Frank White." Hillary Rodham became Mrs. Bill Clinton for the comeback, Hillary Rodham Clinton thereafter. Her rationale that "it meant more to them"—Arkansans—"than it did to me" was the Clintons' all-purpose recipe for compromise as they kept ties with their old comrades but discarded many of their old ideals.

Still, the makeover must have been wrenching. Rodham family lore had it that Hillary decided as a nine-year-old to keep her last name when she married. Her friend Eleanor Acheson remembered that "to her" keeping the name "was an act of self-worth." Now, to mollify Arkansan Neanderthals, Hillary streaked her brown hair blond, stuck contact lenses in her eyes, and began "dressing for success" in that way she and her sisterhood detested. Radical feminists particularly resented such blond, peppy "ladyness" as "a reflection of gender power and the invisibility that marriage brings to women." Ultimately, Hillary's feminism proved as elusive as her husband's liberalism—she returned to this set of first principles when convenient.

Like his wife, Bill Clinton sprang from warring cultural heritages. Time spent in the Georgetown-Yale-Oxford stratosphere tempered but did not wipe out his Southern sensibilities. His family life compressed the pain of a William Faulkner epic or a 1960s anti-family screed into one short story filled with his own possible bastardy, his father's death, his stepfather's drinking and wife-beating, his mother's divorce and triple widowhood, his own adultery and alleged cocaine use. And yet his mother, who spent up to ninety minutes a day putting on her makeup, raised her son to maintain appearances. "Inside my head I construct an airtight box," she said. "Inside is love and friends and optimism. Outside is negativity, can't do-ism and any criticism of me and mine."

Bill learned his lessons well. Photos of Billy Blythe in his cowboy hat—or, after his stepfather moved in, Bill Clinton in his band uniform—did not reveal the tumult. His best friend in high school had no idea the Clinton household was so volatile.

Naturally, Bill developed an elusive relationship with the truth. Even his great moment of self-revelation, in which he described how he forced his stepfather to stop beating his mother, may have been imagined. This wish-fulfillment contradicted his testimony at the time that Roger Clinton "threatened to mash my face in if I . . . went to my mother's aid."

Bill Clinton never lost his head amid the passions of his college years. He re-mained focused on the goal he articulated in an infamous 1969 letter to his ROTC colonel: "to maintain my political viability within the system. For years I have worked to prepare myself for a political life characterized by both practical political ability and concern for rapid social progress." Such a sober statement was typical of a man who later said, "I always wondered if I'd want to be sixteen when I was forty because I never felt like I got to complete my childhood." This mix of prematurely aged child of dysfunction and perpetual adolescent explains his attraction to a sober, powerful and well-bred woman dubbed "Sister Frigidaire" in high school. Both were willing to compromise but remained con-vinced of their own righteousness—a distinguishing trait of their class.

In the media's simple world, Bill's tacit admission of adultery meant that the Clintons' marriage could not be "good." More accurately, the Clinton marriage combined aspects of a frontier marriage and a peer marriage. When Bill's mother first met Hillary, she recoiled from this Yankee know-it-all with "no makeup. Coke-bottle glasses. Brown hair with no apparent style." Vir-ginia Cassidy Blythe Clinton Dwire Kelley had raised Bill to desire "beauties in the classic Hot Springs beauty-pageant mold." Bill chided his mother, "Look I want you to know that I've had it up to *here* with beauty queens. I have to have somebody I can talk with." "Sister Frigidaire" would civilize "Elvis" Clinton, as a lady should. At the same time, the Clintons built a "peer marriage" where he could relinquish the "provider role" and share a "deep friendship." "The woman I marry is going to be very independent," his friend Carolyn Yeldell Staley remembers Bill saying. "She needs to have her own interests and her own life." Whereas other women worshiped Bill and never left him alone, Staley noted that when Bill and Hillary enter "a room, they go their separate ways. She . . . never drew her identity from him."

Such equality and familiarity between spouses often dulled passion. Pop psychologists preached, "Nice is not romantic." Bill said he often told Hillary when they were courting that "I would like being old with her"—an asexual tribute to a girlfriend. Married to a feminist "Madonna," Bill still chased "sex goddesses." This pattern seems to have begun when Bill and Hillary started dating. It intensified after Bill became the boy-wonder governor. "This is fun," his Whitewater partner Susan McDougal recalls Governor Clinton say-ing. "Women are throwing themselves at me. All the while I was growing up, I was the fat boy in the Big Boy jeans."

Hillary, too, seems to have mixed modern and traditional models in choosing a husband and coping with his infidelity. Her harsh father's high standards made his firstborn stoic and perfectionist. Hillary the Methodist good girl imbibed the Sixties' idealism, not its libertinism. She always wanted to balance "family, work and service." As a feminist who hid her beauty behind her "brainiac" demeanor, Hillary wanted equality and passion. Besides, this formidable woman recalled, "He wasn't afraid of me." Hillary remembered watching friends in high school "beginning to cut back on how well they did or the courses they took, because that's not where their boyfriends were. And I can recall thinking, 'Gosh—why are they doing that?'"

Still, Hillary ended up as one of those "Smart Women" who made "Foolish Choices," in the words of the 1985 bestseller. These "bad boy" types made exciting boyfriends but difficult husbands. Her cohort gradually, painfully rediscovered the bourgeois strictures against adultery and divorce.

The Clintons' bouts were legion and legendary. "You couldn't sustain that level of irritation if it were an arrangement," one friend winced. The Clinton marriage endured at least two major crises, when Bill lost the governorship in 1980 amid attacks on his "hippie" wife and gossip about his womanizing, and after the four-term governor aborted his presidential run in 1987 because of his "Gary Hart problem." Bill had prepared Hillary for what she might hear. When he said in his surprising public announcement that he would not run, "I need some family time; I need some personal time," his tough wife cried. Four years later, on "60 Minutes," Bill said, "If we had given up on our marriage . . . three years ago, four years ago, you know . . . I wouldn't be half the man I am today." A week later Hillary told *Newsweek*, "If Bill Clinton and I had been divorced three or four years and he were running for president, no one would ask him anything." These coincidental hypotheticals suggest the depth of the crisis. "My strong feelings about divorce and its effects on children have caused me to bite my tongue more than a few times during my own marriage and to think instead about what I could do to be a better wife and partner," Hillary later admitted.

Shrewdly, the Clintons made the campaign a referendum on George Bush's mudslinging in 1988 and his incompetence at the helm. A candidate of questionable moral fiber had to focus on "the economy, stupid." Hillary called the attacks on her man "the daughter of Willie Horton." "We are banking on the fact that the voters will care about jobs, the economy, and what happens in this country—not on our marriage," she said. Bill defined addressing issues as a mark of character; only policy fidelity counted.

Traumatized by Michael Dukakis's haplessness in 1988, both Clintons were determined to counterpunch. Hillary condemned the double standard that exposed her husband and ignored rumors of George Bush's affair. Using the language of the Sixties, Hillary told the journalist Gail Sheehy that "the Establishment—regardless of party—sticks together. They're gonna circle the wagons on [Bush's alleged girlfriend] Jennifer Fitzgerald and all these other people." When *Vanity Fair* published the interview in May, it rendered the quotation as "Jennifer ———." Never before had a presidential candidate's spouse attacked her husband's rival so directly and so viciously.

Hillary's nuclear attack on campaign protocols injured both the Clintons and the Bushes. Her claim that she had been speaking "off the record" with a well-known reporter perpetuated her reputation as a viper and as an unguided conversational missile. In this ugly attack Hillary exposed the will to power that motivated her, drew Bill to her, and kept her with Bill despite the humiliations. In undercutting Bush's claim to be a family man, damning him with modern America's everybody-does-it ethic, Hillary gave reporters the opening they needed. Headlines screaming "HILLARY'S REVENGE," "HILLARY GOES TABLOID," and "BILL'S WIFE DISHES THE DIRT" put Bush's "mistress" on the media map. Although even Gail Sheehy said that the "rumors . . . have never been proved," they now circulated enough for "respectable" reporters to detail them.

At first, the Clintons promoted Hillary as Bill's greatest political asset. "If I get elected president, it will be an unprecedented partnership, far more than Franklin Roosevelt and Eleanor," Bill averred. "They were two great people, but on different tracks. If I get elected, we'll do things together like we always have." "We care about the same issues and values and concerns," Hillary proclaimed. "We are a partnership." She did not believe that the First Ladyship was "a job" and insisted: "We ought to let individuals have the right to be who they are."

Though the Clintons dismissed talk of a "co-presidency," Republicans used the term, knowing that it triggered fears about designing women. Richard Nixon, in his guise as an elder statesman, once again slighted his own wife when he warned, "If the wife comes through as being too strong and too intelligent, it makes the husband look like a wimp." Others gleefully skewered "the Lady Macbeth of Little Rock" and "the Winnie Mandela of American politics." As a result, 40 percent of voters viewed Bill as a "fast-talking," "wishy-washy" pol, and his wife as "being in the race for herself" and "going for the power." Soon the campaign needed to appear traditional, and yet do so with Hillary's help. Clinton's consultants proposed "events where Bill and Hillary can 'go on dates with the American people.'" Hillary traded in her power suit for an apron, challenging Mrs. Bush to a chocolate-chip cookie baking contest.

For a supposedly rigid ideologue, Hillary Clinton proved remarkably elastic. In what was billed as "the Year of the Woman," this woman—and her man—would do anything to win. As the consultants rewrote her lines, Hollywood stylists from her friend Linda Bloodworth-Thomason's sitcom "Designing Women" redid her look. One cartoon showed Chelsea clutching her mother's side as Mrs. Clinton yammered: "Hi there! I'm Hillary Clinton— the *new* Hillary Clinton! Do you want a homemade cookie? Do you like my new hair style? Do you want to hear about my family values?"

As slippery as they were, the Clintons protected their daughter from much of the hoopla. For years they had inoculated Chelsea against mudslinging by imitating Bill's critics at the dinner table. After Chelsea watched the "60 Minutes" interview, Bill asked tentatively, "What did you think?" "I think I'm glad that you're my parents," the twelve-year-old responded. Although they posed with her for a convention-eve *People* cover story and marched her around Madison Square Garden, the Clintons vetoed the consultants' attempts to showcase Chelsea. During the administration, the Clintons would also show remarkable restraint and skill in maintaining some of the teenager's privacy.

The Clintons' "two for the price of one" pitch and Hillary's makeover blurred the cultural battle lines. Some feminists like Letty Cottin Pogrebin acknowledged, "When we elect a President we get a governing couple; more precisely, when we elect a man we give his wife power. . . . I count a smart First Lady as a bonus." Others like Bella Abzug mourned Hillary's retreat, saying, "We ought to have reached the stage where we accept women for what they are, not try to put them in some cookie cutter." Andrew Sullivan of *The New Republic* snapped, "On her own, she'd never be elected president of the United States, and her attempt to get there by virtue of her marriage is not only an insult to all the women candidates who have the temerity actually to run for office but a worrying sign of a creeping Clinton court." Most voters agreed: only a quarter wanted to see Hillary in the Cabinet, as Bill once contemplated, 58 percent wanted a traditional First Lady, and 66 percent approved of her continuing her law career.

The polls suggested that most Americans accepted the two-career couple. When it came to the presidency, however, they wanted perfect and perfectly traditional couples. The "Republican Mother" remained more alluring than a First Feminist. A First Lady could have a project or a profession, but not power.

While Hillary Clinton continually impressed people with her poise, ultimately she was too poised. Her refusal to acknowledge any conflicts, any sacrifices, or any sense of loss appeared disingenuous, which did not help a husband whose sincerity was already in doubt. Anxious to prove that she was not a passive, pathetic political wife, she went overboard. Saying that "as far as I'm concerned, the main reason I'm interested and involved in this campaign is because of the issues I'm involved in" lacked credibility unless she was indeed a Lady Macbeth.

During the general election campaign, both Clintons emerged as shape-shifters—each varying their respective images as the enterprise demanded, but never appearing fully human. Bill Clinton projected opposing archetypes well enough that enough voters overlooked the inconsistency. One day the "good ole boy" boasted about his 1965 Mustang and imitated Elvis, but the next night he might be the New Age feminist, calling attacks against Hillary "an attack on women who are independent, strong-minded and who work for a living." Hillary also ranged widely. One morning, she would play the homemaker on ABC's "Home Show." In the afternoon, she would appeal to "all working women" by talking about being "engaged in the same kind of juggling act that most women I know are." That night, she might be the power-networker, raising millions from adoring women professionals. In the short term, in an increasingly fragmented media world where the big three networks no longer dominated, such shape-shifting worked.

Bill Clinton's victorious election campaign fused the old politics with the new. The focus on the economy, combined with the call to "Put People First" and the commitment to win at all costs, mimicked Franklin D. Roosevelt's hard-headed synthesis of progressivism and populism. Clinton's New Covenant, like the New Deal, made the Democrats the party of government programs engineered to help "the forgotten man," now the forgotten person. Bill Clinton, like Franklin Roosevelt, attracted devoted aides who were willing to bully opponents. Watching Clinton work a crowd—making the eye contact, shaking the hands, slapping the backs, glistening with sweat, glorying in the people—evoked images of Huey Long, William Jennings Bryan, and Andrew Jackson.

Yet this old-fashioned demagogue was a carefully packaged commodity fluent in the visually driven patois of television. He was a celebrity prompted by consultants, stage-managed by advertising executives, advised by the Ivy League aristocracy, and blessed by the Hollywood royalty. A son of the television age, a product of the consumer culture, the first president raised on "Howdy Doody" and Crest commercials, he knew that the way to reach Americans was to entertain them. This modern sorcerer confessed on "60 Minutes," played saxophone for Arsenio Hall, and bared his soul at the Democratic National Convention. Fittingly, he was best known not for a phrase but a gesture—the way he telegraphed empathy by thoughtfully, mournfully biting his lip. In Arkansas his skills as an old pol earned him the nickname "Slick Willie"; his identity as a yuppie prince was inextricably linked to his wife and earned the sobriquet "Billary."

In 1992 Hillary Clinton first saved this remarkable politician's campaign, then repeatedly endangered it. Unlike Barbara Bush, she never offered her husband an easy wellspring of mass support. At the end of the campaign, 50 percent in a Gallup poll approved of Mrs. Clinton, 29 percent disapproved. She was a polarizing figure, with 42 percent saying she came closer to their values and lifestyle than previous First Ladies and 41 percent disagreeing. A quarter feared she would have too big a role in the Clinton White House. Hillary proved particularly popular with college-educated women, urbanites, minorities, and women between eighteen and twenty-nine years old. These would be her core supporters throughout the Clinton years. Only 41 percent of the women born between 1943 and 1962—the baby-boom cohort—felt closer to her lifestyle and values, while 47 percent of those in her own generation did not. Class identity and the remnants of Franklin Roosevelt's old New Deal coalition had proved more powerful than a media-generated fantasy about a cohesive generation rising to power.

II

Although Bill only won 43 percent of the popular vote, the Clintons felt vindicated. They believed they had a mandate to emphasize issues over character, to stiff-arm the press, to reclaim the "zone of privacy" Hillary demanded on "60 Minutes," and to establish a co-presidency. Indeed, the term "co-presidency," which was mentioned in one article in 1987, would appear in more than ninety-two thousand articles in 1993.

The new president had big plans for his wife. "I would be derelict in my duty to the United States if I did not use her," he insisted. He said that the one person he wanted in the room when key decisions were made—his Bobby Kennedy—was "Hillary." Hillary also expected a broad grant of power commensurate with her talents, her experience, her contributions to Bill's victory, and her sacrifices over the years. The Clintons contemplated Hillary as chief of staff or "principal domestic adviser." Others argued: "You can't do that. It'll destroy her. It'll destroy us. It'll mean she's co-President."

Instead, Bill assigned Hillary his biggest challenge, just as he had done in Arkansas when they tackled the school system. The President said she would chair his Task Force on National Health Reform—with six Cabinet members reporting to her—because "she's better at organizing and leading people from a complex beginning to a certain end than anybody I've ever worked with in my life." Hillary later said that Bill wanted the operation "run out of the White House . . . instead of having to referee fights" over "turf." Like Richard Nixon, Bill Clinton mistrusted Cabinet government. And with more power flowing into the White House, it was only natural to divert some to the missus.

The elite media approved. This approach was "more honest" than lurking behind the scenes, the *New York Times* editorialized. "She will stand *with* her man, or maybe ahead of him." Many women, especially professionals, toasted Hillary's rise. Her new job—and her office in the West Wing, close to the President—"is not just breaking a glass ceiling but knocking down a thick wall," Eleanor Clift rejoiced in *Newsweek*. *Ladies' Home Journal* praised Hillary for ushering in "the age of the smart woman."

Ever the good student, Hillary read biographies of her forty-three predecessors, paying particular interest to Eleanor Roosevelt. Hillary held imaginary "conversations with" Eleanor, asking, "How did you put up with this?" Eleanor would "answer," "You're just going to have to get out there and do it, and don't make any excuses." Unfortunately, Hillary was misled by historians' obsession with power. Having learned that "Hillary's Merely the Latest in a Long Line of Partners Who Pitch In," or that "Before Hillary, There Was Eleanor," she underestimated the delicacy of her new position. Betraying a dangerous inability to learn from critics, she would say, "If you lived your life trying to make sure that nobody ever criticized you, you would probably never get out of bed—and then you'd be criticized for that."

As a mark of the newfound confidence, Hillary's press secretary, Lisa Caputo, said her boss would be known as Hillary Rodham Clinton. The "ladylike" phase was over. Hillary Rodham Clinton had arrived.

Such arrogance, though, was dangerous. While polls now showed that 63 percent of those surveyed liked Hillary, 59 percent opposed a major policy role for her. A vast majority, 70 percent, wanted a "traditional First Lady." Inaugural celebrations of "the Dynamic Duo" eclipsed campaign warnings about Mrs. Clinton's image as "an empowered Nancy Reagan." "The voters aren't getting what they were told they were getting," Mickey Kaus complained in *The New Republic*. Addressing Hillary's cheerleaders—including 57 percent of women under age forty who applauded her power grab—Kaus warned, "Nepotism is not feminism."

Hillary and her sixteen aides established what would be known as "Hillaryland." This enclave included an unprecedented three aides honored with White House commissions; in contrast, the vice president's staff had one. Hillary viewed her chief of staff, Margaret Williams, formerly of the Children's Defense Fund, as equal to the President's chief of staff. The White House operations subsumed many minor functions to limit the number of aides assigned to the First Lady.

Among her loyal aides, Hillary could indulge her softer, girlish, and midwestern "okey-dokey artichokey" sides. She mothered her aides, found them dates, fixed their collars, celebrated their birthdays, and joked frequently. "Hillaryland" was a calm island in a White House notorious for infighting and staff turnover. After three years, only two of the original staffers would have left, one because her mother took ill.

Hillary and her minions originally conceived of their "shop" as a policymaking center oriented toward health care and children's issues. But as Margaret Williams acknowledged in one of her many Whitewater depositions, the staff ended up focusing on "press work" rather than policy matters, given "the press interest in Mrs. Clinton, from the hats that she wears to what she says on health care." As the controversies multiplied, the office would function even more like a war room than a think tank.

Initially, Hillary and her staff were overwhelmed by the President's promise to submit health care legislation "within one hundred days of our taking office." Ira Magaziner, a former Rhodes scholar but a Washington novice, coordinated the twenty-eight committees and five hundred experts. The labyrinthine process had "working groups," "tollgates," and "clusters" established to keep the information flowing in a way that only a social reformer turned millionaire business consultant could love. Meanwhile, the First Lady focused on the big picture and the political marketing. As she breezed in and out of meetings, barking orders, decisions were made too hastily. "After the meeting last evening, I talked for a moment with the First Lady to try to underline the key importance of the purchasing cooperatives," Princeton professor Paul Starr told Magaziner in early February. "And before I could finish a sentence, she said, 'But we need cost containment.' And then she ran off. . . . We need some time to talk this out."

Even as Mrs. Clinton attracted praise for her mastery of detail and her poised presentations, her role complicated an already Sisyphean endeavor. When she first met the task force, Hillary acknowledged the awkwardness: "I don't want you to think because I'm the president's wife it's not OK to tell me what you think. I want everything on the table." But her zeal, her temper, and her status inhibited subordinates. Too many aides wondered, "Do I want to take on the President's wife?" In an era of brittle gender relations, the ambitious liberal men working for the Clintons feared that disagreeing with a woman would seem anti-feminist. As a result, the leading critic among the economic experts was the head of the Council of Economic Advisers, Laura D'Andrea Tyson, despite her relatively low standing in the pecking order. "She was one of the only people who could speak up because of the gender thing," one aide noted. "The others just felt, 'Why should we get into this?'"

Less subtly, the First Lady's ambiguous legal status caused trouble even before Bill released their 1,364-page Rube Goldberg scheme to restructure one-seventh of the American economy. In February 1993 opponents filed suit, charging that the First Lady's presence made the task force a "federal advisory committee," forced by a 1972 law to conduct business in public. After all, she was not a government employee, since hiring her would have violated the "Kennedy rule" against nepotism. At the same time, another federal law prevented "unpaid consultants" from serving at all.

Characteristically, the Clintons tried to argue both ways. The Justice Department claimed that Congress's authorization of offices and staff made the First Lady the "functional equivalent of a federal government employee." The President's lawyers also noted First Ladies' "longstanding tradition of public service" as "advisers and personal representatives for their husbands." Yet when Republicans challenged Mrs. Clinton's health-related investments, White House Counsel Bernard Nussbaum said "the First Lady, like the President, is not covered by the conflict-of-interest statutes and regulations" applied to government workers.

Republicans enjoyed their revenge. They had endured twelve years of ethical nitpicking brought on by the adversarial culture's hostility to the establishment, the media's penchant for scandal, and the Democrats' take-no-prisoners opposition to the Reagan and Bush administrations. Recalling Clinton's search for an attorney general who employed legal domestic help, one conservative jeered that "Bill Clinton, of all people, may have problems with an un-documented worker"—Hillary Clinton.

The First Lady's status confused the courts. In March 1993 a federal district court judge chided the President for "precipitat[ing] a constitutional confrontation" and ruled that "the First Lady is not an officer or employee of the Federal government." In June, the Washington, D.C., Court of Appeals reversed the lower-court ruling, finding that the law funding the East Wing treated "the presidential spouse as a de facto officer or employee." Given the President's "implicit authority to enlist his spouse in aid of the discharge of his federal duties," the sunshine law did not "apply to the Task Force merely because Mrs. Clinton is a member." The court did not say whether she was subject to conflict-of-interest laws.

The litigation was distracting and demoralizing. A federal judge branded Magaziner's crafty attempt to distinguish the working group from the task force "misleading," and the U.S. Attorney considered prosecuting Magaziner for contempt of court or perjury. The ambiguous nature of the First Lady's position, the novelty of a political wife investing the family money, and the new tendency to criminalize political conflict—as well as the Clintons' instinctive refusal to address such difficult issues directly—worsened the strain. Hillary Clinton wanted the deliberations closed to the press because she remained bitter about the 1992 campaign. "In retrospect, I think that was a mistake, because it was the most inclusive legislative process in modern history," the President later said. Even though the task force met with 572 different organizations in three months, frustrated reporters blasted the "secret" process.

"Sooner or later Hillary & Co. will have to choose: Is she Betty Crocker or Eva Peron?" one *Boston Globe* columnist teased after the district court decision. In fact, few observers in the early days of the administration doubted the co-president's power. She had a prominent seat at all key meetings. The President asked repeatedly: "What do you think, Hillary?"

Hillary was supposedly Bill's backbone. "If I didn't kick Bill Clinton's ass every day, he wouldn't be worth anything," she had told one press secretary back in Little Rock. Aides joked about "Hillary's Alzheimer's . . . forget everything else but remember the grudge." Among the President's men—and often with the President—the overworked First Lady was brisk, even ferocious. In Arkansas, many of the state troopers hated working for the imperious Mrs. Clinton. Rumors that the First Lady threw a lamp at Bill perpetuated her reputation. Still reeling from the campaign, always too fearful of "the Establishment," she demanded that aides plumb the leak. The resulting White House paranoia alienated the Secret Service, accelerated a ham-handed purge of the travel office, and may have prompted a review of confidential FBI background reports that would have Republicans in 1996 scolding the Clintons for their "enemies list."

"Friends of Hillary" were as prominent in the Clinton administration as the "Friends of Bill." The First Lady had been one of five key people vetting major appointments. Her boss from the Nixon impeachment proceedings, Bernard Nussbaum, was White House counsel. His top assistant was one of her two closest friends from the Rose law firm, Vince Foster. Her other comrade, Webster Hubbell, was the number two man at the Justice Department. Hillary handpicked at least two Cabinet secretaries and helped flood the executive branch at the subcabinet level with liberal activists. Her West Wing office was called the "left wing" as moderates blamed her for the "diversity jihad" that held up many appointments in the search for women and people of color.

Hillary, of course, dismissed these claims. She never crossed her husband in public and rarely acknowledged her power. At a public appearance in Texas, Bill Moyers asked her, "What is it like to govern?" Hillary answered, "It's been exhilarating, frustrating, eye opening"—then paused and added, "Just to set the record straight, I'm not really governing either." Governor Ann Richards interjected, "If you believe that, I've got a bridge I'd like to show you."

Hillary Rodham Clinton's image during those first hundred days—steely, principled, efficient, and shrewish—came straight from what one feminist scholar called the "dauntingly homogeneous bank of imagery to be drawn on whenever women look like they are stepping into the political arena." It contrasted with the stumbling, temporizing, ineffectual impression Bill made. As usual, one stereotype fed off the other. As reporters mocked the President for backtracking on gays in the military and deserting controversial appointees, the legend of Hillary the powerhouse grew. The President confirmed the oft-published tale that when Chelsea took ill she told the school nurse to call her father, not her mother. Wags had Chelsea saying, "She's very busy working on health care and all sorts of other important things"; Bill said he was just easier to reach by phone.

Intoxicated by her success and sobered by her father's stroke in March, Hillary seized her "white glove pulpit" to try to reshape American values. Speaking at the University of Texas in Austin, she demanded a "politics of meaning." After the Reagan-era paroxysm "of selfishness and greed. . . . all of us face a crisis of meaning," she said. She sought "a new ethos of individual responsibility and caring. . . . a new definition of civil society which answers the unanswerable questions posed by both the market forces and the governmental ones." This gambit to heal the social consequences of the 1960s revolt without repudiating its ideals culminated in May when the cover of the *New York Times Magazine* featured an ethereal First Lady dressed in white. Michael Kelly's article about her "new Reformation" was titled "SAINT HILLARY."

Hillary's fusion of 1950s nostalgia, Methodist altruism, and the 1960s cultural critique answered her husband's call for a "third way" between liberalism and conservatism. In college, she had wondered about being "a mental conservative and a heart liberal." Her "politics of meaning" showed that the rebels of the 1960s were moralistic and, like most radicals, suffused with their own nostalgic conservatism. "There's a very strange conservative strain that goes through a lot of New Left, collegiate protests that I find very intriguing because it harks back to a lot of the old virtues, to the fulfillment of original ideas," the first student to deliver a commencement address at Wellesley College—Hillary Rodham—had said in 1969.

This First Lady fascinated reporters. In her honor, *Parade* focused "an issue on one person . . . for the first time." In May, a *People* cover story on how "Hillary Clinton—mom, wife, policy wonk—redefines the First Lady," pictured a whimsical First Lady stretching back from the White House balcony: the same pose a *Time* cover story celebrating Nancy Reagan's rise used in 1985. *People* also gave Mrs. Clinton the high compliment Mrs. Reagan only earned after four years, calling her "Her Own Woman."

Hillary Rodham Clinton, however, was too much her own woman. In public the First Lady often neglected her primary task—supporting the President. Her "politics of meaning" speech, her *New York Times Magazine* solo turn, barely mentioned Bill. One poll would find that 52 percent believed she had more input into "her" health plan than he did, while only 4 percent said he had more of a say than she did.

The build-up culminated in September, when Mrs. Clinton testified before Congress for the still-to-be-released health care program. "This is as big as it comes. This is Eleanor Roosevelt time," one aide exulted. In more than 130 meetings with legislators Hillary had hewed to the script—"search[ing] for consensus," as Magaziner put it, and emphasizing "security, cost control, prevention, quality, choice: these are non-threatening, non-aggressive middle-class themes."

The First Lady also played the gender card. She began by saying she was "here as a mother, a wife, a daughter, a sister, a woman." She mentioned her mother and Mrs. Roosevelt repeatedly. Her alternately authoritative, fawning, and charming performance prompted a rare standing ovation. When Hillary had testified for the Clintons' Arkansas education reforms back in 1983, one legislator had smirked, "it looks like we've elected the wrong Clinton." A decade later, national legislators were equally condescending. The crusty Dan Rostenkowski said, "I think in the very near future the President will be known as your husband." The First Lady smiled politely. Such accolades led the *New York Times* to rejoice, in a telling choice of words, that the First Lady "captivated and dominated two usually grumpy House committees."

The President was also on a roll that autumn. In August 1993, his $496 billion deficit-reduction package squeaked through Congress. In September, days before Hillary testified, Bill pitched the health care plan to Congress. When the TelePrompTer initially fed him the wrong speech, his eloquent improvisation enhanced his legend as a master salesman who was smarter and more sincere than Ronald Reagan. In November, Clinton muscled the NAFTA treaty through the Senate and rendered a moving tribute to Martin

Luther King, Jr., in Memphis, calling on African-Americans to help stop the violence in America's cities. Bill had discovered the president's bully pulpit; he, too, could play politics with old-fashioned virtues.

The Clintons planned to celebrate the year's triumphs at thirty-two Christmas parties in December. On December 10, *People* interviewed the First Couple for its year-end issue. The President listed all his accomplishments. Both laughed at the talk of a co-presidency. Bill blasted opponents who "don't want to take on my policies, so they think they can hurt me politically by acting like Hillary has too much power or too much influence." *People's* editors selected photographs of an ebullient couple at work and at play, dancing cheek to cheek under a gleaming chandelier. With Bill's popularity pushing 60 percent—and Hillary's nearly 70 percent—his Presidency had finally hit its stride. Looking back on that period, Hillary recalled, "We thought we had a real window." She did, however, ask Bill, "What's in their arsenal now?"

Although the barrage of criticism caused them to back away from the term, the Clintons had fashioned a formidable co-presidency. In public, both "searched for consensus" and sought to make their power-sharing arrangement appear reasonable. In one year, the Clintons—particularly Hillary—had seemingly evolved from shape-shifters to integrated "human beings" perfectly suited for "this post-modern age," as Hillary put it. Shills for *Vogue* and feminist writers praised her as a total woman "who does it all," a model for modern women in all their complexity as they worked if they chose to, and nurtured if they pleased. "For women of my generation, it's a relief to have a First Friend in the White House," the yuppie playwright Wendy Wasserstein said. Unfortunately for the Clintons, this moment of triumph was fleeting. By the time their December 10 interview reached the newsstands, his Presidency and the public's perception of their marriage were once again mired in muck. Within months, health care reform would be dead, and—despite the Cassandras who said First Ladies were not accountable—Hillary would be fired as co-president.

III

On Monday, December 20, 1993, Clinton's presidency unraveled. The evening before, CNN broadcast interviews with two Arkansas state troopers describing what they claimed were Governor Clinton's sexual escapades, and charging that the President tried to silence one of their colleagues with a job offer. That day, the *American Spectator* published a lurid exposé of a libertine governor and his profane, neglected wife who supposedly yelled during one of their many shouting matches: "I need to be f——ed more than twice a year." The Clintons had "more a business relationship than a marriage," the journalist David Brock charged. Meanwhile, the *Washington Times* alleged that Clinton aides removed Whitewater files from Vince Foster's office after he committed suicide in July—ostensibly because criticism of the travel office purge depressed him. "Troopergate," "Travelgate," and "Whitewatergate" became linked. As pundits merrily searched for a new scandal-connoting suffix, Clinton aides scrambled to defend their boss. Political consultant Paul Begala told George Stephanopoulos, "I think I'm going to throw up."

Both Clintons were devastated. The President found it particularly hard to endure such accusations with his mother and mother-in-law visiting for the holidays. Still, he had spent his life coping with emotional messes. It was Hillary the goody-goody who was unequipped. She first tried directing her rage toward the press. On Tuesday, she reprised her campaign paranoia that "the Establishment" was after them and charged: "I find it not an accident that every time he is on the verge of fulfilling his commitment to the American people, and they are responding—whether it's forging ahead in the polls in New Hampshire or now with very high popularity—out comes yet a new round of these outrageous, terrible stories that people plant for political and financial reasons." This statement did not reach the Olympian heights Barbara Bush ascended to when George was besmirched, nor did it refute the charges.

Such controversy proved irresistible to a "media industry" that knew "that emotional pornography is where the money is," as Stephen Carter of Yale said. By 1996 there would be 36 books and 1,264 articles written about Hillary, and more than 16,000 articles about her husband—most of them negative. In contrast, there had been only 13 books and 149 articles about Barbara Bush, and 8,771 articles about George. Bill and Hillary Rodham Clinton, the king and queen of the "Sixties kids," were particularly vulnerable to attack from the dyspeptic extremists who filled airtime cheaply in America's booming "political talk industry." The shameless populists of talk radio and of desktop broadsides lacked the advertising pressures, nonpartisan poses, and professional scruples that tempered network shows like "60 Minutes." When his claim that Foster was murdered in an apartment Hillary owned proved false, Rush Limbaugh shrugged, "That's what it said in the fax." The rumors were overwhelming and conflicting: Hillary the witch was a lesbian, Hillary the lawyer was Foster's lover, Hillary the "feminazi" was frigid. With politics as Roman circus, the pun was the thing: "Heil Hillary," the critics would cry, as they attacked "Shrillary's" attempt to bring on "Big Sister."

The hysteria, and the accelerated "news cycle" spinning stories around the clock, contaminated all journalism. "To make my story fresh, I have to look for an angle—and an angle, by definition, is subjective," Jack Farrell of the *Boston Globe* confessed. "And since the prevailing ethos of journalism is to be skeptical about sources of power, the angle is almost always critical." Journalists in the 1950s like Walter Lippmann and James Reston had played to the Washington elite; modern reporters "play[ed] to the masses" and recycled all kinds of garbage, mourned Howard Kurtz, the *Washington Post*'s media critic.

Even as she retreated, Hillary Rodham Clinton paid dearly for overstepping her boundaries. She became the great scapegoat of the Clinton adminis-tration. As with Nancy Reagan, many preferred to attack the assertive, power-hungry wife who made a career out of protecting her husband than the accommodating, nimble husband who made a career out of being likable. Like Ronald Reagan, Bill Clinton projected a breezy masculinity that ap-pealed to many men and women. Reporters depicted him as a lumbering, bearlike empath with gargantuan appetites. Bill could be soft yet tough—his bad-boy image rounding his New Age emoting, "Bubba" balancing out the policy wonk. Hillary Rodham Clinton, however, was an outlaw. Her assault on traditional sex roles saddled her with the worst of the career-women stereo-types, somehow combined with the worst of the "Stepford wife" caricature.

Wild charges of murder, drug-running, and influence-peddling mixed with assaults on Hillary's liberalism. Even those who did not share Rush Limbaugh's conservatism reveled in the jokes that reversed traditional assumptions by hailing the President "and her husband," or citing Hillary's alleged comment after seeing an ex-boyfriend managing a gas station that, if he had stuck with her, he would be running the country and Bill would be pumping gas. More demeaning were the stories about trysts, separate bedrooms, and shouting matches. The opposition was so ugly, so sexist that the Clintons found it easy to dismiss all their critics and revert to the aggressive and sanctimonious posture that worked in 1992.

The intensity of this high-tech witch burning suggested that in addition to failing to live up to the standards of Camelot, the Clintons' co-presidency struck some of their fellow citizens as threatening and un-American. Millions still built their assumptions about American morality and destiny on the tradi-tional sex roles. The warnings about Hillary's "dangerous sexuality," the attacks on her "feminine credentials," the trivialization of her motives, and the "unnat-ural" imagery were classic feminist illustrations of "our gendered concept of governance." The Celtic legend of the royal court that originated in the Dark Ages was more popular than the Clintons' home-grown, egalitarian partner-ship. The verdict was clear—most Americans still yearned for Camelot; they rejected the co-presidency.

The Clintons united in rage. Theirs was the angriest administration since Richard Nixon's. Both the President and First Lady ranted repeatedly against aides, reporters, and each other. Instead of seducing their new class cohorts, the Clintons froze out reporters. Hillary was particularly hostile. "Hillary Clinton is the first First Lady to have a legitimate policy role in the Administration, and she is the first one I have covered out of five who has totally ignored and avoided the White House press corps," ABC's Ann Compton complained in February 1994. Mrs. Clinton avoided interviews, often barred reporters from her plane, and bristled if they approached. Naturally, reporters retaliated.

Whitewater became largely Hillary's problem. As a partner in the Rose law firm, she had been the "boss" of the money. She knew her position was pre-carious—and may have realized just how much embarrassing information could emerge. Deputy Treasury Secretary Roger Altman noted that Mrs. Clinton "doesn't want [an independent counsel] poking into 20 years of public life." As a result she stonewalled, opposing the appointment of a special prosecutor and repeatedly downplaying her role to investigators. "It's not even a scandal—it's not a scandal," she said revealing a Nixonian tendency to repeat untruths. "A failed land transaction."

Travelgate, too, fell more heavily on her. While Bill's image as a tough pol could possibly have been enhanced by patronage power plays in the travel office, news that Hillary demanded the firings of longtime staffers to get "our people in" would prove she was the "yuppie wife from hell." For that reason, she had a White House lawyer tell the General Accounting Office she "had no role in the decision to terminate the employees"—even though aides would testify of fearing "there would be hell to pay if" they ignored her brusque instructions: "We need our people in. We need the slots." Even more embarrassing was the fact that this daughter of the Sixties, this aspiring philosopher appalled by Reaganite "greed," made $99,537 in cattle futures off a $1,000 investment in nine months. "It is the curse of the '60s generation to be continually judged by what they said and believed at 19 or 20 years old," Ellen Goodman sighed.

Hillary's refusal to come clean, due partly to her sanctimony and partly to her profession, undermined her moral, political, and legal standing. Just as Iran-Contra was a peculiarly conservative scandal—with legal niceties sacrificed on the altar of excessive patriotism—Whitewater was peculiarly liberal, with legal niceties sacrificed for the sake of reform. Hillary and her aides, like so many Reaganites before them, set off the classic post-Watergate tripwires. The possible crimes of the cover-up, suborning perjury, obstructing justice, would overshadow the original sins. In the media's "gotcha" culture, where reporters did not distinguish between high crimes and misdemeanors, the irony of Hillary's role investigating Watergate delighted them and erased any sense of proportion. One cartoon showed a blond woman in a suit with jowly cheeks, flashing a V-for-victory sign: "Hillary Rodham Nixon."

Throughout the winter of 1994 the revelations came, the Clintons' popularity softened, and their health care initiative died. Hillary took out her fury on conservative Democrats and members of the medical establishment who dared to differ with her. Compromise became impossible. The combination of both Clintons' political fumbles and a shrewd, multimillion-dollar lobbying effort turned the great health care debate into a political lynching. As the Clintons lost control of the health care debate, the two powerful streams in modern American ideology that defeated the co-presidency merged. Cartoons of the "evil queen" offering up a Pandora's box of "socialized medicine" linked ancient and modern obsessions about government power and powerful women. Partisan Republicans and jilted reporters described an out-of-control, crusading radical feminist and her henpecked, secretly liberal husband imposing another arrogant, expensive Great Society failure on the American people.

Hillary Rodham Clinton became the rare First Lady who was less popular than her husband. From February to March 1994, his approval rating dropped 11 points to 47 percent, while 45 percent disapproved of the job Bill was doing as President. Hillary's unfavorability rating soared from 29 percent in February to a plurality of 42 percent in March. Even when Bill's numbers would rise slightly beginning in January 1995, hers would continue to plunge.

Republicans assembled the modern politician's torture chamber of over-lapping congressional and criminal investigations. Being a "Friend of Bill"— and especially a friend of Hillary—seemed more a curse than a blessing. Foster was dead. Hubbell was on his way to jail. Nussbaum would resign in disgrace. Margaret Williams and other loyalists would be saddled with six-figure legal bills and threatened with indictment. The Clintonistas took up the plaintive post-acquittal cry of Ronald Reagan's first secretary of labor, Raymond Donovan: "Where do I go to get my reputation back?"

Still, Hillary's people did not abandon her. They circled their wagons around their boss, muttering about the barbarians outside and Bill's "white boys" down the hall. They were so committed to Hillary that West Wing aides often had to remind them that the main goal was to serve the President, not his wife.

Surprisingly, from all indications—and it was an incredibly porous White House, with staffers as garrulous as their commander in chief—Bill and Hillary pulled together during the crisis. They still had their eruptions, and Paula Corbin Jones's sexual harassment suit in May 1994 would deepen the strain and humiliation—but their marriage strengthened. They took refuge in Chelsea and in each other. To the extent that both suffered from some of Hillary's sins, their mutual accounts were better balanced. "I do not believe for a moment that she has done anything wrong," Bill Clinton would say about his wife. "I have . . . I . . . I . . . just," he faltered and chose to speak generally rather than specifically, ". . . if the rest of the people in this country . . . had a character as strong as hers, we wouldn't have half the problems we've got here."

On March 24, the President convened a prime-time news conference to stop the hemorrhaging. He offered a slippery, New Age apology tailor-made for the modern media. He had learned "that there may or may not be a dif-ferent standard than I had seen in the past, not of right and wrong; that doesn't change, but of what may appear to be right or wrong. And I think, that you'll see that, like everything else, this administration learns and goes on." As for his controversial wife—it was time for another makeover.

On April 22, 1994, Hillary Rodham Clinton donned a sensible pink suit and met reporters in the cozy confines of the State Dining Room. She wanted to put this "embarrassing" money-losing affair that "keeps being beaten like the deadest horse there is . . . into a proper perspective." She echoed Bill's post-modernist apology by explaining that her commitment to "measuring up to the standards you set for yourself" and her "sense of privacy . . . led me to per-haps be less understanding than I need to [be] of both the press and the public's interest as well as right to know." The problem was one of appearances and access. She painted a homey picture of her father teaching her "the stock tables" and, like so many members of her elite, defined her money-making ploys as attempts to "create some financial security for our family." Republicans speculated for greed, but Hillary and her pals did it for their children. Always keen, she said people misunderstood her conflicting statements because "I've been traveling, and I'm more committed to health care than anything else I do."

At one point, the crisp yet warm First Lady joked that her "zone of privacy" was being "rezoned." The change was more dramatic than that. As she abandoned the co-presidency she played shamelessly to working women, especially the women paid to cover her. "It's a little difficult for us as a country maybe to make the transition of having a woman like many of the women in this room, sitting in this house," she said. "So I think the standards or to some extent, the expectations of the demands have changed."

Mrs. Clinton had to know that this Friday afternoon press conference, which convened as Richard Nixon lay dying, would not galvanize the public. What NBC's Andrea Mitchell called an "unprecedented extraordinary performance" was directed at reporters. Hillary Rodham Clinton was ready to take on her job as First Lady. The new image would mollify the 49 percent who thought she had too much power and the 62 percent who thought she should not make policy. Back in 1982, Mrs. Reagan sang at the Gridiron to prove she was hip; twelve years later, Mrs. Clinton had to prove she was an old-fashioned midwestern girl in a mixed-up, modern world.

The 1994 Clinton collapse was as dramatic as Richard Nixon's fall in 1973, Lyndon Johnson's in 1965, and Harry Truman's in 1950. In November, when the Republicans recaptured Congress, the rout was complete. Congressman Newt Gingrich had cleverly nationalized the elections so that even when voters repudiated individual congressmen by slim margins, Republicans could claim an anti-Clinton mandate. The President of the United States would soon whine that he was still relevant, while his wife retreated into the land of safe projects and soothing nostrums. "A good wife isn't always advising," a humbled Maggie Williams confessed.

Hillary no longer positioned herself next to the President in meetings, but she still had Bill's ear. She encouraged him to move to the center, as he had done after his 1980 defeat. At her urging, he hired the mastermind of that comeback, Dick Morris, who soon had the President "triangulating" positions, balancing "tax and spend" libertine liberals against heartless conservatives. To the extent that the President would rehabilitate himself for the 1996 campaign, he would do it singly, without Hillary's advocacy.

Compelled, as always, to seduce, Bill apologized to businessmen for raising their taxes and endorsed columnist Ben Wattenberg's lacerating critique of the Clinton administration for forgetting that "Values Matter Most." The President decided he wanted to be "The Good Father," not the bad boy. With the help of his chief of staff, Leon Panetta, the baby-boomer President began imposing discipline on his freewheeling staff and on himself. At his 1996 State of the Union speech, the first president to be born into an American social welfare state—the draft-dodging, non-inhaling poster boy of 1960s liberalism, the architect of one of the most ambitious presidential stabs at social engineering in American history—declared that "the era of big government is over."

Curiously, at a time when the national conversation turned more and more to the problem of America's "character-starved culture"—when George Gallup, Jr., for example, found Americans "more concerned about the state of morality and ethics in their nation than at any other time in the six decades of scientific polling"—most tolerated a President whose integrity they doubted. Clinton and his minions continued to play politics cleverly. They lambasted flawed exposés such as *Unlimited Access,* written by former FBI agent Gary Aldrich, hoping to break the chain of evidence at its weakest point. And the President continued to play the role of the nation's moral leader. Just as they deviated in their daily lives from the moral standards they swore by, many Americans distinguished between this President's private life and his public calls for morality, sobriety, and respect for women. Clinton benefited from a renewed appreciation of the culture of appearances in which public morality obscured private indiscretions, and a weariness with a culture of exposure that mixed private libertinism with a lurid, cynical public Victorianism.

The First Lady also triangulated, although this time she left her name and hair color alone. "My first responsibility," she now said, "is to do whatever my husband would want me to do that he thinks would be helpful to him . . . whatever it takes to kind of be there for him." The retreat was stunning, even as her supporters rejected the notion of a "new Hillary." "No, she's not running health care, but we're not doing health care," Representative Pat Schroeder said in March 1995. "She's remaining active in the things she really cares about, like spending time with her adolescent daughter."

Just as Mrs. Reagan had done, Mrs. Clinton navigated between gender feminism and tradition to celebrate what she called "family feminism." "We need to understand that there is no one formula for how women should lead their lives," Hillary preached. A feminist, she said, is a person who supports "equal political, social and economic rights for women," and not the "rejection of maternal values, nurturing children, [or] caring about the men in your life." As the first First Lady to speak at the Pentagon, she emphasized the importance of respecting women's "choices" and their freedom "not to be stereotyped." In celebrating women's contributions she singled out "not only those done by generals, but those done by mothers, sisters, daughters, all of us."

Even more than Mrs. Reagan had done, Mrs. Clinton defined the attacks on her as an assault on all strong women. Kenneth Walsh of *U.S. News and*

World Report noted that this First Lady "talked mostly to idolizing groups of working women, liberals, social activists, feminists and earnest achievers," ignoring "working-class folks . . . homemakers . . . conservatives." The "a lot of people don't like a strong woman" defense resonated with these professional women who stood by their champion. Yet the rebuttal undercut Hillary's—and her sisters'—demands to be treated equally and ignored the serious, mounting charges of misconduct.

The repackaged First Lady helped establish the Mother Teresa Home for Children in Washington, D.C. She also denounced Gingrich's call for more orphanages as "big government interference," battled for soldiers suffering from "Gulf War syndrome," promoted mammograms to fight breast cancer, redid the Blue Room, and followed in Jackie Kennedy's footsteps with a well-publicized pilgrimage to India and Pakistan. Unlike Mrs. Kennedy, Hillary took her daughter along—posing for cloying mother–daughter travelogue scenes—and visited the poor.

The Clintons offered a model of marriage that triangulated between the 1950s' lifeless perfectionism and the 1990s' dysfunctional cynicism. "Bill and I have always loved each other," Hillary insisted. "No marriage is perfect, but just because it isn't perfect doesn't mean the only solution is to walk off and leave it. A marriage is always growing and changing." Rejecting radical feminists who denounced marriage and traditionalists who disregarded alternative lifestyles, Hillary said, "This is my choice. This is how I define my personhood—it's Bill and Chelsea."

As her heroine Eleanor Roosevelt had done, Hillary Rodham Clinton began writing a syndicated column about "the human dimension of our lives." In "Talking It Over," a chatty and sensible woman familiar with the concerns of working women emerged. "I wake up every morning trying to figure out how to mesh my responsibilities to my family, my public duties and the friend who might be stopping by for dinner," she said. The incongruous image of the savvy lawyer blathering about her "corny" devotion to her husband repelled Maureen Dowd. The *New York Times* pundit quipped that Mrs. Clinton "has a talent for taking on the aspects of those she once scorned," proving to be as secretive as Richard Nixon, as greedy as Ronald Reagan, and as domestic as "the women who bake cookies."

Now, when the First Lady's actions edged toward the controversial, the White House shuddered. Her plans to go to China for the United Nations Fourth World Conference on Women enraged conservatives. Clinton's rival, Senator Bob Dole, said she was condoning oppression out of loyalty to "this misguided conference and its left-wing ideological agenda." Once there, her pointed denunciation of human rights abuses—clearly directed at her Chinese hosts—proved that Mrs. Clinton was not a patsy. A *New York Times* editorial said the speech "may have been her finest moment in public life." Yet her husband undermined her heroism by claiming that "there was no attempt to single any country out."

Throughout 1994 and 1995 Bill kept a certain public distance from his wife, even as they spent more time together in the private quarters. He felt guilty about the suffering his ambitions had caused her. "Insofar as there's been any misunderstanding" about desiring a co-presidency, he said, "it's probably my fault, because I asked her to do a job that probably nobody should ever have been asked to do." He insisted, however, that "she didn't advocate a position or push an issue that I didn't agree with." Despite the distance, after the Oklahoma City bombing in April 1995, Hillary and Bill acquitted themselves in their Reaganesque star turns as America's chief mourners.

Finally, in January 1996, when Hillary's book tour was marred by new evidence of her role in Travelgate and the surprise reappearance of her firm's Whitewater billing records in the White House Book Room adjacent to her private office, with her fingerprints, Bill rallied around his wife. Echoing Harry Truman, he regretted he could not punch William Safire for calling Hillary a "congenital liar." Clinton enjoyed defending his wife against her foibles—and saw his popularity surge as hers declined.

Hillary's 1996 book, *It Takes a Village,* was the most dramatic mark of her makeover. In her now-infamous *New York Times Magazine* portrait, the saintly philosopher had mused, "I hope one day to be able to stop long enough actually to try to write down what I do mean." This bucketful of bromides, suggesting that "Security Takes More Than a Blanket" and "Child Care Is Not a Spectator Sport," was a pale reflection of those ideas. The power-player and thinker of 1993 had become the mom and aphorist of 1996. She was still trying to synthesize liberalism and conservatism. She mourned that children suffered "from violence and neglect, from the breakup of families, from the temptations of alcohol, tobacco, sex, and drug abuse, from greed, materialism, and spiritual emptiness." This was Hillary the good, the devout Methodist, the faithful wife, the "authoritative" mom, and the crusader for children—the safest of all First Lady projects.

In this oddly denatured book, even some of her signature stories over the years were gussied up or diluted. She had often told how when she was four, her mother forced her to confront the neighborhood's female bully, and Hillary ended up walloping her nemesis and impressing the locals. "I can play with the boys now!" Hillary rejoiced. In her book, "the neighborhood kids" tormented the "new kid on the block," until Dorothy Rodham forced her daughter to stay outside. "When they challenged me again, I stood up for myself and finally won some friends." Such trimming gave the book a forced, saccharine quality.

Although this best-seller fit alongside *To Love a Child* and *Millie's Book,* it was a milestone in American cultural history. Equal parts Martha Stewart, Nancy Reagan, and Jane Addams, it reflected the odyssey of an elite that rejected traditional mores only to rediscover them. Hillary publicized studies showing—to much surprise—that divorce harms kids, drugs are destructive, promiscuity is degrading, and that "every child" needs an "intact, dependable family." Even while prescribing a government program for every problem and validating alternative families, she proclaimed, "Every society requires a critical mass of families that fit the traditional ideal."

This makeover had to be painful for Hillary Clinton as she embraced what feminists scorned as the "acceptable face of femininity." One Arkansan recalled that back in 1980, Hillary found it particularly depressing "to have made all those sacrifices for him and then to be blamed for his defeat." She often advised other political wives, "Don't ever lose your own identity in this process. Don't lose yourself to your husband's career." Yet in the White House, Hillary was sacrificing her dreams of a co-presidency and still shouldering the blame, as she became the first First Lady to testify before a grand jury and, with 54 percent disapproving at the start of the 1996 election year, the most unpopular First Lady in history.

Bill Clinton had always played on the edge between disaster and triumph, but his Presidency was more than even he could take. The euphoric co-presidency of 1993 had degenerated into a dysfunctional and controversial partnership, then a subdued alliance. In 1996 Bill Clinton faced the possibility of becoming the first Democratic President since Franklin Roosevelt to serve two terms, while Hillary Clinton faced the possibility of becoming the first First Lady ever indicted. Both Clintons often looked shell-shocked. It was hard to believe that after a career devoted to accumulating power instead of money, they might lose the Presidency and their reputations over financial sloppiness.

By 1996, however restored the Clinton presidency may have seemed, the Clinton co-presidency had become tragic. As a couple, this President and First Lady would enter the history books tarred by scandal, defined more by Gennifer Flowers and Whitewater than by their talents or accomplishments. In 1994, Clinton's own White House Counsel had identified thirty-nine possible scandals in a twelve-page "Task List." At the 1996 convention, Hillary was reduced to defending "the family" and repeatedly invoking "my husband" and "my daughter"; Bill basked in the talk of a miraculous comeback—without his co-president's help.

Bill and Hillary had burst onto the national scene with the potential to become mythic figures. Both were smart, successful, and idealistic. Democrats resented the degree of personal calumny the First Couple endured. The Clintons, their cronies, and their policies should have been judged in the court of public opinion, not in federal court. "I wasn't ready for how cruel this city can be," Hillary sighed, blasting Republican mudslinging and media scavenging.

Yet blaming Republicans for the debased level of discourse ignored the lessons of the postwar presidents. The Clintons' White House was dramatically different than the one the Trumans inherited from the Roosevelts. It was now at the center of American popular culture as well as American politics. Studies estimated that more than 20 percent of the evening news focused on the goings-on at 1600 Pennsylvania Avenue. Twenty-four hours a day, news and talk shows pelted Americans with tidbits about the First Couple. The president had become the nation's master storyteller and celebrity-in-chief. A nation searching for a new civil religion sought answers by scrutinizing presidential character. Harry Truman believed that presidential power is "the power to persuade"; Bill Clinton saw that the power of the modern president is the power to perform. Yet, while being saturated with information about the president and about politics, half of the electorate did not vote and over three-quarters despised politicians. Even as they tuned in, Americans tuned out to the constant carping about his affairs, her hairdos, and their finances.

The Clintons' America was also dramatically different. A culture of exposure had displaced the culture of appearances. Vulgarity rather than gentility reigned; openness supplanted discretion; and diversity, not conformity, was the order of the day. The rigid scripts both men and women had followed were discarded, leaving millions confused. From the Peeping Tom lens of America's omniscient media came a portrayal of this "shining city on a hill" as a tawdry cesspool of crime and corruption, of poverty and great wealth, of materialism and carnality, of celebrities, maniacs, and hack politicians. Tourists walking outside the White House no longer wore standard-issue jackets and ties for men and dresses for the ladies, but a bewildering and colorful array of unisex T-shirts, tank tops, shorts, jeans, baseball caps, and earrings. Inside, air conditioners hummed, computers clicked, faxes buzzed, phones rang, and televisions squawked. This electronic cacophony serenaded a richer, healthier, and more comfortable but somehow less human America.

It was, however, a more humane America in many ways, best exemplified by the fact that the women in the White House were not just maids and secretaries, and the African-Americans were not just domestics and handymen. Female visitors were more likely to wear power suits than white gloves. White House staffers were more likely to have been raised in a suburb, educated at a world-class university far from home, scarred by crime, traumatized by divorce, befriended by their spouses, and enlightened by overseas travel. They were more likely than their predecessors to think of families as dysfunctional, churches as hypocritical, community as virtual, the nation as imperfect, and God as dead. Many male staffers wanted to be nurturing fathers without relinquishing traditional macho prerogatives; many of the women wanted to be savvy professionals without abdicating their roles as wives and mothers. Yearning for self-fulfillment on the job and at home, the staffers' vocabulary was one of hearing, sharing, caring, being, and feeling.

Addicted to false polarities, reporters described the 1996 election as a generational clash between the exemplar of this America and a refugee from Truman's era, between Bill Clinton the yuppie empath and Bob Dole the grizzled World War II hero. Herein reporters at least acknowledged the existence of the other America that rarely generated headlines—where 96 percent believed in God and 71 percent still belonged to a church, where the middle class was broader, richer, prouder, freer, and happier than anywhere else in the world and at any time in human history. Bill Clinton was shrewder than his journalist peers. He knew he could not abandon these people, just as Bob Dole was not so much the Luddite that he eschewed polls and consultants, spurned the yuppie Republicans Ronald Reagan recruited, or censured Arnold Schwarzenegger films when condemning the media plague of violence. After all, it was the supposedly old-fashioned Republican warhorse who had the female chief of staff and the second wife who had served in two Cabinets.

In fact, the battle between Senator Dole and President Clinton was yet another chapter in Americans' tortured search for a new consensus in the wake of the 1960s. Partially a civil war between the new class and the heartland, it was also a contest of reigning sensibilities with blurred battle lines. Both Elizabeth Hanford Dole and Hillary Rodham Clinton resorted to a stealth strategy of low public profiles, soothing rhetoric, apparent disinterest in power, and frilly covers to their hard-driving careers. Yuppies had values too, while in the 1990s churchgoing couples in the Midwest divorced, had abortions, wore Nikes, and watched Tim Allen—a recovering drug addict whose 1994 Disney blockbuster, *The Santa Clause,* portrayed St. Nick as a bumbling, remote, materialistic single father whose son helped him get in touch with his own "inner child." As the Clintons played for the center with a family agenda, they showed that baby-boom Democrats also yearned for an America of faith and values and moral certitude. Bill Clinton, in all his sloppy contradictions and wishy-washiness, was an accurate barometer of the country he led, illustrating the yearnings, the excess, the orthodoxy, and the ingenuity that was and is America.

All these contradictions and changes in culture, in politics, and in society helped facilitate the rise of the presidential couple. The rejection of the First Couple linked the Clintons' world with the Trumans'—and their predecessors. Even in the 1990s, most Americans still did not want to "buy one, get one free."

IV

In America, it seems, every successful campaign requires brochures picturing a happy family. For years politicians have publicized the personal to establish an image and to score political points. The history of the presidential couples shows that in an information age with a bureaucratic government, such political identity-building is essential. With diminished political parties, omnipresent media, and a bankrupt government, presidents lead as much through exhortation as legislation, as much through personal example as political action. In an age of growing balkanization, the First Couple offers the country a focal point—as an inspiring standard or an inviting target. The personalized mom-and-pop presidency makes a large and alienating government seem more accessible; it offers a source of political capital; it provides the president with an arena where he can exert control; it appeals to a public convinced that morality matters in politics; and it is absolutely relevant in an age where government increasingly intrudes on previously private decisions.

No doubt, the chain of causation is actually the reverse. Because politicians endure such scrutiny, because so many barriers have fallen, politicians try to make the best of a bad situation and at least score points. No modern president has kept his life as private as he and his wife would like. The latitude which Presidents Roosevelt and Kennedy enjoyed has disappeared.

Again and again, the politicization of the presidential marriage has proved dangerous. Focusing on the presidential marriage, and the First Lady, created new areas of vulnerability for America's chief executives. Critics now had two targets for the price of one. The natural gap between a couple's image and the torrid or pedestrian realities of their lives became fodder for reporters scavenging for headlines. The Gresham's law of modern media politics could turn the health care debate into a referendum on Bill and Hillary Clinton, as scandal-mongering and personalities drove out substantive debate. In a skeptical culture where basic values were in transition, personalizing the presidency took away too much of the magic that leaders needed to arouse faith. In June 1993 *Time* mocked the new, accessible, open chief executive as "THE INCREDIBLE SHRINKING PRESIDENT."

Modern presidential couples had to work out the dilemmas of marriage on an excruciatingly public stage. Polls showed that Americans were split between couples trying to create new protocols in a "peer marriage" like the Clintons—and the Doles—and a growing number who remained committed to traditional arrangements. Bedeviling questions about power, equality, and priorities were superimposed on the daily crises that came with running the White House, overseeing the Executive Branch, and leading the most powerful nation on earth.

As their husbands coped with awesome responsibilities, First Ladies struggled to define their roles. Their dilemmas were the poignant conflicts of the modern American woman writ large. The demands were pressing and conflicting. First Ladies were told to champion feminism while upholding tradition. They were told to sell government programs to a citizenry that demands such programs but hates government. They were told by reporters that the media reflects popular attitudes and that popularity is all important, when the media's agenda diverged from that of the populace and high poll ratings for the First Ladies did not always win votes for their husbands.

The mixed messages, however, were all on the surface. The fact has remained that First Ladies are not elected, and the public does not want them to act as if they were. Hillary Rodham Clinton—proud graduate of Wellesley and Yale Law School, twice named one of the hundred most influential lawyers in the nation, her husband's presumptive co-president, involved in a sophisticated attempt to solve a central domestic problem, dogged by Whitewater and Travelgate, and best-selling author—was most often asked two questions in correspondence and in her travels: "How's Chelsea?" and "How's Socks?"—the latter being the "first" cat.

The experience of the last half-century suggests that the First Lady has greater potential to hurt than help. More voters are likely to refuse to vote for a president because they dislike his spouse than are likely to vote for him because they like his wife. The safest public position for presidential spouses, therefore, is a benign smile buttressed by discreet behavior behind the scenes.

When they have thrived, most First Ladies have done so at their husbands' expense. Betty Ford, Rosalynn Carter, Nancy Reagan, and Hillary Rodham Clinton were perceived as strong-willed independent women at the "cost" of their husbands, who were derided as being weak, wimpish, not in control. The ancient fear of Delilah endures in our age of space travel and the Internet.

It should not be surprising that the most popular First Lady since Jackie Kennedy was the most traditional one, Barbara Bush. Like Mrs. Kennedy, Mrs. Bush tolerated a certain aristocratic distance in her marriage and never appeared interested in seizing power or currying public favor. She was "half Eleanor, half Bess," engaged in some issues but aware of her place. As a result, she was extraordinarily popular—and powerful.

Few presidents get elected without herculean efforts from their wives. As a result, many wives view life in the White House as payback time, an opportunity to assert themselves after years of self-sacrifice. Reporters encourage this self-assertion, knowing it makes good headlines. Most such actions beyond the scope of the traditional First Lady projects, though, are politically dangerous and threaten to eclipse the president. Nancy Reagan, Rosalynn Carter, and Hillary Rodham Clinton provoked firestorms when they confused political duties with a license to rule.

Their examples, and the more successful relationships forged by the Bushes and the Johnsons, bring up the shopworn problem of the title "First Lady." Today a president no longer needs a First Lady to reign over Washington society but a First Consort. In its noun form, "consort" refers to "a husband or wife, a spouse," "the spouse of a royal person," and "one vessel or ship accompanying another." It also means an "accord or agreement," just as its verb form means to associate, to keep company, to agree, or to harmonize. Modern presidents most need a spouse who can consort with them, accompany them on their exhausting journey at the focal point of American life, and "harmonize," helping to build an appealing political identity while offering encouragement and support.

All marriages, be they good or bad, present a public face to the world that is partly fiction. All couples choose how much of their real lives to present to the world—and to acknowledge to themselves. The impression politicians convey about their marriages are doubly suspect, because the normal fictions are embellished by the political needs to conform to certain ideals.

At the same time, a look at the presidential couples since the Trumans suggests that the private life is revealing but not determining. The marriage tells us some things about the man and the president, but it does not tell us the full story. The scheming, foul-mouthed, vicious Richard Nixon of the Watergate tapes bears little resemblance to Pat Nixon's shy, courtly, and awkward husband. Both sides must be considered together.

Today, First Ladies cannot be kept in the parlor and dispatched to make tea and bake cookies. Just as Jackie Kennedy defined her husband's administration a week after it ended so tragically, modern First Ladies have often functioned as makeup, highlighting particular aspects of their husbands' time in office. Bess Truman emphasized her husband's small-town integrity; Mamie Eisenhower, her husband's benign reign; Lady Bird Johnson, her husband's radical attempt to solve America's problems; and Barbara Bush, her husband's commitment to a "kinder, gentler," WASPier nation. Sometimes the makeup streaked, and First Ladies were seen as reflecting their husband's failings. Pat Nixon reflected her husband's coldness; Betty Ford, her husband's ineptitude; Rosalynn Carter, her husband's starchiness; Nancy Reagan, her husband's greed; and Hillary Clinton, her husband's New Left ideals despite the New Democratic veneer, as well as his political promiscuity.

Criticism of the First Lady, however, does not always damage her husband. Public approval can be a zero-sum game. If Jackie Kennedy at times attracted too much public adulation, she also drew the barbs about aristocratic tastes and inherited wealth Jack otherwise might have received. With Nancy Reagan typed as the greedy "Dragon Lady," Ronnie seemed more benign and less radical than he actually was. Similarly, Hillary Rodham Clinton served as a lightning rod for Bill, who thereby kept his distance from his own administration's more radical initiatives and his complicity in the Whitewater morass. This dynamic intensified the competition between the mates. Even though their destinies were always linked, their particular political needs often clashed.

In today's "consort" co-presidency, the president and First Lady do not share power; they do, however, collaborate on creating a joint identity that exploits their celebrity and reflects the values they wish to uphold—or deem it expedient to embrace. Every presidency is a psychodrama and a sociodrama, a compelling personal story projected against a vision for the nation. The president is the star and the First Lady, not the vice president, is the co-star. The First Lady's crew includes a press secretary, advance people, a special projects coordinator, and a social secretary—in short, a team of public relations specialists to project the president's message and to protect the First

Lady when she jousts with the media, hosts at the White House, or meets the public through letters, speeches, and travel.

Some caution that this quest for popular leadership is undemocratic, destabilizing, and distracting. Charisma is the enemy of institutions, Garry Wills warns, too specific and too volatile to ensure the kind of continuity necessary from one administration to the next. Presidents should be judged on their policies instead of their personalities, defined by their achievements rather than their spouses. In this anarchic, individuated world, however, charisma is one of the few forces that can bind our ersatz community together. And in our post-party age, presidents have great power but few constraints or "markers" to identify them. Now more than ever, Americans need public leaders, inspiring couples who can serve as role models and as links for a quarter of a billion people who spend most of their time avoiding each other except when they venture out to shop in the mall.

The pressures to create a co-presidency, with all its paradoxes, are so great—and the potential benefits for a president seem so alluring—that few since Jackie Kennedy have been able to resist. Many have learned the hard way about the enduring ambivalence regarding this unelected woman and power. The Carters, the Reagans, and now the Clintons have articulated a rationale for a cooperative co-presidency, but they have not sold it to the people. A First Lady has to be assertive but not aggressive, prominent but not overbearing, creative but not controversial—like most women at work, but actually more so because she is not at work but in her husband's office.

These complex cultural and institutional demands are further muddied by the emotional baggage couples bring to the presidency. White House life often upsets whatever equilibrium has been established over the years. Serving as president and First Lady is so demanding, and the scrutiny so intense, that no one ever seems prepared for it despite any number of years in a governor's mansion, the U.S. Senate, or even the vice president's residence. Faced with these unprecedented demands and the intense pressure, the president and his wife end up improvising, changing the way they have worked together through years of marriage—with the whole world watching, and the press ready to pounce on any misstep.

As "companionate marriages" have become more egalitarian, the First Couples, like everyone else, struggled for a new equilibrium. The decades-long negotiations between George and Barbara Bush, Gerald and Betty Ford, or Richard and Pat Nixon reflect the combined impact of World War II, suburbanization, mobility, and women's liberation on American marriages. The Nixons discovered that their public facade did them little good; Jerry Ford indulged his wife's outspokenness, even at the cost of his Presidency; and Ronald Reagan and George Bush usually took pride in their wives' successes, although both occasionally stood firm to remind their wives—and the world—just who was boss. Among the reasons Reagan refused to cancel his ill-advised homage to the Nazi SS graves in Bitburg and was slow to fire Don Regan as chief of staff was to prove he was not henpecked.

Despite the extraordinary tensions all these selfish, ambitious, and overextended couples experienced, none of them divorced. Clearly, politics helps explain this remarkable record of fidelity during a divorce epidemic. Even as their peers sacrificed their families on the altar of self-fulfillment, these couples were unwilling to commit political suicide. But studying these ten marriages as they fluctuated over the years teaches the resilience of such relationships when they are viewed as being "till death do us part." Marriages ebb and flow, fracture and heal. The Eisenhowers' marriage ruptured during World War II; the Nixons' marriage wilted during Watergate; and the Fords' marriage was sorely tested before, during, and after his Presidency. And yet, these three couples persevered and saw their marriages recover. Mamie and Ike renewed their love affair in the White House, as did Bill and Hillary; Pat and Dick healed together when they left the White House, as did Jerry and Betty. Even Jackie and Jack had warm moments together after their infant son died, a potential healing process aborted by Jack's murder.

The experiences of these presidential couples suggest that by being "imprisoned" in a marriage, couples often can make it work. These stories also illustrate the benefits of living in a culture of appearances; people's commitment to a public fiction can change the private reality. Both Reagans admitted that their relationship started slowly and tumultuously, but their common commitment to making their union what Ronnie called "an adolescent's dream of what a marriage should be" turned a shotgun wedding into one of the great love stories of late twentieth-century America.

These lessons about marriage and about the proper role of the First Consort have broader implications as well. In the United States today, the presidency and marriage are undergoing similar crises—both are suffering from a loss of authority, of credibility. Modern American culture is hooked on cynicism. We are addicted to debunking, to doubting, to sneering. We need to give ourselves and our leaders a break. Some distance, some secrecy, and some appearances can be constructive. Just as husbands and wives choose to build useful fictions about each other and about their relationships, so too can citizens choose to build useful fictions about their leaders and their government. A step toward a culture of appearances, away from the culture of the exposé, would be a welcome one. We need to "see heroes," as Jackie Kennedy hoped we would. Camelot, like strong marriages and successful democracies, requires a leap of faith—and an occasional suspension of disbelief, motivated by the confidence that ideals such as love, justice, and virtue can and will ultimately triumph.

"I NEVER PROMISED YOU
A ROSE GARDEN"

Advice for the First Couple

I t all seemed so familiar. The poised First Lady sat across from Larry King during May, one of TV's critical sweeps months—both she and Larry were too savvy to waste her appearance on an ordinary night. Her heavy gold jewelry gleaming, her blond hair perfectly coiffed, she answered questions thoughtfully, smoothly, effectively. This was not the tigress who had spawned countless stories about her influence, but a pussycat. This was not a modern, powerful First Lady for a feminist age, but the embodiment of mainstream middle-class values: loyal, deferential, community-oriented, and empathetic. She spoke about how nasty the attacks on her had been and called for civility in public discourse. She sounded hurt and surprised that her critics were so mean. She had no interest, no angle beyond helping "my husband" and representing the United States of America.

Experienced pro that she was, she pooh-poohed sugestions that she wielded power or that she represented an alternative faction in the White House. Accusations against her were all misunderstandings that her silly critics exaggerated. All she wanted to talk about was her benign yet surprisingly popular crusade for America's kids. As often as she could, she mentioned "my husband" and defended his Presidency. Her appeal was gracious and directed to her core constituency—women.

Even though her body language and the crook of her neck occasionally betrayed her bitterness and her determination, it was hard not to be charmed by this warm, poised woman. When Larry asked her a personal question, her smiling refusal to "answer any questions" of that nature seemed just about right.

Surprisingly, by the spring of 1996, Hillary Rodham Clinton, Wellesley '69, Yale Law '72, feminist, activist, and notorious "McGovernik," had morphed into one of the great anti-feminists of her age, Nancy Reagan. In keeping with the protocols of the exclusive sorority to which she belonged, Mrs. Clinton refused to offer any advice to her successors. She said, as her predecessors had, that her job was an idiosyncratic one, that she "would not prejudge how somebody would fulfill their responsibilities," even as she took solace in the fact that all "starting with Martha Washington" had been abused. That statement was as disingenuous as her performance on Larry King, and in the White House overall.

Hillary Rodham Clinton betrayed many of her longtime political allies as she tried to fulfill her duty to her husband. Her discomfort was palpable as she avoided saying that she was not a liberal, but would not admit that she was; as she avoided admitting she was a scapegoat for feminism, but would not deny that she was not. Yet even as she steered the conversation away from policy, she revealed her true self. She told Larry that her best preparation for what she endured in Washington "was playing sports with boys in my neighborhood growing up." She got "used" to their "razzing," and "that's why I urge girls to play competitive sports with boys at an early age." This feminist critique of Washington's ugly "gotcha" culture masquerading as an innocuous childhood reminiscence betrayed a contempt toward men, an anger that she learned to repress but could not suppress.

For the fourth time in a row, a bold, idiosyncratic, headstrong First Lady had regressed toward the mean. The converging public images of these very different women underline the unspoken, yet quite definitive job description for First Lady of the United States. Those who violated the protocols risked the kind of witch hunts Nancy Reagan and Hillary Rodham Clinton endured. Future First Couples would be well-advised to study their predecessors' experiences and skip a painful and ugly readjustment. Presidential couples in the modern era can succeed—even thrive—if they learn the right lessons from history.

DON'T BE YOURSELVES; BE WHO THEY WANT YOU TO BE.

Hillary Rodham Clinton—and most of her predecessors—urged each member of a presidential couple to "make the choices that are right" for them. While the admonitions not to be a phony and not to go against one's self-interest are well-taken, presidential couples must accept their roles as cultural leaders weaving together a national fantasy. First Couples should give the American people the love story they desire. The presidential spouse needs to symbolize the warm, traditional marriage she and the president have established—despite working around the clock to get elected—and give a warm-hearted facade to a welfare state that has grown increasingly complex, bureaucratic, and impersonal.

Furthermore, First Couples slight their constituencies at their peril. Reporters have particular demands, as do the white-gloved brigade for Republicans and working women for Democrats. It is better to fulfill these demands, or at least some of them, than to disappoint. Given the growing demands on political wives in the wake of women's liberation, it is no wonder Helen Jackson, the wife of the two-time presidential candidate Senator Henry Jackson, sighed in 1976, "It takes a lot more energy now than when all we did was drink tea and shake hands with the ladies."

SUPPORT EACH OTHER, RELY ON EACH OTHER, BUT DON'T FORGET WHO'S BOSS.

The combined effect of presidents "living above the store" and having the "loneliest job in the world" has done wonders for most marriages in the White House. Mamie Eisenhower, Lady Bird Johnson, and Betty Ford were particularly pleased to have their peripatetic husbands home for dinner most nights. Presidents need their spouses as a "safe haven" amid the constant scramble for power among aides and the fawning approach most visitors take. The sensitive spouse sees what the president needs and provides it: Eleanor Roosevelt was her crippled husband's roving "eyes and ears"; Lady Bird Johnson was her volatile husband's island of "se-ren-i-ty"; and Pat Nixon often left her solitary husband alone. Because Nancy Reagan saw that aides often clammed up in the presence of the leader of the free world, she functioned as a conduit, telling her passive husband what she thought he needed to hear and that no one else was bold enough to tell him. All these women remembered that their primary task was to support the president. When Bess Truman went off for weeks at a time to Missouri, and when Hillary Clinton created an alternative power center with aides more devoted to her than him, their respective husbands—and the nation—suffered.

LET THE WHITE-GLOVE PULPIT RESONATE WITH THE BULLY PULPIT.

It took the outpouring of public affection after her mastectomy for Betty Ford to realize she had what Nancy Reagan would call the "white-glove pulpit" to shape American attitudes. Mrs. Ford used her opportunity to undercut her husband and endanger his Presidency. Presidential spouses, though, can play a critical role as the president's chorus. Jackie Kennedy's call for a stylish America echoed her husband's call for a new frontier, and Hillary Rodham Clinton's "politics of meaning" at least attempted to illustrate her husband's call for individual responsibility and a "third way" between 1960s libertinism and 1980s selfishness. Mrs. Clinton's characteristic error—at first—was to emphasize her views and her struggles, rather than *their* views and their vision as central to *his* administration.

TREAT THE SPOUSE'S PROJECT AS AN INTEGRAL PART OF THE ADMINISTRATION.

Modern First Ladies have learned that to define their husbands well they need to define themselves, usually with a special project. The project should be uncontroversial at worst; at best, it should illuminate an aspect of the president's agenda, just as Lady Bird Johnson's beautification campaign advanced Lyndon's Great Society with a cleverly disguised program that was more radical than it appeared, or Nancy Reagan's "Just Say No" campaign against drugs advanced Ronnie's conservative restoration. The project should touch on an area of interest to women, allowing the First Lady to function as a special emissary to them. In doing so, the radical ideology of "gender feminism" is best avoided; the uplifting message of female—and individual—self-fulfillment is the order of the day.

THE LESS POWER YOU SEEM TO WANT, THE MORE YOU'LL GET AND THE MORE POPULAR YOU SHALL BE.

For someone derided as an anti-feminist throwback, Barbara Bush understood the sexist discomfort with powerful women—and especially with powerful First Ladies—better than many feminists. Many female politicians have succeeded in overcoming the Lady Macbeth stereotype; the First Lady is less likely to succeed, though, considering her unelected, pseudo-monarchical position in a democracy terrified of government power and monitored by a media addicted to controversy. By explaining that she never meddled in George's affairs, and he never meddled in hers, Barbara Bush became one of the most popular and effective First Ladies in the modern era. She followed the rule of the Southern belle, which Rosalynn Carter used as her favorite quotation in her junior college yearbook: "There is great ability in knowing how to conceal one's ability." Yet in the White House, Rosalynn, along with Nancy Reagan and Hillary Rodham Clinton, spurned the advice and suffered a drop in popularity and effectiveness.

NEVER CRITICIZE THE PRESIDENT, UNLESS YOU BOTH AGREE IT'S CONVENIENT.

Both Rosalynn Carter and Pat Nixon frustrated reporters for years with their stubborn refusal to criticize their husbands. When Rosalynn finally criticized Jimmy during the 1980 campaign, it was part of a transparent attempt to build up her husband as a statesman. She chided him for spurning her advice to play the demagogue and for hewing to principle despite the political consequences. The Nixons were more subtle; Dick had Pat confront him about his failure to appoint a woman to the Supreme Court and his dithering on the Equal Rights Amendment to give women a sense that someone in the White House represented their interests.

PIONEERS BELONG IN THE WILD WEST, AND POSSIBLY THE WEST WING,
BUT CERTAINLY NOT THE EAST WING.

Considering that she is an unelected figure, he is the head of state, and they live in a political culture most comfortable with consensus, when in doubt the First Couple should play to the cultural center. In a nation wracked by "culture wars," the presidential couple should find a DMZ by offering a benign, soothing role model. The safety zone to which the First Couple retreats can remind Americans of common ties and central values.

In the nineteenth century, Henry James noted that the United States was a country with "no sovereign, no court, no personal loyalty, no aristocracy, no church, no clergy, no army, no diplomatic service, no country gentlemen, no palaces, no castles." Since then the country has acquired more nationalizing influences, more anchors, but Americans today look to the presidential couple for reassurance and stability. Try to give it to us. We need it.

WHEN IN DOUBT, GO RETRO.

In today's world, women are not the only ones bewildered by mixed messages about sex roles. Both presidents and First Ladies are bombarded by conflicting demands: she is supposed to be independent but deferential, he is supposed to be sensitive but strong. No president can afford to look like a wimp, but excessive machismo can be controversial and dangerous, as Lyndon Johnson and Richard Nixon learned in Vietnam.

However individual citizens choose to live their private lives, most Americans hold the First Couple to a higher and more old-fashioned standard. Most would still rather have John Wayne than Jerry Seinfeld in the Oval Office. There is no room for self-doubt or indecision when navigating this ship of state. Jimmy Carter the farmer and George Bush the oil wildcatter learned that for all their macho achievements in the military and in rugged outdoor professions, occasional uncertainty in office defined them as wimps. Ronald Reagan, the *faux* warrior and career actor, appeared tough because he never questioned himself or his actions. Gradually, throughout his first term, Bill Clinton the draft evader and policy wonk learned that Americans prefer tough talk, nostalgic moralizing, and resolute action to New Age psychobabble, tidbits about underwear preference, and reasoned moderation that might seem wishy-washy.

NOTHING IS TRIVIAL AND THE PERSONAL IS POLITICAL,
BUT DON'T TAKE THE POLITICAL PERSONALLY.

In recent years, Bill Clinton was mocked for frequenting McDonald's, Hillary Clinton was teased for teasing her hair, and George Bush was blasted for being fascinated with a supermarket scanner. In contrast, Barbara Bush was deified for wearing fake pearls, Nancy Reagan changed her image with a two-and-a-half-minute skit, and Ronald Reagan rescued his flagging reelection campaign by quipping that he would not make an issue of Walter Mondale's age. Hillary

Clinton attributed the obsession with minutiae to "24-hour news filling all those minutes and hours, so that things that would never have been paid attention to ... 10 years ago, are now more important than they should be." But John Kennedy had exploded at rumors that he posed for *Gentlemen's Quarterly,* and Harry Truman's mother had asked him about the hordes of reporters who greeted her in Washington: "Harry, if you are President, why can't you shoo all these people away?"

In a therapeutic culture where personal tidbits are considered revealing, the First Couple must always be on guard. When the inevitable leaks occur, it is a mistake to overreact. Reporters are only doing their job and will do it even more zealously if they get a rise out of you or you dare to confront them. The First Couple can protect what Hillary Clinton called its "zone of privacy" by creating an illusion of exposure. Presidents and their spouses can just say no to certain topics, as long as they appear forthcoming in other matters. By defining boundaries, the Clintons protected Chelsea more effectively than the Carters protected Amy. They also distracted reporters with tidbits about their own marriage. In 1996 Bob Dole began sharing his feelings about his war injuries, but he refused to discuss his divorce—and properly so. Even the reclusive Bess Truman realized the need to purchase privacy when she told a woman reporter about Margaret's plans to stay longer in Missouri, muttering to her secretary about newswomen, "God only knows what they may be saying. I'd prefer telling her it's *none of their d——business."*

YOU GET ONE MEA CULPA; USE IT WELL.

Petty scandals and minor controversies are inevitable. Fortunately, Americans—especially reporters—are suckers for confessions. The Clintons could have derailed the Whitewater inquisitors with a suitably weepy press conference in which they volunteered embarrassing information and asked for forgiveness. Instead, they repeatedly confessed retroactively to each disclosure, altering their stories so many times that a perjury indictment and a stench of dishonesty seemed difficult to avoid.

TAKE THE LONG-TERM VIEW OF YOUR MARRIAGE.

While reporters describe marriages in all-or-nothing terms as wonderful or horrible, most marriages lie somewhere in between (except, of course, for this author's truly idyllic match). Marriages ebb and flow, rupture and heal. The Eisenhowers survived the war and the Kay Summersby episode; the Nixons survived Watergate; and the Trumans survived the White House.

The president should acknowledge the many sacrifices the presidential spouse makes but defer payment until after the administration ends. Dwight Eisenhower thanked Mamie with the extravagant Gettysburg renovations during his Presidency. Harry Truman mollified Bess by retiring to Independence rather than running for the Senate. And Richard Nixon tried to compensate for some of his high marital crimes by excusing Pat from any public appearances after the resignation, be it one of the dinners he threw to rehabilitate his reputation or greeting trick-or-treaters at Halloween.

KEEP UP APPEARANCES—YOU SET THE STANDARD NOW,
AND YOUR MARRIAGE BELONGS TO HISTORY.

Imagine if you will, how unnerving it will be if the Clintons ever divorce. Even if it is decades after their time in the White House ends, it will mock all their statements of mutual devotion and prove all the cynics right. As Stephen Carter of Yale says, "The marriage vow is an undertaking to alter the future, to realize one's humanity by liberating oneself from a variety of possible eventualities." Presidential marriages resonate and can alter many people's futures. Rather than confirming our culture of negativity, lead us toward a culture of faith. As the Reagans discovered after their rocky start, your marriage and our country just might live up to the billing.

A NOTE ON SOURCES

There are hundreds of books about the presidency and dozens about First Ladies, but this is the first attempt to analyze the history of the presidential couple. Books about First Ladies traditionally have taken a breathy, sycophantic tone, focusing more on tea served and china bought than on policy or politics. Historical interest in First Ladies has increased lately, thanks especially to Lewis Gould, who just edited the encyclopedic *American First Ladies: Their Lives and Their Legacies* (New York, 1996), and to Doris Kearns Goodwin, who analyzed the marriage of Franklin and Eleanor Roosevelt so effectively in *No Ordinary Time* (New York, 1994). Still, most modern authors—be they traditional or feminist—are too concerned with justifying the First Lady's power. Most of these works fall into a progressive mold, celebrating the emergence of First Ladies in our supposedly more enlightened times (see, for example, Carl Sferrazza Anthony, *First Ladies: The Saga of the Presidents' Wives and Their Power,* 2 vols., New York, 1990–1991; and Betty Boyd Caroli, *First Ladies,* New York, 1987). Such works often tend to ignore the respective presidents and their relationship to the First Ladies, much as most books about the presidents ignore the wives.

Studying the presidential couple exacerbates what Stephen Skowronek in *The Politics Presidents Make* (Cambridge, MA, 1993) identifies as one of the critical problems in presidential scholarship: how to trace lines of development in a highly idiosyncratic institution. Marriages are individual and volatile, with few formulas or clear patterns emerging over time. Good marriages have followed bad marriages in the White House; strong marriages like the Trumans' have been strained there, while problematic marriages like the Eisenhowers' have healed. There is no correlation between having a successful marriage and a successful administration, especially when the definition of marital success is even murkier and more fluid than the definition of presidential success. Yet this book argues that there is an institutional dimension to the history of the First Couple, as evidenced by the growth of the East Wing and the unspoken but clear assumptions that have shaped the actions of the recent married partners in the White House.

While this work has benefited from the many biographers and historians who have tilled the same soil, it relies most on the vast collections in the Truman, Eisenhower, Kennedy, Johnson, Nixon, Ford, Carter, and Reagan presidential libraries, as well as the Richard Nixon Presidential Materials Project. Budget cuts and different priorities have hindered the cataloguing of the White House Social Files so essential to a study of First Ladies. Nevertheless, a treasure trove remains in these libraries, which are ably and good-naturedly administered by a corps of effective if underfunded archivists. Some of the material made available to me had never been requested by other researchers or was catalogued specifically at my request.

Often, one collection in each library proved particularly useful. The Mamie Doud Eisenhower White House Social Files in the Dwight D. Eisenhower Library contain hundreds of short notes Mrs. Eisenhower wrote to her friends and benefactors, illustrating the way Mamie grounded and distracted her husband; the vast social files in the Lyndon B. Johnson Library show how central Lady Bird Johnson was in her husband's administration; H. R. Haldeman's notes of his daily meetings with President Nixon in the Richard Nixon Presidential Materials Project offer a running commentary on Nixon's efforts to have his family outdo John Kennedy's; and the Sheila Rabb Weidenfeld Papers in the Gerald Ford Library chronicle the extraordinary press interest in Mrs. Ford—which, I argue, proved so detrimental to Gerald Ford's 1976 reelection effort.

With each succeeding presidency, and almost exclusively for the Bush and Clinton chapters, I was able to rely on the increasingly intrusive press and increasingly responsive First Couples. The candor imposed on modern presidential couples helped compensate for the limited archival resources now available. Modern presidents and First Ladies must submit to countless journalistic interrogations. As we all do, they develop pat answers and favorite stories; often their phrasing and word choice will not vary from year to year or decade to decade. With so many of these interviews available, and with little prospect that I would succeed in freeing these practiced professionals from their conversational ruts, I did not attempt to interview any of the subjects of this book. The limited potential gains did not justify the degree to which my historical distance might be compromised by meeting some—but not all—of these individuals.

To limit the notes, I have usually referenced only material cited directly in the text. Instead of using numbered notes, I have keyed each citation to its respective page number and the first two or three words in the quotation or phrase being referenced.

A GUIDE TO ABBREVIATIONS IN NOTES

NEWSPAPERS AND PERIODICALS

AtCon	*Atlanta Constitution; Atlanta Journal and Constitution*
BH&G	*Better Homes and Gardens*
BosG	*Boston Globe*
BosH	*Boston Herald*
BosTr	*Boston Traveler*
ChiDN	*Chicago Daily News*
ChiT	*Chicago Tribune*
CR	*Congressional Record*
DetFP	*Detroit Free Press*
FamW	*Family Weekly*
GH	*Good Housekeeping*
KCS	*Kansas City Star*
LAT	*Los Angeles Times*
LHJ	*Ladies' Home Journal*
LouCJ	*Louisville Courier Journal*
Nwswk	*Newsweek*
NYDN	*New York Daily News*
NYP	*New York Post*
NYT	*New York Times*
NYTM	*New York Times Magazine*
SatEP	*Saturday Evening Post*

SFChr	*San Francisco Chronicle*
SLGD	*St. Louis Globe-Democrat*
SLPD	*St. Louis Post-Dispatch*
TNR	*The New Republic*
USNWR	*U.S. News & World Report*
WasP	*Washington Post*
WasS	*Washington Star*
WasT	*Washington Times*
WDN	*Washington Daily News*
WSJ	*Wall Street Journal*
WWD	*Women's Wear Daily*

LIBRARIES AND INSTITUTIONS

DDE Lib.	Dwight D. Eisenhower Library, Abilene, KS
GRF Lib.	Gerald R. Ford Library, Ann Arbor, MI
HST Lib.	Harry S. Truman Library, Independence, MO
JC Lib.	Jimmy Carter Library, Atlanta, GA
JFK Lib.	John Fitzgerald Kennedy Library, Boston, MA
LBJ Lib.	Lyndon Baines Johnson Library, Austin, TX
RN Lib.	Richard Nixon Library and Birthplace, Yorba Linda, CA
RN PMP	Richard Nixon Presidential Materials Project, National Archives, College Park, MD
RR Lib.	Ronald Reagan Library, Simi Valley, CA

ADDITIONAL ABBREVIATIONS

AMG	Alfred M. Gruenther
AMS	Arthur M. Schlesinger, Jr.
Arch AV	Audiovisual Collection, National Archives
BB	Barbara Bush
BC	Bill Clinton
BF	Betty Ford
BWT	Bess Wallace Truman
BWT VF	Bess Wallace Truman, Vertical Files, HST Lib.
CS	Constance Stuart
DDE	Dwight D. Eisenhower
DDE Names	Name Series, Ann C. Whitman File, DDE Papers as President, DDE Lib.
DDE PPF	President's Personal File, White House Central Files, DDE Lib.
DDE Pre	DDE Pre-Presidential Papers, DDE Lib.
DDE WHCF	White House Central Files, DDE Lib.

EE	Edgar Eisenhower
ER	Eleanor Roosevelt
GB	George Bush
GRF	Gerald R. Ford
GRF AV	Audiovisual Collection, GRF Lib.
GRF WHSoc	White House Social Office Central Files, GRF Lib.
GRF WHSoc-Subject	White House Social Office Central Files, Subject File, GRF Lib.
HJ	Hamilton Jordan
HRC	Hillary Rodham Clinton
HRH	H. R. Haldeman
HRH Notes	Richard Nixon to HRH in Haldeman's Notes, HRH Files, White House Special Files, RN PMP
HST	Harry S. Truman
HST AV	Audiovisual Archives, HST Lib.
HST Fam	Family Correspondence File, HST Papers, HST Lib.
HST OF	Official File, HST Papers, HST Lib.
HST PSF	President's Secretary's Files, HST Papers, HST Lib.
HST Soc	Social Correspondence File, HST Papers, HST Lib.
JBK	Jacqueline Bouvier Kennedy
JC	Jimmy Carter
JC AV	Audiovisual Archives, JC Lib.
JC Chron	Speechwriters Chronological File, JC Lib.
JC HJ	Hamilton Jordan Files, Chief of Staff, Staff Office Files, JC Lib.
JC PHF	President's Handwriting File, Office of Staff Secretary, JC Lib.
JC VF	Vertical Files, JC Lib.
JC WHCF	White House Central Files, JC Lib.
JFK	John Fitzgerald Kennedy
JFK AV	Audiovisual Archives, JFK Lib.
JFK Per	Personal Papers, JFK Papers, JFK Lib.
JFK POF	President's Office Files, Presidential Papers, JFK Lib.
JFK Pre	Pre-Presidential Papers, JFK Papers, JFK Lib.
JFK WHCF	White House Central Files, JFK Lib.
JFK WHSoc	White House Social Files, JFK Lib.
JNE	Julie Nixon Eisenhower
LaBJ	Lady Bird Johnson
LBJ	Lyndon Baines Johnson
LBJ AV	Audiovisual Collection, LBJ Lib.
LBJ CF	Confidential File, White House Central Files, LBJ Lib.
LBJ Liz-A	Alpha Files, Elizabeth Carpenter, White House Social Files, LBJ Lib.
LBJ Liz-S	Subject Files, Elizabeth Carpenter, White House Social Files, LBJ Lib.

LBJ Ref	Reference Files, LBJ Lib.
LBJ SN	LBJA, Selected Names File, LBJ Lib.
LBJ WHCF	White House Central Files, LBJ Lib.
LBJ WHSoc-A	Alpha File, White House Social Files, LBJ Lib.
LBJ WHSoc-B	Beautification Files, White House Social Files, LBJ Lib.
LBJA	LBJ Archives, LBJ Lib.
Liz	Elizabeth Carpenter
MDE	Mamie Doud Eisenhower
MDE MSS	MDE Papers, DDE Lib.
MDE WH	MDE, White House Social Office Files, DDE Lib.
MJM	Mary Jane McCaffree
MMT	Margaret Truman
MSE	Milton S. Eisenhower
NR	Nancy Reagan
PFC	President Ford Committee Records, GRF Lib.
PN	Pat Nixon
RFK	Robert F. Kennedy
RFK Pre	RFK Pre-Administration Papers, JFK Lib.
RN	Richard Nixon
RN HRH	HRH Files, White House Special Files, RN PMP
RN News	Annotated News Summaries, President's Office Files, RN PMP
RN POF	President's Office Files, RN PMP
RN PPF	President's Personal Files, RN PMP
RN WHSoc	White House Central Files, Subject Files, Social Affairs, RN PMP
RR	Ronald Reagan
RR AV	Audiovisual Archives, RR Lib.
RR News	White House News Summaries, RR Lib.
RSC	Rosalynn S. Carter
RSC VF	RSC Vertical Files, JC Lib.
SRW	Sheila Rabb Weidenfeld
WHCA	White House Communications Agency
WHORM	White House Office of Records Management, RR Lib.
WHSF	White House Special Files

Note: All other abbreviations are internal codes specific to the collections.

COLLECTIONS CITED

The Trumans

Audiovisual Archives, HST Lib.
Biographical, President's Secretary's Files, HST Lib.
Clark Clifford Papers, HST Lib.

Eben Ayers Papers, HST Lib.
Family Correspondence File, HST Papers, HST Lib.
Harry S. Truman Papers as President, HST Lib.
Longhand Notes, President's Secretary's Files, HST Lib.
Mary Paxton Keeley Papers, HST Lib.
Mary Ethel Noland Papers, HST Lib.
Miscellaneous Historical Documents Collection, HST Lib.
Official File, HST Papers, HST Lib.
Personal, President's Secretary's Files, HST Lib.
President's Secretary's Files, HST Papers, HST Lib.
Reathel Odum Papers, HST Lib.
Social Correspondence File, HST Papers
Speech File, President's Secretary's Files, HST Lib.
Vertical Files, HST Lib.

The Eisenhowers

Alfred M. Gruenther Papers, DDE Lib.
Ann C. Whitman Papers, DDE Lib.
Campaign Series, Ann C. Whitman File, DDE Papers as President, DDE Lib.
DDE Pre-Presidential Papers, 1916–1952, Principal File, DDE Lib.
Howard McCrum Snyder Papers, DDE Lib.
James C. Hagerty Papers, DDE Lib.
Mamie Doud Eisenhower Papers, Personal Correspondence, DDE Lib.
Mamie Doud Eisenhower Papers, SHAPE Series, DDE Lib.
Mamie Doud Eisenhower Papers, White House Social Office Files, DDE Lib.
Mary Jane McCaffree Papers, DDE Lib.
Name Series, Ann C. Whitman File, DDE Papers as President, DDE Lib.
President's Personal File, White House Central Files, DDE Lib.
White House Central Files, DDE Lib.
Young and Rubicam, Inc. Papers, DDE Lib.

The Kennedys

Arthur M. Schlesinger, Jr., Papers, JFK Lib.
Audiovisual Archives, JFK Lib.
Audiovisual Collection, National Archives
August Heckscher, White House Staff Files, JFK Lib.
John Kenneth Galbraith Papers, JFK Lib.
Personal Papers, JFK Papers, JFK Lib.
Pierre Salinger, White House Staff Files, JFK Lib.
Pre-Presidential Papers, JFK Lib.

President's Office Files, Presidential Papers, JFK Lib.
RFK Pre-Administration Papers, JFK Lib.
Theodore C. Sorensen Papers, JFK Lib.
Theodore H. White Papers, JFK Lib.
White House Social Files, JFK Lib.
White House Central Files, JFK Lib.

The Johnsons

Alpha Files, Elizabeth Carpenter, White House Social Files, LBJ Lib.
Alpha File, White House Social Files, LBJ Lib.
Audiovisual Collection, LBJ Lib.
Beautification Files, White House Social Files, LBJ Lib.
Bill Moyers Papers, Office Files of White House Aides, LBJ Lib.
Confidential File, White House Central Files, LBJ Lib.
Ellen Cooper Papers, LBJ Lib.
Family Correspondence, Lyndon B. Johnson Papers, LBJ Lib.
Fred Panzer, Office Files of White House Aides, LBJ Lib.
Handwriting File, Special Files, LBJ Lib.
Harry Middleton, Office Files of White House Aides, LBJ Lib.
Horace Busby, Office Files of White House Aides, LBJ Lib.
House of Representatives Papers, LBJ Lib.
Lyndon Baines Johnson Archives, 1934–1967, Selected Names File, LBJ Lib.
Lyndon Baines Johnson Archives, 1927–1963, Subject File, LBJ Lib.
Melvin Winters Papers, LBJ Lib.
Nash Castro Papers, LBJ Lib.
Office of the President File, Special Files, LBJ Lib.
Reference Files, LBJ Lib.
Statements of Lyndon Baines Johnson, Special Files, LBJ Lib.
Subject Files, Elizabeth Carpenter, White House Social Files, LBJ Lib.
White House Central Files, LBJ Lib.

The Nixons

Audiovisual Collection, National Archives
Alexander M. Haig Files, WHSF, RN PMP
Annotated News Summaries, President's Office Files, RN PMP
Confidential Files, WHSF, RN PMP
Dwight Chapin Files, WHSF, RN PMP
H. R. Haldeman Files, WHSF, RN PMP
John W. Dean Files, WHSF, RN PMP

John D. Ehrlichman Files, WHSF, RN PMP
Patrick J. Buchanan Files, WHSF, RN PMP
President's Personal Files, WHSF, RN PMP
President's Office Files, WHSF, RN PMP
Richard Nixon Scrapbook, RN Library and Birthplace
Ronald L. Ziegler Files, WHSF, RN PMP
Susan Porter Files, Staff Member and Office Files, RN PMP
White House Central Files, Subject Files, Social Affairs, RN PMP

The Fords

Audiovisual Collection, GRF Lib.
David Gergen Files, GRF Lib.
Elizabeth O'Neill Files, GRF Lib.
Eric Rosenberger and Douglas Blaser Files, GRF Lib.
Michael Raoul-Duval Files, GRF Lib.
Patricia Lindh and Jeanne Holm Files, GRF Lib.
President Ford Committee Records, GRF Lib.
Richard Cheney Files, GRF Lib.
Robert Teeter Papers, GRF Lib.
Robert Hartmann Papers, GRF Lib.
Ron Nessen Papers, GRF Lib.
Sheila Rabb Weidenfeld Files, GRF Lib.
Susan Porter Files, GRF Lib.
White House Central Files, GRF Lib.
White House Social Office Central Files, GRF Lib.
White House Social Office Central Files, Subject File, GRF Lib.

The Carters

Achsah Nesmith, Presidential Speechwriters, JC Lib.
Advance Office Files, JC Lib.
Audiovisual Archives, JC Lib.
Daniel Malachuk Files, White House Office of Administration, JC Lib.
Hamilton Jordan Files, Chief of Staff, Staff Office Files, JC Lib.
Hugh Carter Files, White House Office of Administration, JC Lib.
Jody Powell Files, Press Office, JC Lib.
Miller Center Interviews, JC Lib.
Peter Bourne Files, Special Assistant for Health Issues, JC Lib.
President's Handwriting File, Office of State Secretary, JC Lib.
Presidential Commission on Mental Health Papers, JC Lib.
Rosalynn Carter Vertical Files

Sarah Weddington Files, Special Assistant for Women's Affairs, JC Lib.
Speechwriters Chronological File, JC Lib.
Speechwriters Subject File, JC Lib.
Staff Office Files, JC Lib.
Vertical Files, JC Lib.
White House Central Files, JC Lib.
White House Central Files, Name File, JC Lib.

The Reagans

Audiovisual Archives, RR Lib.
Edwin A. Meese Files, Staff and Office Files, RR Lib.
Ellen Bradley Files, Staff and Office Files, RR Lib.
Mabel Brandon Files, Staff and Office Files, RR Lib.
Michael Deaver Files, Staff and Office Files, RR Lib.
Michael Baroody Files, Staff and Office Files, RR Lib.
Nancy Reagan Chronological Files, Michael Deaver Files, RR Lib.
Nancy Reagan Vertical Files, RR Lib.
White House Office of Records Management, RR Lib.
White House Alpha File, RR Lib.
White House News Summaries, RR Lib.

The Clintons

Clinton White House, Interdepartmental Working Group, National Archives, College Park, MD.
Hillary Rodham Clinton Website
(http://www1.whitehouse.gov/WH/EOP/First_Lady/html/who.html).

ORAL HISTORIES CITED

Bess Abell, LBJ Lib.
Henry Aurand, DDE Lib.
Eben Ayers, HST Lib.
Letitia Baldrige, JFK Lib.
Roberta Barrows, HST Lib.
Rhonda Bush, JC Lib.
Kathryn Cade, tape, JC Lib.
Elizabeth Carpenter, LBJ Lib.
Leslie Carpenter, LBJ Lib.
Lillian Carter, JC Lib.
Jimmy Carter and Rosalynn Smith Carter, National Park Service Interview

Henry Chiles, HST Lib.
George Christian, LBJ Lib.
Clark M. Clifford, LBJ Lib.
Jacqueline Cochran, DDE Lib.
Virginia Durr, LBJ Lib.
Milton S. Eisenhower, DDE Lib.
Tom Evans, HST Lib.
Sharon Francis, LBJ Lib.
Wallace H. Graham, HST Lib.
James C. Hagerty, DDE Lib.
Stephen Hess, DDE Lib.
Katherine G. Howard, Columbia Oral History Project
Henry Hirshberg, LBJ Lib.
Betty Hughes, LBJ Lib.
Albert Jacobs, DDE Lib.
Hamilton Jordan, JC Lib.
Mary Paxton Keeley, HST Lib.
Jacqueline Bouvier Kennedy, JFK Lib.
Gwendolyn B. King, RN PMP
Herbert G. Klein, RN PMP
Sigurd S. Larmon, DDE Lib.
Edward D. McKim, HST Lib.
Arthur Nevins, DDE Lib.
Mary Ethel Noland, HST Lib.
Reathel Odum, HST Lib.
Mize Peters, HST Lib.
Betty Pope, JC Lib.
Jody Powell, JC Lib.
Dan Quill, LBJ Lib.
Elizabeth Rowe, LBJ Lib.
Pierre Salinger, JFK Lib.
Emily Crow Selden, LBJ Lib.
Willard Slappey, JC Lib.
Ellis D. Slater, DDE Lib.
George Smathers, JFK Lib.
Allie Smith, JC Lib.
Jerrold Smith, JC Lib.
Merriman Smith, DDE Lib.
Connie Stuart, RN PMP
Connie Stuart, exit interview, RN PMP
Willie Day Taylor, LBJ Lib.
Allethea Smith Wall, JC Lib.
Ann C. Whitman, DDE Lib.

NOTES

**PROLOGUE. SEARCHING FOR PERFECT COUPLES
IN THE SHADOW OF FDR AND ER**

Page

2   used as early as . . . : William Safire, *Safire's Political Dictionary*, rev. ed. (New York, 1978), p. 231.

2   "Presidential trademark": *Nwswk*, 8 Nov. 1948, p. 13.

2   celebrities: See Lewis Gould, "First Ladies," *American Scholar* 55 (1986): 528–535.

2   Rorschach test: See, for example, Lewis Gould, "Modern First Ladies in Historical Perspective," *Presidential Studies Quarterly* 15 (Summer 1985): 537; Ann Lewis in *Vanity Fair*, June 1994, p. 154.

2   rise of feminism: See Betty Boyd Caroli, *First Ladies* (New York, 1987), p. 279. Carl Sferrazza Anthony, *First Ladies*, 2 vols. (New York, 1990–1991), 2:443.

2   "officer or employee . . .": *Association of American Physicians and Surgeons, Inc. et al. v. Hillary Rodham Clinton et al.*, 997 F.2d 898, 904 (U.S. App. D.C. 22 June 1993).

3   "A good wife . . .": *Life*, 7 Jan. 1952, pp. 33, 44.

3   "Politics today . . .": *LHJ*, Oct. 1960, p. 73.

3   "anti-image": John Demos, *Past, Present, and Personal* (New York, 1986), p. 37.

3   "two for the . . .": Judith Warner, *Hillary Clinton* (New York, 1993), p. 164.

4   image-building, not power-sharing: For the latest "systematic" and "quantitative" look at the First Lady's power in a journal dedicated to a "Reassessment of Presidents and First Ladies" see Karen O'Connor, Bernadette Nye, and Laura Van Assendelft, "Wives in the White House: The Political Influence of First Ladies," *Presidential Studies Quarterly* 26 (Summer 1996):835–853.

5   "domesticated": Paula Baker, "The Domestication of Politics: Women and American Political Society, 1780–1920," *American Historical Review*, 89 (June 1984): 620–647. Robert L. Griswold, *Fatherhood in America* (New York, 1993), p. 7.

5   "personifies the . . .": Westbrook Pegler in U.S. Congress, House, 77th Cong., 2nd. sess., 19 Jan. 1942, *Appendix to CR*, 88:A154.

5   "you don't elect . . .": ER press conference, 19 Dec. 1938, Betty Houchin Winfield,

"Anna Eleanor Roosevelt's White House Legacy," *Presidential Studies Quarterly,* 18 (Spring 1988): 340.

5   "an almost . . .": ER in Elliott Roosevelt with James Brough, *An Untold Story* (New York, 1973), p. 40.

5   "business partners": James Roosevelt with Bill Libby, *My Parents* (Chicago, 1976), p. 101.

6   "trial balloon": ER, *This I Remember* (New York, 1949), p. 164.

6   "glorious . . .": ER in James R. Kearney, *Anna Eleanor Roosevelt* (Boston, 1968), p. 276.

6   "spur": ER, *Remember,* p. 349.

6   "a hair shirt": William Chafe, "Biographical Sketch," in Joan Hoff-Wilson and Marjorie Lightman, *Without Precedent* (Bloomington, IN, 1984), p. 11.

6   "You kiss . . .": Doris Kearns Goodwin, *No Ordinary Time* (New York, 1994), p. 539.

6   Many heard . . . : Frank Friedel, *Franklin D. Roosevelt: Launching the New Deal* (Boston, 1973), p. 291.

6   "breed": Liz Carpenter, *Ruffles & Flourishes* (Garden City, NY, 1970), p. 113.

6   although society reporters . . . : Allida M. Black, *Casting Her Own Shadow* (New York, 1996), p. 25.

6   "You are the interpreters . . .": ER press conference, 6 Mar. 1933, Maurine H. Beasley, *Eleanor Roosevelt and the Media* (Urbana, IL, 1987), pp. 38, 187.

6   "managed to conceal . . .": Elliott Roosevelt, *Untold,* p. 308.

7   inching away from . . . : See Alan Brinkley, *The End of Reform* (New York, 1995), pp. 265, 267.

7   "progressive social . . ." Joseph P. Lash, *Eleanor and Franklin* (New York, 1971), pp. 823, 843, 842.

7   "fire-fighting . . .": ER, *Remember,* pp. 231, 240.

7   "was glad to . . .": Anna Rosenberg in Lash, *Eleanor and,* p. 829.

7   "plain, ordinary . . .": ER in Blanche Wiesen Cook, *Eleanor Roosevelt,* vol. 1, *1884–1933* (New York, 1992), 1:472.

7   "humanitarian . . .": Susan Ware, "ER and Democratic Politics," in Hoff-Wilson and Lightman, *Without Precedent,* pp. 56, 53.

7   "maternal values . . .": See Theda Skocpol, *Protecting Soldiers and Mothers* (Cambridge, MA, 1992), p. 318.

7   "white glove . . .": NR, "Remarks for Associated Press Publisher's Luncheon," 4 May 1987, p. 6, F95-109, WHORM.

8   By 1939 . . . : Winfield, "ER," p. 333.

8   "that people . . .": ER, *Remember,* p. 164.

8   "I don't want . . .": Lash, *Eleanor and,* p. 829.

8   "on the job": *NYT,* 30 Sept. 1941, p. 28.

8   "every activity . . .": ER, *Remember,* pp. 230–231.

8   "I can't take . . .": Goodwin, *No Ordinary,* p. 324.

8   her power: For recent celebrations of her influence see Joseph P. Lash, "Foreword," p. vii, and Lois Scharf, "ER and Feminism," p. 232 in Hoff-Wilson and Lightman, *Without Precedent.* See Goodwin, *No Ordinary,* for a more balanced but still sympathetic view.

8   "Cabinet minister . . .": Chafe, "Biographical," p. 11.

8   "and tend to . . .": Goodwin, *No Ordinary,* p. 204.

8   "grew up in . . .": Donnie Radcliffe, *Simply Barbara Bush* (New York, 1989), p. 13.

9   "too tall . . .": Cook, *ER,* 1:1.

9   "He is the one . . .": *SatEP,* 24 Aug. 1940, p. 28.

9   "First things . . .": ER, *Remember,* p. 162.

9   "further socialize . . .": Representative Eugene Cox in Lash, *Eleanor and,* p. 837.

9   "if the communities . . .": *NYT,* 11 Feb. 1942, p. 15.

9   "instructions in . . .": *NYT,* 7 Feb. 1942, p. 1.

9   "unfavorable press": ER, *Remember,* p. 238.

9   "a woman . . .": U.S. Congress, House, 77th Cong., 2nd. sess., 9 Feb. 1942, *CR,* 88:1155.

9   "as an assistant . . .": Lash, *Eleanor and,* p. 841.

9   "as long as . . .": ER, *Remember,* p. 250.

10   "to go on . . .": Cook, *ER,* 1:15–16.

10   "small and . . .": Lash, *Eleanor and,* p. 842.

10   "I guess . . .": ER press conference, Mar. 1942 in Beasley, *ER and Media,* p. 150.

10   "Lead your . . .": *NYT,* 20 Apr. 1924, 9:2.

10   "convinced me . . .": ER, *Remember,* p. 261.

10   "keeping quiet . . .": Lash, *Eleanor and,* p. 845.

10   hate mail . . . : Tamara K. Hareven, *Eleanor Roosevelt* (Chicago, 1968), p. 273.

10   "the most . . .": Goodwin, *No Ordinary,* p. 371.

10   "She exercised . . .": Elliott Roosevelt and James Brough, *Mother R.* (New York, 1977), p. 44.

10   "absolutely no . . .": Goodwin, *No Ordinary,* p. 471.

10   "He was a . . .": Elliott Roosevelt, *Untold,* p. 354.

10   "lived those . . .": ER, *Remember,* pp. 350–351.

11   Roosevelt helped forge . . . : See, for example, Barbara Kellerman, *The Political Presidency* (New York, 1984); Samuel Kernell, *Going Public* (Washington, DC, 1986); Theodore J. Lowi, *The Personal President* (Ithaca, 1985). For an alternate view see Richard Pious, *The American Presidency* (New York, 1979), p. 16.

11   "rather bleak": Anthony, *Ladies,* 1:486.

11   "even if . . .": ER, "Wives of Great Men," *Liberty,* 1932, quoted in Cook, *ER,* 1:424.

11   "like many other . . .": *LHJ,* Apr. 1945, p. 33.

11   "It is wonderful . . .": Cook, *ER,* 1:19.

12   "that there . . .": RSC, BF in Anthony, *Ladies,* 1:470.

12   "idolized . . .": RR, *An American Life* (New York, 1990), p. 66.

12   common ideals . . . : On uniformity see Robert S. Lynd and Helen Merrell Lynd, *Middletown* (San Diego, 1929, 1956), pp. 490–491; Warren Susman, *Culture as History* (New York, 1984), pp. 150–210.

12   middle-class prosperity . . . : On consumerism and prosperity see Jackson Lears, *Fables of Abundance* (New York, 1994); on gentility see Richard Bushman, *The Refinement of America* (New York, 1992); on morality see Gertrude Himmelfarb, *The Demoralization of Society* (New York, 1995), p. 261.

12   except Betty . . . : Betty Bloomer studied dance on the Bennington College campus but was not enrolled.

13   "In this as . . .": Rebekah Baines Johnson to LBJ, c. 10 Apr. 1937, Box 1, Family Correspondence, LBJ Lib.

13   "Lives of . . .": RN, *In the Arena* (New York, 1990), p. 84.

13   "I look around . . .": Richard Reeves, *President Kennedy* (New York, 1993), p. 14.

13   "men are God's . . .": Lynd and Lynd, *Middletown,* p. 118.

13   "programmed for . . .": John A. Clausen, *American Lives* (New York, 1993), p. 10.

13   "Now, Nancy . . .": NR with William Novak, *My Turn* (New York, 1989), pp. 76–77.

13   "companionate marriage": Steven Mintz and Susan Kellogg, *Domestic Revolutions* (New York, 1988), p. xvi.

13   " 'Let well . . .": Lynd and Lynd, *Middletown,* p. 120.

13   bargain: see Alan Ehrenhalt, *The Lost City* (New York, 1995), p. 3. For one of many dissenting opinions, see Stephanie Coontz, *The Way We Never Were* (New York, 1992).

14   average life-span . . . : *Historical Statistics of the United States* (Washington, DC, 1975), p. 55.

14   "enablers": See *Current Health,* Jan. 1992, p. 24.

14   "washing, ironing . . .": *Collier's,* 9 July 1954, p. 34.

14   "Life was . . .": JNE, *Pat Nixon: The Untold Story* (New York, 1978), p. 238.

14   common culture: On this "high . . . degree of cultural unity," even in a diverse, polyglot society, see William L. O'Neill, *A Democracy at War* (New York, 1993), p. 8.

14   the artist . . . : Susman, *Culture as History,* p. 194.

14   "How America . . .": *LHJ,* Mar. 1942, pp. 107, 112.

15 "defense haircut . . .": *LHJ,* May 1942, p. 28.

15 Nearly one-third . . . : *Historical Statistics,* p. 134.

15 "History! . . ." Theodore H. White, *In Search of History* (New York, 1978), p. 523.

15 "other little . . .": *Life,* 6 Dec. 1963, p. 160.

16 "little . . . naked . . .": Theodore H. White, "Original Hand-written Notes of 'Camelot' Interview with Mrs. Kennedy," pp. 4, 5, Theodore H. White MSS, JFK Lib.

16 "line from . . .": *Life,* 6 Dec. 1963, p. 160.

16 "for him . . .": White, *Search,* p. 523.

16 "closest thing . . .": White, "Camelot," p. 5.

17 "we" generation: Ambrose in O'Neill, *Democracy,* p. 432.

17 "values matter . . .": See Ben Wattenberg, *Values Matter Most* (New York, 1995); George Lakoff, *Moral Politics* (Chicago, 1996), p. 240.

17 a preoccupation . . . : See Michael J. Sandel, *Democracy's Discontent* (Cambridge, MA, 1996), p. 6.

17 "housekeepers for . . .": See Skocpol, *Protecting Soldiers,* p. 51.

CHAPTER 1. "JUST THE WIFE OF THE PRESIDENT"

Page

19 "REQUEST IMMEDIATE . . .": Adam Clayton Powell to HST, 1 Oct. 1945, HST OF 93.

19 "If you . . .": Powell to BWT, 11 Oct. 1945, p. 2, HST OF 93.

20 "decided she . . .": MMT, *Bess W. Truman* (New York, 1986), p. 279.

20 "lengthy discussion . . .": Diary, 12 Oct. 1945, Box 16, Eben Ayers MSS, HST Lib.

20 "racial discrimination . . .": HST to Powell, 12 Oct. 1945, Box 43, HST Soc.

20 "that the invitation . . .": BWT to Powell, 12 Oct. 1945, Box 43, HST Soc.

20 "Why not?": *ChiT,* 13 Oct. 1945, pp. 24, 8.

20 "MRS. TRUMAN . . .": *Denver Post,* 13 Oct. 1945, p. 1.

20 "gives sanction . . .": *WDN,* 13 Oct. 1945, p. 5.

20 "a public institution . . .": *NYT,* 13 Oct. 1945, p. 17.

21 "that damn . . .": Robert J. Donovan, *Conflict and Crisis* (New York, 1977), p. 148. See also Charles V. Hamilton, *Adam Clayton Powell, Jr.* (New York, 1991), p. 165.

21 Junior Jaycees': *Birmingham News,* 11 Oct. 1945, p. 2.

21 "TRUMAN ASSAILS . . .": *WasS,* 12 Oct. 1945, p. 1.

21 "American . . .": *KCS,* 13 Oct. 1945, p. 10.

21 "the Hitler philosophy . . .": U.S. Congress, House, 79th Cong., 1st sess., 24 Oct. 1945, *CR,* 92:10026.

21 "communistic attacks . . .": 16 Oct. 1945, *CR,* 91:9675.

21 "policy of . . .": 18 Oct. 1945, *CR,* 91:9791.

21 "the patriotic and . . .": U.S. Congress, Senate, 79th Cong., 1st sess., 26 Oct. 1945, *CR,* 92:10074.

22 "this recent controversy . . .": *KCS,* 15 Oct. 1945, p. 1.

22 "because of its . . .": *WasP,* 18 Oct. 1945, B1.

22 "the war hasn't . . .": *NYP,* 15 Oct. 1945, p. 20.

22 "condone[d]": Edward Rosenhahn to BWT, 15 Oct. 1945, Box 125, HST Soc.

22 "stand on . . .": Frances E. Nease to BWT, 13 Oct. 1945, Box 125, HST Soc.

22 "The American public . . .": Mrs. Edwin S. Schweig to BWT, 13 Oct. 1945, pp. 1–2, Box 125, HST Soc.

22 "Thank God . . .": Mrs. Boell to BWT, 18 Oct. 1945, Box 125, HST Soc.

22 "All this horror . . .": Mrs. Charlotte Rosenthal to BWT, 12 Oct. 1945, Box 125, HST Soc.

22 tea with . . . : A. R. Smith to BWT, 17 Oct. 1945, Box 125, HST Soc.

23 "At last . . .": C. C. Brown, telegram, 15 Oct. 1945, HST OF 93.

23 "One has to . . .": Susie M. Baird to BWT, 22 Oct. 1945, p. 3, Box 125, HST Soc.

23 "cheap . . .": E. A. Roberts to BWT, 12 Oct. 1945, Box 125, HST Soc.

23 "that you stay . . .": Lillian A. Chambers to BWT, 22 Oct. 1945, Box 125, HST Soc.

23   "I agree . . .": MMT, *BWT,* p. 279.

23   "Much damage . . .": Ibid.

23   "the battle . . .": *Miami Herald,* 9 Sept. 1945, D1.

23   "profoundly . . .": *WDN,* 25 Nov. 1946, p. 39.

24   "For Heaven's . . .": Evelyn Peyton Gordon, "Some Advice to Debutantes," *WDN,* c. Spring 1946, BWT VF.

24   twenty Army trucks: David McCullough, *Truman* (New York, 1992), p. 382.

24   "Well, what . . .": *NYTM,* 10 Apr. 1949, 6:7.

24   "After a diet . . .": Alonzo L. Hamby, *Man of the People* (New York, 1995), p. 298.

24   "people's President . . .": CBS "Person to Person," 27 May 1955, HST AV.

24   "their pencils . . .": Helen Brown in Carl Sferrazza Anthony, *First Ladies,* 2 vols. (New York, 1990), 1:517.

24   former teacher: See, for example, *WasS,* 15 Apr. 1945, B1.

24   "her preferred . . .": *ChiT,* 13 Apr. 1945, p. 2.

24   "maidless": *WasS,* 13 Apr. 1945, A6.

24   "new and . . .": *ChiDN,* 13 Apr. 1945, p. 17.

24   "model wife": *Providence Evening Bulletin,* 13 Apr. 1945, p. 8.

24   "trim": Ibid.

25   "plump": *ChiDN,* 13 Apr. 1945, p. 17.

25   "A career . . .": Ibid.

25   "helped . . .": *WasS,* 13 Apr. 1945, A6.

25   "She is . . .": *ChiDN,* 13 Apr. 1945, p. 17.

25   "NEW FIRST . . .": *ChiDN,* 13 Apr. 1945, p. 17.

25   "childhood . . .": *WasS,* 13 Apr. 1945, A6.

25   "I cannot . . .": *ChiT,* 13 Apr. 1945, p. 2.

25   "Four Eyes": Mize Peters OH, p. 11. See also Mary Ethel Noland OH, p. 58.

25   "sissy": McCullough, *Truman,* p. 45.

25   "town schooling": William Hillman, *Mr. President* (New York, 1952), p. 159.

25   "a little . . .": HST in *NYT,* 7 Nov. 1950, p. 17.

25   "She never . . .": Richard Lawrence Miller, *Truman* (New York, 1986), p. 40.

25   "top-drawer": See Mary Paxton Keeley OH, p. 23.

25   "the queenliest woman . . .": Alfred Steinberg, *The Man from Missouri* (New York, 1962), p. 35.

25   tomboy: Henry Chiles OH, p. 19.

26   "your grandfather . . .": MMT, *BWT,* p. 234.

26   "Well, I saw . . .": Ibid., p. 32.

26   "clodhopper": HST to BWT, 19 Nov. 1913 in Robert H. Ferrell, ed., *Dear Bess* (New York, 1983), p. 143.

26   "empty head[ed]": HST to BWT, [18] July 1912, p. 1, Box 1, HST Fam.

26   frontier tradition: See David Donald, "The Folklore Lincoln," *Lincoln Reconsidered,* rev. ed. (New York, 1961), p. 154.

27   "I really . . .": HST to BWT, 5 Sept. 1911 in Ferrell, *Bess,* p. 45.

27   "become engaged . . .": HST to BWT, 28 Apr. 1915 in Ferrell, *Bess,* p. 182.

27   "a guy . . .": HST to BWT, 19 Nov. 1913 in Ferrell, *Bess,* p. 145.

27   "that I was . . .": Robert H. Ferrell, ed., *The Autobiography of Harry S. Truman* (Boulder, CO, 1980), p. 41.

27   "It really . . .": HST to BWT, 20 Oct. 1918, pp. 3, 4, Box 4, HST Fam.

28   "companionate marriage": Steven Mintz and Susan Kellogg, *Domestic Revolutions* (New York, 1988), p. xvi.

28   democratic love story: See Richard L. Bushman, *The Refinement of America* (New York, 1992), p. 423.

28   "silly": BWT to Mary Ethel Noland, 23 Nov. 1944, p. 4, Box 1, Mary Ethel Noland MSS, HST Lib.

29   "my girl": HST to BWT and MMT, 18 July 1930, Box 5, HST Fam.

29   "Don't spank . . .": HST to BWT, 4 May 1933, Box 5, HST Fam.

29 "sentimental": HST to BWT, 19 Nov. 1913 in Ferrell, *Bess,* p. 145.

29 "never": Tom Evans OH, 3:599.

29 "warmth and hospitality": *KCS,* 9 June 1935, A2.

29 "cooped up": MMT with Margaret Cousins, *Souvenir* (New York, 1956), p. 37.

29 "like a . . .": HST to BWT, 18 June 1935 in Ferrell, *Bess,* p. 363.

29 "I am so . . .": BWT to Mary Ethel Noland, undated, Box 1, Noland MSS.

30 job holders: HST to BWT, 17 June 1936 in Ferrell, *Bess,* p. 387.

30 "genius": HST to BWT, 23 July 1935 in Ferrell, *Bess,* p. 373.

30 "He never . . .": Reathel Odum OH, pp. 134–135.

30 "untold and yeoman . . .": HST to BWT, 17 June 1940 in Ferrell, *Bess,* p. 437.

30 "seeing the senator . . .": "Mrs. Truman Spurns Active Campaign Role," *Kansas City Journal,* c. 1940, clipping, BWT VF.

30 "But Mommy . . .": HST to BWT, 1 May 1942 in Ferrell, *Bess,* p. 475.

30 "When a man . . .": HST to BWT, 28 June 1942 in Ferrell, *Bess,* p. 480.

30 Truman understood . . . : See Edward D. McKim OH, p. 99; Lewis B. Schwellenbach to HST, 13 Apr. 1945, Box 307, HST PSF.

31 "that I had . . .": HST to BWT, 12 July 1943 in Ferrell, *Bess,* p. 495.

31 "I've talked . . .": MMT, *Souvenir,* p. 64.

31 could not afford: Jonathan Daniels, *The Man of Independence* (Philadelphia, 1950), p. 231.

31 too minor: Ibid.

31 "I've had . . .": Evans OH, 2:335.

31 "a dozen senators . . .": Ibid., 2:335a.

31 "every effort": Ferrell, *Autobiography,* p. 87.

31 "Are we going . . .": MMT, *Souvenir,* p. 68.

31 "gloomy Victorian . . .": *Life,* 21 Aug. 1944, p. 77.

31 "Certainly my wife . . .": Frank McNaughton and Walter Hehmeyer, *This Man Truman* (New York, 1945), p. 183.

31 "Marg has gone . . .": BWT to Noland, 30 Mar. 1945, p. 2, Box 1, Noland MSS.

32 "It is a . . .": HST to Emmy Southern, 13 May 1945 in Robert H. Ferrell, ed., *Off the Record* (New York, 1980), p. 23.

32 "President Truman . . .": *NYTM,* 30 Nov. 1952, 6:14.

32 "Harry, if you . . .": *NYT,* 23 May 1945, p. 21.

32 "a valet . . .": HST to Noland, 24 Sept. 1950, Noland MSS.

33 "sobsister": HST to Ethel Noland, 1 Nov. 1918, in Monte M. Poen, *Letters Home by Harry Truman* (New York, 1984), p. 47.

33 Knowing that . . . : Maurine H. Beasley, *Eleanor Roosevelt and the Media* (Urbana, IL, 1987), p. 57.

33 "I don't know . . .": Frances Perkins in Jhan Robbins, *Bess & Harry* (New York, 1980), pp. 80–81.

34 "began her . . .": *NYT,* 16 May 1945, p. 17.

34 "Mrs. Truman . . .": Robbins, *Bess & Harry,* p. 82.

34 "All questions . . .": Eben A. Ayers, memorandum, 18 May 1945, Box 3, Reathel Odum MSS, HST Lib.

34 "in the long run . . .": HST in Hillman, *Mr. President,* p. 11.

34 "any use . . .": BWT to Reathel Odum, 22 Oct. 1969, Box 3, Odum MSS.

34 "Am hoping for . . .": BWT to Bess Furman, 16 Apr. 1948, Box 5, Odum MSS.

34 "leading hostess": *WasS,* 15 Apr. 1945, B1.

34 "Woman's real . . .": *McCall's,* Jan. 1951, pp. 26, 52.

35 "nobody . . .": MMT, ed., *Where the Buck Stops* (New York, 1989), pp. 257, 256.

35 Bess Truman sponsored . . .: See "List of Organizations . . ." in Box 5, Odum MSS.

35 "one of these . . .": BWT to HST, 12 Nov. 1946 in MMT, *Letters from Father* (New York, 1981), p. 185.

35 "Bess was . . .": HST to Mary Truman, 1 Nov. 1947 in Poen, *Letters,* p. 214.

35 "dinner hour . . .": *WasS,* 16 Nov. 1945, B6.

35 "America's most ornate . . .": *NYTM,* 20 Feb. 1949, 6:12.
35 "We have watched . . .": Mary L. Johnson to HST, 2 Feb. 1950, pp. 1, 2, Box 325, HST PSF Personal.
35 "an item . . .": *SatEP,* 30 Nov. 1946, p. 22.
36 "I have a . . .": HST to MMT, 22 Dec. 1946 in MMT, *Letters from Father,* p. 87.
36 the ritual: HST to BWT, 3 Oct. 1947, p. 1, Box 8, HST Fam.
36 "that he had . . .": *NYT,* 1 Aug. 1949, p. 20.
36 "demonstrative . . .": HST to BWT, 18 Nov. 1913 in Ferrell, *Bess,* p. 144.
36 "wasn't happy . . .": HST Diary, 7 July 1945 in Ferrell, *Off the Record,* p. 49.
36 "I'm sorry . . .": HST to BWT, 6 July 1945 in Ferrell, *Bess,* p. 517.
37 "I spent the . . .": HST to BWT, 29 July 1945 in Ferrell, *Bess,* p. 522.
37 "It isn't polls . . .": HST, "Polls . . . ," pp. 1–2, Box 334, Longhand Notes, HST PSF.
37 "relapsed into . . .": MMT, *Souvenir,* p. 109.
37 "bedlam": BWT to Reathel Odum, 8 June 1945, Box 5, Odum MSS.
37 "merry-go-round": BWT to Madeline [Mahoney], 30 July 1945, #660, Miscellaneous Historical Documents Collection, HST Lib.
37 "None of this . . .": *Collier's,* 9 Feb. 1952, p. 60.
37 "Imagine a President's . . .": Ibid.
37 "President Truman forever! . . .": Robbins, *Bess & Harry,* p. 110.
37 "What was Eddie . . .": Odum OH, p. 72.
37 "was scared . . .": Roberta Barrows OH, pp. 92–93.
38 "one of the . . .": *NYT,* 26 Dec. 1945, p. 1.
38 "It's a very . . .": MMT, *BWT,* p. 281.
38 "I had never . . .": MMT, *First Ladies* (New York, 1995), pp. 77–78.
38 "You can never . . .": HST to BWT, 28 Dec. 1945 in Ferrell, *Bess,* p. 524.
38 "one of the . . .": MMT, *First Ladies,* p. 78. See also Hamby, *Man,* p. 344.
38 "babying the Soviets": Daniels, *The Man,* p. 310.
39 "the real riot . . .": Ibid.
39 "cordial meeting": James Byrne, *All in One Lifetime* (New York, 1958), p. 343.
39 "such a letter . . .": Ibid., p. 402.
39 "vastly exaggerate . . .": Dean Acheson, *Present at the Creation* (New York, 1969), p. 136; Hamby, *Man,* p. 345.
39 turbulent Christmas: Ibid. See also HST, *Memoirs,* 2 vols. (Garden City, NY, 1955–1956) 1:549–552; Donovan, *Conflict,* pp. 159–161.
39 Typically Bess awoke . . . : Hamby, *Man,* pp. 467–468.
39 "Three Musketeers": Lillian Rogers Park, *My Thirty Years Backstairs at the White House* (New York, 1961), p. 275.
39 "If I expressed . . .": MMT, *Letters from Father,* p. 26.
39 "Mrs. T . . .": Form letter, "This will acknowledge . . . ," Box 3, Odum MSS.
40 "relieve[s] . . .": Memorandum to Reathel Odum, 4 Apr. 1946, Box 4, Odum MSS.
40 "small-townish . . .": *Pittsburgh Post-Gazette,* 16 Apr. 1946, p. 6.
40 "got out . . .": *Life,* 22 Apr. 1946, p. 45.
40 "Pledge . . .": *NYT,* 7 June 1946, p. 22.
40 "set a good example": Robbins, *Harry & Bess,* p. 98.
40 "It was nice . . .": HST to BWT, 16 Sept. 1946, p. 3, Box 8, HST Fam.
40 "even when . . .": HST to BWT, 18 Nov. 1946 in Ferrell, *Bess,* p. 540.
40 "get awfully . . .": BWT to Mary Paxton Keeley, 8 Jan. 1946, pp. 2–3, Box 1, Mary Paxton Keeley MSS, HST Lib.
40 "but my conscience . . .": BWT to Helen [Souter], 17 Sept. 1946, p. 1, #572, Miscellaneous Historical Documents Collection, HST Lib.
41 175 days: Hamby, *Man,* p. 483.
41 "press boys": HST to BWT, 2 Mar. 1948 in Poen, *Letters,* p. 233.
41 "more fun . . .": Evelyn Peyton Gordon, "If President Isn't Entitled to Vacation, Who Is?" *WDN,* clipping, BWT VF.
41 "absolute privacy": HST to BWT, 22 Aug. 1946 in Ferrell, *Bess,* p. 533.

41 "I go swimmin' . . .": Ken Hechler, *Working with Truman* (New York, 1982), p. 114.

41 "crackpots . . .": HST to BWT, 19 Sept. 1946 in Ferrell, *Bess,* p. 538.

41 "greatest ambition . . .": Clifford in Irwin Ross, *The Loneliest Campaign* (New York, 1948), p. 9.

41 "I'd be much . . .": HST to BWT, 24 Sept. 1947, p. 2, Box 8, HST Fam.

41 "that he did . . .": Robert H. Ferrell, ed. *Truman in the White House: The Diary of Eben A. Ayers* (Columbia, MO, 1991), p. 242.

41 "the welfare . . .": HST, *Memoirs,* 2:17.

42 "Better tell . . .": BWT to Reathel Odum, c. 11 Oct. 1946, Box 5, Odum MSS.

42 "terse, tart . . .": *Time,* 10 Nov. 1947, p. 24. See also *Nwswk,* 10 Nov. 1947, p. 16.

42 Wallgren introduced . . .: MMT, *BWT,* p. 320.

42 "to run . . .": Robbins, *Bess & Harry,* p. 123.

42 "people's crusade": HST remarks, 28 Oct. 1948, Box 7, Speech File, HST PSF.

42 "And now . . .": *NYer,* 9 Oct. 1948, pp. 63–64.

43 "Mrs. Truman . . .": "Recollections of the 1948 Campaign," p. 4, Box 23, Clark Clifford MSS, HST Lib.

43 "Truman ladies . . .": *Nwswk,* 8 Nov. 1948, p. 13.

43 "It never occurred . . .": MMT, *Souvenir,* p. 215.

43 "It put . . .": *Nwswk,* 8 Nov. 1948, p. 13.

43 "children of the sturdy . . .": John M. Crane, *The Pictorial Biography of HST* (Philadelphia, 1948), pp. 12, 3 in Box 298, Biographical, HST PSF.

43 "her husband's . . .": Ibid., p. 12.

43 "Mrs. Average . . .": *Smithfield* (NC) *Herald,* 22 Oct. 1948, p. 12.

43 "Our job . . .": MMT, *Souvenir,* p. 235.

43 "Good morning . . .": *NYT,* 27 Sept. 1948, p. 15.

43 "I don't seem . . .": BWT to Mary [Paxton Keeley], 2 Aug. 1948, Box 1, Keeley MSS. See also, Hamby, *Man,* p. 476.

44 "more noises . . .": HST to MMT, 11 Aug. 1948 in Poen, *Letters,* p. 223.

44 "The President's . . .": *Look,* 1 Mar. 1949, p. 56; *Collier's,* 12 Feb. 1949, p. 63.

44 "Dignity, reserve . . .": *Collier's,* 12 Feb. 1949, p. 63.

44 "self-effacing . . .": *Look,* 1 Mar. 1949, p. 56; *McCall's,* Apr. 1949, p. 18.

44 "She doesn't try . . .": *Look,* 1 Mar. 1949, p. 55.

45 "demure housewife . . .": *Collier's,* 12 Feb. 1949, p. 65.

45 "simple American . . .": *McCall's,* Apr. 1949, p. 98.

45 "in-depth": *Life,* 11 July 1949, p. 89.

45 "comparative wealth": *McCall's,* Apr. 1949, pp. 96–97.

45 "finest things . . .": *NYT,* 16 Aug. 1949, p. 1.

45 "does not . . .": *SatEP,* 30 Nov. 1946, p. 23.

45 "wishes to . . .": Statement, 6 Mar. 1947, Box 43, HST Soc.

45 "so they . . .": HST to Judge F. Ryan Duffy, 1 Dec. 1947, Box 325, Personal, HST PSF.

45 "Would she . . .": *Life,* 8 Sept. 1947, p. 42.

45 "a career in which . . .": *NYTM,* 19 June 1949, 6:12.

46 "is really *interested* . . .": BWT to Mary Paxton Keeley, 14 Apr. 1947, Box 1, Keeley MSS.

46 "the womanly ideal . . .": HST to Thomas E. H. Black, 15 Mar. 1951, Box 325, Personal, HST PSF.

46 "business failure . . .": HST to BWT, 29 June 1949 in Ferrell, *Off the Record,* p. 158.

46 "Remember . . . The Blackstone . . .": Ibid., p. 159.

46 "eight years . . .": HST Diary, 16 Apr. 1950 in Ferrell, *Off the Record,* p. 177.

46 "sure that . . .": MMT, *BWT,* p. 353.

47 "had something . . .": HST to Ethel Noland, 13 Sept. 1950 in Ferrell, *Off the Record,* pp. 199, 198.

47 "name . . .": HST to Ethel Noland, 17 Nov. 1950 in Ferrell, *Off the Record,* pp. 190–191.

47 "I've worked . . .": HST Diary, 9 Dec. 1950 in Ferrell, *Off the Record,* p. 204.

47 "To err . . .": See, for example, Robert H. Ferrell, *Harry S. Truman, A Life* (Columbia, MO, 1994), p. 218.

47 "averageness": *Life,* 10 Dec. 1951, p. 36.

48 "cannot sing . . .": *Time,* 18 Dec. 1950, p. 17.

48 "was the varnish . . .": HST Diary, 9 Dec. 1950 in Ferrell, *Off the Record,* p. 204.

48 "I've made . . .": HST to Nellie and Ethel Noland, 8 Sept. 1949 in Ferrell, *Off the Record,* p. 164.

48 "paid mental . . .": Monte M. Poen, *Strictly Personal and Confidential* (Boston, 1982), p. 9.

48 "guttersnipe . . .": HST to Paul Hume, 6 Dec. 1950 in Hamby, *Man,* p. 478.

48 "It was Harry . . .": MMT, *BWT,* p. 366.

48 "Well I've had . . .": HST Diary, 9 Dec. 1950 in Ferrell, *Off the Record,* p. 204.

48 "stuffed . . .": HST to Barbara Heggie, 20 Dec. 1950 in Ferrell, *Off the Record,* p. 205.

48 "The President's . . .": *New York Enquirer,* 11 Dec. 1950, clipping, Box 325, Personal, HST PSF.

49 "The trouble . . .": MMT, *Harry S. Truman* (New York, 1973), p. 503.

49 "Mrs. Wallace always . . .": Arthur Prettyman in Robbins, *Bess & Harry,* pp. 136–137.

49 "It is lovely . . .": Madge G. Wallace to Mary Paxton Keeley, 29 Apr. 1946, Box 1, Keeley MSS.

49 "treated her . . .": Wallace H. Graham OH, p. 61.

49 "the grandmother . . .": See, for example, 29 Feb. 1952 and 4 Mar. 1952, Box 333, Longhand Notes, HST PSF.

49 "piled high . . .": BWT to Madeline Mahoney, c. 1951, p. 2, #600, Miscellaneous Historical Documents Collection.

49 "My wife . . .": Meeting with Stevenson, 4 Mar. 1952, Box 333, Longhand Notes, HST PSF.

50 "would like . . .": *NYT,* 24 Mar. 1952, p. 1.

50 "Nothing could . . .": *DetFP,* 25 Mar. 1952, p. 6.

50 "Suddenly her step . . .": Robbins, *Bess & Harry,* p. 153.

50 "made one . . .": *KCS,* 29 June 1952, A17.

50 "No one, but . . .": Ibid.

50 "take those invisible . . ." Dorothy McCardle, *WasP,* c. 1952, BWT VF.

50 "one of the . . .": *Chicago Sun Times,* 7 Dec. 1952, p. 41.

51 "form its manners . . .": Benjamin Rush in Linda Kerber, *Women of the Republic* (Chapel Hill, NC, 1980), p. 230.

51 "The nicest thing . . .": Robert Ruark, *LouCJ,* 11 Jan. 1951, p. 7.

51 "The contrast between . . ." *SLPD,* c. 5 Dec. 1952, clipping, Box 299, Biographical, HST PSF.

51 "I don't care . . .": Raymond Lonergan, "Millions Listen to Truman's Final Talk," clipping, c. Jan. 1953, BWT VF.

51 "humanness": *Forbes,* 15 June 1952, p. 15.

51 "He's the only . . .": Henry McLemore, "Applauds President After Talking to Him," c. 4 Apr. 1947 in Box 307, Personal, HST PSF.

51 "That home town . . ." Ferrell, *Autobiography,* p. 109.

51 "If this is . . .": HST, *Mr. Citizen* (New York, 1960), p. 24.

52 "No kibitzing . . .": CBS, "Person to Person," 27 May 1955.

52 "She was . . .": Ibid.

53 all interactions: Erving Goffman, *The Presentation of Self in Everyday Life* (New York, 1959), pp. 15–17, 30, 233.

CHAPTER 2. "IKE IS MY CAREER"

Page

54 "Please, if . . .": Nanette Kutner to Bill [Robinson], 7 Nov. 1952, Box 25, MDE WH.

54 "I got . . .": MDE to Nanette Kutner, 15 Nov. 1952, Box 25, MDE WH.

55 smaller than the office: DDE, *At Ease* (Garden City, NY, 1967), p. 73.

55   "Father was . . .": Ibid., p. 31.
56   "We were . . .": Ibid., p. 33.
56   "Our family . . .": Ibid., p. 37.
56   wrote down the names: Ibid., p. 52.
56   maladies: Fred I. Greenstein, *The Hidden-Hand Presidency* (New York, 1982), pp. 39–40.
56   "tough cooky": Kenneth S. Davis, *Soldier of Democracy* (Garden City, NY, 1945), p. 85.
56   "the grin . . .": R. G. Tonkin in *SatEP,* 3 May 1952, p. 19.
56   "bawled like . . .": MSE OH, p. 25.
56   At one dance: DDE, *At Ease,* pp. 9–10.
57   "The management . . .": Alden Hatch, *Red Carpet For Mamie Eisenhower* (New York, 1956), p. 51.
57   "belle of . . .": *Coronet,* Aug. 1951, p. 57.
57   "the woman-hater . . .": DDE, *At Ease,* p. 113.
58   "just about . . .": Steve Neal, *The Eisenhowers* (Lawrence, KS, 1978, 1984), p. 35.
58   "the boys . . .": Alden Hatch, *Red Carpet,* p. 62.
58   "You know . . .": *American Magazine,* June 1948, p. 35.
58   "He simply . . .": Neal, *Eisenhowers,* p. 36.
58   "all those lounge . . .": JNE, *Special People* (New York, 1977), p. 198.
58   "did not . . .": MDE, "If I Were a Bride Today," *True Confessions,* Nov. 1954, p. 16, in Box 542, PPF 2, DDE WHCF.
58   "a nobody . . .": Hatch, *Red Carpet,* p. 73.
58   finally had brothers: Davis, *Soldier,* p. 164.
58   "Come now . . .": Hatch, *Red Carpet,* p. 81.
58   the worst: Davis, *Soldier,* p. 166.
58   "Dwight has . . .": EE to MDE and DDE, 27 June 1956, Box 11, DDE Names.
58   "never heard . . .": DDE, *At Ease,* p. 31.
59   In his memoir . . . : Ibid., p. 123.
59   "Your husband . . .": MDE, "If I Were a Bride," p. 19.
59   "You're not . . .": Lester David and Irene David, *Ike and Mamie* (New York, 1981), pp. 66–67.
59   "you must . . .": Ibid., p. 66.
59   "Just for that . . .": *McCall's,* Nov. 1950, p. 114.
59   "although parting . . .": David, *Ike and Mamie,* p. 94.
59   "spoiled brat": MDE, "If I Were a Bride," p. 160.
59   "Half the . . .": "How the Eisenhowers Budget," Box 9, Campaign Series, Ann C. Whitman File, DDE MSS, DDE Lib.
60   "first real home": MDE to Josephine Bay, 22 Aug. 1955, Box 3, MDE WH.
60   "the greatest disappointment . . .": DDE, *At Ease,* p. 181.
60   "recovered . . . had to learn": DDE to EE, 14 Dec. 1956, Box 11, DDE Names.
60   "It was ironic . . .": *American Magazine,* June 1948, p. 104.
60   "You mean . . .": David, *Ike and Mamie,* pp. 91–92.
60   "The office . . .": *American Magazine,* June 1948, p. 35.
60   "I'll go . . .": Hatch, *Red Carpet,* p. 103.
60   "minimum accommodations . . .": Robert H. Ferrell, ed., *The Eisenhower Diaries* (New York, 1981), p. 35.
61   "Only a man . . .": DDE to MSE, 3 Jan. 1939 in Stephen Ambrose, *Eisenhower,* 2 vols. (New York, 1983, 1984), 1:104.
61   "They never . . .": JNE, *Special,* p. 201.
61   "first and most . . .": MDE, "If I Were a Bride," pp. 16, 19.
61   "I never . . .": JNE, *Special,* p. 202.
61   "It would have . . .": Neal, *Eisenhowers,* p. 38.
61   "full credit . . .": David, *Ike and Mamie,* p. 22.
61   "The loving relationship . . .": DDE, *Letters to Mamie,* John S.D. Eisenhower, ed. (Garden City, NY, 1978), p. 11.

61   "There were a . . .": JNE, *Special,* p. 199.

61   "encapsulated life . . .": Lewis Mumford in James Howard Kunstler, *The Geography of Nowhere* (New York, 1993), p. 10.

62   "Ike was . . .": JNE, *Special,* p. 194.

62   "Don't you . . .": David, *Ike and Mamie,* p. 13.

62   "Gen. Ike's . . .": Clipping, c. 1943, Box 2, Personal Correspondence, MDE MSS. See also Susan M. Hartmann, *The Homefront and Beyond* (Boston, 1982), p. 23.

62   "American soldiers . . .": DDE to EE, 26 Sept. 1944, Box 172, DDE Pre.

62   500 to 700: William L. O'Neill, *A Democracy at War* (New York, 1993), p. 252.

62   "Soooooo—. . .": Gladys and Cecil Brooks to DDE, 10 May 1943, p. 6, Box 8, DDE Pre.

62   "attempt at . . .": DDE to MSE, 10 July 1944, p. 1, Box 174, DDE Pre.

63   ugly black hairnet: Doris Kearns Goodwin, *No Ordinary Time* (New York, 1994), p. 204.

63   "a nervous wreck": *American Magazine,* June 1948, p. 105.

63   "entirely too personal": DDE to Harry C. Butcher, 12 Oct. 1945, Box 16, DDE Pre.

63   "one of the . . .": *Life,* 13 Oct. 1952, p. 157.

63   "her nerves . . .": Frances "Mike" Moore to DDE , 16 May 1942, Box 175, DDE Pre.

63   proved less abstemious: Merriman Smith OH, pp. 11–13.

63   "calamitous": DDE to Ruth Butcher, 6 Apr. 1943, Box 16, DDE Pre.

63   "over three . . .": DDE to MDE, Teletype message to Stoner via Tully, 14 Dec. 1943, Box 173, DDE Pre. See also MDE to DDE, from Ordway signed Marshall, 18 Jan. 1943.

64   "rather lonely . . .": DDE to MSE, 24 July 1942, Box 174, DDE Pre.

64   "feminine companionship": DDE to Frances "Mike" Moore, 4 Dec. 1942, Box 175, DDE Pre.

64   "Kay, there's nobody . . .": David, *Ike and Mamie,* p. 147.

64   "Leave Kay . . .": Ambrose, *Eisenhower,* 1:418.

64   "Of course, I don't . . .": David, *Ike and Mamie,* p. 158.

64   "I love you . . .": Neal, *Eisenhowers,* p. 176.

64   "Stop worrying . . .": David, *Ike and Mamie,* p. 159.

64   "Apparently you . . .": DDE to MDE, 29 Sept. 1945 in David, *Ike and Mamie,* p. 159.

64   Ike feared: DDE to Kay Summersby, 28 July 1948, Box 112, DDE Pre.

65   Harry Truman: Merle Miller, *Plain Speaking* (New York, 1973), pp. 367–369.

65   Three years later . . . : See Kay Summersby Morgan, *Past Forgetting* (New York, 1976).

65   "no one . . .": DDE, *Letters,* p. 11.

65   most historians: See, for example, Ambrose, *Eisenhower,* 1:285–286.

65   "Some men . . .": DDE to John Eisenhower, 26 Feb. 1943, Box 173, DDE Pre.

65   "having done . . .": DDE to Frances "Mike" Moore, 29 Apr. 1945, Box 175, DDE Pre.

66   "changed terrifically": JNE, *Special,* p. 202.

66   "Neither of us . . .": Carl Sferrazza Anthony, *First Ladies,* 2 vols. (New York, 1990), 1:504.

66   "belonged to . . .": JNE, *Special,* p. 202.

66   "my three . . .": David, *Ike and Mamie,* p. 112.

66   first fur coat: Ambrose, *Eisenhower,* 1:439.

66   "It seems . . .": DDE to MSE, 19 Dec. 1949, Box 174, DDE Pre.

66   "We had almost . . .": Howard Snyder, "Draft," pp. 14–15, Howard McCrum Snyder MSS, DDE Lib.

66   "the possible volume . . .": DDE to Thomas J. Watson, 14 June 1947, Box 122, DDE Pre.

66   "Ho Hum . . .": MDE to Margaret Chick, note on envelope of Anne Kennedy to MDE, 27 Mar. 1946, Box 173, DDE Pre.

66   "stay out . . .": Jock Lawrence to General Lanham, memorandum, 10 Apr. 1951, Box 2, SHAPE Series, MDE MSS.

66   "there is about . . .": John Gunther, *Eisenhower* (New York, 1951, 1952), pp. 5–6.

66   "woman behind . . .": *American Magazine,* June 1948, pp. 34–35.

66 "a whole . . .": MDE, "A Wife's Big Job," clipping, Charlotte C. Marsh to MDE, 30 Mar. 1952, Box 1, SHAPE Series, MDE MSS.

67 "a good wife . . .": *Coronet,* Aug. 1951, p. 56. See also Ethel Klein, *Gender Politics* (Cambridge, MA, 1984), p. 44.

67 20 million . . . : Hartmann, *Homefront,* p. 8.

67 "her pet . . .": *Coronet,* Aug. 1951, p. 61.

67 "As an American . . .": "Message from Mrs. Eisenhower . . ." 3 Jan. 1952, Box 35, MDE WH.

67 she posed: *McCall's,* Nov. 1950, p. 30.

67 "the all-important . . .": DDE to Bill Robinson, 24 Nov. 1951, Box 99, DDE Pre.

67 "These days . . .": DDE to MSE, 27 May 1952, Box 174, DDE Pre.

67 would blossom: Still, it is an oversimplification to call their relationship "happy, uncomplicated, and old-fashioned." See Ambrose, *Eisenhower,* 2:29.

67 politicization of domestic life: See Elaine Tyler May, *Homeward Bound* (New York, 1988), pp. 10–11; Stephen J. Whitfield, *The Culture of the Cold War* (Baltimore, 1991), pp. 12, 14.

68 "behind": *SatEP,* 27 Sept. 1952, p. 32.

68 "Thru the articles . . .": Helen E. Williams to MDE, c. Apr. 1952, Box 2, SHAPE Series, MDE MSS.

68 "this whole business . . .": DDE to Clifford Roberts, 19 May 1952, Box 98, DDE Pre.

68 "would never . . .": MDE to Florence E. Witter, 7 Aug. 1950, Box 173, DDE Pre.

68 "Bill, what . . .": Ellis Slater OH, p. 11.

68 "My mind . . .": MDE to Mrs. C. R. Lehner, 21 Apr. 1952, Box 1, SHAPE Series, MDE MSS.

68 "If each . . .": Marquis Childs, *Eisenhower* (New York, 1958), p. 138.

68 only 31 percent: *Time,* 2 June 1952, p. 21.

68 "Well, I know . . .": M. Smith OH, p. 10.

68 never posed: Katherine G. Howard OH, 5:479.

69 "If he's . . .": Ibid., 5:355, 436.

69 "THEY LIKE . . .": *Life,* 13 Oct. 1952, p. 149.

69 "I leave all . . .": *BosH,* 4 Nov. 1952, p. 3.

69 "Of course the . . .": *Life,* 13 Oct. 1952, p. 158.

69 "talked lady-talk": *New York Journal-American,* 9 Nov. 1952, L6.

69 "the sweetheart": Howard OH 1:73.

69 "The Sunshine . . .": See "Campaign Memorabilia," Box 5, MJM MSS, DDE Lib.

69 "Mamie . . .": "Eisenhower News of Special Interest to Women," 12 May 1952, No. 4.

69 "win the crowd . . .": Merlo J. Pusey, *Eisenhower the President* (New York, 1956), p. 26.

69 "This feeling . . .": *Life,* 13 Oct. 1952, p. 150.

69 "Mamie won't . . .": *Time,* 2 June 1952, p. 21.

69 "all the highly . . .": *Life,* 13 Oct. 1952, p. 158.

70 "I do all . . .": Howard OH, 5:415.

70 "All they talked . . .": Ambrose, *Eisenhower,* 1:546.

70 "Politics is . . .": James C. Hagerty OH, p. 44.

70 often shelter . . .: See Greenstein, *Hidden Hand,* p. 64.

70 "astonished": DDE to William H. Burnham, 13 Sept. 1952, Box 3, DDE Names.

70 "out of character": MDE to Marjorie Davies, 11 Oct. 1952, Box 10, MDE WH.

70 "all-important . . .": MDE to Nanette Kutner, 10 Nov. 1952, Box 25, MDE WH.

70 "a bunch of . . .": *BosH,* 4 Nov. 1952, p. 3.

70 "Fashion needs . . .": *Daily Times Herald* (Dallas), 3 Nov. 1952, 6:5.

70 "Mamie must . . .": David, *Ike and Mamie,* pp. 178–179.

70 "I think she . . .": AMG to DDE, 1 Nov. 1952, Box 1, AMG MSS.

70 "You're doing . . .": Albert Jacobs OH, p. 25.

70 "You are a dear . . .": MDE to AMG, 17 Nov. 1952, Box 15, MDE WH.

71 "HISTORY KNOWS . . .": T. D. Deforest to MDE, 14 Nov. 1961, Box 1, Personal Correspondence, MDE MSS.

71 Mamie was upstairs: Ellis Slater, *The Ike I Knew* (privately published, 1980), p. 27.

71 "NOW . . .": *Life,* 13 Oct. 1952, p. 150.

71 "will eventually . . .": DDE to EE, 26 Sept. 1944, Box 172, DDE Pre.

71 "convictions": DDE, *White House Years,* 2 vols. (Garden City, NY, 1963–1965), 1:51.

71 "You always have . . .": Ambrose, *Eisenhower,* 2:41.

72 "a real homey . . .": *WasP,* 21 Jan. 1953, p. 1.

72 "This is a different . . .": Jay Franklin, *Republicans on the Potomac* (New York, 1953), pp. 18–19.

72 "a remarkable woman . . .": *New York Journal-American,* 9 Nov. 1952, L6.

72 "that the home . . .": *Wichita Eagle,* clipping in Mrs. William W. McCammon to MDE, c. 28 Nov. 1952, Box 28, MDE WH.

72 "invaluable . . . indispensable . . .": DDE quoted in Wilton B. Persons to Shirley M. Baronie, 2 Apr. 1959, Box 547, PPF2, DDE WHCF.

72 "Mamie's biggest . . .": David, *Ike and Mamie,* pp. 240–241.

72 "Ike and I . . .": MDE to Charlotte Duruz, 2 Mar. 1953, Box 12, MDE WH.

72 "A smile . . .": MDE to Louise Caffey, 10 June 1953, Box 5, MDE WH.

72 "White House takes . . .": MDE to Maud Hurd, 7 Aug. 1953, Box 21, MDE WH.

72 107-room . . .: *BH&G,* Aug. 1960, p. 48.

72 "I am never . . .": MDE to Nell Woodruff, 14 Feb. 1953, Box 47, MDE WH.

72 "little violet": Eileen Archibold to MDE, 4 May 1953, p. 3, Box 2, MDE WH.

73 "meet[ing] . . .": MDE to William H. Burnham, 19 May 1953, Box 5, MDE WH.

73 sponsored dozens: Barbara [Eisenhower?] to Mr. [Thomas] Stephens, 12 Mar. 1959, Box 547, PPF2, DDE WHCF.

73 "I feel that . . .": MDE to Mrs. Doris Beam, 4 Feb. 1954, Box 3, MDE WH.

73 "Who was . . .": Clipping, 7 Nov. 1960 in BWT VF.

73 "Well, I'm glad . . .": *LAT,* 3 Feb. 1956, p. 6.

73 "personal involvement . . .": MJM to Mrs. J. L. Paterson [draft], c. 12 Mar. 1956, Box 544, PPF2, DDE WHCF.

73 "not take part . . .": MJM to Max Chambers, 7 July 1954, Box 542, PPF2, DDE WHCF.

73 no speeches: MJM to Ancher Nelsen, 12 Apr. 1954, Box 542, PPF2, DDE WHCF.

73 "make out of town . . .": Ferne Hudson to Homer H. Gruenther, 12 May 1958, Box 546, PPF2, DDE WHCF.

73 "ironclad": James C. Hagerty to Mrs. Harold S. Talbott, 1 Apr. 1953, Box 540, PPF2, DDE WHCF.

73 "precedent . . .": James C. Hagerty to MJM, 30 Mar. 1955, Box 543, PPF2, DDE WHCF.

73 "look after Ike": "Mamie Eisenhower," clipping, 28 Nov. 1952 in Bess McCammon to MDE, Box 28, MDE WH.

73 "Every woman . . .": E. K. Thompson to Henry Luce, 26 Apr. 1958, Box 35, MDE WH.

73 "Do let . . .": Helen Reid to MDE, 19 June 1958, p. 2, Box 36, MDE WH.

73 "denied access . . .": Murray Snyder to MJM, 31 Jan. 1955, Box 35, MDE WH.

73 "on stale . . .": Fleur Cowles to MJM, 28 Jan. 1955, Box 35, MDE WH.

74 "respond to any . . .": MDE statement, 21 Mar. 1953, Box 41, MDE WH.

74 "constant merry-go-round . . .": MDE to William H. Burnham, 19 May 1953, Box 5, MDE WH.

74 "that every woman . . .": Ambrose, *Eisenhower,* 2:72.

74 "Now look here . . .": Slater, *Ike I Knew,* p. 36.

74 "Mrs. Eisenhower has . . .": Murray Snyder to Miss Rogers, 7 Apr. 1953, Box 540, PPF2, DDE WHCF. See also Betty Boyd Caroli, *First Ladies* (New York, 1987), p. 218.

74 "IKE'S MAMIE . . .": *ChiT,* 26 Sept. 1954, 1:2.

74 "as gracious . . .": Henry Aurand OH, pp. 25–26.

74 requests . . . : See file "February 1953," Box 540, PPF2, DDE WHCF. See also Paula Baker, "The Domestication of Politics," *American Historical Review,* 89 (June 1984):620–647.

75 "Propped up . . .": *BH&G,* Aug. 1960, p. 79.

75   "words in my . . .": MDE to Grace Gruenther, 15 July 1954, Box 16, MDE WH.

75   "mulling over . . .": MDE to AMG, 26 Aug. 1953, Box 15, MDE WH.

75   "brought me . . .": MDE to Louise Cannon, 9 Apr. 1953, Box 6, MDE WH.

75   "the purple . . .": MDE to Louise Caffey, 4 Sept. 1956, Box 5, MDE WH.

75   "The latest news . . .": MDE to Louise Caffey, 31 Mar. 1954, Box 5, MDE WH. See also *NYT,* 31 Mar. 1954, p. 1.

75   "Because of the Israeli . . .": MDE to Mabel McKay, 20 Feb. 1957, Box 29, MDE WH.

76   "walked with . . .": *Minneapolis Tribune,* 27 Sept. 1954, p. 1.

76   "This is a slave's . . .": DDE to EE, 3 Feb. 1954, Box 11, DDE Names.

76   "At last I've . . .": David, *Ike and Mamie,* p. 194.

76   "and pat Ike . . .": Ambrose, *Eisenhower,* 2:29.

76   "and each time . . .": JNE, *Special,* p. 203.

76   "To me . . .": MSE OH, 1:13–14.

76   "rebuild that . . .": DDE to William Pawley, 3 Aug. 1953, Box 25, DDE Names.

76   "to give her . . .": DDE to MSE, 23 Apr. 1953, Box 12, DDE Names.

76   "Mamie occasionally . . .": DDE, *At Ease,* p. 359.

77   "dream house": MDE to Rosamond Berry, 16 Aug. 1955, Box 3, MDE WH.

77   "loath to leave . . .": MDE to Mrs. Josephine Bay, 22 Aug. 1955, Box 3, MDE WH.

77   "No man . . .": Kenneth T. Jackson, *Crabgrass Frontier* (New York, 1985), p. 231.

77   "I never pretended . . .": JNE, *Special,* p. 203.

77   "Sometimes I feel . . .": Ambrose, *Eisenhower,* 2:75.

77   "ward off . . .": MDE to Maud Hurd, 7 Aug. 1953, Box 21, MDE WH.

77   "complete rest . . .": MDE to Louis Caffey, 16 Sept. 1953, Box 5, MDE WH.

77   "Today is . . .": MDE to Caroline Walker, 26 Aug. 1953, Box 44, MDE WH.

78   "be alone . . .": MDE to Kurt and Peggy Heilbronn, 18 Nov. 1961, Box 1, MDE Personal Correspondence, MDE MSS.

78   "I am almost . . .": DDE to AMG, 26 Feb. 1953, Box 1, AMG MSS.

78   "Anglo-Saxon . . .": DDE to Bill Robinson, 12 July 1951, p. 3, Box 99, DDE Pre.

78   "Makes one . . .": Ferrell, *Diaries,* p. 145.

78   "congenial friends": Slater, *Ike I Knew,* p. 83.

78   "boss of the money": Marty Snyder, *My Friend Ike* (New York, 1956), p. 207.

79   "Each mention . . .": *Minneapolis Tribune,* 13 July 1957, p. 20.

79   "the outstanding American . . .": Slater OH, p. 22.

79   "the informality . . .": DDE to Cliff Roberts, 25 July 1957, Box 28, DDE Names.

79   "the boss": Slater, *Ike I Knew,* p. 151.

79   "but the only . . .": Priscilla Slater in Slater, *Ike I Knew,* p. 57.

79   "These evenings . . .": Sherman Adams, *Firsthand Report* (New York, 1961), p. 428.

79   ritualized . . . : Michael Kimmel, *Manhood in America* (New York, 1996), p. 214.

80   "never been . . .": Slater, *Ike I Knew,* p. 74.

80   "beautiful, intelligent . . .": DDE to John Eisenhower, 18 Jan. 1947, Box 173, DDE Pre.

80   "far more . . .": Ferrell, *Eisenhower Diaries,* p. 294.

80   "gabfests . . .": DDE to Mrs. R. F. Lucier, 20 Oct. 1943, Box 69, DDE Pre.

80   "Where are . . .": Ambrose, *Eisenhower,* 2:29.

80   never called . . . : Gwendolyn King OH, p. 8.

80   "most devoted . . .": Slater, *Ike I Knew,* p. 178.

80   Ann had grown: See Robert J. Donovan, *Confidential Secretary* (New York, 1988), pp. 14–15, 161–162; Ann Whitman OH, pp. 18–19; Jacqueline Cochran OH, pp. 187–188, 206, 251–252.

80   "One of the . . .": DDE to MSE, 12 Sept. 1955, Box 12, DDE Names.

80   "feminine, really luscious . . .": Priscilla Slater in Slater, *Ike I Knew,* pp. 57–58.

80   "Mamie wants . . .": Ambrose, *Eisenhower,* 2:73.

81   "years of endurance . . .": DDE to Everett and Kate Hughes et al., 4 June 1949, Box 173, DDE Pre.

81   "It's the levity . . .": Slater, *Ike I Knew,* p. 184.

81 "Cheer Water": AMG to MDE, 21 June 1956, Box 16, MDE WH.

81 "my favorite . . ." MDE to Gracie and AMG, 16 Nov. 1961, Box 3, AMG MSS.

81 "bring[ing] me . . .": MDE to AMG, 25 June 1956, Box 16, MDE WH.

81 five hundred cases: See "Alcohol," Bulk Mail, DDE WHCF.

81 "that colored . . .": Kendall K. Hoyt to Charles Willis, 23 Sept. 1953, Box 541, PPF2, DDE WHCF.

81 "boozed it . . .": *National Enquirer,* 7 June 1959, clipping, Letter of Helen T. Geyser, 23 June 1959, Box 547, PPF2, DDE WHCF.

81 "a downright lie": James C. Hagerty to Ernie Barbush, 14 July 1959, Box 547, PPF2, DDE WHCF.

81 "nurse an old-fashioned . . .": Smith OH, p. 13. See also King OH, p. 11.

81 "the things he . . .": Slater, *Ike I Knew,* p. 28.

81 "How different . . .": Ibid., p. 71.

81 "the office of . . .": DDE to MSE, 9 Oct. 1953, Box 12, DDE Names.

81 "Have you no . . .": Emile de Antonio and Daniel Talbot, *Point of Order!* (New York, 1964), p. 95. For a contrasting view see Greenstein, *Hidden Hand,* chap. 5.

82 "The only reason . . .": DDE to EE, 17 Sept. 1956, Box 11, DDE Names.

82 "colored . . .": Slater, *Ike I Knew,* p. 149.

82 "the militant . . .": Cliff Roberts to DDE, 23 July 1952, Box 27, DDE Names.

82 bemoaned the divorce . . . : Slater, *Ike I Knew,* pp. 200–201.

82 "so-called human interest": DDE to MSE, 9 Oct. 1953, p. 3, Box 12, DDE Names.

82 "things of importance . . .": DDE to Bill Robinson, 4 Aug. 1954, Box 29, DDE Names. See also Craig Allen, *Eisenhower and the Mass Media* (Chapel Hill, NC, 1993), pp. 6–9.

82 "important and established . . .": *WasS,* 7 Jan. 1954, A20.

82 "a production . . .": *SatEP,* 26 May 1956, pp. 27, 119.

83 In 1958, pollsters: George H. Gallup, *The Gallup Polls,* 3 vols. (New York, 1972) 2:1569.

83 a plurality approved . . . : Ibid., 2:1116–1117.

83 "said he assumed . . .": *WasP,* 26 Sept. 1955, p. 2.

84 "Don't you put . . .": Hagerty OH, 4:290.

84 "Tell the truth . . .": DDE, *White House,* 1:538.

84 "the ideal wife . . .": Harry A. Bullis to MDE, 10 Nov. 1955, Box 5, MDE WH.

84 "deputy husband": Laurel Thatcher Ulrich, *Good Wives* (New York, 1980, 1982), p. 38.

84 "You are a gallant . . .": Helen Reid to MDE, 29 Nov. 1957, Box 36, MDE WH.

84 "Funny thing . . .": Adams, *Firsthand,* p. 188.

84 "When he feels . . .": MDE to Benjamin F. Caffey, 6 Oct. 1955, Box 5, MDE WH.

85 "We conversed . . .": DDE, *White House,* 1:542.

85 "I have tried . . .": MDE to Joshena Ingersol, 29 Sept. 1955, Box 22, MDE WH.

85 "Mamie, above all . . .": DDE, *White House,* 1:542.

85 "underwent an operation . . .": "Mrs. Eisenhower's Operation, 8-6-57," James C. Hagerty statement, 6 Aug. 1957, Box 5, James C. Hagerty MSS, DDE Lib.

85 "a gynecologist . . .": *Des Moines Register,* 7 Aug. 1957, p. 1.

85 Dr. Snyder told . . . : Ambrose, *Eisenhower,* 2:281.

85 Mamie insisted . . . : Arthur Nevins OH, pp. 72–73.

85 "Mamie's judgment . . .": Slater, *Ike I Knew,* p. 108.

85 "Mamie simply . . .": DDE to Nettie Jones, 17 Dec. 1955, Box 20, DDE Names.

86 "Mamie is a wonderful . . .": DDE to Harry Bullis, 2 Oct. 1956, Box 3, DDE Names.

86 "the vital importance . . .": *The Crusader,* issue no. 4, in Box 5, Young and Rubicam, Inc. MSS, DDE Lib.

86 "to enforce integration . . .": Ambrose, *Eisenhower,* 2:420.

86 "that all this anti-Negro . . .": Slater, *Ike I Knew,* p. 158.

86 "Alleged inter-service . . .": DDE to Harry Butcher, c. 7 Nov. 1957, Box 3, DDE Names.

87 only 17 . . .: 26 June 1953, Gallup, *Polls,* 2:1151.

87 "overdoing": *USNWR,* 23 Aug. 1957, p. 61.

87   "part-time": *America,* 14 Feb. 1959, p. 565.

87   "luxurious beauty . . .": *Life,* 10 Mar. 1958, p. 54.

87   "I think when . . .": *SFChr,* 26 Feb. 1958, p. 10.

87   Harry Truman . . . : Childs, *Eisenhower,* p. 276.

87   "squirrel cage": MDE to Eileen Archibold, 5 Nov. 1957, Box 2, MDE WH.

87   "deal almost . . .": Ed Wimmer to MDE, 2 Apr. 1957; MJM to Wimmer, 3 July 1957, Box 546, PPF2, DDE WHCF.

87   "entered the store . . .": Ida Kaufman to DDE, 24 Sept. 1958; Henry Roemer McPhee to Ida Kaufman, 15 Oct. 1958, Box 546, PPF 2, DDE WHCF.

88   "the last years . . .": Stephen Hess OH, pp. 31–32.

88   "younger than . . .": *BH&G,* June 1955, p. 70.

88   "Grandma Lives . . .": *National Business Woman,* Aug. 1957, p. 7.

88   "the worst year . . .": Slater, *Ike I Knew,* p. 180.

88   "contract . . . fallible . . .": *McCall's,* Apr. 1955, p. 91.

88   "The Eisenhowers . . .": *BH&G,* Aug. 1960, p. 49.

88   "Barbara has been . . .": MDE to Betsy Whitney, 16 Dec. 1959, Box 45, MDE WH.

89   "does not like . . .": DDE to Sigurd Larmon, 13 Oct. 1956, Box 20, DDE Names.

89   "the next President . . .": RN, 28 July 1960 in Gregory Bush, *Campaign Speeches of American Presidential Candidates* (New York, 1976, 1985), p. 105.

89   "was not up . . .": Ambrose, *Eisenhower,* 2:602.

89   A month after . . .: 13 Jan. 1961, Gallup, *Polls,* 3:1701.

89   "my constant problems": DDE to Elivera Doud, 13 July 1959, Box 9, DDE Names.

90   "It was wonderful . . .": Betsy Whitney to MDE, 4 Mar. 1953, Box 45, MDE WH.

CHAPTER 3. THE KENNEDYS

Page

91   *"Vive Zha-kleen! . . .":* BosG, 1 June 1961, p. 18.

91   "De Gaulle and . . .": Thomas C. Reeves, *A Question of Character* (New York, 1991), p. 298.

91   "secret weapons . . .": *BosTr,* 12 June 1961, p. 16.

92   "He savaged . . ." Richard Reeves, *President Kennedy* (New York, 1993), p. 172.

92   "For the . . ." Ibid., p. 174.

92   "if I . . .": Alistair Horne, *Harold Macmillan,* 2 vols. (New York, 1989), 2:290.

93   "individuals with . . .": Rose Fitzgerald Kennedy, *Times to Remember* (Garden City, New York, 1974), p. 79.

93   "a good-sized . . .": Ibid.

93   "the architect . . .": Ibid., p. 57.

93   "the perfect . . .": Doris Kearns Goodwin, *The Fitzgeralds and the Kennedys* (New York, 1987), p. 419.

93   "America's best known . . .": *New York World Telegram,* 7 Dec. 1940, Box 1, JFK Per.

94   "rather spoils . . .": Nigel Hamilton, *JFK: Reckless Youth* (New York, 1992), p. 683.

94   "Once I . . .": Henry James quoting JFK in Hamilton, *Reckless Youth,* p. 358.

94   "The thing . . .": John White in T. C. Reeves, *Character,* p. 58.

94   "It's certainly . . .": Hamilton, *Reckless Youth,* p. 618.

94   "politics and . . .": Herbert Parmet, *Jack* (New York, 1980), p. 259.

94   "there are . . .": Benjamin C. Bradlee, *Conversations with Kennedy* (New York, 1975), pp. 201–202.

94   "thoroughbred . . .": C. David Heymann, *A Woman Named Jackie* (New York, 1989), p. 26.

95   taste . . . : Richard L. Bushman, *The Refinement of America* (New York, 1992), p. 96.

95   "prissy . . ." Edith Beale in Heymann, *Jackie,* p. 63.

95   "Not to . . .": William Manchester, *Portrait of a President,* rev. ed. (Boston, 1962, 1967), p. 87.

95   "a regal . . .": Heymann, *Jackie,* p. 69.

95   "hang around . . .": Ibid., pp. 90, 99.
95   "Which First . . .": Ibid., p. 97.
95   "I can feel . . .": Paul B. Fay, Jr., *The Pleasure of His Company* (New York, 1966), p. 152.
96   "Daddy, do . . ." Hamilton, *Reckless Youth,* p. 753.
96   "Men who . . .": "News Release for Weekly Papers," c. 1946, Box 98, JFK Pre.
96   "Women compose . . .": Hamilton, *Reckless Youth,* p. 765.
96   "matinee . . .": *McCall's,* Aug. 1957, p. 118.
96   "Every woman . . .": *NYP,* 31 July 1956, p. 21.
97   "MASSACHUSETTS *NEEDS* . . .": *"Massachusetts Needs JFK as U.S. Senator,"* c. 1952, Box 135, JFK POF.
97   "What is . . .": *SatEP,* 13 June 1953, p. 27.
97   "the family . . .": *Nwswk,* 9 July 1956, p. 29.
97   "part of . . .": *NYP,* 31 July 1956, p. 4.
97   "Potentially America's . . .": *ChiDN,* 18 Mar. 1957, p. 14.
97   "The Senate's . . .": *SatEP,* 13 June 1953, p. 27.
97   "A politician . . .": Lem Billings quoting Joseph P. Kennedy in Heymann, *Jackie,* p. 117.
98   "a very . . .": *McCall's,* Aug. 1957, p. 123.
98   "He's not . . .": Ibid.
98   "put the . . .": Kitty Kelley, *Jackie Oh!* (Seacaucus, NJ, 1978), p. 29.
98   "since Jack . . .": Heymann, *Jackie,* p. 125.
98   too scrawny . . . : Ralph G. Martin, *A Hero for Our Time* (New York, 1983), p. 79.
98   "I have . . .": *Life,* Aug. 1995, p. 35.
98   "most eligible . . .": *Greenfield Record Gazette,* 25 June 1953, p. 9.
98   "No man . . .": Heymann, *Jackie,* p. 127.
98   A *Life* . . . : Kenneth P. O'Donnell and David F. Powers, *Johnny We Hardly Knew Ye* (New York, 1972, 1973), p. 108.
98   "perfect couple": Clark Clifford with Richard Holbrooke, *Counsel to the President* (New York, 1991), p. 361.
98   "little peach": Earl E. T. Smith to JFK, 25 June 1953, Box 479a, JFK Pre.
98   "She has . . .": Rev. A. C. Zabriskie to JFK, 1 July 1953, Box 479a, JFK Pre.
98   "risky": Paul E. Morgan to JFK, 25 June 1953, Box 479a, JFK Pre.
98   "GREATEST BLOW . . .": Red Fay to JFK, 29 June 1953, Box 479a, JFK Pre.
99   "But watch . . .": Manchester, *Portrait,* p. 87.
99   "means the . . .": JFK to Red Fay, July 1953 in Fay, *Pleasure,* p. 160.
99   magazine rights: John T. McCullough to JFK, 9 July 1953, Box 486; John T. McCullough to JFK, 29 July 1953, Box 479a, JFK Pre.
99   "vulgar": Laurence Leamer, *The Kennedy Women* (New York, 1994), p. 434.
99   "the Senator . . .": Evelyn Lincoln, *My Twelve Years with John F. Kennedy* (New York, 1965), p. 41.
99   "think of . . .": Kennedy, *Times to Remember,* p. 351.
99   "storybook . . .": Warner Path News, "People in the News," c. Sept. 1953, IFP 16, JFK AV.
99   "the public . . .": Leamer, *Kennedy Women,* p. 494.
99   "the Deb": Goodwin, *Fitzgeralds and Kennedys,* p. 890.
99   "the rah-rah . . .": T. C. Reeves, *Character,* p. 113.
99   "when she . . .": Lem Billings in Goodwin, *Fitzgeralds and Kennedys,* p. 893.
100 "He would . . .": Kennedy, *Times to Remember,* p. 352.
100 "a normal . . ." Heymann, *Jackie,* p. 166.
100 "send": See Lincoln, *Twelve Years,* p. 48.
100 "Which requires . . .": CBS, "Person to Person" with Edward R. Murrow, 30 Oct. 1953, TNC 183, JFK AV.
100 "If I . . .": *Time,* 2 Dec. 1957, p. 18.
100 "unusual qualification . . .": Theodore C. Sorensen to Ken Hechler, pp. 1–2, 31 July 1956, Box 810, Senate Papers, JFK Pre.
100 "The American . . .": Betty Spalding in Martin, *A Hero,* p. 144.

100 "My wife . . .": Heymann, *Jackie,* p. 172.

101 "In some . . .": *NYP,* 30 July 1956, p. 21.

101 "'the All . . .": Sargent Shriver to Joseph P. Kennedy, 18 July 1956, p. 4, Box 810, JFK Pre.

101 "Kennedy is . . .": Doris Fleeson, "Push Kennedy for Vice President," clipping, Box 810, JFK Pre.

101 "from 1/6 . . .": Theodore Sorensen, "The Democratic Nominee for Vice President in 1956," Box 810, JFK Pre.

101 "Just whatever . . .": NBC, "Outlook" with Arthur Barrio, 16 Aug. 1956, TNN 10B, JFK AV.

101 "during the . . .": *McCall's,* Aug. 1957, p. 125.

101 "national celebrity": *BosH,* 13 Aug. 1956, p. 19.

101 "His was . . .": *BosH,* 18 Aug. 1956, p. 1.

101 "SENATOR KENNEDY . . .": *BosH,* 25 Aug. 1956, p. 1.

101 "seemed . . . needed him": George Smathers OH, p. 188.

102 "nervous tension . . .": Heymann, *Jackie,* p. 191.

102 "What else . . .": Kelley, *Jackie Oh!,* p. 57.

102 "Ladies Day . . .": "Dem Ladies Mob 'Elvis' Kennedy," clipping, c. 1956, Box 521, JFK Pre.

102 too much status . . .: Martin, *A Hero,* p. 144.

102 "A vital . . .": *Omaha World Herald,* 21 July 1957, quoted in Victor Lasky, *JFK* (New York, 1963, 1966, 1977), p. 251.

102 "When Jackie . . .": O'Donnell and Powers, *Johnny,* pp. 162–163.

102 "lithe brunette . . .": *Boston Evening American,* 8 Oct. 1958, p. 4.

102 "the petite . . ." *Trentonian,* 10 Oct. 1958, Box 19, Theodore C. Sorensen MSS, JFK Lib.

102 furtive . . . : Parmet, *Jack,* p. 452.

103 "HIS GREATNESS . . .": "Why You Should Re-Elect John F. Kennedy," Box 19, Sorensen MSS.

103 "The John F. Kennedy . . .": "The John F. Kennedy Story," Box 19, Sorensen MSS.

103 "whenever the . . .": "Memorandum—Radio and TV," Box 20, Sorensen MSS.

103 In April 1957 . . . : NBC, "Jackie Kennedy, Home Show," 19 Apr. 1957, TNN 11, JFK AV.

103 "I'll take . . ." "The U.S. Senator John F. Kennedy Story," 1958, PPP 64, JFK AV.

103 "At Home . . .": "At Home with the Kennedys," 28 Oct. 1958, IFP 130, JFK AV.

103 "She is . . .": *Trentonian,* 10 Oct. 1958.

103 "Kennedy's strength . . .": Charles L. Bartlett, ed., "News Focus," 16 Aug. 1959, Box 27, JFK POF.

103 "the early . . .": Leslie Carpenter OH, p. 16.

104 "a good . . .": Louis Harris and Associates, "A Survey of Issues and Images in Wisconsin," June 1958, p. 10, Box 819, JFK Pre.

104 Catholic couple: Larry J. Sabato, *Feeding Frenzy* (New York, 1991), p. 37; Heymann, *Jackie,* pp. 226–227.

104 "felt that . . .": Theodore H. White, *The Making of the President 1960* (New York, 1960), p. 380.

104 "always . . .": Louis Harris and Associates, "A Study of Voter Attitude in West Virginia of Presidential Preferences," Jan. 1960, p. 25, Box 818, JFK Pre.

104 "personality element . . .": Louis Harris and Associates, "A Study of the Presidential Election in South Carolina," June 1960, p. 17, Box 818, JFK Pre.

104 "youth and . . .": Louis Harris and Associates, "A Survey of the Race for President in 1960 in the State of California," Mar. 1958, p. 7, Box 815, JFK Pre.

104 "how to . . .": "Campaign Reflections," unsigned memorandum, c. Sept. 1960, Box 535, Senate Files, General Files, JFK Pre.

104 "junior executives . . .": *NYP,* 8 Aug. 1960, p. 39.

105 "When you . . .": CBS, "Presidential Countdown. Mr. Kennedy: A Profile," 19 Sept. 1960, p. 4, Box 1027, JFK Pre.

105 "lovely aspirants . . .": *Life,* 10 Oct. 1960, p. 150.

105 "stunning egghead": *Nwswk,* 22 Feb. 1960, p. 29.

105 "by no . . .": *Nwswk,* 17 Oct. 1960, p. 34.

105 "pace setter": *USNWR,* 8 Aug. 1960, pp. 67–68.

105 "self-discipline[d]": *Nwswk,* 22 Feb. 1960, p. 28.

105 "a suburban . . .": *Look,* 27 July 1954, p. 23.

105 "large and . . .": *Time,* 29 Feb. 1960, p. 27.

105 "the super-duper . . .": *Nwswk,* 22 Feb. 1960, pp. 28–29.

105 "I think . . .": *USNWR,* 8 Aug. 1960, p. 66.

105 "We both . . .": *Nwswk,* 22 Feb. 1960, p. 29.

105 "Pat's only . . .": *Life,* 10 Oct. 1960, p. 150.

105 "the best-known . . .": *Time,* 29 Feb. 1960, p. 25.

106 "Whatever you . . .": *Nwswk,* 17 Oct. 1960, p. 31.

106 "pull some . . .": Bradlee, *Conversations,* p. 28.

106 "turn to . . .": Roger Tubb memorandum, 26 Sept. 1960, Box 37, RFK Pre.

106 "It's the . . .": *Life,* 10 Oct. 1960, p. 150.

106 "She breathes . . .": *Life,* 24 Aug. 1959, p. 80.

106 "Acapulco": Ibid.

106 "keeps seeing . . .": JBK, "Campaign Wife", 27 Oct. 1960, Box 1034, JFK Pre.

106 "shocking pink": *USNWR,* 21 Nov. 1960, p. 78.

106 "I couldn't . . .": *Life,* 26 Sept. 1960, p. 18.

106 "in general . . .": Louis Harris and Associates, "Nixon Before Labor Day," 25 Aug. 1960, pp. 15–17, Box 48, RFK Pre.

107 "to appoint . . .": JFK, New York, 5 Nov. 1960, Box 1035, JFK Pre.

107 "New Frontier . . .": *NYT,* 12 Aug. 1960, p. 6.

107 "so totally . . .": Liz OH, 1:31.

107 "four major . . .": "DNC Press Release," 11 Oct. 1960, Box 1035, JFK Pre.

107 "To express . . .": See "cool," *Dictionary of American Slang* (New York, 1975), p. 121.

107 Professor McLuhan . . . : Marshall McLuhan, *Understanding Media* (New York, 1964), pp. 42, 261, 269.

107 "an occasion . . .": John Kenneth Galbraith to JBK, 16 Sept. 1960; JBK to Galbraith, 24 Sept. 1960, Box 74, John Kenneth Galbraith MSS, JFK Lib.

108 "Oh, Bunny . . .": White, *Making, 1960,* p. 30.

108 "Okay, girls . . .": Bradlee, *Conversations,* p. 32.

108 "struggle against . . .": T. C. Reeves, *Character,* p. 233.

108 "This Administration . . .": Heymann, *Jackie,* p. 279.

108 "poise . . .": Kennedy, *Times to Remember,* p. 399; Pierre Salinger, *With Kennedy* (Garden City, New York, 1966), pp. 73, 139–144; T. C. Reeves, *Character,* p. 250.

108 "Have you . . .": R. Reeves, *President Kennedy,* p. 35.

109 "Jacqueline Bouvier . . .": *USNWR,* 21 Nov. 1960, p. 78.

109 "I'm never . . .": O'Donnell and Powers, *Johnny,* p. 268.

109 "Running our . . .": *BosG,* 15 Jan. 1961, p. 5.

109 "an old . . .": NBC, "The World of Jackie Kennedy," 1962, TNN 1, JFK AV.

109 "AMERICA'S 2 QUEENS . . .": *Photoplay,* June 1962, cover.

109 The movie colony . . . : See Ronald Brownstein, *The Power and the Glitter* (New York, 1990), pp. 144–145, 155.

109 the best-selling . . . : *ChiDN,* 3 Oct. 1963, p. 14.

109 "Inaugural day . . .": Mrs. L. J. Morand to JBK, 24 Jan. 1961, p. 3, Box 701, JFK WHSoc.

109 "Jackie Kennedy look . . .": *BosTr,* 10 Jan. 1961, p. 40.

110 "Women everywhere . . .": Mrs. Lorraine G. Trester to JBK, 31 Jan. 1961, Box 701, JFK WHSoc. See also Joseph B. Lieves to JBK, 6 July 1962, Box 701, JFK WHSoc.

110 "the best . . .": *Boston Record American,* 29 Dec. 1961, p. 4; *Newsday,* 8 Jan. 1962, clipping in A. Babcock to JBK, Box 36, JFK WHSoc.

110 "There are . . .": JBK to James V. Spadea, 17 Sept. 1960, Box 701, JFK WHSoc.

110 "discreetly": Letitia Baldrige to Janet A. Des Rosiers, 19 Sept. 1961; Letitia Baldrige to Madame Jackie Givinchy, 3 Aug. 1960, Box 701, JFK WHSoc.

110 "Just make . . .": JBK to Oleg Cassini, 13 Dec. 1960 in Oleg Cassini, *In My Own Fashion* (New York, 1987), p. 310.

110 "American Gothic . . .": *Boston Evening American,* 20 Jan. 1961, p. 3.

110 "my motivating . . .": *BosG,* 15 Jan. 1961, p. 5.

110 "If you . . .": NBC, "World of JBK."

110 "the Happy . . .": Betty Friedan, *The Feminine Mystique* (New York, 1963), pp. 28, 30.

110 "It is . . .": *NYT,* 20 Jan. 1962, p. 14.

110 "The President . . .": David Butler in Manchester, *Portrait,* p. 234.

110 "is a real . . .": *Minneapolis Star,* 19 July 1961, clipping, Mrs. Howard Cameron to JBK, 19 July 1961, Box 97, JFK WHSoc.

111 "a candid . . .": CBS, "A Day in the Life of President Kennedy," 17 Feb. 1961, TNC 194, JFK AV; NBC, "JFK Report #2," with Edwin Neumann, 11 Apr. 1961, TNN 260, JFK AV.

111 "We couldn't . . .": T. C. Reeves, *Character,* p. 250.

111 "most extraordinary . . .": *BosG,* 12 Apr. 1961, p. 8.

111 "We interviewed . . .": Helen Thomas, *Dateline: White House* (New York, 1975), p. 8; Salinger, *With Kennedy,* p. 315.

111 "My two . . .": Mrs. R. A. Cameron to JBK, 29 Jan. 1961, pp. 1–2, Box 97, JFK WHSoc.

111 "the enormous . . .": Louis Harris and Associates, "Reaction to Kennedy During the First 60 Days of His Administration," Mar. 1961, pp. 22–23, Box 105, JFK POF.

111 "found it . . .": Salinger, *With Kennedy,* p. 119.

111 "that things . . .": JFK to Stan Carey, 20 Feb. 1963, Box 680, PL JFK WHCF.

112 "Negroes are . . .": R. Reeves, *President Kennedy,* p. 357.

112 "There is . . .": NBC, "Interview with Mrs. John F. Kennedy," 24 Mar. 1961, transcript pp. 4–5, Box 463, JFK WHSoc.

112 "the 'hothouse . . .": *USNWR,* 7 Oct. 1963, p. 72.

112 "Is President . . .": *BosG,* 15 Apr. 1961, p. 1.

112 "Just as . . .": *McCall's,* Feb. 1962, p. 26.

112 "official . . .": *USNWR,* 5 Feb. 1962, p. 19.

112 "a saddle . . .": James N. Giglio, *Presidency of JFK* (Lawrence, KS, 1991), p. 271.

112 "President's wife . . .": JBK to Bonnie Angelo, 16 Apr. 1962, Box 753, JFK WHSoc.

112 "People must . . .": *WasP,* 21 Jan. 1963, B4.

113 "minimum information . . .": Giglio, *Presidency,* p. 271.

113 "His 'coolness' . . .": AMS, *A Thousand Days* (Boston, 1965), p. 115.

113 "What do . . .": David Halberstam, *The Powers That Be* (New York, 1979), p. 506.

113 "harpies": Thomas, *Dateline,* p. 7.

113 "Poor Jack . . .": Heymann, *Jackie,* p. 273.

113 "The boss . . .": Thomas, *Dateline,* p. 10.

113 "Say hello . . .": Giglio, *Presidency,* p. 271.

113 "low man on . . .": Helen Thomas, *Dateline,* p. 5.

113 "women were treated . . .": Ben Bradlee, *A Good Life* (New York, 1995), p. 298.

113 "was news . . .": Thomas, *Dateline,* pp. 12, 8.

113 "to avoid . . .": "White House Gag is On," clipping, with letter, Kitty Cole to Letitia Baldrige, c. 8 June 1962, Box 753, JFK WHSoc.

113 "the rudest . . .": Heymann, *Jackie,* p. 379.

113 One guest . . . : *USNWR,* 9 Apr. 1962, pp. 57–58.

113 "The Private . . .": *GH,* Feb. 1963, pp. 74, 165–166. See also Robert G. Deindorfer to Pierre Salinger, 16 Aug. 1962, JFK WHCF.

114 "the practice . . .": JFK news conference, 21 Feb. 1963, Joseph P. Berry, Jr., *JFK and the Media* (Lanham, MD, 1987), p. 1.

114 "an air . . .": JFK to Henry Luce, 8 Aug. 1961, Box 31, JFK POF.

114 "Ted Sorensen . . .": Stanley Tretick to JFK, 19 July 1962, Box 705, PP5/Kennedy, Caroline, JFK WHCF.

114 "We'd better . . .": R. Reeves, *President Kennedy,* p. 475.

114 "Mrs. Jacqueline . . .": *New York Journal American,* 23 Dec. 1961, p. 1.

114 "a guided . . .": Eldridge Cleaver, *Soul on Ice* (New York, 1968), p. 181.

114 "COMMUNISTS CAN . . .": Raymond J. Conner to JFK, 24 Dec. 1961, Box 706, PP5/JBK, JKF WHCF.

114 Kennedy's people . . . : Pierre Salinger to JFK, 23 Dec. 1961, Benjamin McKelway to Salinger, 25 Dec. 1961, France Leary telegram, undated, all in Box 10, Pierre Salinger MSS, JFK Lib.

115 "grabbing their . . .": Garry Wills, *Kennedy Imprisonment* (New York, 1981, 1982), p. 35.

115 "keep our . . .": R. Reeves, *President Kennedy,* p. 102.

115 "Is there . . .": Berry, *Media,* p. 2.

115 "resplendent": AMS, *Thousand Days,* p. 277.

115 "No . . . I . . .": R. Reeves, *President Kennedy,* p. 93.

115 "political . . .": *USNWR,* 17 Sept. 1962, p. 42.

115 "Despite himself . . .": AMS, *Thousand Days,* p. 259.

115 "image . . .": Dean Acheson to HST, 18 July 1961, in David McCullough, *Truman* (New York, 1992), p. 980.

115 "My God . . .": AMS, *Thousand Days,* p. 295.

115 "There's an . . .": Ibid., p. 289.

115 "one of . . .": O'Donnell and Powers, *Johnny,* p. 311.

116 "Jesus, it's . . .": R. Reeves, *President Kennedy,* p. 106.

116 "It is . . .": AMS, *Thousand Days,* p. 840.

116 "wants to . . .": Hugh Sidey, *JFK, President* (New York, 1964), p. 47.

116 "whatever the . . .": "Interview with Mrs. JFK," p. 6.

116 "to make . . .": Clifford, *Counsel,* p. 364.

116 "dentist office . . .": JBK to H. F. du Pont, 21 Nov. 1962, Box 947, JFK WHSoc.

116 "a woman's . . .": *BosG,* 27 May 1962, p. 18.

117 "Do you . . .": J. B. West, *Upstairs at the White House* (New York, 1973), pp. 191–192.

117 "brilliant . . . the renovation . . .": JBK to du Pont, 21 Nov. 1962.

117 "horrible wrinkles . . .": JBK to Clifford, 3 Nov. 1963 in Clifford, *Counsel,* p. 367.

117 "I think . . .": Evelyn Lincoln to Larry O'Brien [JBK dictated], 23 Jan. 1963, Box 62, JFK POF.

117 "I want . . .": Sidey, *JFK,* p. 283.

117 "Jack and . . .": Clifford, *Counsel,* p. 365.

117 "Oh, Dr. King . . .": Harris Wofford, *Of Kennedys and Kings* (Pittsburgh, 1980, 1992), p. 128.

118 "Just forget . . .": Letitia Baldrige OH, p. 52.

118 "Quarreling over . . .": Salinger, *With Kennedy,* p. 88.

118 "relationship between . . .": CBS "A Tour of the White House," 14 Feb. 1962, TNC 164, JFK AV; transcript of interview, p. 12, Box 701, JFK WHSoc.

118 "Jacqueline Kennedy . . .": "News Nielsen," Henry Rahmel to Pierre Salinger, 12 Mar. 1962, Box 706, PP5/JBK, JFK WHCF.

118 "the most successful . . .": Pierre Salinger OH, p. 117.

118 "a charming . . .": *BosG,* 16 Feb. 1962, p. 22.

118 "fragile loveliness . . .": *BosG,* 15 Feb. 1962, p. 18.

118 "I approve . . .": Sidey, *JFK,* p. 280.

118 Bradlees sensed: Bradlee, *Conversations,* pp. 57–58.

119 "I think . . .": "World of JBK."

119 middle class . . .: Ben J. Wattenberg, *The Real America,* rev. ed. (New York, 1974, 1976), pp. 51, 52, 85.

119 "the average . . .": *NYT,* 20 Jan. 1962, p. 14.

119 "an empty . . .": "World of JBK."

119 "Nothing quite . . .": *USNWR,* 3 Apr. 1961, p. 66.

119 "It was . . .": *LHJ,* Mar. 1964, p. 59.

119   "It's bound . . .": Charles Bartlett to JFK, undated, Box 28, JFK POF. See also *BosTr,* 21
         Feb. 1962, p. 26.
119   "a part . . .": R. Reeves, *President Kennedy,* p. 476.
120   "general ferment . . .": BD [Biddle Duke?] to August Heckscher, 21 Nov. 1962, Box 40,
         August Heckscher MSS, JFK Lib.
120   "In case . . .": Letitia Baldrige to Evelyn Lincoln, 17 Feb. 1961, Box 62, JFK POF.
120   "Now, Jackie . . .": Kelley, *Jackie Oh!,* pp. 188–189.
120   "My family . . .": Jim Bishop, *A Day in the Life of President Kennedy* (New York, 1964),
         p. 53.
120   "about family . . .": Ibid., p. 56.
120   "Jack has . . .": Lasky, *JFK,* p. 693.
120   "She did . . .": Bishop, *A Day in the Life,* p. 23.
121   "had one . . .": Letitia Baldrige to Mrs. John E. Davis, 18 July 1962, Box 906, JFK
         WHSoc.
121   Jack once scribbled . . . : Christopher Andersen, *Jack and Jackie* (New York, 1996), p. 189.
121   comic book: *Caroline Kennedy* (Derby, CT, 1961), Box 705, PP5/Caroline Kennedy,
         JFK WHCF.
121   "You'll find . . .": Fred Blumenthal, "A Working Weekend with the President," clipping,
         Autumn 1963, Box W-9, AMS MSS, JFK Lib.
121   "That's your . . .": Martin, *A Hero,* p. 317.
121   "Come on . . .": William Miller, *Fishbait* (Englewood Cliffs, NJ, 1977), p. 298.
122   Lincoln's Birthday: R. Reeves, *President Kennedy,* p. 464.
122   "the responsibility . . .": Ibid., p. 154.
122   "What are . . .": Martin, *A Hero,* p. 132.
122   "The president . . .": Andersen, *Jack and Jackie,* p. 330.
122   "Tell her . . .": R. Reeves, *President Kennedy,* pp. 154–155.
122   "civil war . . .": Baldrige in Carl Sferrazza Anthony, *First Ladies,* 2 vols. (New York,
         1991), 2:50.
122   "with the women": R. Reeves, *President Kennedy,* p. 82.
122   "Good night . . .": Sidey, *JFK,* p. 95.
123   "the art . . .": "Jacqueline Kennedy's Asian Tour," Mar. 1962, USG 1–16, JFK AV.
123   nearly four hundred thousand . . . : Government of India, Overseas Communication
         Service, New Delhi, 24 Mar. 1962, Box 705, PP5/JBK, JFK WHCF.
123   "You are . . .": CBS, "Jackie's Journey to India" with Walter Cronkite, 16 Mar. 1962,
         TNC 205, JFK AV.
123   "It feels . . .": *BosTr,* 30 Mar. 1962, p. 14.
123   Anticommunists . . . : See David Lawrence column, *BosTr,* 16 Mar. 1962, p. 18.
123   Moralists . . . : See Mrs. James Haller to JBK, 19 Mar. 1962, Box 6, JFK WHSoc.
123   "Has it . . .": Mr. and Mrs. Paul W. Ober to Pierre Salinger, 11 Mar. 1962, Box 706, JFK
         WHCF.
123   "is mostly . . .": *NYT,* 25 Mar. 1962, p. 3.
123   "Jesus Christ . . .": Kelley, *Jackie Oh!,* p. 187.
123   "The closer . . .": Elizabeth S. Cowles to JBK, 6 Apr. 1962, Box 257, JFK WHSoc.
123   "I was . . .": Dolores E. B. Parry to JBK, 30 Mar. 1962, Box 257, JFK WHSoc.
124   "Of course . . .": Vivian Kopritz to JBK, 26 Mar. 1962, Box 257, JFK WHSoc.
124   "Our First . . .": Mrs. O. P. Bowen to JBK, 26 Apr. 1962, Box 257, JFK WHSoc.
124   "Are you . . .": A. Babcock to JBK, 5 May 1962, Box 36, JFK WHSoc.
124   excesses undermined: *LAT,* 17 July 1961, p. 3.
124   "the peacock . . .": *ChiT,* 13 Apr. 1962, p. 26.
124   "DOES THIS . . .": Concerned Citizens of America Committee to JBK, Aug. 1962, Box
         706, JFK WHSoc.
124   "Has something . . .": Mrs. H. E. Bellomy to JFK, 27 Aug. 1962, Box 906, JFK
         WHSoc.
124   "It appears . . .": *NYDN,* 26 Aug. 1962, p. 4.
124   "I'm just . . .": Mrs. F. D. Carter to JBK, 16 Oct. 1962, Box 906, JFK WHSoc.

125   "A Harvard . . .": Lasky, *JFK*, p. 725.

125   "A LITTLE . . .": Heymann, *Jackie*, p. 356.

125   "headlong national . . .": Barry Goldwater, *Goldwater* (New York, 1988), pp. 130, 139.

125   "We're having . . .": Peter Collier and David Horowitz, *The Kennedys* (New York, 1984), p. 359.

125   "People told . . .": T. C. Reeves, *Character*, p. 237.

125   "good looks . . .": George Gallup, "Gallup Poll on Mrs. Kennedy," 8 Oct. 1962, clipping, Box W-9, AMS MSS.

126   "He was completely . . .": John White in Parmet, *Jack*, p. 94.

126   "if I . . .": T. C. Reeves, *Character*, p. 202.

126   "We're a . . .": R. Reeves, *President Kennedy*, p. 291.

126   "he was heartily . . .": Hamilton, *Reckless Youth*, p. 359.

126   "will help . . .": Wills, *Kennedy Imprisonment*, p. 26.

126   "Happy Birthday . . .": Manchester, *Portrait*, p. 89.

126   Nostalgic for . . . : On underlying causes see, for example, Ethel Klein, *Gender Politics* (Cambridge, MA, 1984), pp. 5–6; William Henry Chafe, *The American Woman* (New York, 1972), p. 247.

127   "housekeepers . . .": Theda Skocpol, *Protecting Soldiers and Mothers* (Cambridge, MA, 1992), p. 51.

127   "Certainly there . . .": Margaret Price, "Women—Role in Government," 8 Dec, 1960, Box 1072, JFK Pre.

127   "everything to . . .": Clayton Fritchey to JFK, 22 July 1963, Box 374, JFK WHCF.

127   "Kennedy never . . .": Heymann, *Jackie*, p. 370.

127   "assume the . . .": Mary C. Rest, 18 Jan. 1962, Box 27, JFK WHSoc.

127   "how you . . .": Mrs. Erma Shapiro to JBK, 6 May 1962, Box 27, JFK WHSoc.

127   "As the mothers . . .": *Parent's Magazine*, Nov. 1963, p. 57. The other magazines were *McCall's, Cosmopolitan, Good Housekeeping, Redbook, Family Circle*, and *Woman's Day*, Nov. 1963. JFK to Robert Stein, 6 Aug. 1963, "HU3 Equality for Women," Box 374, JFK WHCF. See also Stein to Pierre Salinger, 13 May 1963, Box 106, JFK POF.

128   "My dear . . .": *Look*, 17 Nov. 1964, p. 95.

128   "She hung . . .": T. C. Reeves, *Character*, p. 400.

128   "the one . . .": Heymann, *Jackie*, p. 386.

128   "Jackie, do . . .": Ibid., p. 389.

128   "impropriety of . . .": Oliver P. Bolton, 88th Cong., 1st sess., 16 Oct. 1963, *CR*, 109:19627.

128   "Does this . . .": Heymann, *Jackie*, p. 393.

128   "Jackie's guilt . . .": Bradlee, *Conversations*, p. 219.

128   "with Sinatra . . .": *Nwswk*, 28 Oct. 1963, p. 20.

129   "I will . . .": JBK to Pamela Turnure, 11 Nov. 1963 in Salinger, *With Kennedy*, p. 304.

129   "to hear him . . .": LBJ, *The Vantage Point* (New York, 1971), p. 1.

129   "It's my . . .": Theodore White, *In Search of History* (New York, 1978), p. 542.

129   "The manner . . .": *LHJ*, Mar. 1964, pp. 58–59.

129   "let them . . .": White, *Search*, p. 544.

129   "Mrs. Kennedy . . .": LaBJ, *A White House Diary* (New York, 1970), p. 10.

130   "if it . . .": Heymann, *Jackie*, p. 409.

130   "And her message . . .": White, *Search*, pp. 538, 543–545.

130   "The knowledge . . .": "JBK Speaks to the Nation Thanking Them for Condolences," 14 Jan. 1964, IFP 6, JFK AV.

130   "Now no . . .": JBK to AMS, 23 Nov. 1965, Box W-7, AMS MSS.

130   "a touch . . .": CBS [WTOP] "JFK One Thousand Days and Ten Years," 11 Nov. 1973, WHCA VTR 6657, Arch AV.

131   sex, power, and . . . : See Wills, *Kennedy Imprisonment*, p. 33; Michael Kimmel, *Manhood in America* (New York, 1996), pp. 268–269.

131   the ideals so grand . . . : See James T. Patterson, *Grand Expectations* (New York, 1996); Robert J. Samuelson, *The Good Life and Its Discontents* (New York, 1995).

CHAPTER 4. "CRAWLING DOWN PENNSYLVANIA AVENUE ON BROKEN GLASS"

Page

133 "high, forbidding . . .": LBJ, *Vantage Point* (New York, 1971), p. 13.

134 "Lady Bird would . . .": Sam Houston Johnson, *My Brother Lyndon* (New York, 1969), p. 108.

134 "Concession, Patience . . .": LBJ, undated notes, desk P38, Box 1, Handwriting File, LBJ Lib.

134 "show horses . . .": Erv Duggan in Merle Miller, *Lyndon* (New York, 1980), pp. 418–419.

134 "was like comparing . . .": Hubert Humphrey in Miller, *Lyndon,* p. 421.

135 "I am suddenly . . .": LaBJ, *A White House Diary* (New York, 1970), p. 17.

135 "been a partner . . .": "Biography of Mrs. LBJ," Box 60, LBJ Liz-S.

135 "I will try . . .": "Mrs. Johnson's Press Releases—1964," 8 Dec. 1963, Box 73, LBJ-Liz S.

135 "dazzling . . .": *Time,* 28 Aug. 1964, p. 20.

135 "You don't sell . . .": *American Heritage,* Dec. 1980, p. 13.

135 "I've got . . .": *GH,* Mar. 1964, p. 37.

135 "voluptuous": *SatEP,* 8 Feb. 1964, p. 24.

135 "pretty as . . .": LaBJ to Ellen Cooper, 13 Mar. 1961, Ellen Cooper MSS, LBJ Lib.

135 "their mouths . . .": C. David Heymann, *A Woman Named Jackie* (New York, 1989), p. 407.

135 "sandwiched in . . .": LaBJ, Diary, p. 69; LaBJ speech, 28 Oct. 1970, p. 3, Box 88, Harry Middleton MSS, LBJ Lib.

135 "to give my . . .": ABC, "A Conversation with the First Lady," 23 Aug. 1964, MP 494, LBJ AV.

135 "to tell him . . .": Clark M. Clifford OH, p. 29.

135 "Lady Bird brought . . .": LBJ, *Vantage,* p. 299.

135 "there next to . . .": Joseph Califano, *The Triumph and Tragedy of Lyndon Johnson* (New York, 1991), p. 28.

136 "Johnson would . . .": McPherson quoted in Myra MacPherson, *The Power Lovers* (New York, 1975), p. 184.

136 "It thrills me . . .": *Coronet,* Feb. 1966, p. 18.

136 "a big political . . .": CBS, "The New President: LBJ," 23 Nov. 1963, MP 521, LBJ AV.

136 "I think . . .": CBS, "The First Lady at Home," 12 Aug. 1964, MP 475, LBJ AV.

136 "I find . . .": ABC, "The View from the White House with Claudia Taylor Johnson," 27 Dec. 1968, WHCA 2949, LBJ AV.

136 "A sturdy political . . .": Jack Valenti, *A Very Human President* (New York, 1975), p. 39.

136 "let's save . . .": *Nwswk,* 28 Dec. 1964, p. 12.

136 "Unfortunately, plans . . .": LaBJ to Brooke Astor, 28 Oct. 1965, Box 83, LBJ WHSoc-A.

136 "the most wonderful . . .": LBJ to Mr. Dee J. Kelly, 28 Oct. 1964, Box 2, Ex TR 1, LBJ WHCF.

136 "my dearest . . .": LBJ to David Dubinsky, 28 Oct. 1964, Box 2, Ex TR 1.

136 "great political . . .": LBJ to Charles S. Robb, 28 Oct. 1968, LBJ Ref.

136 comic book: *Lyndon B. Johnson* (New York, 1964), Box 10, Ex FG1, LBJ WHCF.

136 "an elusive private . . .": *Nwswk,* 28 Dec. 1964, p. 12.

136 "working partnership": *McCall's,* Feb. 1964, p. 4.

136 "a woman who . . .": *Nwswk,* 28 Dec. 1964, p. 14.

136 "marriage, like . . .": Ibid.

136 "I'm not . . .": *Time,* 28 Aug. 1964, p. 21.

137 "he-men": Liz OH, 5:12.

137 "Oh, he makes . . .": Betty Hughes OH, 1:58.

137 "Mrs. Johnson has . . .": Liz OH, 5:8–9.

137 "I don't . . .": Liz speech, 15 Apr. 1965, Box 1, Office of the President File, LBJ Lib.

137 "the greatest . . .": Liz OH, 3:45.

137 "SCHEDULE STIRS . . .": *USNWR,* 27 Jan. 1964, p. 16.

137 "I wanted . . .": Richard Goodwin, *Remembering America* (Boston, 1988), p. 271.

137 "The bet we . . .": LaBJ, *Diary,* p. 156.

137 "tea poisoning": Ibid., p. 138.

137 "Mrs. Johnson didn't . . .": Liz OH, 2:33.

137 "problem that . . .": Betty Friedan, *The Feminine Mystique* (New York, 1963), p. 11.

137 "egalitarian marriage": Sheila Rothman, *Woman's Proper Place* (New York, 1975), p. 6; Steven Mintz and Susan Kellogg, *Domestic Revolutions* (New York, 1988), p. xvi.

138 "chief purpose . . .": *SatEP,* 22–29 Dec. 1962, pp. 27–28, 32. See also William Henry Chafe, *The American Woman* (New York, 1972), p. 231.

138 "natural woman . . .": LaBJ speech, 9 June 1964, p. 1, Box 73, LBJ Liz-S.

138 Southern belles: Anne Firor Scott, *The Southern Lady* (Chicago, 1970); Eugene D. Genovese, "Toward a Kinder and Gentler America," Carol Blesser, *In Joy and in Sorrow* (New York, 1991), pp. 125–134.

138 "a wife . . .": LaBJ speech, 9 June 1964, pp. 1–3, Box 73, LBJ Liz-S.

138 "If given . . .": LaBJ speech, 24 June 1964, p. 4, Box 73, LBJ Liz-S.

138 "JFK, with . . .": Eric Goldman, *The Tragedy of Lyndon Johnson* (New York, 1969), p. 11.

138 "unabashedly in . . .": LBJ in Miller, *Lyndon,* p. 545.

138 "A woman's place . . .": *SatEP,* 27 June 1964, p. 86.

139 "extra careful . . .": Ibid.

139 "prowomen feeling": Katie Louchheim in Miller, *Lyndon,* p. 547.

139 "the great untapped . . .": Luci Baines Johnson in Miller, *Lyndon,* p. 544.

139 "In a day . . .": LBJ to Alice Brown, 17 Jan. 1965, Box 12, LBJ SN.

139 "the harem": George Reedy, *Memoir* (New York, 1982), p. 36.

139 "more women . . .": Robert Dallek, *Lone Star Rising* (New York, 1991), p. 189.

139 "Move over . . . Ah've had . . .": MacPherson, *Power Lovers,* pp. 185–186.

139 "You have . . .": *People,* 2 Feb. 1987, p. 35.

139 "In the Lyndon . . .": Reedy, *Memoir,* p. 31.

140 "I infiltrate": Goldman, *Tragedy,* p. 357.

140 "in a few . . .": LBJ, *Vantage,* p. 98.

140 "I was not . . .": Ibid., pp. 95, 97.

140 "Your 'war' . . .": Mrs. Charles Muehlstein to LBJ, 16 May 1964, Box 64, Ex PP5/LaBJ, LBJ WHCF.

140 she traveled . . .: "Fact Sheet on Mrs. Johnson's Travels . . . ," c. 1964, Box 73, LBJ Liz-S.

140 "The hustings . . .": *NYDN,* 9 Aug. 1964, p. 4.

140 "serenity . . .": "First Lady at Home."

140 "a sounding board . . .": "Conversation with the First Lady."

141 President's film . . . : "LBJ: Campaign Special," 1964, MP 648, LBJ AV.

141 "When I . . .": Mrs. William Howard Gardener to LBJ, 12 Aug. 1964, Box 64, Ex PP5/LaBJ, LBJ WHCF.

141 "Mrs. Johnson represents . . .": Douglass Cater to LBJ, 18 Aug. 1964, Box 62, Ex PP5/LaBJ, LBJ WHCF.

141 "a link between . . .": *Weekly Digest,* 6 Sept. 1964, 48:10 in PP5/LaBJ, 9/1/64–9/20/64, LBJ WHCF.

141 "early sun-ups . . .": "Handy Facts on the Johnson Ladies" in Box 88, Middleton MSS.

141 "subdued": Horace Busby to Liz, 2 Oct. 1964, Box 18, Horace Busby MSS, LBJ Lib.

141 "They didn't want . . .": Bess Abell OH, p. 13.

141 With 55 . . .: D. Elaine Sellers, "It's All Smiles Aboard 'Special,'" clipping, *Story of the Lady Bird Special,* p. 2, Box 2, TR1/LaBJ, LBJ WHCF.

141 "I am fond . . .": *Whistle Stop,* 13 Oct. 1964, Box 12, LBJ Liz-S.

141 "We are . . .": Liz, *Ruffles & Flourishes* (College State, TX, 1993), pp. 154–155.

142 "It's a new . . .": *New Orleans States-Item,* clipping, *Lady Bird Special,* p. 5.

142 "You've put . . .": 31 Dec. 1964, Box 4, Handwriting File, LBJ Lib.

142 "Lady Bird . . .": *Charleston Post-Courier,* 27 Sept. 1990, p. 3, LBJ Ref.

142 "chivalry is not . . .": Scooter Miller in Miller, *Lyndon,* p. 483.

142 "one of the . . .": LaBJ to G. G. Cromwell, 31 Oct. 1964, Box 1329, LBJ WHSoc-A.

142 "packed the bag . . .": LaBJ to Barbara McAden, *Lady Bird Special,* p. 7.

142 "warrior . . .": David Hackett Fischer, *Albion's Seed* (New York, 1989), p. 676.

142   the eight-year-old: Dallek, *Lone Star,* p. 37.
142   "There was nothing . . .": Doris Kearns, *Lyndon Johnson and the American Dream* (New York, 1977), p. 26.
143   The first night: Ibid., p. 76.
143   "it was high . . .": Henry Hirshberg OH, p. 8.
143   "For Bird . . .": Goldman, *Tragedy,* p. 344.
143   "I see something . . .": LBJ to LaBJ, in "A National Tribute to Lady Bird Johnson On the Occasion of Her Sixty-Fifth Birthday," 11 Dec. 1977, pp. 4, 5, LBJ Lib.
143   "richest man . . .": Robert A. Caro, *The Years of LBJ: The Path to Power* (New York: 1982), p. 294.
143   most likely . . . : Ibid., p. 297.
144   "holier, more . . .": Sara Josephine Hale, "Empire Woman," in Mary Beth Norton, *Major Problems in American Women's History* (Lexington, MA, 1989), p. 114. See also Patricia Limerick, *The Legacy of Conquest* (New York, 1987, 1988), pp. 48, 53; Carl Degler, *At Odds* (New York, 1980), pp. 47–49.
144   "looked like . . .": Virginia Durr OH, p. 10.
144   "She's as purty . . .": *USNWR,* 2 Dec. 1963, p. 16.
144   "the family nurse . . .": LaBJ to Mrs. M. R. Curtis, 12 Dec. 1963, Box 1621, LBJ WHSoc-A.
144   "give way . . .": Durr OH, p. 10.
144   "undoubtedly the most . . .": LaBJ interview with Blake Clark for *Reader's Digest,* c. summer, 1963, p. 6, Box 60, LBJ Liz-S.
144   "My father . . .": Ibid., p. 3.
144   "feudal . . .": LaBJ interview with Clark, p. 9.
144   "for every . . .": LaBJ interview with Henry Brandon, for *NYTM,* Aug. 1967, Box 60, LBJ Liz-S.
144   "she wanted . . .": Eugenia Lassater in *Time,* 28 Aug. 1964, p. 22.
144   "people in . . .": LaBJ interview with Clark, p. 13.
144   "repulsive": LaBJ in Miller, *Lyndon,* p. 52.
144   "excessively thin . . .": LaBJ interview with Clark, p. 11.
144   "I just knew . . .": *NYTM,* 10 Sept. 1967, p. 49.
145   "I've always . . .": LBJ interview with Blake Clark for *Reader's Digest,* 3 July 1963, p. 1, Box 60, LBJ Liz-S.
145   "he told me . . .": Caro, *Path,* pp. 298–299.
145   "I just thought . . .": LaBJ in Miller, *Lyndon,* p. 62.
145   "Hmmm. You've . . .": LaBJ interview with Clark, p. 13.
145   "his ears . . .": Emily Crow Selden OH, 2:7.
145   "We either . . .": LaBJ interview with Clark, p. 16.
145   "I hope . . .": Dan Quill OH, pp. 4–5, 10, 30. See also Hirshberg OH, pp. 7, 10.
145   "the prettiest girl . . .": Goldman, *Tragedy,* p. 345.
145   "than my own . . .": LaBJ to Melvin and Anita Winters, 23 Jan. 1959, Melvin Winters MSS, LBJ Lib.
145   "Bird . . . are you . . .": Kearns, *LBJ,* p. 88.
145   "Mein Herr": *Woman's Day,* Dec. 1967, p. 89.
146   "Why, darlin' . . .": Mary Hardesty in Miller, *Lyndon,* p. 433.
146   "emotional and affectionate": LBJ to George Brown, 27 Apr. 1947, Box 12, LBJ SN.
146   "She's the greatest . . .": *Woman's Day,* Dec. 1967, p. 89.
146   "Never shall I . . .": LBJ to LaBJ, 17 Aug. 1935, "Tribute," p. 8.
146   "beehive": LaBJ interview with Clark, p. 20.
146   "called my Daddy": Ibid., pp. 21–22.
146   "I kept that . . .": Caro, *Path,* p. 408.
146   "a nightmare": *Woman's Day,* Dec. 1967, p. 94.
146   "larger than . . .": Elizabeth Rowe OH, 1:14.
146   "I was always . . .": Kearns, *LBJ,* p. 83.
146   "I remember Alice . . .": Caro, *Path,* p. 490.

146 "I could never . . .": Ibid., p. 492.

147 "I felt terribly . . .": Kearns, *LBJ,* p. 98.

147 "fondly . . .": "The Home Movies of LaBJ," HM 3, 1941 Senate Campaign, p. 5, LBJ AV; LaBJ interview with Clark, p. 23.

147 "This was a sadness": *Woman's Day,* Dec. 1967, p. 95.

147 "business school . . .": LaBJ to Reese Lockett, 5 Feb. 1942, Box 74, Subject File, LBJA.

147 "LBJ. To be . . .": See "Alice Glass," LBJ Ref.

147 "scared": LaBJ interview with Clark, p. 24.

147 "First you *use* . . .": LBJ to LaBJ, in "Tribute," p. 12.

147 "strange new . . .": LaBJ to Jerry Winkle, 15 Apr. 1942, Box 37, House of Representatives MSS, LBJ Lib.

147 "two of the . . .": LaBJ to George Brown, 26 Mar. 1942, Box 12, LBJ SN.

147 "Lyndon-Johnson quitting . . .": LaBJ to Mrs. E. M. Cape, 3 Mar. 1942, Box 14, LBJ SN.

148 "More and more . . .": LaBJ to A. J. Wirtz, 13 Mar. 1942, Box 37, Subject File, LBJA.

148 "You certainly . . .": Jane Ickes to LaBJ, c. Mar. 1942, Box 74, Subject File, LBJA.

148 "the best damn . . .": Jim [Blundell?] to "My Dear Friends . . . ," 27 Apr. 1942, Box 37, House of Representatives MSS.

148 "If Bird keeps . . .": Jim [Blundell] to LBJ, c. spring, 1942, p. 2, Box 37, House of Representatives MSS.

148 "What changes . . .": LaBJ to L. E. Jones, 4 May 1942, Box 74, Subject File, LBJA.

148 "the grandest day . . .": LaBJ to Ben Crider, 16 July 1942, Box 16, LBJ SN.

148 "We'll see . . .": Robert Caro, *The Years of LBJ: Means of Ascent* (New York, 1990), pp. 69–70.

148 World War II . . . : Susan M. Hartmann, *The Homefront and Beyond* (Boston, 1982), pp. 23–24; D'Ann Cambell, *Women at War With America* (Boston, 1984), pp. 236–237.

148 "one of the . . .": LaBJ interview with Clark, pp. 25–26.

148 "He told her . . .": *Woman's Day,* Dec. 1967, p. 95.

148 "Every woman . . .": Ibid.

148 "full time": LaBJ in *WSJ,* 23 Mar. 1964, p. 1.

148 "running the . . .": LBJ to JC Kellam, 25 June 1943, Box 22, LBJ SN.

149 "She's any man's . . .": Lewis L. Gould, *Lady Bird Johnson and the Environment* (Lawrence, KS, 1988), p. 20.

149 "can't do . . .": Caro, *Means of Ascent,* p. 299.

149 "the most wonderful . . .": Dallek, *Lone Star,* p. 326.

149 "All I could . . .": *Time,* 28 Aug. 1964, p. 22.

149 "an efficient woman . . .": *Life,* 25 June 1956, p. 121.

149 "to compartmentalize . . .": Bess Abell in Miller, *Lyndon,* pp. 430–431.

149 "With all . . .": *Reader's Digest,* Nov. 1963, p. 5.

150 "de-privileged . . .": Willie Day Taylor OH, p. 22.

150 "worst feature . . .": "New President."

150 "Lyndon said . . .": LaBJ to J. J. Pickle, 4 Aug. 1955, Box 30, LBJ SN.

150 "home base": "First Lady at Home."

150 "Thank God . . .": Rowe OH, 2:20.

150 "little scrawny . . .": Dallek, *Lone Star,* p. 572.

150 "traded a career . . .": Press release, Citizens for Johnson National Committee, c. 1960, LBJ Ref.

150 "I'm not deeply . . .": *Austin American Statesman,* 3 Apr. 1960, pp. 1, 4.

150 "charming and business-wise": Press release, Citizens for Johnson c. 1960.

150 "major crisis . . .": LBJ interview with Clark, pp. 5–6.

150 "the Hill . . .": "Conversation with the First Lady."

151 "would sit . . .": JBK OH, pp. 12–13.

151 "Lady Bird carried . . .": *Time,* 28 Aug. 1964, p. 23.

151 "to help . . .": Gould, *Lady Bird,* pp. 12–13.

151 "Uncle Cornpone": Goldman, *Tragedy,* p. 18.

151 "more about . . .": *SatEP,* 8 Feb. 1964, p. 20.

151 "a wonderful man . . .": *NYTM,* 15 Dec. 1963, 6:73.
151 "I married . . .": ABC, "The View from the White House with LaBJ," 27 Dec. 1968, 2949, LBJ AV.
151 "Lyndon saw . . .": *Reader's Digest,* Nov. 1963, p. 2.
151 "bullied, shoved . . .": *San Antonio Express,* 25 Apr. 1983, C1.
151 "millions upon . . .": Kearns, *LBJ,* p. 219.
152 "before the aura . . .": Wilbur J. Cohen in Miller, *Lyndon,* p. 497.
152 "more of each": LaBJ interview with Drew Pearson, 16 Nov. 1967, Box 60, LBJ Liz-S.
152 "pillow talk": Califano, *Triumph,* p. 235.
152 "I came very . . .": Lewis Gould, "Lady Bird Johnson and Beautification" in Robert A. Divine, ed., *The Johnson Years, Volume Two* (Lawrence, KS, 1987), p. 172.
152 "In her quiet . . .": Miller, *Lyndon,* p. 432.
152 "Sometimes I'd like . . .": *Coronet,* Feb. 1966, p. 18.
152 "shake hands . . .": Liz OH, 3:43.
152 "She wanted . . .": Abell OH, p. 2.
152 "power . . .": Califano, *Triumph,* p. 85.
152 "if I take . . .": LaBJ, *Diary,* p. 255.
153 "Next time . . .": Ibid., p. 299.
153 "bad physical . . .": Gould, *Lady Bird,* p. 2.
153 "Beauty is . . .": LaBJ speech, 1 Oct. 1965, p. 2, Box 60, LBJ Liz-S.
153 "environmental quality": Sharon Francis OH, 2:58.
153 "New Conservation": Vaughn Davis Bornet, *The Presidency of Lyndon B. Johnson* (Lawrence, KS, 1983), p. 138.
153 "a combination . . .": LaBJ speech, 1 Oct. 1965, p. 2.
153 "Getting on . . .": "Tribute," p. 23; LaBJ, *Diary,* p. 233.
154 "revitalize parks . . .": Report to the President for the First Lady's Committee for a More Beautiful Capital," Box 22, LBJ WHSoc-B.
154 "A conversation between . . .": Emily Post, *Emily Post's Etiquette* (New York, 1965), p. 40.
154 "Lady Bird's business": Bornet, *LBJ,* p. 136.
154 "Laurance Rockefeller . . .": *NYT,* 3 July 1967, p. 1.
154 "to produce . . .": LBJ speech, 25 May 1965, p. 1, Box 79, Bill Moyers MSS, LBJ Lib.
154 "the beautification expert . . .": LBJ speech, 8 May 1967, Doug Cater, Memos for the President: "National Youth Administration," Box 326, Fred Panzer MSS, LBJ Lib.
154 Johnson commanded . . . : LBJ to Luther Hodges, 21 Jan. 1965, Box 5, Handwriting File, LBJ Lib.
154 The major . . . : *LAT,* 13 Sept. 1965, 2:6.
154 "Why that's Lady . . .": *WasP,* 7 Oct. 1965, G11.
155 "If we don't . . .": Francis OH, p. 55.
155 "continued on her . . .": *LAT,* 13 Sept. 1965, 2:6.
155 "No one . . .": Liz to LaBJ, 4 Oct. 1965, Box 14, LBJ WHSoc-B.
155 "this remarkably tenacious . . .": John L. Sweeney in Miller, *Lyndon,* pp. 429–430.
155 "one of the . . .": *ChiT,* 22 Sept. 1965, p. 22.
155 Congressman Robert Dole . . . : U.S. Congress, House, 89th Cong., 1st sess., 7 Oct. 1965, *CR,* 3:26306.
155 "when one chooses . . .": 8 Oct. 1965, *CR,* 3:26423.
155 "It is a . . .": Bornet, *LBJ,* p. 142.
155 "Impeach Lady Bird . . .": Gould, *Lady Bird,* p. 165.
155 "conservation": LBJ, *Vantage,* pp. 336–339.
155 "and he never . . .": Califano, *Triumph,* p. 85.
156 "A visit . . .": ABC, "A Visit to Washington with Mrs. LBJ on Behalf of a More Beautiful America," 25 Nov. 1965, MP 1052, LBJ AV.
156 "most appealing . . .": Mrs. Charles Draper to LBJ, 27 Nov. 1965, Box 15, LBJ Liz-A.
156 "sow some . . .": LaBJ, *Diary,* p. 298.
156 "somewhat . . .": Ben J. Wattenberg, *The Real America,* rev. ed. (New York, 1976), p. 226.
156 "exquisite edition[s]": LaBJ to Mary Lasker, 1 June 1965, Box 1340, LBJ WHSoc-A.

156 "this job allows . . .": LaBJ to Mr. Lankford Curtis, 9 June 1964, Box 1980, LBJ WHSoc-A.

156 "We didn't . . .": George Christian OH, 2:1.

156 "I tried . . .": Ibid., p. 4.

157 They needed . . . : See, for example, Bess Abell to Marvin Watson, 13 July 1965, Box 62, PP5/LaBJ; Marvin Watson to LBJ, 30 May 1967, Box 70, FG 11-8-1, LBJ WHCF.

157 "In an economy . . .": Liz to Marvin Watson, 19 July 1965 and 20 July 1965 in Liz, *Ruffles,* pp. 298–300.

157 Carpenter found: C.A. Sither to Marvin Watson, 15 Sept. 1967, Box 76, FG 11-8-1, LBJ WHCF.

157 prompted President . . . : LBJ memorandum to the Director of the Secret Service, 7 Nov. 1968, Box 64, Ex PP5/LaBJ, LBJ WHCF.

157 "With Mrs. . . .": *SFChr,* 16 July 1964, p. 37.

157 "eyes-and-ears . . .": *NYT,* 1 Mar. 1964, p. 54.

157 "I don't believe . . .": *Coronet,* Feb. 1966, p. 18.

157 They proposed . . . : Francis OH, 4:11.

158 "eyes and ears for . . .": *Life,* 13 Aug. 1965, p. 60.

158 "focus[ed] the interest . . .": *WasS,* 6 Nov. 1967, C6.

158 "I can report . . .": Walt W. Rostow to LBJ, 12 June 1967, Box 63, Ex PP5/LaBJ, LBJ WHCF.

158 "how many miles . . .": *NYT,* 27 Dec. 1968, p. 16.

158 "do not consider . . .": Bess Abell to Arthur Waxman, 28 July 1966, Box 2128, LBJ WHSoc-A.

158 "The marriage . . .": Simone Poulaine to Liz (with enclosure from Chet Haga), 4 May 1966, Box 78, PP5/Presidential Family, LBJ CF.

158 "Please! Each . . .": Mrs. R. J. Adams to LBJ and LaBJ, 22 May 1966, Box 62, LBJ Liz-A.

159 "uncelebrated middle-class . . .": *WasP,* 7 Aug. 1966, p. 1.

159 "the No. 1 story . . .": Liz to LBJ et al., 26 Apr. 1966, Box 78, PP5/LaBJ, LBJ CF.

159 "We have gotten . . .": Liz to LBJ, 3 Aug. 1966, Box 63, Ex PP5/LaBJ, LBJ WHCF.

159 "the American people . . .": Clark Clifford to LaBJ, 9 Aug. 1966, Box 353, LBJ WHSoc-A.

159 "She has come . . .": *National Observer,* 24 Apr. 1967, p. 14.

159 "total woman . . .": *Redbook,* July 1965, pp. 12, 20.

159 "Something is lacking . . .": *National Observer,* 24 Apr. 1967, p. 1.

160 "Lady Bird was . . .": Goldman, *Tragedy,* p. 375.

160 "current of feeling . . .": LaBJ, *Diary,* p. 452.

160 "Hey, hey LBJ . . .": *WasP,* 7 Aug. 1966, p. 1.

160 "I myself . . .": LaBJ, *Diary,* p. 449.

160 "swat[ting] Lady Bird . . .": *Time,* 28 Aug. 1964, p. 21.

161 "astonishing . . .": Jack Valenti to LBJ and Bill Moyers, 14 July 1965, Box 11, FG LBJ WHCF.

161 "a good picture . . .": Liz to LBJ, 4 Dec. 1964, Box 1, LBJ Office of the President File.

161 "ugly problem[s]": Valenti to LBJ and Moyers, 14 July 1965.

161 "quality of life": Fred Panzer to LBJ, 18 Sept. 1967, p. 1, Box 82, PR 16, LBJ CF.

161 "to grow . . .": LaBJ speech, 9 Oct. 1967, p. 5, Box 74, LBJ Liz-S.

161 "probably a mistake . . .": LaBJ, *Diary,* pp. 636–637.

161 "garden club": LaBJ to Sylvia Porter, 28 Dec. 1965, Box 14, LBJ Liz-A.

161 "Education-children . . .": Stewart L. Udall to LaBJ, 18 Mar. 1966, Box 2016, LBJ WHSoc-A.

162 "the minds . . .": Mrs. Vera Dunn to LaBJ, 24 Oct. 1967, Box 159, LBJ WHSoc-A.

162 "the biggest legislative. . . .": *NYT,* 3 July 1967, p. 8.

162 "a leisurely, civilized . . .": LaBJ, *Diary,* pp. 740, 764.

162 "Everyone is . . ." *LouCJ,* 6 July 1968, A4.

162 "garden club . . .": Allan Temko in *NYT,* 3 July 1967, p. 8.

163 "unfortunate, ill-considered . . .": "Statement of President Johnson," 23 Aug. 1968, Box 15, LBJ WHSoc-B.

163   "Thank you . . ." Nash Castro memorandum, 18 Dec. 1968, Box 3, Nash Castro MSS, LBJ Lib.

163   "the First Lady . . .": Joseph Califano to LaBJ, 30 Sept. 1968, Box 64, PP5 LBJ WHCF.

163   "gimmick . . .": LaBJ, *Diary,* p. 797.

163   "What Citizens . . .": Liz to LBJ and LaBJ, 26 Dec. 1967, Box 45, LBJ Liz-S.

164   "What do we . . .": "Remarks at First Lady's Luncheon for Women Doers," 18 Jan. 1968, pp. 6, 32, Box 45, LBJ Liz-S.

164   "ready to beat . . .": Francis OH, 2:37.

164   "Anybody who's . . .": "Remarks at First Lady's Luncheon," p. 33.

164   "violent . . .in her own . . .": "Telephone Calls—Carpenter's Office," 19 Jan. 1968, p. 1, Box 45, LBJ Liz-S.

164   "a stormy Thursday . . .": LaBJ to Mrs. Eugene Meyer, 24 Jan. 1968, Box 45, LBJ Liz-S.

164   "ears . . . are somewhat . . .": *Variety,* 24 Jan. 1968, p. 2.

164   "Hooray for Eartha . . .": "A Voter" to LaBJ, Box 1305, LBJ WHSoc-A.

165   "the most affluent . . .": Louis Harris and Associates, "The Harris Survey," 18 Apr. 1966, Box 82, PR16, LBJ CF.

165   "Stop cultivating . . .": Mrs. Shirley Almanza to LaBJ, 20 Jan. 1968, Box 1305, LBJ WHSoc-A.

165   "THE FIRST LADY . . .": Darlene Feldman to LBJ, 21 Jan. 1968, Box 1306, LBJ WHSoc-A.

165   "There seems . . .": *Houston Post,* 31 Jan. 1968, clipping, Box 63, PP5/LaBJ, LBJ WHCF.

165   "the quality . . .": *WasP,* 21 Jan. 1968, B6.

165   "was typical . . .": WBC, "News 4 Washington: Nancy Dickerson Report," 18 Jan. 1968, WHCA #127, LBJ AV.

165   "If Mrs. Johnson . . .": *Variety,* 24 Jan. 1968, p. 71.

165   "After all . . .": "Lady Bird Is Upset," UPI dispatch, Box 63, PP5/LaBJ, LBJ WHCF.

166   "pushing against . . .": LaBJ, *Diary,* p. 689.

166   "Surely the war . . .": *NYT,* 27 Dec. 1968, p. 16.

166   "Why don't people . . .": Goldman, *Tragedy,* p. 524.

166   "there had never . . .": Walt Rostow to LBJ and LaBJ, 25 Dec. 1968, Box 1790, LBJ WHSoc-A.

166   "endure": LaBJ, *Diary,* p. 569.

166   "in all our . . .": LBJ, *Vantage,* p. 429.

166   "to deescalate . . .": *Public Papers of LBJ* (Washington, DC, 1970), p. 470.

166   "wasn't really . . .": *NYT,* 27 Dec. 1968, p. 16.

167   "What role . . .": LBJ press conference, 31 Mar. 1968, p. 6, Box 80, Harry Middleton MSS, LBJ Lib.

167   "action . . . has not . . .": LBJ speech, 31 Mar. 1968; President's Remarks, alternate draft, McPherson, 29 Mar. 1968, both in Box 274, LBJ Statements. For final draft see *Papers of LBJ,* pp. 469–470.

167   a resurgent conservatism . . . : See Alan Brinkley, "The Problem of American Conservatism," *American Historical Review,* 99 (Apr. 1994): 409–429.

167   "The speech was . . .": LaBJ, *Diary,* p. 710.

CHAPTER 5. "STAND BY YOUR MAN"

Page

168   On election . . . : See JNE, *Pat Nixon: The Untold Story* (New York, 1978), pp. 246–247; RN, *RN,* 2 vols. (New York, 1978), 1:409–413.

169   "three words . . .": RN, *RN,* 1:15.

169   "honesty . . .": Earl Mazo, *Richard Nixon* (New York, 1959, 1960), p. 25.

169   "Richard always . . .": *Time,* 25 Aug. 1952, p. 13.

169   Dick distinguished . . . : Fawn M. Brodie, *Richard Nixon* (New York: 1981), p. 39.

169   "in her whole . . .": RN, *In the Arena* (New York, 1990), p. 87.

169   "He wasn't . . .": Jessamyn West in *Baltimore Sun,* 6 Dec. 1970, K1.

170   "to be *three* . . .": Hannah Nixon in *GH,* June 1960, p. 212.

170   "Show me . . .": RN, *RN,* 1:24.

170   "never could . . .": *Life,* 14 Dec. 1953, p. 151.

170   "beautiful and vivacious . . .": RN, *RN,* 1:28.

170   "Her life . . .": RN, *Arena,* p. 232.

170   "a quietly . . .": PN in *SatEP,* 6 Sept. 1952, p. 17.

170   "didn't want . . .": ABC, "A Visit with the First Lady," Virginia Sherwood, 12 Sept. 1971, 4649, Arch AV.

170   "stood out . . .": Dr. Frank Baxter in *Time,* 29 Feb. 1960, p. 26.

170   "had not lived yet": JNE, *Pat,* p. 41.

171   "You are a great . . .": Ibid., p. 68.

171   Pat began . . . : PN in *SatEP,* 6 Sept. 1952, p. 19.

171   "It reminds . . .": *Collier's,* 9 July 1954, p. 32.

171   In the Quaker . . . : David Hackett Fischer, *Albion's Seed* (New York, 1989), pp. 490, 485.

171   "just a gypsy . . .": JNE, *Pat,* p. 73.

171   "our Quaker principles": RN, *RN,* 1:31.

171   "a student . . .": CBS, "Nixon: A Self-Portrait," 17 May 1972, [original broadcast, 4 Nov. 1968], 5380, Arch AV.

171   "the break point": Ibid.

171   Three of four . . . Richard Polenberg, *War and Society* (New York, 1972), p. 55.

171   "break down . . .": *The Sports Program* (Annapolis, MD, 1943), p. 4.

171   "the longest . . .": Roger Morris, *Richard Milhous Nixon* (New York, 1990), p. 244.

171   "Coming back . . .": JNE, *Pat,* p. 77.

171   "Please say . . .": Ibid., p. 81.

171   "Dear Plum": Ibid., p. 79.

172   almost a million . . . : Susan M. Hartmann, *The Homefront and Beyond* (Boston, 1982), p. 56.

172   "to the winning . . .": Morris, *RMN,* p. 236.

172   "Your job . . .": JNE, *Pat,* p. 79.

172   "A woman is . . .": Doris Kearns Goodwin, *No Ordinary Time* (New York, 1994), p. 413.

172   "These many . . .": JNE, *Pat,* p. 83.

172   "learned how . . .": Lucille Parsons in Morris, *RMN,* pp. 251–252.

172   "I could see . . .": *Time,* 29 Feb. 1960, p. 26.

172   "our candidate . . .": *San Marino Times,* 23 Jan. 1969, p. 1. See also Morris, *RMN,* pp. 270–282.

172   "working wife . . .": "Elect Richard M. Nixon . . ." PPS 1.225, RN Lib.

172   "will grow . . .": Morris, *RMN,* p. 289.

173   "that Pat . . .": RN to Murray Chotiner, 4 Apr. 1950, memorandum, PPS 3/400, RN Lib.

173   "know what . . .": Tom Wicker, *One of Us* (New York, 1991), p. 43. See also JNE, *Pat,* p. 92.

173   "The vote . . .": Postcard, PPS 3/53, RN Lib.

173   "Julie honey . . .": *Time,* 25 Aug. 1952, p. 15.

173   "My husband . . .": *WasP,* 14 July 1952, p. 15.

173   "seemed to have . . .": *Time,* 25 Aug. 1952, p. 13.

174   "special treat": PN in *SatEP,* 6 Sept. 1952, p. 93; *Time,* 25 Aug. 1952, p. 15; *American Weekly,* 24 Aug. 1952, p. 5.

174   "If you . . .": RN, *Six Crises* (Garden City, NY, 1962), p. 87.

174   "Why do . . .": RN, *RN,* 1:124.

174   "I just . . .": RN, *Crises,* pp. 113–117.

174   "like a wax . . .": PN in *LHJ,* Nov. 1962, p. 118.

174   "the character . . .": Clipping, *Long Beach Independent-Telegram,* RN scrapbook, RN Lib.

174   "the wife . . .": PN in *LHJ,* Nov. 1962, p. 118.

174   "Dick and Pat . . .": *ChiT,* 1 Oct. 1952, p. 12.

175   "A Dollar . . .": *Westporter* (CT) *Herald,* 25 Sept. 1952, p. 1, RN scrapbook.

175   "Pat and I . . .": RN, *Crises,* p. 124.
175   "You do . . .": *Life,* 27 July 1954, p. 23.
175   thrifty, sober . . . : Warren Susman, *Culture as History* (New York, 1984), p. xx.
175   "homebody in the . . .": *Life,* 27 July 1954, p. 23.
175   "I love . . .": *NYT,* 11 Dec. 1957, p. 10.
175   "sometimes moody": PN in *LHJ,* Nov. 1962, p. 57.
175   "All the useless . . .": JNE, *Pat,* p. 162.
175   "Here, take . . .": Brodie, *RN,* p. 473.
175   "Why can't . . .": *LHJ,* Feb. 1960, p. 157.
175   "I've got . . .": *Life,* 14 Dec. 1953, p. 160.
175   "Some people . . .": JNE, *Pat,* p. 189.
176   "assistant President": *Life,* 14 Dec. 1953, p. 146.
176   "Any time . . .": JNE, *Pat,* p. 158.
176   "discuss politics . . .": *NYT,* 21 Aug. 1956, p. 15.
176   "anxiety, suppressed . . .": *McCall's,* Aug. 1958, p. 80.
176   photo spread: *Life,* 27 July 1954, p. 23.
176   "I must be . . .": RN, *Crises,* pp. 219, 218, 220.
176   "I think . . .": JNE, *Pat,* p. 187.
177   "The trips . . .": *NYTM,* 30 Oct. 1960, p. 112.
177   "My husband . . .": *NYT,* 27 July 1960, p. 19.
177   "I never . . .": *Nwswk,* 17 Oct. 1960, p. 31.
177   "in on . . .": *NYT,* 11 Sept. 1960, p. 48.
177   "Pat Week . . .": JNE, *Pat,* pp. 189–190.
177   "would snap . . .": Ibid., p. 198.
177   "I always . . .": PN in *LHJ,* Nov. 1960, p. 54.
177   "find it . . .": RN, *Crises,* p. 405.
177   "involved more . . .": RN in *GH,* Mar. 1962, p. 160.
177   "disillusioned . . .": JNE, *Pat,* p. 204.
177   "seemed unexciting . . .": RN, *RN,* 1:286.
177   "the first private . . .": PN in *LHJ,* Nov. 1962, p. 57.
177   "already . . .": Herbert G. Klein OH, p. 21.
177   "Let's be . . .": *LHJ,* Nov. 1962, p. 57.
178   "Bravo . . .": JNE, *Pat,* pp. 213, 216.
178   "six-year vacation": *WasS,* 31 July 1970, D1.
178   "Miss Ryan . . .": JNE, ed., *Eye on Nixon* (New York, 1972), p. 100.
178   "a failure . . .": JNE, *Pat,* p. 227.
178   "oldest friends . . .": RN, *RN,* 1:344, 361.
178   "The public image . . .": *GH,* July 1968, p. 188.
178   "a volunteer . . .": *NYT,* 3 July 1968, p. 30.
179   "I may be dying . . .": *GH,* July 1968, p. 188; *Nwswk,* 2 Dec. 1968, p. 31. See *Time,* 29 Feb. 1960, p. 25.
179   "the public man's . . .": *Nwswk,* 2 Dec. 1968, p. 31.
179   "I never had time . . .": *New York,* 28 Oct. 1968, p. 35.
179   "happy . . . were deeply . . .": "Nixon: A Self-Portrait."
179   "my father . . .": JNE, *Pat,* p. 248.
179   "A President . . .": RN to HRH, 11 Dec. 1970, p. 4, Box 229, RN HRH.
179   "to really convey . . .": RN to HRH, 1 Mar. 1971, Box 3, RN PPF.
179   "little acts . . .": 21 Jan. 1971, Box 43, HRH Notes.
179   "we come across . . .": RN to HRH, 11 Dec. 1970, p. 2.
180   "We should . . .": HRH, *The Haldeman Diaries* (New York, 1994), p. 287.
180   "When Presidents . . .": NBC, "Today," 15 Mar. 1971, 4220–4221, Arch AV.
180   "it is a bit . . .": CS to Rose Mary Woods, 29 Mar. 1972, Box 35, RN PPF.
180   "hypo . . .": RN to Ron Ziegler, 15 Mar. 1973, Box 162, RN HRH; William Safire, *Safire's Political Dictionary,* rev. ed. (New York, 1978), p. 410.
180   "TV just . . .": RN to HRH, annotation, 26 Feb. 1971, Box 32, RN News.

180   "nothing [was] . . .": 6 Sept. 1970, Box 42, HRH Notes.
180   "*no* substance": 8 Mar. 1971, Box 43, HRH Notes.
180   "need to do . . .": 6 Sept. 1970, Box 42, HRH Notes.
180   Security concerns . . . : Colonel James D. Hughes to Charles Stuart, 14 Oct. 1969, Box 53, RN HRH.
181   "great asset": Herb Klein to HRH, 2 July 1971, Box 172, RN HRH.
181   "RN's room . . .": RN to PN, 25 Jan. 1969 in Bruce Oudes, ed., *From: The President* (New York, 1989), p. 11.
181   "call PN": 24 June 1971, Box 43, HRH Notes.
181   The President made . . . : See 2 Sept. 1969, 7 Oct. 1969, Box 40, HRH Notes.
181   "She was swaying . . .": JNE, *Pat,* p. 279.
181   "I looked . . .": Ibid., p. 255.
182   "get PN . . .": 27 Jan. 1969, Box 39, HRH Notes.
182   "I just want . . .": PN interview, 14 Dec. 1969 in Box 31, RN News.
182   "Project A": *NYT,* 18 Feb. 1969, p. 44.
182   "policies and principles": "First Family Staff Operations Manual," Nov. 1972, p. 2, Box 3, Ronald L. Ziegler MSS, RN PMP.
182   citizens credited . . . : Gwendolyn B. King OH, p. 19.
182   "is very busy . . .": Liz Carpenter OH, 3:43–44.
182   "tragic epitome . . .": *LHJ,* Sept. 1969, p. 88.
182   "feminine spirit . . .": Ibid.
182   "many people . . .": *NYTM,* 13 Sept. 1970, 6:26–27, 147.
182   "If the President . . .": *Baltimore Sun,* 6 Dec. 1970, K1.
183   "warm and loving. . .": *NYTM,* 13 Sept. 1970, p. 145.
183   The growing appetite . . . : Anthony Smith, *Goodbye Gutenberg* (New York, 1980), p. 19.
183   "how men and . . .": Ben Bradlee, *A Good Life* (New York, 1995), p. 298.
183   "Pat is really . . .": RN, PN in *GH,* Feb. 1971, p. 66.
183   "New Journalism": See *Saturday Review,* 12 Feb. 1966, p. 65; Michael Schudson, *Discovering the News* (New York, 1978), pp. 187–188. For an attack see Dwight Macdonald, "Parajournalism, or Tom Wolfe and His Magic Writing Machine," in Gerald Howard, ed., *The Sixties* (New York: 1982, 1991), p. 459.
183   name recognition: *Nwswk,* 30 Nov. 1970, p. 19.
183   "delightful"; "star quality": *McCall's,* Jan. 1971, pp. 103, 105.
183   "live-wire celebrity"; "unfettered expression": *Nwswk,* 30 Nov. 1970, p. 19.
183   Pat saw . . . : JNE, *Pat,* pp. 393–394.
184   "too good . . .": 20 Feb. 1971, pp. 3–4, Box 43, HRH Notes.
184   "in those small": "Volunteering—the In-Thing," Box 11, Susan Porter MSS, RN PMP.
184   "small projects . . ": *NYT,* 15 June 1969, p. 28.
184   "every woman . . .": PN in *LHJ,* Sept. 1969, p. 93.
184   "Few pursuits . . .": Mrs. Eugene Morrison to PN, 2 Mar. 1970, Box 12, Porter MSS.
184   helping poor . . . : See Coral Schmid to CS, 5 Sept. 1970, Box 11, Porter MSS.
184   "since most . . .": CS to HRH, 20 Jan. 1970, Box 56, RN HRH.
184   "vest pockets . . .": *NYT,* 19 June 1969, p. 29.
184   "model of . . .": *Time,* 27 June 1969, p. 19.
184   "If she keeps . . .": *LHJ,* Sept. 1969, p. 90.
185   "working trip": CS to Dwight Chapin, 17 Feb. 1970, Box 209, RN HRH.
185   "overall objective": HRH to CS, 22 June 1970, Box 11, Porter MSS.
185   "be photographed . . .": David Parker to HRH, 10 Sept. 1971, Box 20, Dwight Chapin MSS, RN PMP.
185   "a touch . . .": CBS, "60 Minutes," 2 Mar. 1971, 4204, Arch AV.
185   "In the White . . .": HRH to Dwight Chapin, 17 Apr. 1969, p. 3, Box 18, Chapin MSS.
185   The President dictated . . . : See, for example, HRH to Nick Ruwe, 9 July 1969, Box 18, Chapin MSS; HRH to Lucy Winchester, 19 Aug. 1969, Box 52, RN HRH; HRH to Lucy Winchester, 14 Apr. 1969, Box 50, RN HRH.
185   "For whatever . . .": Bob Dole to RN, 4 Feb. 1969, Box 4, Ex SO 1 RN WHSoc.

185 "Pat Nixon is . . .": *NYTM,* 8 Mar. 1970, 6:42.
185 "the Kennedys got . . .": HRH to Herbert Klein, 30 Nov. 1970, Box 68, RN HRH.
185 "anecdotalists": John Andrews to Staff Secretary, 24 June 1971, Box 94, RN POF.
186 "build her . . .": 30 June 1969, Box 39, HRH Notes.
186 "slip . . .": 12 July 1969, p. 9, Box 40, HRH Notes.
186 "badly organized . . .": *Nwswk,* 2 June 1969, p. 85.
186 "West Wing males . . .": Charles Stuart to John Ehrlichman, 3 Sept. 1969, p. 4, Box 191, RN HRH.
186 "PN thing . . .": 8 Aug. 1969, Box 40, HRH Notes.
186 "chief of staff . . .": "Notes on Conversation with Lenore Haag," 14 Aug. 1969, Box 67, John D. Ehrlichman MSS, RN PMP; "Notes on Conversation with Rex Scouten," 25 Aug. 1969, Box 17, Ehrlichman MSS.
186 "Mrs. Nixon has . . .": Stuart to Ehrlichman, 3 Sept. 1969, pp. 23, 1–6.
186 "all of the positive . . .": Ibid., pp. 5–6.
187 "Mrs. Nixon's role . . .": Ibid., pp. 16, 21.
187 "favorable publicity": Ibid., p. 1.
187 "the official spokesman . . .": "First Family Staff Manual," p. 1. See also "Proposed Table of Organization—First Lady Personal Staff," Box 17, Ehrlichman MSS.
187 "triangle . . . and I could . . .": CS OH, p. 12.
187 "She matters . . .": Ibid., p. 47.
187 "have just one . . .": *USNWR,* 22 Dec. 1969, p. 13.
187 Gallup's list: *NYT,* 31 Dec. 1969, p. 9.
188 "an asset . . .": Harry S. Dent to RN, 8 July 1969, Box 2, POF, President's Handwriting, RN PMP.
188 "the largest . . .": *NYTM,* 13 Sept. 1970, 6:139.
188 "Mrs. Nixon's Wardrobe . . .": CS to HRH, 20 Nov. 1969, Box 54, RN HRH; *NYT,* 18 Nov. 1969, p. 50; *NYT,* 20 Nov. 1969, p. 52.
188 "The Selling . . .": *National Observer,* 9 Mar. 1970, Box 11, Porter MSS.
188 "pull the Jewish . . .": 9 Mar. 1970, p. 5, Box 41, HRH Notes.
188 "new . . . unwound": *Time,* 16 Mar. 1970, p. 13.
188 "warm": *Nwswk,* 16 Mar. 1970, p. 35.
188 "ready for . . .": 20 June 1970, p. 4, Box 41, HRH Notes.
188 "make a real . . .": 23 June 1970, p. 4, Box 41, HRH Notes.
188 "little check . . .": *Nwswk,* 13 July 1970, p. 45.
188 "To have President . . .": *Time,* 13 July 1970, p. 11.
188 "the first . . .": Ibid.
189 she demanded mess . . . : See CS to HRH, 14 Jan. 1970; HRH to CS, 23 Jan. 1970, both in Box 56, RN HRH.
189 "The attached . . .": CS to PN, 8 Feb. 1972, Box 1, Porter MSS.
189 "Suggest a meeting . . .": HRH to Alexander Butterfield, annotation on CS to HRH, 17 Feb. 1971, Box 18, Chapin MSS.
189 "persistent and . . .": King OH, p. 52.
189 *"must sell . . .":* 2 Aug. 1971, Box 43, HRH Notes.
189 "You see . . .": Butterfield in Gerald S. Strober and Deborah Hart Strober, *Nixon: An Oral History of His Presidency* (New York, 1994), pp. 36–37.
189 "questions of . . .": CS OH, p. 27.
189 "about Tricia . . .": CS to Pat Buchanan, c. Mar. 1970, Box 14, Patrick J. Buchanan MSS, RN PMP.
189 "the most requested . . .": CS Exit OH, p. 27.
190 Pat offered . . . : See 7 Sept. 1971, 1 June 1971, 20 Apr. 1971, all in Box 43, HRH Notes.
190 "I do not . . .": RN in *USNWR,* 22 Mar. 1971, p. 29.
190 "blind . . . to . . .": *Parade,* 31 Oct. 1971, p. 3.
190 "a group of women . . .": Jim Keogh memorandum, 10 July 1969, Cabinet Meeting, pp. 7–8, Box 78, RN POF.
190 "I want . . .": *WasP,* 3 Dec. 1970, G7.

190   President joked . . . : *Parade,* 31 Oct. 1971, p. 7.
190   "an affluent . . .": Ibid., p. 3.
191   "women's libbers . . .": NBC, "Today," 15 Mar. 1971.
191   "make political . . .": 8 Sept. 1970, Box 42, HRH Notes.
191   "being a political . . .": 14 Oct. 1970, Box 82, RN POF.
191   "proud of . . .": *Parade,* 31 Oct. 1971, p. 5.
191   "the silliest . . .": *Nwswk,* 23 Jan. 1989, p. 25.
191   "Women have . . .": *USNWR,* 19 May 1969, p. 18.
191   "to separate . . .": Marianne Means quoted in 21 Feb. 1973, p. 19, Box 48, RN News.
191   "get a story . . .": 13 Oct. 1971, Box 44, HRH Notes.
191   "We tried . . .": JNE, *Pat,* p. 321.
191   "scored another . . .": HRH, *Diaries,* p. 447.
192   feared that . . . : See Memorandum for the President, c. Sept. 1971, Box 33, John Dean MSS, RN PMP.
192   a note: JNE to RN, 1 Feb. 1972, Box 8, RN PPF.
192   "Last night . . .": Rose Mary Woods to John Ehrlichman, 2 Feb. 1972, Box 35, Confidential Files, WHSF, RN PMP.
192   a letter . . . : RN to Hugh Scott, 18 Mar. 1972, Box 33, Dean MSS.
192   "your adherence . . .": Mrs. Paul L. Carver to RN, 24 Jan. 1969, Box 4, SO1 RN WHSoc.
192   "want to think . . .": *Time,* 3 Jan. 1972, p. 19.
192   "the embodiment . . .": *Nwswk,* 8 Dec. 1969, p. 46.
192   "They should . . .": CS to HRH, 20 July 1970, Box 164, RN HRH.
192   "an 'anti-image' . . .": John Demos, *Past, Present, and Personal* (New York, 1986), p. 37.
192   Tricia admitted . . . : *USNWR,* 19 May 1969, p. 18.
192   "No, I don't . . .": *NYT,* 12 Apr. 1970, p. 78.
192   "appendages to . . .": *NYT,* 21 Mar. 1971, 4:2.
193   "full effort . . .": CS to HRH, 30 Oct. 1969, Box 53, RN HRH.
193   "introvert . . .": *USNWR,* 22 Mar. 1971, p. 29.
193   "We both . . .": *Time,* 14 June 1971, p. 13.
193   "human side": *Time,* 29 Mar. 1971, p. 12.
193   "the biggest . . .": HRH to Alexander Butterfield, 22 Mar. 1971, Box 157, RN HRH.
193   "too emotional": 20 Mar. 1971, Box 43, HRH Notes.
193   "keep a hard . . .": HRH to Butterfield, 22 Mar. 1971.
193   "to elope": *Time,* 29 Mar. 1971, p. 11.
193   "It may be . . .": CBS, "June Wedding at the White House: a Preview," 11 June 1971, 4436, Arch AV.
193   "America's First . . .": 21 June 1971, Box 43, HRH Notes.
193   "were beautifully . . .": RN, *RN,* 1:629.
193   "to begin . . .": HRH, *Diaries,* p. 361.
193   News of . . . : RN, *RN,* 1:629; *NYT,* 13 June 1971, p. 1.
194   "improving the quality . . .": CS to HRH, 27 July 1971, Box 10, Porter MSS.
194   "first pick . . .": "Visit With the First Lady."
194   his diplomatic . . . : See Stephen E. Ambrose, *Nixon,* 3 vols. (New York, 1987–1991), 2:477.
194   "Pat Nixon has changed . . .": *Time,* 6 Dec. 1971, p. 15.
194   "Christmas at . . .": WTOP, "Christmas at the White House with JNE," 24 Dec. 1971, 4913, Arch AV.
194   "the image . . .": Charles Colson to RN, 19 Jan. 1972, pp. 1–2, Box 91, RN HRH.
195   "she was not . . .": WHCA, "Summary of PN to Africa" 13 Jan. 1972, 4968, Arch AV.
195   "The TV coverage . . .": RN to PN, 4 Jan. 1972, Box 5, RN PPF.
195   "the first lady . . .": 10 Jan. 1972, p. 9, Box 37, RN News.
195   "If we can't . . .": Doug Hallett to Charles Colson, 12 Jan. 1972, in Oudes, *From: The President,* p. 355.
195   "She is an . . .": Charles Colson to RN, 19 Jan. 1972, Box 91, RN HRH.
195   "Thought you'd . . .": JNE, *Pat,* p. 333.

195   "big league": 2 Mar. 1972, Box 45, HRH Notes.

195   "bourgeois": JNE, *Pat,* p. 334.

195   "the picture . . .": "Presidential Guidance: Notes on Meeting with Henry Kissinger and HRH, 14 Oct. 1971," 15 Oct. 1971, pp. 3, 1, Box 179, RN HRH.

196   "good for . . .": 11 Oct. 1971, Box 44, HRH Notes.

196   "goes, she . . .": HRH, *Diaries,* p. 443.

196   "events interesting . . .": PN annotation on HRH to PN, c. Oct. 1971, Box 32, Chapin MSS.

196   "Of course . . .": *NYDN,* 25 June 1972, p. 111.

196   "the week . . .": RN, *RN,* 2:52.

196   "unusual world . . .": 2 Mar. 1972, Box 45, HRH Notes.

196   "every minute . . .": *Time,* 6 Mar. 1972, p. 14.

196   "pictorially . . .": *NYDN,* 25 June 1972, p. 111.

196   "average . . . a typical . . .": *Sioux Falls Argus-Leader,* 6 Jan. 1972, p. 4, Box 5, RN PPF.

196   "ideal . . . a bit . . .": "First Lady, Gracious Envoy"; "A Personable First Lady," both in "Summary of First Family Activities," 1969–1972, Box 19, Porter MSS.

196   "the No. 1 . . .": *Time,* 9 Oct. 1972, p. 20.

196   "75% of . . .": David Parker to HRH, 1 July 1972, Box 100, RN HRH.

196   would travel . . . : 2 Nov. 1972, p. 16, Box 45, RN News.

196   "President Nixon continues . . .": NBC, "News," 18 Sept. 1972, on WHCA, "15 Sept. to 21 Sept. 1972," Tape II, 5782, Arch AV.

197   "twinned": "Political Media Analysis," 19 Sept. 1972, p. 1, Box 43, RN News.

197   "Women of . . .": "Fact Sheet: Brunch Honoring the First Lady," 17 Aug. 1972, Box 11, Porter MSS.

197   "Tribute to . . .": "Pat: A Tribute to the First Lady," 21 Aug. 1972, MVF VCR 049, Arch AV.

197   "graceful and . . .": RN, *RN,* 2:173.

197   "the White House . . .": *Nwswk,* 2 Oct. 1972, p. 17.

197   "All I know . . .": *USNWR,* 2 Oct. 1972, p. 31.

197   "it doesn't develop . . .": HRH, *Diaries* p. 616.

198   "The only question . . .": *Time,* 9 Oct. 1972, p. 14.

198   "trouper": *USNWR,* 2 Oct. 1972, p. 31.

198   "I do . . .": *Time,* 9 Oct. 1972, p. 17.

198   "Never before . . .": Ibid., pp. 14, 17.

198   McGovernites: Ambrose, *Nixon,* 2:580.

198   Pat headed: *NYT,* 31 Dec. 1972, p. 19.

198   "The only sour . . .": RN, *RN,* 2:218.

198   "We shall . . .": Ibid., 2:263–264.

198   "Pat did not . . .": Ibid., 2:265–266.

198   "I've been campaigning . . .": CS OH, pp. 18–19.

199   "slogan or phrase . . .": Coral Schmid to PN, in JNE, *Pat,* p. 364.

199   "It's so quiet . . .": *The Fort Worth Press,* 1 May 1973, p. 12. See also CS OH, p. 21; King OH, p. 28.

199   "overworked . . .": JNE, *Pat,* p. 361.

199   Pat scotched . . . : *GH,* July 1976, p. 128; JNE, *Pat,* p. 363.

199   "double standard": RN, *Arena,* p. 37.

199   "cancer within . . .": Gerald Gold, ed., *The White House Transcripts* (New York, 1973), p. 30.

200   "Mother's trying . . .": JNE, *Pat,* p. 367.

200   "felt as if . . .": RN, *RN,* 2:385.

200   "I hope . . .": JNE, *Pat,* p. 369.

200   "She was marvelous . . .": *McCall's,* Oct. 1973, pp. 84, 134.

200   Dick summoned . . . : JNE, *Pat,* p. 372.

200   "her father's . . .": *Nwswk,* 16 July 1973, p. 24.

200   "balance . . .": WTTG, "Panorama with JNE," 25 Oct. 1973, 6622, Arch AV.

201   "Richard Nixon could . . .": *Nwswk,* 14 Oct. 1974, p. 39.

201   "Is the President . . .": Holmes Alexander, "An Eisenhower Speaks for a Nixon," for release 14 Feb. 1974, McNaught Syndicate, Box 17, Alexander Haig MSS, RN PMP.

201   "Ed and I . . .": Tricia Nixon Cox in *LHJ,* Apr. 1974, p. 136.

201   "Everything's going . . .": PN in May 1973, p. 17, RN News.

201   "My mother . . .": *McCall's,* Oct. 1973, p. 84.

201   "I keep . . .": Ibid., p. 137.

201   "No matter . . .": JNE, *Pat,* p. 417.

201   "knew all . . .": Helen Thomas, *Dateline: White House* (New York, 1975), pp. 238–239, 227.

201   "unique phenomenon . . .": *McCall's,* Jan. 1974, pp. 124, 12.

202   "sleeps well": CBS, "Evening News," 28 Jan. 1974, Walter Cronkite interview with PN, WHCA, 6770, Arch AV.

202   "that the conservation": David N. Parker to PN, 8 Nov. 1973, Box 10, Porter MSS.

202   "all of this . . .": NBC, "Nightly News," 11 Mar. 1974, WHCA, "Weekly News Summary," 6836, Arch AV.

202   "the mood . . .": reporter, PN in JNE, *Pat,* p. 402.

202   "should talk . . .": Roger Ailes to HRH, memorandum, May 1970, in King OH, p. 47.

202   "the public . . .": King OH, p. 47.

203   "should have . . .": *GH,* July 1976, p. 130.

203   "My mother's . . .": JNE, *Pat,* pp. 409–410. See also p. 380.

203   "'cloth coat' . . .": Lawrence Stern in *The Fall of a President* (New York, 1974), p. 151.

203   "profoundly disturbing . . .": *NYT,* 29 May 1974, pp. 1, 24.

203   "puzzled": CBS, "Evening News," 12 May 1974, WHCA, "Weekly News Summary," 6939, Arch AV.

203   "No . . . Why . . .": *Detroit News,* 9 Aug. 1974, E1.

203   "You know . . .": *GH,* July 1976, p. 127.

203   "lifelong bride . . .": *WasP,* 9 Aug. 1974, NIX:15.

203   five hundred letters: King OH, p. 40.

203   Four months . . . : *GH,* Jan. 1975, p. 14; *NYT,* 2 Jan. 1975, p. 35.

203   Pat Nixon would remain . . . : RN, *Arena,* pp. 231–232.

203   quarter of a million . . . : JNE, *Pat,* p. 450.

203   "How can . . .": *GH,* July 1976, p. 130.

203   "Most people . . .": RN, *Arena,* p. 232.

203   "ordeal": *Time,* 7 Oct. 1974, pp. 15–22.

203   "If there . . .": JNE, *Pat,* p. 407.

203   "*was* drinking . . .": Ibid., p. 392.

204   "had seen . . .": Michael Schudson, *Watergate in American Memory* (New York, 1992), p. 12.

204   "Politics is . . .": *Time,* 9 Oct. 1972, p. 20.

204   "Dick has . . .": PN, Drown in JNE, *Pat,* p. 417.

204   "In the pre-Watergate . . .": Ibid.

204   "With us . . .": Jonathan Aitken, *Nixon* (Washington, DC, 1993), p. 518.

204   "But why? . . ." JNE, *Pat,* p. 418.

204   "I don't know . . .": Ibid., p. 420.

204   "and see . . .": RN, *RN,* 2:652.

204   "her head . . .": Ibid., 2:669.

204   "Well, I . . .": JNE, *Pat,* p. 421.

204   "Ollie, we're . . .": *GH,* July 1976, p. 130.

204   "Our hearts . . .": JNE, *Pat,* p. 424.

204   "Oh, Dick . . .": Ibid., p. 426.

204   "Always remember . . .": RN, *RN,* 2:688.

204   "he knew that . . .": *GH,* July 1976, p. 128.

204   "would have . . .": JNE, *Pat,* p. 428.

205   "would be too . . .": RN, *Arena,* p. 17.

206   "The image . . .": *Time,* 7 Oct. 1974, p. 21.
206   "those first . . .": RN, *Arena,* p. 44.
206   "You have only . . .": JNE, *Pat,* p. 443.
206   "to spend . . .": *GH,* July 1976, p. 133.

CHAPTER 6. THE FORD INTERREGNUM

Page

207   analysis of presidential . . .: Stephen Skowronek, *The Politics Presidents Make* (Cambridge, MA, 1993), p. 411.
208   peppy classics . . . : "Inquiries (1)," Box 4, Elizabeth O'Neill MSS, GRF Lib.
208   "A successful . . .": GRF, "Material from the writing of *A Time to Heal,*" GRF Lib.
208   "We run . . .": Eric Rosenberger, 27–29 June 1975, Eric Rosenberger and Douglas Blaser MSS, GRF Lib.
208   "Our job . . .": Eric Rosenberger to Larry Speakes and Ray Zook, 23 Feb. 1976, p. 3, Rosenberger/Blaser MSS.
208   "some women . . .": *SLGD,* 20 Sept. 1974, A13.
208   beyond her . . . : Nancy M. Howe to Sue Errington, 20 Sept. 1974, Box 2, O'Neill MSS.
208   "the President . . .": *NYT,* 13 Aug. 1974, p. 20.
208   "transcended the . . .": *Time,* 5 Jan. 1976, p. 6.
209   "drilling in . . .": Clipping [UPI], 23 June 1975, Box 21, Patricia Lindh and Jeanne Holm MSS, GRF Lib.
209   "Go ahead . . .": GRF, "The Ford Presidency," in Bernard J. Finestone and Alexej Ugrinsky, *Gerald R. Ford and the Politics of Post-Watergate America,* 2 vols. (Westport, CT, 1993), 2:670; Robert T. Hartmann, *Palace Politics* (New York, 1980), pp. 294–295.
209   "I had never . . .": SRW, *First Lady's Lady,* (New York, 1979), p. 146.
209   "Because we . . .": BF in *McCall's,* Feb. 1975, p. 142.
209   "an ideal . . .": BF with Chris Chase, *The Times of My Life* (New York, 1978), p. 189.
209   "reminded me . . .": *WasS,* 2 Oct. 1974, A13.
209   a growing sophistication . . . : James T. Patterson, *The Dread Disease* (Cambridge, MA, 1987), p. 258.
209   "It's a . . .": *NYT,* 4 Oct. 1974, p. 16.
210   "saved many . . .": Mrs. Ronald Warren to BF, 7 Feb. 1975, p. 2, Box 21, GRF WHSoc-Subject.
210   "remarkable . . .": Mrs. Harvey L. Lowenthal to BF, 1 Oct. 1974, Box 13, GRF WHSoc-Subject.
210   "Lying in . . .": BF, *Times,* p. 194.
210   "reborn": *McCall's,* Feb. 1975, p. 99.
210   "This is . . .": Ibid., pp. 142–143.
210   "policy and . . .": Nancy M. Howe to Hallie Mitchell, 30 Sept. 1974, Box 2, O'Neill MSS.
210   "A liberated . . .": *NYT,* 8 Nov. 1975, p. 32.
210   "defin[e] Mrs. Ford's . . .": SRW, *Lady,* p. 69.
210   "Your stressing . . .": SRW to BF, undated, Box 47, SRW MSS.
211   "Oh, I'm . . .": SRW, *Lady,* pp. 86–87.
211   "I must . . .": Sen. William Harris (R–IL) in *LAT,* 18 Feb. 1975, 4:6.
211   "dangerous, anti-family . . .": Mr. and Mrs. Robert W. Lee to Congressman Herbert Harris, 15 Feb. 1975, Box 5, PP5/1 GRF WHCF.
211   "using taxpayers' . . .": *LAT,* 18 Feb. 1975, 4:1.
211   "BETTY FORD GET . . .": Bruce Cassiday, *Betty Ford* (New York, 1978), p. 123.
211   "BETTY FORD FAILS . . .": Clipping in "International Women's Year" file, 1974–77, Box 4, O'Neill MSS.
211   "Betty is . . .": Jean Rogers to First Lady's Office, 15 May 1975, Box 37, Robert Hartmann MSS, GRF Lib.
211   "right . . .": *LAT,* 18 Feb. 1975, 4:1.

211   "Why not . . . ?": *Women's Work,* Jan.–Feb. 1976, p. 20.

211   "to stick . . .": *LAT,* 18 Feb. 1975, 4:1.

211   "Speech Freedom . . .": *DetFP,* 24 Feb. 1975, A6.

211   "self-expression gives . . .": *Providence Bulletin,* 26 Feb. 1975, clipping, Box 47, SRW MSS.

211   "To deny . . .": *LAT,* 27 Feb. 1975, 2:6.

211   "play 'wife . . .": "BF Speaks Out," Ann Arbor, MI, 24 Feb. 1975, clipping, Box 47, SRW MSS.

211   "Those who . . .": *Tampa Tribune,* 21 Feb. 1975, A13.

212   "to stop . . .": Ioana Martinke to BF, 24 Feb. 1975, Box 6, O'Neill MSS.

212   "Consider yourself . . .": Linda Goolsbee to BF, c. Mar. 1975, Box 6, O'Neill MSS.

212   Within three weeks . . . : See BF Mail Analysis, Box 39, SRW MSS.

212   "absolutely delighted . . .": *LAT,* 18 Feb. 1975, 4:1.

212   "a disaster . . .": SRW, *Lady,* p. 102.

212   "take informational . . .": Don Hewitt, *Minute by Minute* (New York, 1985), p. 27.

212   "current manners . . .": Charles Montgomery Hammond, Jr., *The Image Decade* (New York, 1981), p. 42. See also Richard L. Rubin, *Press, Party, and Presidency* (New York, 1981), p. 149.

212   "really": SRW, *Lady,* p. 102.

212   "nobody at . . .": SRW in *Parade,* 25 Apr. 1976, p. 4.

212   Reporters were . . . : Study, Reuven Frank in Edward Jay Epstein, *News From Nowhere* (New York, 1973), pp. 14, 206, 4.

213   "drinking problem": Hewitt, *Minute,* p. 101.

213   "occasionally, with . . .": "Mrs. Ford Composite Tape," 9 Jan. to 3 Dec. 1975, F758, GRF AV.

213   "My dad . . .": *Nwswk,* 18 Oct. 1976, p. 42.

213   "Well, I . . .": ABC, "Barbara Walters Interview with President and Mrs. Ford," 6 Dec. 1976, transcript, p. 4, Box 55, Ron Nessen MSS, GRF Lib.

213   "Look, you . . .": *Christian Science Monitor,* 7 Aug. 1975, p. 23.

213   "I told my . . .": CBS, "60 Minutes," 10 Aug. 1975, F388, GRF AV.

213   "swinging gal": Mrs. Don E. Farkas to BF, 20 Apr. 1975, Box 24, GRF WHSoc-Subject.

213   "Briefly, I . . .": BF, *Times,* p. 33.

214   "ready for . . .": James Cannon, *Time and Chance* (New York, 1994), p. 46.

214   "It taught me . . .": *SatEP,* Sept. 1976, p. 120.

214   "I'm Leslie . . .": GRF, *A Time to Heal* (New York, 1979), p. 48; Cannon, *Time and Chance,* p. 14; "Growing Up in Grand Rapids," clipping, p. 34, Box 1, O'Neill MSS.

214   "comes as . . .": Coach Gettings, interview, 18 Aug. 1976, "Sound Roll Transcripts," Box E41, PFC.

214   "deeply in . . .": GRF, *Time to Heal,* p. 56.

214   "would never . . .": Cannon, *Time and Chance,* p. 31.

214   "When are . . .": GRF, *Time to Heal,* p. 62.

215   "handsome blond . . .": BF, *Times,* pp. 46, 48.

215   "low-key": GRF, *Time to Heal,* p. 32.

215   "I'd like . . .": Ibid., p. 65.

215   "admitted that he . . ." BF, *Times,* p. 53.

215   "complete farce . . .": Ibid., p. 61.

215   "a combination . . .": *NYDN,* 10 Jan. 1965, p. 4.

215   "thinking man's . . .": *Pittsburgh Press,* 9 Feb. 1965, p. 29.

215   "a man's . . .": *Los Angeles Herald Examiner,* 15 July 1964, Box 60, SRW MSS.

215   "the prettiest . . .": *Holand Evening Sentinel,* 12 May 1954, Box 60, SRW MSS.

215   "as good-looking . . .": Bill Henry, "Now Maybe Ford for President," c. Jan. 1965, clipping, Box 60, SRW MSS.

215   pictured: See, for example, *Grand Rapids Press,* 4 Oct. 1962, p. 21; *Pittsburgh Press,* 9 Feb. 1965, p. 29; *WasP,* 17 Jan. 1965, F6; *LHJ,* Apr. 1961, pp. 76–77.

215   "the secret . . .": *DetFP,* c. 1965, clipping, Box 60, SRW MSS.

215 "The Congress . . .": BF, *Times,* p. 123.
215 "the ego . . .": *Nwswk,* 7 Oct. 1974, p. 32.
216 "but mostly . . .": BF, *Times,* p. 123.
216 "a warm . . .": Cannon, *Time and Chance,* p. 74.
216 "The loneliness . . .": BF, *Times,* p. 122.
216 A photo: *WasP,* 17 Jan. 1965, F6.
216 "a sounding . . .": *LouCJ,* 31 July 1974, A6.
216 "It siphoned . . .": BF, *Times,* p. 124.
216 "weather the . . .": GRF, "Material from writing *Time to Heal.*"
216 "We would . . .": Cannon, *Time and Chance,* p. 89.
216 Americans were ashamed . . . : Joseph Veroff, Richard Kulka, Elizabeth Douvan, *Mental Health in America* (New York, 1981), p. 266.
216 "there was . . .": BF, *Times,* p. 127.
216 "a lot . . .": Ibid., p. 125.
216 Studies were . . . : Barbara Sinclair Dockard, *The Women's Movement,* 2nd ed. (New York, 1975, 1979), p. 63; Alfreda P. Inglehart, *Married Women and Work* (Lexington, MA, 1979), pp. 42, 45.
216 "My hands . . .": GRF, *Time to Heal,* p. 83.
217 "Are you . . .": *WWD,* 15 Oct. 1973, p. 8.
217 "Is it . . .": *The Journal,* 8 Nov. 1973, B3, clipping, Box 60, SRW MSS.
217 "If I could . . .": *WWD,* 15 Oct. 1973, p. 8.
217 "It's all . . .": Ron Nessen, *It Sure Looks Different From the Inside* (Chicago, 1978), p. 4.
217 "It had . . .": *LAT,* 19 Oct. 1973, p. 1.
217 "Otherwise, I . . .": *WWD,* 12 Apr. 1974, p. 4.
217 "I live . . .": *WasP,* clipping, c. 1973, Box 60, SRW MSS.
217 "As I . . .": *McCall's,* May 1974, p. 138.
217 "a successful . . .": *BosG,* 21 July 1974, p. 72.
217 "loneliness and . . .": *South Bend Tribune,* 30 Dec. 1973, S1.
217 "You can't . . .": *LouCJ,* 31 July 1974, A6.
217 "husbands come . . .": *National Star,* clipping, c. Jan.–Apr. 1974, Box 61, SRW MSS.
218 "when my . . .": In her memoirs Betty admits, "I started seeing a psychiatrist twice a week" in 1965; BF, *Times,* p. 124; *LouCJ,* 31 July 1974, A6; *WWD,* 28 Dec. 1973, p. 9; *DetFP,* 19 Oct. 1973, C1; *LAT,* 19 Oct. 1973, p. 1; *NYP,* 15 Dec. 1973, p. 21.
218 "two years . . .": *LouCJ,* 31 July 1974, A6; *WWD,* 28 Dec. 1973, p. 9; *NYP,* 15 Dec. 1973, p. 21.
218 "my problems . . .": BF to National Association of Mental Health Centers, 2 Nov. 1974, Box 3, SRW MSS.
218 for once . . . : Hartmann, *Palace Politics,* p. 131.
218 "would fall . . .": GRF, *Time to Heal,* pp. 9–10.
218 "the saddest . . .": BF, *Times,* p. 1.
218 "break down": GRF, *Time to Heal,* p. 32.
218 "straight talk . . .": *USNWR,* 19 Aug. 1974, p. 74.
218 "In other . . .": *WasP,* 10 Aug. 1974, A1.
218 "openness and . . .": *USNWR,* 19 Aug. 1974, p. 74.
218 "Mr. Nice Guy": *NYDN,* 22 Aug. 1974, p. 62.
218 "close-knit . . .": "Betty Polls and Surveys," Box 39, SRW MSS.
219 "The nation's. . . . a plain . . .": *WasS,* 10 Aug. 1974, B1.
219 "typical . . .": "BF Just Isn't Perfect Political Wife," c. Aug. 1974, Box 61, SRW MSS.
219 "I do . . .": *Youngstown Daily Vindicator,* 24 Sept. 1974, p. 21.
219 "more folksy": *BosG,* 9 Aug. 1974, p. 33.
219 "instead of an . . .": *Vogue,* Sept. 1974, p. 269.
219 "FORDS MOVE . . .": *SLGD,* 21 Aug. 1974, A16.
219 "We've been . . .": *W,* 23 Aug. 1974, p. 5.
219 "the same . . .": Ibid.
219 "Middle America . . .": *McCall's,* Sept. 1975, p. 30.

219   "Life is . . .": *SLGD,* 20 Sept. 1974, A13.

219   "the traditional . . .": Dockard, *Women's Movement,* p. 73.

219   "building blocks . . .": John Demos, *Past, Present, and Personal* (New York, 1986), pp. 37–38.

219   "Divorce has . . .": *Parade,* 26 Oct. 1975, p. 4.

219   "much conduct . . .": *The American Scholar,* Winter 1993, p. 19. See also, *TNR,* 22 Nov. 1993, "Defining Deviancy Up," which describes what happened to the Nixons, whereby their "wholesome" behavior was deemed abnormal.

219   "a credit . . .": National Republican Congressional Committee, *Wives Manual* (Washington, DC, 1972), pp. 3–5, 10.

220   "This behavior . . .": Nancy M. Howe to Mary M. Huston, 13 Sept. 1974, Box 1, O'Neill MSS.

220   "The Relentless . . .": *Time,* 7 Oct. 1974, p. 15.

220   habit of . . . : *Dynamic Maturity,* Jan. 1976, p. 13.

220   "meant a . . .": NBC, "Today," 15 Aug. 1974, p. 3, transcript, Box 37, SRW MSS.

220   "This does . . .": *Time,* 7 Oct. 1974, p. 20.

220   "the very . . .": Winnie McLendon to Jerry ter Horst, Aug. 1974, pp. 1–3, in Ron Nessen to Jerry Jones, 10 July 1975, Box 130, Nessen MSS.

220   "I've been . . .": *Nwswk,* 19 Aug. 1974, p. 30.

220   "What would . . .": BF, *Times,* p. 168.

220   "'hippie' or . . .": Teresa R. Vidal to BF, 18 Aug. 1974, Box 29, GRF WHSoc-Subject.

220   "pants suits . . .": Opal Edwards to BF, 6 Sept. 1974, Box 14, GRF WHSoc-Subject.

220   "highly undignified . . .": Mrs. Randolph Richards to BF, 19 Aug. 1974, Box 14, GRF WHSoc-Subject.

220   "helluva": Mr. W. L. Helton to BF, 13 Sept. 1974, Box 14, GRF WHSoc-Subject.

220   "It seems . . .": Howard R. Miller to BF, 10 Sept. 1974, Box 14, GRF WHSoc-Subject.

220   "Many people . . .": "Today," 15 Aug. 1974, p. 2.

221   "lobby": *NYTM,* 8 Dec. 1974, 6:87.

221   "Now their . . .": *Current Events,* 28 Feb. 1975, p. 7.

221   "light-hearted response": Mara S. Perrott to Gisele F. Anderson, 30 May 1975, Box 12, GRF WHSoc-Subject.

221   "sexist attitudes": *LHJ,* Jan. 1975, p. 116.

221   "Uhhh, you know . . .": *WWD,* 30 Aug. 1974, p. 4.

221   "sex appeal": Hewitt in *TV Guide,* 20 Oct. 1973, p. 16.

221   Safer asked . . . : CBS, "60 Minutes," 10 Aug. 1975, F388, transcript, pp. 1–13, Box 6, SRW MSS.

222   "You just . . .": SRW, *Lady,* p. 172.

222   he stormed . . . : *NYDN,* 29 Dec. 1975, p. 32.

222   "I can't . . .": *SLGD,* 20 Sept. 1974, A13.

222   "to try . . .": The Staff to GRF, 1 May 1976, Box 132, Nessen MSS.

222   "SUSAN HAVING . . .": *Herald-Journal* (Logan, UT), 11 Aug. 1975, p. 1.

222   "endorsed premarital . . .": *Virginian Gazette,* 11 Aug. 1975, p. 1.

222   "nothing . . . not yet . . .": CBS, "Evening News," 11 Aug. 1975, BF Composite Tape, 9 Jan. to 3 Dec. 1975, F758, GRF AV.

223   On "Today" . . . : NBC, "Today," c. 17 Aug. 1975, BF Composite.

223   "us to . . .": "First Lady Draws Praise from Episcopalian," clipping, Box 62, SRW MSS.

223   "I thought, wow . . .": *Chicago Sun-Times: Two,* 14 Aug. 1975, p. 75.

223   "to rewrite . . .": *Sentinel Star,* 17 Aug. 1975, B9.

223   "the super-policemen . . .": *WasP,* 25 Aug. 1975, A21.

223   On popularity see *Columbia Journalism Review,* Nov.–Dec. 1975, p. 16.

223   "Betty meant . . .": *NYT,* 26 Aug. 1975, p. 17.

223   "Betty Ford freely admits . . .": *McCall's,* Sept. 1975, pp. 93, 120, 122, 124.

224   "MRS. FORD DOES . . .": CBS, ABC reports, BF Composite Tape, F758.

224   "you never . . .": *Interview* 6:9, Sept. 1975, p. 16. On Steve Ford see SRW, *Lady,* p. 402.

224   "be very . . .": GRF in clipping, [UPI], 8 Oct. 1975, Box 40, SRW MSS.

224 "announcement . . .": *SatEP,* Sept. 1976, p. 64.

224 "private identity": Mrs. James A. Wilcox to BF, 11 Aug. 1975, Box 459, "Con" Bulk Mail Samples, GRF WHSoc.

224 "You are . . .": quoted in Myra G. Gutin and Leesa E. Tobin, " 'You've Come a Long Way, Mr. President': Betty Ford as First Lady," in Finestone and Ugrinsky, *Gerald R. Ford and Politics,* p. 623.

224 "Miss America . . .": *Chicago Sun-Times: Two,* 14 Aug. 1975, p. 75.

224 "Truth is . . .": Girard T. Bryant to BF, 26 Aug. 1975, Box 439, "Con" Bulk Mail Samples, GRF WHSoc.

224 "doormat[s]": Laurie Ruby to BF, 22 Aug. 1975, Box 12, GRF WHSoc-Subject.

224 "if I . . .": Mrs. Charles Sec to BF, 28 Aug. 1975, Box 4, Exec, PP5-1, GRF WHCF.

225 "gray, no-woman's . . .": *LHJ,* Nov. 1975, p. 118.

225 Forty-four percent . . . : Dennis A. Gilbert, *Compendium of American Public Opinion* (New York, 1988), p. 324.

225 "Any president . . .": Anne L. Brown to GRF, 11 Aug. 1975, Box 458, "Con" Bulk Mail Samples, GRF WHSoc.

225 "Permissive sex . . .": Mrs. Paul D. King et al., 26 Aug. 1975, Box 459, "Con" Bulk Mail Samples, GRF WHSoc.

225 "God is . . .": Jeanne M. Griffiths, 12 Aug. 1975, Box 458, "Con" Bulk Mail Samples, GRF WHSoc.

225 "lived twenty-six . . .": BF Form Letter, Sept. 1976, Box 1, O'Neill MSS.

225 "profession . . .": BF, "Remarks to the Homemakers Association," 26 Sept. 1975, pp. 2, 3, 7, Box 7, SRW MSS.

225 "one of . . .": *WasP,* 10 Nov. 1975, B9.

225 "I certainly . . .": *People,* 29 Dec. 1975–5 Jan. 1976, p. 16.

225 "trademark": *Women's Work,* Jan.–Feb. 1976, p. 18.

225 "Woman of . . .": *Nwswk,* 29 Dec. 1976, p. 19.

226 *People . . . : People,* 29 Dec. 1975–5 Jan. 1976, p. 16.

226 "If only . . .": Richard S. Dawson, Jr., to BF, 25 Aug. 1975, Box 443, "Pro" Bulk Mail Samples, GRF WHSoc.

226 "Gerald Ford is much . . .": *Dallas Morning News,* clipping, Box 12, GRF WHSoc-Subject.

226 The First Lady's mail . . . : Staff Secretary to GRF, 1–29 Aug. 1975, Box 3, WH 4-1 Mail, GRF WHCF, 12975.

226 "We think . . .": William J. Gordy to Harold Calloway, 13 Aug. 1975, Box 80, PFC.

226 "Your statements . . .": Mrs. John Richard Ghilon to BF, 11 Aug. 1975, Box 458-459, "Con" Bulk Mail Samples, GRF WHSoc.

226 Reagan's core . . . : Earl Black and Merle Black, *The Vital South* (Cambridge, MA, 1992), pp. 273–279.

226 "the new morality . . ." *LAT,* 20 Sept. 1975, p. 5.

226 "Betty or . . .": Pamphlet in Box 12, Susan Porter MSS, GRF Lib.

227 "hasn't the . . .": Market Opinion Research, Aug. 1976, p. 3, Box 54, Robert Teeter MSS, GRF Lib.

227 "Unlike her . . .": *Parade,* 25 Apr. 1976, p. 4.

227 "stole the . . .": *NYDN,* 29 Dec. 1975, p. 32.

227 "the change . . .": *Time,* 28 July 1975, p. 7.

227 "carries about . . .": *Nwswk,* 24 Nov. 1975, p. 30.

227 *Time* chronicled . . . : *Time,* 5 Jan. 1976, p. 33. See also John Robert Greene, *The Presidency of Gerald R. Ford* (Lawrence, KS, 1995), p. 62.

228 "the country's leading . . .": Earl Wilson in *Time,* 5 Jan. 1976, p. 33.

228 "Since you . . .": R. Schlosser to GRF, 14 Aug. 1975, Box 458, "Con" Bulk Mail Samples, GRF WHSoc.

228 "accident-prone . . .": *People,* 29 Dec. 1975–5 Jan. 1976, p. 19.

228 "close friend . . .": *NYT,* 16 Dec. 1975, p. 10.

228 "a beautiful . . .": *NYT,* 15 Dec. 1975, p. 31.

228 "private behavior . . .": *NYT,* 21 Dec. 1975, 4:1.

228 "Jack Kennedy's . . .": *Time,* 29 Dec. 1975, pp. 10, 11.

228 "presidential performance": *NYT,* 23 Dec. 1975, p. 23.

229 "a kind . . .": *Nwswk,* 29 Dec. 1975, p. 14.

229 "a shocking . . .": *National Enquirer,* 2 Mar. 1976, p. 4.

229 "I never . . .": Harris Wofford, *Of Kennedys and Kings* (Pittsburgh, 1980, 1992), p. 492.

229 The 1975 disclosures . . . : On the refusal of the general public to believe these revelations, see Thomas Brown, *JFK: History of an Image* (Bloomington, Indiana, 1988), pp. 70–77.

229 "He enjoys . . .": *Nwswk,* 24 Nov. 1975, p. 32; *The Media Report,* 21 Nov. 1975, p. 1.

229 "publicly": *The Media Report,* 21 Nov. 1975, p. 1.

229 Aides called . . . : Paul Theis to Ron Nessen, 18 Dec. 1975, Box 127, Nessen MSS; Ron Nessen to Dick Cheney, 18 Dec. 1975, 25 Nov. 1975, both in Box 127, Nessen MSS; interview with Robert T. Hartmann, 27 Jan. 1976, p. 22, Box 129, Hartmann MSS.

229 "Character will . . .": *The Media Report,* 21 Nov. 1975, p. 1.

229 "What used . . .": *WasP,* 25 May 1976, C3.

229 "a man . . .": *ChiT,* 6 June 1976, 1:4.

230 In an increasingly . . . See Richard Sennett, *The Fall of Public Man* (New York, 1974, 1976); Christopher Lasch, *The Culture of Narcissism* (New York, 1978).

230 "moral leader": George Van Cleeve to David Gergen, undated, Box 2, David Gergen MSS, GRF Lib.

230 "neighborhood, community . . .": William J. Barrody, Jr. to GRF, 17 Sept. 1975, pp. 2, 4, 5, Box 9, Richard Cheney MSS, GRF Lib.

230 "the first . . .": SRW, *Lady,* p. 248.

231 "It's physical . . .": Mary McGrory, "BF Out Front with Most Everyone," clipping, c. Feb. 1975, Box 4, Exec, PP5-1, GRF WHCF.

231 "the President's biggest . . .": See, for example, Barbara Walters, c. Feb. 1976 on "BF and Sons" Summary Tape, 12 Jan.–19 Aug. 1976, 83-11-19, GRF AV.

231 "individuals rather . . .": *People,* 4 Mar. 1974, p. 2.

231 "ELECT BETTY'S . . .": BF, *Times,* p. 258.

231 Mrs. Ford received . . . : *Star,* 12 Apr. 1976, clipping, Box 39, SRW MSS.

231 "sick . . . became so . . .": BF, *Times,* p. 255.

231 "He used . . .": *Nwswk,* 29 Dec. 1975, p. 23.

231 "never to . . .": *The Presidential Campaign,* vol. 2, *Gerald Ford* (Washington, DC, 1978), p. 2.

231 As Secret Service . . . : CBS, "Evening News," c. June, 1976, "BF and Sons" Summary Tape.

231 she enjoyed 71 . . . : *ChiT,* 9 Aug. 1976, p. 3.

232 A widely . . . : *Nwswk,* 30 Aug. 1976, p. 29.

232 "sleazy little . . .": *Tulsa World,* clipping, c. Aug. 1976, Box 27, SRW MSS.

232 "I just think . . .": *Time,* 30 Aug. 1976, p. 31.

232 "Mrs. Ford, too, . . .": Elizabeth O'Neill to Mary H. Martin, 28 Sept. 1976, Box 1, O'Neill MSS.

232 "ticket splitters": "Campaign Plan," p. 80, Box 13, Michael Raoul-Duval MSS, GRF Lib.

232 "family campaign . . .": ABC, "News," c. 18 Aug. 1976 on "BF and Sons" Summary Tape.

232 "not only . . .": NBC, News Coverage, "GOP Convention," 19 Aug. 1976, F658, Tape 7, 1 of 2, GRF AV.

232 "the television . . .": President Ford Convention Film, transcript, undated, p. 2, Box 27, SRW MSS.

233 One scene: "Sound Roll Ford Family Lunch," pp. 75, 76, Box E41, PFC.

233 "principal task . . .": "Campaign Strategy," Aug. 1976, p. 3, Box 13, Raoul-Duval MSS.

233 "sometimes a . . .": *NYT,* 29 Sept. 1976, p. 22.

233 "What a . . .": GRF, *Time to Heal,* p. 431.

233 "the emphasis . . .": *NYT,* 29 Sept. 1976, p. 22.

233 "There's no . . .": *LAT,* 30 Aug. 1976, p. 6.

233 "to communicate him . . .": *ChiT,* 17 Aug. 1976, 3:1.
233 "I am not . . .": *WasS,* 22 Aug. 1976, E3.
233 "educating me . . .": *LHJ,* Oct. 1976, p. 86.
233 "Betty has had . . .": ABC, GRF with Harry Reasoner, transcript, 6 Sept. 1976, p. 22, Box 55, Nessen MSS.
234 "Jerry couldn't . . .": *LAT,* 1 Oct. 1976, p. 7.
234 "When I . . .": *WasP,* 19 Oct. 1976, A19.
234 "Mom, did . . .": BF, *Times,* pp. 272, 273.
234 "crestfallen": Cannon, *Time and Chance,* p. 409.
234 "nice person . . .": Greene, *Presidency of GRF,* p. 69.
234 "My advice . . .": *WWD,* 18 June 1976, p. 1.
234 "*still* did . . .": SRW, *Lady,* p. 417.
235 "male chauvinism": Ibid.
235 From a cross-section . . . : See *GH,* Jan. 1975, p. 20; *LAT,* 2 Jan. 1975, p. 2; *WasS,* 17 Dec. 1975; *GH,* Jan. 1977, pp. 42, 44, all clippings in Box 39, SRW MSS. George Gallup, *The Gallup Poll: Public Opinion, 1972–1977* (Wilmington, DE, 1978), p. 943.
235 65 percent . . . : *National Enquirer,* 14 Sept. 1976, p. 21.
235 "the polarization . . .": Gregory Bush, *Campaign Speeches of American Presidential Candidates, 1948–1984* (New York, 1976, 1985), p. 247.

CHAPTER 7. "WHO ELECTED HER?"

Page

236 "rigid Baptist faith": *NYT,* 30 Sept. 1976, p. 41.
236 "impossible standards . . .": Robert Scheer in G. Barry Golson, ed., *The Playboy Interview* (New York, 1981), pp. 486–488.
236 "NOW, THE *REAL* . . .": Ibid., pp. 460, 463. *Playboy,* Nov. 1976, cover.
237 *Playboy* embodied . . . : James T. Patterson, *Grand Expectations* (New York, 1996), p. 358.
237 the Carter homestead . . . : JC, *Why Not the Best?* (Nashville, 1975), p. 13.
237 "the greatest day . . .": JC/RSC OH, pp. 139–140.
237 "my life on . . .": JC, *Why,* p. 13.
237 "Hot . . .": "JC Biography," p. 8, Office of Media Liaison to White House Staff, 5 Dec. 1977, Box 3, Advance Office, JC Lib.
237 "hunger[ing] . . .": JC, *Always a Reckoning* (New York, 1995), p. 99.
237 "that we thought . . ." JC/RSC OH, p. 200.
237 "feeling of . . .": JC, *An Outdoor Journal* (New York, 1988), p. 37.
237 "it would have . . .": Ibid., p. 13.
237 "terribly sensitive . . .": "Mrs. James Earl Carter, Sr." in "Lillian Carter," JC VF.
237 "centered almost . . .": JC, *Why,* pp. 14, 32, 19.
237 "We were very . . .": JC/RSC OH, p. 6.
238 "We grew up in . . .": RSC OH, p. 16. See also Willard Slappey OH, p. 36.
238 "go to Annapolis": JC/RSC OH, p. 9.
238 "planned my . . .": JC, *Why,* p. 42.
238 "the saddest . . .": Lillian Carter OH, p. 33.
238 "assume some . . .": JC, *Turning Point* (New York, 1992), p. 19.
238 "There was . . .": Hugh Carter with Frances Spatz Leighton, *Cousin Beedie and Cousin Hot* (Englewood Cliffs, NJ, 1978), p. 112.
238 "a naive . . .": JC, *Turning,* p. xix.
238 "I think . . .": Lillian Carter OH, p. 53.
238 "You've got . . .": *WasP,* 26 Oct. 1976, A6.
238 "If you were . . .": RSC, *First Lady from Plains* (New York, 1984), p. 62.
238 "for myself . . .": JC, *Why,* p. 133.
238 "born again": Richard Quebedeaux, "Conservative and Charismatic Developments of the Late Twentieth Century," in Charles H. Lippy and Peter W. Williams, eds., *Encyclopedia of the American Religious Experience* (New York, 1988), 2:963, 972; Grant Wacker,

"Searching for Norman Rockwell: Popular Evangelism in Contemporary America," in Leonard Sweet, ed., *The Evangelical Tradition in America* (Macon, GA, 1984), p. 294.

239 "'You show . . .'": JC, *Why,* p. 98.

239 "our kind . . .": "Sumter County Residents Know . . ." Sept. 1970, "JC Governor," JC VF. See also Randy Sanders, "The Sad Duty of Politics," *Georgia Historical Quarterly,* 76 (Fall 1992): 621.

239 "president of what?": *LHJ,* Aug. 1976, p. 73.

239 "All you . . .": HJ, *Crisis* (New York, 1982), p. 17.

239 "My childhood . . .": RSC, *First,* p. 15.

239 "that you can . . .": "Life with Mother," "RSC," JC VF.

239 "appear to . . .": RSC, *First,* p. 17.

240 "felt very guilty": *Book Digest,* Apr. 1978, p. 37.

240 "had visions . . .": RSC, *First,* p. 19.

240 "building bodies . . .": JC/RSC OH, p. 23.

240 "She was beautiful . . .": RSC, *First,* p. 18.

240 "never paid . . .": For JC's version, see *Why,* p. 62. For RSC, see *First,* pp. 21–22. For both, see JC/RSC OH, p. 340.

240 "seventeen real . . .": Allie Smith OH 2:26.

240 "I never did . . .": JC/RSC OH, p. 16.

240 "War brides . . .": *LHJ,* Mar. 1942, p. 110.

240 "a child": ABC, "Barbara Walters," 14 Dec. 1975, C16, JC AV.

240 "very domineering . . .": Kandy Stroud, *How Jimmy Won* (New York, 1977), p. 106.

240 "Divorce was . . .": JC and RSC, *Everything to Gain* (New York, 1987), p. 74.

241 "studied . . .": RSC, *First,* p. 24.

241 "resourceful, efficient . . .": Anne Briscoe Pye and Nancy Shea, *The Navy Wife* (New York, 1942), p. 131.

241 "felt overwhelmed . . .": RSC, *First,* pp. 25–26.

241 "a cheerful . . .": Pye and Shea, *Navy,* pp. 192, 132.

241 "She loves . . .": Ibid., p. 133.

241 "violently": JC, *Why,* p. 64.

241 "But Jimmy . . .": RSC, *First,* p. 33.

241 "because no . . .": James Wooten, *Dasher* (New York: 1978), p. 217; RSC, *First,* pp. 35–36.

241 "I was just . . .": Betty Glad, *Jimmy Carter* (New York, 1980), p. 70.

241 "a hard teacher . . .": *LHJ,* Mar. 1979, p. 101.

241 "was a rare . . .": JC/RSC OH, p. 156.

241 "I was doing . . .": RSC, *First,* p. 37.

241 "never really . . .": Wooten, *Dasher,* p. 232.

242 "Can't we . . .": RSC, *First,* p. 39.

242 "Everything that . . .": JC/RSC OH, p. 31.

242 "grew together . . .": RSC, *First,* p. 41.

242 "would have . . .": JC, *Turning,* p. 55.

242 "felt very . . .": Glad, *JC,* p. 70.

242 "more a political . . .": RSC, *First,* p. 50.

242 "I wasn't . . .": Ibid., p. 54.

242 "we had to . . .": RSC, "The Perspective of the First Lady," in Kenneth W. Thompson, ed., *The Carter Presidency* (Lanham, MD, 1990), p. 228.

242 "It's just . . .": Jerrold Smith OH, p. 34. See also Allethea Smith Wall OH, p. 21.

242 "If it appears . . .": *ChiT,* 17 Sept. 1978, p. 23.

243 "Every time . . .": RSC, *First,* p. 63.

243 "the hardest thing . . .": *New York,* 22 Nov. 1976, p. 56.

243 "stylistic populist": Sanders, "Sad Duty," p. 623; "'Hi Neighbor,'" 3 Nov. 1970, pamphlet, JC Governor, JC VF.

243 "I want . . .": RSC, *First,* p. 69.

243 "panicked": RSC OH, p. 8.

243 "from the simpler . . .": RSC, *First,* p. 86.
243 "come and visit": Victor Lasky, *Jimmy Carter* (New York, 1979), p. 100.
243 "hadn't planned . . .": RSC, *First,* pp. 90, 72–73, 87. See also RSC OH, p. 14.
243 "I would never . . .": RSC, *First,* p. 87.
243 "a First Lady can . . .": Ibid., p. 90.
244 "I am for it . . .": Ibid., pp. 92–93.
244 "a team": JC, *Keeping Faith* (New York, 1982), p. 18.
244 "The things . . .": RSC OH, p. 20.
244 "my campaign . . .": JC, "Letter to Friends," 4 Dec. 1974, *The Presidential Campaign,* vol. 1, *Jimmy Carter* (Washington, 1978), p. 2.
244 "There must . . .": JC, *Why,* p. 154.
244 "Peanut Brigade": See Betty Pope OH, p. 16.
244 "How can . . .": *NYTM,* 26 Sept. 1976, 6:76.
245 "most detailed . . .": *WasP,* 30 Sept. 1976, A27.
245 "a substitute . . .": Leslie Wheeler, *Jimmy Who?* (Woodbury, NY, 1976), p. 158.
245 "I'm not . . .": Ibid., p. 159.
245 "make friends": Edna Langford and Linda Maddox, *Rosalynn* (Old Tappan, NJ, 1980), p. 48.
245 "I can call . . .": RSC, waiter in Stroud, *How Jimmy Won,* p. 101.
245 "That's one . . .": SRW, *First Lady's Lady* (New York, 1979), p. 296.
245 "tough-minded . . .": Wheeler, *Jimmy Who?,* p. 159.
245 "does nothing . . .": CBS, "Dinah!" c. Oct. 1976, C22, JC AV.
245 "do you have . . .": Ibid.
246 "My mother . . .": JC, *Keeping Faith,* p. 545.
246 "became the darling . . .": "Lillian Carter," *Current Biography,* Jan. 1978, p. 12.
246 "define [a] white . . .": Jody Powell, "Farewell to a Great Lady," 4 Nov. 1983, "Lillian Carter," JC VF.
246 "work with . . .": *NYTM,* 26 Sept. 1976, 6:90.
246 He admitted . . . : Stroud, *How Jimmy Won,* p. 136.
246 "I sound . . .": Peter Meyer, *James Earl Carter* (Kansas City, 1978), p. 144.
246 "When Jimmy . . .": Carter, *Cousin Beedie,* p. 292.
246 "———": *NYTM,* 26 Sept. 1976, 6:78.
246 "Jimmy talks . . .": RSC, *First,* p. 132.
247 "I trust . . .": Stroud, *How Jimmy Won,* p. 357.
247 "If I had . . .": Ibid.
247 "a very personal . . .": ABC, "Barbara Walters," 14 Dec. 1976.
248 "governing with . . .": Patrick H. Caddell, 10 Dec. 1976, pp. 1, 3, 37–40, Box 4, Jody Powell MSS, JC Lib.
248 "we won . . .": *New York,* 22 Nov. 1976, p. 52.
248 "always say . . .": JC annotation on Rich Hutcheson to JC, 26 Jan. 1977, Box PP-2, PP 5-1, JC WHCF.
248 "to do justly . . .": JC, *Vital Speeches of the Day,* 43 (15 Feb. 1977):258–259; see also JC, *Keeping Faith,* p. 19.
248 "We communicated . . .": JC, *Keeping Faith,* p. 18.
249 "Holding hands . . .": *FamW,* 3 June 1984, p. 13.
249 "delightful, like . . .": David R. Beisel, "A Psychohistory of Jimmy Carter," Lloyd de Mause and Henry Ebel, *Jimmy Carter and American Fantasy* (New York, 1977), p. 60.
249 "national family . . .": *Time,* 3 Jan. 1977, p. 29.
249 "rural Camelot": Glad, *JC,* p. 361.
249 "strengthen . . . unlike some . . .": "Carter Administration Family Initiatives," Jan. 1979, JC Lib.
249 "This is home . . .": *Time,* 15 Aug. 1977, p. 24.
249 "needs": Mary Hoyt and Nancy Bingaman, "Report on the Functions and Organization of the Office of the First Lady," 6 Jan. 1977, p. 1, Box 1, Daniel Malachuk Administration Files, JC Lib.

249 "working White House . . .": Ibid., pp. 28, 26.

249 "substantive . . . an active . . .": Ibid., pp. 26, 27.

250 "work for . . .": See "Rosalynn's Staff," clipping, 21 Feb. 1978, Box 29, Hugh Carter MSS, JC Lib.

250 "assistance and . . .": "Public Law 95-570," 2 Nov. 1978, Box 7, Malachuk MSS.

250 "Rosalynn Carter Wants . . .": *WasS,* 11 Dec. 1976, A10.

250 "Projects, Issues . . .": Kathryn Cade OH.

250 "my one . . .": RSC, *First,* pp. 258, 257.

250 "the chairperson": Ellen Metsky to Doug Huron, 15 Feb. 1977, Box 28, Peter Bourne MSS, JC Lib.

250 "if she remained . . .": John M. Harmon to Douglas B. Guron, 18 Feb. 1977, p. 1, FG 287, Box FG 216, JC WHCF.

250 "avoid being . . .": Edwin S. Kneedler to John M. Harmon, 17 Feb. 1977, p. 7 in Harmon to Guron, 18 Feb. 1977.

250 Conflict-of-interest . . . : Richard Harden to Bert Lance, 4 Feb. 1977, Box PP-2, PP5-1, JC WHCF.

251 "first opportunity . . .": Peter Bourne to RSC, 6 Dec. 1976, p. 1, Box 28, Bourne MSS.

251 "media attention . . .": Ibid., p. 12.

251 "dismissed as . . .": RSC, *First,* p. 258.

251 "captive audience . . .": RSC, 15 Sept. 1977, p. 1, Box 25, Presidential Commission on Mental Health MSS, JC Lib.

251 "major": RSC, *First,* p. 260. See also Press Release, 15 May 1979, Box 46, JC Chron.

251 "greatest disappointment": RSC, *First,* p. 271.

251 "did just . . .": Ibid.

252 "serious . . .": Ibid., p. 272.

252 "I am a relatively . . .": RSC, 26 Apr. 1979, Box 44, Sarah Weddington MSS, JC Lib.

252 Two opposing conceptions . . . : Donald G. Mathews and Jane Sherron De Hart, *Sex, Gender, and the Politics of ERA* (New York, 1990), p. xi.

252 "the most impassioned . . .": Hugh Carter to RSC, week ending 25 Nov. 1977, Hugh Carter MSS.

252 "This confusion . . .": Hugh Carter to RSC, 24 Feb. 1978, Box 104, Hugh Carter MSS.

252 "to move women . . .": Sarah Weddington to JC and RSC, 27 Mar. 1979, Box S0-02 S03, JC WHCF.

252 "early childhood . . .": "Carter Administration Family Initiatives," Jan. 1979, pp. 1–5.

252 "keen political antennae": HJ, *Crisis,* pp. 358–359.

252 "I am a political . . .": RSC, "Women and America," 26 Apr. 1979, Box 44, Weddington MSS.

252 "Ros, Comment, J.": See, for example, Memorandum to the President, 22 Jan. 1979, Box 116, JC PHF.

253 "What do . . .": RSC in Thompson, *Presidency,* p. 231.

253 "Some things . . .": *NYT,* 30 May 1978, B1.

253 "I don't even . . .": Interview with JC, 29 Nov. 1982, p. 54, Miller Center Interviews, JC Lib.

253 "I would lose . . .": ABC, "Interview with Barbara Walters," 14 Dec. 1978, transcript, pp. 5–6, Box 38, JC Chron.

253 "I don't hesitate . . .": Ibid., p. 6.

253 "working lunch . . .": JC, *Keeping Faith,* p. 56.

253 "save these . . .": RSC, *First,* p. 145.

253 "contact master . . .": See "Contact Master List," 13 Jan. 1981, JC Lib.

254 "Rosalynn spends . . .": HJ to JC, 16 July 1979, p. 7, Box 34, JC HJ. See RSC, *First,* p. 152.

254 "secretaries, people . . .": RSC in Thompson, *Presidency,* p. 225. See also *FamW,* 3 June 1984, p. 13.

254 "presumptuous . . .": *Time,* 31 July 1978, p. 13.

254 "theirs is no . . .": *WasP,* 25 June 1978, K2.

254 "The Latins . . .": RSC, *First,* p. 177.

254   "was *determined* . . .": RSC, *First,* p. 178.
254   "I've always . . .": See, for example, ABC, "First Lady on the Go," 13 June 1977, C113, JC AV; NBC, "Today" with Mrs. Carter, 14 June 1977, C114, JC AV.
255   "substantive bilateral . . .": Rhonda Bush OH.
255   "Jimmy's policy": "First Lady on the Go."
255   "In Peru . . .": Ibid.
255   "reflected the growing . . .": RSC, *First,* p. 199.
255   "eyes and ears": "Interview with Walters," transcript, pp. 5–6.
255   "an Imperial . . .": *NYT,* 15 June 1977, A20. See also Jack Anderson, "Amateurs Running Foreign Policy," clipping, Box 42, Powell MSS; *USNWR,* 6 June 1977, p. 36.
255   "Have you felt . . .": "First Lady on the Go."
255   "What gives . . .": "Today" with RSC.
255   "unelected kin . . .": *Nwswk,* 20 June 1977, p. 100.
256   "Who elected . . .": *NYT,* 15 June 1977, A20.
256   "the wife of . . .": Ibid.
256   "She talked . . .": *NYT,* 6 July 1977, pp. 1, 9.
256   "my Eleanor": *WasP,* 22 Jan. 1978, H6.
256   "More than . . .": *WasP,* 25 June 1978, K2, K3.
256   "fuzzy": *AtCon,* 1 Aug. 1978, A6.
256   "whether or not . . .": *WasP,* 25 June 1978, K1–K5.
257   "There is great . . .": *National Enquirer,* 11 Jan. 1977, p. 10.
257   "That's their . . .": *WasP,* 22 Jan. 1978, H6.
257   That first year . . . : Ibid.
257   "always . . .": *AtCon,* 29 Oct. 1978, A21.
257   Most Washington . . . : Edward Jay Epstein, *News from Nowhere* (New York, 1973), p. 206.
257   "most of the important . . .": *Society,* Mar.–Apr. 1980, p. 2.
257   "traditional life . . .": *Working Woman,* July 1980, p. 29.
257   "I do not think . . .": RSC, 26 Apr. 1979, Box 44, Weddington MSS.
257   "Mrs. Carter's rating . . .": Patrick H. Caddell to RSC, 30 July 1977, pp. 1, 3, 5, 6, Box 42, Powell MSS.
257   her mail . . .: Rhonda Bush to Kit Dobelle, 8 Feb. 1980, Box 7, Malachuk MSS.
258   Gallup's ten . . .: George Gallup, 25 Dec. 1980, WHCF Name File, JC Lib.
258   for 46 months . . .: John Orman, *Comparing Presidential Behavior* (New York, 1987), p. 165.
258   "new man": Michael Kimmel, *Manhood in America* (New York, 1996), p. 270.
258   "Jimmy Carter first . . .": *WSJ,* 11 May 1984, p. 30. See also Orman, *Comparing Behavior,* p. 168.
259   "The mood . . .": RSC, 19 Jan. 1979, pp. 1–3, Box 116, JC PHF.
259   "problems we . . .": JC, *Vital Speeches of the Day,* 45 (1 Feb. 1979): 226, 228–229.
259   "at least six . . .": Hedley Donovan to JC, 24 Oct. 1979, Box 154, JC PHF.
259   "are the good . . .": HJ OH, p. 5.
259   "permanent Washington": Jody Powell OH, p. 28.
259   "mistake . . .": RSC in Thompson, *Presidency,* p. 229.
259   "it never . . .": Interview with JC, 29 Nov. 1982, pp. 21–22.
259   "look in Rosalynn's . . .": *WasP,* 25 June 1978, K5.
260   "Too many . . .": JC annotation on HJ et al. to JC and RSC, 29 Dec. 1978, Box 114, JC PHF.
260   "the ceremonial . . .": JC, *Keeping Faith,* p. 30.
260   "to look every . . .": *WasP,* 20 Jan. 1977, p. 5.
260   "very cynical": RSC in Thompson, *Presidency,* p. 229.
260   "Jimmy and I . . .": RSC, 2 Feb. 1978, Box 42, Powell MSS.
260   "We didn't . . .": "Interview with Walters," transcript, p. 17.
260   "the sad duty . . .": JC, *Why,* p. 7.
260   "a more caring society": *NYT,* 20 Mar. 1979, A16.

260 "for the Age . . .": RSC, *First*, p. 268.
260 "cult of true . . .": Barbara Welter, "The Cult of True Womanhood, 1820–1860," *American Quarterly* 18 (1966): 151–174.
260 "heart": Chris Matthews, "Draft Remarks for Governor Graham's Introduction of RSC," 16 Nov. 1979, Box 28, Speechwriters Subject File, JC Lib.
261 "the caution . . .": *WasP,* 24 Apr. 1978, A23.
261 "moment in . . .": BF with Chris Chase, *Betty: A Glad Awakening* (Garden City, NY, 1987), p. 39.
261 "I have found . . .": *LAT,* 25 Apr. 1978, 2:4.
261 "unaffected directness": *SFChr,* 30 Apr. 1978, Punch:1.
261 "make it possible . . .": RSC, *First*, p. 95.
261 "are not weak . . .": *WasP,* 21 June 1978, A2.
261 "sincerity and caring . . .": Peter Bourne to RSC, 22 June 1978, Bourne MSS.
261 "as assisting . . .": *WasP,* 25 June 1978, K1–K2.
262 "Joan Mondale is . . .": Ibid., K3.
262 "Joan of Art . . .": *NYTM,* 26 Feb. 1978, 6:17.
262 "If Rosalynn . . .": *Nwswk,* 4 Sept. 1978, p. 18.
262 "She's created . . .": *WasP,* 25 June 1978, K3, K5.
262 "I don't think . . .": *WasS,* 28 Jan. 1979, F2.
262 "a great deal . . .": Achsah Nesmith to Jim [Fallows?], c. 1978, Box 1, Nesmith Speechwriting MSS, JC Lib.
262 "his own man": *Nwswk,* 18 Sept. 1978, p. 33.
262 "tea party lady": *AtCon,* 1 Aug. 1978, A1, A6.
262 press relations . . .: Ibid.
262 "pretty much . . .": Cade OH.
262 "The relationship . . .": *WasP,* 25 June 1978, K3.
263 "I don't believe . . .": RSC, *First*, p. 226.
263 "so they . . .": JC, *Keeping Faith*, pp. 327–328.
263 "no compatibility . . .": Ibid., p. 327.
263 "a partner . . .": Ibid., p. 346.
263 "It was a relief . . .": RSC, *First*, p. 234.
264 Pat Caddell urged . . .: Patrick H. Caddell to JC, 12 July 1979, Box 50, JC Chron.
264 "Nobody wants . . .": RSC, *First*, p. 286. See also JC, *Keeping Faith*, p. 115.
264 "The decision . . .": Interview with JC, 29 Nov. 1982, p. 66.
264 "Rosalynn and I . . .": JC, *Keeping Faith*, p. 115.
264 "every segment . . .": JC, 15 July 1979, p. 1, Box 50, JC Chron.
264 "intense reassessment": JC, *Keeping Faith*, p. 118.
264 "heart was . . .": RSC, *First*, p. 287.
264 "fragmentation and . . .": JC, 15 July 1979, pp. 6, 10.
264 "If you and . . .": HJ to JC, 16 July 1979, Box 34, JC Chron.
265 "the second most . . .": *Time,* 7 May 1979, p. 22.
265 "we realized . . .": *LAT,* 26 July 1979, 1:16.
265 "Clearly, the Carters . . .": *NYDN,* 29 July 1979, p. 5.
265 "the dessert . . .": *Tampa Times Tribune,* 25 July 1979, C1.
265 "the administration's . . .": Ibid., p. 1.
265 "I just have . . .": *WasS,* 26 July 1979, D2.
265 "the people . . .": *NYDN,* 29 July 1979, p. 57.
265 "Goddam it . . .": *WasS,* 3 Aug. 1979, A11.
265 "visions of . . .": *WasS,* 26 July 1979, D2.
265 Rosalynn's approval . . .: *Nwswk,* 6 Nov. 1979, p. 38.
265 Masculinity had to be . . . : Kimmel, *Manhood*, p. 270.
265 "precious relationship . . .": *NYDN,* 29 July 1979, p. 60.
265 "henpecked . . .": *WasS,* 3 Aug. 1979, A11.
266 "The First Lady . . .": *WasP,* 4 Oct. 1979, p. 19.
266 "I think that . . .": *WasP,* 6 Oct. 1979, B2.

266 "To the many . . .": *WasS,* 21 Oct. 1979, D5.
266 "The President's Partner": *Nwswk,* 6 Nov. 1979, p. 36.
266 "Lady Macbeth . . .": Ibid., p. 38.
266 "The Imperial . . .": *Washington Weekly,* 6 Nov. 1979, clipping, JC VF.
266 "I am a taxpayer . . .": Letter of Louise LeFort, 25 Nov. 1979, Box PP-4, PP5-1, JC WHCF.
266 "You keep . . .": Mrs. J. McCarthy to JC, Mar. 1980, Box PP-4, PP5-1, JC WHCF.
266 "It's going . . .": *WasS,* 21 Oct. 1979, D5.
267 "It was a gnawing . . .": Interview with JC, 29 Nov. 1982, p. 53.
267 "call attention . . .": RSC, *First,* p. 278.
267 "too dangerous . . .": Langford, *Rosalynn,* p. 15.
267 "another example . . .": Cade OH.
267 "some concrete action": Langford, *Rosalynn,* p. 15.
267 "extraordinary example . . .": Cade OH.
267 "the eagerness . . .": Langford, *Rosalynn,* pp. 16–17.
267 "*we should . . .*": Richard Moe to HJ, 12 Nov. 1979, Box 41, JC HJ.
267 "Get Jody . . .": JC annotation, Jim McIntyre and Henry Owen to JC, 31 Oct. 1979, Box 155, PHF.
267 "brought my family . . .": Interview with JC, 29 Nov. 1982, p. 74.
268 "the scrawny . . .": *WasS,* 6 Nov. 1980, C4.
268 "if Lady Bird . . .": *FamW,* 12 Oct. 1980, p. 5.
268 "Jimmy should . . .": RSC, *First,* p. 313.
268 "caution government . . .": Memorandum for Heads of Executive Departments and Agencies, 1 Oct. 1980, Box PP-2, PP5, JC WHCF.
268 "a virtuoso . . .": *WasS,* 20 Oct. 1980, D1.
268 "I had to keep . . .": RSC, *First,* p. 317.
268 "Don't you . . .": CBS, "60 Minutes," with President and Mrs. Carter, 10 Aug. 1980, C1184, JC AV.
269 "the principals . . .": Les Francis to HJ and Tim Kraft, 2 June 1980, Box 79, JC HJ.
269 "It's their Presidency": *FamW,* 12 Oct. 1980, p. 5.
269 "greetings from . . .": *WasS,* 28 Oct. 1979, A30.
269 "call this week-end . . .": RSC to Tim Kraft, 7 Nov. 1979, Box 155, JC PHF.
269 "I prefer . . .": JC to Governor Bob Graham, 10 June 1980, Box PP-4, PP5-1, JC WHCF.
269 "Don't trade . . .": Hal Gulliver to JC, 27 Apr. 1980, Box PP-4, PP5-1, JC WHCF.
269 "demagogic": "Rosalynn Carter Says Bombing of Iran Would Have Helped Jimmy," AP clipping, 30 Apr. 1984, RSC VF.
269 "the right thing . . .": RSC, *First,* p. 304.
269 Both understood: "Rosalynn Carter Says Bombing of Iran Would Have Helped Jimmy," AP clipping, 30 Apr. 1984, RSC VF.
270 "with crucial . . .": "60 Minutes," 10 Aug. 1980.
270 "I don't like . . .": Ibid.
270 "reconciliation strategy . . .": JC annotation, on Richard Moe and Anne Wexler to HJ, undated, 1980, Box 79, JC HJ.
270 "I could . . .": *FamW,* 12 Oct. 1980, p. 5.
270 "no matter . . .": *Newark Star-Ledger,* 22 July 1980, p. 29.
270 "She is just . . .": *WasS,* 20 Oct. 1980, D3.
270 "no simple . . .": Second debate, 28 Oct. 1980, in Richard Harwood, ed., *The Pursuit of the Presidency 1980* (New York, 1980), pp. 363, 384.
271 "Who's running . . .": *LHJ,* Aug. 1984, p. 68.
271 "Damn, damn . . .": RSC, *First,* p. 321.
271 "somewhat artificial . . .": JC and RSC, *Everything,* pp. 6, xiii.
271 "and walk . . .": Betty and John Pope to JC and RSC, 6 Nov. 1980, WHCF Name File.
271 "Sometimes Helmut . . .": RSC, *First,* p. 326.
271 "Isn't this . . .": *LHJ,* Aug. 1984, p. 72.

271   "the closest working . . .": Frontispiece of RSC, *First.*
271   "More than . . .": *AtCon,* 13 May 1984, H8.

CHAPTER 8. "DOING EVERYTHING WE CAN"

Page

273   "always impl[y] . . .": *WasP,* 19 Aug. 1984, A9.
273   "What? . . .": *WasP,* 2 Aug. 1984, A28.
273   "I wasn't . . .": Ibid.
274   "Look. We . . .": Patti Davis, *The Way I See It* (New York, 1992), pp. 11, 242.
274   "Ronald . . .": RR, *An American Life* (New York, 1990), p. 21.
274   "If my father . . .": RR with Richard C. Hublen, *Where's the Rest of Me?* (New York, 1965), p. 14.
274   "loved three . . .": Ibid., p. 11.
274   "Life is . . .": *WSJ,* 8 Oct. 1980, p. 1.
274   "We hang . . .": *Time,* 5 Jan. 1981, p. 14.
274   "the perfect . . .": Bill Thompson in Anne Edwards, *Early Reagan* (New York, 1987), p. 65.
274   "you couldn't . . .": RR, *American,* pp. 46, 59.
274   "and my fraternity . . .": Ibid., p. 75.
274   Dutch told . . . : Laurence Leamer, *Make-Believe* (New York, 1983), p. 97.
275   "likeable, clean-cut American": Anne Edwards, *Early Reagan,* p. 154.
275   "it was a fantasy . . .": RR, *American,* pp. 84, 83.
275   "poor man's . . .": RR in *Photoplay Combined with Movie Mirror,* Aug. 1942, p. 45.
275   "Mr. Norm . . .": Ibid., p. 44.
275   "We'll lead . . .": Leamer, *Make-Believe,* p. 119.
275   "one of . . .": Frank Van Der Linden, *The Real Reagan* (New York, 1981), p. 59.
275   "Now I'm . . .": *Photoplay,* Jan. 1945, p. 23.
275   "The monastery . . .": RR, *Where's,* p. 11.
275   "This learning . . .": *Photoplay,* Apr. 1948, p. 113.
275   "I *was* divorced . . .": *People,* 29 Dec. –5 Jan. 1981, p. 24.
276   "and I couldn't . . .": Joe Santley quoted in Leamer, *Make-Believe,* p. 148.
276   "*But Nancy* . . .": RR, *American,* p. 122.
276   "backstage baby . . .": NR with William Novak, *My Turn* (New York, 1989), p. 69.
276   "Nancy Robbins . . .": Leamer, *Make-Believe,* p. 34.
276   "armchair psychologists . . .": NR, *My Turn,* pp. 69–70.
276   "my father . . .": NR in *McCall's,* June 1983, p. 81.
276   "Nancy's social . . .": Leamer, *Make-Believe,* p. 46.
276   "majored in English . . .": NR, *My Turn,* p. 82.
276   "the Glamour Girl . . .": Leamer, *Make-Believe,* pp. 59–60.
277   "lead the life . . .": Lee Edwards, *Reagan* (San Diego, 1967), p. 61.
277   "the most glamorous . . .": NR, *My Turn,* p. 86.
277   "to have a successful . . .": Leamer, *Make-Believe,* p. 70.
277   "I had always . . .": NR, *My Turn,* p. 90.
277   "one of the things . . .": Ibid., p. 95.
277   "everything wrong": *GH,* June 1985, p. 241.
277   "Do you want . . .": NR, *My Turn,* p. 100.
277   "Go ahead . . .": Ibid., p. 103.
277   just decided . . . : RR, *Where's,* p. 269.
277   "squeeze[d] in": NR in *McCall's,* June 1983, p. 133.
277   "By then . . .": NR, *My Turn,* p. 101.
277   "Your mother . . .": Davis, *Way I See,* p. 25.
277   "difficult": NR, *My Turn,* p. 103.
277   "From the start . . .": RR, *American,* p. 123.
277   "the Dragon Lady": Michael Reagan, *On the Outside Looking In* (New York, 1988), p. 84.

278   "preferred my mother's . . .": Davis, *Way I See,* pp. 33–34.

278   "presidential couple . . .": NR, *My Turn,* p. 123.

278   "A woman isn't . . .": James T. Patterson, *Grand Expectations* (New York, 1996), p. 364.

278   "My life . . .": NR, *My Turn,* p. 93.

278   "Wow, everything's . . .": Davis, *Way I See,* p. 73.

278   "Not a day . . .": Leamer, *Make-Believe,* p. 191.

279   "If Ronnie . . .": *Nwswk,* 28 Apr. 1980, p. 33.

279   a recognition . . . : Edwards, *Reagan,* p. 85.

279   "He has *two* . . .": Davis, *Way I See,* p. 105.

279   "the most difficult . . .": *Redbook,* July 1981, p. 62.

279   "Nancy, people . . .": *Look,* 31 Oct. 1967, p. 40.

279   "a stopgap . . .": Ibid., p. 38.

280   "How do you . . .": Ibid., p. 42.

280   "Sex is not . . .": Helene Von Damm, *Sincerely Ronald Reagan* (Ottawa, IL, 1976), pp. 95–96.

280   "Yes, dear . . .": Bill Boyarsky, *The Rise of Ronald Reagan* (New York, 1968), p. 6.

280   "I simply don't . . .": *USNWR,* 8 Mar. 1976, p. 16.

280   "the most powerful . . .": *Time,* 24 Nov. 1975, p. 23.

281   "peer marriage": Pepper Schwartz, *Love Between Equals* (New York, 1994), pp. 4–5.

281   "You're really . . .": CBS, "60 Minutes," with NR, 20 Dec. 1981, R5643, RR AV.

281   "never seen . . .": *NYT,* 5 Apr. 1980, p. 7.

281   "When you . . .": *New York,* 28 July 1980, p. 14.

281   "She never . . .": *WasP,* 1 May 1980, F20.

281   "as close . . .": Peter Hannaford, *The Reagans* (New York, 1983), p. 292; see also pp. 228–229.

281   "Campaigning and . . .": *New York,* 28 July 1980, p. 16.

281   "Give me . . .": *People,* 17 Nov. 1980, p. 45.

281   "They had eyes . . .": Hannaford, *The Reagans,* p. 290.

281   "when they . . .": *Time,* 24 Nov. 1975, p. 23.

282   "was all sweetness . . .": *WasP,* 1 May 1980, F2. See NR with Bill Libby, *Nancy* (New York, 1980).

282   "Ronald Reagan's . . .": *New York,* 28 July 1980, p. 14.

282   "mostly women . . .": *LHJ,* Oct. 1980, p. 111.

282   "part of . . .": *NYTM,* 26 Oct. 1980, 6:45.

282   "shamelessly goody-two-shoes . . .": *New York,* 28 July 1980, pp. 16, 14.

282   "equal rights . . .": *LHJ,* Oct. 1980, p. 111.

282   "soften": John Sears in *NYTM,* 26 Oct. 1980, 6:100.

282   "glare at . . .": *LHJ,* Oct. 1980, p. 111.

282   "My biggest . . .": NR, *My Turn,* p. 36.

282   "Nancy, you . . .": Chris Wallace, *First Lady* (New York, 1986), p. 83.

282   "I don't often . . .": *NYT,* 26 Oct. 1980, p. 41.

283   "No, no . . .": *WasP,* 10 Nov. 1980, D1.

283   "If I were . . .": *WasP,* 1 May 1980, F3.

283   "Obviously we . . .": *NYT,* 5 Apr. 1980, p. 7.

283   "You can't . . .": *Nwswk,* 21 Dec. 1981, p. 27.

283   "more emphasis . . .": American Council of Life Insurance, "Monitoring the Attitudes of the Public 1983," in Dennis A. Gilbert, *Compendium of American Public Opinion* (New York, 1988), p. 138.

283   "spic and span . . .": Daniel Yankelovich, *New Rules* (New York, 1981), p. 96.

283   "THE NEW . . .": *People,* 17 Nov. 1980, p. 44.

283   "more Rodeo . . .": *NYDN,* 13 Nov. 1980, p. 43; *WasP,* 11 Nov. 1980, B1.

283   "still . . . cringe": NR, *My Turn,* p. 36.

283   When Nancy suggested: *Nwswk,* 22 Dec. 1980, p. 14.

283   "Why can . . .": Professor Caryl Rivers in *New Orleans Times-Picayune,* 15 Feb. 1981, 4:15.

284   "First Companion . . .": *LAT,* 16 Jan. 1981, 2:11.

284   "a policy decision . . .": "Transition of the wife of the President-elect," OA 5097, p. 16, Edwin A. Meese MSS, RR Lib.

284   "It's a hard . . .": *People,* 17 Nov. 1980, p. 47.

284   "I'll be me": *New York,* 28 July 1980, p. 15.

284   "redecorating the . . .": *People,* 29 Dec.–5 Jan. 1981, p. 25.

284   "I don't like . . .": *People,* 19 Jan. 1981, pp. 38, 40.

284   "perhaps . . .": *People,* 17 Nov. 1980, p. 47.

284   "very special . . .": See Bill Adler, *Ronnie and Nancy* (New York, 1985); Leamer, *Make-Believe; 50 Plus,* Feb. 1986, p. 20; *NYT,* 7 May 1986, p. 1.

284   "I love you . . .": Adler, *Ronnie and Nancy,* pp. 104–105.

284   "gave old . . .": *NYDN,* 13 Nov. 1980, p. 57.

284   "main characteristics . . .": *Time,* 5 Jan. 1981, p. 15.

285   "fatherly . . .": David Stockman, *The Triumph of Politics* (New York, 1986, 1987), pp. 12, 119.

285   after the first hundred . . . : "The Reagan Presidency After 100 Days," 28 Apr. 1981, 018542CA, Box 1, PR 015, WHORM.

285   tragic tradition . . . : See C. Vann Woodward, *The Burden of Southern History,* rev. ed. (Baton Rouge, LA, 1968), p. 190.

285   "Critics who . . .": *Nwswk,* 9 Mar. 1981, p. 27.

285   "old fashioned . . .": *WasS,* 4 Mar. 1981, C1. See also *Nwswk,* 21 Dec. 1981, cover story and 17 Nov. 1980, cover story.

286   "That the first . . .": *WasP,* 2 Dec. 1981, A26.

286   "more ceremonial . . .": Judy Mann in *WasP,* 20 Nov. 1981, B1, B19.

286   "everything . . .": Sheila Tate in *NYT,* 17 Nov. 1985, p. 14.

286   "I wish . . .": *Redbook,* July 1981, p. 64.

286   drifted off . . . : *WasS,* 4 Mar. 1981, C1.

286   "Honey, I . . .": ABC, "Barbara Walters Special," with NR, 2 June 1981, R247, RR AV.

286   "I love you": Leamer, *Make-Believe,* p. 318.

286   "Nothing can . . .": NR, *My Turn,* p. 11.

286   "I think you . . .": "Barbara Walters Special," with NR.

286   "I have a new . . .": George Mitrovich to Mabel H. Brandon, 3 June 1981, 031491, Box 19, PR 016-1, WHORM.

287   "You are right . . .": RR to Sam Harrod, 4 Feb. 1982, 058987, Box 12, PR 016, WHORM.

287   "today's media . . .": *Washington Journalism Review,* Dec. 1982, p. 26. See also *Public Opinion,* Oct.–Nov. 1981, p. 42. Herbert J. Gans offered a tendentious critique of these polemical articles in *Columbia Journalism Review,* Nov.–Dec. 1985, p. 29. For liberal complaints about right-wing media bias see Mark Hertsgaard, *On Bended Knee* (New York, 1988, 1989).

287   "I don't mean . . .": *Redbook,* July 1981, p. 64.

287   the nation's elite: On the "values gap" between masses and elites, see John Kenneth White, *The New Politics of Old Values* (Hanover, NH, 1988), p. 41.

287   only 23 percent . . . : *WasP,* 25 Nov. 1981, C1.

287   "lovely, lovely . . .": *ChiT,* 17 Jan. 1982, 9:12.

287   "She dresses . . .": *Washingtonian,* July 1981, p. 109.

287   "Good Heavens . . .": *WasP,* 28 Dec. 1981, A19.

287   "I and many . . .": *WasP,* 2 Dec. 1981, A26.

287   "silly . . .": *WasP,* 24 Oct. 1981, B1.

287   "fresh look . . .": "60 Minutes" with NR.

288   "bum rap": *WasP,* 25 Nov. 1981, C3.

288   "Last year . . .": *NYT,* 19 Feb. 1982, B5.

288   "all major . . .": Sheila Tate to West Wing Scheduling Committee, 29 Dec. 1981, CFOA 152, NR Chronological Files, Michael Deaver MSS, RR Lib.

288   "national release": Wendy Borcherdt to Shirley Hudson Allison, 13 July 1982, OA 7112, Michael Baroody MSS, RR Lib.

288   *"no more . . ."*: Muffie Brandon to George Stevens, Ann Wrobleski, 10 Dec. 1982, Box 7176, Mabel Brandon MSS, RR Lib.

288   "hard news": Betty Cole Dullert to Sheila Tate, 3 Jan. 1985, OA 10867, Michael Deaver Files, RR Lib.

288   "more suitable . . .": Sheila Tate to Ginny Frizzi, 25 Jan. 1982, 056454, Box 2, PR016, WHORM.

288   Senate Finance . . . : Max Friersdorf to Michael Deaver et al., 29 Jan. 1981, Box 13528, Ellen Bradley MSS, RR Lib. See also "Suggested Talking Points," 20 Mar. 1981, for Luncheon with Wives of Top Democratic and Republican Leaders and Ranking Members, 23 Mar. 1981, in Box 13528.

288   "She has derived . . .": *NYT,* 16 Jan. 1982, p. 15.

288   "no longer . . .": Elaine D. Crispen to Mrs. Marjorie Behr, 24 Feb. 1982, 062058, Box 11, PR 01402, WHORM.

289   overlapping frumpy . . . : NR, *My Turn,* pp. 41–42.

289   off the record: AP and UPI wire services provided a short description, and major newspapers including the *NYT, WasP,* and the *ChiT* had minor items about the skit. 29 Mar. 1982, A-3, Box 14, RR News.

289   Now they loomed . . . : Compare "Polishing the Image," *WasP,* 19 Feb. 1982, D1 to "NR on the Road in Iowa," *WasP,* 6 Aug. 1982, D1.

289   The program grew . . . : "The Reagan Record on the Family and Traditional Values," 9 Aug. 1988, p. 20, 576686, Box 63, FG 001, WHORM.

289   "To love . . .": NR in *SatEP,* Mar. 1982, p. 81.

289   She released . . .: NR with Jane Wilkie, *To Love a Child* (Indianapolis, 1982), p. xi.

289   "a Betty Ford issue": *TNR,* 16–23 Sept. 1985, p. 18.

289   "depressing . . .": *NYT,* 14 Sept. 1986, p. 27.

290   "Money does . . .": NR interview in *USNWR,* 31 May 1982, p. 50.

290   "Government didn't . . .": WTTG, "Merv Griffin Show," 6 Oct. 1982, R1119, RR AV. On why this moralistic appeal inspired conservatives and frustrated liberals see George Lakoff, *Moral Politics* (Chicago, 1996), pp. 186–187.

290   "I became . . .": Letter quoted in the Entertainment Industries Council, Inc., "Nancy": "The Entertainment Industry Salutes the First Lady," 26 Sept. 1985, NR Vertical Files.

290   "But Mrs. Reagan . . .": Staff notes for Wendy Toler to John T. Schuler, 24 Aug. 1988, WH Alpha File, JSN [2 of 18], RR Lib.

290   "Well why . . .": *GH,* Jan. 1987, p. 64.

290   simplistic: For an attack on the program, see *Washington Monthly,* May 1992, p. 18.

290   "a marked change . . .": Entertainment Industries Council, "Nancy."

291   In the episode . . .: NBC, "Diff'rent Strokes," with Mrs. Reagan, 19 Mar. 1983, 20:00–20:30, RR AV.

291   "the most significant . . .": Carlton Turner to NR, 1 Feb. 1983, 127555PD, Box 5, PR 016, WHORM.

291   "You radiated . . .": Burt Reynolds to NR, c. Mar. 1983, 136120, Box 20, PR 016-012, WHORM.

291   "constructive hypocrisy": *ChiT,* 30 Oct. 1995, p. 11.

291   Reporters treated . . .: See 26 Apr. 1985, Box 43, B5, RR News.

291   "a mother-to-mother . . .": *NYT,* 25 Apr. 1985, C1.

291   "Because there . . .": *Time,* 14 Jan. 1985, p. 27.

291   "Well, I'm sure . . .": WTTG, "Merv Griffin Show" with RR and NR, 27 Sept. 1983, 21:00–22:00, R1630 B, RR AV.

291   "If a wife . . .": *LAT,* 30 Mar. 1982, p. 1.

292   a sea change: "Drug Use Decreasing—Trends Promise a Real Success," 18 Mar. 1983, 1292225C, Box 13, FG 001, WHORM. On NR and the "Revival of Abstinence," see David F. Murto, *The American Disease* (New York, 1987), pp. 270–273.

292   "total nominal . . .": "Ten Myths That Miss the Mark," Issue Alert, 2 Mar. 1983, 118188PD, Box 11, FG 001, WHORM.

292   new government . . .: "The Reagan Accomplishments: The First Six Years," 16 Dec. 1986, pp. 4, 5, 44117755, Box 46, FG 001, WHORM.

292   "They portray . . .": *NYT,* 14 Oct. 1984, p. 28.

293   "Christmas in . . .": George Stevens, Jr., to Michael Deaver, 5 Apr. 1982, Box 7176, Brandon MSS; NBC, "Christmas in Washington," 13 Dec. 1982, R1210, RR AV.

293   "the Great . . .": RR, Eizenstat in Stephen Skowronek, *The Politics Presidents Make* (Cambridge, MA, 1993), pp. 409, 412.

293   "The public . . .": Richard B. Wirthlin to NR, 21 Oct. 1981, p. 1, OA 10872, Deaver MSS.

293   By 1984 . . .: Eleanor Smeal and Associates, "Maximizing the Women's Vote '84," Jan. 1984, pp. 23–24, 200446PD, Box 4, PR015, WHORM.

294   "provide an . . .": Elizabeth Fox-Genovese, *Feminism is NOT the Story of My Life* (New York, 1996), p. 11. See also Betty Friedan, *The Second Stage* (New York, 1981), p. 22; Donald G. Mathews and Jane Sherron De Hart, *Sex, Gender, and the Politics of ERA* (New York, 1990), pp. 152–153; Kristin Luker, *Abortion and the Politics of Motherhood* (Berkeley, 1984), pp. 162–163.

294   "hormone" gap: Boyarsky, *Rise of RR,* p. 20. See also Bella Abzug with Mimi Kelber, *Gender Gap* (New York, 1984), p. 90.

294   "recognize and . . .": "Gender Gap," 19 Nov. 1982, President's Weekly Update, 22 Nov. 1982, 10901425C, Box 10, FG001, WHORM.

294   a characteristically . . .: Robert Dallek, *Ronald Reagan* (Cambridge, MA, 1984), p. 82.

294   "I'm not . . .": NR in *LHJ,* Oct. 1980, p. 111.

294   "there are . . .": *LHJ,* May 1985, pp. 200, 138.

294   "Feminism is . . .": *McCall's,* Nov. 1985, p. 178. On the difficult question of what constitutes feminism, see Nancy Cott, "What's in a Name? The Limits of 'Social Feminism,'" *Journal of American History,* Dec. 1989, 76:809–829.

294   "the hell . . .": *NYT,* 1 June 1972, p. 43.

294   "the most satisfying . . .": *Cosmopolitan,* Nov. 1980, p. 284.

294   "seem caught . . .": *NYTM,* 26 Oct. 1986, 6:29.

294   "I consider . . .": NR in *SatEP,* Sept. 1981, p. 34.

294   "I can't imagine . . .": *NYT,* 23 Aug. 1984, p. 24.

294   "is in reality . . .": James F. Bender, "The Trouble with Most Brides," *American Magazine,* Oct. 1948, p. 42.

294   "it can be . . .": ABC, "Barbara Walters Special," with RR and NR, 24 Mar. 1986, R3132B, RR AV.

295   "Thinking of . . .": *NYTM,* 26 Oct. 1986, 6:32.

295   "The Revolution . . .": *Time,* 9 Apr. 1984, p. 74.

295   "still . . . happy . . .": *LHJ,* May 1985, p. 138.

295   NBC surveyed . . .: NBC, "NBC Special: The First Lady, Nancy Reagan," 24 June 1985, R2729B, RR AV.

295   highest favorability . . .: Richard Wirthlin to NR, 6 Oct. 1982, 10844, Box 2, PR 015, WHORM.

295   "women's equality . . .": Susan Faludi, *Backlash* (New York, 1991), p. 230.

295   "universal sisterhood": Alice Echols, *Daring to Be Bad* (Minneapolis, 1989), p. 203. For working-class resentments, see Luker, *Abortion,* pp. 162–163.

295   Reagan captured . . .: Nelson W. Polsby and Aaron Wildavsky, *Presidential Elections,* 8th ed. (New York, 1991), pp. 337, 186; *Public Opinion,* Oct.–Nov. 1985, 8:51.

296   "equity feminism . . .": Christina Hoff Sommers, *Who Stole Feminism?* (New York, 1994), p. 22.

296   "seen as guaranteeing . . .": Naomi Wolf, *Fire with Fire* (New York, 1993), pp. 67, 68. See also Katie Roiphie, *The Morning After* (Boston, 1993, 1994), pp. 5, 121.

296   reporters celebrated . . .: See *Time,* 14 Jan. 1985, p. 24; *NYT,* 26 Mar. 1985, p. 20.

296   "Nancy Reagan at the peak . . .": "NBC Special: NR." See also Ed Rollins with Tom DeFrank, *Bare Knuckles and Back Rooms* (New York, 1996), pp. 97, 137.

297   "prerogatives . . . seemed so . . .": Donald T. Regan, *For the Record* (New York, 1988), pp. 290–292.

297   "You just . . .": *USNWR,* 29 July 1985, p. 24.

297   "whisper peace . . .": *WasP,* 23 Oct. 1984, C12.

297   "tone . . . down": NR, *My Turn,* p. 64.

297   "stirring up . . .": RR, *American,* p. 378.

297 "I'm worried . . .": Ibid., p. 379.

297 "Are you going . . .": Hedrick Smith, *The Power Game* (New York, 1988), p. 376.

297 "to have a checkup . . .": NR, *My Turn*, pp. 278–279.

298 "to say it . . .": Ibid., p. 282; Larry Speakes to Donald Regan, 6 Aug. 1985, Box 30, 35461D, PR016-04, WHORM; *WasT,* 8 Aug. 1985, A7, Box 45, RR News.

298 "Mrs. President": *USNWR,* 29 July 1985, p. 24.

298 "reassuring serenity . . .": *WasP,* 17 July 1985, A15.

298 "as a proven . . .": *WasP,* 18 Nov. 1985, B1.

298 "as usual": Regan, *For the Record,* p. 300.

298 "they're not . . .": *WasP,* 18 Nov. 1985, B9.

299 "if women . . .": *WasP,* 21 Nov. 1985, C14.

299 "style wars": *Nwswk,* 2 Dec. 1985, p. 34.

299 "I really think . . .": *WasP,* 21 Nov. 1985, C14.

299 "Who does . . .": Regan, *For the Record,* p. 314.

299 "the pleasure . . .": "Barbara Walters" with RR and NR.

299 "You'll meet . . .": Ibid.

299 "reality-based . . .": Tom Rosenstiel, *Strange Bedfellows* (New York, 1993), p. 26.

300 "I tried . . .": "Barbara Walters" with RR and NR.

300 "master narrative": James Fallows, *Breaking the News* (New York, 1996), p. 171.

301 "Number One . . .": See "Number One National Problem," 19–21 Sept. 1986 in "Anti-Drug Crusade: Attitudes and Opportunities for Change," 439787, Box 10, PR015, WHORM.

301 "I had my first . . .": RR, *American,* pp. 501–502.

301 "Are you . . .": Regan, *For the Record,* p. 69.

301 "Usually in . . .": Peggy Noonan, *What I Saw at the Revolution* (New York, 1990), p. 163.

301 "get off . . .": For rumor see *BosG,* 9 Dec. 1986, p. 16.

301 "journalistic firestorm": RR, *American,* p. 527.

301 His job approval . . . : *NYT,* 3 Mar. 1987, pp. 1, 11.

302 "unhappy . . .": RR, *American,* p. 532.

302 "I don't believe . . .": NR, *My Turn,* p. 109.

302 "possible ways . . .": Dennis Thomas to Donald T. Regan, 16 Jan. 1987, 484685, FG 001, WHORM.

302 "You are not . . .": *NYT,* 21 Feb. 1987, p. 32.

302 "seemed uninterested . . .": Regan, *For the Record,* p. 71.

302 "the leader . . .": "NBC Special: NR."

302 calling Nancy . . .: Noonan, *What I Saw,* p. 163; *WasP,* 12 June 1987, D2.

302 "time . . .": Regan, *For the Record,* p. 90. See also NR, *My Turn,* p. 326.

302 "troubled by . . .": RR, *American,* p. 537.

303 "Reagan Caught . . .": *NYT,* 21 Feb. 1987, p. 32.

303 "Who is . . .": *Time,* 9 Mar. 1987, p. 28.

303 "the world . . .": *ChiT,* 24 Feb. 1987, 1:3.

303 *"That does it . . .":* RR, *American,* pp. 538, 537.

303 "I thought . . .": Regan, *For the Record,* p. 98.

303 "flustered . . . Mr. President . . .": Jane Mayer and Doyle McManus, *Landslide* (Boston, 1988), p. 382.

303 "in weeks": NR, *My Turn,* p. 333.

303 "the leak . . .": RR, *American,* p. 539.

303 "At a time . . .": *NYT,* 2 Mar. 1987, p. 17.

304 "Nancy Reagan's . . .": *NYT,* 3 Mar. 1987, p. 1.

304 "the most vicious . . .": NR, *My Turn,* p. 333.

304 "convey a . . .": Frederick J. Ryan to Howard Baker, Jr., 5 Mar. 1987, 464563, Box 49, PR007, WHORM.

304 "gets her hackles . . .": *NYT,* 3 Mar. 1987, pp. 1, 11.

304 "despicable fiction . . .": *WasP,* 5 Mar. 1987, B1, B2.

304 only 24 . . .: *NYT,* 3 Mar. 1987, p. 1.

304 "Americans were . . .": RR, *American,* p. 541.

304   "Regan once . . .": *LAT,* 4 Mar. 1987, p. 4.
305   "not one of . . .": *NYT,* 8 Mar. 1989, 4:5.
305   "self-proclaimed . . .": *AtCon,* 12 Mar. 1987, A23.
305   "Spousal advice . . .": *NYT,* 4 Mar. 1987, p. 30.
305   Phil Donahue . . .: NR, *My Turn,* p. 335.
305   63 percent . . .: *WasP,* 11 Mar. 1987, C1.
305   woman with whom . . .: *WasP,* 11 June 1987, C1.
305   "There are those . . .": NR, "Remarks for Associated Press Publisher's Luncheon," 4 May
      1987, pp. 1, 16, 6, 10, 14–15, F95-109, WHORM.
306   marital partnership . . .: Steven Mintz and Susan Kellogg, *Domestic Revolutions* (New
      York, 1988), p. 186.
306   "cultural materialist": Maxine L. Margolis, *Mothers and Such* (Berkeley, 1974), p. 3.
306   "What could . . .": *NYT,* 25 May 1988, p. 22.
306   "Only a damn . . .": *WasP,* 13 May 1988, A23.
306   "main adviser . . .": *WasP,* 11 Mar. 1988, A25.
306   "She has made . . .": *McCall's,* Mar. 1988, p. 60.
306   "part of the deal": *WasP,* 13 May 1988, A23.
306   "When they go . . .": *WasP,* 10 June 1988, D3.
306   "In the waning . . .": *Commonwealth,* 24 Apr. 1987, p. 231.
307   "an official . . .": *LHJ,* Aug. 1987, p. 69.
307   "if being . . .": *Ms.,* July 1988, p. 66.
307   "Do your own . . .": *NYT,* 15 Jan. 1989, p. 20.
307   poll confirmed . . .: *LHJ,* Sept. 1988, p. 90.
307   "after playing . . .": *NYT,* 12 Mar. 1987, A31.
307   "I confess . . .": RR, *American,* p. 693.
307   "I couldn't . . .": *WasP,* 4 Dec. 1987, D8.
308   "set us back . . .": *NYT,* 5 Mar. 1988, p. 6.
308   the number . . .: *NYT,* 1 Nov. 1987, p. 44.
308   "there was nothing . . .": RR, *American,* pp. 696–697.
308   "That was . . .": *McCall's,* Mar. 1988, p. 143.
308   "terrible, terrible": *WasP,* 4 Dec. 1987, D1.
308   "henpecked, manipulated . . .": *TNR,* 23 Mar. 1987, p. 12.
308   to endure . . .: Michael Deaver, *Behind the Scenes* (New York, 1987); Reagan, *On the
      Outside;* Larry Speakes, *Speaking Out* (New York, 1988).
308   "no policy . . .": *Nwswk,* 16 May 1988, p. 20.
309   "America's most . . .": Kitty Kelley, *Nancy Reagan* (New York, 1991), p. 528.
309   "benefited from the . . .": Paul Maslin in Michael Duffy and Dan Goodgame, *Marching
      in Place* (New York, 1992), p. 43.
309   "diminutive, designer-sheathed": *NYT,* 15 Jan. 1989, p. 1.
309   "brought all . . .": *WasP,* 10 May 1988, A6.
309   "ole boys . . .": *NYT,* 25 May 1988, p. 22.
309   "The warmest . . .": RR, *American,* p. 724.
309   "peer marriage . . .": Schwartz, *Love,* p. 17.
310   "ordinary people . . .": *NYT,* 11 Apr. 1991, A25.
310   they complained . . .: See Mintz and Kellogg, *Domestic Revolution,* p. 236. On abortion,
      see Luker, *Abortion,* pp. 216–217; and E. J. Dionne, *Why Americans Hate Politics* (New
      York, 1991), p. 341.

CHAPTER 9. PERFECT COUPLE, IMPERFECT PRESIDENT

Page

311   "much to . . .": BB, *Barbara Bush* (New York, 1994), p. 18.
311   "begged and . . .": Ibid., p. 22.
311   "storybook . . .": GB with Victor Gold, *Looking Forward* (New York, 1987, 1988), pp.
      31, 27, 26.
312   "secretly engaged": BB, *BB,* pp. 20, 22.

312   "'Tisn't often . . .": *Meet Me in St. Louis* (1944).

312   "I knew . . .": *TNR,* 9 Nov. 1992, p. 29.

312   "You shouldn't . . .": *Nwswk,* 19 Oct. 1987, p. 32.

312   "I chose . . .": BB, *BB,* p. 26.

312   "conservative kitsch . . .": Sidney Blumenthal, *Pledging Allegiance* (New York, 1990), p. 267.

312   "I do not . . .": *Nwswk,* 23 Jan. 1989, p. 25.

313   "I don't fool . . .": *NYT,* 11 Dec. 1988, p. 42.

313   "running the . . .": *WasP,* 15 Jan. 1989, F6.

313   "a wavemaker": *People,* 21 Nov. 1988, p. 56.

313   "lobby George . . .": *LAT,* 15 Jan. 1989, p. 1.

313   "down-to-earth": *Nwswk,* 16 Jan. 1989, p. 32; *Time,* 23 Jan. 1989, p. 22; *NYT,* 15 Jan. 1989, p. 1; *WasP,* 14 Nov. 1988, B1; *AtCon,* 18 Nov. 1992, D4.

313   "GOODBYE FIRST . . .": Quoted in *NYT,* 11 Dec. 1988, p. 42.

313   "the kind . . .": *WasP,* 14 Nov. 1988, B6.

313   "Bush was the real . . .": *Atlantic,* Aug. 1992, p. 24.

314   "a WASPy . . .": *Nwswk,* 23 Jan. 1989, p. 24.

314   "WASP virtues": Richard Brookhiser, *The Way of the WASP* (New York, 1991), p. 153.

314   "dream—high . . .": GB acceptance speech, *Congressional Quarterly Weekly Report* 20 Aug. 1988, 46:2356.

314   She could not . . . : *LAT,* 7 Aug. 1988, 1:18.

314   "all-rounder": Richard Ben Cramer, *What It Takes* (New York, 1992), pp. 90–91.

315   "a very happy . . .": *WasP,* 20 Jan. 1989, F34.

315   "really mean . . .": *Vanity Fair,* Aug. 1992, p. 124.

315   "being bad . . .": Margaret Hemphill in *NYT,* 11 Dec. 1988, p. 42.

315   "a green . . .": ABC, "The Next President with David Frost," 6 Dec. 1987, 0030, RR AV.

315   "have nothing . . .": BB, *BB,* pp. 16–18.

315   "I married . . .": *People,* 21 Nov. 1988, p. 57.

315   "It all . . .": *McCall's,* Sept. 1988, p. 85.

315   "to talk . . .": *TNR,* 9 Nov. 1992, p. 28.

315   "Nothing will . . .": *WasP,* 20 Jan. 1989, F34.

315   "never . . .": *McCall's,* Sept. 1988, p. 85.

316   "George was in some . . .": BB, *BB,* p. 56.

316   "She always . . .": *Time,* 23 Jan. 1989, p. 24.

316   "I really love . . .": *LAT,* 7 Aug. 1988, p. 17.

316   "Bar, are . . .": *Nwswk,* 22 June 1992, p. 36.

316   "dormant . . .": Cramer, *What It Takes,* pp. 242–243.

316   "Nothing . . .": Ann Grimes, *Running Mates* (New York, 1990), p. 189.

316   "There's nothing . . .": Gail Sheehy, *Character* (New York, 1988), p. 170.

316   "fell apart": *People,* 21 Nov. 1988, p. 57.

316   "George held . . .": *Time,* 23 Jan. 1989, p. 25.

316   "genuine closeness . . .": BB, *BB,* p. 48.

317   "Learn to . . .": GB, *Looking Forward,* pp. 12–13.

317   "Where would . . .": James A. Baker III, *The Politics of Diplomacy* (New York, 1995), p. 17.

317   "emphasize the . . .": *National Review,* 1 Dec. 1964, p. 1053.

317   "I took . . .": Fitzhugh Green, *George Bush* (New York, 1991), p. 91.

317   "cancer, leukemia . . .": Cramer, *What It Takes,* p. 421.

317   "rules of leadership . . .": GB, *Looking Forward,* p. 94.

317   "one of the . . .": *NYT,* 5 Nov. 1970, p. 37.

317   "At least . . .": *WasP,* 27 Oct. 1970, A1.

318   "Where do . . .": Cramer, *What It Takes,* p. 15.

318   "Would the . . .": BB, *BB,* p. 61.

318   "Look at . . .": *NYT,* 22 Feb. 1981, p. 42.

318   "I now . . .": BB, *BB,* p. 65.

318   "Perle Mesta Bush": Ibid., p. 266.

318 "the enforcer": *WasT,* 13 Oct. 1992, E5.

318 "Not brains . . .": *Time,* 22 Aug. 1988, p. 26.

319 "ten most . . .": *New York,* 3 Jan. 1972, p. 32.

319 "adorable, chunky . . .": BB, *BB,* p. 82.

319 "Were we . . .": Ibid., p. 80.

319 "Boy, you . . .": Sheehy, *Character,* p. 176.

319 "wants to . . .": HRH, *The Haldeman Diaries* (New York, 1994), p. 795.

319 "I wouldn't . . .": Cramer, *What It Takes,* p. 614.

319 "the stench": Robert Mosbacher in *WasP,* 9 Aug. 1988, A10.

319 "journey into . . .": GB, *Looking Forward,* p. 128.

319 "missed being . . .": BB, *BB,* p. 108.

319 "I think . . .": Cramer, *What It Takes,* p. 754; photo in GB, *Looking Forward.*

319 "I'm sitting . . .": Sheehy, *Character,* p. 176.

320 "there was . . .": GB, *Looking Forward,* p. 152.

320 "that I hadn't . . .": *People,* 21 Nov. 1988, p. 58.

320 "'code' told . . .": BB, *BB,* p. 135.

320 "taught me . . .": *LAT,* 7 Aug. 1988, pp. 17, 18.

320 "personal, eye-to-eye . . .": GB, *Looking Forward,* p. 185.

320 "a big family . . .": BB, *BB,* p. 141.

320 "'blowing his . . .": Ibid.

320 "Oh, Lord . . .": *Time,* 22 Aug. 1988, p. 22.

320 "I will . . .": *USNWR,* 22 Aug. 1988, p. 16.

320 "should help . . .": BB, *BB,* p. 145.

320 "What are . . .": Ibid., p. 149.

320 "her matronly . . .": *WasP,* 18 Oct. 1980, B5.

320 "the children . . .": BB, *BB,* p. 147.

321 "I'll work . . .": *WasP,* 18 Oct. 1988, B1.

321 "have loved . . .": C-SPAN, "National Federation of Republican Women, Luncheon with Mrs. Bush and Mrs. Reagan," 23 Aug. 1984, R2159, RR AV.

321 "insulting . . .": *NYT,* 22 Feb. 1981, p. 42.

321 "I am not running . . .": *LHJ,* July 1986, p. 131.

321 "I don't . . .": *NYT,* 22 Feb. 1981, p. 42.

321 "I'm not going . . .": *People,* 21 Nov. 1988, p. 55.

321 "We tried to . . .": GB, Sydney H. Schanberg in *NYT,* 20 Oct. 1984, p. 23.

322 "not like . . .": *NYT,* 9 Oct. 1984, p. 29.

322 "go to bat . . .": *NYT,* 15 Oct. 1984, B5.

322 "the Cliff Barnes . . .": NBC, "Nightly News," 1 Nov. 1984, in Vice President composite, 1 Nov. 1984 to 25 Feb. 1985, R2555, RR AV.

322 "testy . . .": "Next President with Frost."

322 "There's no . . .": Sheehy, *Character,* p. 156.

323 "GEORGE BUSH . . .": *Nwswk,* 19 Oct. 1987, cover.

323 "the honor . . .": Michael Duffy and Dan Goodgame, *Marching in Place* (New York, 1992), pp. 21–22.

323 "Family, kids . . .": Peggy Noonan, *What I Saw at the Revolution* (New York, 1990), p. 300.

323 "What is . . .": *Time,* 22 Aug. 1988, p. 21.

323 "more a . . .": "Next President with Frost."

323 "down on . . .": Cramer, *What it Takes,* p. 578.

323 "I'll do . . .": *Life,* Oct. 1988, p. 108.

324 "It is not fair . . .": CBS, "Evening News," 25 Jan. 1988, with Dan Rather in Vice President composite videotape, 15 Jan. to 25 Jan. 1988, R4990, RR AV.

324 "combat": ABC, "Evening News," 26 Jan. 1988 in R4990.

324 "didn't sleep . . .": *AtCon,* 3 Feb. 1988, A10.

324 "The poet . . .": *People,* 21 Nov. 1988, p. 58.

324 "despite herself . . .": Grimes, *Running Mates,* p. 54.

324 "asinine . . ." *AtCon,* 24 Feb. 1988, A8.

324 "If they . . .": *AtCon,* 29 May 1988, A12.

324 "I'm the luckiest . . .": *McCall's,* Sept. 1988, p. 82.

324 "How [do] you . . .": Grimes, *Running Mates,* p. 54.

324 "What's wrong . . .": *AtCon,* 29 May 1988, A1.

324 "Well, I'd . . .": CBS, "Evening News," 25 June 1988, R5342, RR AV.

325 Mrs. Bush would travel: Grimes, *Running Mates,* p. 144.

325 "No. 1 trick . . .": *USA Today,* 7 Nov. 1988, A11.

325 "secret weapon . . .": *AtCon,* 29 May 1988, A12; *WasP,* 5 June 1988, F1.

325 "What you . . .": C-SPAN, "Interview with BB, 1 Sept. 1988," 9 Oct. 1988, R5682, RR AV.

325 "I'm not going . . .": CBS, "This Morning," 20 Oct. 1988, R5717, RR AV.

325 "When you . . .": Duffy and Goodgame, *Marching,* p. 110.

325 "Wimp, WASP . . .": *WasP,* 10 July 1988, C1.

325 "Big A . . .": *Nwswk,* 29 June 1987, p. 6. See also Larry Sabato, *Feeding Frenzy* (New York, 1991), pp. 96, 175.

325 "very sexually . . .": *Life,* Oct. 1988, p. 112.

326 "the domestic . . .": *People,* 21 Nov. 1988, p. 59.

326 "I'm a feeler . . .": *LAT,* 7 Aug. 1988, p. 18.

326 "you know . . .": *WasP,* 15 Aug. 1988, C6.

326 "We weren't saints . . .": GB acceptance, 46:2353, 2355.

326 "very mainstream": *People,* 30 Jan. 1989, p. 56.

326 During a live . . . : *BosG,* 16 Aug. 1988, p. 13.

326 "extraordinary special . . .": *LAT,* 19 Aug. 1988, 1:13.

326 "gender gap . . .": *NYT,* 19 Aug. 1988, A26.

326 "compassion": *BosG,* 30 Oct. 1988, p. 22.

327 "you'd like . . .": *NYT,* 12 Oct. 1988, A24.

327 "place his . . .": *Time,* 30 Jan. 1989, p. 23.

327 "THE 'LIBERATION' . . .": *Nwswk,* 16 Jan. 1989, p. 28.

327 "I have never . . .": *Nwswk,* 23 Jan. 1989, p. 25.

327 "What speech?" . . . : *WasP,* 15 Jan. 1989, F6.

327 "Just kidding . . .": *Time,* 23 Jan. 1989, p. 26.

327 "and did . . .": *Nwswk,* 23 Jan. 1989, p. 25.

328 "I'll take . . .": *BosG,* 21 Dec. 1988, A11.

328 "Show me . . .": *Houston Post,* 15 Jan. 1989, A17.

328 "Every time . . .": *Time,* 23 Jan. 1989, p. 25.

328 "There we go . . .": *WasP,* 15 Jan. 1989, F6.

328 "feels a lot . . .": Lois W. Banner, *In Full Flower* (New York, 1992), p. 356. See also Barbara MacDonald, "Outside the Sisterhood: Ageism in Women's Studies," *Women's Studies Quarterly,* Spring–Summer, 1989, p. 6.

328 "social X-ray": Tom Wolfe, *Bonfire of the Vanities* (New York, 1987), p. 13.

328 "a local . . .": *ChiT,* 29 Jan. 1989, 5:2.

329 "absolutely devastate[d] . . .": BB, *BB,* p. 148.

329 "I don't . . .": *Vogue,* Aug. 1989, pp. 314–315. See also Banner, *In Full Flower,* p. 296.

329 "morning people": *LHJ,* July 1986, p. 131; BB, *BB,* p. 265.

329 56 percent . . . : *USA Today,* 21 Apr. 1989, A1.

330 "don't have . . .": Charles Kolb, *White House Daze* (New York, 1994), p. 6.

330 "You've got . . .": *Vanity Fair,* Aug. 1992, p. 123.

330 "You can't . . .": Anna Perez in *WasP,* 2 Jan. 1991, B9.

330 "I think . . .": *Vanity Fair,* Aug. 1992, p. 122.

330 "generous . . . gracious . . .": BB to LaBJ, 2 May [no year], Box 279, LBJ WHSoc-A.

330 "If you close . . .": *WasP,* 2 May 1989, D3.

330 "Obviously I . . .": BB, *BB,* p. 253.

330 "I hate . . .": *WasP,* 2 Jan. 1991, B9.

331 "Somehow I . . .": Ibid.

331 "For 43 years . . .": *People,* 21 Nov. 1988, p. 54.

331   "I stay . . .": *AtCon,* 9 Apr. 1989, p. 18.
331   "She's not . . .": *WasP,* 24 Feb. 1989, C1.
331   Growing up . . . : *Nwswk,* 19 Oct. 1987, p. 32.
332   "People try . . .": *People,* 4 Aug. 1980, p. 22.
332   "Bush and his policies . . .": Suzanne Gordon in *BosG,* 22 Apr. 1990, A24.
332   "abortion, pro . . .": BB, *BB,* p. 275.
332   "Both George . . .": Ibid., p. 153.
332   "that each . . .": Ibid., p. 272.
332   "I don't . . .": *WasP,* 2 May 1989, D3.
332   "the causes . . .": *ChiT,* 29 Oct. 1989, 5:10.
332   "useful . . . it reflects . . .": BB, *BB,* p. 275.
332   publication of . . . : BB, *Millie's Book* (New York, 1990).
333   "executive business . . .": *ChiT,* 29 Oct. 1989, 5:1.
333   "having the . . .": *LHJ,* Mar. 1990, p. 229.
333   "I *love* . . .": Ibid.
333   "She has . . .": *BosG,* 6 June 1990, p. 14.
333   "I probably . . .": *LHJ,* Mar. 1990, pp. 229–230.
333   "dinosaur": Grimes, *Running Mates,* p. 57.
333   "This is . . .": *WasP,* 21 Jan. 1990, p. 14.
333   "a woman . . .": *Commonweal,* 15 June 1990, p. 408.
333   "does not voice . . .": *USNWR,* 28 May 1990, p. 32.
333   "nurturing women . . .": *BosG,* 22 Apr. 1990, A21.
334   "whining, unshaved . . .": *BosG,* 26 Apr. 1990, p. 41.
334   "these little . . .": *AtCon,* 25 Apr. 1990, E1.
334   "longtime feminist[s] . . .": Suzanne Gordon in *BosG,* 22 Apr. 1990, A21, A24.
334   More than three-quarters . . . : *BosG,* 17 May 1990, p. 7.
334   "these young . . .": *Glamour,* Aug. 1990, p. 132.
334   "putting too . . .": BB, *BB,* p. 338.
334   "You need . . .": *Vital Speeches* 56 (1 July 1990): 549.
334   "official cause . . .": *Time,* 11 June 1990, p. 21.
334   Polls showed . . . : Grimes, *Running Mates,* p. 136.
334   "I think . . .": *Redbook,* May 1991, p. 44.
334   "very, very proud . . .": *LAT,* 9 June 1990, A22.
334   "our No. 1 asset": *WasT,* 1 Oct. 1990, A3.
335   "take a definitive . . .": *BosG,* 3 June 1990, p. 25.
335   "people don't . . .": *CSM,* 16 Feb. 1989, p. 14.
335   "R & R at . . .": BB, *BB,* p. 353.
335   "callous and . . .": *NYT,* 23 Aug. 1990, A23.
336   "I am really . . .": *USNWR,* 22 Aug. 1988, p. 12.
336   "Meanwhile we . . .": BB, *BB,* pp. 355–356.
337   "Some typical . . .": *People,* 1 Oct. 1990, p. 84.
337   "It's very . . .": Ibid., p. 85.
337   "I love . . .": BB, *BB,* pp. 361, 385, 389–390, 395.
337   "calmly . . . I know . . .": Ibid., p. 385.
337   commander in chief: See, for example, *USNWR,* 31 Dec. 1990–7 Jan. 1991, p. 22.
337   "man of the year": *Time,* 7 Jan. 1991, pp. 18–26.
337   "To feel . . .": *People,* 30 Dec. 1991–6 Jan. 1992, p. 38.
338   "he lost . . .": BB, *BB,* p. 326.
338   "Remembering how . . .": Ibid., p. 410.
338   "If you played . . .": *WasT,* 7 June, 1991, A9.
338   "I think . . .": *Vanity Fair,* Aug. 1992, p. 178.
338   "What's the . . .": Robert Bly in Susan Faludi, *Backlash* (New York, 1991), p. 310. On the "soft male," see Bly in *Iron John* (Reading, MA, 1990) p. 2.
339   "Keep Barbara . . .": Mary McGrory in *WasP,* 12 Apr. 1992, C5; *WasT,* 13 Oct. 1992, E5.
339   "Message: I care": *WasP,* 7 Feb. 1992, B4.

339   "I got . . .": Duffy and Goodgame, *Marching,* p. 106.
339   "WE LIKE . . .": *WasP,* 7 Feb. 1992, B1.
339   "if you . . .": Ibid., B4.
339   "to my . . .": *WasP,* 12 Apr. 1992, C5.
339   "When you've . . .": *LAT,* 31 May 1992, M3.
339   "half-Eleanor . . .": Ibid.
340   "centerpiece of . . .": Mary Matalin and James Carville, *All's Fair* (New York, 1994), p. 201.
340   back-to-back . . . : *Nwswk,* 24 Aug. 1992, p. 27.
340   "advising [Bill] Clinton . . .": *ChiT,* 14 Aug. 1992, pp. 1, 4.
340   "I'm not a . . .": PBS–NBC, Republican National Convention coverage, 18 Aug. 1992.
340   "conversation . . . There is . . .": *Vital Speeches,* 58 (15 Sept. 1992): 718.
341   "what accomplishment . . .": Ibid.
341   "Grandma America": *WasT,* 13 Oct. 1992, E1.
341   "that the way . . .": *NYT,* 9 Aug. 1992, 4:17.
341   "in trotting . . .": *NYT,* 21 Aug. 1992, A24. See also Peter Hart in *WasT,* 20 Aug. 1992, A10.
341   "personal-emotional . . .": *WasT,* 23 Aug. 1992, B3.
341   "prickly": *Nwswk,* 22 June 1992, p. 34.
341   "She's a . . .": *Vanity Fair,* Aug. 1992, p. 122.
341   "that hurt me": *TNR,* 9 Nov. 1992, p. 30.
341   "hallmark picture . . .": *TNR,* 5 Oct. 1992, pp. 13–16.
342   As voters worried . . . : See Gil Troy, *See How They Ran,* rev. ed. (Cambridge, MA, 1991, 1996), pp. 270–271.
342   "far and . . .": Edward J. Rollins in *Vanity Fair,* Aug. 1992, p. 120.
342   "She is . . .": *NYT,* 19 Aug. 1992, A15.
342   "What big . . .": *WasP,* 9 Oct. 1992, B2.
342   the wives' impact . . . : *USNWR* poll in *LAT,* 24 July 1992, E1; *SFChr,* 29 Sept. 1992, A4.
342   "worn": *USNWR,* 24 Aug. 1992, p. 26.
342   "restore the . . .": *WasT,* 13 Oct. 1992, E1.
342   "Hers is . . .": *WasP,* 9 Oct. 1992, B2.
342   "The last . . .": *People,* 3 Oct. 1994, p. 145.
343   "We've done . . .": John Podhoretz, *Hell of a Ride* (New York, 1993), p. 50.
343   "OK, let's . . .": Marlin Fitzwater, *Call the Briefing!* (New York, 1995), p. 362.
343   "There will . . .": Matalin and Carville, *All's Fair,* p. 472.

CONCLUSION. "DATES WITH THE AMERICAN PEOPLE"

Page

344   The average age . . . : Ben J. Wattenberg, *The Birth Dearth* (New York, 1987), pp. 124, 126.
344   "Never have . . .": Judith Warner, *Hillary Clinton* (New York, 1993), p. 75.
344   "her own name": Virginia Clinton Kelley with James Morgan, *Leading with My Heart* (New York, 1994), p. 236.
344   "Look, if . . .": David Maraniss, *First in His Class* (New York, 1995), p. 247.
345   "All we ever . . .": BC to Carolyn Yeldell Staley in Maraniss, *First,* p. 342.
345   "he combined . . .": HRC in *Parade,* 11 Apr. 1993, p. 6.
345   ruining her life: Peter Edelman referred to in *Vogue,* Dec. 1993, p. 232.
345   "I had no . . .": *People,* 17 Feb. 1992, p. 43.
345   "urge to heroism": Ernest Becker, *The Denial of Death* (New York, 1973), p. 4. See also Maraniss, *First,* p. 345.
345   The fertility . . . : The actual numbers are 3.6 in 1960, 1.8 in 1975. Baby-boom fertility peaked in 1957. Ben J. Wattenberg, *The First Universal Nation* (New York, 1991), p. 85.
345   "our generation": BC, "Announcement Speech," 3 Oct. 1991, Bill Clinton and Al Gore, *Putting People First* (New York, 1992), p. 197.

346 "a new kind . . .": Ibid., pp. 191, 187.

346 "Buy one . . .": *Vanity Fair,* May 1992, p. 143.

346 "If you vote . . .": *WasP,* 10 Mar. 1992, E2.

346 only 28 percent . . . : *Time,* 4 Jan. 1993, p. 41.

346 "I'm not some . . .": Warner, *Hillary,* p. 185.

346 "They don't have . . .": Roger Morris, *Partners in Power* (New York, 1996), p. 440.

346 "I wish . . .": *Time,* 27 Jan. 1992, p. 44.

346 "electability problem . . .": James Stewart, *Blood Sport* (New York, 1996), p. 213.

347 "I suppose . . .": Warner, *Hillary,* p. 185.

347 this "New Age" . . . : On modern man's "fear of the wimp" see Michael Kimmel, *Manhood in America* (New York, 1996), p. 298.

347 "Bill: stop . . .": *NYT,* 26 Mar. 1992, A23.

347 a symbol of . . . : See Anne Firor Scott, *The Southern Lady* (Chicago, 1970), p. 230.

347 "the overbearing yuppie . . .": *NYT,* 18 May 1992, A15.

347 "new class . . .": Peter Steinfels, *The Neoconservatives* (New York, 1979), p. 287; Christopher Lasch, *The Revolt of the Elites and the Betrayal of Democracy* (New York, 1995), pp. 6, 34, 28.

347 "Yuppie": See *Time,* 9 Jan. 1984, p. 66; Marissa Piesman and Marilee Hartley, *Yuppie Handbook* (New York, 1983). For Ralph Whitehead's critique and description of less affluent baby-boom "new collars," see *ChiT,* 9 July 1985, C1.

347 only 28 percent: George H. Gallup, *The Gallup Poll,* 3 vols. (New York, 1972), 3:2196.

348 "I'm too . . .": *NYT,* 18 May 1992, A15.

348 "the women's movement . . .": Julianne Malveaux in *LAT,* 22 Mar. 1992, M5.

348 "prevailing, acquisitive . . .": *Life,* 20 June 1969, p. 31.

349 "family, church on . . .": *GH,* Jan. 1993, p. 98.

349 "straight out of . . .": Hillary Rodham Clinton, *It Takes a Village* (New York, 1996), pp. 20, 156.

349 "that feminist . . .": *ChiT,* 31 Jan. 1992, 1:10.

349 "it meant more . . .": *Time,* 27 Jan. 1992, p. 19.

349 Rodham family . . . : Morris, *Partners,* p. 115.

349 "to her . . .": *People,* 17 Feb. 1992, p. 43.

349 "ladyness . . .": Mary Ellen Guy, "Hillary, Health Care, and Gender Power," Georgia Duerst-Lahti and Rita Mae Kelly, eds., *Gender Power, Leadership and Governance* (Ann Arbor, MI, 1995), p. 248.

349 possible bastardy: On questions about "the timing of the conception of William Jefferson Blythe III," see Maraniss, *First,* p. 28.

349 alleged cocaine use: Morris, *Partners,* pp. 325–326.

349 "Inside my . . .": Kelley, *Leading,* p. xvii.

349 His best friend . . . : Carolyn Yeldell Staley in Maraniss, *First,* p. 41.

349 elusive relationship . . . : Morris, *Partners,* p. 50.

350 "threatened to . . .": Meredith L. Oakley, *On the Make* (Washington, DC, 1994), p. 30.

350 "to maintain . . .": BC to Colonel Eugene J. Holmes, 3 Dec. 1969, Maraniss, *First,* p. 202.

350 "I always . . .": BC in *Vanity Fair,* May 1992, p. 214.

350 "no makeup . . .": Kelley, *Leading,* p. 203.

350 "peer marriage": Pepper Schwartz, *Love Between Equals* (New York, 1994), pp. 16, 111, 17.

350 "The woman I . . .": Maraniss, *First,* p. 117.

350 "a room . . .": *People,* 25 Jan. 1993, p. 55.

350 "Nice is not . . .": Connell Cowan and Melvyn Kinder, *Smart Women/Foolish Choices* (New York, 1985), p. 97; Schwartz, *Love,* p. 15.

350 "I would like . . ." *NYer,* 30 May 1994, p. 62.

350 "This is fun . . .": Stewart, *Blood,* p. 70.

350 harsh father's . . . : See Morris, *Partners,* pp. 114–115.

351   "family, work . . .": *AtCon,* 31 May 1992, G7.
351   "He wasn't . . .": *Vanity Fair,* May 1992, p. 214.
351   "beginning to . . .": *WasP,* 10 Mar. 1992, E2.
351   "Smart Women . . .": Cowan and Kinder, *Smart Women,* p. 105.
351   "You couldn't . . .": *NYTM,* 17 Jan. 1993, p. 26.
351   "I need . . .": Maraniss, *First,* p. 443.
351   "If we . . .": *Vanity Fair,* May 1992, p. 217.
351   "If Bill Clinton . . .": *Nwswk,* 3 Feb. 1992, p. 22.
351   "My strong . . .": HRC, *Village,* p. 43.
351   "the daughter . . .": *Vanity Fair,* May 1992, p. 147.
351   "We are banking . . .": *AtCon,* 31 Jan. 1992, A9.
351   Bill defined addressing . . . : *Time,* 20 July 1992, p. 20.
351   "the Establishment . . .": *Vanity Fair,* May 1992, p. 147.
352   "off the record": Mary Matalin and James Carville, *All's Fair* (New York, 1994), p. 298.
352   "HILLARY'S REVENGE . . .": Warner, *Hillary,* p. 188.
352   "rumors . . . have . . .": *Vanity Fair,* May 1992, p. 147.
352   "If I get . . .": Ibid., p. 144.
352   "We care about . . .": *People,* 17 Feb. 1992, p. 42.
352   "a job": *Harper's Bazaar,* July 1992, p. 91.
352   "If the wife . . .": *WasP Magazine,* 1 Nov. 1992, p. 12.
352   "the Lady Macbeth . . .": *American Spectator,* Aug. 1992, p. 25.
352   "fast-talking . . .": *NYT,* 14 Nov. 1992, p. 1.
352   "events where . . .": *BosG,* 4 Feb. 1996, p. 25.
352   "Hi there . . .": *WasT,* 23 Aug. 1992, B3.
353   "What did . . .": Linda Bloodworth-Thomason in *People,* 20 July 1992, p. 78.
353   "two for . . .": *Glamour,* Aug. 1992, p. 269.
353   "When we . . .": *NYT,* 8 June 1992, A15.
353   "We ought . . .": *ChiT,* 14 July 1992, p. 12.
353   "On her own . . .": *TNR,* 22 June 1992, p. 42.
353   only a quarter . . . : *USNWR,* 27 Apr. 1992, p. 35.
353   and 66 percent . . . : *WasP Magazine,* 1 Nov. 1992, p. 12.
353   "Republican Mother": Linda K. Kerber, *Women of the Republic* (Chapel Hill, NC, 1980), p. 284.
353   "as far as . . .": *WasP Magazine,* 1 Nov. 1992, p. 24.
353   "an attack . . .": *TNR,* 15 Feb. 1993, p. 6.
354   "all working . . .": *People,* 20 July 1992, p. 71.
354   carefully packaged commodity . . .: On commodification, see Robert Westbrook, "Politics as Consumption: Managing the Modern American Election," chap. 5 in Richard Wightman Fox and T. J. Jackson Lears, eds., *The Culture of Consumption* (New York, 1983); on modern America's "show business discourse," see Neil Postman, *Amusing Ourselves to Death* (New York, 1985).
354   sorcerer: Jackson Lears, *Fables of Abundance* (New York, 1994), p. 75.
354   50 percent in . . . : George Gallup, Jr., *The Gallup Poll: Public Opinion 1992* (Wilmington, DE, 1993), pp. 194–197.
355   "zone of privacy": Warner, *Hillary,* p. 171.
355   "I would be . . .": *USNWR,* 25 Jan. 1993, p. 46.
355   "Hillary": *Time,* 4 Jan. 1993, p. 37.
355   "principal domestic . . .": Haynes Johnson and David S. Broder, *The System* (Boston, 1996), p. 98.
355   "she's better . . .": *NYT,* 26 Jan. 1993, p. 1.
355   "run out . . .": Johnson and Broder, *System,* pp. 99, 98.
355   "more honest . . .": *NYT,* 27 Jan. 1993, A22.
355   "is not just . . .": *Nwswk,* 1 Feb. 1993, p. 38.
355   "the age . . .": *LHJ,* Apr. 1993, p. 146.

355 "conversations with . . .": *People*, 10 May 1993, p. 83.

355 "Hillary's Merely . . .": Carl Anthony in *WasP*, 31 Jan. 1993, F1; Blanche Wiesen Cook in *LAT*, 17 Jan. 1993, M1.

356 "If you lived . . .": *Redbook*, Mar. 1993, p. 123.

356 Lisa Caputo, said . . . : *NYT*, 14 Feb. 1993, p. 33.

356 63 percent of . . . : *USNWR*, 25 Jan. 1993, p. 50.

356 "the Dynamic Duo": *Time*, 4 Jan. 1993, p. 36.

356 "an empowered . . .": *NYT*, 8 Feb. 1993, A14.

356 "The voters . . .": *TNR*, 15 Feb. 1993, p. 6. The same poll found that only 43 percent of the men under forty approved. *AtCon*, 21 Feb. 1993, F3.

356 Hillary could indulge . . . : *Nwswk*, 15 Jan. 1996, p. 22. See also *NYer*, 26 Feb.–4 Mar. 1996, p. 125.

356 "press work . . .": Deposition of Margaret A. Williams, 20 July 1994 in U.S. Congress, Senate, Committee on Banking, Housing and Urban Affairs, *Depositions of White House Officials in Response to S. Res. 229*, 103rd Cong., 2nd sess., 1994, 5:236–237.

356 "within one hundred . . .": Johnson and Broder, *System*, pp. 100, 113.

357 "After the meeting . . .": Paul Starr to Ira Magaziner, 7 Feb. 1993, Box 3308, Clinton White House, Interdepartmental Working Group, National Archives, College Park, MD.

357 "I don't want . . .": *AtCon*, 21 Feb. 1993, F3.

357 "Do I want . . .": Johnson and Broder, *System*, p. 101.

357 "She was one . . .": *Nwswk*, 4 Oct. 1993, p. 50.

357 "functional equivalent . . .": *Association of American Physicians and Surgeons, Inc. et al. v. Hillary Rodham Clinton et al.*, 997 F.2d 898, 902, 904 (U.S. App. D.C. 22 June 1993).

357 "the First Lady, like . . .": Gregory S. Walden, *On Best Behavior* (Indianapolis, 1996), p. 87.

358 "Bill Clinton, of all . . .": *BosG*, 26 Feb. 1993, p. 15.

358 "precipitat[ing] a . . .": *American Physicians v. HRC*, 813 F. Supp. 90 (D.D.C. 1993).

358 "the presidential . . .": *American Physicians v. HRC*, 997 F.2d 905, 910–911. Eventually, in September 1994, the White House opened 230 boxes of documents from the "working group" to end the litigation.

358 Magaziner's crafty . . . : Walden, *On Best Behavior*, pp. 120–121.

358 "In retrospect . . .": Johnson and Broder, *System*, p. 142.

358 572 different organizations . . . : James Fallows, "A Triumph of Misinformation," *Atlantic Monthly* (Jan. 1995), p. 28.

358 "Sooner or later . . .": *BosG*, 15 Mar. 1993, p. 13.

358 "What do . . .": *Time*, 10 May 1993, p. 33.

358 "If I didn't . . .": HRC to Julie Baldridge in Stewart, *Blood*, p. 91.

358 "Hillary's Alzheimer's . . .": *LAT Magazine*, 23 May 1993, p. 15.

358 many of the state . . . : *American Spectator*, Jan. 1994, p. 25.

358 "enemies list": *Nwswk*, 24 June 1996, p. 40.

359 helped flood . . . : Ben J. Wattenberg, *Values Matter Most* (New York, 1995), pp. 247–248.

359 "left wing": *WasT*, 6 May 1993, G1.

359 "diversity jihad": *USNWR*, 25 Jan. 1993, p. 47.

359 "What is it . . .": *People*, 10 May 1993, p. 86.

359 "dauntingly homogeneous . . .": Suzanne Dixon, "Conclusion—The Enduring Theme: Domineering Dowagers and Scheming Concubines," in Barbara Garlick, Suzanne Dixon, Pauline Allen, eds., *Stereotypes of Women in Power* (New York, 1992), p. 222.

359 "She's very . . .": *BosG*, 6 Apr. 1992, p. 14.

359 "of selfishness and . . .": HRC, 6 Apr. 1993 in *Tikkun*, May–June 1993, p. 8.

359 "new Reformation . . .": *NYTM*, 23 May 1993, 6:22.

359 "a mental conservative . . .": Donnie Radcliffe, *Hillary Rodham Clinton* (New York, 1993), p. 62.

360   "There's a . . .": *Life,* 20 June 1969, p. 31. See also the Port Huron Statement on "American values," "American virtue," "making values explicit," and the search for "a meaning in life that is personally authentic." "Agenda for a Generation" in Robert D. Marcus and David Burner, eds., *America Firsthand,* 2 vols. (New York, 1989), 2:296–299.

360   "an issue . . . ": *Parade,* 11 Apr. 1993, p. 4.

360   "Hillary Clinton—mom . . .": *People,* 10 May 1993, p. 83. See also *Time,* 14 Jan. 1985, p. 24.

360   One poll would . . . : *USNWR,* 31 Jan. 1994, p. 46.

360   "This is as . . .": *NYT,* 29 Sept. 1993, A18.

360   "search[ing] for consensus . . .": Magaziner to HRC in Johnson and Broder, *System,* p. 16.

360   "here as a . . .": *NYT,* 29 Sept. 1993, A18.

360   "it looks . . .": Lloyd R. George in Oakley, *On the Make,* p. 285.

360   "I think . . .": *NYT,* 29 Sept. 1993, A18.

360   "captivated and . . .": Ibid., A1.

361   "don't want . . .": *People,* 27 Dec. 1993–3 Jan. 1994, pp. 39, 44–45.

361   "We thought we . . .": Johnson and Broder, *System,* p. 256.

361   "human beings . . .": *NYTM,* 23 May 1993, p. 65.

361   "who does it all": *BosG,* 12 Dec. 1993, A6. See also Katha Politt in *NYT,* 3 Oct. 1993, 4:1.

361   "For women . . .": *Harper's Bazaar,* Jan. 1994, p. 39.

361   "I need to . . .": *American Spectator,* Jan. 1994, pp. 28, 22.

362   "I think I'm . . .": Elizabeth Drew, *On the Edge* (New York, 1994), p. 384.

362   "I find . . .": *BosG,* 22 Dec. 1993, p. 12.

362   "media industry . . .": Stephen L. Carter, *Integrity* (New York, 1996), p. 95. See also Thomas E. Patterson, *Out of Order* (New York, 1993).

362   "Sixties kids": Rush H. Limbaugh III, *See I Told You So* (New York, 1993), p. 143.

362   "political talk . . .": James Fallows, *Breaking the News* (New York, 1996), pp. 92–93.

362   "That's what it . . .": Johnson and Broder, *System,* p. 277.

362   "Heil Hillary . . .": Ibid., p. 281; *Nwswk,* 15 Nov. 1993, p. 34; *Nwswk,* 1 Nov. 1993, p. 24.

362   "To make my . . .": Kenneth T. Walsh, *Feeding the Beast* (New York, 1996), p. 239. See also Howard Kurtz, *Hot Air* (New York, 1996), pp. 4, 10.

363   Millions still built . . .: Lori D. Ginzberg, *Women and the Work of Benevolence* (New Haven, 1990), p. 216.

363   "dangerous sexuality": Arlene W. Saxonhouse, "Introduction—Public and Private: The Paradigm's Power," in Garlick et al., *Stereotypes of Women,* p. 7.

363   "feminine credentials . . .": Dixon, "Conclusion," pp. 215, 218.

363   "our gendered concept . . .": Guy, "Hillary and Gender Power," p. 254.

363   "Hillary Clinton is the first . . .": Ann Compton in Walsh, *Feeding the Beast,* p. 159.

364   "doesn't want . . .": "Testimony of Roger Altman," 2 Aug. 1994, in U.S. Congress, Senate, Committee on Banking, Housing and Urban Affairs, *Hearings Relating to Madison Guaranty S & L and the Whitewater Development Corporation—Washington, DC Phase,* 103rd Cong., 2nd sess., 1994, 3:421.

364   "It's not . . .": *Nwswk,* 21 Mar. 1994, p. 35.

364   "had no role . . .": Neil Eggleston to GAO, 6 Apr. 1994; Draft Memorandum from David Watkins, undated, both in Gregory S. Walden, "Recent Disclosures Regarding the First Lady," 11 Jan. 1996, Addendum to Walden, *Behavior,* pp. 1, 3.

364   "We need our . . .": *NYT,* 29 Feb. 1996, A21.

364   "It is the . . .": *BosG,* 3 Apr. 1994, p. 63.

364   "Hillary Rodham Nixon": *AtCon,* 11 Mar. 1994, A16.

364   Cartoons of the . . . : Theda Skocpol, *Boomerang* (New York, 1996), pp. 153, 151.

365   his approval rating . . . : Stewart, *Blood,* p. 418.

365   Hillary's unfavorability. . . : *Nwswk,* 21 Mar. 1994, p. 35.

365 "Where do . . .": *NYer,* 26 Feb.–4 Mar. 1996, p. 130.

365 "I do not . . .": *AtCon,* 11 Mar. 1994, A17.

365 "that there may . . .": Stewart, *Blood,* p. 420.

365 "embarrassing . . .": "Press Conference by the First Lady," 22 Apr. 1994, in U.S. Congress, Senate, Committee on Banking, Housing and Urban Affairs, *White House Document Production in Response to S. Res. 229,* 103rd Cong., 2nd sess., 1994, 9:1590, 1587, 1588, 1591, 1596.

366 "unprecedented extraordinary . . .": *WasP,* 23 Apr. 1994, G1.

366 the 49 percent. . . : *USA Today,* 26 Apr. 1994, A4.

366 "A good wife . . .": *Esquire,* Mar. 1994, p. 52.

366 "Values Matter . . .": Wattenberg, *Values,* pp. 239–267.

367 "The Good Father": *Nwswk,* 12 Feb. 1996, p. 32.

367 "character-starved culture . . ." Don E. Eberly, George Gallup, Jr., in Don E. Eberly, *The Content of America's Character* (Lanham, MD, 1995), pp. 6, ix. See also New York Times/CBS News Poll in *NYT,* 16 July 1996, A15; Gary Aldrich, *Unlimited Access* (Washington, DC, 1996).

367 "My first . . .": *USNWR,* 27 Feb. 1995, p. 36.

367 "new Hillary": *AtCon,* 18 Feb. 1995, A7.

367 "No, she's . . .": *BosG,* 9 Mar. 1995, p. 20.

367 "family feminism": *NYer,* 26 Feb.–4 Mar. 1996, p. 126.

367 "We need to . . .": HRC, "Remarks to the United Nations Fourth World Conference on Women," Beijing, China, 5 Sept. 1995, p. 3; HRC Website (http://www1.whitehouse.gov/WH/EOP/First_Lady/html/who.html).

367 "equal political . . .": *GH,* Jan. 1993, p. 99.

367 "choices . . .": HRC, "Remarks at Pentagon Celebration of Women's History Month," Washington, DC, 1 Mar. 1995, pp. 3–4, HRC Website.

368 "talked mostly to . . .": Walsh, *Feeding the Beast,* p. 171.

368 "a lot of people . . .": *Nwswk,* 1 July 1996, p. 23.

368 "big government . . .": *Nwswk,* 16 Jan. 1995, p. 22.

368 "Bill and I . . .": *Glamour,* Aug. 1992, p. 269.

368 "the human dimension . . .": *NYDN,* 23 July 1995, p. 2.

368 "corny": HRC, *Evening Standard,* 9 Oct. 1995, p. 12.

368 "has a talent . . .": *NYT,* 10 Aug. 1995, A19.

368 "this misguided . . .": *ChiT,* 3 Sept. 1995, 1:3.

368 "may have been . . .": *NYT,* 6 Sept. 1995, A24.

369 "there was no . . .": *BosG,* 7 Sept. 1995, p. 24.

369 "Insofar as . . .": *People,* 25 Dec. 1995–1 Jan 1996, p. 112.

369 "congenital liar": *NYT,* 8 Jan. 1996, A27. See also *NYT,* 10 Jan. 1996, A11.

369 "I hope one . . .": *NYTM,* 23 May 1993, 6:25.

369 "Security Takes . . .": HRC, *Village,* pp. 128, 221, 11.

369 "I can play . . .": Radcliffe, *HRC,* p. 35.

369 "When they . . .": HRC, *Village,* p. 153.

370 "every child . . .": Ibid., pp. 41, 50.

370 "acceptable face . . .": Dixon, "Conclusion," p. 216.

370 "to have made . . .": John Brummett, HRC in *Mother Jones,* Nov.–Dec. 1993, p. 37.

370 54 percent . . . : *LAT,* 25 Jan. 1996, A1.

370 "Task List": "Task List—December 13, 1994, in U.S. Congress, House, 104th Cong., 2nd Sess., 11 Sept. 1996, *CR,* 142: H10213–H10215.

370 "I wasn't ready . . .": Steve Gunderson and Rob Morris with Bruce Bawer, *House and Home* (New York, 1996), p. 221.

370 Studies estimated that . . . : See Frederic T. Smoller, *Six O'Clock Presidency* (New York, 1990), p. 45.

371 "the power to persuade": Richard Neustadt, *Presidential Power and the Modern Presidents* (New York, 1990), p. 28. See also Stephen Skowronek, *The Politics Presidents Make*

(Cambridge, MA, 1993); Samuel Kernell, *Going Public* (Washington, 1986); Howard Gardner, *Leading Minds* (New York, 1995), p. 9.

371   over three-quarters . . . : Skocpol, *Boomerang,* p. 109.

371   Yearning for . . . : Steven Mintz and Susan Kellogg, *Domestic Revolutions* (New York, 1988), p. 205; Christopher Lasch, *The Culture of Narcissism* (New York, 1978), pp. 7–21.

371   where 96 percent . . . : Dennis A. Gilbert, *Compendium of American Public Opinion* (New York, 1988), pp. 303, 309.

373   "THE INCREDIBLE . . .": *Time,* 7 June 1993, cover.

373   Americans were split . . . : *American Demographics,* Aug. 1990, p. 28.

374   Delilah: Simon Schama in *NYer,* 30 Jan. 1995, p. 34.

374   "half Eleanor . . .": *LAT,* 31 May 1992, M3.

374   "consort": *Random House College Dictionary,* rev. ed. (New York, 1982), p. 287.

374   how much of their . . . : See Erving Goffman, *Presentation of Self in Everyday Life,* (New York, 1959), pp. 8–9.

376   Charisma is the enemy . . . : Garry Wills, *The Kennedy Imprisonment* (New York, 1981, 1982), p. 195.

376   in this anarchic . . . : See Richard Sennett, *Fall of Public Man* (New York, 1974, 1976).

APPENDIX. "I NEVER PROMISED YOU A ROSE GARDEN"

Page

378   "answer any . . .": CNN, "Larry King Live," interview with HRC, 20 May 1996, transcript by Journal Graphics, Inc., pp. 8, 4, 7, 3.

380   "It takes . . .": *NYT,* 12 Apr. 1976, pp. 1, 24.

382   "no sovereign . . .": Henry James quoted in David Donald, *Lincoln Reconsidered,* 2nd ed. (New York, 1961), p. 235.

382   "24-hour news . . .": HRC on "Larry King," p. 7.

384   "The marriage vow . . .": Stephen Carter, *Integrity* (New York, 1996), p. 134.

ACKNOWLEDGMENTS

In the four years it took me to research and write this book about political partnership, I have benefited from all kinds of alliances. At The Free Press, Joyce Seltzer first pitched this idea as we had lunch together with marriage on the mind—I had just become engaged. I thank Joyce for entrusting me with this venture. Bruce Nichols took over the project and made it his own. On every page I can see improvements thanks to his energy, his insight, his keen eye for narrative detail, and his sure-footed instinct for the broader historical and political implications. I am grateful for his support and his friendship. I also thank the rest of the Free Press/Simon & Schuster team, especially Norah Vincent; Chris Kelly, the copy editor; and Edith Lewis, who once again shepherded my manuscript through the production process with wisdom and grace.

While it is fashionable to lament that students today are not what they used to be, this book could not have been completed without a corps of crackerjack assistants. For two years Jeffrey P. Heynen was my eyes and ears in Washington, tracking down all kinds of bizarre requests with great intelligence and good humor. In a burst of pre-Commencement efficiency and enthusiasm, Nigel A. DeSouza, Kelly K. Matsumoto, and Lee Anne M. Wallace organized the notes, then Lee Anne took on the formidable job of cite-checking with a great eye for detail. Peter M. Hendricks, Edward P. Kohn, and Aviva Poczter also helped out at critical junctures. I thank them as well as all the McGill students who helped me clarify my ideas and endured the hurried office hours and terminal exhaustion caused by my rush to meet my publisher's deadline.

For their insights and their friendship, I thank my colleagues at McGill University. Professors Leonard Moore, Suzanne Morton, and A. R. Riggs interrupted summer vacations to read the manuscript, and offered perceptive comments. Dean Carman Miller and Professor John Zucchi have ably chaired the History Department during this time of budgetary cataclysm. Georgii Mikula, Mary McDaid, Joan Pozer, and Celine Coutinho keep the department running and have helped in numerous ways over the years. Marion Dukaczewski administered the generous three-year grant I was lucky enough to receive from the Social Science and Humanities Research Council of Canada. The project would have taken much longer without such assistance. An internal Humanities Research Grant from McGill's Faculty of Graduate Studies and Research in 1993 helped jump-start my efforts.

Researching in the presidential libraries is the archival equivalent of flying first class—although sometimes the libraries even pay your fare. A Moody Grant from the Lyndon Baines Johnson Foundation, a Gerald Ford Foundation Grant, and a Harry S. Truman Library Institute Grant were most helpful. I especially thank Liz Safly and Denis Bilger of the Harry S. Truman Library; Maura Porter and June Payne of the John F. Kennedy Library; Claudia Anderson and Linda Hanson of the Lyndon Baines Johnson Library; Susan Naulty of the Richard Nixon Library and Birthplace; David Horrocks and Leesa Tobin of the Gerald R. Ford Library; Robert Bohanan, Jim Herring, David J. Stanhope, and James A. Yancey, Jr., of the Jimmy Carter Library; and Catherine Sewell of the Ronald Reagan Library for their gracious and unstinting assistance. I thank their many helpful colleagues as well as the librarians at the Dwight D. Eisenhower Library; the Nixon Presidential Materials Project at the new National Archives facility in College Park, Maryland; the Franklin D. Roosevelt Library in Hyde Park, New York; the Jacob Javits Collection at the State University of New York in Stony Brook, New York; St. John's University Library in Jamaica, New York; the McGill University Library in Montreal; Harvard University's Widener Library in Cambridge, Massachusetts; and the New York Public Library in New York City.

Permission to quote and reproduce material also came from Louis Harris and Associates, Inc., the Republican National Committee, Theodore C. Sorensen, the *Washington Post*, and the Bush Presidential Library, where Mary Finch proved particularly helpful.

My former dissertation advisers, David Herbert Donald and Alan Brinkley, continue to offer friendship and inspiration. I am especially grateful to Alan for taking the time to read and comment on a draft of the manuscript. I only hope this book can meet the high standards both set with their own work.

For various favors large and small I thank Sonia Asiman, my friends in Boston who gave me a "home away from home," Maya Abi-Chaker, Wendy Felson and David Goodman, Angela Fortugno, Steven B. Greenberg, Rochelle Hahn and Professor Kenneth S. Breuer, Stephen Hess, Professor Peter Hoffmann, Susan Kaplan and Matt Gerson, Diane Mullins, the 1995 inhabitants of 514 Crown View Drive who gave me and my wife a tour of the Fords' old home in Alexandria, Virginia, Diane Pardillo, Alice Rhee, Joel Rosenfeld, Jack Rosenfeld, Amy Sheon and Marvin Krislov, Lesley Stahl, and Michael Seth Wolfson. My proofreading brigade of Annie Adams, Linda Adams, Ted Frankel, Ted Kohn, Dr. Jason Szabo, Bernard Dov Troy, Dr. Tevi Troy, Lee Anne Wallace, and Barbara Weinstein caught many errors—the rest, alas, are my own.

Annie and Marcel Adams have welcomed me warmly into their spirited clan. They, their children, their children's families, and Mrs. Susie Cohen have supplied friendship, support, enthusiasm—and proofreading.

Among countless other gifts, my parents, Elaine and Bernard Dov Troy, have provided an inspiring example of how a marriage can survive and thrive over decades. My grandparents, Leon and Charlotte Gerson, served as a living link to the lost world of appearances and common standards. I regret that my grandmother did not live to see this book published.

My brothers, Dr. Tevi Troy and Dan Troy, and my sister-in-law, Dr. Cheryl Horowitz Troy, are great friends, warm hosts, impressive role models, political sparring partners, able critics, and constant sources of assistance, encouragement, and diversion.

Last but certainly not least, I wish to thank my "first lady" and best friend, Linda Adams, for helping me every step of the way. I am sorry that in writing about these overworked and preoccupied husbands, I became one myself. While I was working night and day on this book, she was giving life to our daughter, Lia Charlotte Adams Troy. Contrary to our society's misplaced priorities, I have no doubt that Linda's achievement is the more remarkable and important one.

INDEX